THE ILLUSTRATED ENCYCLOPEDIA OF ARCHITECTS AND ARCHITECTURE

THE ILLUSTRATED ENCYCLOPEDIA OF ARCHITECTS AND ARCHITECTURE

Edited by
DENNIS SHARP

WHITNEY LIBRARY OF DESIGN
An imprint of Watson-Guptill Publications
New York

A QUARTO BOOK

First published in 1991 in the United States by
Whitney Library of Design,
an imprint of Watson-Guptill Publications,
a division of BPI Communications, Inc.,
1515 Broadway, New York, N.Y. 10036

Library of Congress Cataloging-in – Publication Data

The Illustrated encyclopedia of architects and architecture/edited by Dennis Sharp.

p. cm.

Includes bibliographical references and index.

ISBN 0-8230-2539-X

1. Architects-Biography-Dictionaries.
2. Architecture-History.
I. Sharp, Dennis
NA40.I45 1991
720 .3-dc20 91-710
CIP

ISBN 0-8230-2539-X

This book was designed and produced by
Quarto Publishing plc
The Old Brewery
6 Blundell Street
London N7 9BH

Senior Editor Christine Davis
Editors Judith Wardman, Susan Berry
Designer Bill Mason
Illustrator Dave Kemp
Picture Manager Sarah Risley
Picture Research Susan Rose-Smith
Art Director Moira Clinch
Art Editor Philip Gilderdale
Publishing Director Janet Slingsby

Manufactured in Hong Kong by Regent Publishing Services Ltd
Typeset by ABC Limited, Bournemouth
Manufactured in Singapore by
Chroma Graphics Limited
Printed by Leefung Asco Printers Limited,
Hong Kong

Acknowledgements

Quarto would like to thank the following for providing photographs, and for permission to reproduce copyright material:

Key: a = above; b = below; l = left; r = right

L & R Adkins: 183 cr; Chloë Alexander: 110; Archivi Alinari: 12 b, 23, 108 a, 212 b, 213 ar; Arcaid: 68, 83, 106 b, 119, 131, 137, 154, 233 b, 243 a; Arkitekturmuseet, Stockholm: 16, 104, 116, 153, 239 cl; Arup Associates: 14, 243 cl; James Austin: 55, 59, 66, 71 r, 95, 188 b, 189 al, 191 ar, 213 al, 239 cr, 240 b, 241; Avery Library, Columbia University: 86 l, 101, 233 ar; Peter Bareham: 25, 235 br; Gunter Behnisch & Partners: 245 b; Tim Benton: 12 a, 70, 129, 214 b, 235 a, 238; Book Art: 40, 41 a, 46 al, 111, 136, 239 b, 243 cr; Buckminster Fuller Institute, Los Angeles (© 1960 The Estate of Buckminster Fuller): 237 b; Photographie Bulloz: 60, 96, 217 a; P. Cayford: 62, 67, 80, 86 r; Martin Charles: 77, 99 r, 212 a, 213 br, 228, 229 c, 236; Moira Clinch: 182, 243 b; Conway Library, Courtauld Institute: 17 b, 37 b, 45, 54 cr, 58, 81, 107 b, 128, 168 l, 192 a, 193 al & br, 214 a; Jeffrey Cook: 69; Peter Cook: 47, 244 a; Catherine Cooke: 34, 106 a; Susan Cunningham: 41 b; Miles Danby: 196 a; Douglas Dickins: 201 bl, 224 b; C M Dixon: 168 r, 172, 174 a, 179 al, 180; Ezra Stoller, Esto: 132; Mary Evans Picture Library: 223 al; GSF Picture Library: 197 al; Giraudon: 72, 94, 103, 123 l; Dimitrios Harissiadis: 175 bl, 177; Malcolm Higgs: 235 cr; Foto Marburg: 20, 123 r, 185 al; Markus Hilbich: 241 al; Angelo Hornak: 31, 32, 33 a, 65, 82, 109, 130, 134 a, 142, 217 cl, 232; The Hutchison Library: 170, 171 al & b, 196 b, 197 ar, cr & b, 199; Instituto de Investigaciones Estéticas: 35 c; Islamic Architecture Archive: 205 c; Hilary James: 185 ar; John James: 184, 185 br, 187 b, 189 br, 191 al, 192 b, 193 br; Japan Information Centre: 208, 209 al; A F Kersting: 15, 19 b, 28, 33 b, 39 c, 43 l, 52, 53 b, 63, 64, 75, 79, 84, 91, 97 a, 100, 112, 113 a, 114, 117 b, 118, 146, 148 b, 156, 185 bl, 186, 187 l, 191 b, 201 br, 203 bl, 205 br, 215 ar & bl, 217 b, 218 a, 219, 220 b, 222, 223 a & bl, 231 al, 229 b; Akademie der Künste: 73, 151, 241 cl; André Laubier: 175 br, 176, 179 bl, 181 br; Douglas McGregor: 219, 223 br; Marlborough Photo Library: 37 a, 226 b, 227 al, 227 br; Garry Martin: 204; Mas: 38, 61, 190; Louise Mereles: 195; Osamu Murai: 150; Museo Archaeologico, Florence: 174 b; Museum of Finnish Architecture: 10 b, 50, 133; Samuel H Kress Collection, National Gallery of Art, Washington: 181 bl; National Portrait Gallery: 11 a, 30, 225 b (by permission of Lord Romsey); Peter Newark: 171 ar; Michael Nicholson: 181 a; Bernard O'Kane: 206, 207; Tomio Ohashi: 209 ar; Paul Oliver: 198; Olympia & York: 120; A & B Peerless· 173 cr, 179 ar, 183 ar, 200 a, 203 br; Josephine Powell: 26, 141; Quarto: 148 a, 173 a, 237; RIBA: 18 c, 22, 88, 127, 138, 145 l, 225 a, 229 a; RIBA (BAL): 10 a, 35 a, 57, 113 b, 124; Georg Riha: 53 a, 76, 99 l, 115 r; Eddie Ryle-Hodges: 51; Yasmin Shariff: 201 a, 203 a & cr; Dennis Sharp: 13, 27, 39 a, 90, 97 b, 105, 107 a, 134 b, 139, 149, 200 b, 202, 234, 235 cl, 240 a, 242, 244 b, 245 a & c; South American Pictures: 115 l; Tange Architects: 209 br; UN: 74; UNESCO (Dominique Roger): 29; University of Virginia Library, Thomas Jefferson Papers: 227 ar; Hiroshi Watanabe: 209 c; Jeremy Whitaker: 11 b, 87; Roger Wilson: 179 br; Frances Wood: 211 a; Xinhua Agency: 210, 211 b.

Whilst every effort has been made to trace and acknowledge all copyright holders, we would like to apologise should any omissions have been made.

Title page picture: Antoni Gaudí, Casa Battló, Barcelona

CONTENTS

THE CONTRIBUTORS

PETER BAREHAM is Senior Lecturer at Brighton Polytechnic School of Architecture and Interior Design. He has a special interest in twentieth-century German design, in particular the work of Dominikus and Gottfried Böhm.
(PB)

DR GEOFFREY BEARD was formerly Director of the Visual Arts Centre at the University of Lancaster. He has written a number of books on architecture and the decorative arts including *Craftsmen and Interior Decoration in England* (awarded the Sir Banister Fletcher Prize), *The National Trust Book of the English House Interior* and monographs on Robert Adam, Sir Christopher Wren and Sir John Vanbrugh.
(GB)

ALAN BLANC is a widely travelled architect and lecturer. Now practising in London, he is also a freelance writer for the *Architects' Journal* and *Building Design* and joint editor of *Steel Construction for Architects*.
(AB)

PETER BLUNDELL JONES is principal lecturer in History and Theory of Architecture at the South Bank Polytechnic, London. He is the author of *Hans Scharoun: A Monograph*. He is currently foreign correspondent for the Swiss magazine *Archithèse* and the Italian magazine *Spazio e Societá*.
(PBJ)

DR IAIN BOYD WHYTE is lecturer in History and Theory of Architecture at the University of Edinburgh. His books include a monograph on Bruno Taut, and he has translated a number of exhibition catalogues and books including *Industrielkultur: Peter Behrens and AEG* (Tilmann Buddensieg). From 1989–90 he was a Getty Scholar and is currently researching Otto Wagner and Berlage for publication at the Getty Center.
(IBW)

JAMES CLARK was in charge of publications at the Royal Institute of British Architects from 1966 to 1971 and is currently a freelance editor and writer.
(JRC)

TIM CLARKE is a specialist writer on architecture and design. Formerly the architecture correspondent for the *Independent*, he now contributes to a variety of architecture and design publications.
(TC)

ROGER CONNAH is an architectural and cultural historian. In 1990 he received the International Architectural Critics Award for his book on the Finnish architect Reima Pietilä, *Fantomas, Fragments, Fictions – an Architectural Journey through the Twentieth Century*.
(RC)

PROFESSOR JEFFREY COOK is a Canadian-trained architect who has written and edited a number of books, including a monograph on Bruce Goff. Known internationally as a proponent of bioclimatic design he is an active member of Passive and Low Energy Architecture and Planning (PLEA) and founding editor of the *Passive Solar Journal*. He holds the Regents Professorship at Arizona State University, Tempe, Az.
(JC)

DR CATHERINE COOKE is widely known as a specialist on Soviet architecture. Her books include *Street Art of the Revolution* and *Architectural Drawings of the Russian Avant-Garde*. She is currently Lecturer in Design at the Open University and a consultant editor of *Architectural Design*.
(CC)

MARK COUSINS is a practising architect and regular contributor to the *Architects' Journal*, who has wide-ranging interests in both architecture and the decorative arts. He has organized a number of exhibitions and is the author of *Twentieth-Century Glass*.
(MC)

CHRISTOPHER DEAN is an architect with his own London-based practice. He has lectured widely in the UK and the US, and is the UK co-ordinator of DOCOMOMO, the recently formed international organization for the protection and conservation of Modern Movement Buildings.
(CD)

PHILIP DREW is an Australian architect, author and architectural critic. His books include *Frei Otto: Form and Structure, Two Towers: Harry Seidler* and *The Architecture of Arata Isozaki*.
(PD)

DAVID HEMSOLL, currently Lecturer in the History of Art at the University of Birmingham, is a specialist in Renaissance and Roman Architecture. He was formerly involved in research at the Warburg Institute, London, for the census of Greek and Roman Antiquities known in the Renaissance.
(DH)

DR JOHN JAMES is a specialist in Medieval architecture. He has published widely and acted as visiting lecturer and Professor in the US, England and France. In 1989 he was appointed Academic Associate Fellow at the University of Melbourne.
(JJ)

IAN LATHAM is editor and publisher of *Architecture Today* which he co-founded in 1989. Previously Deputy Editor of *Building Design*, he has written and contributed to many books and publications. His monograph *Joseph Maria Olbrich* was published in 1980.
(IL)

PROFESSOR ROBERT MACLEOD is Head of Architecture at Brighton Polytechnic School of Architecture and Interior Design. Trained as an architect at the University of British Columbia (UBC), he did his research work at the Courtauld Institute, London. He was Director at the Advanced Institute of Architectural Studies, York, and Head of School at UBC. He is the author of two studies of the Scottish architect Charles Rennie Mackintosh.
(RM)

GARRY MARTIN is an Australian architect with a specialist interest in art history and archaeology who has travelled widely throughout the Islamic world. He has been involved in many building projects in the Middle East and has lectured and written extensively on Islamic architecture.
(GM)

JOHN McKEAN is Head of Interior Design at Brighton Polytechnic School of Architecture and Interior Design and has been active as a visiting lecturer all over Europe. His books include *Learning from Segal: Walter Segal's Life, Work and Influence*, and monographs in the ADT *Architecture in Detail* series.
(JM)

LOUISE NOELLE, former editor of *Arquitectura/México*, is a researcher at the National University of Mexico. In 1988 she was named Honorary Academician of the Society of Mexican Architects.
(LN)

PAUL OLIVER writes and lectures on traditional and indigenous architecture based on his researches throughout the world. Formerly Deputy Head of the School of Architecture at Oxford Polytechnic, his books include *Shelter in Africa* (as contributing editor) and *Dwellings: The House Across the World*. A fellow of the Royal Anthropological Institute, Paul Oliver is also editor of the forthcoming *Encyclopedia of Vernacular Architecture of the World*.
(PO)

BRIGID PEPPIN studied art history at Birkbeck College, London University
(BP) and is a freelance lecturer in art history, specializing in British nineteenth-century art and architecture.

POLLY POWELL is a book editor and writer specializing in architecture and
(PP) the decorative arts. She is the co-author of *Fifties and Sixties Style* and *An Introduction to Twentieth-century Architecture.*

DONALD PROWLER is a practising architect and member of the architectural
(DP) faculty at both Princeton University and the University of Pennsylvania. He is the author of *Modest Mansions.*

YASMIN SHARIFF is a practising architect. She studied Indian Archaeology at
(YS) the School of Oriental and African Studies, London University, and writes and lectures on Indo/Islamic architecture.

PROFESSOR DENNIS SHARP is the author and editor of many books including
(DS) *Modern Architecture and Expressionism* and *Twentieth Century Architecture: A Visual History* (1991). He now edits *World Architecture,* the journal of the International Academy of Architecture from whom he holds the title of Professor of Architecture. He runs his own architectural firm in London. In 1991 the Academie d'Architecture, Paris, awarded him their Silver Medal for his architectural writings.

VLADIMÍR ŠLAPETÁ studied architecture at the Czech Technical University in
(VS) Prague where he is now Vice-Dean of the Architecture Faculty. He is also Head of the Architecture Department of the Prague National Museum of Technology. He is the author of *Czech Functionalism 1918–1938* and *The Brno Functionalists.*

CATHERINE SLESSOR has worked as a technical editor on the *Architects'*
(CS) *Journal* and was voted Architectural Journalist of the Year 1990 by the International Building Press. She is currently a freelance architectural writer.

FAY SWEET is a London-based freelance journalist and author specializing
(FS) in design and architecture. She is a regular contributor to magazines and newspapers including the *Independent, Independent on Sunday, Building Design and Interior Design.*

DR CHRISTOPHER TADGELL is Senior Lecturer in Architectural History at the
(CT) Canterbury School of Architecture. His main fields of research are French classical and Indian architecture; his books include *Ange-Jacques Gabriel, France: Baroque and Rococo Architecture* (ed. Blunt), and *Architecture in India.*

GIORGIO VERRECCHIA is a translator and interpreter for publications such as
(GV) *Art International* and the *AA Quarterly.* He translated Manfredi Tafuri's *Teorie e storia dell'architettura* into English.

HIROSHI WATANABE is a Japanese architectural critic. He has written widely
(HW) for US and Japanese publications including *Progressive Architecture, Art in America* and *Japan Architect.* He is the translator of *Space in Japanese Architecture* (Mitsuo Inoue).

DR FRANCIS WOOD is currently curator in charge of the Chinese section at
(FW) the British Library. Her books include *A Companion to China* and *The Blue Guide to China,* and she is currently working on a book about Chinese domestic architecture.

HOW TO USE THIS BOOK

The book comprises two main sections. Section One provides an A-Z of architects' biographies; this is fully cross-referenced to Section Two, a spread-by-spread visual of the history of architecture and ideas.

BIOGRAPHICAL DICTIONARY

- The use of CAPITALS denotes an architect with a separate entry in the Biographical Dictionary.
- Other notable architects are denoted by the use of **bold** type.
- Standard abbreviations are used as follows: c14 (fourteenth century) N European (North European); all other abbreviations are listed in the Glossary.

☐ List of major buildings/projects includes dates of commencement of a scheme to final construction. In some instances it has only been possible to state the year of completion.

▷ A select bibliography is given for each architect; where applicable books by the individual architects are listed first.

▷ A cross-reference at the end of an entry refers to the appropriate essay in Section Two, placing the architects in an historical context.

ARCHITECTURE AND THE HISTORY OF IDEAS

- The use of CAPITALS in the introductory essay denotes an architect with an entry in the Biographical Dictionary. The reader may therefore refer to Section One for further biographical information.

GLOSSARY OF TERMS AND ABBREVIATIONS

- Architectural styles, movements, terms and abbreviations are here fully defined and explained.

INDEX

- Includes entries for major buildings and projects.

EDITOR'S INTRODUCTION

Architecture is a complex and multi-faceted subject, and one which is frequently surrounded by an aura of mystique. This book aims to bring architecture's many faces into focus, and provide an invaluable source of reference not just to those with a special interest in architecture, but to a broad-based general readership. Both a documentary history of ideas and a biographical dictionary, it fills an obvious gap in the current literature available.

Section One, the Biographical Dictionary, provides full biographical information on architects from many periods and countries. Each entry provides a clear, concise account of the architect's life and work, including birth and death places and a list of major buildings and projects for reference. Dates are given from the commencement of a scheme to final completion; work that may have been destroyed, abandoned or altered is also included. Each entry concludes with a select bibliography for further reading.

Biographical entries are fully cross-referenced to Section Two of the book, a series of visual essays which places architects in their context within the history of architecture and ideas. This section examines the development of national and international movements and isolates new trends, as well as discussing the techniques of building and the materials and methods of construction. The approach here is historical rather than merely stylistic, and examines architectural developments in the light of changing goals and intentions, changes in cultural attitudes and fashions as well as new developments in building technology. These aspects are dealt with as a reflection of architecture's wide role in society. In this section, a conscious effort has been made not to isolate non-Western material nor to devalue it. It appears, therefore, within the broadly chronological sequence of buildings and events.

Over 400 illustrations have been chosen to provide both contemporary and recent views; these also include a number of plans and drawings. An additional feature is the newly-compiled glossary of architectural terms and abbreviations. This includes technical descriptions, acronyms, architectural groups and organizations as well as brief summaries of the chief stylistic changes and movements. The book concludes with a general bibliography and very full index which includes entries for buildings, architects and practices.

All contributions have been prepared by specialist authors and scholars, many of whom are renowned in their own particular fields of architectural study and have brought well tested knowledge and up-to-date scholarship to the work they have done. This specialist input has meant the introduction of valuable and original material, thus providing a unique source of information on architects and architecture on an international basis.

A major problem with a book such as this is knowing where to begin in terms of personalities, dates and sources. After much discussion about the veracity and reliability of information on early architects it was decided to omit from the biographical section those architects who were active before the 1550s, with one notable exception: Vitruvius. Although still an enigma to many scholars, Vitruvius is widely regarded as the patron name of architecture of all periods and without whom the definition of the building art as "commodity, firmness and delight" would be without its initial inspiration.

To encompass within 256 pages not only biographies of twentieth-century and historical figures but an overall history of architectural development, is not an easy task. The obvious temptation constantly to add names to an already full list of architects has had to be restrained. In a few cases the choices we have made may well cause surprise. This choice, however, was never arbitrary, and we have aimed throughout to achieve a balance between the historical and the contemporary whilst maintaining a broad international scope. The result, I believe, is an invaluable source of information not just for those with a special interest in architecture but for a broad-based general readership with a growing desire for more knowledge on the subject.

When this project was first mooted we had little idea of its enormity. Those involved, at all levels of production, are deeply indebted to Senior Editor Christine Davis for her skill, patience, fortitude and unflagging enthusiasm for the whole project. The expertise and tact of sub-editor Judith Wardman proved invaluable, and the exhaustive search by picture researcher Susan Rose-Smith for new and original material is much appreciated.

I would also like to thank all those specialist authors who took time off from their own original projects – or temporarily deviated from their academic or professional duties and commitments – in order to apply themselves to this project. They are all fully acknowledged by name elsewhere, but I would like to add my thanks to each and every one of them.

DENNIS SHARP

LONDON, MAY 1991

1

BIOGRAPHICAL DICTIONARY

AALTO (Henrik Hugo) Alvar

b. Kuortane, Finland, 1898; d. Helsinki, 1976.

The singular figure who established modern architecture in Finland. He studied at Helsinki Polytechnic, graduating in 1921 with all possible honours. His early work showed the familiar signs of a developing Neo-Classicism, but he ruptured the architectural scene in 1929 with his Internationalist-inspired entry for Paimio Sanatorium in the W of Finland. The obvious recall and refinement of LE CORBUSIER into the iconography of the Modern Movement as it was then developing, and the functionalist leap in scale from the domesticated-constructivist reference of the Turun Sanomat Building (1927-9) make Paimio the seminal building for Finnish architecture. As so often throughout Aalto's immense œuvre, his Mediterranean affinities, the Greek and Italian predilections, allowed a remarkable and consistent refinement of the Finnish cultural environment. Many of Aalto's buildings in Finnish towns established a dignity and scale absent both before and after. The white period of "literal functionalism", a cleansing of both national romanticist excess and Neo-Classical limpidity, an absolute explosion

Alvar Aalto

into the rather provincial architectural scene, is nowhere better indicated than in the ill-fated Viipuri Library of 1935. This pivotal building displayed the source and what was to come in later projects. But it would be a mistake to claim a neat identification for Aalto's architectonics so early on: the Villa Mairea (1939) indicated the transformation of romance as it moved into the Finnish landscape. Buildings that in Central Europe lacked regional discipline were given a privilege by Aalto in the Finnish space. It is this transition from the universal versions of modern architecture found in almost all Central European towns and cities to the Italianate refinements Aalto made that left such an influence on Finnish architecture and planning. Where planning was, and still remains, pocket-handkerchief plot isolation, Aalto's complex village semiotics (Säynätsalo, Seinajoki, Jyväskylä, Otaniemi) reinforced the domestic cluster whilst introducing a much-needed complexity to Finnish towns. Possibly because Aalto was neither theoretician nor teacher, his range and output were immense. His work abroad, significant for the response to site, material and form, can be seen best in the projects in Germany, America and Sweden. A useful exercise is to trace Aalto's projects back to the functionalist-hygiene model (the streamlined Paimio) leading to the later marble-clad versions; or then the softer, more ambiguous statements, a lyricism from Viipuri and Mairea into the later red-brick statements (Pensions Institute, Helsinki, 1956, and The House of Culture, 1958). Often at work on multi-

Alvar Aalto, Town Hall, Säynätsalo, 1950–2

ple projects Aalto intermingles ideas and details; an activity that might be said to have led to less rigour in later buildings. It is no surprise that Aalto remains the admired master of many different types of architects, and, like Eliel SAARINEN and PIETILÄ, no doubt his reputation will survive eras of strict rationalism and indiscriminate pluralism.

□ Paimio Sanatorium, Finland, 1929. Viipuri Library, 1935. Villa Mairea, 1939. Baker Dormitory, MIT, 1948. Town Hall, Säynätsalo (1950-52). Sunila Factory, 1954. Pensions Institute, Helsinki, 1956. Opera House, Essen, 1961-89. Cultural Centre, Wolfsburg, 1964. Mount Angel Library, Oregon, USA, 1970. Finlandia Hall, Helsinki, 1975. Riola Church, Italy, 1979.

▷ Alvar Aalto, "The Humanizing of Architecture", *Architectural Forum*, Dec. 1940. Karl Fleig, *Alvar Aalto* (3 vols., 1963, 1971, 1978), Zürich 1983-4. Goran Schildt, *Alvar Aalto: The Early Years*, New York, 1984, and *Alvar Aalto: The Decisive Years*, New York, 1986. W. C. Miller, *Alvar Aalto, A Bibliography*, Illinois, 1976. David Paul Pearson, *Alvar Aalto and the Internationalist Style*, London, 1989. RC

▷ *see also pp238-9*

ABRAMOVITZ Max

see Harrison and Abramovitz

ADAM Robert

b. Kirkcaldy, Fife, 1728; d. London, 1792.

Unquestionably Scotland's most famous architect and one of the most celebrated of British architects. He formed a fertile repertory of new ideas on a visit to Italy (1754-8), and at his return to London he was determined to become the leader of classical revival in England in architecture and decoration. His ability to select and use motifs from the classical antique in an original way led to his success, and his interior designs are one of the finest expressions of C18 artistic achievement. Adam had decided, whilst still in Italy, to measure the ruins of the Roman emperor Diocletian's palace at Spalatro. This experience helped him to abstract the essential details of antiquity, and then infuse them with a personal slant composed of many component pieces. Robert was the second surviving son of **William Adam** (1689-1748). Himself the son of a builder,

Robert Adam

William had become one of the first strictly classical architects working in Scotland. He owed a little to the two principal architects of the previous generation, Sir William Bruce (*c.*1630-1710) and James Smith (*c.*1645-1731), and he used architectural forms as they did, from a wide variety of sources. This gave a "vigorous and sometimes over-dressed character" to the façades of his houses. The same might, unfairly, be said of his son's interior schemes. The most unusual of the interior wall treatments Robert created were those which were based on Etruscan vase decoration. The Etruscan Dressing Room at Osterley Park, Middlesex (1775-6), is the only substantial survival of at least eight such rooms; its fans, palmettes, painted pedestals, urns, sphinxes and roundels of disporting classical figures make a unique pattern. It breaks with the servitude to antiquity in an original way. Adam decorative schemes are associated with a lavish use of colour. This can be observed not only in the actual settings but in their surviving drawings. Some nine thousand of these survive (Sir John Soane's Museum, London), and often surprise by their strength and clarity of colour. The Adam style was created by a true eclectic who incorporated lightness, smallness of ornament, colour, and archaeological, Italian, French and Renaissance influences. That it has enjoyed lasting approval is due to the quality of Robert Adam's directing, if ruthless, mind, which was backed by superb craftsmen and, thanks to his acute business sense, by a family firm to supply all the building materials needed.

□ Hatchlands, Surrey, 1758-61. Harewood House, Yorks., 1759-71. Kedleston Hall, Derbyshire, 1760-70. Osterley Park, Middx, 1761-80. Syon House, Middx, 1762-9. Nostell Priory, Yorks., 1766-70. Newby Hall, Yorks., 1767-80. Saltram, Devon, 1768-9. Chandos House, 2 Queen Anne Street, London, 1771. Royal Society of Arts, London, 1772-4. 20 St James's Square, London, 1772-4. 20 Portman Square, London, 1775-7.

▷ Robert Adam, *The Ruins of the Palace of the Emperor Diocletian at Spalatro in Dalmatia*, 1764; *The Works in Architecture of Robert and James Adam*, 1773-9, 1822. William Adam, *Vitruvius Scoticus*, 1810. John Fleming, *Robert Adam and his Circle in Edinburgh and Rome*, London, 1962. Geoffrey Beard, *The Work of Robert Adam*, London, 1978. John Gifford, *William Adam*, Edinburgh, 1989. GB

Robert Adam, Syon House, 1762–9, Great Hall

ALBERTI Leon Battista

b.Genoa, 1404; d. Rome, 1472.

Leading Renaissance architect, the first theorist of Humanist art. Though born in Genoa, Leon Battista, illegimate son of Benedetto Alberti, belonged to an important Florentine family, exiled, for political reasons, from their city since 1387. His father moved to Venice and Leon Battista studied Latin and Greek in Padua and, subsequently, canon law in Bologna, where he obtained a degree in 1428. In

1429 he was at last able to enter Florence after the Alberti were given back their civil rights. He then visited several Italian towns and settled in Rome in 1443. The year 1447 marked a turning-point in Alberti's life, when the new Pope Nicholas V asked him to take part in the restoration of the ancient buildings in Rome and the great reconstruction of the city. Alberti's ideas found a sympathetic ear in the humanist Pope. Alberti the architect was the product of his own studies and research rather than of a traditional coaching as disciple to one or more masters. A very prolific author, from an early comedy, through philosophy and mathematics, to a late consideration of grammatical reforms, he brought to all his projects an extraordinary intellectual application, seldom matched before or since. His two main writings are *De Pictura* (1435), in which he clearly states the importance of painting as a base for architecture – "can anyone doubt ... painting is ruler of the arts?" (Book II) – and *De Re Aedificatoria* (*c.*1450), his theoretical masterpiece, the first treatise on architecture since the Roman VITRUVIUS. Like Vitruvius's *De Architectura*, Alberti's text consisted of ten books – half homage, half challenge to his illustrious predecessor. Unlike Vitruvius, Alberti is concerned with new ways of doing, rather than simply recording what has been done. Vitruvius tells how buildings were built and Alberti how they should be built, asking also for a new and higher social standing for the architect. The ten books of *De Re Aedificatoria* remained the classic treatise on architecture from C16 to the C18 (the first English edition was published in 1726); virtually every leading architect over this long period was indebted to it. It was with the Tempio Malatestiano in Rimini (*c.*1450) that Alberti became a fully fledged practical architect. The Tempio, meant to be a new enclosure for the old church of San Francesco, was never completed, but the façade and sides show a strict re-creation of ancient sources in which the shapes seem to turn the wall into an enormous sculpture. Between 1444 and 1451 Alberti built the Palazzo Rucellai, Florence, where the interest in the typology of the house he expressed in the treatise is revealed in the fusion of Florentine and Latin tradition. But it is in the façade of Santa Maria Novella, Florence (1458-71), that we find perhaps his best achievement: the pre-existing and newly added parts of the building merge into a clear statement of the new principles. All in all, as Franco Borsi has said "...a personality that was as aggressive on the intellectual level as it was prudent and elusive on the practical".

Leon Battista Alberti, Palazzo Rucellai, Florence, 1444–51

□ Palazzo Rucellai, Florence, 1444-51. Tempio Malatestiano (S. Francesco), Rimini, *c.*1450. Santa Maria Novella, Florence, 1458-71. Rucellai Chapel, S. Pancrazio, Florence, 1460-67. S. Sebastiano, Mantua, 1460. Sant'Andrea, Mantua, 1470. Santissima Annunziata (Tribuna), Florence, 1470.

▷ Leon Battista Alberti, *On Painting and Sculpture*, ed. and trans. Cecil Grayson, London 1972; *On the Art of Building in Ten Books*, tr. Joseph Rykwert, Neil Leach and Robert Tavernor, New Haven, 1988. Franco Borsi, *Leon Battista Alberti*, tr. Rudolf G. Carpanini, Oxford, 1977. GV

▷ *see also pp212-3*

ALEIJADHINO

b. Ouro Preto, 1738; d. 1814.

Brazil's greatest Baroque architect and sculptor. Antonío Francisco Lisboa, known as "O Aleijadhino" (the little cripple), was the illegitimate son of a Portuguese stonemason and an African slave. He originally trained as a stonemason, apprenticed to his father and registered as a fully fledged craftsman in 1766. At that time, in the absence of an established architectural body, stonemasons were responsible for the design of churches, hiring other craftsmen to develop the basic plans as required. In 1766 Aleijadhino's father died while working on the church of Sao Francisco de Assis in Ouro Preto, leaving his son to complete the job. Aleijadhino went on to work on a succession of churches in the rich gold-mining province of Minas Gerais (SE Brazil). A true Baroque artist and superlative craftsman, his work combines sinuous and emotionally charged sculptural decoration with the traditionally simple form of Lusitanian church design. His childhood enthusiasm for biblical scriptures provides the inspiration for many of his sculptures and interior church decorations. At the age of 39 he contracted a debilitating disease which left his hands and feet horribly disfigured; despite this he continued to work with his carving tools strapped to his hands.

Aleijadhino, Church of Sao Fransisco de Assis, Ouro Preto, 1766–76

□ Sao Francisco de Assis Church, Ouro Preto, 1766-76. Nosso Senhor do Bom Jesus de Matosinhas Church, Congonhas do Campo (sanctuary, courtyard and statuary), 1777-1805.

▷ Rodrigo José Ferreira Bretas, *Antonio Francisco Lisboa – O Aleijadhino*, Rio de Janeiro, 1951. John Bury, "Estilo Aleijadhino and the Churches of Eighteenth Century Brazil", *Architectural Review*, 111, Feb. 1952. CS

ALEOTTI Giovanni Battista

b. L'Argenta, 1546; d. Ferrara, 1636.

Influential Italian architect, engineer and writer of the early C17. Very little is known of his formal education, but his sphere of influence included architecture, hydraulic engineering, stage design, military engineering and the formulation of theoretical and technical studies. Aleotti first rose to prominence in the city of Ferrara, where his early patron, Duke Alfonso II d'Este, secured several prestigious commissions for him in the years 1575-97. In 1598 he was appointed City Architect for Ferrara. Aleotti's technical understanding was considerable, and his advice and expertise were much in demand in cities such as Rome, Modena, Venice and Piacenza. His most celebrated project is undoubtedly the Teatro Farnese, Parma, often cited as an early model for the modern theatre. The commission from Ranuccio I Farnese was part of an elaborate celebration to mark an impending marriage between the rival families of the Farnese and the Florentine Medici. The initial conversion of the armoury in the Pilotta, Palazzo Nuovo, required only a few months' work, but the internal decoration was to take almost ten years. Aleotti's design was the first to use stage wings to facilitate set changes, heralding the development of the box theatre.

□ Santa Maria del Quartiere, Parma, 1604. S. Carlo, Ferrara, 1613-23. Teatro Farnese, Parma, 1618-28.

▷ Per Bjurstrom, *Giacomo Torelli and Baroque Stage Design*, Stockholm, 1961. Margarete Baur-Heinhold, *The Baroque Theatre*, New York, 1967. Bruno Adorni, *L'Architettura Farnesiana a Parma 1546-1630*, Parma, 1974.

MC

ARCHER Thomas

b. Umberslade, Warwicks., 1668; d. Hale, Hants., 1743.

Distinguished English architect, strongly influenced by the Baroque architecture of Italy, which he studied at first hand. The son of a country gentleman, Archer was educated at Trinity College, Oxford, and then travelled in Europe (1691-5). On his return, he used his connections to secure the post of Court Groom in 1705 and, ten years later, the more lucrative sinecure of Controller of Customs at Newcastle. He took up architecture in his mid-thirties, without any formal training or apprenticeship. Initially he was appointed as one of the Commissioners for the Building of Fifty New Churches under the Act of 1711, but failed to replace VANBRUGH when the latter was dismissed in 1713 and reinstated the following year. A competent draughtsman and designer, Archer worked privately for members of the aristocracy on large town houses such as Harcourt House (1725) and Russell House (1716-17) in London. He was influenced by the Italian Baroque of BORROMINI and BERNINI, which he encountered during his excursions to Rome, and was more familiar with continental Baroque than his contemporaries HAWKSMOOR and Vanbrugh. His work is distinguished not only by his literal adoption of mature Roman Baroque motifs, but also by his manipulation of space and his taste for the curved plane, as exemplified by his two London churches (St John's, Smith Square and St Paul's, Deptford) and Chettle House in Dorset. A man of considerable property, Archer was buried on his estate in Hale, Hants., under the north transept of the estate's church, which he had renovated during his lifetime, and opposite a monument of his own design.

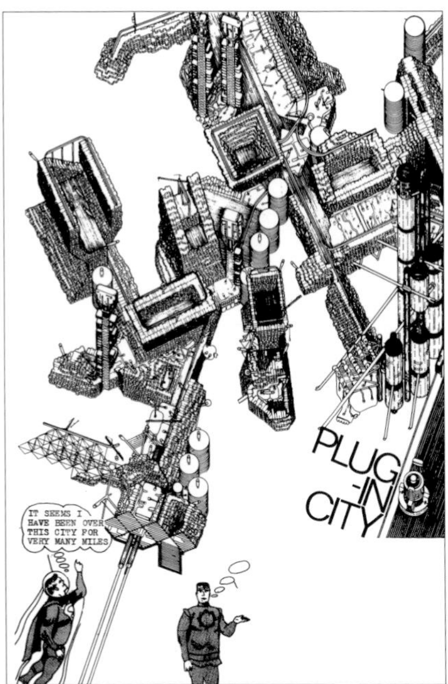

Archigram/Peter Cook, Plug-in-City, 1964–6, project

□ Chatsworth House, Derbyshire (N front), 1704-5. Garden Pavilion, Wrest Park, Beds., 1709-11. Birmingham Cathedral, 1710-15. Chettle House, Dorset, from 1711. St Paul's Church, Deptford, London, 1713-30. St John's Church, Smith Square, London, 1713-30.

▷ Kerry Downes, *English Baroque Architecture*, London, 1966. Marcus Whiffen, *Thomas Archer: Architect of the English Baroque*, Los Angeles, 1973.

CS

ARCHIGRAM

Established 1961.

A loose-knit collective of radical British architects, initially consisting of Warren Chalk (1927-87), Peter Cook (b. 1936), Dennis Crompton (b. 1935), David Greene (b. 1937), Ron Herron (b. 1930), Mike Webb (b. 1937). In 1961 the group issued the first instalment of its occasional journal *Archigram*, a two-page propaganda newssheet-cum-manifesto describing a position that might now be referred to as aesthetic technocratic idealism. Most of the members of the group were closely associated with the Architectural Association School, London, but over the following years some of them took up academic positions elsewhere, notably the USA. However, the residual group – Cook, Herron, Chalk, Crompton – remained as teachers at the AA. Archigram has been described as the pop group of modern architecture; throughout its history its ambitious slide, light and music shows have had a strong following. The group's first major project was the controversial "Living City" exhibition held in 1963 at the ICA, London, an organization of which Peter Cook was later to act for a short time as Director (1972-4). Archigram's *Lieber Meister* and guru was the distinguished British architectural critic and historian Reyner Banham, who contributed much to the international and lasting credibility of the group as well as of its individual designers. Herron and Cook have had successful one-man exhibitions and collective shows with other Archigram members. Both have also pursued successful professional careers, with Herron's Imagination building in Store Street, London (1989) reaping a harvest of architectural awards. The group was never formally constituted, but has exerted a tremendous influence, particularly on students. (Archigram Architects, comprising Cook, Herron and Crompton, ran from 1969 to 1975.) It was left to individual members to produce issues of *Archigram* magazine, which was issued between 1961 and 1970, when it ceased because of escalating production costs. Its story is told in Peter Cook's *Archigram* anthology (1974).

□ Fulham Study, 1963. Plug-in City by Peter Cook, 1964-6. Walking City by Ron Herron, 1964. Cushicle project by Mike Webb, 1966-7. Instant City by Peter Cook, 1969-70, and Inflatable Suit House by Greene, 1968. The Archigram Capsule, Expo70, Osaka, Japan. Summer Casino, Monte Carlo, 1971. Exhibit for Malaysia, Commonwealth Institute, London, 1973.

▷ The journal *Archigram* was published from London 1961-70. *Living City* (exhibition catalogue), London, 1963. Peter Cook, *Architecture, Action and Plan*, London, 1967; *Archigram*, London 1974. DS

▷ *see also pp240-41*

D'ARONCO Raimondo

b. Gemona, Italy, 1857; d. San Remo, 1932.

Leading Italian Art Nouveau architect. After apprenticeship to a stonemason in Austria, he attended classes at the Accademia delle Belli Arte at Venice. From 1880 to 1892 he taught at various institutions, while extending his professional reputation with a series of ambitious competition entries. In 1892 he was summoned to Istanbul by Sultan Abdul Hamid to design the 1st National Ottoman Exhibition. Though this was cancelled because of a severe earthquake, D'Aronco remained in Istanbul as an official architect. He rebuilt the damaged city and subsequently designed a library complex at Yildiz and other works in a free "Arte Nova" style inspired both by Turkish architectural forms and by the Austrian Secession. Meanwhile he won (1900) the competition to design the 1902 Turin International Exhibition of the Decorative Arts. His pavilions (the construction of which he monitored by daily letters from Istanbul) used exposed building materials and a freely inventive vocabulary to create a visual counterpoint to the radical political ideals with which the new art was associated. He returned to Italy in 1908 and reverted to a classical style for the Palazzo Comunale, Udine. Elected to the Italian Parliament in 1910, he was an Associate of the Politecnico of Naples and Vice-Superintendent of excavations at Pompeii (1911-17).

□ International Exhibition of the Visual Arts, Turin, 1902. Main Pavilion, Udine Exhibition, 1903. Italian Embassy Summer Residence, Therapia, 1905. Library, Yildiz, 1907. Palazzo Comunale, Udine, 1908-30.

▷ Manfredi Nicoletti, *Raimondo d'Aronco*, Milan, 1955; *D'Aronco e l'Architettura Liberty*, Italy, 1982. BP

ARUP ASSOCIATES

Established London, 1963.

Sir **Ove Arup** (b. Newcastle upon Tyne, 1895; d. London, 1988) was undoubtedly the foremost engineer of his generation. The firm of Arup & Partners was founded in 1946 as structural consultants and has played a significant role in the realization of many major projects. Arup Associates, formed in 1963 by Arup, the architect **Philip Dowson** (b. Johannesburg, 1924) and others, was intended to operate as a multi-disciplinary office embracing not only architecture and quantity surveying but also structural, mechanical and electrical engineering, all within one core organization, thus achieving a greater degree of control and efficiency. The firm now numbers over 50 offices and approximately 3000 staff worldwide. Such overwhelming success was principally due to the personal vision of Ove Arup, who maintained his belief in architectural pragmatism, where design is essentially a practical fulfilment of society's needs. His own academic career at Copenhagen University embraced not only civil engineering but also philosophy and mathematics. It was his desire to look beyond the narrow confines of a single profession which led to his role within the Modern Architecture Research Group (MARS) and subsequent collaborative projects with Berthold LUBETKIN and the Tecton Group during the 1930s.

□ Kingsgate Footbridge, Durham, 1963. Wolfson Building, Oxford, 1964-7. Maltings Concert Hall, Snape, Suffolk, 1967. Bush Lane House, London, 1970-76. Lloyds Headquarters Building, Chatham, 1977-80.

▷ Ove Arup, *Ove Arup and Partners 1946-86*, London, 1986. Michael Brawne, *Arup Associates – the Biography of an Architectural Practice*, London, 1983. MC

ASAM BROTHERS

Cosmas Damian Asam, b. Benediktbeuern, 1686; d. Munich, 1739. Egid Quirin Asam, b. Tegernsee, 1692; d. Mannheim, 1750.

German brothers who were the leading exponents of Bavarian Baroque architecture. During their lifelong partnership the Asam brothers showed themselves to be architects of great innovation and sensi-

Above: Sir Ove Arup, Kingsgate Footbridge, Durham, 1963

Right: Asam brothers, Church of St Johann Nepomuk, Munich, 1733–40

tivity, although neither received any formal architectural training (Cosmas Damian originally studied painting at the Accademia di S. Luca in Rome, while Egid Quirin trained in Munich with the sculptor Andreas Faistenberger from *c.*1714 to 1716). Sons of a Bavarian painter, the brothers did not emerge from provincial obscurity until they visited Rome (1711-14), where they eagerly absorbed the stylistic principles of Italian Baroque. Their reasons for turning to architecture are undocumented, but their built output was relatively small, totalling just four churches, executed between 1714 and 1738, plus numerous individual commissions for frescoes and sculptures. However, the main body of their work was concerned with "baroquizing" the interiors of existing churches – whether medieval ones, such as the Cathedral at Freising, or contemporary ones completed by other architects, such as the enormous Swiss pilgrimage church at Einsiedeln. Their churches and interiors display the sublimely melodramatic and emotionally charged influence of Roman Baroque ingeniously adapted to Bavarian settings.

□ Benedictine Abbey, Weltenberg, 1716-35. Cathedral, Freising (interior decoration), 1723-4. Benedictine Abbey, Einsiedeln, Switzerland (interior decoration), 1724-6. St Johann Nepomuk, Munich, 1733-40.

▷ Henry-Russell Hitchcock, *Rococo Architecture in Southern Germany*, London, 1968. Bernard Rupprecht and Wolf von der Mulbe, *Die Brüder Asam: Sinn und Sinnlichkeit im Bayerischen Barock*, Regensburg, 1980. CS

▷ *see also pp218-19*

ASHBEE Charles Robert

b. London, 1863; d. nr Sevenoaks, 1942.

Leading member of the Arts & Crafts movement. He was educated at King's College, before becoming a pupil of BODLEY & GARNER, one of the most effective Gothic Revival practices of the day. Ashbee's commitment to the Arts & Crafts ideals was a natural outcome of his training under Bodley. In 1888 he founded the Guild and School of Handicraft in the East End of London, where he established training in the arts and crafts, particularly the design and manufacture of furniture. In 1902 he moved the entire establishment to Chipping Campden in Gloucestershire with a total Guild membership of 50 plus some hundred dependants. He thus anticipated by one year the establishment in nearby Sapperton of the workshops of Ernest Gimson and the brothers Barnsley. His architectural work is firmly bedded in the Arts & Crafts tradition, with a spareness and restraint not always characteristic of VOYSEY or BAILLIE SCOTT. In his pursuit of the Arts & Crafts ideals he is notable for two particular characteristics: he was almost unique in drawing attention to the work of the brothers GREENE and Frank Lloyd WRIGHT in America; and in his essay *Should We Stop Teaching Art?* (1911) he drew attention to the changing nature of industrial patronage and client organization.

□ Magpie and Stump House, Chelsea, London, 1897. 37 Cheyne Walk, 72-4 Cheyne Walk, 38-9 Cheyne Walk, London, variously between 1897 and 1899. 52 industrial cottages around Birchfield Road, Ellesmere Port, Cheshire, 1906. Byways, Yarnton, Oxford, 1907. Villa San Giorgio, beside San Pancrazio Church, Taormina, Sicily, 1907. 1049-1054 Squirrel's Heath Avenue, Romford, Essex, 1911.

▷ C. R. Ashbee, *Should We Stop Teaching Art?*, London, 1911; *Modern English Silverwork* (1909, reprinted London, 1974). A. Crawford, *C. R. Ashbee, Architect, Designer, and Romantic Socialist*, New Haven and London, 1985. Fiona McCarthy, *C. R. Ashbee in the Cotswolds*, London, 1981. RM

ASPLUND Erik Gunnar

b. Stockholm, 1885; d. Stockholm, 1940.

Sweden's leading C20 architect. He began his career as a painter but later studied architecture at the Royal Institute of Technology, Stockholm (1905-9) and worked privately under TENGBOM, Westman and ÖSTBERG. He also travelled widely in Sweden and other parts of Europe and entered a number of competitions, winning two for school buildings in 1912 and 1913. In 1913 he also won first prize for the extension for the Law Courts, Gothenburg, a project he completed in 1937. In 1914, with Sigurd LEWERENTZ, he won the international competition for the Stockholm South

Cemetery at Enskede, where two of his most famous buildings reside. In the years 1912-18 he also worked as an architectural teacher, and he edited a Swedish architectural magazine 1917-20. In 1920 he visited the USA to research public libraries for his Stockholm City Library commission. He designed his Skandia Cinema, Stockholm, in the early 1920s. However, by the end of the decade he, too, had become a committed Modernist like Sven MARKELIUS and Lewerentz. He designed the layout for the Stockholm Exhibition in 1930; the Paradise Restaurant that he built was a *tour de force*. The exhibition itself contained many buildings, including a modern housing section which sought to point the way "to a new architecture and a new life". He was a signatory to the *Acceptera* manifesto of 1931. Aplund moved away from Modernism soon after the exhibition had closed indicating a sympathy towards stripped Nordic classicism. During the period from 1931 until his death he produced many competion entries, a number of which were premiated. He was professor of architecture at the Royal Institute of Technolkogy, Stockholm, and during this last decade built a number of structures, including the impressive Crematorium at the Wood land Cemetery, Enskede. After the war the

Gunnar Asplund, City Library, Stockholm, 1920–28

legacy of his work received international acknowledgment whilst the work of his former colleague, Sigurd Lewerentz, began to assume great architectural significance.

□ Gothenburg law Courts (extension and rebuilt) 1913, 1925, 1934-7. First prize and commission, Woodland Cemetery, Stockholm South Burial Ground, Skogskyrkogarden, (with S. Lewerentz), 1915. Woodland Chapel, Stockholm South Burial Ground, 1918-20. Stockholm City Library, 1920-28. Skandia Cinema, Stockholm, 1922-3. Town Plan for the area around Observatory, Stockholm, 1923. Project for 1925 Paris Exhibition, 1924. Cemetery at Kviberg, Gothenburg (competition first prize) Stockholm Exhibition, 1928-30. Bredenberg department store, Stockholm, 1933-5. Crematorium at the Woodland Cemetery, Stockholm, 1935-40.

▷ Bruno Zevi, *Erik Gunnar Asplund,* Milan, 1948. Stewart Wrede, *The Architecture of Gunnar Asplund*, Cambridge, Mass., 1980. *Gunnar Asplund 1885-1940: The Dilemma of Classicism*, Architectural Association, London, 1988. Holmdahl, C. and S. I. Lind and K. Odeen, *Gunnar Asplund Architect 1885–1940*, Stockholm, 1950 (re-issued 1986). DS

▷ *see also pp238-9*

BAILLIE SCOTT Mackay Hugh

b. near Ramsgate, 1865; d. Brighton, 1945.

British architect whose long career was almost exclusively concerned with the design of the smaller country house and its furnishings, and was supplemented by wide publication of his work in Europe and America as well as at home. He was initially trained at the Royal Agricultural College, Cirencester, with a view to managing his father's estates in Australia, but after graduation he decided on a career in architecture and was articled to the Bath City Architect, Major Charles E. Davis. This seems to have been a singularly unhelpful preparation, except for some experience gained in recording Roman pavings and in the restoration of some churches in N Somerset. Baillie Scott's career extended over a fifty-year period from 1889 to 1939, producing almost 300 building designs (from 1919 with A. Edgar Beresford), but its chief interest lies in his domestic work up to 1907, which, published and promulgated by Hermann MUTHESIUS and Alexander Koch in Germany and by W. Shaw Sparrow, Raffles Davison and Baillie Scott himself in England, reached a wide international audience. As a more comprehensive and

M. H. Baillie Scott, White Lodge, Wantage, Berks, 1898-99.

richer manifestation of the English "Free School" than VOYSEY, Baillie Scott's work influenced the Deutscher Werkbund through Muthesius, and almost certainly the Chicago School and early work of Frank Lloyd WRIGHT. The chief characteristics of his mature work were a commitment to cosy romantic rural detail, married to an interesting and assured handling of open planning and the disposition of internal space. Scott's reputation has unjustly suffered in that he continued to work well into the period of the Modern Movement without either adopting the paucity of that movement's programme for design or moving significantly from the position he had reached during the first decade of the C20.

□ Semi-detached houses, Douglas, Isle of Man, 1895-6. School and Master's house, Peel, Isle of Man, 1897. White Lodge, Wantage, Berkshire, 1898-9. Bill House, Selsey-on-Sea, Sussex, 1907. Sandy Holt, Blackhills Road, Esher, Surrey, 1931-2.

▷ M. H. Baillie Scott. *Houses and Gardens*, London, 1906. M. H. Baillie Scott and A. Beresford, *Houses and Gardens*, London, 1933. James D. Kornwolf, *M. H. Baillie Scott and the Arts and Crafts Movement*, Baltimore and London, 1972. RM

▷ *see also pp228-9*

BAKEMA Jacob Berend

see Van den Brock & Bakema

BAKER Sir Herbert

b. Cobham, Kent, 1862;
d. Cobham, 1946.

British architect who received many important international commissions, for which he developed a largely classical "Colonial" style. Baker was trained in Victorian times, but his career only developed well into the C20. He began his architectural training in the office of Arthur Baker but, at the age of twenty, joined Sir Ernest George's practice, where he met LUTYENS. At the suggestion of Cecil Rhodes, Baker moved to South Africa, where he completed a number of important state buildings. In 1912 Baker and Lutyens won one of the most important commissions of the period: to design the state buildings at New Delhi. At a time when the seeds of Modernism were being sown throughout Europe and America, Baker chose to design in a High Edwardian style with its feet firmly in the classical vocabulary of the Baroque. After the First World War he returned to practise in England, where he was knighted (1923) and awarded the RIBA Royal Gold Medal (1927).

□ Groote Schur, South Africa, 1890. Stonehouse, Johannesburg, South Africa, 1902. Government House and Union Buildings, Pretoria, South Africa, 1905 onwards and 1910-13. Legislative Buildings, New Delhi, from 1912. Bank of England, London, 1921. War Memorial Cloister, Winchester College, Winchester, 1922-4. India House, London, 1925. South Africa House, London, 1930.

▷ Herbert Baker, *Plas Mawr, Conway, North Wales*, London, 1888; *Cecil Rhodes by his Architect*, London 1934. PP

Sir Herbert Baker, Legislative Buildings, New Delhi, 1912

BARRAGÁN Luis

b. Guadalajara, Jalisco, Mexico, 1902;
d. Mexico City, 1988.

Key Mexican pioneer of "regionalism" in architecture. He studied engineering in his native city and graduated in 1924. In 1925-6 he travelled widely in Europe, where his future development was shaped by the Moorish architecture in S. Spain, Mediterranean constructions, Ferdinand Bac and his gardens, the theories of Frederick KIESLER, and particularly LE CORBUSIER's conferences. After his return to Mexico he accomplished some works in the International Style, but it was only in 1945, when he planned a series of gardens, and in 1947, with the design of his house, that his own style shone through. Thus he was able to achieve a synthesis of diverse teachings, together with his memories of small towns in the State of Jalisco, without forgetting the influence of two artists, Jesús Reyes Ferreira and Mathias Goeritz. Goeritz is of unique importance for his *Emotional Architecture* manifesto in 1953; Barragán adopted the term to define his own work. His architecture is interested in vernacular roots and is at the same time a quest for spiritual considerations, exalting beauty and harmony with nature. These concerns are evidenced by massive constructions, thick walls and small openings, by the use of artisan materials, thick textures and bright colours of popular extraction. Light and water are of particular importance in Barragán's compositions.

☐ Houses for the Prieto family (1950), the architect himself, Tacubaya (1947), and the Gálvez (1959), Egestrom (1968) and Gilardi (Tacubaya, 1976) families. Chapel of the Sacramentarian Capuchins (Capilla para las Capuchinas Sacramentarias), Mexico City, 1955. Jardines del Pedregal (1950) and Las Arboledas (1959). Torres de Ciudad Satélite, (in collaboration with Mathias Goeritz), 1957.

▷ Emilio Ambaz, *The Architecture of Luis Barragán*, New York, 1976. Enrique De Anda (ed.), *Luis Barragán, clásico del silencio*, Colombia, 1989. LN

BARRY Sir Charles

b. London, 1795; d. London, 1860.

Leading British Neo-Classical architect of the C19 whose career was crowned with the winning of the national competition for the Houses of Parliament. The son of a successful London stationer, Barry was articled, at the age of 15, to a firm of Lambeth surveyors. After unusually extensive travels in Greece, Turkey, and Egypt, he became one of the most successful practitioners of the day, drawing on a diversity of styles, including Greek, Italian Renaissance, and Elizabethan. His use of the early C16 Italian palaces as his models for the Travellers' Club (1833-7) and Reform Club (1835) influenced later urban developments in London and Edinburgh. The articulation of the buildings as free-standing entities, with massive cornice capping an elevation in which equal dominance was given to the ground floor and the first, was a marked departure from Georgian precedent. Barry's winning of the competition for the Houses of Parliament with major input from A. W. N. PUGIN in 1836 started a preoccupation which was to dominate the rest of his life. The continued participation of Pugin, to a degree which is still not certain, cast a shadow of contention over his work which did not end with Pugin's death. He was awarded the RIBA Gold Medal in 1850 and knighted in 1852.

☐ St Peter's Church, Brighton, 1824–8. Travellers's Club, London, 1833–7. Reform Club, London, 1835. Houses of Parliament, London competition 1836; 1839-52. Highclere House, Hants., 1842. Cliveden, Bucks., 1850–51.

▷ Alfred Barry, *Memoir of the Life and Works of Sir Charles Barry*, 1867 (reprinted 1970). RM

Sir Charles Barry, Houses of Parliament, London, 1836–52, drawing

BARTNING Otto

b. Karlsruhe, 1883; d. Darmstadt, 1959.

Remembered primarily as one of the major German Evangelical church architects of his generation. Educated at the Technische Hochschule, Berlin-Charlottenburg, and the Technische Hochschule, Karlsruhe, he commenced practice in 1905 and continued working until 1951. He designed his first church in 1906. He held a lifelong interest in the Lutheran liturgy. His aesthetic development was reflected in the ideas and aspirations of the early 1920s. There were firstly "Arts & Crafts" buildings in the Gothic manner, studies in Expressionism and finally designs where detail and decoration were stripped down to the minimum. Bartning's commitment to Expressionism included membership of the Novembergruppe and the Arbeitsrat für Kunst (Workers' Council for Art) from 1918. Later, he became a member of "Der Ring". A number of his Expressionist projects were published, including some villas. This period culminated in the famous "Sternkirche" project of 1921, a polygonal star-shaped church with a tiered floor under a multiple shell roof of timber construction. Though it was not erected, these themes were returned to in the built projects that followed. From 1926 to 1953 he built or reconstructed some 130 churches, including his celebrated Steel Church in Cologne (1929). Bartning's mature designs built in the 1920s and 30s

Otto Bartning, Star Church, 1921, section and plan

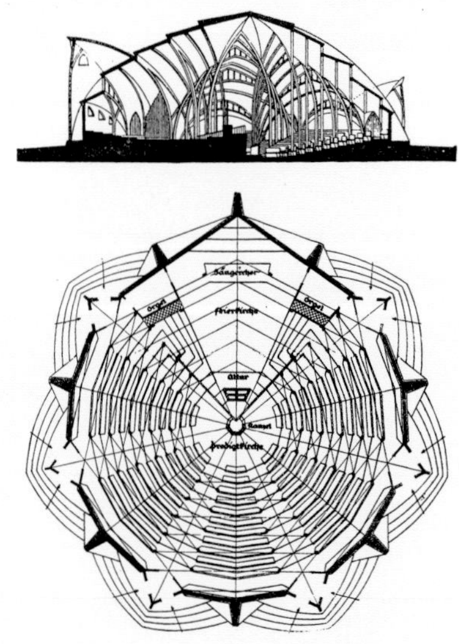

reveal considerable talents in merging Expressionism into the mainstream of Modernism. His *Vom neuen Kirchbau* (1919) was a most influential book in its time. From 1951 until his death he was President of the BDA. After the Bauhaus moved to Dessau Bartning was appointed Director of the Bauhochschule in Weimar, 1925-9. Never a member of the Nazi party he did however remain in Germany during the war years and in 1946 became Chairman of the reconstituted German Werkbund.

□ Sternkirche (project), 1921. Danish Church, Berlin, 1922. Steel Church, Pressa, Cologne, 1929. Rundkirche, Essen, 1929. Evangelical Church, Dornbirn bei Bregenz, Austria, 1931. Gustav-Adolf Evangelical Church, Berlin, 1931-3. St Mark's Evangelical Church, Baden, Karlsruhe, 1935. Evangelical Churches at Chemnitz, St Blasien, Stetten am Heuberg, 1936-9. After the Second World War, approximately 50 churches utilizing bomb rubble for concrete, with roofs of light timber trusses.

▷ Otto Bartning, *Vom neuen Kirchbau*, Berlin, 1919; *Was ist Bauen?*, Stuttgart, 1952; *Kirchen*, Vol. II, Munich, 1959. Hans Meyer, *Der Baumeister Otto Bartning und die Wiederentdeckung des Raumes*, Heidelberg, 1951. DS

BASEVI George

b. 1794; d. Ely, 1845.

An early C19 London-based architect whose classical work reflected the transition from Georgian repose to Victorian restlessness. Usefully connected to the wealthy D'Israeli and Ricardo families, Basevi was articled to Sir John SOANE (1810-16) and studied at the Royal Academy Schools. After travelling in Italy, Greece and Turkey (1816-19), he set up practice in London, and during the following decades designed several of the most fashionable terraces and squares of brick and stucco in the expanding suburbs of Belgravia, Kensington and Pimlico. For the Fitzwilliam Museum at Cambridge he created a Corinthian façade that epitomized and probably helped to stimulate the early Victorian shift from Neo-Classical restraint towards a more Baroque exuberance.

George Basevi, Fitzwilliam Museum, Cambridge, 1836–45

□ Belgrave Square, London (apart from the corner mansions), 1825-40. For the Thurloe estate: Alexander Square etc., 1827-30; Thurloe Square, 1843. For the Trustees of Dr Smith's Charity: Pelham Crescent and Place, Brompton (now Egerton) Crescent, Walton Place, from 1833. Fitzwilliam Museum, Cambridge, 1836-45. Conservative Club, St James's, London (with Sidney Smirke), 1843-4. Country houses: Gatcombe Park, Glos. (alterations), *c.* 1820; Painswick House, Glos., 1827-32.

▷ Dorothy Stroud, *The Thurloe Estate*, London, 1959; *The South Kensington Estate of Henry Smith's Charity*, London, 1975. BP

DE BAUDOT Joseph Eugène Anatole

b. Sarrebourg, 1834; d. Paris, 1915.

French architect who links the rationalist theories of VIOLLET-LE-DUC and Modernism. He began his training in the atelier of LABROUSTE and then went to study under Viollet-le-Duc. For the rest of his long career he was an exponent of V-l-D's rationalist and structuralist doctrines of Gothic architecture against the intuitive academic Beaux-Arts tradition exemplified by GARNIER's triumphant Paris Opéra. Baudot's masterpiece, the church of Saint-Jean-de-Montmartre (1894-1904), uses Gothic ribs in reinforced concrete and is reminiscent of the work of HORTA and other Art Nouveau architects. By the time it was completed, PERRET had already built his flats in the rue Franklin in Paris and the novelty of concrete construction had passed. For the remaining ten years of his life, Baudot created a large number of imaginative schemes which grew out of the theories of Viollet-le-Duc and anticipate some of the schemes of Pier Luigi NERVI.

□ Saint-Lubin, Rambouillet, 1865-9. Lycée Lakanal, Sceaux, 1882-8. Lycée Victor Hugo, Paris, 1894-6. Saint-Jean de Montmartre, Paris, 1894-1904.

Anatole de Baudot, Saint-Jean-de-Montmartre, Paris, 1894–1904

▷ Anatole de Baudot, *L'Architecture, le Passé, le Présent*, Paris, 1916. E. E. Viollet-le-Duc, *Entretiens sur L'Architecture*, Paris, 1863-72. TC

BBPR Studio

Established 1932.

Early protagonists in the introduction of modern architecture to Italy, BBPR were also one of the first practices to reject dogmatic Modernism in favour of a more considered contextualist approach. Gianluigi Banfi (1910-45), Lodovico Belgiojoso (b. 1900), Enrico Peressutti (1908-73) and Ernesto Nathan Rodgers (1909-69) had studied together at the Milan Polytechnical Institute, where all four had submitted hard-edged Modernist thesis projects. They formed a partnership in 1932 at a time when the Rationalists held sway and the Fascists held power. They fought for the resistance movement in the Second World War, and later provided a focus for the post-war surge in Italian design. BBPR employed a contextualist approach which could accommodate the partners' belief in architecture's *adherence to circumstance*. This shifting of priorities was intended not to deny the continuity of Modernism but to emphasize the importance of integrating new buildings into the existing city fabric. This demanded a respect for history and a concern for symbolism and allusion. BBPR's mature work of the 1950s and 60s demonstrates their heightened awareness of the surrounding context and anticipates more recent developments within the architectural profession.

Heliotherapy Clinic, Legnano, 1938. Sforza Castle Museum, Milan, 1954-6. Torre Valasca, Milan, 1955-8. Piazzale Meda Offices, Milan, 1969. Chase Manhattan Bank, Milan, 1969.

Renato Pedio, *Architettura – In the Barracks of the Geometry of Death*, Rome, 1980. Antonio Pavia, *BBPR a Milano*, Milan, 1982. G. Jamona, *Casabella: The Architecture of Continuity*, Milan, 1982. MC

BEHNISCH Günter

b. Dresden, 1922.

Contemporary German architect whose firm's work is seen as part of the organic tradition in modern architecture. Trained at the Technical University, Stuttgart, he worked in 1951 for a year with local architect Professor Rolf Gutbrod before commencing practice on his own account. In 1967 he formed Günter Behnisch and Partner, which operates today with over 50 architects. The 1960s work was largely concerned with prefabricated school building. Growing disillusion with this kind of rigidly systematized construction forced Behnisch into a new direction: to seek out free, more varied, flexible forms and more ecologically balanced designs. Thus he revivified an interest in the organic/functional tradition in Modernism which harks back to SCHAROUN and HÄRING and which Gutbrod had been closely identified with. The idea that "new techniques and new materials lead to new orders and new possibilities" is central to Behnisch's thinking and is demonstrated effectively in such schemes as the Library for the Catholic University at Eichstadt (1985-7), the remarkable-looking solar-responsive Hysolar Institute at the University, Stuttgart (1986-7), and the Postal Museum of Frankfurt-am-Main (won in competition in 1982). His best-known project is the Olympic Park created at Munich for the 1972 Olympic Games, on which Frei OTTO was consulted on the oversailing lightweight roofs.

Olympic Park, Munich, 1969-72. Secondary School, Schufersfeld in Lorch, 1975-87. Hans Keller House (Lutheran), Stuttgart, 1983-4. Library, University of Eichstadt, 1985-7. Hysolar Institute, University of Stuttgart, 1986-7. Postal Museum, Frankfurt, 1982-90.

Behnisch and Partner, Stuttgart, 1975. Günter Behnisch, "Das neue ist nicht Alte", *Deutsche Bauzeitung*, Sept. 1987. C. Kandzia (ed.) *Behnisch and Partner: Designs 1958-87*, Stuttgart, 1988. DS

see also pp244-5

BEHRENS Peter

b. Hamburg, 1868; d. Berlin, 1940.

A key figure in the transition from Jugendstil to industrial Classicism who played a central role in the evolution of German architectural Modernism. Originally trained as a painter, Behrens was a founder member of the Munich Secession in 1893. In the late 1890s he abandoned painting in favour of graphic and applied arts, and was invited to the Artists' Colony at Darmstadt in 1899. Together with Joseph Maria OLBRICH, Behrens was a leading spirit in the Colony, both as designer of his own house and organizer of theatrical events with markedly Nietzschean overtones. A period as Director of the Kunstgewerkeschule in Düsseldorf (1903-7) coincided with a marked swing in Behrens's own

Peter Behrens

work towards geometric abstraction, with strong references to the Florentine proto-Renaissance. Typical products of this transitional period are the Tietz Store in Düsseldorf (1905-6), the Tonhaus at the 1906 Cologne Exhibition, and a crematorium at Delstern, near Hagen

AEG TURBINE FACTORY, Berlin

This large-scale building was one of a number of industrial projects designed by Peter Behrens, who acted as combined architect and industrial design consultant for the great German electrical combine AEG. Built in 1909, its three-pin arched structure and huge glazed side walls represented an important practical and aesthetic breakthrough in early modern architecture. They provide a telling contrast to the classically handled gable end which, despite appearances, is not a masonry finished structure but an early example of the use of reinforced concrete construction. This contrasts effectively with the great framed metal window on the end.

(1906-7). In the years 1907-14, Behrens was employed as artistic adviser to the AEG in Berlin, and his work of this period reveals an attraction to the intellectual rigour of C19 Prussian Classicism. Behrens's principal activity in Berlin was graphic, product and architectural design for the AEG, for which he created the world's first corporate image. Behrens's first major building for the firm was the celebrated Turbine Factory in Berlin-Moabit (1909), which combined a temple-like gable front with a hinged steel frame in a successful fusion of the Classical canon with the structural demands of a highly-mechanized industrial plant. Several other factories followed, together with workers' housing and recreational buildings. The Neo-Classical revival that was latent in the industrial buildings found a climax in the German Embassy at St Petersburg (1911-12), whose giant-order columns and marble-clad vestibule evoked the works of Langhans and SCHINKEL. The significance of Behrens's example can be adjudged from the list of assistants from the AEG years, which included Walter GROPIUS, Ludwig MIES VAN DER ROHE, and LE CORBUSIER. In the aftermath of the First World War, Behrens reassessed his architectural language in designing the office building for the IG Farben dyeworks at Hoechst, near Frankfurt (1920-24), a lyrical essay using coloured brick and glass in a distinctly neo-medievalist spirit. This development, which relates to post-war German Expressionism, lingered in two glazed exhibition pavilions of 1925. A return to the cubic forms of "Neues Bauen" appeared in the apartment blocks built in Vienna between 1925 and 1929, and in his house at the Weissenhof Estate, Stuttgart (1927). The large blocks in Behrens's successful competition project for the rebuilding of Alexanderplatz, Berlin (1929-31) had the banded windows and streamlined mouldings favoured by the international Modernists of the younger generation, a style used again by Behrens in his last major commission, for a tobacco factory in Linz, Austria. Fortunately for his subsequent reputation, Behrens's monumental AEG building for Albert Speer's North-South axis in Berlin remained unbuilt.

☐ Festival Theatre, Darmstadt, 1900. Behrens House, Darmstadt, 1901. Pavilions at the North West German Art Exhibition, Oldenburg, 1905. Tietz Store, Düsseldorf, 1905-6. Tonhaus, Cologne Exhibition, 1906. Crematorium, Delstern, near Hagen, 1906-7. AEG Turbine Factory, Berlin-Moabit, 1909. AEG High-Voltage Factory, Berlin-Wedding, 1909-10. AEG Small-Motor Factory, Berlin-Wedding, 1910-13. AEG Workers' Housing, Hennigsdorf, 1910-11. German Embassy, St Petersburg, 1911-12. Factories, Offices and Water Tower for Frankfurter Gas Company, Frankfurt, 1911-12. AEG Assembly Hall for Large Machines, Berlin-Wedding, 1912. Head Office for IG Farben Hoechst Dyeworks, Hoechst, near Frankfurt, 1920-24. House, "New Ways", Northampton, 1923-5. Viennese Pavilion, Exposition des Arts Décoratifs, Paris, 1925. Pavilion for the Union of German Mirror-Glass Manufacturers, Cologne, 1925. House at the Weissenhof Estate, Stuttgart, 1927. Lewin House, Berlin, 1929-30. AEG Administration Building, Berlin, 1937-9.

▷ Alan Windsor, *Peter Behrens: Architect and Designer 1868-1940*, London, 1981. Tilmann Buddensieg and Henning Rogge, *Industriekultur: Peter Behrens and the AEG*, Cambridge, Mass., 1984. Bernard Buderath (ed.), *Peter Behrens: Umbautes Licht*, Frankfurt and Munich, 1990. IBW

BELLUSCHI Pietro

b. Ancona, Italy, 1899.

Prolific American Modernist architect and academic. He became chief designer in the American firm of A. E. Doyle during the 1930s. Belluschi served in the Italian army from 1917 to 1920, and graduated in engineering at the University of Rome in 1922. He then studied in the US, receiving a degree in civil engineering from Cornell University (1924). Following a short spell as a mining engineer in Idaho, he joined the Portland-based firm of A. E. Doyle, one of the leading architectural practices in NW America. From 1928 to 1943 Belluschi was chief designer, becoming a partner in 1933 and then taking over the practice under his own name ten years later. In 1951 he became Dean of Architecture and Planning at the prestigious Massachusetts Institute of Technology, a post he occupied until 1965. During his early years in Oregon, Belluschi designed numerous commercial buildings in the evolving International Style, culminating in his masterpiece, the Equitable Building in Portland. Significant in terms of technological development as well as design, it is one of the earliest applications of a taut-skinned curtain-wall cladding system. In an architectural career spanning more than 50 years, Belluschi designed over 1000 buildings. In 1972 he was awarded the AIA Gold Medal.

☐ Finley Mortuary, Portland, Oregon, 1936-7. Equitable Building, Portland, Oregon , 1945-8. Julliard School of Music, New York (with Eduardo Catalano), 1955-70. Symphony Hall, San Francisco (with Skidmore Owings & Merrill), 1975-80.

▷ Camillo Gubitosi & Alberto Izzo, *Pietro Belluschi: Edifici e progetti 1932-1973*, Rome, 1974.

CS

BENTLEY John Francis

b. Doncaster, 1839; d. London, 1902.

The architect of Westminster Cathedral, London. In 1857, after working for engineering and building supply firms, Bentley joined the London office of Henry Clutton, a Gothic Revival architect whom he followed into the Roman Catholic church in 1861. He set up in practice in 1862 and during the following decades designed houses, a distillery, a school, churches, church extensions, and monasteries in a range of styles, including many varieties of Gothic and Renaissance and an eclectic vernacular deriving from Norman SHAW. An admirer of STREET and BUTTERFIELD, he believed that past styles should be freely adapted and combined in modern buildings, but that the intrinsic qualities of the construction materials must also be visually expressed. Therefore he consistently opposed the hidden structural use of iron. Bentley's design for Westminster Roman Catholic Cathedral was based, at Cardinal Vaughan's insistence, on the Byzantine churches of Italy. In the resulting basilica and campanile, built inexpensively of brick on what was then a back-street site, he achieved maximum impact by means of height, exterior colour and detail, and interior magnitude. Bentley was a member of the Art Workers' Guild (*see* TOWNSEND), and his furnishings and decorations reflected this affiliation. Nominated for the RIBA Gold Medal in 1902, he died the day before the award was to be confirmed.

☐ St Johns Seminary, Hammersmith, London, 1876-84. Church of the Holy Rood, Watford, 1883-90. St John Beaumont College, Old Windsor, 1888. Westminster Cathedral, London, 1895-1903.

▷ Halsey Ricardo, *John Francis Bentley*, 1902 (in *Victorian Architecture*, ed. Peter Ferriday, London, 1963). Winefride de L'Hôpital, *Westminster Cathedral and its Architect*, London, 1919. BP

BERLAGE Hendrik Petrus

b. Amsterdam, 1856; d. The Hague, 1934.

Father of Modern architecture in the Netherlands and chief mediator between the Traditionalists and the Modernists. He studied architecture under Gottfried SEMPER at the Zürich Institute of Technology during the 1870s, then returned to Holland for a short while before commencing an extensive European study tour. In the early 1880s he entered into partnership with Theodore Sanders in Holland and subsequently produced a vast amount of projects, most practicable but some clearly utopian. Throughout his professional life he was a prominent member of local, national and international societies and organizations, including CIAM, and was a prolific writer, widely published in Dutch and German magazines. He visited the USA in 1911 and on his return reported to Zürich architects about the work of RICHARDSON and SULLIVAN, and particularly what he had seen of Frank Lloyd WRIGHT's new buildings. These had a remarkable effect on his own work, as can be seen in the beautiful Municipal Museum at The Hague (1919-35). Berlage's theories, enshrined in his articles and books, inspired all the Dutch Modernists, including members of *De Stijl*, the "Expressionistic" Amsterdam School and the New Objectivists of the 1930s, who deeply respected this paternal figure. He became the mediator between the long-standing Dutch Traditionalists and the various avant-garde Moderns. He was consistently honoured for his architecture and received the British Royal Gold Medal in 1932.

□ Stock Exchange, Amsterdam, 1896-1903. Plan: Amsterdam South, 1900-1917. Holland House, Bury Street, London EC3, 1914-16. St Hubertus Hunting Lodge, Otterlo, 1914-20. Municipal Museum, The Hague, 1919-35. Christian Science Church, The Hague (with P. Zwart), 1925-6.

▷ Berlage's famous Zürich lectures, *Grundlagen und Entwicklung der Architektur* were published in Rotterdam, 1911 (in Dutch and English, 1912). P. Singelenberg, *H. P. Berlage: Idea and Style. The Quest for Modern Architecture*, Utrecht, 1972. Sergio Polano, *Henrik Petrus Berlage: Complete Works*, London, 1988. DS

H. P. Berlage, Stock Exchange, Amsterdam, 1896–1903

BERNINI Giovanni Lorenzo (Gianlorenzo)

b. Naples, 1598; d. Rome, 1680.

Creator of the Baroque. Prolific universal artist, painter, sculptor, architect and poet. He was trained in Naples by his father, who was a notable Florentine sculptor. The family settled in Rome *c.*1606 and the brilliant young Bernini came to the attention of the future Pope Urban VIII (1623-44), under whom he emerged as architect. Bernini spent his entire career in Rome and became pre-eminent under Alexander VII (1655-67). Bernini transformed the Renaissance tradition of the universal artist-genius into the style which came to be known as Baroque – a fusion of the arts of architecture, sculpture and painting to create new forms, which above all created a dramatic impact and involved the spectator. Bernini's first fully Baroque work was his Baldacchino (1624-33), the canopy over St Peter's Tomb in St Peter's, Rome. As contemporaries recognized, it transcends categories: it is conceived both architecturally and as a work of sculpture. Bernini later (1658-65) created the architectural and sculptural setting for the papal throne; the theatrical use of light had been anticipated in the Cornaro Chapel (1645-52), one of his most famous works. The Baroque was the expression of the resurgence of the Catholic Church during the Counter-Reformation and communicates the power of the church and the mystery of religion. Bernini, a devout Catholic, used various devices to create mystery and drama: the false perspective of the Scala Regia (1663-6) – the stairway to the papal apartments – creates a large architectural trompe-l'oeil, heightened by a concealed light source. At the bottom of the stairs a statue of the Emperor Constantine looks, at the moment of his conversion, across the architectural space towards the golden Cross. This introduction of psychological tension and dramatic movement across the architectural space is typical, and the effect is repeated at S. Andrea al Quirinale, one of Bernini's three churches, all of which experiment with central planning. Bernini, like MICHELANGELO, thought of himself primarily as a sculptor, and amongst his secular work his virtuoso skills created other new forms in his marvellous series of fountains. Another of his important architectural innovations was the evolution of a type of palace façade articulated by massive pilasters above a rusticated

Gianlorenzo Bernini, Piazza of St Peter's, Rome, 1656–67

base; these are seen in his Louvre project and the Palazzo Chigi-Odescalchi (1664-6). In his revolutionary creation of the Baroque Bernini used classical elements but in completely new forms and a new framework of curves, diagonals and ovals. However, in contrast to his neurotically gifted contemporary BORROMINI, Bernini maintained a continuity with the serenity of the Renaissance, best seen in his most important single architectural work, the symbolic anthropomorphic "arms" of the colonnades forming the Piazza in front of St Peter's.

☐ Santa Bibiana, Rome (restoration), 1624-6. Baldacchino, St Peter's, Rome, 1624-33. Barcaccia fountain, Piazza di Spagna, Rome, 1627-9. Palazzo Barberini, Rome, 1629-*c.*1640. Triton Fountain, Rome, 1642-3. Cornaro Chapel, Santa Maria della Vittoria, Rome, 1645-52. Four Rivers Fountain, Rome, 1647-51. Piazza di San Pietro, Rome, 1656-67. Cathedra Pietri, St Peter's, Rome, 1657-66. S. Andrea al Quirinale, Rome, 1658-70. Scala Regia, Vatican, 1663-6. Louvre Palace, Paris (unexecuted), 1664-5; Palazzo Chigi-Odescalchi, Rome, 1664-6.

▷ H. Hibberd, *Bernini,* Harmondsworth, 1965. R. Wittkower, *Art and Architecture in Italy: 1600 to 1750,* Harmondsworth, 1958. TC

▷ *see also pp218-19*

BIBIENA FAMILY

see Galli da Bibiena

BIJVOET & DUIKER

Johannes Duiker, b. The Hague, 1890; d. Amsterdam, 1935.
Bernard Bijvoet, b. Amsterdam, 1889; d. Haarlem, 1979.

Dutch radical modernists of the 1920s. They were students at the Delft School of Architecture and achieved early fame by winning the competition for the Fine Art State Academy in 1919. Although not built, this scheme set a high standard, showing much influence of F. L. WRIGHT. This quality of work was realized by the series of individual houses by the sea at Kijkduin. This was followed shortly by the dramatic functional competition entry for the Chicago Tribune Tower (1922). But it was the small, timber-framed house at Aalsmeer in 1924 which broke most new ground and established the intense purposefulness of a new architecture. It was in the same year that the long and fruitful association with their clients the Diamond Workers Union began. This culminated in the building of the "Zonnestraal" sanatorium, started in 1927. This, in R. Vickery's words, "stands as the canonical building of *'De nieuwe Zakelijkheid'* [the new functionalism]". Duiker built Zonnestraal largely without Bijvoet, who in 1925 had moved to Paris and where he co-operated with Pierre Chareau on the "Maison de Verre", which undoubtedly has conceptual links with Duiker's individual buildings. The engineer J. Wiebenga joined Duiker in 1926 and contributed much to the structural clarity of the work. Duiker wrote with distinction and edited *De 8 en Opbouw*, the chief vehicle for Dutch Rationalism. Several housing projects followed Zonnestraal, chiefly the "Nirwana" flats at The Hague (1927), based on the American formula for service flats, and schemes for tall cluster blocks. In 1928 Duiker began work on the open-air school in Amsterdam which is probably his best-known work and demonstrated, in the original glazing system, the most "dematerialized" external surface. The early 30s saw the preparation of several cinema schemes and, in 1934, the completion of the Cineac, Amsterdam, in Peter Smithson's words, "the constituent monument to Dutch Constructivism". Duiker's final work, completed after his death by Bijvoet, was the Gooiland hotel and theatre at Hilversum (the hotel has recently been sympathetically restored for use as an arts centre). Bijvoet resumed practice in Holland in partnership with Professor G. H. M. Holt in 1947 after a further period in France. A number of theatre projects were undertaken, including a national opera house. Duiker claimed no style yet he subsumed Constructivism, Rationalism and "de nieuwe Zakelijkheid" into one understanding.

Johannes Duiker, Open-air School, Amsterdam, 1928

☐ Terrace houses and shops, Thomsonplein, The Hague, 1918. Terrace housing, J. v. Oldenbarneveldelaan, The Hague, 1920. Villas, Kijkduin, The Hague, 1922. Technical School, Scheveningen, 1922, 1929, 1931. Villa, Aalsmeer, 1924. Factory, Diemerburg, 1924-5. Chemist Shop, Haltestraat, Zandvort, 1925. Block of Flats, "Nirwana", The Hague, 1927. Sanatorium, "Zonnestraal",

Hilversum, 1928. Open-air School, Amsterdam, 1928. Cinema, "Cineac", Amsterdam, 1934. Hotel and Theatre "Gooiland", Hilversum, 1936.

▷ J. Duiker (ed. and contrib.), *De 8 en Opbouw*, Contributors to *Bouwkindig Weekblad*. J. Duiker, *Hoogbouw*, Brussels, Rotterdam, 1930. *L'Architecture Vivante*, Paris, 1924, 1925 and 1926. J. B. van Loghan, *Bowen*, Rotterdam, 1932. Jelles and Alberts, *Forum*, Vol. 16, No.1, 1962; Vol. 22, Nos. 5 and 6, 1971 and 1972. R. Vickery, "Bijvoet and Duiker", *AA Quarterly*, Vol. 2, No.1, 1970; "Bijvoet and Duiker" *Perspecta* (Yale), Nos. 13 and 14, 1971. J. Boga, *Bijvoet and Duiker, 1890-1935*, Zürich, n.d. W. de Jong, "Jan Duiker, and the preservation of the heritage of the 20's" in *Architecture and Construction in Russia*, No. 6, 1990.

CD

BINDESBØLL Michael Gottlieb Birkner

b. Ledøje, Denmark, 1800; d. Copenhagen, 1856.

Danish designer of public buildings, including the remarkable Thorvaldsen Museum in Copenhagen. Bindesbøll studied engineering in Copenhagen from 1815 and attended the Danish Royal Academy of Art from 1823. In 1822-3 he travelled in Germany (where he was impressed by SCHINKEL's work) and visited Paris; in 1833-4, after winning the Academy's Gold Medal and a travelling stipend, he went to Munich (where he admired the romantic Neo-Classicism of KLENZE'S Glyptothek), and from there to Rome, Naples, Athens, and Istanbul. In Rome he met the Danish Neo-Classical sculptor Bertel Thorvaldsen (1768 or 1770-1844) and exhibited designs for a museum of his work; returning to Copenhagen, he won this commission in a limited competition. The extraordinary building that resulted (converted from a former warehouse) was designed in a simplified neo-Greek manner. Bindesbøll emphasized the flatness of the external wall-surfaces, which, without orders, were punctuated by tapering full-height window and door embrasures and supported polychromatic frescoes by Jørgen Sonne. The effect was an exhilarating synthesis of structure and ornament. For subsequent projects, Bindesbøll used an eclectic range of styles including Baltic Gothic, "Rundbogenstil" and various forms of neo-vernacular, selected as appropriate and freely modified in the interests of function.

□ Thorvaldsen Museum, Copenhagen, 1839-44. Church, Hobrø, 1850-52. City Halls at Thisted, 1851-3, Flensburg, 1852, Stege, 1853-4, and Naestved 1855-6. Oringe Hospital, 1853-7. Medical Association Housing Project, Copenhagen, 1853. Veterinaer School, Copenhagen (main block), 1856-8.

▷ Tobias Faber, *Danish Architecture*, Copenhagen, 1978.

BP

BLONDEL Jacques François

b. Rouen, 1705; d. Paris, 1774.

Influential C18 French architectural theorist, teacher and writer. Born into a family of architects, Blondel learned to draw and engrave while studying architecture with his uncle, Jean François Blondel, and subsequently with the French Rococo architect Gilles Marie Oppenord. He travelled extensively through France, gaining an intimate knowledge and understanding of the national culture and sources of traditional French design. In 1746 he founded his own school of architecture in Paris, where he lectured before being appointed professor at the Académie Royale de l'Architecture (1762). His best-known work was a sophisticated plan for the reorganization of the French city of Metz (of which only three sides of the Place d'Armes survives), but his real reputation was established through a lifetime of teaching and writing. He also published papers and reports for the Académie, gave Sunday lectures and conducted guided tours. But the true measure of a teacher is his pupils, and Blondel's included BOULLÉE, LEDOUX and CHAMBERS. His theories were based on the need for rational analysis which emphasized the notion of *convenance* (suitability, decorum), with architecture as a public and visible expression of order. His ideas reflect his taste for traditional forms, despite the contemporary challenge of Neo-Classicism and progress tempered by reason. A prolific writer and inspirational teacher, he died, after a long illness, in his beloved classrooms in the Louvre.

▷ Jacques François Blondel, *De la Distribution des Maisons de Plaisance...*, originally published 1737-8 (reprinted Farnborough, England, 1967); *Discours sur la Manière d'Etudier l'Architecture...*, Paris, 1747; *Discours sur la Nécessité de l'Etude de l'Architecture...*, Paris, 1754. Jacques François Blondel and Pierre Patte, *Cours d'Architecture...* (9 volumes), Paris, 1771-7. Alan Brabham, *The Architecture of the French Enlightenment*, Berkeley, California, 1980.

CS

BODLEY George Frederick

b. Hull, 1827; d. Water Eaton, Oxon., 1907.

One of the most accomplished and influential of mid-Victorian church architects. He studied under George Gilbert SCOTT (1845-*c.* 1850) and practised from 1860. Between 1869 and 1898 he was in partnership with **Thomas Garner** (1839-1906); they collaborated on projects until 1884 but from then on worked individually. Bodley was influenced during the 1850s by the ideas of John RUSKIN and G. E. STREET. His early churches, often for Tractarian patrons, were based on C13 examples, but from the 1870s he preferred a synthesis of Gothic styles. His buildings were known for their refinement of proportion and detail. He paid much attention to interior furnishing and decoration, and was the first to commission stained glass from William MORRIS. For secular projects the partnership used styles other than Gothic, often "Queen Anne". Bodley was awarded the RIBA

J. F. Blondel, designs from Maison de Plaisance, *1837-8*

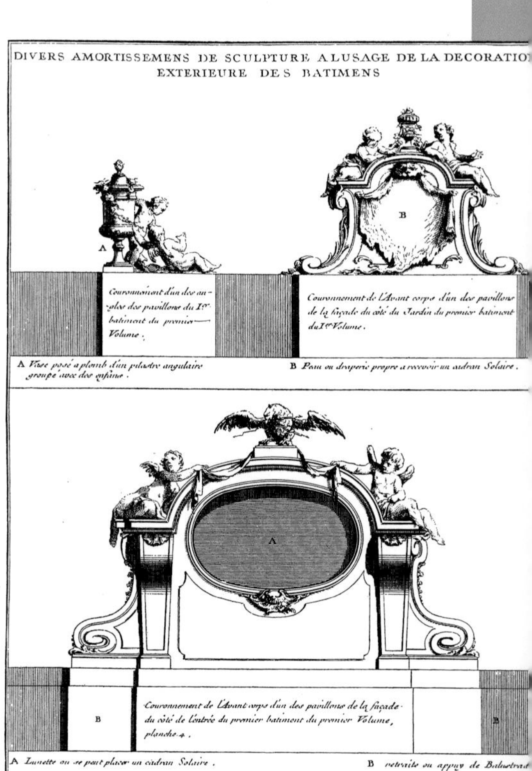

Gold Medal in 1899and an Hon. DCL by Oxford University in 1907. He was also the Diocesan architect for Leicester.

☐ Churches: St John the Baptist, France Lynch, Glos., 1855-7; All Saints, Selsley, Glos., 1859-62; St Martin-on-the Hill, Scarborough, Yorks., 1861-3 (and vicarage, 1867); Holy Angels, Hoar Cross, Staffs., 1871-7; St Augustine, Pendlebury, Lancs., 1874; St Mary, Clumber, Notts., 1886-9; St Mary, Eccleston, Cheshire, 1894-9; Holy Trinity, Prince Consort Road, London, 1902; Cathedral of SS. Peter and Paul, Washington DC, 1906 (built posthumously 1910-76). Secular: Master's Lodge, University College, Oxford, 1876-9; 3 Chelsea Embankment, London, 1879.

▷ B. F. L. Clarke, *Church Builders of the 19th Century*, London, 1938. David Cole, *Handlist of the Works of British Architects*, Vol. 1, London, 1972.

BP

BOFFRAND Gabriel Germain

b. Nantes, 1667; d. Paris, 1754.

The most celebrated French court architect of the early C18, successor to LE VAU and precursor of the Neo-Classicists. The son of a provincial architect/sculptor, Boffrand travelled to Paris to work for the royal building organization at the Place Vendôme. By the turn of the century he had achieved the elevated position of archival curator and project manager under Jules HARDOUIN-MANSART. His reputation rests principally on the construction and modernization of a series of grand Parisian *hôtels* or town houses, built primarily for the vast legion of ambassadors and ministers connected with the French court. In 1719, however, this speculative venture collapsed and resulted in Boffrand's financial ruin. His subsequent workload was largely administrative; for example, he acted as adviser to the Prince Bishop of Würzburg for the design of the Residenz by NEUMANN. He also completed a number of influential interiors in the highly fashionable Rococo style, the most famous being the oval salons in the corner pavilion of the Hôtel de Soubise.

☐ Hôtel LeBrun , Paris, 1700. Château of Lunéville, 1702-22. Hôtel d'Amelot, Paris, 1712-14. Hôtel de Torcy, Paris (now the German Embassy), 1713-15. Hôtel de Soubise, Paris, 1732-9.

▷ Emil Kaufmann, *Architecture in the Age of Reason*, Cambridge, 1955. Wolfgang Hermann, *Laugier and 18th Century French Theory*, London, 1962. Wend Kalnein and Michael Levey, *Art and Architecture in 18th Century France*, Harmondsworth, 1972. MC

BOGARDUS James

b. The Catskills, New York, 1800; d. New York, 1874.

A key figure in the development of the American skyscraper, having registered a patent for the first complete iron building in 1849. Bogardus's engineering background stemmed from his apprenticeship to a watchmaker and developed through a series of mechanical inventions for clocks and mill machinery during the 1830s and 40s. He won a competition in Britain for a mechanical engraving machine which was used in the production of the first "penny black" stamps. His interest in ironwork followed his investment in a New York foundry for structural and decorative iron (1848). By 1854 the Bogardus works could provide entire façades with an open framework of cast-iron columns and components with clear span windows (floor to ceiling) together with spine columns and a floor-beam framework that was the earliest application of rolled wrought-iron beams in the USA. The pioneer buildings constructed in the New York area with these patents in the years 1848-55 included Bogardus's own foundry (1848-9). Between 1850 and 1880 the construction methods patented by Borgardus were followed in buildings throughout the USA, including department stores, offices and warehouses. He also produced prophetic designs for the Crystal Palace of the New York Exposition (1853) together with ideas for free-standing towers which foreshadowed skyscraper buildings with curtain walls as the outer envelope.

☐ Bogardus's own foundry, New York, 1848-9. Laing Stores, New York, 1848. Fire Tower, New York, 1851. Harper & Bros. Printing Plant, New York, 1855. McCullough Shot Tower, New York, 1855.

▷ James Bogardus, *Cast Iron Buildings: Their Construction and Advantages*, New York, 1858. S. Giedion, *Space, Time and Architecture*, Oxford, 1967. AB

BOHIGAS Oriol

see Martorell-Bohigas-Mackay

BÖHM Dominikus

b. Jettingen, 1880; d. Cologne, 1955.

Leading figure in the revival of C20 German Catholic church architecture following the widespread devastation and deep spiritual trauma of the First World War. That period of reappraisal focused attention on the importance of the Liturgy and the active participation of the congregation with the priest during the Mass. Böhm's own deep spirituality informed all his work and reflected the new awareness within the Roman Catholic Church. He studied at the Technische Hochschule in Stuttgart under Theodor Fischer before establishing a private practice in Cologne (1903). He became professor at the Kunstge-

Dominikus Böhm, Church of Christ the King, Mainz-Bischofsheim, 1924–6

werbeschule in Offenbach and served in the army during the First World War. His son Gottfried BÖHM worked with him from 1947. The bulk of Dominikus Böhm's work is restricted to churches and associated ecclesiastical buildings. He pioneered the concept of the single-volume, open-plan church, and although Dominikus Böhm's work often tends towards Expressionism, it is always allied to a strong feeling for geometry and a love of materials.

□ War Memorial Church of John the Baptist, Neu-Ulm, 1921-6. Church of Christ the King, Mainz-Bischofsheim, 1924-6. Church of St Engelbert, Cologne-Riehl, 1930-32. Mary Queen of Heaven Church, Cologne-Marienburg, 1953-4.

▷ Josef Habbel (ed.) *Dominikus Böhm – ein deutscher Baumeister*, Regensberg, 1943. August Hoff, Herbert Muck and Raimund Thoma, *Dominikus Böhm*, Munich, 1962. Hugo Schell, *20th Century Church Architecture in Germany*, Munich, 1974. MC

BÖHM Gottfried

b. Offenbach-am-Main, 1920.

Internationally esteemed third-generation Modern architect, untainted by fashion, whose extensive and individual oeuvre anticipated subsequent architectural developments in Germany. He has received many honours and prizes. The son of Dominikus BÖHM, he graduated from the Munich Technische Hochschule in 1946 and for another year studied sculpture at the Munich Academy of Fine Arts. Apart from a period in 1951, when he travelled and worked in the USA, he worked in his father's office from 1947 until 1955, when his father died and he took over the direction of the office. Subsequently he designed a large number of buildings, including churches, museums, theatres, cultural and civic centres, offices and housing, most of them notable for the uncompromising way they integrate old and new work, and for their breathtaking internal spaces. Böhm's work has evolved through distinct phases which have been linked by a consistent attitude and approach summed up by his term "connections", be it materials, buildings, or a building and its setting. He has won the Grande Médaille d'Or de l'Académie d'Architecture (1983), the Fritz Schumacher Prize for Architecture, Hamburg (1985) and the Pritzker Architecture Prize (1986).

□ Restaurant and Hotel in Castle Ruins, Bonn-Bad Godesberg, Germany, 1956. Parish Church, Cologne-Schildgen, 1958. Pilgrim Church, Neviges, and Bensberg City Hall, 1964. City Hall, Bocholt, 1977. Citizens' Centre, Bergisch-Gladbach, 1980. Town Hall, Rheinberg, 1980. Züblin HQ, Stuttgart, 1984. Saarbrücken Castle Restoration for Regional Government Office, 1987.

▷ *Architecture + Urbanism*, special issue (March 1978) and feature (September 1990). *Zusammenhänge-Der Architekt Gottfried Böhm*, Kunsthalle Bielefeld, 1984. Svetlozar Raèv (ed.) *Gottfried Böhm*, Stuttgart and Zurich, 1988. Veronika Darius, *Der Architekt Gottfried Böhm, Bauten der sechziger Jahre*, Düsseldorf, 1988. PB

BORROMINI (CASTELLI) Francesco

b. Bissone, Lugano, 1599; d. Rome, 1667.

Controversial and influential Baroque architect. As a child he learnt the craft of the stone cutter from his father, Giovanni Domenico Castelli. Still extremely young (9 or 10), he continued his craft in Milan. In 1619 he moved to Rome with Lombard relatives engaged in the works on St Peter's and soon joined them. During this initial period in Rome he changed his name to Borromini, perhaps to avoid being confused with other workers from the N of Italy of the same name. His first major influence came from Carlo MADERNO, distant relative and official architect to St Peter's. Borromini began work under Maderno simply as a stone cutter, but by 1620-21 he had begun to take over drafting and some designing. In 1629 the much older and more traditional Maderno died, and Borromini joined the workshop of his more exciting contemporary BERNINI. Under Bernini he worked as a draughtsman on the half-sculptural, half-architectural baldacchino of St Peter's. In collaborating with Bernini he found greater freedom of expression, in spite of

Francesco Borromini, S. Ivo alla Sapienza, Rome, 1642-62

Mario Botta, Casa Rotunda, Stabio, Switzerland, 1981

a long-lasting resentment between the two. In 1634 he began his independent activity as architect with the reconstruction of the monastery and church of S. Carlo Borromeo (alle Quattro Fontane), which, according to Paolo Portoghesi, shows "a dynamic genesis, through a process of 'spatial synthesis or compenetration'". S. Ivo alla Sapienza (1642-62) is a small church but of great impact with its drumless dome and skilful use of hidden lighting. But it was only after the death of Urban VIII (1644), with the new Pope Innocent X, that Borromini consolidated his prominent position, a rise in his fortunes which corresponded to Bernini's decline. It reached its height with the pontificate commissions for renovating S. Giovanni in Laterano (1647-50, remarkable for the use of archaic elements in the new Baroque space) and Piazza Navona and carried on to include the major late works of S. Andrea delle Fratte (1653-65) and the Collegio di Propaganda Fide (1647-62), including the very significant small church of the Re Magi. Borromini's architecture springs from the contrast between convention and freedom, with an underlying ethical attitude resulting from his social and historical commitment. He accepts tradition as a useful past experience but not necessarily as source of unshakable rules; in short, as Bernini said of him, he was "a good heretic". He was a typical product of the Baroque culture, and his position and importance followed the ups and downs of the style. His works were later studied by FISCHER VON ERLACH, Konrad Rudolf and Lucas von Hildebrandt during their visits to Rome. GUARINI transferred Borromini's architecture to Turin and Sicily. Through von Erlach it reached Vienna as that city was rebuilt after the siege of 1683, and then passed to Munich, Dresden, Berlin, Prague and, via Spain, even Latin America. Whatever its popularity, "*Borrominismo*" will always conjure up organic continuity of curved surfaces, imaginative patterns of brickwork and countless other architectural details.

☐ S. Carlo alle Quattro Fontane, Rome (including dormitory, refectory, various cells and a library), 1634-42. Oratory and Residence of the Filippini, Rome (from work started by Maruscelli, 1637-50. S. Ivo alla Sapienza, Rome, 1642-62. S. Giovanni in Laterano, Rome, 1647-50. Collegio di Propaganda Fide, Rome 1647-62.

▷ Paolo Portoghesi, *Borromini nella cultura europea*, Rome, 1964. Rudolf Wittkower, *Studies in the Italian Baroque*, London 1967, 1975. Anthony Blunt, *Borromini*, Harmondsworth, 1979. GV

▷ *see also pp218-19*

BOTTA Mario

b. Mendrisio, Switzerland, 1943.

Influential Swiss architect whose work embodies the tenets of the Italian Neo-Rationalist movement and local craft traditions. Educated at primary school in Genestrerio and secondary school in Mendrisio in the Italian-speaking canton of Ticino (S Switzerland), Botta trained as a technical draughtsman (1958-61) and then studied at the Liceo Artistico, Milan (1961-4), and the Istituto Universitario di Architettura in Venice (1965-9). He subsequently worked as an assistant in LE CORBUSIER's office (1965) and with Louis KAHN (1969), and is now in private practice based in Lugano. Botta has built almost exclusively in Switzerland, but he has earned an international reputation with his library for the Capuchin convent in Lugano (1976-9), Craft Centre in Balerna (1977-9) and Administration Building for the Staatsbank in Fribourg (1977-82). In his attempts to reconcile traditional architectural symbolism with the severe but rational codes of the Modern movement, Botta is principally identified with the Italian Neo-Rationalist group (the Tendenza), whose other members include Aldo ROSSI and Luigi Snozzi. Botta's work is characterized by a respect for topographical conditions and regional sensibility coupled with an emphasis on craftsmanship and geometric order, as embodied by the Casa Rotunda at Stabio (1981). He is an honorary fellow of the Bund Deutscher Architekten (1983) and the AIA (1984).

☐ Secondary School, Morbio Inferiore, Switzerland, 1972-7. Library of the Capuchin Convent, Lugano, 1976-9. Craft Centre, Balerna, Switzerland, 1977-9. Administration Building, Staatsbank, Fribourg, Switzerland, 1977-82. Casa Rotunda, Family House, Stabio, Switzerland, 1981. Theatre, Chambéry, France, 1987.

▷ Italo Rota (ed.) *Mario Botta: Architecture and Projects in the 70's*, Milan, 1979. Pierluigi Nicolin, *Mario Botta: Buildings and Projects 1961-1982*, New York, 1984. CS

BOULLÉE Etienne Louis

b. Paris, 1728; d. 1799.

Visionary French designer. Boullée spent all his life in Paris and began his career as a painter. He taught at the Ecole des Ponts et Chaussées and later became a professor at the Académie d'Architecture. He saw few of his architectural designs built but his theories and drawings were widely publicized. He admired the unfussy, bold lines of Neo-Classical styles of architecture and in his writings, including the *Essai sur l'Art* (unpublished until 1953), pleaded for an architecture which was felt as much as it was reasoned and which would achieve grandeur through scale, geometry and purity. In his designs Boullée restricted himself to the use of simple, geometrical shapes, such as pyramids, spheres and cylinders. His most noted drawings were for the Tomb of Newton (1784) which envisaged a sphere 150m (500ft) high emerging from a drum base. The vast cavernous interior was to house the sarcophagus containing Newton's remains. The great scale and startling simplicity of Boullée's projects won him many admirers, including his students Jean François Thérèse Chalgrin (1739-1811), designer of the Arc de Triomphe, and the influential theorist Jean Nicolas Louis DURAND.

☐ Hôtel Alexandre, Paris, 1766-8. Tomb of Newton, 1784.

▷ *Visionary Architects: Boullée, Ledoux, Lequeu*, Houston, Texas, 1967. Jean Marie Perouse de Montclos, *Boullée*, New York, 1974. Helen Rosenau, *Boullée and Visionary Architecture*, London, 1976. FS

BRAMANTE Donato

b. Monte Asdrualdo (now Fermignano) near Urbino, 1444; d. Rome, 1514.

Architect and painter, one of the main personalities of Italian Renaissance architecture. Unlike other major figures (LEONARDO, RAPHAEL, MICHELANGELO), few facts are known about his life and training. From a very young age he learnt painting under Mantegna and Piero della Francesca and probably had contact with artists and architects working at nearby Urbino. His first documented activity is in 1477, on the frescoes of Palazzo Podestà in Bergamo; then he was in the service of the Sforzas as "ingegnerius et pinctor" in Milan, where in 1482 he was in charge of the reconstruction of S. Satiro. In Milan in the 1490s an extraordinary, mutually enriching meeting took place between Bramante and Leonardo, Giuliano da SANGALLO, Francesco di Giorgio and the mathematician Luca Pacioli. Almost certainly because of the French invasion of Milan and the fall of the Sforzas, Bramante moved to Rome in 1499. Among the many (uncertain) attributions, the first documented commission was from Oliviero Carafa, Cardinal of Naples, for the cloister of Santa Maria della Pace (1500). In November 1503 Julius II became the new Pope, and Bramante almost immediately became engaged in the renewal of the Vatican complex as interpreter of the Pope's triumphal and political vision of the renewal of the empire ("renovatio imperii"). During his 14 years in Rome, most of Bramante's work was commissioned by Julius II until the Pope's death in 1513 (Bramante died a year later), with the two notable exceptions of the circular Tempietto of S. Pietro in Montorio and the Palazzo Caprini (the House of Raphael). Bramante's original plan for St Peter's was only partially carried out and subsequently was so much changed that only the great spiral stair remains. Already in his early work Bramante changed conventional architectural space by inserting illusionistic features more typical of painting and stage settings. In his Roman projects, particularly those for St Peter's, he achieved the "grand manner" which directly (through followers and disciples such as Sangallo, PERUZZI, SANSOVINO, SANMICHELE, Raphael) and indirectly (through PALLADIO, SERLIO, Pierre Lescot etc.) became Cinquecento Mannerism. Historically, his importance is due to the way he inspired and influenced contemporary and successive architects rather than through the original buildings he designed, few of which survived unaltered: "Bramante... inventor...of...good architecture buried until the time of Julius II" (Serlio, Book IV).

Donato Bramante, Santa Maria delle Pace, Rome, 1500

☐ Canonica of S. Ambrogio, Milan, 1492. Santa Maria della Pace (cloister), Rome, 1500. Tempietto of S. Pietro in Montorio, Rome, c. 1502. St Peter's, Rome (demolition and partial reconstruction of the old basilica), 1505. Palazzo Caprini (House of Raphael), Rome, 1508-9.

▷ Arnaldo Bruschi, *Bramante architetto*, Bari, 1969; *Bramante*, London, 1977. Fert Sangiorgi, *Bramante hasdrubaldino*, Urbino, 1970. G. Milanesi (ed.), *Le opere di Giorgio Vasari*, Florence, 1973: see *Vasari's Lives*, tr. and ed. G. du C. de Vere, London, 1912-15.

GV

▷ *see also pp214–15*

BREUER Marcel

b. Pécs, Hungary, 1902; d. New York, 1981.

One of the most famous Bauhaus graduates, who in a long career embraced a wide spectrum of design and adapted his skills to differing situations in Europe and the USA. He was educated at Allami Foreaiskola, Pécs, and at the Bauhaus, Weimar, where he graduated in 1924. He taught at the Bauhaus, Dessau, until 1928 and practised in Berlin 1928-31. After a brief spell in London, in partnership with

UNESCO HEADQUARTERS, Paris

Marcel Breuer's work on the huge UNESCO building in Paris (built in 1953) was to be the realisation of the architect's long-held ideas about the sculptural possibilities offered by reinforced concrete. The most striking feature of the UNESCO complex is the enormous "Y"-shaped office and conference room block. Where the spurs meet, the corners are concave and give the building's great sweeping walls a satisfying curvilinear shape. The design also allows easy circulation inside and an optimum use of the office space. The use of concrete excited Breuer who described it as acting "not only as the support of the building, but also as the enclosure, the form. Concrete is not bones alone, but also bones, muscles and skin combined."

F.R.S. YORKE (1935-6), Breuer emigrated to the USA, with an appointment as associate professor at Harvard (1937-46) and a working arrangement with Walter GROPIUS (until 1941). His New York office, established in 1946, continued until his retirement *c.*1976. Marcel Breuer, the youngest of the pioneer Modernists, was instrumental in shifting the bias of the Bauhaus from the "Arts & Crafts" to "Art & Technology". His key role as furniture designer led to the commission for fitting out the new Bauhaus at Dessau (1925). Many pieces of modern, tubular steel furniture in use today can trace their origins back to the Breuer experiments in the mid-20s. His early experience of coupling design with teaching led to another inspirational period at Harvard, where his students included Philip JOHNSON, Paul RUDOLPH, John Johanson and Harry SEIDLER. The early projects in the USA were largely domestic, but in 1952 Breuer was selected with NERVI and Zehrfuss as architect for the UNESCO HQ in Paris, and this breakthrough into prestigious work carried the practice into the international field. Breuer's buildings were always distinguished by attention to detail and to clarity of expression vis-à-vis the different functional elements. He can be said to be the last of the true functionalist architects.

☐ Prototype steel Furniture and fitting out the Bauhaus, Dessau, 1924-8. Harnischmacher House, Wiesbaden, 1932. Doldertal Apartments, Zürich, for GIEDION (with Roth Brothers), 1935-6. Work in England with F.R.S. Yorke: Isokon Laminated Furniture; Gane's Exhibition Pavilion, Bristol; Civic Centre of the Future (project), 1936. Wheaton College Art Centre, Norton, Mass., (with Walter Gropius), 1938. Gropius House, Lincoln, Mass. (with Walter Gropius), 1938. Breuer House, Lincoln, Mass., 1939. Wartime Housing, New Kensington, Pittsburgh (with Walter Gropius), 1943. Co-op Dormitory, Vassar College, New York, 1950. UNESCO Headquarters, Paris, France (with Nervi and Zehrfuss), 1952-8. St John's Abbey and University, Collegeville, Minn. (with H. Smith), 1953-70. Institute for Advanced Study Housing, Princeton, NJ (with R.F. Gatje), 1954-7. De Bijenkorf Store, Rotterdam (with A. Elzas), 1957. US Embassy, The Hague, 1958. Convent of the Annunciation, Bismarck, N Dakota (with H. Smith), 1959. Flaine Ski Resort, Haute Savoie, France (with R. F. Gatje), 1960s. IBM Research Centre, Le Gaude, Var, France (with R. F. Gatje), 1961. Whitney Museum, New York (with H. Smith), 1966. Third Power Plant, Grand Coulee Dam, Washington State (with H. Smith), 1968-77. Yale University Engineering Building, New Haven, Conn., 1969. Cleveland Museum of Art, Cleveland, Ohio (with H. Smith), 1970. Australian Embassy, Paris (with Harry Seidler and M. Jossa), 1975. Federal Courthouse and Offices, Columbia, S Carolina (with H. Beckbard and others), 1977.

▷ Marcel Breuer, "Where do we stand?" *Architectural Review*, April 1935.
Marcel Breuer Architect (exhibition catalogue), New York, 1949. Peter Blake (ed.), *Sun and Shadow*, New York, 1955. Cranston Jones, *Marcel Breuer 1921-62*, London, 1962. Tician Papachritou, *Marcel Breuer, New Buildings & Projects*, New York, 1970. AB

▷ *see also pp238–9*

BRINKMAN Johannes Andreas

see Van der Vlugt & Brinkman.

VAN DEN BROEK & BAKEMA

Established 1948.

Dutch Functionalist partnership influenced by the ideals of *De Stijl* and the International Style. **Jacob Berend Bakema** (b. Groningen, 1914; d. Rotterdam, 1981) was educated at the Technikum in his native Groningen, followed by sessions at the Architectural Academy in Amsterdam and the Technical University in Delft. As a student he spent some time in the office of Cornelius VAN EESTEREN and the municipal architects' department in Rotterdam. In 1948 he established a partnership with **Johannes Hendrik van den Broek** (b. Rotterdam, 1898; d. The Hague, 1978), and they quickly became an influential force in contemporary Dutch architecture. Van den Broek also studied at the Delft Technical University, from which he graduated in 1924. He sat up his own practice in Rotterdam in 1927 and was in partnership with J. A. BRINKMAN from 1937. Over the years the practice gradually expanded, employing up to 200 people. Control of design, however, always lay with the principals. The output was equally prolific and covered housing, shops, schools, churches and offices. Van den Broek and Bakema were influenced by the philosophical ideals of *De Stijl* and Functionalism. Bakema in particular was also known as a social architect, giving consideration to the function of architecture within society. His influential theories and writing were widely circulated both in Holland and abroad. The partnership's most important work is the Lijnbaan shopping street in Rotterdam, an open pedestrian arcade flanked by low-rise buildings which recreate the intimacy and scale of the original streets destroyed during the war. Later projects such as the Town Hall in Terneuzen and the Psychiatric Hospital in Middelharnis display a positive, modern quality which owes much to Constructivism.

□ Shopping Centre Lijnbaan, Rotterdam, 1949-54. Town Hall, Terneuzen, 1963-72. Psychiatric Hospital, Middelharnis, 1973-4.

▷ Jacob Bakema, *Towards an Architecture for Society*, Delft, 1963. Camillo Gubitosi and Alberto Izzo, *Van den Broek/Bakema*, Rome, 1976. CS

DE BROSSE Salomon

b. Verneuil-sur-Oise, 1571; d. 1626.

French architect of the C17 whose style influenced the leading classicist François MANSART. De Brosse was trained by his architect father and then by his uncle, Jacques II Androuet DU CERCEAU. His completion of the Verneuil château (1600-1608) was inspired by engravings of VIGNOLA. Appointed architect to the crown in 1608, he spent the next ten years working on a series of Parisian *hôtels* and châteaux. Blérancourt château in Picardy was of the Italian H-block design (with Lescot-inspired elevations) that was later to influence Mansart. Coulommiers-en-Brie (1613) follows the Verneuil plan and has much in common with de Brosse's Luxembourg Palace (1614), celebrated chiefly for its entrance and pavilions. Inspired by Philibert DELORME's three-tier frontispiece at the Château of Anet and Vignola's Roman masterpiece, the Gesù, de Brosse's design for St Gervais, Paris, combining a high Gothic nave and a classical façade, proved an inspired solution to the problem of integrating Gothic and classical styles. His last important work was the completion of the Palais de Justice, Rennes, begun in 1618 by Mansart's brother-in-law, Germain Gaultier. Much of de Brosse's work was destroyed or redesigned, but his interest in elevational composition was to have a profound effect on the style of Mansart, the most important French architect of the next generation.

□ Château of Verneuil, Oise, 1600-1608. Château of Blérancourt, Aisne, *c.* 1611-*c.* 1619. Church of St Gervais, Paris (W front), 1616. Palais du Parlement, Rennes (principal front and rooms; now Palais de Justice), 1618.

▷ Reginald Blomfield, *A History of French Architecture, from the Reign of Charles VII till the Death of Mazarin*, London, 1911. Anthony Blunt, *Art and Architecture in France 1500-1700*, Harmondsworth, 1953, 1973. Rosalys Coope, *Salomon de Brosse and the Development of the Classical Style in French Architecture from 1565-1630*, London, 1972. CS

▷ *see also pp216–17*

BROWN Lancelot ("Capability")

b. Kirkharle, Northumberland, 1716; d. London, 1783.

The nickname "Capability", which came from Brown's mannerism of referring to the "capabilities" of places or situations, is also an appropriate comment on the outstanding abilities of this gardener turned architect to transform English landscape into Art. Following the apprenticeship practice of the time, he was first trained as a gardener at Sir William Loraine's estate (1732-9), which led to work at Stowe for Lord Cobham until 1749. On the death of his patron Brown commenced independent practice as both gardener and architect. His talents in both capacities made him the most important designer of English landscape in the C18. His official appointments included Master Gardener for the Royal Household (from 1764). His executed projects are extremely numerous, probably over 140, many of them after 1770 in partnership with Henry HOLLAND (who later married Brown's daughter).

"Capability" Brown

□ Croome, Worcs. (both house and parkland), 1750-52. Warwick Castle (renovated) and parkland, 1750-52. Petworth Park, Sussex, 1754. Blenheim Park, Oxon, 1766. Claremont, Surrey (both house and park), 1770. Also landscaping at Alnwick, Longleat and Prior Park, and involvement at Kew Gardens (the Rhododendron Walk) and Richmond Park, London.

▷ Christopher Hussey, *English Gardens and Landscape, 1700-1750*, London, 1967. Dorothy Stroud, *Capability Brown*, London, 1984. AB

BRUNELLESCHI Filippo

b. Florence, 1377; d. Florence, 1446.

Architect, sculptor and engineer who was the main initiator of stylistic changes in Renaissance architecture. He began his training in Florence as apprentice goldsmith with the Silk Guild in 1398 and matriculated as master in 1404. By 1401-2 he was well enough established as a sculptor to enter the competition for the second bronze door of the Florence Baptistery (won by GHIBERTI). He was active as a sculptor for most of his life, but the bronze relief he produced for the competition (now in the Bargello, Florence) is considered to be one of his best. He began his architectural career in 1404 as adviser for Santa Maria Novella, although he continued to work mostly as an engineer until he began his involvement with the cupola of Santa Maria del Fiore, the project around which the greater part of his active life revolved (1417-34). Brunelleschi's work at Santa Maria del Fiore shows his inventiveness as engineer (he designed special lifting machinery) as well as architect. The magnificent size of the double-skinned cupola and its complexities (built in successive "fishbone" layers) make its still medieval lines less obvious and overshadow some of his other and perhaps more original buildings. The lantern (1436) combines the delicacy of goldsmith's work with the strength to tie the cupola ribs together. As terminations of the octagon, four *tribune morte* (blind

Filippo Brunelleschi, Ospedale degli Innocenti, Florence, 1419

tribunes; 1438) enhance the plastic value of the structures below the drum. Brunelleschi's multiple activities are also reflected in several projects of military architecture and engineering, e.g. the Pisa fortifications. He was the first architect to employ mathematical perspective, to work out its rules and to redefine Gothic and Romanesque space according to measurable proportions. His portico at the Ospedale degli Innocenti (Orphanage) in Florence (1419) is often cited (in spite of its Romanesque and late Gothic elements) as the first Renaissance building. The church and sacristy of S. Lorenzo (*c.* 1418) are milestones of the "new style"; the sacristy was the prototype for centrally planned Renaissance buildings. The Church of Santo Spirito (*c.* 1436) is perhaps Brunelleschi's finest example of ideal symmetry and beautifully balanced lighting. Unlike ALBERTI, Brunelleschi seemed unwilling to organize and put down his theories in writing, almost certainly in order not to give away his hard-won secrets. Recent criticism has moved away from the stereotyped view of Brunelleschi as "father of the Renaissance".

☐ Santa Maria del Fiore, Florence (cupola, lantern and *tribune morte*), 1417/18-1446. S. Lorenzo, Florence (church and sacristy), *c.* 1418. Ospedale degli Innocenti, Florence, 1419. Church of Santo Spirito, Florence, *c.* 1436.

▷ Antonio Manetti, *The Life of Brunelleschi*, ed. Howard Saalman, tr. Catherine Enggass, Penns., 1970. G. C. Argan, *Brunelleschi*, Milan, 1955, 1978. Isabelle Hyman, *Brunelleschi in Perspective*, Englewood Cliffs, NJ, 1974. Carlo Ragghianti, *Filippo Brunelleschi: un uomo, un universo*, Florence, 1977. GV

▷ *see also pp212–13*

DOME OF SANTA MARIA DEL FIORE, Florence

The engineering feat represented by the cupola of Florence cathedral staggered Brunelleschi's contemporaries. The architect's ingenious solution to the problem of how to cover the cathedral crossing involved a double-shell dome using a system of vertical ribs tied by horizontal arches.

"Fishbone"-bonded brickwork (derived from Roman building techniques) was used instead of stone for the upper parts of the dome as this was lighter whilst maintaining stability. Work began in 1420, and the top was closed in 1436, when the elegant lantern was built to complete it.

BULFINCH Charles

b. Boston, Mass., 1763; d. Boston, 1844.

Leading American architect and civic planner of the Federal period. After graduating in mathematics and perspective from Harvard (1781), Bulfinch travelled in Europe (1785-7), studying modern buildings in England (where the work of WREN and CHAMBERS, the WOODS in Bath, and the ADAM brothers impressed him), France and Italy. He practised professionally after his return to Boston. The ambitious but financially unsuccessful Tontine Crescent (1793-4) was his first translation of English town-planning concepts into an American setting. Soon after designing the Massachusetts State House (distantly influenced by Chambers's Somerset House), Bulfinch was appointed permanent Chairman of the Board of Selectmen in Boston and Police Superintendent (1799). During the next eighteen years the city was transformed under his direction, with new roads and wharves, and an array of administrative, commercial, educational, residential, penal and religious buildings in a dignified classical style that became increasingly detached from its European sources. Summoned to Washington by President Monroe, Bulfinch succeeded LATROBE as architect of the Capitol (1818-30).

Charles Bulfinch, Massachusetts State House, Boston, 1793–1800

☐ Massachusetts State House, Boston, Mass., 1798. Harrison Grey Otis houses, 1800 and 1806. India Wharf, Boston, 1803-7. Church of Christ, Lancaster, Mass., 1816-17. State Capitol, Augusta, Maine, 1829-32.

▷ Charles Place, *Charles Bulfinch, Architect and Citizen*, Boston, Mass., 1925, 1968. Harold Kirker, *The Architecture of Charles Bulfinch*, Cambridge, Mass., 1989. BP

BUNSHAFT Gordon

see Skidmore, Owings & Merrill.

BURGES William

b. London 1827; d. 1881.

A highly imaginative Victorian architect whose appetite for the exotic resulted in a richly decorated Medieval style. Burges attended King's College School with Dante Gabriel Rossetti, and the Pre-Raphaelite brotherhood of painters (of whom Rossetti was one) were later to have a profound influence on his work. Other early influences included the work of A. W. N. PUGIN and Japanese and Indian art before he focused on c13 French Gothic architecture as the epitome of architectural perfection. He worked in the office of Edward Blore (an exponent of the Gothic Revival) and then for Matthew Digby Wyatt, leaving in 1851 to form a loose partnership with Henry Clutton. Once Burges had devised his highly ornate and colourful style (which he applied to fixtures and fittings with equal generosity), he stuck to it despite a swing in fashion away from the Gothic Revival. In the 3rd Marquis of Bute he found an enlightened patron who gave him the opportunity to let his creative talents run wild, producing at Cardiff Castle a riot of polychrome Medievalism.

☐ St Finbar's Cathedral, Cork, Ireland, 1863-76. Chapel and hall, Worcester College, Oxford, 1864-79. Additions to Cardiff Castle, Wales, begun 1866. Speech room at Harrow School, Middlesex, 1872-7. Trinity College, Hartford, Connecticut, built to his designs 1873-82. Castle Coch, near Cardiff (remodelling), *c.*1875. Tower House, Melbury Road, Kensington, London, 1875-81.

▷ J. Mordaunt Crook, *William Burges and the High Victorian Dream*, London, 1981. J. Mordaunt Crook et al., *The Strange Genius of William Burges*, Cardiff, 1981. PP

BURLE MARX Roberto

b. Sao Paulo, Brazil, 1909.

Leading figure in the evolution of a contemporary approach to landscape design within the rigorous intellectual parameters of the Modern Movement. Burle Marx studied painting, architecture and music at the Escola Nacional de Belas Artes in Rio de Janeiro and then spent two years in Berlin, where he found inspiration at the Dahlem Botanical Gardens. He returned to Brazil in 1930 to pursue his ambition to fashion landscape into a form of three-dimensional painting. His first project was in 1932 for a house designed by Lucio COSTA. Only two years later he was appointed director of parks and gardens in Recife, where he created Brazil's first ecological garden. The recreational development at Pampulha (1943) gave him the opportunity to collaborate with Brazil's foremost architect, Oscar NIEMEYER. Since the 1950s he has operated from a rambling farmstead outside Rio de Janeiro, where he cultivates indigenous flowers and plants, many of them biologically engineered in his own greenhouses. His rich palette of colours is the result of his extensive knowledge of horticulture but it is an innate flair for mathematics and the manipulation of form which elevate his gardens to the level of abstract art.

☐ Roof Gardens of the Ministry of Education Building (now Palacio da Cultura), Rio de Janeiro, 1938. Pampulha Park and Gardens, Belo Horizonte, 1943. Odette Monteiro Gardens, Petropolis, 1947-8. Del-Este Park, Caracas, 1956. UNESCO Gardens, Paris, 1963.

▷ Pietro Maria Bardi and M. Gautherot, *The Tropical Gardens of Burle Marx*, New York, 1964. Flavio Motta, *Roberto Burle Marx e a nova visao da paisagem*, Sao Paulo, 1984. MC

BURLINGTON Lord

Richard Boyle, 3rd Earl of Burlington and 4th Earl of Cork, b. Yorkshire, 1694; d. Londesborough, 1753.

Patron of the arts and champion of English Palladian style. His Grand Tour to Italy (1714-15) roughly coincided with the publication of LEONI's English edition of PALLADIO's Four Books (1715-16) and CAMPBELL's *Vitruvius Britannicus* (1715), and Burlington subsequently embarked on a mission to revive the true architecture of VITRUVIUS as interpreted by Palladio. Campbell replaced James GIBBS as architect on Burlington House, and by the early 1720s Burlington himself was a practising architect, employed mostly by fellow members of the aristocracy. He was also Lord Treasurer of Ireland, Lord Lieutenant of the East and West Ridings of Yorkshire, a Privy Councillor and a director of the Royal Academy of Music. Working strictly in accordance with the principles of Palladio, Burlington's first coup was the dormitory of Westminster School, and his last major work, the Assembly Rooms, York, was an exact reproduction of Palladio's Egyptian Hall based on Vitruvius. By 1730 Palladianism was the leading style in England and Burlington chief arbiter of taste. Through the Office of Works Burlington was also able to influence his protégé William KENT's designs for Horse Guards, the Royal Mews and the Treasury Building. Although most of Burlington's work was later pulled down or redesigned, he was undoubtedly very influential in the development of English Neo-Classicism. But his simple faith lacked critical analysis, and his strict reproductions lacked imagination, interpretation and taste.

☐ Dormitory, Westminster School, London, 1722-30. Northwick Park, Worcs., 1728-30. Chiswick House, London (with William Kent), *c.*1730. Assembly Rooms, York, *c.*1731-2.

▷ F. Saxl and Rudolf Wittkower, *British Art and the Mediterranean*, London, 1969. *Apollo of the Arts: Lord Burlington and his Circle* (exhibition catalogue), Nottingham 1973. Rudolf Wittkower, *Palladio and English Palladianism*, London, 1974. CS

BURNHAM & ROOT

Established 1873.

American architects who played an important part in the development of the Chicago School during the late C19. **Daniel Hudson Burnham** (b. Henderson, New York, 1846; d. Heidelberg, 1912) and **John Wellborn Root** (b. Georgia, USA, 1850, d. 1891) first met in 1872 in the Chicago offices of Carter, Drake and WRIGHT, where both were working as architectural draughtsmen. Despite a privileged background, Burnham's early career was dogged by rejection (by both Harvard and Yale universities) and a restlessness which led to a succession of jobs in small architectural offices in Chicago, plus a short spell as a silver speculator in Idaho. By contrast Root had followed a more conventional path, studying at Oxford and taking an engineering degree at the University of New York. The two formed a partnership which successfully combined the reciprocal qualities of Root's idealism and Burnham's pragmatism. In 1874 they obtained their first major commission from stockyard magnate John B. Sherman, whose influence led to a string of further residential commissions from various Chicago luminaries. However, Burnham's ultimate goal lay in the creation of big architecture for big business, epitomized by monumental skyscrapers such as the Monadnock Building (1889-90), the 22-storey Masonic Temple (1890-92) – the world's tallest building at the time – and the Fuller Building in New York (1903). These and others display the ordered functionalism and strong vertical articulation characteristic of Louis SULLIVAN and the Chicago School. After Root's premature death (1891) Burnham concentrated on town and area planning. His District of Columbia plan marked the start of comprehensive town planning in America and was followed by many others.

☐ Sherman House, Chicago, 1874. Monadnock Building, Chicago, 1889-91. Masonic Temple, Chicago, 1890-92. Fuller (also known as the Flatiron) Building, New York, 1903.

▷ Donald Hoffmann, *The Architecture of John Wellborn Root*, Baltimore, 1973. Thomas S. Hines, *Burnham of Chicago, Architect and Planner*, 2nd ed., Chicago, 1979. CS

▷ *see also pp226–7, 232–3*

Burnham & Root, Fuller (Flatiron) Building, New York, 1903

BURTON Decimus

b. London, 1800; d. London, 1881.

The most talented protégé of John NASH, whose own work maintained the classical imagery associated with the Regent's Park development. His father, James Burton, a builder and architect, was one of the speculators backing Nash's building plans, and Decimus's first accredited designs were for Cornwall and Clarence Terraces (1821 and 1823). His formal education at the Royal Academy School was followed by a brief professional spell with Nash. He was then in practice from 1823 until his retirement in 1864.

Alongside COCKERELL, HARDWICK and SMIRKE, Burton represents the continuing thread of English academic classicism in the first half of the C19. He was the architect most seriously engaged in glass and iron construction, and is best remembered for his innovative designs for conservatories, with PAXTON at Chatsworth (1837-40) and with the Dublin engineer Richard Turner for the Palm House at Kew Gardens (1844-8), the building which brought fame to Burton and Turner. Burton's family background led to continued involvement with run-of-the-mill speculative work at the Calverley Estate, Tunbridge Wells (1827-40), Upper Norwood (1830s), Fleetwood, Lancs. (1835-43), as well as planning schemes for Brighton, St Leonards and Hastings. His better-known "public works", such as the Hyde Park Screen, the designs for Regent's Park, and the Athenaeum, follow closely with the Nash connection.

☐ Hyde Park Screen, London, 1825. Colosseum, Regent's Park, London, 1825. Athenaeum, London, 1827-30. Grove House, Regent's Park, 1823-7. Palm House and Home Farm, Chatsworth, Derbyshire (with Paxton), 1832-48. Phoenix Park, Dublin (with Turner), 1834-49. Palm House and Temperate House, Kew Gardens (with Turner), 1844-8 and 1859-63.

▷ John Summerson, *Georgian London*, London, 1945; *The Life and Works of John Nash, Architect*, London, 1980. AB

▷ *see also pp222–3*

Decimus Burton, Palm House, Kew Gardens, Surrey, 1844–8

BUTTERFIELD William

b. London, 1814; d. London, 1900.

One of the most original of the Gothic Revival architects, known for his use of constructional polychromy. The son of a chemist, he trained as a builder, then studied architecture under E. L. Blackburne (1833-6) and worked for W. and H. W. INWOOD. In 1842, soon after setting up in practice, he aligned himself with the newly formed Ecclesiological movement (a radical Anglo-Catholic group within the Church of England), marking out the ecclesiastical character of his subsequent career. At All Saints, Margaret Street (1849-59), his first and most influential church, Butterfield expounded the Ecclesiological doctrine that the planning and design of churches must symbolize the spiritual functions of sacrament and worship. At the same time the harsh structural geometry of All Saints, its boldly variegated exterior and interior surfaces, and inventive use of manufactured materials announced Butterfield's personal commitment to reinterpreting the Gothic language in contemporary terms. His theoretical position thus formed a striking contrast to the medievalism of PUGIN, though he shared Pugin's concern for furnishings and interiors. Butterfield's later buildings retained both the uncompromising "ugliness" (Summerson) and the functional planning of his early work. Professionally and personally solitary, he had few pupils. His work was greatly admired by Philip WEBB. He received the RIBA Gold Medal in 1884.

All Saints, Margaret Street, London, 1849-59. Balliol Chapel, Oxford, 1854-7. Milton Ernest Hall, Bedfordshire, 1854-8. Rugby School (additions), 1858-84. All Saints, Babbacombe, Devon, 1865-74. Keble College, Oxford, 1867-83. St Augustine, Queen's Gate, London, 1870-77. Anglican Cathedrals in Perth (Scotland), 1847, Adelaide (Australia), 1847-78, Melbourne (Australia), 1877-86.

John Summerson, *Heavenly Mansions*, London, 1948. Peter Ferriday (ed.), *Victorian Architecture*, London, 1963. Paul Thompson, *William Butterfield*, London, 1981.

BP

see also pp228–9

CAMERON Charles

b. London, mid-1740s; d. St Petersburg (Leningrad), 1811/12.

British architect, creator of integrated building and landscape compositions that brought English aesthetic ideas to the Imperial Russian court of Catherine the Great. He was apprenticed as a carpenter by his father, a builder, but in the early 1760s he was hired, on the basis of his drawing skills, by Isaac WARE to check PALLADIO's Roman baths measurements for republication. This led to his own more interpretative study, *Baths of the Romans* (published in London 1772) and thence to an invitation to Russia in 1779 when Catherine the Great sought expertise for creating a Roman-style baths complex at Tsarskoe Selo Palace. He was chief architect to Catherine at Tsarskoe Selo, and to her heir Paul at nearby Pavlovsk, till the former's death in 1796, when he was dismissed by Paul. In 1803 he was re-employed into imperial service by Alexander I as chief architect to the admiralty, but he was dismissed in 1805 in favour of ZAKHAROV. At Tsarskoe Selo Palace Cameron created a series of superb interiors with ADAMesque Classicism, chinoiserie etc. as well as pavilions and promenades forming a stage-set for Catherine's new Enlightenment ideas. With elements from William KENT and other British designers, Catherine's park became an allegory of her foreign policy, and Sofia model town demonstrated a new-Neo-Palladian urbanism for Russia. At Pavlovsk Cameron introduced the English Palladian villa and park, widely replicated later throughout Russia.

Charles Cameron, Catherine the Great's Bedchamber, Tsarskoe Selo, 1780-8, detail

Tsarskoe Selo (now Pushkin): Baths and Agate Pavilion, 1780-85; Cameron Gallery, 1783-6; Private apartments and reception rooms, 1780-87. Sofia model town, 1780-85. Pavlovsk: Palace and park, 1781-7. St Andrew's Cathedral, Kronstadt, 1804 (redesigned by Zakharov). Oranienbaum Naval Hospital, 1804-5.

T. Talbot-Rice in *Charles Cameron* (exhibition catalogue), Edinburgh and London, 1967, pp.7-24. I. Rae, *Charles Cameron*, London, 1971. D. Shvidkovsky, *England in Russia: British Architects Build for the Tsars*, London, 1991.

CC

CAMPBELL Colen

b. Boghole, Scotland, 1676; d. London, 1729.

Successful founder of English Palladianism (*see* PALLADIO), author of the influential book *Vitruvius Britannicus*. Campbell's origins are obscure and nothing is known of his education, although he claimed to have studied architecture both in England and abroad. He has traditionally been seen as a great architectural pioneer; his Wanstead House was a hugely successful precedent for a succession of

Colen Campbell, Wanstead House, Essex, c. 1714–20

Whig country houses in the Palladian style. However, the Earl of Shaftesbury's earlier call for a new national style is one indication that the English Palladian reaction against the continental Baroque – which was associated with absolutism – was already in motion. Campbell grasped the needs of the English Whig aristocracy and had an instinct for the simple box-like composition. He consolidated this success through his book *Vitruvius Britannicus*. The Palladian style lent itself to "literary transmission", through outline engravings, and this in turn reinforced the trend to geometrical outlines and simple classical details. *Vitruvius Britannicus,* in fact, featured the older native Baroque tradition of WREN and VANBRUGH alongside Palladianism. Campbell's own designs for Mereworth, which is based on Palladio's famous Villa Rotonda, incorporates elements of the Baroque and diverges from the more dogmatic plainness of the other great Palladian, Lord BURLINGTON.

☐ Shawfield Mansions, Glasgow, 1711-12. Wanstead House, Essex, *c.*1714-20. Rolls House, Chancery Lane, London, 1717-24. Ebberston Lodge, Scarborough, Yorks., 1718. Gateway to Burlington House, Piccadilly, London, 1718-19. 31-33 Old Burlington Street, London, 1718-23. Stourhead, Wilts., *c.*1720-24. Mereworth Castle, Kent, *c.*1722-5.

▷ Colen Campbell, *Vitruvius Britannicus or The British Architect*, 1716-25. H. E. Stutchbury, *The Architecture of Colen Campbell*, Manchester, 1967. P. Breman and D. Addis, *Guide to Vitruvius Britannicus*, New York, 1972. R. Wittkower, *Palladio and English Palladianism*, London, 1974. TC

VAN CAMPEN Jacob

b. Haarlem, 1595; d. Randenbroek, near Amersfoort, 1657.

Dutch painter and – as architectural designer – the leading practitioner of C17 international classicism in the Netherlands. Trained as a painter in his birthplace, he seems to have visited Venice and the Veneto between 1615 and 1621, becoming acquainted with Vincenzo SCAMOZZI and studying the work of PALLADIO. On returning home, he began designing buildings for clients, although the execution was left to others, under his supervision. His French-influenced palace in The Hague for the Dutch grandee Jan Mauritius of Orange-Nassau, the Mauritshuis (1633, completed with altered plan in 1655 and recently restored), later became the world-famous painting gallery. Other notables commissioned Palladian palaces from him in The Hague, and after being appointed government architect he designed the Amsterdam Town Hall (1648-65, now the royal palace). Van Campen's assured handling of the classical idiom reflected and projected the confidence of the Dutch in their newly independent and wealthy republic.

☐ Mauritshuis, The Hague, 1633-55. Noordeinde Palace, The Hague, 1640. Nieuwe Kerk, Haarlem, 1645. Amsterdam Town Hall (now Royal Palace), 1648-65.

▷ P. T. A. Swillens, *Jacob van Campen*, Assen, 1961. Catalogue of the Royal Palace exhibition, Amsterdam, 1982. JRC

▷ *see also pp216–17*

CANDELA Felix

b. Madrid, 1910.

Nicknamed "The Shell Builder" because of his extensive exploration of the structural possibilities of lightweight concrete roof construction, often using complex curve forms to exploit the tensile strengths within this versatile material. He entered Madrid's Escuela Superior de Arquitectura in 1927, graduated in 1935, and worked for a year as an engineer before enlisting with the Republican forces in the struggle against Franco. He was later interned and eventually emigrated to Mexico in 1939, adopting Mexican nationality in 1941. Candela believes that strength should come not from mass but from form, and while expanding this concept he has developed a coherent philosophy towards shell structures. His obsession with the thin shell vault and the hyperbolic paraboloid paralleled the ideas of Buckminster FULLER in the US, and he is often compared with PROUVÉ and NERVI in terms of being a master-builder; he was frequently obliged to combine the roles of architect, structural engineer and contractor in order to further his experiments in aesthetic form and constructional methods. However, he viewed the engineer as a poet, essentially one possessing the intellectual breadth to design not only great cathedrals but also low-cost single-family housing.

Felix Candela, Church of the Miraculous Virgin, Mexico City, 1953–5

□ Cosmic Ray Pavilion, Ciudad Universitaria, Mexico City, 1951. Church of the Miraculous Virgin, Navarte, Mexico City, 1953-5. Xochimilco Restaurant, Mexico City, 1958. Chapel, Lomas de Cuernavca, 1958-9. Olympic Stadium, Mexico City, 1968.

▷ Max Cetto, *Modern Architecture in Mexico*, New York, 1961. Colin Faber, *Candela – The Shell Builder*, London, 1963. Clive Bamford Smith, *Builders in the Sun – Four Mexican Architects*, New York, 1967. MC

CARDINAL Douglas

b. Calgary, Alberta, 1934.

Canadian-born architect, of part-American-Indian extraction, with an interest in architecture as an art form in harmony with nature and the living environment but designed by computers. He graduated as an architect from Texas University, Austin, in 1963 and commenced his own practice in Edmonton, Canada, in 1964. He moved his office to Ottawa in 1985 largely to deal with the exigencies of the celebrated Museum of Civilization he built in Hull, Quebec, between 1981 and 1989. This building, sculpted, as the architect says, "by the winds and glaciers", is split into two distinct low-lying, organically shaped elements. It overlooks one of the finest panoramas in North America, Ottawa's patrician Parliament Hill. Cardinal's earlier buildings, although all much smaller, have the same dynamic form basis and employ local indigenous materials.

□ St Mary's Church, Red Deer, Alberta, 1967. Grande Prairie Regional College, Grande Prairie, Alberta, 1970-74. Government Services Centre, Ponoka, Alberta, 1977. Canadian Museum of Civilization, Hull, Quebec, 1981-9.

▷ Trevor Boddy, *The Architecture of Douglas Cardinal* (with an extensive selection of Cardinal's own writings), Edmonton, 1989. DS

▷ *see also pp244–5*

DE CARLO Giancarlo

b. Genoa, 1919.

Designer, planner and theorist whose mature Modern architecture links CIAM ideals with late C20 reality. He trained as an architect in Milan (Dip.Ing. 1942) and Venice (Dip.Arch. 1949) in a time of political turmoil which formed his own philosophy. In a long and independent career, an unswerving libertarian socialism, with its intellectual strength, underpins all his planning and design. De Carlo's built works, like his rare theoretical essays, are complex. "Understanding is something for which you have to suffer in order to obtain it at any depth," he commented in 1979. A pragmatic idealist, he enjoys the place of conflict in the development of his architecture, which is centred in participation (itself inherently conflictual), in its context and in dialogue with its past. De Carlo shows a rare mastery in reading historic places (the people, politics and buildings), transforming and liberating them, then stitching them together with new insertions. His political independence (rare in post-war Italy) has limited his built œuvre and his academic standing. But his own vehicles, the journal *Spazio e Società* and his master class, the International Laboratory of Architecture and Urban Design (ILAUD), and the support of his Team 10 colleagues, have calmly ridden against the tide of the "tendenza" or "Post-Modernism".

□ Buildings for Urbino University, 1952-82. Housing in Matera, 1957, Urbino, 1965, Terni, 1972 and Venice, 1986. Art School, Urbino, 1972. Reconstruction of Renaissance *rampa* (1980) and C19 theatre (1984) in Urbino. Masterplans and buildings for Reggio Emilia (with Albini, 1948), Urbino (1958/64), Padua (1960), Volterra (1961), Dublin University, Ireland (1964), Plovdiv, Bulgaria (1969), Pavia University (1972-5), Pistoia (1986), Catania University (1988), Sienna University Sports Centre (1990).

▷ Giancarlo de Carlo, "The situation of contemporary architecture", in O. Newman (ed.), *CIAM '59 in Otterlo*, London, 1959; *Urbino, the History of a City and Plans for its Redevelopment*, Padua, 1966, MIT, 1970; "Reflections on the Present State of Architecture", *AA Quarterly*, Vol. 10, No. 2, 1978. F. Brunetti and F. Gesi, *Giancarlo de Carlo*, Florence, 1981. See also: *GDC: Architettura, Città, Universita: Disegni*, Florence, 1982. L. Rossi, *Grancarlo de Carlo*, Milan, 1988. JM

DU CERCEAU FAMILY

Jacques Androuet du Cerceau (the Elder), b. c. 1515, d. 1585; Jean-Baptiste Androuet du Cerceau, b. c. 1547, d. 1590; Jacques Androuet du Cerceau (the Younger), b. 1550, d. 1614; Charles Androuet du Cerceau, d. 1606; Jean Androuet du Cerceau, b. c. 1585, d. 1649.

Distinguished dynasty of French architects, designers, engravers and decorators who brought the Renaissance style to the Fontainebleau court. Jacques the Elder produced some of the most famous architectural books of the period, based on measured drawings. Less is known about his work as an architect, though he was involved in a number of churches and châteaux. Jacques the Younger was responsible for several châteaux and the Grand Gallery at the Louvre; Jean built the Luxembourg Palace and the Hôtel de Sully.

□ Jean Baptiste Androuet du Cerceau: Pont Neuf, Paris, 1578. Jacques Androuet du Cerceau the Younger: Grand Gallery, Louvre, Paris, 1605-13. Jean Androuet du Cerceau: Luxembourg Palace, Paris (with de BROSSE), *c.* 1614; Hôtel de Sully, Paris, 1632.

▷ J. Androuet du Cerceau the Elder, *Grotesques*, 1550; *Livres d'architecture . . .*, c. 1571–9; *Arabesques*, 1586. W. H. Ward, *French Chateaux and Gardens of the XVIth Century*, 1909; *Architecture of the Renaissance in France*, 1912. DS

CHAMBERS Sir William

b. Gothenburg, Sweden, 1723; d. London, 1796.

An outstanding "official architect" whose reputation as "a prodigy for genius, for sense and good taste" was earned early. His architecture blends concerns with Palladianism – symmetrical, well-ordered façades – with, in the interiors, early forms of Neo-Classicism, learned in Italy. The son of a Scottish merchant who had established himself in Gothenburg, Chambers was educated in England and returned to Sweden at the age of sixteen to enter the service of the Swedish East India Company. This is the first clue to his unusual career, for travelling out to Bengal and China gave him an almost unrivalled knowledge of Oriental art. By 1749 he had saved enough money from these spirited labours to make architecture his "sole study and profession". Travelling to study in Paris he journeyed on to Italy and was there by the autumn of 1750. There he not only studied under drawing masters, including the influential Charles-Louis Clérisseau (1721-80), but absorbed ideas current at the French Academy in Rome. These were concerned with observing antiquity and developing ways of giving it new and influential forms in contemporary decoration. In 1755 Chambers returned to England with a

Sir William Chambers, the Pagoda, Kew Gardens, Surrey, 1757–62

wife and an infant daughter. As with his rival Robert ADAM, commissions were at first few, but Chambers' ferocious talent came early to the notice of Lord Bute, who recommended him as architectural tutor to the Prince of Wales, the future George III. This was an auspicious start to his long patronage by the royal family. Augusta, the Dowager Princess of Wales, mindful of the drawings Chambers had made in Rome for a mausoleum to her husband Frederick Louis, Prince of Wales (d. 1751), asked him in 1757 to lay out the gardens of her Surrey house at Kew. Many bridges, temples and the celebrated Pagoda (1761-2) were built and in 1763 were further set out, fulsomely, in a book by Chambers. With Lord Bute's patronage, as with Adam, Chambers had been appointed in 1761 as one of the Joint Architects of the King's Works. By 1769 he was so indispensable an official architect that he was appointed Comptroller of the King's Works. When the office was reorganized in 1782 he became both Surveyor-General and Comptroller. Chambers' architecture divides into three unequal representations. Firstly the public buildings, and pre-eminently Somerset House in the Strand, London, which dominated his last twenty years (1776-96); secondly a number of town houses in London, Edinburgh and Dublin; finally the country houses: at least forty-five commissions, from 1757 onwards. All were controlled by an able and sympathetic architect.

□ Kew Gardens, Surrey: The Orangery; Pagoda, 1757-62. Charlemont House, Dublin, 1763-75. Woburn Abbey, Beds. (S Wing and certain interiors), 1767-72. Melbourne House, Piccadilly, London, 1771-4. Dundas House, Edinburgh, 1771-4. Milton Abbey House, Dorset (in Gothic style), 1771-6. Somerset House, Strand, London, 1776-96.

▷ William Chambers, *Designs of Chinese Buildings...*, 1757; *Treatise on Civil Architecture*, 1759, 1768, 3rd ed. 1791, title altered to *A Treatise on the Decorative Part of Civil Architecture*; *Plans, Elevations, Sections...of the Gardens and Buildings at Kew*, 1763. J. Harris, *Sir William Chambers*, London, 1970. GB

CHERMAYEFF Serge Ivan

Sergius Ivan Issakovitch,
b. Grozny, North Caucasus, 1900.

Pioneer practitioner of the Modern Movement in Britain and prominent American educator. He was sent to England at the age of 12 to be educated firstly in London then at Harrow School, where he gained (but did not take up) a scholarship to Cambridge University. The Russian Revolution put a stop to his family's financial support and he entered the army. Later he started out as an interior designer and subsequently worked largely for the then progressive furniture firm of Waring & Gillow before establishing his own architectural practice in 1930. After 1934 he executed a number of commissions with Eric MENDELSOHN, the most significant of which was the entertainment complex at Bexhill-on-Sea. This early work looks not just to Western European prototypes, but also to Russian Constructivist architecture. In 1940 he emigrated to the USA, where he became involved both in practice and in teaching, as Art Department Chairman, Brooklyn College (1942), and later President of the New Bauhaus in Chicago (1946). He remained active as a small-scale practitioner until he moved to Cambridge, Mass., where he opened an office with Hayward Cutting in 1953. He took up a professorship at Harvard the same year; in 1962 he transferred to Yale. His two major books on community architecture and planning followed.

Serge Chermayeff (with Erich Mendelsohn), 64 Old Church St, Chelsea, London, 1935–6

□ Cambridge Theatre, London (interior), 1930. BBC interiors, London, 1932-4. De La Warr Pavilion, Bexhill-on-Sea, Sussex (with Mendelsohn), 1934-5. Nimmo House, Chalfont St Giles, Bucks. (with Mendelsohn), 1935. 64 Old Church St, Chelsea, London, 1935-6. W. & A. Gilbey offices, London, 1937. ICI Research laboratory, Manchester, 1938. Own house (Bentley Wood), Halland, Sussex, 1939. Payson House, Portland, Maine, 1952.

▷ Serge Chermayeff and Christopher Alexander, *Community and Privacy: Toward a New Architecture*, New York, 1963, Harmondsworth, 1966. Serge Chermayeff and Alexander Tzonis, *Shape of Community: Realization of Human Potential*, Baltimore, Md., and Harmondsworth, 1971. R. Plunz (ed.), *Design and the Public Good: Selected Writings by Serge Chermayeff*, Cambridge, Mass., 1982. DS

CHURRIGUERA FAMILY

José Benito Churriguera, b. Madrid, 1665; d. Madrid, 1725. Joaquin Churriguera, b. Madrid, 1674; d. Salamanca, 1724. Alberto Churriguera, b. Madrid, 1676; d. Madrid, c. *1740.*

Spanish family of architects and craftsmen who developed the sumptuous, highly decorative "Churrigueresque" style. Their father, José Rates y Dalmau (d. 1684), was a Catalan sculptor, employed by King Philip IV to design wooden altarpieces for churches around the country. His highly elaborate style, which incorporated elements of native South American art, was one of the formative influences on his sons' architectural development. The eldest son, José Benito, originally followed in his father's footsteps by designing altarpieces. His huge altarpiece at the Church of San Esteban in Salamanca (1692-4) is a design of great power and coherence, featuring twisting and elaborate "Salomonic" columns. His principal work of architecture was a new town, Nuevo Baztan, planned and built between 1709 and 1713. José's brother Joaquin also started out designing altarpieces for churches and was eventually appointed master of the works at Salamanca Cathedral in 1714. Joaquin's later work includes the Collegio de Calatrava in Salamanca, which was eventually completed by his younger brother Alberto. Alberto de Churriguera's early years were over-shadowed by his more experienced brothers, but he gradually developed into a leading talent in his own right. In 1725 he succeeded Joaquin at Salamanca Cathedral and three years later commenced work on the Plaza Mayor, the main square in Salamanca. His last works (churches at Orgaz and Rueda) remained unfinished, but typify his individual interpretation of the Spanish Rococo style.

Alberto Churriguera, Church of Santo Tomas, Rueda, 1738–40

□ José Benito: Altarpiece, Church of San Esteban, Salamanca, 1692-4. Town of Nuevo Baztan, 1709-13. Joaquin: Collegio de Calatrava, Salamanca, 1717. Alberto: Plaza Mayor (S, E and W sides), Salamanca, 1729-33; Parish Church, Orgaz, 1731-8; Church of Santo Tomas, Rueda, 1738-40.

▷ Alfonso Rodriguez Gutierrez de Ceballos, *Los Churriguera*, Madrid, 1971. CS

COATES Wells Wintemute

b. Tokyo, 1895; d. Vancouver, 1958.

Leading Modernist architect in Britain in the 1930s and founder, with E. Maxwell FRY, of the English Modern Architecture Research (MARS) Group (1933). The son of Canadian Christian missionaries serving in Japan, he received his early education in Tokyo. Later, he studied science and engineering at the university in Vancouver. By all accounts he was destined for a career in science, and he obtained a PhD in engineering from London University (1924); nonetheless, he took up journalism and sought part-time work with the architectural firm of Adams and Thompson, where he met Maxwell Fry. His first design projects

Wells Coates, Embassy Court, Brighton, 1935

were mainly for shops and exhibition stands, although by the early 1930s he was working for the property developer Jack Pritchard on a series of houses of the minimal type. He designed the modern "Isokon" Lawn Road Flats, Hampstead, 1932-4. This scheme, with 10 Palace Gate, Kensington, and the Embassy Court luxury flats at Brighton, are among his best buildings; all are in the Corbusian manner. He was a member of Herbert Read's loose-knit "Unit One" and was featured in the publication of the same name. He was also active in CIAM. He worked extensively for the BBC, producing studios in Broadcasting House, London, in the interwar period and an experimental "Telekinema" as part of the Festival of Britain in 1951. Earlier, after creating the MARS Group in 1933 he designed the Group's major exhibition in London in 1938. In the 1950s he formed an architectural and planning practice with Jaqueline Tyrwhitt and spent his rather unsuccessful last years in Canada.

☐ Lawn Road Flats, London NW3, 1932-3. Sunspan House design (with D. Pleydell-Bouverie), 1934. Embassy Court, Brighton, 1935. 10 Palace Gate, Kensington, London, 1938. "Telekinema", South Exhibition, London (incorporated later into the National Film Theatre), 1951.

▷ S. Cantacuzino, *Wells Coates*, London, 1978. Laura Cohn (ed.), *Wells Coates*, Oxford, 1979. DS

▷ *see also pp238-9*

COCKERELL Charles Robert

b. London, 1788; d. London, 1863.

The most scholarly and original classical architect of his generation in Britain. He studied under his father, the architect **Samuel Pepys Cockerell** (1754-1827), and was briefly an assistant to Robert SMIRKE. In 1810-15 he was in Greece, where he discovered the Aegina and Phigalea Marbles (now respectively in the Munich Glyptothek and the British Museum), and in 1815-17 he was in Italy. He practised in London from 1818 to 1859, succeeding his father as Surveyor to St Paul's Cathedral (1819-57) and SOANE as Surveyor to the Bank of England (1833-57). To his buildings he brought a detailed understanding of Greek and Roman architecture and sculpture, and an expressive but disciplined vigour recalling WREN

C. R. Cockerell, Taylorian Institute, Oxford, 1841–5

and HAWKSMOOR, whose work he admired. He was also influenced by contemporary French architecture, and was an early advocate of cast-iron construction. His reputation declined during the Gothic upsurge of the 1850s, but was rehabilitated during the Baroque revival of the 1880s and 1890s. Cockerell was Professor of Architecture at the RA (1840-56) and was a member of the Academies of Paris, Rome, Munich, and Copenhagen. He received the RIBA's first Royal Gold Medal (1848) and was its first professional President (1860).

☐ University Library, Cambridge (unfinished), 1840. Ashmolean Museum and Taylorian Institute, Oxford, 1841-5. Bank of England branches at Manchester, 1844-5, Bristol, 1844-6, and Liverpool, 1844-7. Liverpool and London Insurance Co., Liverpool, 1856-7.

▷ C. R. Cockerell, *Antiquities of Athens and other places of Greece, Sicily etc.*, London, 1830. E. M. Dodd, *Charles Robert Cockerell* (in *Victorian Architecture*, ed. Peter Ferriday, London, 1963). David Watkin, *The Life and Work of C. R. Cockerell*, London, 1974. BP

CODERCH Y DE SENTMENAT José Antonio

b. Barcelona, 1913; d. Barcelona, 1984.

Dynamic Spanish architect and urban design theorist. Coderch was trained at the Escuela Tecnica Superior de Arquitectura in Barcelona (1929-40), but between 1936 and 1939 his education was interrupted by the Spanish Civil War, in which he served as a lieutenant. Following the war he worked in the offices of the Director General of Architecture in Madrid for two years, going on to hold similar positions in Barcelona and Sitges. An energetic practising architect from 1947 until his death, Coderch originally collaborated with fellow Barcelona architect Manuel Vallas Verges. In his urban design and housing projects he always believed in putting human problems first. His career began with two notable but unexecuted designs – the Las Forcas housing project, Sitges (1945), and Ugalde House, Caldetas (1951), but success eventually followed with the Cocheras flats (completed in 1968) and The Barcelona Trade Office Building which draws inspiration from MIES VAN DER ROHE. In an article entitled "There are no geniuses that we need now" (published in the Italian magazine *Domus* in 1961) Coderch imagined the architect as a detached professional, with a recognized duty to serve society. True to his principles, Coderch attempted to produce "truly living works", unhindered by the dogma and confusion of style. Sadly, his extraordinary last achievement – an extension to the Barcelona School of Architecture – was unrealized.

☐ Trade Office Building, Barcelona, 1965. Cocheras Housing Block, Sarria, Barcelona, 1968. French Institute Building, Barcelona, 1972.

▷ J. A. Coderch, *Architecture and Urbanism* (special issue), Feb. 1976. Javier Ortega, Antón Capitel, *J. A. Coderch 1945-1976*, Madrid, 1978. Toshiaku Tange, "The Dilemma of Coderch", *Architecture and Urbanism*, April 1978. CS

CONNELL, WARD & LUCAS

Established 1933.

Modern English architectural practice, formed in 1933 and disbanded in 1939. Its work was based on a simple interpretation of the "white" Corbusian cubic Modern architecture, with emphasis on the potential of thin self-supporting reinforced concrete construction. **Amyas Douglas Connell** (b. New Zealand, 1900; d. London, 1980) began his career as an articled pupil but emigrated to England to continue his architectural training at University College, London. In 1926 he won the prestigious RIBA Rome Prize, which led to a commission for a large villa for the Director of the British School in Rome, at Amersham, Bucks. (1929-31). This controversial house can be viewed as the last of the great British villas or as the first "modern" one. Known as *High and Over* and finished in the white "concrete" Le Corbusian style it proved offensive to conservative architectural circles in Britain at the time. Connell worked in East Africa after the war, first in Tanganyika (Tanzania) and later in Nairobi, Kenya, where he designed the award-winning Aga Khan Platinum Jubilee Hospital as well as the new Parliament Buildings. In Nairobi he was founder partner with his son of TRIAD, a firm of architects that is still extant. **Basil Ward** (b. New Zealand, 1902; d. Ambleside, 1978) joined Connell in practice in London in 1932. Ward was the apologist and philosopher of CWL, who was placed second in the 1926 Rome Prize after Connell. When CWL closed in 1939 and after war service in the Royal Navy, Ward became a partner in Murray Ward and Partners. He was also Lethaby Professor of Architecture, Royal College of Art, London. In the mid-1960s he retired to Cumbria, taking up teaching appointments at Manchester Polytechnic and Lancaster University. **Colin Lucas** (b. London, 1906, d. London, 1988) was educated at Cambridge University. After a period with his own building company he became a member of the Modernist Unit 1 led by Herbert Read. He joined CWL in 1933. In the post-war period he acted as a team leader of the Development Group, LCC (later GLC) Architect's Department. After retirement he took up painting and held a number of exhibitions in London.

□ By Connell: "High and Over", Amersham, Bucks., 1929-31; Cordon Bleu School, London, 1931. By Connell and Ward: New Farm, Grays Wood, Surrey, 1932. By Connell, Ward & Lucas: Sun House Estate, Amersham, Bucks., 1934; Parkwood Estate, Middx., 1935; Kent House, London, 1935; House (66 Frognal), London, 1936-8; House (6 Temple Gardens), Herts., 1938; House (26 Besborough Road), London, 1939.

▷ "Connell, Ward and Lucas; 1927-1939", *AA Journal* 72, No. 806, 1956. Basil Ward, "Connell, Ward and Lucas", in Dennis Sharp (ed.), *Planning and Architecture*, London, 1967.

DS

▷ *see also pp238-9*

Connell & Ward, New Farm, Haslemere, 1932

CORREA Charles

b. Hyderabad, India, 1930.

Correa's architecture, planning and writing well illustrate the dilemmas facing the western-trained architect in an indigenous and sensitive culture such as that of northern India. Educated at the University of Michigan and MIT, graduating in 1955, he has had a private practice in Bombay since 1958. Returning to India, Correa, like DOSHI, shows careful development, understanding and adaptation of Modernism in his early works. A tight, small-scale village community, a domestic architecture with echoes of LE CORBUSIER characterize Correa's early works, which were systematic attempts to explore a local vernacular and a modern environment. Such sensitivity, low-cost village semiosis and community strategies are best seen in the Gandhi Memorial in Ahmedabad (1963). Correa continued this exploration whilst searching for new patterns and techniques, a new landscape, which included radical urban thinking and the concern, beyond cliché, for the demographic problems of a country like India. Correa's land-use planning and community studies and projects have continually tried to go beneath the surface of hackneyed Third World solutions. The late 70s and 80s have seen Correa take on more important larger projects using a fuller semiotic approach; sign, form and colour are influenced by Rajastani village symbolism. The best examples are the Cidade de Goa Hotel (1982) and the more challenging and innovative addition to Connaught Circus in the centre of Delhi, the LIC Building (1988). A cosmopolitan, having lectured all over the world, he was awarded the RIBA Royal Gold Medal (1984), the Aalto Medal and in 1990 the UIA Gold Medal.

□ Sports Complex, Ahmedabad, India, 1960. Gandhi Memorial Museum, Ahmedabad, 1963. Boyce Houses, Bombay (project), 1964. Tara Housing, Delhi, 1975. Salvacao Church, 1977. Crafts Museum, Delhi, 1977. Cidade de Goa Hotel, Goa, 1982. Indira Gandhi International Airport, Delhi, 1986. LIC Building, Delhi, 1988.

▷ Charles Correa, *The New Landscape*, India, 1985. S. Cantacuzino, *Charles Correa*, Singapore and London, 1984.

RC

Charles Correa, Boyce Houses, Bombay, 1964, project

CORTONA Pietro Berrettini da

b. Cortona, 1596; d. Rome, 1669.

One of the pioneers, with BERNINI and BORROMINI, of Roman Baroque, with a taste for dramatic composition and grandiose planning. He was trained as a painter, and his earliest architectural works reveal an unexpected boldness. The Villa Pigneto was one of the earliest examples of a concave façade, and the slightly concave front of SS. Martina e Luca predates that of Borromini's S. Carlo alle Quattro Fontane. Several works reveal Cortona's Tuscan origins and his debt to MICHELANGELO; the recessed columns inside SS. Martina e Luca, for example, recall those of the Laurentian Library. The highly sculptural and dynamic approach to wall articulation explored here, with its emphasis on the close packing of columns and other elements in tightly unified composition, becomes one of the hallmarks of Cortona's architecture. His masterpiece, the façade of Santa Maria della Pace, extends the two-storey church front around the sides of the remodelled piazza as a gradual crescendo from the flat articulation at the sides to the bold projection of the columnar portico in a series of inter-related and complementary curves.

□ Villa Pigneto, Rome, *c.*1625 (destroyed). SS. Martina e Luca, Rome, from 1635. Santa Maria della Pace, Rome (façade), from 1656. Santa Maria in Via Lata, Rome (façade), 1658-62.

▷ K. Noehles, *La Chiesa di SS Luca e Martina nell' Opera di Pietro da Cortona*, Rome, 1970. R. Krautheimer, *The Rome of Alexander VII*, Princeton, 1985.

DH

▷ *see also pp218-9*

COSTA Lucio

b. Toulon, 1902.

Often hailed as the man who first introduced the rigorous tenets of the Modern Movement to a still slumbering Brazil. He attended a variety of educational establishments and graduated, with a diploma in architecture from the Escola Nacional de Belas Artes, Rio de Janeiro, in 1924. Initially he fostered the burgeoning Neo-Colonial Revival which swept across Brazil in the 1930s. Costa was appointed director of the Escola Nacional de Belas Artes and immediately dismantled the moribund Beaux-Arts curriculum; in its place he introduced the revolutionary concepts of the European avant-garde but politics intervened and he was quietly eased out after only one year. He shared LE CORBUSIER's penchant for *brise-soleil* and *pilotis* and invited the celebrated Swiss architect to act as consultant on the Ministry of Education and Health project, designed in conjunction with Oscar NIEMEYER. His most enduring legacy, however, will be the competition-winning city plan for the new capital Brasilia.

□ Ministry of Education and Health, Rio de Janeiro, 1937-43. Park Hotel, Friburgo, 1944. Parque Eduardo Guinle Apartments, Rio de Janeiro, 1948-54. Masterplan for Brasilia, 1957.

▷ L. Costa, *The Architect and Contemporary Society*, Venice, 1952. J. O. Gazenco and M. M. Scarone, *Lucio Costa*, New York, 1956. H. Mindlin, *Modern Architecture in Brazil*, Buenos Aires, 1959.

MC

COX Philip

b. Sydney, 1939.

Australian architect whose work is underpinned by technology and a strong sense of the importance of relating built form to landscape in an ecologically responsible manner. He studied architecture at Sydney University and then worked with Bruce Rickard (1962-3) and Ian McKay (1963-6). His early houses were neo-Wrightian, but the St Andrews Presbyterian Preparatory College, Leppington (1964), and C. B. Alexander Presbyterian Agricultural College, Paterson (1966), designed in association with McKay, marked an important step in Australian awareness. In practice on his own since 1967, Cox's designs maintained their loyalty to WRIGHT, but this orientation was to be challenged by an increased interest in historical restoration and research into early Australian colonial architecture and vernacular building traditions. His architecture is susceptible to external style shifts; this accounts for a certain eclectic facility and a reliance on structural effects. In his later, carefully integrated tensile works with partners Taylor and Richardson, he has brought a greater technical sophistication to bear, exemplified by the Yulara Tourist Village, Ayers Rock, with its simple saddle shade canopies, Sydney Football Stadium and the Exhibition Halls at Darling Harbour.

Lucio Costa, Ministry of Education and Health, Rio de Janeiro, 1937-43

□ Hawkins house, Cheltenham, NSW, 1969. National Sports Stadium, Bruce, Canberra, 1977. Yulara Tourist Village, Ayers Rock, NT, 1984. Sydney Football Stadium, 1988. Exhibition Halls, Darling Harbour, NSW, 1988.

▷ Philip Cox and C. Lucas, *Australian Colonial Architecture*, Melbourne, 1978. Philip Cox, J. Freeland and W. Stacey, *Rude Timber Buildings in Australia*, Sydney, 1980. *Australian Architects 1: Philip Cox*, Canberra, 1984. PD

CRAM Ralph Adams

see Goodhue & Cram.

CUBITT Thomas

b. Buxton, Norfolk, 1788; d. Dorking, 1855.

Victorian builder and developer. Born in relative poverty, Cubitt trained as a carpenter in London. In 1815 he set up as a building contractor, and during the post-Waterloo expansion of London he emerged as the leading speculative developer of new middle- and upper-middle-class suburbs. His success was founded on his innovative system of employing tradesmen on a permanent wage rather than on a jobbing basis, on his acquisition of extensive workshops and warehousing, and on the fact that most of his developments were planned and designed "in house" by himself or his brother **Lewis Cubitt** (1799-1883). The brick and stucco villas and terraces that he erected between 1820 and 1850 were shrewdly calculated to fill market needs – solidly built, well provided with services, and ornamented in accordance with social expectations. Cubitt's pre-eminence as a residential builder was acknowledged when the Queen and Prince Albert enlisted him (rather than any professional architect) to design and construct their Italianate seaside villa, Osborne House. He also built the entrance wing of Buckingham Palace to the designs of Edward Blore (whose inattention to practical detail confirmed Cubitt's lifelong distrust of working to outside specifications). Cubitt took an active interest in London's infrastructure, especially smoke abatement, the provision of public parks, and sewage disposal; he also advised on the Metropolitan Buildings Act of 1855.

□ London: parts of Highbury Park, Stoke Newington, Bloomsbury, Belgravia, Clapham Park, Pimlico. Brighton: part of Kemp Town. Polesden Lacey House, Surrey, 1824. Osborne House, Isle of Wight (with Prince Albert), 1845-8.

▷ Hermione Hobhouse, *Thomas Cubitt, Master Builder*, London, 1971. BP

CUYPERS Petrus Josephus Hubertus

b. Roermond, Holland, 1827; d. 1921.

The most prolific and influential Dutch architect of the C19. Cuypers studied architecture at the Antwerp Academy, Belgium, graduating in 1849 with the Prix d'Excellence, and briefly in Paris. He set up in practice in Roermond in 1850 and moved to Amsterdam in 1865. The establishment in 1853 of a Roman Catholic episcopal hierarchy in Holland stimulated a demand for new churches; Cuypers responded with a succession of free Gothic designs, influenced in a general way by PUGIN, but above all by VIOLLET-LE-DUC's insistence on the primacy of structure to the Gothic language, and on the honest use of materials. In 1852 Cuypers set up a studio to produce ecclesiastical furnishings and sculpture in accordance with these principles. For secular commissions, whether private or institutional, he usually adopted a Renaissance manner, selecting Dutch versions of the style in brick for the Rijksmuseum and the Central Station in Amsterdam, his most prominent works. As a medieval restorer, he believed that the reinstatement or insertion of architecturally "correct" features was often preferable to the conservation of existing fabric, an approach that won substantial public and government support. He founded and taught art history at the Rijksmuseum-school. Pioneer modern architects such as Lauwericks and Wijdeveld trained in his office.

□ St Catherina, Eindhoven, 1859-67. "Posthoorn-Kerk", Amsterdam, 1860-63. St Jacobus, The Hague, 1875-8. Rijksmuseum, Amsterdam, 1876-85. St Hippolytus, Delft, 1884-6. Central Station, Amsterdam, 1885-9. Haarzuylen Castle, Utrecht (restoration and extension), 1890.

▷ *Het Werk van Dr P. J. H. Cuypers 1827-1917*, Amsterdam, 1917. BP

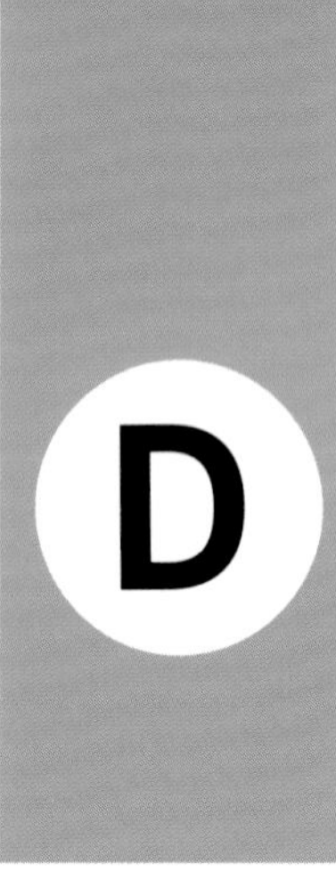

DANCE George, the Younger

b. London, 1741; d. London, 1825.

English Neo-Classical architect. Dance absorbed the rudiments of architecture from his father, George Dance the Elder, who was Clerk of Works in the City of London. He studied in Rome and imbibed the principles of European Neo-Classicism. On returning to London he became his father's assistant and shortly after won a competition for the rebuilding of All Hallows Church, where his innovative and radical simplifying of the classical orders shocked contemporary critics. He became Clerk of Works on the death of his father (1768). In one of his first development projects, for a site near the Minories, Dance was responsible for introducing to London the crescent and circus – urban forms which John WOOD had adapted from Roman amphitheatres and applied in Bath. Dance's most famous building was probably Newgate Gaol, which was widely imitated in England. However, because of the demanding nature of his position (from which he retired in 1815) Dance had little time for work outside the city and there is little evidence for any wider international impact of his work. His most important influence was undoubtedly on SOANE, who was his pupil

Deane & Woodward, University Museum, Oxford, 1855–61

Above: George Dance the Younger, the Guildhall, London, 1788–9

for two years and who later acquired all his architectural drawings.

□ All Hallows Church, London, 1765-7. Crescent, Circle and Square, Minories, London, 1767-8. Newgate Gaol, London, 1768-85. Giltspur Street Compter, London, 1787-9. Guildhall, London (façade), 1788-9. St Bartholomew-the-Less, London, 1789. Alterations to Mansion House, London, 1795.

▷ D. Stroud, *George Dance, Architect: 1741-1825*, London, 1971. TC

DEANE & WOODWARD

Established 1851.

Irish partnership which played a key part in the Ruskin-inspired revival of Gothic architecture in Victorian England. The firm of Deane & Woodward was an offshoot from the Dublin-based practice of Thomas Deane, father of **Thomas Newenham Deane** (b. Cork, 1828; d. 1899). Deane Jr had been educated at Trinity College Dublin before joining his father's practice in 1850. There he met **Benjamin Woodward** (b. Tullamore, 1816; d. 1861), who had originally trained as an engineer. His enthusiasm for medieval architecture had led him to change professions; he entered Thomas Deane's office in 1845. Both Deane and Woodward were made partners in 1851. Their first major building was Trinity College Museum (1852-7), which established the character of Victorian Gothic architecture in line with the tenets of RUSKIN. In practice this involved the creation of a monumental building based on a regular, almost classical plan form, with a richly embellished exterior. Deane and Woodward went on to design a number of buildings in Oxford, notably the Oxford Museum (1855-61), the first Gothic public building in Victorian England since the Houses of Parliament. In this case Ruskin was active in the development of the decorative scheme of the building. After Woodward died (1861), Deane continued to practise on his own, mainly in Dublin and Oxford. In 1878 he formed a new partnership with his son, Thomas Manly Deane, who subsequently took over the practice.

□ Trinity College Museum, Dublin, 1852-7. Oxford Museum, Oxford, England, 1855-61. Oxford Union, Oxford, 1857-9.

▷ Stefan Muthesius, *The High Victorian Movement in Architecture 1850-1870*, London, 1972. Eve Blau, *Ruskinian Gothic: The Architecture of Deane and Woodward, 1845-61*, Princeton, 1981. CS

Title page to L'Architecture de Philibert de l'Orme, *1568*

DELORME (DE L'ORME) Philibert

b. Lyon, c.1510; d. Paris, 1570.

Prolific and inventive designer of châteaux, fortifications and public buildings, who taught France the classical style – lucid, rational and regular. He was the son of a building contractor in Lyon and from the age of 15, while studying for the church, managed his father's business in his absence. The experience helped to give him, as heir to medieval traditions of masonry, his enormous practical ability. In 1533 he went to Rome to continue his clerical studies, and while there he took an enthusiastic interest in archaeology and the new architectural fashions in Italy, making friends with leading scholars and architects. Back in France, determined to pursue a career in architecture, he won the patronage of King Henri II and the royal family, who rewarded him with church preferments. Among many works for his royal employers are the tomb of François I in the abbey of St Denis, Paris, and large parts of the château of Fontainebleau. He built the château of Anet (largely destroyed in the French Revolution) for the King's mistress Diane de Poitiers.

Château of Anet, 1547-52. Château of Fontainebleau, 1548-59. Tomb of François I, St Denis, Paris, 1549-58.

Philibert Delorme, *Nouvelles inventions pour bien bastir et à petits frais (New Designs for Good Low-cost Building)*, Paris, 1561; *L'Architecture de Philibert de l'Orme*, Paris, 1568. Anthony Blunt, *Philibert de l'Orme*, London, 1958. JRC

DINKELOO John

see Roche & Dinkeloo

VAN DOESBURG Theo

C. E. M. Kupper (who also used the pseudonyms Aldo Camini and I. K. Bronset), b. Utrecht, 1883; d. Davos, Switzerland, 1931.

Founder of *De Stijl* in Holland, he was the sustaining intellectual of the movement; painter, architect and theoretician, editor of the periodical *De Stijl* which, after the departure of Mondrian in 1925 from the movement, became the unique vehicle for his theory of the fundamental unity of the arts. During military service (1914-16) Van Doesburg experienced crucial changes in his artistic work and developed an abstract cubism closely related to early Mondrian. He collaborated with J. J. P. OUD and Jan Wils, with whom he founded the group *De Spinx* in 1916. *De Stijl* was founded in 1917 by Van Doesburg with Mondrian, Huszar, Oud and Kok. In 1918 the *De Stijl* manifesto was published which led Van Doesburg to tour Germany in 1920, where he met GROPIUS. He lectured at the Bauhaus, where he continued to publish *De Stijl.* He had close associations with the Dadaists and wrote at this time under the name of Aldo Camini. During 1923 and 1924 Van Doesburg developed his "neo-plastic" aesthetic of mass with VAN EESTEREN and exhibited with him and RIETVELD in Paris and Nancy. It was during this period that he developed his "contra compositions" and introduced Elementarism, and its concern with geometrical form, to *De Stijl.* In 1926 Van Doesburg was commissioned to redesign the Aubette restaurant in Strasbourg. This was his canonical achievement of fusing painting and architecture. In 1928 Van Doesburg returned to Paris where, with Van Eesteren, he designed and built the Studio House at Meudon-val-Fleury. This was intended to be the new *De Stijl* Centre. The simultaneous compositions were produced at this time. Soon after the completion of the Studio and the establishment of the new group "Abstract-Creation", Van Doesburg travelled to Switzerland where he died. In the words of Allan Doig: "from tectonic painting developed a constructive architecture; from an ideal and utopian theory developed a practice which, although initially modest, became increasingly influential in the 1920's".

Restaurant "l'Aubette", Strasbourg, 1926. Studio House, Meudon-val-Fleury, 1929-31.

Writings by Van Doesburg are numerous. A useful summary appears in *De Stijl: Visions of Utopia* (see below). See especially *De Stijl* 1917-31. J. J. Sweeny (ed.), *Theo Van Doesburg* (exhibition catalogue), New York, 1947. H. L. C. Jaffe, *De Stijl 1917-1931. The Dutch Contribution to Modern Art*, Amsterdam, 1956. B. Gay, *De Stijl* (Camden exhibition catalogue), London, 1968. M. Friedman (ed.), *De Stijl: 1917-1931 Visions of Utopia*, Oxford, 1982. E. Van Straaten, *Theo Van Doesburg 1883-1913*, The Hague, 1983. C. Bocktaad (ed.), *Neo Plasticism in Architecture*, Delft, 1983. A. Doig, *Theo Van Doesburg*, Cambridge, 1986. E. Van Straaten, *Theo Van Doesburg, Painter and Architect*, The Hague, 1988. CD

DOMENECH Y MONTANER Lluis

b. Barcelona, 1850; d. Barcelona, 1923.

Spanish architect, historian and leading figure in the Catalan *Modernismo* movement. A contemporary of GAUDI, Domènech received his diploma from the Escuela Tecnica Superior de Arquitectura in Madrid in 1873. The principles of *Modernismo* – a potent mixture of Art Nouveau, the Modern style, the Jugendstil and the Secession – were first established by Domènech in his article "In Search of a National Architecture" (1878). The movement's aim was to make a rational transition from late C19 eclecticism to a modern idiom without sacrificing the essential characteristics of national Catalan identity. Domènech's early works are eclectic, but a hotel constructed in 83 days for the Barcelona Universal Exposition of 1888 was based on a modular system which anticipated some of the technological processes of industrialization. The Palau de la Musica Catalana (1905-8) and the Hospital de Sant Paul (1902-10), both in Barcelona, were produced during the central and most important period of Domènech's career. The Palau de la Música combines a radical, modern purity in its iron and glass structural form, with decorative ceramic embellishment of Art Nouveau origin. The Hospital de Sant Paul makes an important urban contribution to the regular street grid of the Barcelona Extension (conceived by the engineer Ildefonso Cerda in 1859). Another hospital, the psychiatric Institute of Pere Mata in Reus (1897-1919), also combines modernity with fragments of national Catalan tradition, especially in the use of Catalan arched vaults and ornamentation. Along with Gaudí, Domènech was an influential figure in the development of Catalan historical, cultural and political identity. Between 1900 and 1919 he was Director of the School of Architecture in Barcelona, which he transformed from a stagnant Neo-Classical institution to a crucible of second-generation Catalan Modernism.

☐ Institute of Pere Mata, Reus, 1897-1919. Hospital de Sant Paul, Barcelona, 1902-10. Palau de la Música Catalana, Barcelona, 1905-8.

▷ Maria Lluisa Borras, *Lluis Domènech y Montaner*, Barcelona, 1970. Oriol Bohigas, *Once Arquitectos*, Barcelona, 1976. CS

▷ *see also pp230-31*

DOSHI Balkrishna Vithaldas

b. Poona, India, 1927.

Cosmopolitan, without ever losing sight of his Hindu origins and Indianness "Doshi" (as he is known) is, along with CORREA, among the most influential architects practising in India today. Educated at J. J. School of Art, Bombay (1946-50), he became senior designer for LE CORBUSIER in Paris for projects in Ahmedabad and Chandigarh. He was in private practice in Vastu-Shilpa, Ahmedabad (1956-77) and as Stein, Doshi & Bhalla since 1977. Responsible for the sensitive adaptation and refinement of modern architecture to the Indian context, Doshi supervised buildings by Le Corbusier and Louis KAHN in Ahmedabad. Emancipation from this vocabulary has allowed Doshi to evolve his own command of the modern-vernacular approach; an architecture beyond stylistic considerations. As thinker and teacher he remains unique in India, his environmental concerns and his urbanism always relevant. He set up the Vastu-Shilpa Foundation for Environmental Design in 1962 and founded the School of Architecture and Planning in Ahmedabad, also designing their premises. The architectonic scale and massing (vaulting), the clear sense of space (courts), mystery and community (water), an attraction to material and the role of incompletion in visual terms for an India ever constructing and decaying, remain thematically strong throughout his work. Doshi's more recent Gandhi Institute of Labour achieves complexity and scale by an exquisite treatment of community and space in a very difficult unenlivened environment. Doshi's thorough professionalism and modest architecture will distinguish him in the future and provide one of the most important models of response for new Indian architecture.

☐ Doshi House, Ahmedabad, India, 1961. Institute of Indology, Ahmedabad, 1962. Institute of Management, Ahmedabad (with Kahn), 1962-74. Tagore Theatre, Ahmedabad, 1967. Srinagar Master Plan (with Stein), 1970. Computer Centre, Hyderabad, 1976, Sangath, 1981. Institute of Management, Bangalore, 1985. Gandhi Institute of Labour, Ahmedabad, 1986.

▷ W. J. R. Curtis, *Balkrishna Doshi: An Architecture for India*, Ahmedabad, 1988. RC

DOWSON Philip

see Arup Associates

DREW Jane

see Fry, Edwin Maxwell

DUDOK Willem Marinus

b. Amsterdam, 1884; d. Hilversum, 1974.

Influential Dutch architect and town planner who, despite completing over 240 projects, is primarily remembered internationally for a handful of beautifully crafted brick buildings from the 1920-30s in the town of Hilversum. After graduating as an engineer from the Royal Military Academy at Breda, Dudok spent the first ten years of his architectural career constructing defensive forts and military barracks for the Dutch army. In 1927 he was appointed City Architect for Hilversum to co-ordinate the expansion of the town and to design the principal public buildings. He also practised privately. Dudok cultivated a highly eclectic approach to architecture. He admired Frank Lloyd WRIGHT and the American Prairie School. He produced a strongly idiosyncratic, and therefore easily recognizable, brick architecture style which hinged upon the dramatic asymmetrical

W. M. Dudok, Town Hall, Hilversum, 1928–30

W. M. Dudok

massing of geometrical forms. Hilversum Town Hall is considered the apotheosis of this particular period. He was awarded the RIBA Gold Medal in 1935. After the Second World War, Dudok produced a number of fine housing schemes in Hilversum and other Dutch towns as well as urban design proposals. He received the AIA Gold Medal in 1955.

□ Public Baths, Hilversum, 1921. Abattoir, Hilversum, 1923. Dutch Hostel, Paris University, 1926-38. Town Hall, Hilversum, 1928-30. "Bijenkauf" Store, Rotterdam, 1928-30. Vondel School, Hilversum, 1929.

▷ G. Friedhoff, *W. M. Dudok*, Amsterdam, 1930. Max Cramer and Hans van Grieken, *W. M. Dudok 1884-1974*, Amsterdam, 1981. Yukio Futagawa (ed.), *Global Architecture* 58, Tokyo, 1981. MC

DUIKER Johannes

see Bijvoet & Duiker

DURAND Jean Nicolas Louis David

b. Paris, 1760; d. Thiais, Val-de-Marne, 1834.

Influential theoretician; Neo-Classical "Rationalist". Durand's parents were poor and he studied architecture through the generosity of patrons. He entered the office of BOULLEE in 1776 and became his favourite pupil. He earned enough to enrol at the Académie d'Architecture and was placed second in the Prix de Rome competitions of 1779 and 1780. In 1795 he became professor of architecture at the recently established Ecole Polytechnique, where he remained until shortly before his death. He built very little, but his introductory lectures to engineering students, published as the *Précis*, were enormously influential and represent the culmination of French "rationalist" architectural thinking. Although he accepted the prevailing Neo-Classical style, it was conventional for Durand, with no expressive function as it had for LEDOUX or Boullée. Instead he reduced architecture to its essentials of structure and geometry, and its utilitarian purpose; for the first time Durand considered architecture in terms of the history of building types. In this way his writing anticipated and helped to create the intellectual foundations of C20 Modernism.

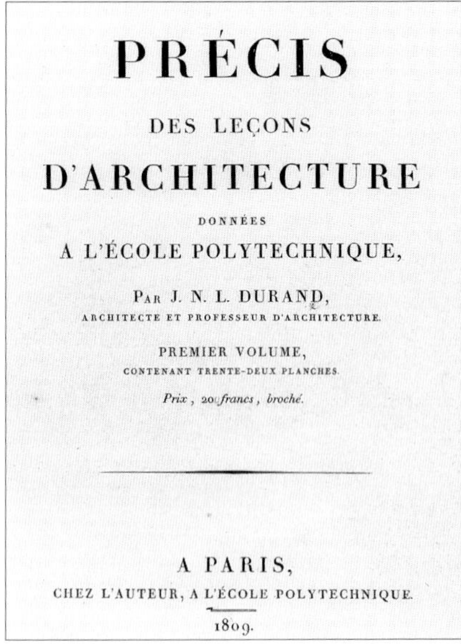

PRÉCIS

DES LEÇONS

D'ARCHITECTURE

DONNÉES

A L'ÉCOLE POLYTECHNIQUE,

PAR J. N. L. DURAND,

ARCHITECTE ET PROFESSEUR D'ARCHITECTURE.

PREMIER VOLUME,

CONTENANT TRENTE-DEUX PLANCHES.

Prix, 20 francs, broché.

A PARIS,

CHEZ L'AUTEUR, A L'ÉCOLE POLYTECHNIQUE.

1809.

J. N. L. Durand, title page to Précis des Leçons d'architecture, *1802–5*

□ Museum project, 1779. Hôtel Lathuille, rue du Faubourg-Poissonière, Paris, 1788. Country house at Thiais, 1825. (See also his *Précis.*)

▷ J. N. L. Durand, *Précis des leçons d'architecture données à l'école Polytechnique*, Paris, 1802-5. Henry-Russell Hitchcock, *Architecture: the Nineteenth and Twentieth Centuries*, Harmondsworth, 1958, 1977. A. Braham, *The Architecture of the French Enlightenment*, Los Angeles, 1980. R. Middleton (ed.), *The Beaux-Arts and Nineteenth Century French Architecture*, London, 1982. Sergio Villari, *J. N. L. Durand*, tr. E. Gottlieb, New York, 1990. TC

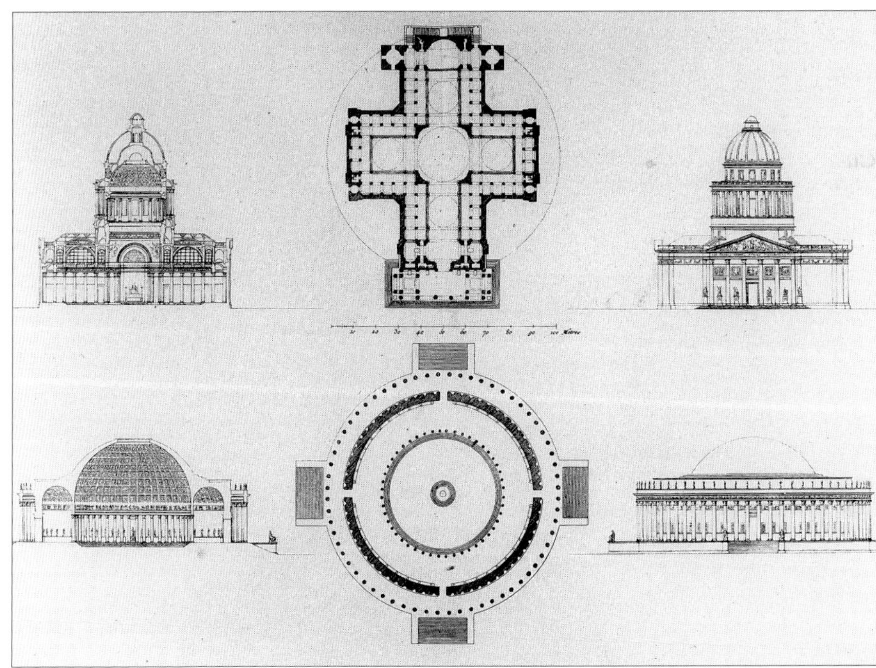

J. N. L. Durand, engravings from Précis des Leçons d'architecture, *1802-5*

EAMES Charles Ormand

b. St Louis, Missouri, 1907; d. St Louis, 1978.

American architect, film-maker, designer and polymath who occupies a unique position in the history of modern design. Eames began his architectural career at Washington University in his home town of St Louis in 1924. A trip to Europe (1929) exposed him to the work and philosophy of the Modern Movement and the following year he established his own firm of Gray and Eames in St Louis. His early work in the 1930s consisted mainly of designs for stained glass, textiles, furniture and ceramics, culminating in 1938 with the award of a fellowship to Cranbrook Academy in Michigan, where he studied under and collaborated with Eero SAARINEN on furniture design. In 1941 Eames moved to California with his second wife, the distinguished painter and sculptor **Ray Kaiser** (b. Sacramento, 1912; d. 1988). Together they made a formidable design partnership and explored many fields with equal success – furniture, photography, architecture and interior design. This was due in part to Eames's analytical, systems-based approach to design problems, which generated unlimited possibilities. Two houses completed between 1945 and 1950, the Eames and Entenza Residences, confirmed his reputation as an architect. Both display a Japanese finesse in their simple, sculptural form and innovative application of modern building components. Eames continued to work as an architect until the mid 1960s, thereafter concentrating his prodigious energies on furniture, film-making and exhibition design.

Charles Eames, Own House, Pacific Palisades, California, 1945–9

□ Charles Eames Residence, Pacific Palisades, California (with Eero Saarinen), 1945-9. John Entenza Residence, Pacific Palisades (with Eero Saarinen), 1945-50. Herman Miller Showroom, Beverly Hills, California, 1947-9.

▷ Arthur Drexler, *Charles Eames: Furniture from the Design Collection*, Museum of Modern Art, New York, 1973. Ester McCoy, "Charles and Ray Eames", *Design Quarterly*, 1975, 98-99. J. Neuhart *et al.*, *Eames Design*, London and New York, 1989. CS

VAN EESTEREN Cornelius

b. Kinderdijk, 1897.

Dutch Modernist architect and town-planner. Van Eesteren came from a family of building contractors in N Holland. Following a conventional secondary education, some drawing lessons and a short spell as a carpenter's apprentice, he turned his attention to architecture and in 1915 joined the practice of Willem Kromhout in Rotterdam. Two years later he gained his architectural diploma from the Rotterdam Academy of Fine Arts and Technical Sciences. He studied at the Hoger Bouwkunstonderwijs in Amsterdam (1919-22) and won the Prix de Rome, which enabled him to visit Germany in 1922 to study brick architecture. He also spent some time at the Bauhaus in Weimar, where he met the painter and architect Theo VAN DOESBURG, a leading figure in the Dutch *De Stijl* movement, which was strongly influenced by the principles of Cubism. In 1923 Van Eesteren worked in Paris with Van Doesburg and met the painter Piet Mondrian. Together they formulated the architectonic principles of Neo-Plasticism. From 1924 to 1927 Van Eesteren worked under Jan Wils and continued his studies in town-planning. By 1929 he had become chief architect in the town-planning department in the City of Amsterdam, supervising the development of the city for the next fifty years. Van Eesteren based much of his work on a plan by BERLAGE prepared in 1917, which he revised and enlarged in accordance with extensive research. He was one of the first planners to analyse the development of a city, and use this information to predict future needs. From 1930 to 1947 he was president of CIAM and professor of town-planning at the Technical University in Delft 1947-67.

□ House, Alblasserdam, 1923. General Extension Plan, Amsterdam, 1929-34.

▷ Hans Ludwig C. Jaffe, *De Stijl 1917-1931: The Dutch Contribution to Modern Art*, Amsterdam, 1956. Reinder Blijstra, *Cornelius Van Eesteren*, Amsterdam, 1971. CS

EIERMANN Egon

b. Neuendorf, 1904; d. Baden-Baden, 1970.

German industrial architect and academic who worked in the International Modern style. Eiermann trained at the Technische Hochschule in Berlin-Charlottenburg (1923-7), studying under the influential Expressionist architect and academic Hans POELZIG. Between 1934 and 1945 he had his own practice in Berlin and served on many competition juries. He was Dean of the Faculty of Architecture at the University of Karlsruhe until 1970. The recipient of numerous design awards, Chairman of the Olympic Buildings Jury for the Munich Games, Eiermann also worked on exhibitions, notably the German Pavilion for the 1958 Brussels World Fair. Many of his commissions during the 1950s and 60s were collaborations with

Egon Eiermann, Kaiser Wilhelm Memorial Church, Berlin, 1959–63

fellow German Modernist Robert Hilgers. Influenced by the Americans, SKIDMORE, OWINGS & MERRILL, Eiermann saw his function as architect "to make visible the order of urban planning down to the smallest structure". But despite his rationalist approach and the rigidity suggested by his attention to detail, Eiermann's work has a lightness and elegance born of inherent plasticity. Typical of his work is the use of the fixed screen, and the placing of functional elements (stairways, lift towers, etc.) on the outer skin of the building but always skilfully integrated within the design.

☐ Handkerchief factory, Blumberg, 1949-51. Neckermann Export Company Building, Frankfurt-am-Main, Germany 1958-61. Kaiser Wilhelm Memorial Church, Berlin, 1959-63. German Embassy, Washington DC, 1959-64. Bundestag, Bonn, 1965-9. IBM Administration Building, Stuttgart, 1967-72. Olivetti headquarters, Frankfurt-am-Main, 1968-72.

▷ "Headquarters of IBM Germany" and "Headquarters of Olivetti Germany", *Architecture and Urbanism 4*, No. 6, 1974. H. Werner Rosenthal, "Egon Eiermann 1904-1970", *RIBA Journal*, Jan. 1978. CS

EIFFEL Alexandre Gustave

b. Dijon, 1832; d. Paris, 1923.

French engineer and bridge builder, whose most notable achievement was the Eiffel Tower, completed in 1899 for the Paris Exhibition. He graduated from the Ecole Centrale des Arts et Manufactures, Paris, in 1855, and joined a Belgian firm which specialized in railway equipment. This provided his first commission, for the Gargonne Bridge, Bordeaux (1860). Independent practice followed in 1864, with ownership of fabrication shops in 1867 and the subsequent career of engineer-contractor. Eiffel was the master of elegantly constructed wrought-iron lattices, which formed the basis of his bridge constructions (42 for French railways) and led to his greatest project, which was self-financed, the 300-m (1000-ft) Eiffel Tower, completed in 1899 for the Paris Exhibition. The tower's concept amounted to four curving and tapered lattice pylons combined with decks to brace the structure; surprisingly the lowermost arches are decorative. The Tower is still owned by the Eiffel family.

☐ Palais des Machines, Paris (arched lattice roof, clear span 480m x 360m; 1575ft x 1180ft), 1867.

EIFFEL TOWER, Paris

The modern world's most celebrated architectural monument, the Eiffel Tower is neither a building nor a utilitarian object. Its purpose was symbolic: it was designed to advertise and to be the central feature of the Paris World Exposition of 1889 on the Champs de Mars. It remained, at 300 m (1000 ft), the world's tallest structure until the Empire State Building was completed in New York in 1929. It was constructed from 12,000 separate prefabricated iron pieces and was held together by 2½ million rivets. It took just over four years to fabricate and some 3000 drawings depicted its 29 sections.

Arched lattice and pylon bridges: Douro, 1875, Garabit (arch span 165m; 540ft), 1883. Pest Station, Budapest, 1877. Bon Marché Store Extension, Paris, 1879. Armature for Statue of Liberty, New York, 1881. Nice Observatory Dome (with Charles GARNIER), 1885. Eiffel Tower, Paris, 1889. Locks for Panama Canal, 1889.

▷ Gustave Eiffel, *Les Grandes Constructions Métalliques*, Paris, 1888; *La Tour Eiffel en 1990*, Paris, 1902. S. Giedion, *Space, Time and Architecture*, Oxford, 1967. Joseph Harris, *The Eiffel Tower*, London, 1975. AB

▷ *see also pp222-3*

EISENMAN Peter

b. Newark, NJ, 1932.

Prominent New York avant-garde critic, architect and theorist. Eisenman studied at Cornell and Columbia Universities and then at Cambridge, England. He taught at Cambridge, Princeton and the Cooper Union in New York, where he was founder director of the Institute for Architecture and Urban Studies, co-ordinating an ambitious programme of lectures, seminars, research and publications. Until recently he has built little but received critical attention for a series of controversial "anti-houses" which flout practicality in an attempt to create an auto- nomous abstract architecture. A 1988 MoMa exhibition in New York defined him and other architects as "Deconstructivist", subverting received ideas about structure and function related to the earlier movement of Constructivism. Eisenman, however, has always sought somewhat obscure parallels between his work in architecture and philosophical ideas and literary theory. His earlier houses were "generated" from the transformation of forms, as structural linguistics holds that language is related to an underlying structure. Latterly in a number of larger commissions he has taken up some of the metaphysical and "anti-humanist" ideas of Post-structuralism or Deconstructionism.

□ House I (Bareholtz Pavilion), Princeton, N J, 1967-8. House II (Falk House) Hardwick, Conn., 1969-70. House III (Miller House), Lakesville, Conn., 1969-71. Apartments, Kochstrasse, Berlin, 1981-7. Wexner Center for the Visual Arts (extension), Ohio State University, Columbus, 1985-9. Bio-Centre, Frankfurt-am-Main, 1987-9. Guardiola House, Bay of Cadiz, Spain, 1988. Convention Center, Ohio, 1989

Peter Eisenman, House VI, Cornwall, Conn., 1972

▷ P. Eisenman, *House of Cards*, New York, 1978. K. Frampton *et al.*, *Five Architects*, New York, 1972. P. Johnson and M. Wigley, *Deconstructivist Architecture*, New York, 1988. C. Jencks, *The New Moderns*, London, 1990. TC

▷ *see also pp244-5*

ELLIS Tom

Thomas Bickerstaff Harper Ellis, b. London, 1911; d. Lancaster, 1989.

Dynamic personality who was the inspirational force in a young practice, established in 1947, Lyons, Ellis, Israel & Gray, which proved to be one of the catalysts in the development of Modern architecture in post-war Britain; the leadership of Tom Ellis also inspired the next generation of committed Modernists. He was educated at the Lancaster School of Art (1933-5) and at the Architectural Association, graduating at the Royal College of Art in London in 1938. His partners Lyons and Israel, both trained part-time at the Polytechnic of Central London, had already achieved competition successes before the war, such as the Wolverhampton Civic Hall (1938-40). The post-war practice was based upon educational buildings, first primary and secondary schools and then, as social priorities changed, colleges and research institutes. The portfolio of work is very extensive and varied, though the taste for exposed concrete and Brutalism may in hindsight seem a cul-de-sac.

□ Schools: Northfleet, Kent (County Modern), 1952; Herne Bay, Kent (Mixed County Secondary), 1954; Peckham Comprehensive, London, 1958; Jordanthorpe, Sheffield, 1959; Weston Park, Southampton, 1960. Old Vic Theatre Annexe, London, 1958. Wolfson Institute, Hammersmith, London, 1961. Commonwealth Building, University of London, 1961. College of Engineering and Science, Polytechnic of Central London, 1970.

▷ Lyons, Israel, Ellis & Gray, *Buildings and Projects 1932-83 Works* IV, London, 1986. AB

ELMSLIE George Grant

see Purcell & Elmslie

EMBERTON Joseph

b. Staffs., 1889; d. London, 1956.

A first-generation architect of the Modern Movement in England. Emberton claimed to have learned nothing from his tutors at the Kensington College of Art (now the Royal College of Art) but he must surely have been influenced by his professor, W. R. LETHABY. In the large London practice of Sir John Burnet, Tait and Lorne, which Emberton joined at the end of the First World War, he gained work experience in both traditional and contemporary idioms, sharing Tait's interest in developments on the Continent, in particular the work of DUDOK. His early commissions already show his elegant use of the staple materials of the Modern Movement – concrete, glass, chromium, welded steel, plywood – although, rather surprisingly, he used brick and plaster for the New Empire Hall, Olympia. International recognition came in 1932, when his Royal Corinthian Yacht Club, Burnham, was included in the International Exhibition of Modern Architecture, staged at the Museum of

Modern Art, New York. At various stages in his career, Emberton was involved in advertising and exhibition design, disciplines that were to influence his other work. After the Second World War, he designed a number of distinguished housing schemes in London.

☐ Kiosks and pavilions at the British Empire Exhibition, London (with P. J. Westwood), 1924-5. Summit House, Red Lion Square, London (with Westwood), 1925. New Empire Hall, Olympia, London, 1929-30. Royal Corinthian Yacht Club, Burnham-on-Crouch, Essex, 1931. Universal House, London, 1933. Pleasure Beach, Blackpool, 1935. Simpson's, Piccadilly, London, 1936. HMV shop, Oxford Street, London, 1939.

▷ Joseph Emberton, *Modern Store Design* (Specification 34), 1932. Rosemary Ind, *Emberton*, London, 1983. PP

ENGEL Carl Ludwig

b. Germany, 1778; d. Finland, 1840.

Architect whose solemn scale and elegance, a modesty without being a plainness, influenced and defined the emerging sensibility within Finnish architecture. His early training was at the Bauakademie in Berlin before he moved to Tallinn in Estonia, where he worked as an architect from 1808 to 1814. His visit to Leningrad in 1815, before settling in Helsinki in 1816, is key to the pocket-Leningrad scale of much of Engel's Helsinki. He quickly became the leading architect in Finland and was appointed Director of Public Housing in 1824. The pattern books prepared during that time were meticulous and had a lasting influence on Finnish planning and urbanism. Though often considered mostly in the Russian Neo-Classical school, Engel's German origins can be seen to provide an element of balance, certainly a restraint, to the Russian tradition. The Lutheran Cathedral defines the heart of Engel's Helsinki; at first more restrained, it is centrally planned on a Greek cross with four porticos outside, a quatrefoil inside. The tall dome emphasizes site and scale – a grandeur completed by the Senate Square. Built between 1818 and Engel's death in 1840, the Senate Square includes the Cathedral, the Senate House (1818-22), the University Building and University Library (1836-45) and is a perfect example of Engel's assimilated Neo-Classicism.

☐ Senate Square, Helsinki, 1818-40. Military Hospital, Helsinki, 1826-32. Lutheran Cathedral, Helsinki, 1830-40. Helsinki City Hall, 1833. Viurila (with Bassi), 1840.

▷ J. M. Richards, *800 Years of Finnish Architecture*, London, 1978; N. E. Wickberg, *Engel*, Berlin, 1970; A. Salokorpi, *Modern Finnish Architecture*, London, 1970. RC

ERICKSON Arthur Charles

b. Vancouver, 1924.

Probably Canada's greatest architect, Erickson was educated at the University of British Columbia and McGill University, Montreal. He started practice in Vancouver in 1953 and now has offices in Vancouver, Toronto and the Middle East. In the second half of the C20 Canada has produced a remarkable renascence of Modernism; the Erickson partnership's unique contribution is its ability to handle large-scale contemporary architecture in the urban context. The unfolding townscape of the Courthouse Complex in Vancouver (1978) and the monumental qualities at Simon Fraser University (1962) reveal considerable skill in adapting and extending principles drawn from LE CORBUSIER. Another thread that runs through the repertoire is lavish house designs, which form a distinguished volume of work. The masterpiece, without doubt, is the superbly detailed Museum of Anthropology, University of British Columbia (1971-7), where the subtle composition of modulated interior spaces provides a perfect setting for the magnificent display of American Indian art.

☐ Simon Fraser University, Burnaby, B C, 1962. MacMillan Bloedel Tower, Vancouver, 1969. Museum of Anthropology, University of British Columbia, Vancouver, 1971-7. National Art Gallery, Ottawa, 1977. New Massey Hall, Toronto, 1978-80. Courthouse and Federal Office Complex, Vancouver, 1978. Napp Laboratories, Cambridge, UK, 1985.

▷ Arthur Erickson, *The Architecture of Arthur Erickson*, Montreal, 1975. AB

ERSKINE Ralph

b. London, 1914.

Anglo-Swedish architect whose humanistic buildings and community schemes are widely admired. Educated firstly at the Quaker School, Saffron Walden, Essex, Erskine later graduated in architecture from the Regent Street Polytechnic,

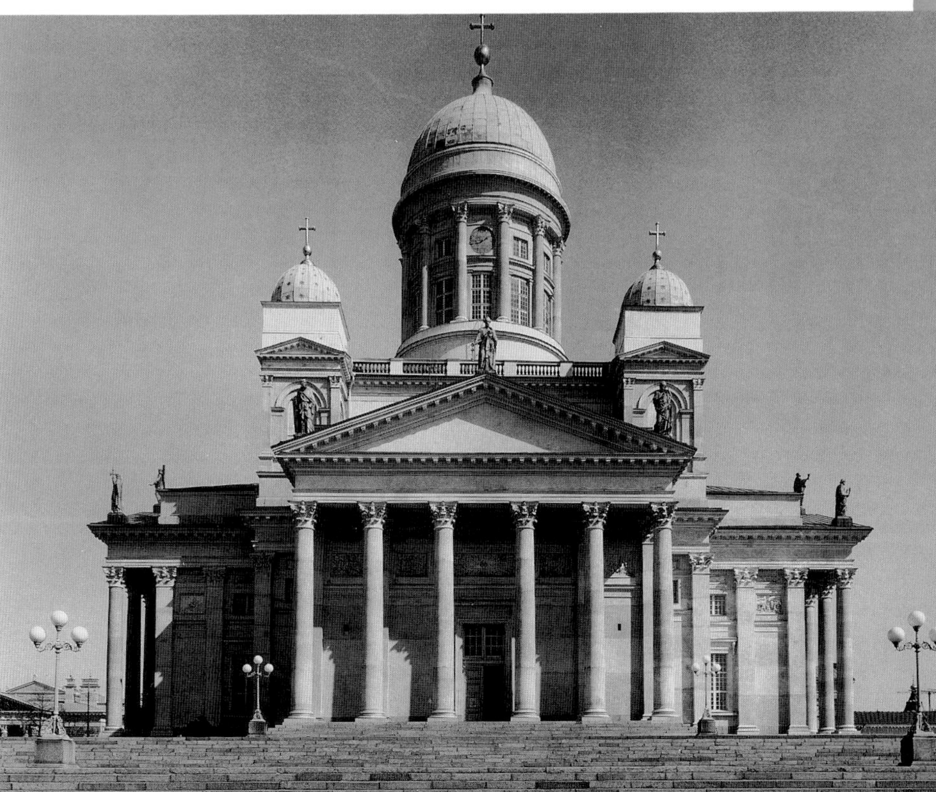

Carl Engel, Lutheran Cathedral, Helsinki, 1830–40

Ralph Erskine, Byker Wall, Newcastle upon Tyne, 1968–82

London (now PCL) in 1938. A year later he went to Sweden and stayed there for a number of reasons: he worked briefly for Weijke and Odeen but remained principally because he was a pacifist and it proved impossible to return to England after the outbreak of war. Thus his career began, and has largely continued, in Sweden, where he built his first traditional timber houses in 1940. A year later he constructed his own timber family cabin in Lissma, Solangen, where he lived and worked close to nature. In 1946 Erskine moved to rented accommodation in Drottningholm. He later stabilized the practice there with a new house and studio (1963) on the Royal Island. Nearby was moored the *Verona*, a Thames barge that also served as offices for many summers. Among his first important projects were studies of architecture for the Arctic and sub-Arctic, a subject on which he addressed the CIAM Congress at Otterlo in 1950. His Ski Hotel at Borgafjäll dates from 1948-50. It incorporated a winter nursery slope on its roof. The Fors Cardboard Factory (1950-51) was widely published internationally. It was followed by a large number of houses, schools, flats and urban-scale planning schemes, including many competition entries. Invited to enter a limited competition for housing at Killingworth, Newcastle upon Tyne, Erskine reinforced his architectural opportunities in Britain which had begun at Clare Hall, Cambridge. The famous Byker redevelopment scheme at Newcastle soon followed, with its strange formal vocabularies and much-publicized approach to user participation and to motorway noise barrier block solutions to housing. The Byker scheme brought new ingredients into the architectural and housing mix, with small terrace units and detached housing combined with larger blocks of flats, one in this case about 1 km (*c.* ½ mile) long and rising to 8 storeys. The shaped profile of the block and the expression of individual units within the frame all took on a special significance, as do – in Erskine's Nordic work – elements like solar catchers and sun balconies. The latter can be found on the façades of the University Library at Stockholm and the former above the refectory roof at St Goran's Hospital. More recently Erskine has been experimenting with complete climatically controlled environments of the building with the Larson offices at Hammersmith, London, and the office tower in Gothenburg.

□ Various house projects including those in Sweden and Lewes, Sussex. Tourist Ski Hotel, Borgafjäll, Avasjo, Lapland (with Rosenvold and Bergström and Staalehoef), 1948. Chemical Works, Gnests (with Wimmerström), 1950. Cardboard Factory, Fors, Avesta, 1950-53. Housing schemes at Frösö, 1953, Tibro, from 1956, Newcastle upon Tyne: Killingworth, 1968, and Byker, 1968-82; Eaglestone, Milton Keynes, 1973. Own house, Drottningholm, 1963. Clare Hall, Cambridge, England, 1968. Vasa Terminal, Stockholm, 1984. Refectory, St Goran's Hospital, Stockholm, 1985-6. Offices, Gothenburg, 1986-9. Larson Office Building, Hammersmith, London (with Vernon Gracie), 1988-91.

▷ Peter Collymore, *Ralph Erskine*, London, 1982. Mats Egelius, *Ralph Erskine Arkitekt*, Stockholm, 1988. "Ralph Erskine", *World Architecture* (special issue), Vol. 6, 1990. DS

VAN EYCK Aldo

b. Driebergen, 1918.

Influential figure in contemporary Dutch architecture. Although born in Holland, van Eyck spent most of his childhood and formative years in England. Educated in London and Somerset 1924-35, later studied at the ETH, Zürich, and in 1967 was invited to join the Delft Technical College as professor. He has lectured extensively throughout Europe and northern America and was a founding member of Team 10. The group, which included Alison and Peter SMITHSON, not only rejected the moribund concept of Functionalism but also attacked the banality of most post-war Modernism. Van Eyck's position as co-editor of the Dutch magazine *Forum* (1959-67) helped to propagate the group's call for a new humanism within architecture. Much of his written work promotes an existential search for archetypal solutions, and this adherence to Structuralist values has informed all of his post-1960s work. His collaboration with Hannie van Eyck, his wife (m. 1943) and Theo Bosch (his partner 1971-82) has generated an architecture which possesses a rare modesty and is imaginative but at the same time understated, approachable and appropriate. He received the RIBA Royal Gold Medal in 1990.

□ Municipal Orphanage, Amsterdam, 1957-60. Protestant Church, Driebergen, 1965. Pastoor van Ars Church, The Hague, 1968-70. Hubertus House, Amsterdam, 1973-78. ESTEC Headquarters, Noordiwijk, 1986.

▷ Reinder Blijstra, *Dutch Architecture after 1900*, Amsterdam, 1966. Alison Smithson (ed.), *Team X Primer*, Cambridge, 1968. Pierluigi Nicolin, "Aldo van Eyck: The Web and the Labyrinth", *Lotus International*, Vol.11, 1976. MC

▷ *see also pp240–41*

F

FILARETE (IL)

Antonio di Pietro Averlino, b. Florence, c. 1400; d. Rome, 1469.

Theorist and propagandist in northern Italy for BRUNELLESCHI's classical style and the doctrines of ALBERTI. The choice of a high-flown *nom-de-plume* (from Greek, meaning roughly "Lover of the Full Life") was sadly indicative of the humanist Averlino's mainly unfulfilled ambitions. After an inauspicious start as designer of doors (1445) for old St Peter's, Rome, which got a bad press from VASARI a century later (and fail to impress modern visitors), he departed for the north. In 1456 he began building the largest hospital in Milan (Albergo dei Poveri di Dio). Its cruciform plan within a square, with a chapel at the hub, carried the seeds of other centrally planned buildings which led up to BRAMANTE's Greek-cross plan for the new St Peter's (1505). Il Filarete's *Treatise* (*c.*1461-4), gives him a more significant place in the history of Renaissance architecture than do his actual buildings.

□ Albergo dei Poveri di Dio, Milan, begun 1456. St Peter's, Rome (doors), 1445.

▷ *Trattato (Treatise) of Filarete*, trans. J. R. Spencer, New York, 1965. JRC

FINSTERLIN Hermann

b. Munich, 1887; d. Stuttgart, 1973.

German Expressionist painter and philosopher with an interest in Dream and Fantasy architecture. After an initial period as a painter and a self-publisher, he studied at Munich University (1914-15). He began making a series of so-called Phantasy portraits after 1918 and a year later commenced work on a series of architectural drawings or *Architeckturtraumen* (architectural dreams), some of which were shown in Behne and GROPIUS's "Exhibition for Unknown Architects" in Berlin, 1919. The same year he exhibited other drawings at the Neumann Gallery, Berlin, for the Arbeitsrat für Kunst. His first architectural drawings were published in the AfK publication *Ja! Stimmen des AfK* (1919). Later in the same year he began his association with Bruno TAUT's Glass Chain group and started publishing widely in the *Frühlicht* publication. His work appealed to architects interested in biomorphic Expressionist tendencies, and until the end of the 1920s he remained closely connected with Berlin avant-garde circles. In 1924 the Dutch magazine *Wendingen* issued a special number on his work and he was mentioned in Platz's *Die Baukunst in der Neuesten Zeit* (1927), although he built nothing. He hardly ever ventured outside Germany and went into obscurity until the 1950s, when his work was rediscovered by a new generation of architectural historians who saw its relevance to organic and the new architecture. Since then it has been extensively written about and exhibited. Most of his original drawings, models and paintings are held in the Staatsgalerie, Stuttgart.

▷ Finsterlin's best-known essay, "Der Achte Tag" (*Frühlicht*, Vol. 11, 1920), appears in English in I. B. White, *The Crystal Chain Letters*, MIT, 1985. "Hermann Finsterlin and *Formspiel*" in Dennis Sharp, *Modern Architecture and Expressionism*, London, 1966. R. Dohl, *Hermann Finsterlin: Eine Annäherung* (catalogue), Stuttgart, 1988. DS

FISCHER Johann Michael

b. Burglengenfeld, 1692; d. Munich, 1766.

The leading ecclesiastical architect of the early C18, a skilled exponent of the exuberant Bavarian school of Rococo. Fischer's early education was guided by

Above: Johann Fischer, Benedictine Church, Ottobeuren, 1744–67

Right: Johann Fischer, Benedictine church, Zwiefalten, 1741–65, interior

his father, a master mason. On completion of his apprenticeship, he travelled extensively in Moravia and Bohemia, arriving in Munich in 1718. Having established an independent reputation, he secured several prestigious commissions from the Wittelsbach princes. Although he completed numerous secular projects, his reputation rests primarily with his ecclesiastical buildings: thirty-two churches and twenty-two monasteries. Fischer's church interiors display a high degree of spatial complexity, often employing a centralized plan, where the cupola is located above the intersection of the nave and the transept. He collaborated closely with many of the leading Rococo artists of his day, including Tiepolo and the ASAM brothers, and his work is characterized by a complex interaction of opposites: construction and illusion, structure and symbolism. His genius lay in the subtle resolution of these forces to create a *Gesamtkunstwerk*.

□ Premonstratensian Church, Osterhofen, 1726-31. St Anne, Munich, 1727-39. Augustinian Priory Church, Diessen, 1732-9. St Michael's Church, Berg-am-Laim, 1738-42. Benedictine Church, Zwiefalten, 1741-65. Benedictine Church, Ottobeuren, 1744-67. Augustinian Church, Altomünster, 1763-7.

▷ Nicolas Powell, *From Baroque to Rococo*, London, 1959. Henry-Russell Hitchcock, *Rococo Architecture in Southern Germany*, London, 1968. Alastair Laing and Anthony Blunt, *Baroque and Rococo – Architecture and Decoration*, New York, 1978. MC

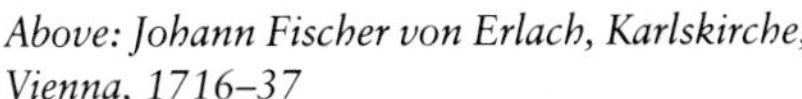

FISCHER VON ERLACH Johann Bernhard

b. Graz, 1656; d. Vienna, 1723.

The undisputed leader of northern European Baroque of the 1680s and 90s – and still showing his mastery of architectural magnificence two decades later. Trained as a sculptor, Fischer went to Rome in the early 1670s and learned the rudiments of architecture from his employers and his acquaintances among the dilettanti and antiquaries there. Even when young he displayed his virtuosity in the design of sculpture, medals and decoration for gardens as well as interiors, and began to work as an architect for wealthy aristocratic patrons. By the time he returned to Austria from Italy (1686) he had already made a fortune. He ascended the top rung of the social and professional hierarchy when he was appointed architectural tutor to the eleven-year-old future emperor Joseph I. Fischer leapt to fame with his designs for the most splendidly spacious of all his buildings, the imperial Schönbrunn Palace outside Vienna. Intended to eclipse Louis XIV's palace at Versailles, the Habsburgs' Schönbrunn was begun (on a smaller scale than originally planned) in 1696. As court architect, Fischer now received numerous commissions from Joseph I, the Austro-German nobility and the Catholic church. For the emperor, Fischer created aloof yet magnificent settings which were grand and unusual enough to project the superiority of the Kaiser over all other ranks of the nobility. His country houses for the aristocracy, on the other hand, combined sumptuous elegance with a more natural living style, and were widely imitated throughout central Europe. This productive period ended with the outbreak of the War of the Spanish Succession (1701-14). The Austrian court's building plans were stifled, and in 1704 Fischer set out for England and Prussia in search of commissions. His brand of grandiose ceremonial architecture did not, however, suit the Protestant inclinations of those countries'

Above: Johann Fischer von Erlach, Karlskirche, Vienna, 1716–37

Entwurff
Einer Historischen ARCHITECTUR,
In Abbildung unterschiedener berühmten Gebäude,
des Alterthums und fremder Völcker,
Umb aus den Geschicht-büchern Gedächtnüß-müntzen, RUINEN, und
eingeholten wahrhafften Abrißen, vor Augen zu stellen.
In dem Ersten Buche
Die von der Zeit vergrabene Bau-arten der alten Juden, Egyptier, Syrer, Perser, und Griechen.
In dem Andern
Alte unbekante Römische.
In dem Dritten
Einige fremde, in- und außer-Europaische, als der Araber, und Türcken, etc. auch neue Persianische, Siamitische, Sinesische, und Japonesische Gebäude.
In dem Vierten
Einige Gebäude von des AUTORIS Erfindung und Zeichnung.
Alles mit großer Mühe gezeichnet und auf eigene Unkosten herausgegeben von Ihr. Kaiser: Mai: Ober-Bau Inspectorn, Johann Bernhard Fischers von Erlachen.
Auch kurtzen Teutschen und Frantzösischen Beschreibungen.
Wien, MDCCXXI

Johann Fischer von Erlach, title page to Entwurf einer historischen Architektur, *1721*

rulers. The death from smallpox of his chief patron, Joseph I, in 1711 was a further blow, but from 1712 onwards, while Fischer was working on the engravings for his massive book, *Entwurf einer historischen Architektur* (*Outline for an Architectural History*), commissions began to come his way again. The advent of peace in 1714 coincided with a competition for a grand church in Vienna dedicated by the new emperor, Charles VI, to St Charles Borromeo. Fischer's design won and his Baroque masterpiece, known universally as the Karlskirche, was built 1716-37. Its oval plan embedded in a reversed Latin cross echoes BORROMINI, whom Fischer had known in Rome. His Hofbibliothek (Imperial Library) in the Hofburg palace, Vienna, also belongs to this period. Becoming ill in 1721, Fischer retired and left the completion of his unfinished projects to his son, Josef Emanuel (1693-1742), who saw them all through after his father's death.

□ Dreifaltigkeitskirche, Salzburg, 1694-1702. Kollegienkirche, Salzburg, 1694-1707. Schönbrunn Palace, Vienna, begun 1696. Karlskirche, Vienna, 1716-37. Hofbibliothek, Vienna, begun 1723.

▷ J. B. Fischer von Erlach, *Entwurf einer historischen Architektur*, Vienna, 1721. H. V. Lanchester, *Fischer von Erlach*, London, 1924. Hans Aurenhammer, *J. B. Fischer von Erlach*, London, 1973. JRC

▷ *see also pp218-19*

FISKER Kay

b. Frederiksberg, Denmark, 1893; d. Copenhagen, 1965.

Danish C20 architect and writer who specialized in public and private housing. Fisker graduated from the school of architecture at the Academy of Fine Arts in Copenhagen (1920), then took up private practice, which led to a partnership with Christian Frederik Møller in 1930. Fisker was professor of architecture at the Copenhagen Academy of Fine Arts from 1936, and became dean of the architectural school in 1941. He was also a visiting professor and lecturer in America, teaching at the Harvard Graduate School of Design and the Massachusetts Institute of Technology. He edited the Danish journal *Arkitekten* and wrote numerous articles and books. Humane in outlook, strongly influenced by VOYSEY, BAILLIE SCOTT and the English town-planners, Fisker played an important part in raising the standards of Danish housing, particularly in the public sector. By nature a traditionalist, opposed to the more extreme tenets of the Modern Movement, Fisker attempted to balance utilitarian function with regional styles, while incorporating certain innovative features in planning and design. Large-scale housing projects such as the Voldparken flats featured limited-storey blocks to avoid monotony, with centralized amenities including garages, shops and recreational space, in the manner of LE CORBUSIER. Fisker's solution for the Vestersohus flats included the characteristic use of informal patterns of fenestration, and the novel introduction of recessed balconies.

□ Aarhus University (with Poul Stegmann until 1937 and with C. F. Moller until 1945), 1932-45. Vestersohus Housing, Copenhagen, 1935. Voldparken Housing and School, Husum, 1945. National Council for Unmarried Mothers Administration Building and Home, Copenhagen, 1955.

▷ Kay Fisker, "The History of Domestic Architecture in Denmark", *Architectural Review*, 104, Nov. 1948; "The Moral of Functionalism", *Magazine of Art*, 43, Feb. 1950. Kay Fisker and Christian Elling, *Danish Architectural Drawings*, Copenhagen, 1961. "Kay Fisker – 70 Years", *Arkitekten*, Special Issue No. 65, Feb. 1963. CS

Carlo Fontana, S. Marcello al Corso, Rome, 1682–3

FONTANA Carlo

b. Como, c.1638; d. Rome, 1714.

Architect, engineer and planner, a representative figure of academic classicism during the last quarter of the C17 in Rome. A nephew of Domenico FONTANA, he moved to Rome in the early 1650s and worked as a draughtsman under Pietro da CORTONA during the building of Santa

Maria della Pace and then under BERNINI on several projects, including the Scala Regia and the Chigi Palace. In 1667 he became *accademico di merito* of the Accademia di S. Luca in Rome; he was made *cavaliere c.*1670 and *principe* of the Accademia in 1616. Fontana was particularly successful in the design of chapels, the best of which is the small masterpiece of Cappella Cybo, with its handsome proportions and dark harmony of black and yellow marbles. His best-known work, however, is the façade of S. Marcello al Corso – a concave front receding in concentric layers. Among his publications on architecture and engineering, *Templum Vaticanum* provides detailed information on St Peter's, particularly the building of the cupola and the raising of the obelisk. In spite of his diverse activity, none of Fontana's works is equal to those of his greater contemporaries such as Bernini or BORROMINI, but they all show a clear architectural balance underlying the liveliness of the Baroque style.

□ Church of Santa Rita, Rome, 1665. Cappella Cybo in Santa Maria del Popolo, Rome, 1683-7. S. Marcello al Corso, (façade), Rome, 1682-3.

▷ Carlo Fontana, *Templum Vaticanum et ipsius origo*, Rome, 1694; *Descrizione della nobilissima cappella del fonte battesimale nella Basilica Vaticana*, Rome, 1697. Rudolf Wittkower, *Art and Architecture in Italy: 1600-1750*, Harmondsworth, 1958, 1973. GV

▷ *see also pp218-19*

FONTANA Domenico

b. Melide, Lake Lugano, 1543; d. Naples, 1607.

Right-hand man to a pope who replanned Renaissance Rome, and designer of the Royal Palace, Naples. He went to Rome *c.*1563 and was later taken up by Cardinal Felice Peretti, for whom he built the Cappella Sistina in Santa Maria Maggiore (1585). In the same year, to Domenico's good fortune, Peretti was elected pope as Sixtus V (1585-90). Together they hastened the transformation of medieval Rome into a modern city. Sixtus had town-planning ideas on a grand scale, with great thoroughfares radiating from Santa Maria Maggiore. Among Domenico's many undertakings for the Pope was an engineering feat that made him more famous at the time than anything else he did: safely shifting the Vatican obelisk from its original position to the centrepoint of the space in front of St Peter's (1586). Sixtus V's cost-cutting successor dismissed Domenico, who migrated to Naples, where he designed a palace for his new patrons, the Spanish governors. Domenico's son, Giulio Cesare Fontana, became royal architect in Naples; Carlo FONTANA, and Carlo MADERNO were Domenico's nephews.

□ Cappella Sistina, Santa Maria Maggiore, Rome, 1585. Lateran Palace, Rome, 1586. Vatican Library, Rome, 1587-9. Royal Palace, Naples, 1600-1602.

▷ Domenico Fontana, *Della trasportatione dell'Obelisco Vaticano*, Part I, Rome, 1590; Part II, Naples, 1603. S. Giedion, *Space, Time and Architecture*, London, 1954. JRC

▷ *see also pp214-15*

FOSTER Sir Norman

b. Manchester, 1935.

Leading British modern architect noted for his High-Tech structures. After service in the RAF he received his architectural training at Manchester University School of Architecture (1956-61) and Yale University (1961-2). One of his first projects, a house for Richard ROGERS's parents, was carried out with his late wife, and former partner, Wendy Foster, and Richard and Sue Rogers, working together as "Team 4". Foster Associates was founded in London in 1967 and has grown into an enormously successful practice, with projects in many parts of the world. Major projects include the controversial Reliance Controls Factory

SAINSBURY CENTRE FOR THE VISUAL ARTS, Norwich

The Sainsbury Centre at the University of East Anglia is a dashing combination of simplicity and complexity. Uncompromisingly High-Tech and machine-like, the building is nevertheless extremely elegant in its detailing. Norman Foster's design, a low-lying, rectangular slab, is constructed from trussed, tubular steel support frames which house the services, thus allowing the central hallway area to remain uncluttered. The exterior of the building is finished in glass and metal ready-made panels, and the roof is fitted with electronically-controlled louvres which can be adjusted to allow the control of a soft, evenly distributed light. Completed in 1978 it stands as an example of the beauty of engineering detail and is one of the key High-Tech modernist buildings in Britain.

(1966-7), the much-admired black glass Willis Faber Dumas offices, Ipswich (1974-5), the Sainsbury Centre for the Visual Arts (1976-8), what was described as the most expensive office building ever constructed, the Hong Kong and Shanghai Bank (1979-85), and the Stansted Airport Terminal (1980-90). Over the years Foster has worked with a number of partners, who are all now well established in their own practices, including Birkin Haward and Michael Hopkins. The "High-Tech" vocabulary of the practice is uncompromising and clear in its exploration of technological innovation: technology produces form. However, Foster is also deeply concerned with architectural details and the craftsmanship that goes into them. Emphasis is often laid on the repetition of industrialized "modular" units in his work. Prefabricated off-site-manufactured elements are frequently employed and specialist components are often specially designed for individual projects, as at Hong Kong. Foster was awarded the RIBA Royal Gold Medal in 1983, and in 1990 the RIBA Trustees Medal was made for the Willis Faber Dumas building, Ipswich. He was knighted in 1990.

☐ Reliance Controls Factory, Swindon, 1966-7. Willis Faber Dumas offices, Ipswich, Suffolk, 1974-5. Sainsbury Centre for the Visual Arts, University of East Anglia, Norwich, 1976-8. Hong Kong and Shanghai Bank, 1979-85. Médiathèque, Maison Carrée, Nîmes, France, from 1984. Airport Terminal, Stansted, Essex, 1980-91. Kings Cross Redevelopment, London, 1988- .

▷ R. Banham (intro.) *Foster Associates*, London 1979. Various authors, *Foster Associates: Buildings and Projects*, 3 vols., London, 1989. DS

▷ *see also pp244-5*

FRY Edwin Maxwell

b. Wallasey, Chesire, 1899; d. Durham, 1987.

First-generation architect of the Modern Movement in Britain. Fry trained at Liverpool University, spending one vacation in the New York office of the architects Carrere and Hastings. He spent the first ten years of his working life with the firm of Adams and Thompson, gradually developing in the early 1930s from a neo-Georgian style to fully fledged Modernism. He was co-founder of the English MARS group. In 1934 he established his own practice, working alongside Walter GROPIUS for a time. His Sun House draws inspiration from the works of continental Modernism, with its smooth white walls, strip fenestration, *pilotis* and general geometric precision. In 1945 Fry set up a partnership with Jane Drew, his second wife. They were joined at various later stages by Lindsey Drake, Denys LASDUN, Frank Knight and Norman Creamer. Fry and Drew earned a reputation for work in tropical climates, culminating in their commission from President Nehru to run the Capital project in Chandigarh, India, where they were responsible for involving LE CORBUSIER on the public buildings.

Maxwell Fry, Sun House, Hampstead, London, 1936

☐ Sun House, Hampstead, London, 1936. Impington Village College, Cambs. (with Walter Gropius), 1936. Levy House, Chelsea, London (with Walter Gropius), 1936. Kensal House, Ladbroke Grove, London, 1937-8. Capital scheme, Chandigarh, India (with Le Corbusier and Jane Drew), 1951-6. University College, Ibadan, Nigeria (with Jane Drew), 1953-9. Pilkington Glass Headquarters, St Helen's, Lancashire, 1963.

▷ E. Maxwell Fry, *Fine Building*, London, 1944; *Architecture for Children*, London, 1944; *Art in a Machine Age*, London, 1969; *Autobiographical Sketches*, London, 1975. H. A. N. Brockman, *Fry, Drew, Knight, Creamer: Architecture*, London, 1978. PP

▷ *see also pp238-9*

FUCHS Bohuslav

b. Všechovice, 1895; d. Brno, 1972.

One of the most important representatives of Czechoslovak functionalism. He studied at the Academy of Fine Arts in Prague with Professor Jan KOTĚRA, in whose studio he then worked for two years. From 1921 to 1923 he had a joint architecture studio with Josef Štěpánek in Prague, then he was invited to Brno by Jindřich Kumpošt, municipal architect of the city. He accepted, moved to Brno and produced his major works there. His early art was influenced by Cubism and Expressionism, and he was also inspired by the Dutch red-brick style until he joined, in the mid-1920s, the white functional movement. A typical feature of his work was the space concept which reached its peak in the Avion Hotel, on a narrow and deep site where by means of staircases and galleries he gave access to views covering four storeys. Fuchs was a Czechoslovak delegate to CIAM, a corresponding RIBA Member, and – from 1945 to 1958 – a professor at the Faculty of Architecture in Brno.

☐ Villa and Power plant, Háj near Mohelnice, 1921-2. Cemetery Funeral Chapel, Brno, 1925. Villas Avion, Viola and Radun Luhačovice, 1926-7. City Pavilion, Brno, 1927-8. Avion Hotel, Brno, 1927-8. Triple House at the Czechoslovak Werkbund Housing Exhibition, Brno, 1927-8. Vesna School and Girls' Home, Brno, 1929-30. Masaryk Student Home, Brno, 1929-30. Municipal Baths, Brno, 1929-31. Moravian Bank (with Arnošt Wiesner), 1929-31. Morava Recreation Home, Tatranská

Lomnica, 1931. Savings Banks Tišnov (with Jindřich Kumpošt) and Třebíč, 1931: Green Frog Thermal Bath, Trenčianske Teplice, 1935-7. Provincial Military Command, Brno, 1936-7. Rail Post Office, Brno, 1938; Vlčina Mountain Hotel, Frenštát), 1940. Department Store, Znojmo (with Kamil Fuchs) 1968-72.

▷ Zdenek Rossmann, *Bohuslav Fuchs 1919-1929*, Basel, 1930. Zdenek Kudelka, *Bohuslav Fuchs*, Prague, 1966. VS

FULLER Richard Buckminster

b. Boston, Mass., 1895; d. Los Angeles, 1983.

American engineer, designer, inventor, mathematician, cartographer, ecologist, poet, thinker: the C20's universal man. Fuller's lifelong task was the search for elegant technical solutions to rationally stated problems, without being prejudiced by experience. This essentially Modernist theme was for Fuller based on the clear moral aim of transferring high scientific capability from the world of weaponry to creative and humane needs. Thus in his remarkable "Dymaxion" house (1927) (the Dymaxion car and map followed), the realistic prototype of a mass-produced house, every design move is based on a radical awareness of engineering principle, the aim of efficiency in world-resource use, and insight into manufacturing processes, all under Fuller's motto of "more with less". Asked to put what he was trying to do into one sentence, Fuller, typically, wrote: "Acutely aware of our beings' limitations and acknowledging the infinite mystery of the a priori universe into which we are born but nevertheless searching for a conscious means of hopefully competent participation by humanity in its own evolutionary trending while employing only the unique advantages inhering exclusively to the individual who takes and maintains the economic initiative in the face of the formidable physical capital and credit advantages of the massive corporations and political states and deliberately avoiding political ties and tactics while endeavoring by experiments and explorations to excite individuals' awareness and realization of humanity's higher potentials, I seek through comprehensive anticipatory design science and its reductions to physical practices to reform the environment instead of trying to reform men being thereby intent to accomplish prototyped capabilities of doing more with less whereby in turn the wealth augmenting prospects of such design science regenerations will induce their spontaneous and economically successful industrial proliferation by world around services' managements all of which chain reaction provoking events will both permit and induce all humanity to realize full lasting economic and physical success plus enjoyment of all the Earth without one individual interfering with or being advantaged at the expense of another." The central exposition of his philosophy can be grasped in the remarkable, rambling but essential lecture *Designing a New Industry* (1945-6) and in *The Critical Path* (New York, 1981), a summary of his views on the evolution of society and its future prospects he did not see much hope for humanity, which he viewed as "moving ever deeper into crisis" brought about by changes in cosmic evolution. Fuller enjoyed considerable success as a visiting lecturer in a number of architectural schools in the USA.

Buckminster Fuller, USA Pavilion, Expo 67, Montreal, 1967

□ Thousands of projects and patented inventions include: 240 "stockade buildings", 1922-7; Dymaxion House, 1927; Dymaxion Car, 1937; Dymaxion Bathroom, 1940; Fuller house, 1946; Geodesic Dome, 1954; Paperboard Frame, Plydome, Catenary, 1959; Energetic/Synergetic Geometry, Dymaxion air-ocean world map, USA Pavilion, Expo 67, Montreal, 1967; Inventory of World Resources and computerized "world game", star tensegrity and non-symmetrical tensegrity structures, 1967-75.

▷ R. Buckminster Fuller, *Transport Magazine*, 1918; *4-D Timelock*, 1927; *Shelter Magazine*, 1930; *Nine Chains to the Moon*, New York, 1938. R. W. Marks, *The Dymaxion World of Buckminster Fuller*, New York, 1960. J. Meller, *The Buckminster Fuller Reader*, London, 1970. M. Pawley, *Buckminster Fuller*, London, 1990. JM

▷ *see also pp236-7*

FURNESS Frank

b. Philadelphia, 1839; d. Medea, Pennsylvania, 1912.

Late C19 American architect of outstanding individuality. After working as a draughtsman in the Philadelphia office of

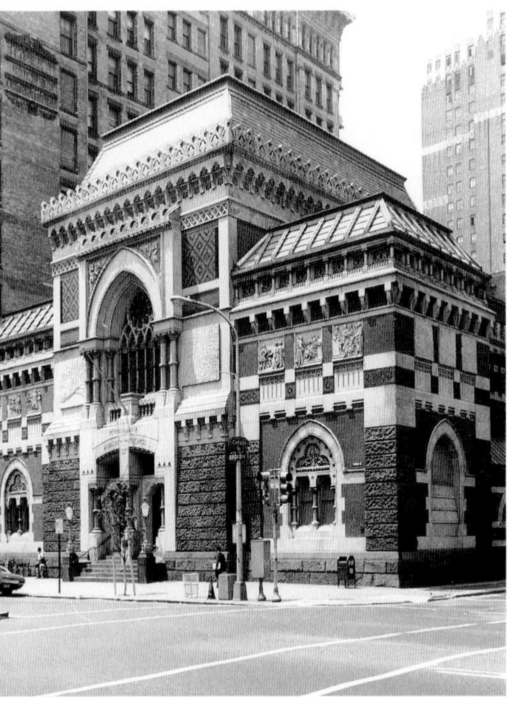

Frank Furness, Pennsylvania Academy of Fine Arts, Philadelphia, 1871–6

John Fraser, Furness studied at the New York atelier of Richard Morris HUNT 1859-61 and (after distinguished service in the Union cavalry during the Civil War) 1864-65/6. He subsequently practised in Philadelphia, in partnership with Fraser and George W. Hewitt (1867-71), with Hewitt (1871-5) and with Allen Evans (from 1881). Furness never travelled abroad; though evidently influenced by the ideas of RUSKIN and VIOLLET-LE-DUC, his eclectic and boldly polychromatic style remained uninhibited by any first-hand experience of European historicism or "taste". He developed a dynamic sculptural freedom in his articulation of form and mass, used unexpected, variegated and sometimes dramatically overscaled detail to give expressive strength to his outlines and surfaces, and knew how to exploit the visual and tactile character of his materials. The late Victorian exuberance of Furness's style proved unpalatable to C20 taste, and few of his buildings have survived unmutilated.

□ All in Philadelphia: Pennsylvania Academy of the Fine Arts, 1871-6. Centennial National Bank, 1876. Provident Life and Trust Co., 1876-9. Kensington National Bank, 1877. First Unitarian Church, 1883-6. Library of the University of Pennsylvania, 1883-91.

▷ James F. O'Gorman, *The Architecture of Frank Furness*, Philadelphia, 1973.

BP

GABRIEL Ange-Jacques

b. Paris, 1698; d. Paris, 1782.

Principal royal architect for most of the reign of Louis XV, who promoted the transition from Rococo to Neo-Classicism through the evolution of the so-called *Style Louis XVI*. Heir to the related architectural dynasties of the MANSARTS and the Gabriels, predominant under Louis XIV and XV, Ange-Jacques was trained by his father, Jacques V, and Robert de Cotte in the establishment of the Premier Architecte at Versailles. He did not follow his father's footsteps on an Italian tour. A member of the Académie Royale de l'Architecture from 1728 and principal assistant to his father as Premier Architecte from 1735, he succeeded his father in that post and as director of the academy in 1742. Gabriel's work may be seen as the practical expression of the fully evolved academic classical principles of which the theoretical works of J. F. BLONDEL provide the most complete elaboration. Responsive to new ideas, his work is a consummate example of the academic ideal of emulation: his was the ability of the great classicist to assimilate the lessons of the past, adapting its models to ever more sophisticated purposes in accordance with the dictates of propriety, through the development of compositional principles derived from the greatest masters, Italian and French. The decorative motifs with which he complemented these principles derived from the same authorities and, like SOUFFLOT's, constituted a rather more extensive repertory of essentially architectonic detail than he had inherited from his immediate predecessors. In its truth to physics, this reflected the attitude of the "progressive" critics of the mid-century who, rejecting the licence of the Rococo, proclaimed the fundamental academic belief that progress depends upon reason and discipline. Its introduction *c.*1750 marked a watershed in Gabriel's development: on the premise that the role of ornament is essentially the articulation of structure, the sumptuous embellishment of his work in the 1740s gave way to the *noble simplicité* most celebrated in the Petit Trianon at Versailles. From 1742 until 1775, Gabriel was engaged in *grands projects* for modernizing and upgrading the architectural dignity of the principal royal residences – Versailles, Fontainebleau, Compiègne. The Fontainebleau and Versailles projects were partially executed from 1749 and 1772 respectively, and Compiègne was entirely rebuilt, largely in accordance with Gabriel's plans, from 1751. He also undertook the rearrangement of the royal apartments in all the King's châteaux – notably Choisy and Bellevue in addition to the above.

□ Pavillon Français and King's private garden at Trianon, Versailles, 1749-50. Hermitage at Fontainebleau, 1749. Hunting pavilion "Le Butard", Vaucresson (near Versailles), 1750. Bourse, completion of Jacques V's Place Royale, Bordeaux, from 1750. Ecole Militaire, Paris, 1751-75. Place Louis XV (de la Concorde), Paris, 1753-75. Completion of the Cour Carrée of the Louvre, Paris, from 1754. Château of St Hubert near Rambouillet, 1755-74. Petit Trianon, Versailles, 1762-8. Hunting pavilion "La Muette" near St Germain, 1766. Opera at Versailles (after the projects evolved since 1742, see above), 1768-70.

▷ F. Fels, *Ange-Jacques Gabriel*, Paris, 1912 and 1924. C. Tadgell, *Ange-Jacques Gabriel*, London, 1978. Y. Bottineau, M. Gallet etc., *Les Gabriel*, Paris, 1982.

CT

LE PETIT TRIANON, Versailles

Begun in 1760 by the royal architect, Ange-Jacques Gabriel, as a retreat for Louis XV's mistress, Mme de Pompadour, in the woods of Versailles, the "Petit Trianon" seems to brush aside the whole frothy fun of 20 years of Rococo as if they had never happened. This faultless example of Classical restraint, balance and elegance looks back both to French principles of nearly a century earlier, and across the channel to the Palladian tradition of contemporary English country houses. Work was continued after Mme de Pompadour's death (1764) by her successor, Mme du Barry. The house really came to life inside and out when taken over in the 1770s by Marie Antoinette, who furnished it in the style seen today. The existence in the house of a top floor for the ladies-in-waiting is concealed from view.

GALLI DA BIBIENA FAMILY

Ferdinando Galli da Bibiena, b. Bibiena (near Bologna), 1657; d. 1743. Francesco Galli da Bibiena, b. Bibiena, 1659; d. 1739.

Italian brothers who co-founded an artistic dynasty of painters, architects and theatre designers in the early c18. The Bibiena family's long list of accomplishments included architecture, interior design and trompe-l'œil painting, and their skills were widely sought after by European nobility. Three generations of Bibienas were employed at various times by the courts of Vienna, Stockholm, Barcelona, Bayreuth, Lisbon and St Petersburg. As well as building theatres and decorating palaces and churches, they also stage-managed elaborate spectacles to accompany royal births, marriages and deaths. Both Francesco and Ferdinando were originally trained as painters, specializing in the complex art of illusionistic trompe-l'œil painting known as *quadratura*. From early days as fresco painters, the brothers graduated to stage design, theatre renovation and church architecture, initially in Italy, then, as their fame spread, further afield. In 1717 Ferdinando became the first imperial theatre architect at the Habsburg court in Vienna; he was assisted by his gifted sons **Alessandro** (1686-1748), **Giuseppe** (1695-1747) and **Antonio** (1697-1774). All were accomplished designers in their own right; Giuseppe designed the sumptuous interior of the theatre at Bayreuth, Antonio completed several theatres in Italy, and Alessandro designed the Mannheim opera house.

□ Francesco da Bibiena: Grossehoftheater, Vienna, 1704. Ferdinando da Bibiena: Church of S. Antonio Abate, Parma, 1712-43. Giuseppe da Bibiena: Markgrafliches Opernhaus, Bayreuth (interior), 1745-8.

▷ Hyatt A. Mayor, *The Bibiena Family*, New York, 1945. CS

GARNER Thomas

see Bodley, George Frederick

Giuseppe Galli da Bibiena, theatre design, c. 1740

Charles Garnier, L'Opéra, Paris, 1860–75, study for façade

GARNIER Charles

b. Paris, 1825; d. Paris, 1898.

Architect of the Paris Opera House and creator of the "Style Napoléon III". Garnier, who came from humble origins, studied in the evenings at the Ecole Gratuite de Dessin. He eventually entered the atelier of Lebas in 1840 and worked as a draughtsman for VIOLLET-LE-DUC. In 1842 he was admitted to the Ecole des Beaux Arts, the institution founded by Napoleon in 1819 whose teaching programme was basically conceived as a preparation for designing monumental public buildings and culminated in the competition for the Grand Prix de Rome. Garnier won the prize in 1848 with a design for a Conservatoire des Arts et Métiers. He spent five years at the French Academy in Rome (1848-54) and seems to have been captivated by the pageantry of Roman society. His architectural education also included a visit to Greece and Turkey in 1852; he made a reconstruction study of the temple of Aegina complete with polychrome decoration, in accordance with Hittorff's theories, which were revolutionizing the understanding of classical architecture and attitudes to colour in architecture. On returning to Paris, Garnier received only a couple of private commissions and accepted several municipal posts, finally as architect of the fifth and sixth *arrondissements*. But in 1860, following HAUSSMANN's extensive replanning of Paris, a public competition for a new opera house was announced, and in 1861 Garnier, though almost unknown, won. The Empress had hoped the commission would go to VIOLLET-LE-DUC, but Garnier's design brilliantly reflected the aspirations of the Second Empire. It was, as Garnier said, the "Style Napoléon III", and became an immediate favourite with the Parisian public for its rich colouring and decoration and glittering sumptuousness. Garnier had a great sense of occasion and the theatrical; the exuberant, but carefully controlled, Baroque interior of the Opéra provided an architectural procession from the street to the auditorium intended to create a "*milieu artistique et même grandiose*". Underneath, however, the planning is extremely logical, not to say functional. The Opéra was built with an electric lift and lighting, and set new standards of comfort and convenience. The circulation is carefully considered, reflecting the hierarchy of Second Empire society, and the order of these internal arrangements is clearly expressed on the exterior. There is a shallow dome over the auditorium and a tall pedimented fly-tower; pavilions on either side are separate entrances for those arriving by carriage and for the Emperor (who fell from power before its completion). The style of the Opéra had many imitators; the Beaux Arts tradition was perpetuated by others, as Garnier himself did not produce anything of comparable importance, though he remained active as a teacher and in professional associations.

□ Conservatoire des Arts et Métiers project, 1848. Chapel, Dampierre, 1855-61. House, rue de Sebastapol, Paris, 1859. L'Opéra, Paris, 1860-75. Dépôt de décors, Opéra, Paris, 1863-9. Villa Garnier, Bordighera, Italy, 1872-3. School, Bordighera, 1874. Maison Hachette, Paris, 1878-80. Casino, Monte Carlo, 1878-81. Observatory, Nice, 1880-88. Panorama Valentino, Paris, 1882-3. Church of Ste Grimonie, La Chapelle-en-Thiérache, France, 1883-7.

▷ S. Tidworth, *Theatres: An Illustrated History*, London, 1973. R. Middleton and D. Watkin, *Neo-Classical and Nineteenth Century Architecture*, New York, 1980.

TC

▷ *see also pp224-5*

GARNIER Tony

b. Lyon, 1869; d. La Bédoule, 1948.

French architect and author of *Une Cité Industrielle*, whose work is mainly to be found in the Lyon area. From 1886 to 1899 he studied consecutively at the Ecoles des Beaux Arts in Lyon and in Paris under Guadet, from whom he inherited a rationalist's turn of mind. He won the Prix de Rome and continued his studies in Rome until 1904, during which time he began his original work on a Cité Industrielle for 35,000 people. His first youthful projects defied the classical tradition in which he had been trained and embraced a primitive kind of continental concrete-finished Modernism. Ultimately he was to publish this seminal work (*Une Cité Industrielle*) in two parts in 1917. His absorption with ideas for an industrial city – which involved zoning and block housing and open spaces – must be compared to epoch-making projects such as Howard's Garden City idea and LE CORBUSIER's Ville Radieuse, which it undoubtedly influenced. Almost everything he did later was to some extent influenced by these notions, whether in the simple way that buildings were expressed in cubic concrete terms, as in some of his *Grands Travaux* for Lyon, or in the way the renderings were done for his numerous competition entries. He was city architect of Lyon 1905-19.

□ Abattoirs de La Mouche, Lyon, 1909-13. Municipal (Olympic) Stadium, Lyon, 1913-16. International Urbanisme Exhibition, Lyon, 1913-14. Lyon-St Etienne Pavilion, Paris Exposition, 1925. Town Hall, Boulogne-Billancourt, 1931-4.

▷ Tony Garnier, *Une Cité Industrielle: étude pour le construction des villes*, Paris, 1917, 2nd ed. 1932 (various foreign-language editions are available); *Les Grands Travaux de la Ville de Lyon*, Paris, n.d. J. Badovici, *L'œuvre de Tony Garnier*, Paris, 1938. D. Weibenson, *Tony Garnier – The Cité Industrielle* (includes extended bibliography), New York, 1979.

DS

GÄRTNER Friedrich von

b. Koblenz, 1792; d. Munich, 1847.

A leading eclectic whose "romantic classicism" was widely influential. Gärtner studied architecture in Munich (1808-12) and then in Karlsruhe and Paris. He visited Italy on a grand tour (1814-17) and England (1819); later he worked in Greece. With von KLENZE, he was employed by Ludwig I of Bavaria, whose ambition to propel himself and his capital Munich to the forefront of art patronage in Germany produced the Ludwigstrasse (1829-40), a triumphal thoroughfare terminated to the north by Gärtner's Siegestor (adapted from the Arch of Constantine), and to the south by his Feldherrenhalle (based on the Florentine Loggia dei Lanzi). Among the other buildings fronting the route, Gärtner designed the university, library and church. Proclaiming Ludwig's role as patron, the secular designs were based on the Medici Palace in Florence, while at the Ludwigskirche, Italian Romanesque and Quattrocento motifs coalesced in a striking twin-towered composition that gave focus and punctuation to the street landscape. Gärtner's two palaces, the Munich Wittelsbacher and the Royal Residence in Athens, were respectively Anglo-Venetian Gothic and Neo-Classical in style. For his other major project, the Saltworks Administration Building, he used a form of "Rundbogenstil".

□ Ludwigskirche, Munich, 1829-44. Bavarian Court and State Library, Munich, 1832-43. Ludwig Maximilian University, Munich, 1835-40. Royal Residence, Athens, 1836-41. Saltworks Administration Building, Munich, 1838-43. Siegestor, Munich, 1843-52. Feldherrenhalle, Munich, 1844.

▷ Klaus Eggert, *Friedrich von Gärtner, der Baumeister König Ludwigs I*, Munich, 1963. Osward Hederer, *Friedrich von Gärtner 1797-1847; Leben, Werk, Schuler*, Munich, 1976. BP

GAUDÍ Antoni y Cornet

b. Reus, Spain, 1852; d. Barcelona, 1926.

One of architecture's most original and unusual talents. The son of a coppersmith, pot and kettle maker, he was working in northern Spain at the time of an enthusiastic revival of all things Catalan, and became absorbed in the idea of producing a style of architecture for the region. He studied at the Escola Superior d'Arquitectura in Barcelona and began his architectural career with a Gothic Revival style for his first major commission – the Casa Vincens in Barcelona (1883-5). As his work progressed, he developed a sinuous, flowing, almost surreal form of design which placed him at the forefront of the Spanish Art Nouveau movement. Gaudí's idiosyncratic and bizarre-looking architecture drew admiration from other avant-garde artists, including his fellow countryman the Surrealist painter Salvador Dali. The emergence of Gaudí's entirely original style is to be found at the Palau Güell in Barcelona (1885-9). Here, under the patronage of a textile businessman, Count Güell, Gaudí was given the opportunity to experiment with unusual, sculpted chimney pots and the use of tiled mosaic. These two features frequently occur in his later work. Such was the suc-

Right: Antoni Gaudí, Sagrada Familia, Barcelona, begun 1884

Below: Antoni Gaudí, Casa Batlló, Barcelona, 1905–7

cess of this house design that Gaudí was invited by Güell to design a workers' community for his textile plant at Santa Coloma de Cervello (Colonia Güell) in 1891. Seventeen years later he worked on the chapel. For Güell he also designed the Park Güell on Barcelona's outskirts. Here glittering, gaudy mosaics of tiles and mirror bedeck the swooping stairways, sculpted benches, the mock Grecian theatre, underground grottoes and curious stone beasts which Gaudí planted in the rural setting. It was full of fantasy, far removed from the original intention of creating an English garden suburb. Gaudí's imagination was also given full rein on two housing projects in Barcelona, the Casa Batlló (1905-7) and the exuberant Casa Mila (1905-7). Both incorporate strong maritime imagery. Casa Batlló has a sculpted façade of waves and fishbone shapes surrounding windows and forming balconies. The exterior was completed with a coral effect of broken ceramic tiles. The sense of the bizarre was continued inside, where no two apartments were the same, and none had straight walls. At the nearby Casa Mila the sculpted façade was further embellished with ornate iron balconies resembling tangles of seaweed. Gaudí's undoubted masterpiece is the unfinished Expiatory Church of the Sagrada Familia in Barcelona, where he worked from 1884 until his tragic death in 1926 when he was knocked down and killed by a tram just outside the building. Work on the church charts the styles Gaudí evolved during his career. At the crypt level a Gothic design is used, but as the building climbs towards the sky the structure passes through an Art Nouveau stage before becoming more surreal and fanciful, finishing in the four intricately carved, open-work cone-shaped spires. Work to Gaudí's designs is still continuing on the church.

□ Casa Vincens, Barcelona, 1883-5. Palau Güell, Barcelona, 1885-9. Workers' community at Santa Coloma de Cervello, Barcelona, 1891, and a chapel at the same site, 1908. Park Güell, Barcelona, 1900-1911. Casa Batlló, Barcelona, 1905-7. Casa Mila, Barcelona, 1905-7. Expiatory Church of the Sagrada Familia, Barcelona, from 1884.

▷ George Collins, *Antoni Gaudí*, New York, 1960. Roberto Pane, *Antoni Gaudí*, Milan, 1964. Ignasi de Sola-Morales, *Gaudí*, New York, 1984. Rainer Zerbst, *Antoni Gaudí*, Cologne, 1988. FS

▷ *see also pp230-31*

Frank Gehry, California Aerospace Museum, Los Angeles, 1982–4

GEHRY Frank O.

b. Toronto, Canada, 1929.

One of the first "punk-style" architects, whose curious, irreverent buildings have been described as "functional sculpture" and Deconstructivist architecture. Although he was born in Canada, Gehry has become synonymous with the American West Coast where he works. He studied at the universities of Southern California and Harvard. His first practice, Frank O. Gehry and Associates, was founded in 1963 and was succeeded in 1979 by the firm Gehry & Krueger Inc. Gehry has held a long fascination for painting and sculpture and first won public acclaim for his chunky corrugated cardboard furniture in 1972. His distinctive exploded-then-reconstructed architectural style began to emerge in the late 1970s, when the design for his home at Santa Monica used corrugated metal, an exposed wooden frame and shields of chain-link fencing. He justifies his unusual use of materials saying "If Jasper Johns and Donald Judd can make beauty with junk materials, then why can't that transfer into architecture?" His off-beat style continued at the Mid-Atlantic Toyota Distributorship Offices, Santa Monica, which contained a maze of odd-shaped offices painted in different colours. The Loyola Law School, Los Angeles, was again idiosyncratic, with its aluminium portico and Romanesque-style chapel made from plywood and glass. Gehry's strangest work is a fish-shaped restaurant in Japan, called "Fishdance", and his most sophisticated is the Vitra Design Museum, Wein am Rhein. The jumble of plain white geometric shapes of the latter resembles a Russian Constructivist sculpture. Inside the museum is a calm top-lit space with galleries linked by bold curving ramps. His work was exhibited as part of the "Deconstructivist Architecture" show at MOMA, New York in 1988.

□ Gehry House, Santa Monica, 1978-9. Mid-Atlantic Toyota Distributorship Offices, Santa Monica, 1978. Loyola Law School, Los Angeles, 1981-4. California Aerospace Museum, Los Angeles, 1982-4. Fishdance Restaurant, Kobe, Japan, 1985. Vitra Design Museum, Wein am Rhein, 1989.

▷ Olivier Boissière, *Gehry, SITE, Tigerman, trois portraits de l'artiste en architecture*, Paris, 1981. Luciano Rubino, *Il Bovindo/5 Frank O. Gehry Special*, Rome, 1984. FS

GEORGE Sir Ernest

b. London, 1839; d. London, 1922.

A late Victorian exponent of the picturesque. While a student at the RA Schools, he won the RIBA Gold Medal for Architecture (1859). He was in partnership with Thomas Vaughan (1861-71), Harold Ainsworth Peto (1876-90) and Alfred Yeates (1893-1919). His early work drew freely on Dutch, Flemish, French and English late Gothic and early Renaissance examples; his red brick and terracotta façades combined decorative flair with an eclectic approach to period detail. His interiors stylishly evoked "olden times", and he became known for his mastery of domestic planning. His later buildings reflected the prevailing fashion for English neo-Baroque. At his death he was remembered mainly as a designer of country houses, but more recently attention has focused on the distinctive residential developments in South Kensington (designed in partnership with Peto), which epitomized the aesthetic of cultivated informality in planned urban scenery. George was a noted watercolourist and published several volumes of topographical etchings. His many architectural pupils included Herbert BAKER and Edwin LUTYENS. He received the Royal Gold Medal for Architecture (1896), was knighted in 1907, and was elected PRIBA 1908-10, ARA 1910, and RA 1917.

☐ St Pancras Church, Rousdon, Devon, 1875. Harrington and Collingham Gardens, Kensington, London, 1881-8. St Andrew's Church, Streatham, London, 1886. Claridge's Hotel, London, 1894-7. Motcombe House, Dorset, 1894-7. Eynsham Park, Oxon., 1900-1904. Crathorne Hall, Yorkshire, 1906-9. Royal Exchange Buildings, Cornhill, London, 1907. Royal Academy of Music, Marylebone, London, 1910.

▷ Ernest George, *Etchings of Old London*, London, 1884. *Country Houses in Essex*, London, 1895. *Inventing Urban Variety* (RIBA Journal, 1984). Mark Girouard, *Sweetness and Light*, Oxford, 1977. BP

GHIBERTI Lorenzo

b. Florence, ?1378/81; d. Florence, 1455.

Leading pioneer of Renaissance sculpture in Florence, and an all-rounder whose buildings, paintings and theoretical writings all added to his reputation in Italy. Although most likely the illegitimate child of a Florentine goldsmith, Bartoluccio, with whom his mother lived from *c.*1380 after leaving the husband (named Ghiberti) she had married in 1370, Lorenzo later asserted his eligibility for public office as the lawful son of Ghiberti, and used his name. Lorenzo grew up in Bartoluccio's workshop, where he learned the skills as sculptor and metalcraftsman which he practised all his life. Winning the competition for the design of gilded bronze doors for the Florence Baptistery (beating even BRUNELLESCHI's entry) brought him early fame in his twenties, and kept him busy until 1420. Young artists who started as assistants in his ever-expanding workshop team included Paolo Uccello, Donatello and MICHELOZO. In 1420, Lorenzo and the only slightly older Brunelleschi were put in charge, on a equal footing, of the construction of the dome for Florence Cathedral, designing the model of it in collaboration. In 1429 they were again commissioned jointly, this time to work on the model for the entire building. In 1447 Ghiberti began writing his *Commentarii*, Book 2 of which has some of the most influential opinions ever written about art. Book 3 was still unfinished when he died.

▷ L. Goldscheider, *Lorenzo Ghiberti*, London, 1949. JRC

GIBBERD Sir Frederick

b. Coventry, 1908; d. Harlow, 1984.

Prolific English architect and town planner who made a major contribution to the development of post-war housing, town planning and landscape design. Gibberd studied with the firm of Crouch, Butterfield and Savage and at the Birmingham School of Architecture (1925-9). He developed a lasting friendship with Modernist F. R. S. YORKE, with whom he toured Europe, and was influenced by LE CORBUSIER and MIES VAN DER ROHE. Gibberd also respected the work of Wells COATES and Berthold LUBETKIN. He set up his London practice in 1930; he was principal of the Architectural Association School (1942-4), chief architect for Harlow New Town in Essex (1946-73), and established the firm of Gibberd and Partners in 1965. Three times winner of the Festival of Britain award, Gibberd was knighted in 1967. He was concerned with overseeing a design through to completion and was keen to emphasize the multi-disciplinary nature of his approach, which encompassed architecture, planning and landscape design. Gibberd's work is characterized by restrained, rectangular massing, although his circular "Crown of Thorns" design for Liverpool Cathedral was a singular exception. Humane in outlook, his work covered housing estates (including post-war prefabs), hospitals, offices, schools and power stations. His designs for shopping centres, notably Harlow, show a regard for centralized amenities and pedestrianization. Gibberd's later work in London includes the Inter-Continental Hotel (1968–75) and the Central London Mosque (1970–77).

Sir Frederick Gibberd, Roman Catholic Cathedral, Liverpool, 1960–67

□ Harlow New Town, Essex, 1946-73. Terminal Building, Heathrow Airport, London, 1950-69. Roman Catholic Cathedral, Liverpool, 1960-67. Inter-Continental Hotel, Hyde Park Corner, London, 1968-75. Central Mosque, Regent's Park, London, 1970-77.

▷ Frederick Gibberd, "Expression in Modern Architecture", *RIBA Journal*, Jan. 1952; *Harlow: The Story of a New Town*, London, 1980. Frederick Gibberd and F. R. S. Yorke, *Modern Flats*, 2nd ed., London, 1961. Tony Aldous, "The Gibberd Touch", *The Architects' Journal*, 167, Jan., 1978. CS

GIBBS James

b. near Aberdeen, Scotland, 1682; d. London, 1754.

London church architect who blended Mannerist, Baroque and Palladian motifs, as well as looking carefully at the soaring church spires designed by Sir Christopher WREN. He drew to perfection, from childhood, and in 1728 produced the most widely used C18 architectural publication. And yet he had started with the seeming disadvantage of being brought up a Catholic in Protestant Scotland. In 1703 he set off to be enrolled as a candidate for the priesthood at the Scots College in Rome. Within a year an over-zealous rector had driven him from the calling into architecture, and he entered the studio of the leading Baroque architect Carlo FONTANA. Gibbs absorbed all he could in Rome. He returned to London in 1709 with a secure training denied to most. It was, however, religion which now threatened to halt his advance, but an important fellow Catholic, the "Architect" John Earl of Mar, saw to his early preferment. He was appointed in 1713 as one of the two surveyors to the commissioners charged with building fifty new churches in London. Gibbs's first public building for them was the Church of St Mary-le-Strand (1714-17), which gave him a "great reputation in his business". But after the changing of the commissioners in 1715, he was dismissed, both as a suspected Tory and as a Scot. In the same year Lord BURLINGTON replaced him with Colen CAMPBELL as architect of Burlington House. His training in Fontana's studio and recognition of his rare ability allowed Gibbs to survive without a salaried post. There was work in plenty from his Tory patrons. And, with a percipience which seems to have been finely observed rather than merely accidental, Gibbs chose the busy years of the 1720s for several achievements. His mentor, Edward Harley, 2nd Earl of Oxford, not only wanted to build a church in Vere Street, London, but needed alterations at his country house, Wimpole, Cambridgeshire. There were also many houses to build for others. Furthermore Gibbs's *Book of Architecture*, issued in 1728, with its elevations of, amongst much else, his London church of St Martin-in-the-Fields, had a great success. As a result of its wide distribution many copies of the St Martin's spire rear up in America and elsewhere.

ST MARTIN-IN-THE-FIELDS, London

In this new (not rebuilt) church of 1722–6, James Gibbs' study of Roman buildings led him to a successful marriage between the traditional steeple form that people felt was expected of a church, and a wide temple portico in the Classical taste. It served as a model for many others. This view from the south-west (opened up after 1820 when the space that is now Trafalgar Square began to be cleared and rebuilt) shows the round-topped side windows with their characteristic decoration – a style which came to be described as "Gibbs surrounds". The ceiling inside the church is still resplendent with original fine plasterwork executed by Italian craftsmen.

□ St Mary-le-Strand, London, 1714-17. St Peter, Vere Street, London, 1721-4. St Martin-in-the-Fields, London, 1722-6. Senate House, Cambridge, 1722-30. St Bartholomew's Hospital, London, from 1730. Radcliffe Library, Oxford, 1737-48.

▷ James Gibbs, *A Book of Architecture*, 1728; *Rules for Drawing the several parts of Architecture*, 1732; *Bibliotheca Radcliviana*, 1747. Terry Friedman, *James Gibbs*, London, 1984. GB

GIEDION Sigfried

b. 1888; d. Zürich, 1968.

Leading historian and staunch advocate of the Modern Movement, whose books were highly influential in shaping the direction of the early movement. The son of a Swiss industrialist, Giedion studied engineering in Vienna before enrolling as a student of art history in 1913. His close friendship with GROPIUS and LE CORBUSIER led to his early involvement with the CIAM, founded in 1928 to act as a unified pressure group for Europe's avant-garde; Giedion was secretary general until the organization disbanded (1956). His most celebrated book, *Space, Time and Architecture*, catalogues the contemporary schism between thought and emotion and analyses the largely unconscious inter-relationship between art and science, architecture and human activity. The popularity of the book necessitated numerous reprints and it quickly acquired honorific status because of its contemporary slant and highly moral stance. Giedion's belief that history was not just "a compilation of facts but an insight into the moving process of life" proved invaluable in the Modernists' quest for a functional solution to the chaos and contradictions within society today.

▷ Sigfried Giedion, *Space, Time and Architecture*, Cambridge, Mass., 1941; *Mechanization takes Command – a contribution to Anonymous History*, New York, 1948; *The Eternal Present – the Beginnings of Architecture*, New York, 1964; *Architecture and the Phenomena of Transition – the Three Space Conception in Architecture*, Cambridge, Mass., 1970. MC

GILBERT Cass

b. Zanesville, Ohio, 1859; d. New York, 1934.

American architect who designed one of the first skyscrapers in New York. Following a brief spell as a draughtsman and carpenter's assistant in St Paul, Minnesota, he enrolled in the Massachusetts Institute of Technology (1878) as a pupil of William Ware. For two years he studied the work of luminaries such as H. H. RICHARDSON, Emerson, BURGES and Sears before undertaking a European tour. On his return he joined the firm of MCKIM, MEAD & WHITE and then set up in partnership with James Knox Taylor in St Paul (1882). The practice's ensuing output was varied but also fairly pedestrian and occasionally derivative. The Minnesota Capitol in St Paul (1895-1903) clearly owes its origins to the National Capitol in Washington. Nevertheless its success catapulted Gilbert into the limelight, with a series of commissions in Boston and New York, including the Brazer Building in Boston (1896) and the Broadway-Chambers Building in New York (1899-1900). In order to carry out the latter commission, Gilbert moved to New York, where he also designed a Gothicized twenty-four-storey office building on West Street, which made imaginative use of mock C14 terracotta details. But Gilbert is principally remembered as the designer of the tallest building in the world at the time, the Woolworth Building (1911-13), standing 760 m high (2430 ft) on Broadway. The lightweight terracotta cladding evoked the medieval glories of European cathedrals, while the soaring, symbolic tower paid tribute to corporate largesse. Gilbert's last Gothic excursion was the New York Life Assurance Building (1925-8). Subsequent works during the early 1930s were competent Classical essays which tended to lack the originality of contemporary Modernists such as Frank Lloyd WRIGHT and MIES VAN DER ROHE.

□ Minnesota State Capitol, St Paul, Minnesota, 1895-1903. Brazer Building, Boston, 1896. Broadway-Chambers Building, New York, 1899-1900. West Street Building, New York, 1905-7. Woolworth Building, New York, 1911-13. New York Life Assurance Building, New York, 1925-8.

▷ Donald Torbet, *A Century of Art and Architecture in Minnesota*, Minneapolis, 1958. Edgar Kaufman Jr, *The Rise of an American Architecture*, New York, 1970. William H. Jordy, *American Buildings and their Architects*, Vol. 3, New York, 1976. CS

GILLY Friedrich

b. Altdamm, near Stettin, 1772; d. Karlsbad (Karlovy Vary), 1800.

As teacher and theoretician, Gilly was a founding father of C19 Prussian Neo-Classicism and forged an essential link with contemporary architecture in revolutionary France. The son of an architect, he studied with Friedrich Becherer at the Akademie der Künste in Berlin and went on to work for Carl Gothard Langhans and Friedrich Wilhelm Erdmannsdorff.

Cass Gilbert, Woolworth Building, New York, 1911–13

Langhans's design for the Brandenburg Gate in Berlin (1785-91), modelled on the Propylaeum in Athens, marked the demise of the late Baroque style that had lingered in Prussia during the reign of Frederick II, and the advent of a new interest in classical precedent. Gilly's intensive study of Egyptian, Greek and Roman antiquity was stimulated by a six-month visit to Paris in 1797. Although he must certainly have encountered the work of BOULLEE and LEDOUX, Gilly was particularly drawn to the designs of François Joseph Bélanger. Among the few buildings constructed to Gilly's design during his short life were the Villa Mölter and Palais Sohns in Berlin, and a mausoleum in Dyhernfurth, near Breslau (only the ruins of the mausoleum survive). Gilly's lasting fame derives from his teaching at the Bauakademie in Berlin – where he was appointed professor for optics, perspective, and architectural drawing in 1799 – and from two unexecuted designs. His projected monument to Frederick the Great on Leipziger Platz, Berlin (1796), takes the form of an octagonal enclosure entered through a massive arched portal topped by a quadriga. At the centre of the enclosure a Doric temple – probably derived from the Greek temples at Agrigento, Sicily – is set on a monumental plinth. In another unrealized project, for a Nationaltheater on the Gendarmenmarkt in Berlin (*c*.1798), Gilly gave a simple, geometric articulation to the principal elements of the theatre: a cubic block for stage and scenery, and a semicircular auditorium. A simplified Doric order appears both on the gable-less portico and in the interior scheme, while the Diocletian window favoured by Bélanger dominates the exterior elevations. As teacher and model, Gilly exerted a great influence on his pupil and natural successor, Karl Friedrich SCHINKEL. With the exception of the Dyhernfurth Mausoleum, now in ruins, none of Gilly's buildings survive.

□ House facade, Jägerstrasse 14, Berlin, 1792. Monument to Frederick the Great, Leipzigerplatz, Berlin (project), 1796. Nationaltheater, Gendarmenmarkt, Berlin (project), *c*.1798. Dairy in park of Schloss Bellevue, Berlin, 1799. Villa Mölter, Tiergartenstrasse 31, Berlin, 1799-1800. Palais Sohns, Behrensstrasse 68, Berlin. Mausoleum, Dyhernfurth, near Breslau.

▷ Alste Oncken, *Friedrich Gilly 1772-1800*, Berlin, 1935; reprinted Berlin, 1981. *Friedrich Gilly und die Privatgesellschaft junger Architekten, 1777-1800* (exhibition catalogue), Berlin, 1984. David Watkin and Tilman Mellinghoff, *German Architecture and the Classical Ideal 1740-1840*, London, 1987. IBW

▷ *see also p220-21*

GIULIO ROMANO

Giuliano Pippi de' Giannuzzi, b. Rome, 1499; d. Mantua, 1546.

The master of architectural unease and dissonance. His designs and murals – in the Palazzo del Tè at Mantua he combined both – mimicked constructional instability (e.g. slabs apparently slipping down) and pushed Mannerism to its limit. Giulio made an early start as a painter, working in RAPHAEL's studio, and was still quite young when he was recognized as his brightest assistant. He was the obvious successor on Raphael's death at only 37 in 1520. Even though Giulio's moody, illusionist designs, especially for ceilings, were usually carried out by mediocre assistants, they impressed PALLADIO and influenced Baroque artists of the C17. In

Giulio Romano, Palazzo del Tè, Mantua, 1526–31

1524 he left Rome for good and went to serve the Gonzaga dynasty at Mantua for the rest of his life. Here he blossomed as an architect, working extensively on the interiors of the Cathedral and the Ducal Palace and, above all, on remodelling the summer residence of the Gonzagas, the Palazzo del Tè. He also designed his own house and improved the city's drainage. He died of fever as he was about to be appointed chief architect of St Peter's, Rome, in succession to SANGALLO.

□ Palazzo del Tè, Mantua, 1526-31. Ducal Palace, Mantua (interior), 1538-9. Cathedral, Mantua (interior), 1544-6. His own house, Mantua, *c*.1544.

▷ Frederick Hartt, *Giulio Romano*, New York, 1958. Egon Verheyen, *The Palazzo del Tè in Mantua: Images of love and politics*, Baltimore, 1977. JRC

▷ *see also pp214-15*

GOČÁR Josef

b. Semtín near Pardubice, 1880; d. Prague, 1945.

Jan KOTĚRA's student at the School of Decorative Arts in Prague and one of the leading representatives of the Cubist Movement in Czech architecture after 1910. From 1924 to 1939 he succeeded Kotěra as professor at the Academy of Fine Arts in Prague. He started his professional career with the Wenke Department Store at Jaroměř, which is an example of early rational architecture. The following Cubist period in his work culminated in the Black Virgin Mary House in Prague and the Sanatorium of Bohdaneč, and left some traces after the First World War in the so-called National Style, especially in the Czechoslovak Legion Bank. In the early 1920s, Gočár was charged with the town-planning of Hradec Králové, East Bohemia, where he constructed a number of public buildings, making the city the best example of modern town-planning in Czechoslovakia. In the late 1920s he joined the functional movement whose principles he applied in his educational work at the Academy of Fine Arts.

□ Wenke Department Store, Jaroměř, 1909-10. Black Virgin Mary House, Prague, 1911-12. Sanatorium, Bohdaneč, 1911-12. Czechoslovak Legion Bank, Prague, 1921-3. Tannery School, Hradec Králové, 1923-4. School complex, Hradec Králové, 1924-7. Czechoslovak National Pavilion, Paris, 1924-5. Agricultural Education House, Prague, 1925-6. Ambrož Choir, Hradec Králové, 1926-7. St Venceslas Catholic Church, Prague, 1927-30. Czechoslovak Rail Administration, Hradec Králové, 1927-32. Czechoslovak Werkbund Housing Estate (three villas), Baba District, Prague, 1932-3. Regional Administration, Hradec Králové, 1935.

▷ Zdeněk Wirth, *Josef Gočár*, Geneva, 1930. Marie Benešová, *Josef Gočár*, Prague, 1958. Olga Herbenová, *Josef Gočár*, Jaroměř, 1983. VS

GOFF Bruce

b. Alton, Kansas, 1904; d. Tyler, Texas, 1982.

American Organic architect of exceptional creativity whose idiosyncratic work spanned the C20. He was apprenticed at the age of 12 to Rush, Endacott and Rush of Tulsa, Oklahoma, and became a partner (1930-33). Self-educated, Goff was among the best informed in avant-garde architecture and post-classical music. Both enriched his free associational and subconscious creativity. Goff's homespun personality protected his intellectual and artistic sophistication. In the Seabees, a navy construction battalion (1942-5), he freely designed for the military, often with ad hoc materials. Without academic credentials he was professor of architecture at the University of Oklahoma, Norman (1946-55), and led that program as a unique design curriculum in creativity. His private practice, distinguished by its pluralistic directions, was always assisted by a small number of apprentices who often constructed his exuberant works. Goff's organic sensitivities to site and client produced an unparalleled diversity of "client" styles. He designed for the blossoming of the "continuous present". Without urban theories but with particularly American convictions about the worth and experience of the individual, most Goff buildings are isolated and inaccessible one-family houses in leafy suburbs of the Great Plains. Their dramatic decorations challenge c20 plainness. But with equal structural clarity and spatial complexity Goff's intimate retreats explored every technique of the century. His public buildings importantly initiated and concluded his career.

□ Public buildings: Boston Avenue Methodist Episcopal Church, Tulsa, OK, 1926. Japanese Pavilion, Los Angeles County Museum (completed posthumously by Bart Prince, 1988). Houses: Ledbetter, Norman, OK, 1947; Ford, Aurora, Illinois, 1949; Bavinger, Norman, 1950-55; Price Studio and Extensions, Bartlesville, OK, 1957, 1966, 1974.

▷ Takenobu Mohri, *Bruce Goff in Architecture*, Tokyo, 1970. Jeffrey Cook, *The Architecture of Bruce Goff*, London and New York, 1978. David G. Delong, *Bruce Goff: Toward Absolute Architecture*, Cambridge, Mass., and London, 1988. JC

GOODHUE & CRAM

Established c.1898.

Idealistic American partnership which explored both Gothic and classical idioms. **Bertram Grosvenor Goodhue** (b. Pomfret, Conn., 1869; d. New York, 1924) began his architectural career at the age of 15 in the New York office of

Bruce Goff, Japanese Pavilion, Los Angeles County Museum, completed 1988

Renwick, Aspinwall and Russell. By 1898 he was established in the partnership of Cram, Goodhue and Ferguson and was collaborating with **Ralph Adams Cram** (b. Hampton Falls, New Hampshire, 1863; d. 1942) on a magazine of criticism entitled *The Knight Errant*. At that time he began to develop an interest in typography and book design and embarked on a series of general horizon-broadening excursions to various parts of the world. The first major building to emerge from the partnership of Cram and Goodhue was All Saints' Church in Ashmont (1892), an imposing Gothic edifice which demonstrated a studied awareness of the principles of medieval design. But the ability to reinterpret Gothic style was only one item in Goodhue's architectural repertoire. His firm's reputation was secured in 1903 with a competition-winning design for a major extension to the US Military Academy at West Point, which integrated the existing mid-c19 Gothic buildings with a series of monumental additions. Goodhue eventually separated from Cram in 1913 and went on to design numerous churches, houses and public buildings, gradually moving away from the dense, dark Gothic style towards a lighter, simpler, almost Romanesque idiom, as exemplified by the National Academy of Sciences in Washington (completed 1924). Towards the end of his career, he developed a more vigorous contemporary freestyle, but ultimately his quest for an architecture which reflected the spirit of its time was fulfilled by a legacy of ideas rather than buildings.

□ All Saints' Church, Ashmont, Mass. (with Frank Ferguson), 1892-1913. United States Military Academy, West Point (additions with Frank Ferguson), 1903-10. National Academy of Sciences Building, Washington DC, 1919-24.

▷ Richard Oliver, *Bertram Grosvenor Goodhue*, New York, 1982. CS

GRAVES Michael

b. Indianapolis, 1934.

One of the major figures of American Post-Modernism. Graves studied at the University of Cincinatti, Ohio, and then at Harvard. He was a fellow at the American Academy in Rome for two years and in 1964 started his own practice in Princeton, NJ. He became a professor at Princeton University in 1972. He first came to prominence through the book *Five Architects* (1972). The members of the "New York Five" were termed "Neo-Modernist" because of their austere reinterpretation of the rational style of LE CORBUSIER in the 1920s. However, at the end of the 1970s, Graves' work evolved away from concern with the roots of Modernism towards a wide-ranging borrowing from architectural history. His borrowings are eclectic; he uses historical forms in a more abstract and decorative way than some other Post-Modern classicists and puts much emphasis on a painterly use of colour. Graves has become an amusing anti-Modern propagandist. Humour is an integral part of his architecture, and much of his recent work, especially for Disney, seems to be a celebration of kitsch.

□ Handselmann House, Fort Wayne, Indiana, 1967. Addition to Benacerraf House, Princetown, NJ, 1969. Fargo-Moorhead Cultural Center (bridge), Minnesota, designed 1977. Kalko House, Green Brook, NJ, designed 1978. Public Services Building, Portland, Oregon, 1982. Humana Corporation Building, Louisville, Kentucky, 1983. Witney Museum Extension Project, NY, from 1985 – . Dolphin and Swan Hotels, Disneyland, 1989. Newark Museum, New York, 1990.

▷ Michael Graves, *Buildings and Projects*, New York, 1982. K. Frampton *et al.*, *Five Architects*, New York, 1972; A. Colquhoun and P. Michael Carl, *Graves*, London, 1979. TC

▷ *see also pp242-3*

GREENE & GREENE

Charles Sumner Greene, b. Brighton, Ohio, 1868; d. Carmel, California, 1957. Henry Mather Greene, b. Brighton, Ohio, 1870; d. Altadena, California, 1954.

American architects who produced in partnership the finest houses of the Arts & Crafts Movement in the USA. The new Manual Training High School of Washington University, St Louis, with its emphasis on craft and the influence of Ruskin and Morris, was their critical educational experience (1886-8). They left MIT School of Architecture (1888-91) with a Certificate of Partial Course because they felt stifled. But two years' apprenticeship in Boston provided familiarity with the "shingle style". Although their partnership began in Pasadena, California, in 1894, their exceptional work was between 1903 and 1909, with the emphasis on the craftsmanship of wood jointry, articulated surfaces, oriental sensitivities and the refinement of the bungalow at all scales. It was a relaxed and tactile regional architecture that celebrated the emerging nature-related lifestyle of Southern California. Each brother practised independently after 1922; Charles moved to Carmel in 1916, leaving Henry in Pasadena. Greene & Greene as a team had complementary and supporting skills that make individual credits difficult. Charles had the vivid imagination and the decorative eye to provide the oriental lift to taper a beam; Henry had the natural sense of order and the conceptual vision. Separately their artistic care was equally highly recognized. "The idea was to eliminate everything unnecessary, to make the whole as direct and as simple as possible but always with the beautiful in mind as the final goal", said Henry. Their finest houses are generous and informal with sleeping porches, portes-cochère and garden patios, matched by refinement in custom furniture.

Greene & Greene, Gamble House, Pasadena, 1908

□ By Greene & Greene (all in Pasadena, California): Bandini House, 1903; Blacker House, 1907; Gamble House, 1908; Culbertson House, 1911. By Charles: James House, Carmel Highlands, California, 1918-23.

▷ Esther McCoy, *Five California Architects*, New York, 1960, 1977. Janann Strand, *A Greene and Greene Guide*, Pasadena, 1974. Randell L. Makinson, *Greene and Greene*: Volume 1: *Architecture as Fine Art*; Volume 2: *Furniture and Related Designs*, Salt Lake City, 1977-9. JC

GREENE Herb

b. Oneonta, NY, 1929.

Inventive Organic architect and painter of vernacular themes and iconic perceptions. Educated at Syracuse University NY and then under Bruce GOFF at the University of Oklahoma (1948–52). Associated with Joseph Krakower, Houston 1954-57, he also worked with Bruce Goff (1950-52) and John Lautner (1952). Greene taught at the University of Oklahoma 1957–1963 and was Professor of Architecture at the University of Kentucky, Lexington, 1963–1982. Since 1982 he has lived in Berkeley, California as consultant on collaborative urban and park projects with Organic emphases on specifics of site and participation of local culture. A scholar on visual perception and the layers of meaning such as in historic photographs or the paintings of Vermeer, Greene is a penetrating image-maker in paint and collage. In these works, dreams and memories, high and low art, vernacular language and learned responses are creatively reconfigured. His most influential building, "Prairie House", successfully combines personal expression with surprising economy. Greene's increasingly complex writing and art advocate a "continuum of many individualized acts of expression symbolic of democratic society and the diversity and indeterminacy of the world".

□ John Joyce House, Snyder, Oklahoma, 1960. Herb & Mary Greene "Prairie House", Norman, Oklahoma, 1961. Earl Cummingham House (with Robert Bowlby) Oklahoma City, 1964. Villa Blanca Farm, Lexington, Kentucky, 1983.

▷ Herb Greene, *Mind & Image. An Essay on Art and Architecture*, Lexington, 1976. *Buildings to Last, Architecture an Ongoing Art*, New York, 1981. JC

Herb Greene, "Prairie House", Norman, Oklahoma, 1961

GRIFFIN Walter Burley

b. Maywood, Illinois, 1876; d. Lucknow, India, 1937.

A leading member of the Prairie School of architects in Chicago. He worked for Frank Lloyd WRIGHT for four years (1901-5) before setting up in practice in association with Barry Byrne. In 1911, the year he married Wright's talented design assistant Marion Lucy MAHONY, Griffin's personal style acquired a new maturity and independence. From 1914 the couple lived in Australia after Griffin won the competition for the layout of the new capital city, Canberra. Griffin pioneered the development of vertical space in contrast to Wright's accentuation of horizontal flow. Openness exists without destroying the box. His interiors are confined rather than spreading, with spatial variety and interest achieved through the manipulation of multi-level space. The work reveals a lifelong preference for solid, compact forms; simple square or rectangular shapes bounded by large confining corner piers; in combination with gable roofs and laterally extended appendages (these appendages are omitted in his later work in Australia). In the Trier centre Neighborhood (1912-13), the Rock Crest-Rock Glen subdivision of Mason City, Iowa (from 1912), and his prize-winning concept for Canberra (1912), Griffin revealed his talent for planning suburban neighbourhoods and cities related to landscape. Unlike Wright's work, Griffin's plans were never mere expansions of smaller unit schemes. His designs were more respectful of nature and, over time, proved more realistic and durable. These schemes mix formal and informal elements and include local flora. Griffin invariably introduced axial roads and paths, to order the meandering spaces. In 1917 Griffin, who used concrete in his houses at a time when Wright was still advocating its use, patented a workable system of concrete blocks (Knitlock), well before the highly publicized concrete-block experiments of Wright in the 1920s for the Millard House, Pasadena. The Australian houses at Castlecrag, Sydney, and in Melbourne tend on the whole to be smaller and cramped internally, though they exhibit the same bold inventiveness in their details and compact solid forms as the American work. Of his Australian output, Newman College at the University of Melbourne (1917), the magnificent interior of the Capitol Theatre, Melbourne (1924) and a series of incinerator structures, notably those at Pyrmont and Willoughby (1934), are the most impressive. From 1935 until his death in 1937, Walter Burley Griffin worked in Lucknow, India, engaged on a bizarre series of projects which celebrate decorative motifs borrowed from the Nawab period of India's history.

□ Designs for federal capital at Canberra, 1912. Newman College, University of Melbourne, 1917. Capitol Theatre, Melbourne, 1924. The U.P. Industrial and Agricultural Exhibition, Lucknow, 1936.

▷ Walter Burley Griffin, *The Federal Capital*, Melbourne, 1913. James Birrell, *Walter Burley Griffin*, Brisbane, 1964. D. Johnson, *The Architecture of Walter Burley Griffin*, Melbourne, 1977. PD

GROPIUS Walter

b. Berlin, 1883: d. Boston, Mass., 1969.

Leading designer and theoretician, founder of the Bauhaus, and subsequently professor at Harvard University, Gropius was one of the most influential figures in C20 architecture. The son of an architect, he studied at the Technical Universities in Munich and Berlin. He joined the office of Peter BEHRENS in 1910 and three years later established a practice in partnership with Adolf Meyer. The example of Behrens's industrial Classicism found an echo in their first important commission, for the Fagus Factory at Alfeld an der Leine (1911-14), a pioneering steel-frame building with a glazed façade wrapped around the corners of the main block. The exposed interior staircases reappeared in the model factory designed by Gropius and Meyer for the 1914 exhibition of the Deutscher Werkbund at Cologne, in the form of glazed stairtowers at each end of the office block. After war service, Gropius became involved with the groups of radical artists that sprung up in Berlin in the winter of 1918-19. In March 1919 he was elected chairman of the Arbeitsrat für Kunst (Working Council for Art), and a month later was appointed Director of the Bauhaus, located initially at Weimar, and subsequently in the Gropius-designed school at Dessau (1925-6). This steel and concrete building gave vigorous external expression to Gropius's ideal of a fusion of hand and intellect, with the technical school and library in one block and the workshops in a separate large block with spectacularly glazed façades. On the upper level of the bridge that linked the two blocks was the Director's office, symbolically joining the worlds of science and craft. A second large commission in Dessau was for an employment office on a semicircular plan (1927-9), which was applauded by Adolf Behne as Gropius's best building. Following the housing for the Bauhaus Masters at

Walter Gropius, Fagus Factory, Alfeld an der Leine, 1911–14

Dessau Gropius designed the Dessau-Törten Estate (1926-8), an experiment in rationalized construction on Taylorist principles. Gropius's commitment to lower-income housing that combined an urban scale with access to light and greenery was further developed in the Dammerstock Estate at Karlsruhe (1928-9), and the two blocks at Siemensstadt, Berlin (1929-30). A commission from Erwin Piscator to design a "variable theatre-instrument" resulted in the unbuilt Total-Theatre (1927), with flexible spaces for stage and auditorium. After leaving the Bauhaus in 1928, Gropius resumed private practice in Berlin before leaving for England in 1934. In partnership with Maxwell FRY, Gropius designed Impington Village College, Cambs. (1938-9). With its two long ranges of single-storey classrooms running in opposite directions from a central block, this design was one of Gropius's most successful schemes of the 1930s. Gropius was appointed to a professorship at Harvard University in 1937, and in the years 1938-41 worked on an impressive series of houses in collaboration with Marcel BREUER. Larger projects from this period were the Pennsylvania Pavilion at the New York World's Fair (1939) and a workers' estate at New Kensington, Pennsylvania (1941-2). In 1945 Gropius founded "The Architects' Collaborative", a small design team that embodied his belief in the value of teamwork. Pre-eminent among the TAC commissions was the Pan American Airways building in New York City (1958-63, in collaboration with Pietro BELLUSCHI and Emery Roth and Sons), an elegant prismatic tower, much criticized at the time for blocking off Park Avenue. The Bauhaus Archive in Berlin (1976-9) was adapted by Alexander Cvijanovic from a design by Gropius originally intended for a site in Darmstadt (1964-8).

□ Fagus Factory, Alfeld an der Leine, 1911-14 (completed 1925). Office and Factory Building, Werkbund Exhibition, Cologne, 1914. Sommerfeld House, Berlin, 1920-21. Otte House, Berlin, 1921-2. Competition project: *Chicago Tribune* Tower, 1922. Bauhaus Building, Dessau, 1925-6. Houses for the Bauhaus Masters, Dessau, 1925-6. Dessau-Törten Estate, 1926-8. Project: Total-Theatre, 1927. Employment Office, Dessau, 1927-9. Project: "Residential Mountains", 1928. Dammerstock Estate, Karlsruhe, 1928-9. Housing blocks, Berlin-Siemensstadt, 1929-30. Project: High-rise apartment blocks, Berlin-Wannsee, 1930-31. Competition project: Palace of the Soviets, Moscow, 1931. Ben Levy House, Chelsea, London (with Maxwell Fry), 1935-6. Impington Village College, Cambs. (with Maxwell Fry), 1936-9. Frank House, Pittsburgh (with Marcel Breuer), 1939-40. Pennsylvania Pavilion, World's Fair, New York, 1939. Aluminium City, New Kensington, Pennsylvania, 1941-2. Graduate Center, Harvard University, Cambridge, Mass., 1948-50. Housing block, Hansaviertel, Berlin, 1955-9. US Embassy, Athens, 1956-61. Comprehensive Plan for the New University of Baghdad, from 1957. Pan American Airways Building, New York, 1958-63.

▷ Walter Gropius, *The New Architecture and the Bauhaus*, London, 1935. James Marston Fitch, *Walter Gropius*, London, 1960. Klaus Herdeg, *Harvard Architecture and the Failure of the Bauhaus Legacy*, Cambridge, Mass., 1983. Winfried Nerdinger, *The Architect Walter Gropius*, Berlin, 1985. IBW

▷ *see also pp234-5, 238-9*

GRUPPO SETTE

Established 1926.

Alliance of seven Milanese architects who called for a new pragmatism within Italian architecture and the rejection of provincial eclecticism and historical revivalism. The original group consisted of Giuseppe TERRAGNI, Luigi Figini, Gino Pollini, Ubaldo Castagnoli (replaced after a few months by Adalberto Libera), Guido Frette, Sebastiano Larco and Carlo Rava. All had studied at the Milan Polytechnic during the early 1920s and reacted against the rather dry, academic emphasis of the Scuola Superiore di Architettura. Their manifesto, published in four parts by the periodical *La Rassegna Italiana*, was both politically and ideologically more moderate than the Futurists' radical stance. Nevertheless, it proved a seminal document in the emergence of Italian Rationalism and proclaimed that "The new architecture, the true architecture, should be the result of a close association between logic and rationality." The group later expanded to become the Movimento Italiano per l'Architettura Razionale (MIAR) but the tense political climate within Mussolini's Italy led to its eventual demise in 1931.

□ Figini and Pollini: Olivetti Buildings, Ivrea, 1934-57; Nursery School, Ivrea, 1939-41. See also TERRAGNI.

▷ Giulia Veronesi, *Difficoltà politiche dell' architettura in Italia 1920-40*, Milan, 1953. Raffaello Giolli, *L'architettura razionale*, Bari, 1972. Silvia Danesi and Luciano Patetta (eds.), *Il razionalismo e l'architettura in Italia durante il fascismo*, Venice, 1976. Bruno Zevi (ed.), *Giuseppe Terragni*, Bologna, 1980. Vittorio Savi (ed.), *Figini e Pollini-architetti*, Milan, 1980. MC

GUARINI Guarino

b. Modena, 1624; d. Milan, 1683.

The most unorthodox and perhaps the most inventive of all C17 architects, he

Guarino Guarini, Palazzo Carignano, Turin, begun 1679

laid the foundations of the Rococo style of architecture. Ordained a Theatine priest in 1648, Guarini was also one of Europe's leading mathematicians, a concern immediately evident in the geometric elaboration of his buildings. He was deeply influenced by the radical planning and detailing of BORROMINI's designs, and was to develop a similar approach combining complexity and inventiveness with a profound feeling for colour and light. His early works, mostly for the Theatines, took him to Sicily and Paris, and perhaps Portugal and Spain (where he may have inspected the ribbed domes of Moorish buildings), but his career was to flourish under the House of Savoy in Turin. His two centrally planned chapels (S. Lorenzo and SS. Sindone) recall Borromini's S. Ivo but are structurally more daring and visually even more exhilarating, being conceived as a towering succession of geometrically intricate zones. Their mystic quality is enhanced by the rich marbles below and the many openings in the delicate upper reaches that flood the interiors with light. Ultimately more influential are Guarini's many longitudinal church designs (e.g. Divina Providenza) with their undulating walls and vaults. These, like much of Guarini's work, were widely circulated through engravings.

☐ Santa Maria della Divina Providenza, Lisbon, *c.*1650. S. Lorenzo, Turin, from 1668. Cappella della SS. Sindone, Turin Cathedral, from 1668. Palazzo Carignano, Turin, from 1679.

▷ G. Guarini, *Architettura Civile*, Turin, 1737 (plates available 1668). P. Portoghesi, *Guarino Guarini*, Milan, 1956. *Guarino Guarini e l'Internazionalità del Barocco*, Turin, 1970. H. Meek, *Guarino Guarini and his Architecture*, New Haven, 1988. DH

▷ *see also pp218-19*

METRO STATION, Paris

So powerful were Guimard's designs for the Paris metro stations between 1898–1904, that they have since become one of the city's instantly recognizable symbols. The fluid, curvilinear shapes employed for balustrades, rails and entrance-ways were achieved in cast iron, but appear to have bubbled to the surface from some mysterious underworld.

The sinuous quality of the metro entrances is all the more surprising in that they consist entirely of metal castings produced in series and assembled in different variations. Guimard's skilful interpretations of organic forms made him a leading exponent of Art Nouveau and creator of the popular "style métro".

GUIMARD Hector

b. Lyon, 1867; d. New York, 1942.

French architect whose idiosyncratic and unorthodox approach to design has become synonymous with the Art Nouveau movement generally and *fin-de-siècle* Paris in particular. On arrival in Paris, aged 15, Guimard spent three years at the Ecole des Arts Décoratifs and a further four years at the Ecole de Beaux Arts. His rather conventional early work was transformed by two contradictory forces: the radical theories of VIOLLET-LE-DUC and the sinuous curves of the Belgian architect Victor HORTA. Guimard's sojourn to Brussels in 1895, which included a visit to Horta's celebrated Hôtel Tassel, proved a revelation. It completely overwhelmed him and inspired a radical re-evaluation of his proposals for an apartment block, Castel Béranger, in the exclusive 16th *arrondissement* of Paris. This single project provoked considerable controversy and heralded the emergence of *le style Guimard.* His innovative approach to design and decoration demanded the extreme abstraction of both natural and organic forms. His fondness for hypertrophic detailing is apparent in his series of celebrated Metro stations with their characteristic twisted form.

☐ Castel Béranger, Paris, 1894-8. Hôtel Guimard, Paris, 1909-12. Metro stations, Paris, 1898-1904. Synagogue, Paris, 1913.

▷ Lanier Graham, *Hector Guimard*, New York, 1970. J. M. Richards and Nikolaus Pevsner (eds.), *The Anti-Rationalists*, London, 1973. Franco Borsi and E. Godoli, *Paris 1900*, Brussels, 1976. Gillian Naylor and Yvonne Brunhammer, *Hector Guimard*, London, 1978. MC

HANSEN Christian Frederik

b. Copenhagen, 1746; d. Copenhagen, 1845.

The most significant Danish architect of his day, who rebuilt Copenhagen and developed an influential variant of Romantic Classicism. Hansen started his architectural education young: he gained entry to the Royal Academy of Fine Arts in Copenhagen at the age of ten and trained under the French Classicist Caspar Frederik Harsdorff, whom he assisted in the rebuilding of Frederik V's chapel at Roskilde Cathedral. In 1779 Hansen won the Gold Medal of the Academy, followed in 1782 by a scholarship which enabled him to study abroad. He spent some time in Italy, which had a noticeable effect on his architectural development. In 1784 he returned to Denmark to begin work as a surveyor in Holstein, a position he occupied for over twenty years. His skills as an architect and administrator eventually led him to succeed Harsdorff, who died in 1799, as superintendent of the rebuilding of some of Copenhagen's outstanding monuments, including the Royal Palace, City Hall and Cathedral. Hansen was appointed director of buildings and professor at the Royal Academy of Fine Arts in 1808 and proceeded to transform the Danish capital's Baroque appearance into a version of elegant Classicism, as embodied by the Palladian model used in the rebuilding of the City Hall and Law Courts. This romantic interpretation of the Classical style was to dominate Danish architecture for successive generations, in an enduring testimony to Hansen's prodigious, if somewhat conservative, influence on fellow countrymen.

□ City Hall and Law Courts, Copenhagen, 1803-16. Christianborg Palace, Copenhagen, 1803-28; Palace Church, 1811. Our Lady Cathedral, Copenhagen, 1810-29.

▷ J. Rubow, *C. F. Hansens Arkitektur*, Copenhagen, 1936. Hakon Lund and Christian L. Küster, *Architekt C. F. Hansen: 1756-1845*, Hamburg, 1968. CS

HARDOUIN-MANSART Jules

b. Beauvais, 1646; d. Marly, 1708.

Foremost architect of the French Baroque period, great-nephew of the esteemed architect François MANSART. His great-uncle not only gave him an education and introduced him to the profession but also bequeathed him all his papers and drawings. A number of his benefactor's ideas were to reappear in later proposals, but his early influences were Louis LE VAU and Libéral Bruant. Initial projects were largely domestic but in 1671 a commission was secured from Louis XIV for a château in the forests of St Germain-en-Laye. In 1675 Hardouin-Mansart was appointed King's Architect and elected a member of the Académie Royal de l'Architecture. His presence at Versailles dated from 1673 but it was another five years before he was granted overall control and could commence his series of extravagant additions and alterations, which included the Hall of Mirrors, the Orangery, the Stables, the Chapel and the Grand Trianon. Hardouin-Mansart's success was due to his consummate skill in the manipulation of scale to create a heightened sense of grandeur. He enjoyed an extensive clientele and was unchallenged as the nation's leading architect for almost thirty years.

Jules Hardouin-Mansart, Place Vendôme, Paris, 1698

□ Hôtel de Ville, Arles, 1675. Château de Versailles, 1678-89. Invalides Chapel, Paris, 1679-91. Place des Victoires, Paris, 1685. Place Vendôme, Paris, 1698.

▷ Anthony Blunt, *Art and Architecture in France 1500-1700*, Harmondsworth, 1953 (revised 1973). Pierre Bourget and Georges Cattaui, *Jules Hardouin-Mansart*, Paris, 1960. Alfred and Jeanne Marie, *Mansart à Versailles*, Paris, 1972. MC

HARDWICK Philip

b. London, 1792; d. London, 1870.

The most distinguished member of a leading English architectural dynasty. He studied architecture at the Royal Academy

Schools and under his father, **Thomas Hardwick** (1752-1829), designer of St Marylebone Church, London. He was in partnership with his father from *c.*1819 and in due course took over the practice. He was surveyor to a number of prominent London institutions, including St Bartholomew's Hospital, St Katharine's Dock Company, the Goldsmiths' Company, and the London and Birmingham Railway Company. Scholarly in approach, he rebuilt the 1702 gateway at St Bartholomew's Hospital and extended the Palladian Stone Buildings at Lincoln's Inn with scrupulous tact. His own buildings demonstrated a wide and judicious understanding of architectural character; he was able to use Greek Doric (the symbolic and monumental Euston Propylaeum), a restrained English Baroque (Goldsmiths' Hall) or picturesque brick Tudor (Lincoln's Inn Hall and Library) with equal aplomb. He won gold medals from RIBA (1854) and at the Paris Exhibition (1855). From 1843 he was partly incapacitated by illness and he handed on most of the practice to his son, **Philip Charles Hardwick** (1820-90), a versatile and productive architect who designed the Great Hall at Euston Station and the Great Western Hotel, London.

□ St Katharine's Dock offices, London (with Thomas Telford), 1827-9. Goldsmiths' Hall, London, 1835. Euston Propylaeum, London, 1836-40. Lincoln's Inn Hall and Library, London (with P. C. Hardwick), 1843-5.

▷ Jane Fawcett (ed.) *Seven Victorian Architects*, London, 1976. BP

HÄRING Hugo

b. Biberach, 1882; d. Göppingen, 1958.

German architect and teacher who completed few buildings but was author of many theoretical texts, and must be counted among the leading theorists of the Modern Movement. He was educated in Stuttgart under the regionalist Theodor Fischer. After a decade in Hamburg, and having built the elaborate Römer House in Ulm (1916-20), he moved to Berlin in the early 1920s. Here he shared an office with Ludwig MIES VAN DER ROHE and they set up the "Ring", an organization of Berlin Modernists which included all the major German figures of the period. It succeeded in its political goal of replacing the conservative city architect with one of its members, Martin Wagner, who commissioned much of the Modernist work built in Berlin in the late 20s. Häring was the Ring's secretary, and organized its exhibitions and publications. In 1925 he published *Wege zur Form*, his most important theoretical essay, and in the same year he built the farm buildings at Garkau, his best-known work, intended and described as an exemplary piece of Functionalism. Häring believed that architectural form should grow out of the nature of a place and an intended task,

Hugo Häring, Siemensstadt housing, Berlin, 1929-31

each project developing and retaining its own essential identity. It was a highly specific approach, completely opposed to that of more orthodox Modernists such as Mies, who sought architectural solutions of general application. Häring spoke of buildings as having organ-like qualities, and is sometimes classified in an Organic tradition of Modernism. Towards the end of the 20s, Häring built housing developments in Berlin, and he had further projects under way when Hitler came to power. Unable to build under the Nazis, he undertook the running of the Reimannschule, a private art school which he renamed Kunst und Werk. When it was bombed in 1943, he returned to Biberach and devoted himself to theoretical questions. After the war he published essays and undertook many projects, but built only a pair of houses for local friends, the Schmitz family. However, many of his ideas saw fruition later in the work of his friend SCHAROUN.

□ Römer House, Ulm, 1916-20. Gut Garkau farm complex, near Lübeck, 1925. Housing at Wedding (1928) and Siemensstadt (1929-31), Berlin.

▷ Hugo Häring, *Fragmente*, Berlin, 1968. Jürgen Joedicke and Heinrich Lauterbach (eds.), *Hugo Häring*, Stuttgart, 1964 (includes many of Häring's essays). PBJ

HARRISON Thomas

b. Richmond, Yorks., 1744; d. Chester, 1829.

Leading figure in the rise of the Greek Revival in Britain during the late C18 and early C19. The son of a joiner from Yorkshire, Harrison's abilities were first recognized by Sir Lawrence Dundas of Aske who financed a sojourn to Italy in 1769-76. While in Rome he was invited by Pope Clement XIV to join the esteemed Accademia di S. Luca and completed a number of hypothetical designs for the Belvedere at the Vatican and the sacristy of St Peter's. On returning to England his first major project was the Skerton Bridge at Lancaster (1783-8), followed by a handful of country houses in the Neo-Classical manner. But Harrison's heightened sense of grandeur and scale were better suited to the design of public institutions, and he constructed a remarkable series of imposing civic buildings with a primitive simplicity and strength of form. Ironically, his own Grand Tour had never reached Greece and he therefore relied heavily on archaeological and didactic publications such as Peter Nicholson's *The Student's Instructor* (1823). Harrison also enjoys some notoriety as the man partly responsible for advising Lord Elgin to "rescue" the Parthenon sculptures.

□ Chester Castle, Cheshire, 1788-1822. Broomhall, Fife, 1796-9. Lyceum Theatre, Liverpool, 1800-1803. Portico Library, Manchester, 1802-6. Anglesey Column, Plas Newydd, 1816-17.

▷ John Summerson, *Architecture in Britain 1530-1830*, Harmondsworth, 1953. J. Mordaunt Crook, *"The Architecture of Thomas Harrison", Country Life*, Vol. 149, London, 1971; *The Greek Revival*, London, 1972. MC

HARRISON & ABRAMOVITZ

Established 1945.

One of the most successful architectural partnerships in post-war America. **Wallace Kirkman Harrison** (b. Worcester, Mass., 1895; d. New York, 1981) began his career in 1916 in the New York offices of MCKIM, MEAD & WHITE. Following some time in Paris, where he passed the Beaux-Arts examination, and a year at the American Academy in Rome, he worked as a draughtsman for Bertram GOODHUE and Raymond HOOD. In 1927 he became a partner in the firm of Helmle & Corbett and participated in the development of the Rockefeller Center in New York, a pioneering multi-level urban centre. **Max Abramovitz** (b. Chicago, Illinois, 1908) joined Helmle & Corbett in 1934, following an undergraduate training at the University of Illinois and a master's degree from Columbia University. The practice of Harrison & Abramovitz was formally established in 1945. Two years later they obtained the commission for the United Nations Headquarters, one of the first skyscrapers to feature a lightweight curtain-wall construction system. During the 1960s they were responsible for another New York landmark, the Lincoln Center for the Performing Arts, in which the various buildings are arranged around a central plaza. Harrison & Abramovitz parted professional company in 1978: Harrison was to practise independently, Abramovitz with Michael Harris and James Kingsland. Harrison was awarded the AIA Gold Medal in 1957.

UNITED NATIONS COMPLEX, New York

The United Nations Headquarters in New York was the result of a long and patient search for a suitable site by Le Corbusier and other international architects and advisors. Eventually a seventeen-acre site was chosen in Manhattan, close by the East River. The UN complex, 1947-51 – which took its final form based on sketches by Le Corbusier, Oscar Niemeyer and Sven Markelius – was predominantly the work of American architect Wallace K. Harrison, who acted as Director of Planning for the whole project. His partner Max Ambramovitz was deputy. The complex consists of two main elements: a huge high-density vertical Secretariat, with almost completely glazed curtain walls, and a contrasting low-lying Assembly block. Between these two is situated a third building, housing press galleries, members' lounges and so on. The space around the buildings is as important as the buildings themselves; the effect of the whole complex arises from the way the main elements are disposed as sculptural objects within a park setting. The complex as a whole remains an impressive monument although clearly flawed by compromise.

□ Rockefeller Center, New York (Harrison with others), 1930-33. United Nations Building, New York (with LE CORBUSIER, Oscar NIEMEYER and Sven MARKELIUS), 1947-53. Lincoln Center for the Performing Arts, New York, 1959-66. Albany Mall State Administrative and Plaza Complex, Albany, NY, 1972-8.

▷ Rem Koolhas, *Delirious New York*, New York, 1978. Carole Herselle Krinsky, *Rockefeller Center*, New York, 1978. Edgar B. Young, *Lincoln Center: The Building of an Institution*, New York, 1980. CS

HAUSSMANN Baron Georges Eugène

b. Paris, 1809; d. Paris, 1891.

Prefect of Paris who directed the modernization of the city under Napoleon III. He was a forceful legally trained civil servant whose abilities induced the new emperor to appoint him to the prefecture (1853-69). Napoleon III's power rested on the fears aroused by the revolution of 1848. He and Haussmann conceived making Paris a magnificent imperial city but also harnessing the new economic forces to carry out public works to ensure popularity and deter insurrections by replacing the narrow streets of the medieval city with boulevards suited to troop movements. Paris was remodelled on the formal precepts of French Baroque: symmetry and regularity, with the vista down each boulevard closed by a monumental public building. There was a huge programme of building, although the only unquestioned architectural masterpiece was GARNIER's Opéra. Miles of new roads were created; new parks were laid out; a new drainage system was laid, and the administrative system was reorganized. For the first time, systematic planning and intervention in a large modern city had been attempted. The new Paris exerted a tremendous influence in C19 Europe and was copied in cities like Rome, Vienna, Brussels and Lyon. The longer-term legacy was the "City Beautiful Movement" of the C20 and its manifestations in the great commercial cities of America and imperial and colonial capitals.

□ Alterations to layout of Paris from 1853, including Place de l'Opéra, Etoile, Place de la Nation and grands boulevards.

▷ L. Benevolo, *History of Modern Architecture*, Vol. I, London, 1960. H. Saalman, *Haussmann: Paris Transformed*, New York, 1971. P. Hall, *Cities of Tomorrow*, London, 1988. TC

HAWKSMOOR Nicholas

b. Notts. (either Ragnall or East Drayton), 1661; d. London, 1736.

English architect whose own buildings are few (he acted so often as a capable colleague alongside Sir Christopher WREN and Sir John VANBRUGH) but show a complete mastery of the orders and knowledge of the work and theories of other major architects. Some of this was in the Gothic style and some in the style of Roman architects of the High Renaissance, such as BRAMANTE. Hawksmoor was "discovered" in Nottinghamshire by the leading plasterer Edward Goudge and introduced to Wren's service in London as a clerk. He was held to have an "early skill and genius in architecture" and worked at enhancing these attributes as Wren's assistant. By 1700 Hawksmoor had become an experienced and indispensable clerk of works to Wren's work for the Crown. He also assisted Vanbrugh from the start of building at Castle Howard (1699) and a few years later at Blenheim Palace, and in both cases he undoubtedly gave firm and experienced action to Sir John's brilliant pencillings, improving the details in all practical aspects. He also emerged alongside him as a major figure in the short history of the English Baroque. What of his own architecture? Hawksmoor never went to Italy but had studied hard all the work of the masters of Antiquity, the Renaissance and the English Middle Ages. He looked at Italian Baroque only through engravings but incorporated from all sources what he needed to fashion into his façades. In 1700 Hawksmoor started the precise remodelling of Easton Neston, Northamptonshire, for Sir William Fermor, later Lord Lempster. He had been involved, like Wren, in earlier work there, but finally by 1702 the great high structure with a lavish use of the giant order was set up. Perhaps

Nicholas Hawksmoor, Castle Howard Mausoleum, Yorks., 1727-42

Nicholas Hawksmoor, Church of St Mary Woolnoth, London, 1716-24

Hawksmoor should be further assessed by his churches, particularly Christ Church, Spitalfields (1714-29). Finally, Hawksmoor's mausoleum at Castle Howard (1729-36), based on the Tomb of Cecilia Metella on the Appian Way, Rome, and, with modification, reared again on a Yorkshire hill as the burial crypt of the Earls of Carlisle. It looks away to the distant S front of Castle Howard, over which Vanbrugh and he had laboured thirty years before.

□ Kensington Palace, London, King's Gallery, 1695-6. Easton Neston, Northants, 1695-1710. Castle Howard, Yorks. (assisting Vanbrugh), 1699-1726. Greenwich Hospital, London, various works, 1699-1703. Blenheim Palace, Oxon (assisting Vanbrugh), 1705-16. Various churches, including Christ Church, Spitalfields, London, 1714-29. All Souls College, Oxford (N Quadrangle), 1726-35. Castle Howard, Yorks.: Pyramid, 1728, Mausoleum, 1727-42.

▷ Kerry Downes, *Hawksmoor*, 2nd ed. London, 1979. GB

▷ *see also pp218-19*

HERTZBERGER Herman

b. Amsterdam, 1932.

Dutch Structuralist architect who emphasizes the importance of social values in building planning and design. After finishing his early training at the Technical University in Delft, Hertzberger returned to his native Amsterdam in 1958 to set up in private practice. He also embarked on a distinguished academic career. He taught at the Academy of Architecture in Amsterdam (1965-70) and since 1970 he has been a professor at the Technical University in Delft. An influential theorist as well as innovative designer, Hertzberger is a leading exponent of Structuralism in the Netherlands, editing (1959-63) the journal *Forum*, which helped to crystallize the tenets of the emerging movement. Central to Structuralist philosophy is the notion of "spatial possibility", by which architecture is used to provide a spatial framework for the creation and encouragement of individual expression among building users. Hertzberger has succeeded in applying this theory to a range of different types of buildings, including housing, schools and offices. His greatest talent lies in his ability to translate such socially inspired ideas into architectural reality. His most important work is the Centraal Beheer Office Building in Apeldoorn, which is based on a grid plan and expresses its social and organizational functions in the form of separate work islands for groups of sixteen employees.

□ 1966-70 "Diagoon" houses, Delft, 1966-70. Centraal Beheer Office Building, Apeldoorn, 1970-72. De Drie Hoven Old People's Home, Amsterdam, 1972-4. Vredenburg Music Centre, Utrecht, 1976-8.

▷ "Herman Hertzberger: Musical Architecture", *Architects' Journal*, London, April 1976. Ids Haagsma *et al.*, *Amsterdamse Bouwen 1880-1980*, Utrecht, 1981. CS

HILBERSEIMER Ludwig Karl

b. Karlsruhe, 1885; d. Chicago, 1967.

Leading German theoretician in the 1920s who exerted considerable influence through his parallel career as planner, teacher, critic and writer. He studied at the Technische Hochschule in Karlsruhe 1906-11. His architectural, political and cultural aspirations were inextricably linked with the avant-garde and he belonged to a variety of groups, including *Arbeitsrat für Kunst, Novembergruppe, Der Sturm* and *Der Ring,* as well as the *Congrès Internationaux d'Architecture Moderne* (CIAM) and the *Deutscher Werkbund.* In 1929 he accepted an invitation to teach at the Bauhaus, but his position as founder and director of the school's City Planning Department was eventually undermined by the rising clamour of the National Socialists and in 1932 he was discharged. The US proved a refuge for many of the Bauhaus tutors, and in 1938 MIES VAN DER ROHE, then director of the Illinois Institute of Technology, appointed Hilberseimer professor of the Department of City and Regional Planning. His reputation rests primarily on his written work, which promotes an uncompromising image of the modern stratified metropolis, where work and housing are rigidly segregated and the cityscape consists of an ordered grid of anonymous high-rise blocks.

□ Weissenhofsiedlung Townhouse, Stuttgart, 1927.

▷ Ludwig Hilberseimer, *Grossstadtbauten,* Hanover, 1925; *Grossstadt-Architektur,* Stuttgart, 1927; *The Nature of Cities,* Chicago, 1955; *Contemporary Architecture – Its Roots and Trends,* Chicago, 1964; *In the Shadow of Mies,* Chicago, 1988. MC

HOFFMANN Josef

b. Pirnitz, Moravia (now Czechoslovakia), 1870; d. Vienna, 1956.

Highly individualistic architect and designer whose work combines the simplicity of craft production with a refined aesthetic ornament. He studied architecture at the Academy of Fine Arts in Vienna, where his teachers included Carl von Hasenauer and Otto WAGNER. He won the prestigious Rome Prize in 1895 and the following year joined the office of Wagner, whose theories of a functional, modern architecture were to have a profound effect on his entire output. He established his own office in 1898 and taught at the Vienna Kunstgewerbeschule (school of applied arts) from 1899 until 1936. A founder member in 1897 of the Vienna Secession, the breakaway group of radical young artists and architects, he was actively involved in the design of its exhibitions and its magazine *Ver Sacrum.* In 1903 he founded the Wiener Werkstätte with fellow Secessionist Koloman MOSER and Fritz Wärndorfer, who financed the enterprise from his family textile business. Hoffmann's earliest Art Nouveau designs were in the characteristic curvilinear Secession style, but he soon found a more personal language based on regular rhythms of grids and squares, influenced in part by the work of Charles Rennie MACKINTOSH, who exhibited at the Secession in 1900. If Hoffmann's early houses in Vienna followed traditional lines, the functional clarity and abstract purity of the Purkersdorf Sanatorium marked him as an important precursor of the Modern Movement. His masterpiece is the Stoclet Palace in Brussels (1905-11), commissioned by a wealthy coal merchant, who described it as "the most perfect house in the world". Its simple volumes are arranged according to the functions of internal spaces, but the detailed design is executed in expensive materials and delineated with rich and symbolic ornament, all by Wiener Werkstätte artists and craftsmen. One of the great early C20 houses, the Stoclet Palace epitomizes its era, the culmination of bourgeois decadence yet contained in a modern guise.

□ Moser and Moll houses, Hohe Warte, Vienna, 1901-3. Sanatorium, Purkersdorf, near Vienna, 1904-6; Palais Stoclet, Brussels, 1905-11. Skywa House, Vienna, 1913-15. Austrian Pavilion, Werkbund Exhibition, Cologne, 1914. Austrian Pavilion, Exposition des Arts Décoratifs, Paris, 1925. Terrace houses, Werkbundsiedlung, Vienna, 1932.

▷ Leopold Kleiner, *Josef Hoffmann,* Berlin, Leipzig and Vienna, 1927. Giulia Veronesi, *Josef Hoffmann,* Milan, 1956. Eduard Sekler, *Josef Hoffmann,* Salzburg, 1982.

Josef Hoffmann, Moser House, Vienna, 1901–3

HÖGER Johannes Friedrich (Fritz)

b. Beckenreihe, 1877; d. Bad Segeberg, 1949.

Early C20 German architect who worked in the Expressionist tradition. A native of northern Germany, Höger studied architecture at the Bauwerkschule in Hamburg between 1897-9. On graduation he worked in the local firm of Lund and Kallmorgen. By 1907 he had established his own office in Hamburg and begun to design a number of small houses which clearly displayed the influence of Hermann MUTHESIUS. However, it was Höger's pride in his north German heritage and its Gothic tradition, coupled with his enthusiasm for locally produced clinker brick (*Backstein*), that was to shape his productive career as an architect. After the First World War he designed a number of office buildings in Hamburg whose clinker-brick façades heralded a renaissance in north German brick architecture. The most significant of these is the Chilehaus, which is possibly the most important example of German Expressionist architecture outside Berlin. The compact lines and angled "prow" of the massive twelve-storey building recall symbolic shipping imagery in the best Expressionist tradition. Höger continued to design until his death, completing several buildings in north Germany, including the Hannover Anzeiger Tower and Rüstringen Town Hall. Although often criticized for his parochial obsession with *Backstein*, he remains one of Germany's most popular architects.

□ "Chilehaus", shipping offices, Hamburg, 1923. Hannover Anzeiger Office Tower, Hanover, 1927-8. Town Hall, Rüstringen, 1929.

▷ "Chile House, Hamburg", *Architectural Review*, Nov. 1925. Wolfgang Pehnt, *Expressionist Architecture*, London and New York, 1973. E. Berkenhagen (ed.) *Fritz Höger, Baumeister-Zeichnungen*, Berlin, 1977. CS

HOLABIRD & ROCHE

Established 1883.

Leading exponents of the Chicago School, active at the turn of this century, Holabird & Roche developed an unpretentious and highly rational approach to the construction of multistorey commercial buildings which were to be seen as the prototype for the early skyscrapers. **William Holabird** (b. New York, 1854; d. Evanston, 1923) spent two years studying engineering at the United States Military Academy before joining William le Baron JENNEY's office in 1872 as a draughtsman. **Martin Roche** (b. Cleveland, 1853; d. Chicago, 1927) served his time as an apprentice cabinetmaker before joining Jenney's office in 1872. Holabird and Ossian Simonds set up a partnership in 1880 and were joined by Roche the following year (Simonds left in 1883). It was 1885 before the practice received its first commission; the breakthrough came with the influential Tacoma Building, which was to become the model for commercial architecture throughout America. The partnership of Holabird & Roche endured for almost 44 years and was responsible for over 72 notable structures, each displaying a homogeneity in design. The practice did, however, progressively refine its essentially functionalist approach by employing subtle detail variations to articulate the repetitive nature of the flat cellular wall.

□ Tacoma Building, Chicago, 1886-9. Old Colony Building, Chicago, 1893-4. Marquette Building, Chicago, 1894-5. La Salle Hotel, Chicago, 1908-9. Rand McNally & Co. Building, Chicago, 1911-12.

▷ Carl Condit, *Chicago 1910-29 – Building Planning & Urban Technology*, Chicago, 1973. J. Zukowsky (ed.), *Chicago Architecture 1872-1922: Birth of a Metropolis*, Chicago, 1987. MC

▷ *see also pp232-3*

HOLDEN Charles

b. Bolton, 1875; d. 1960.

British architect who appreciated and absorbed the principles of Modernism without abandoning traditional architectural values. During a time as articled pupil Holden studied at the Manchester Technical School before joining the London Arts & Crafts architect C. R. ASHBEE. In 1899 he joined H. Percy Adams, first as his chief assistant and then as his partner (from 1907), designing institutional buildings including the Belgrave Hospital and the BMA in London (with integrated sculpture by Jacob Epstein). Along with Herbert BAKER and Edwin LUTYENS, he designed a number of First World War cemeteries, which consolidated Holden's taste for severe, geometric but fundamentally classical form. His work for the London Underground is similarly powerful, his later designs being influenced by a trip in 1930 (with Frank Pick of London Underground) to Holland, Germany and Scandinavia, where he saw the work of Erik Gunnar ASPLUND. For the Senate House of London University, Holden used his favourite material, Portland stone, and drew on his knowledge of American skyscrapers for its overall design.

□ Belgrave Hospital for Children, Kensington, London, 1900-1903. Bristol Central Reference Library, 1905-6. British Medical Association, (BMA), London (now Zimbabwe House), 1907-8. London Underground stations (many in association with S. A. Heap), 1924-37. London Transport Headquarters, Broadway, London SW1, 1927-30. Senate House and other buildings, London University, Bloomsbury, London, 1931-7. National Library of Wales, Aberystwyth, Dyfed, Wales, 1933. Birkbeck College, Students' Union Building and Warburg Institute, London University, 1952-8.

▷ Nikolaus Pevsner, *Studies in Art, Architecture and Design*, London, 1942. Gavin Stamp and John Harris, *Silent Cities*, London, 1977. PP

Charles Holden, Arnos Grove Underground station, London, 1931–3

HOLLAND Henry

b. London, 1745; d. London, 1806.

English architect of the C18 whose work was clearly influenced by PALLADIO and French Neo-Classicism. The eldest son of a prosperous London builder, Holland trained under his father, and in 1770 became an assistant to the distinguished architect and landscape gardener Capability BROWN. Holland quickly came to the notice of potential clients, producing a design for Brooks's Club and a layout for Hans Town in Chelsea. These were quickly followed by his most famous work, Carlton House in London, which he enlarged and altered for the Prince of Wales. Holland also built the Marine Pavilion in Brighton, which was later transformed into the Royal Pavilion by John NASH. Although many of his external designs remained basically Palladian in origin, his interiors reflect a strong French Neo-Classical influence in their refined simplicity and elegance. Ill-health ultimately prevented Holland from carrying out any work after 1803, and he died three years later at Sloane Place, the house he had built for himself as part of the Hans Town development.

□ Brooks's Club, London, 1776-8. Hans Town development, Chelsea, London (including Sloane Street, Hans Place, Cadogan Place and Holland's own house), 1777. Carlton House, London (enlargement and additions), 1783-96. Marine Pavilion, Brighton, Sussex, 1786-7.

▷ Dorothy Stroud, *Henry Holland: His Life and Architecture*, London, 1966. CS

HOOD Raymond Mathewson

b. Rhode Island, 1881; d. 1934.

American architect who, in his short career, produced some of the landmarks of Chicago and New York skyscraper design. Hood studied at Brown University and the Massachusetts Institute of Technology before joining the Boston firm of Cram, GOODHUE and Ferguson. He left to study at the Ecole des Beaux Arts in Paris, travelling regularly between Europe and America before finally settling in New York in 1914. However, it was eight years before he worked on a major commission: with John Mead Howells he won the competition to design an office building for *The Chicago Tribune*, producing a tower with fine Gothic detailing. The American Radiator Building is also Gothic in design, dramatically heightened by its black brick façade and gilding to the top. Many commissions followed, each one moving further away from the Gothic idiom until, with the *Daily News* Building (in partnership with Howells), little trace is left, its place taken by a pared-down geometric monumentality. With a team of distinguished architects (including his partner J. André Fouilhoux), Hood worked on the Rockefeller Center, pioneering multi-block city planning. The McGraw-Hill Building, with its horizontal bands of windows and its mighty structure hung from a steel frame, looks forward to Miesian tower blocks of the 1950s and 1960s.

☐ *Chicago Tribune* Tower (with John Mead Howells) 1924. American Radiator Building, New York, 1924. National Radiator Building, London (with J. Gordon Reeves), 1928. *Daily News* Building, New York (with John Mead Howells), 1930. Rockefeller Center, New York (with L. A. Reinhard and H. Hofmeister, H. W. Corbett, W. K. HARRISON and W. H. McMurray, and J. A. Fouilhoux), 1930-33. McGraw-Hill Building, New York (with Fouilhoux and F. Godley), 1931.

▷ Raymond M. Hood, *Raymond M. Hood*, New York, 1931. Walter H. Kilham, Jr, *Raymond Hood, Architect*, New York, 1973.

PP

HORTA Victor

b. Ghent, 1861; d. Brussels, 1947.

Leading Belgian Art Nouveau architect. He began his education in Ghent with music studies at the Conservatoire, transferring after a year to the Ghent Académie des Beaux Arts to study drawing, textiles and architecture. He went to Paris in 1878 to work with the architect Jean Dubuysson; on returning to Belgium, he qualified as an architect from the Académie des Beaux Arts in Brussels. He worked for an important Neo-Classical architect, Alphonse Balat (1884-5), and started in independent practice in 1886. His creative power was at its zenith from 1893-1903, a period when he designed more than thirty major projects. The First World War interrupted the first phase of his career; he moved first to London and then to the USA (1916-18). His teaching career overlapped with practice and spanned the years 1892-1931, ending as Professor and finally Director of the Université Libre in Brussels. He had a third role as a Neo-Classical designer when Art Nouveau was no longer in fashion. He was created a Baron in 1932. The Austrian critic Ludwig Hevesi wrote of the Tassel House in 1898: "It is most simple and logical...altogether new and just as delightful. But – and note this – there is in it not the faintest echo of any of the historical styles...No detail derives from anything at all in existence." Many of Horta's buildings have been needlessly destroyed, including the most imaginative glass-and-iron structure of the time, the Maison du Peuple, Brussels. His former assistant, Jean Delhaye, made valiant efforts to protect the remaining heritage and secured the Horta residence as a permanent museum with decorations, furniture and fittings.

☐ Three houses in rue des Douze Chambres, Ghent, 1887. In Brussels: Museum of Natural History (project), 1887; Tassel House (first use of iron in Horta's work), 1892; Solvay House (first design fitted throughout with furniture), 1895-1900; Winssinger House, 1895-6; Maison du Peuple, 1896-9; Deprez House, 1897; Atelier Victor Horta (now the Horta Museum), 1898; Aubecq House, 1900; A l'Innovation department store, 1901; Max Hallet House, 1903; Palais des Beaux Arts (in reinforced concrete frame), 1922-8. Also Grand Bazaar, Frankfurt, 1903.

▷ Victor Horta, *Considérations sur l'art moderne*, Brussels, 1925; *L'Enseignement architectural et l'Architecture moderne*, Brussels, 1926. Robert L. Delevoy, *Victor Horta*, Brussels, 1958. F. Borsi and P. Portoghesi, *Victor Horta*, Rome, 1969, New York, 1990. *Art Nouveau, Belgium/France* (exhibition catalogue), Institute for Arts, Rice University, 1976.

AB

▷ *see also pp230-31*

HOWE & LESCAZE

Established 1929.

Partnership lasting from 1929 to 1934 which was the spearhead in introducing the International Style to the east coast of the USA. **George Howe** (b. Worcester, Mass., 1886; d. Cambridge, Mass., 1955) had an education and training that combined American and European elements: Harvard (1904-7) and the Ecole des Beaux Arts in Paris (1908-12). He started his Philadelphia practice in 1916 and produced a range of eclectic designs that ran the gamut from Neo-Classic to Normandy Rustic. **William Lescaze** (b. Geneva, 1896; d. New York, 1969) was educated in Geneva and under Karl MOSER at the ETH, Zürich, graduating in 1919; he emigrated to the USA in 1920 and worked in Cleveland and New York. Howe & Lescaze completed the first truly modern skyscraper, the Philadelphia Savings Fund Society Building, Philadelphia, in 1932. This seminal design demonstrated for the first time the tenets of International Modernism,

William Lescaze, Dartington village development, Devon, 1931–8

applied both to the exterior and to the interior detailing. As with many partnerships, it is difficult to pin down the precise role of each architect, but the general view is that Howe provided the client with the basic concept plus direction of the project, whilst Lescaze was responsible for the detailing. Lescaze was also a significant figure in introducing the Modern Movement to England following his appointment in 1930 to Dartington Hall development, Devon.

☐ Howe & Lescaze: Philadelphia Savings Fund Society Building, 1929-32. Lescaze: Dartington

Village development, Devon (offices, headmaster's house etc.), 1930-38.

▷ William Lescaze, *On Being an Architect*, New York, 1942. Robert A. M. Stern, *George Howe: Towards a Modern American Architecture*, New York and London, 1975. AB

▷ *see also pp232-3*

HUNT Richard Morris

b. Brattleboro, Vermont, 1827; d. Newport, Rhode Island, 1895.

Internationally known designer of mansions and public buildings; heir to European architectural tradition while committed to furthering the architectural profession in America. In 1846-54 Hunt studied at the Ecole des Beaux Arts in Paris (the first American to do so), and assisted Lefuel on extensions to the Louvre. On his return to the USA he worked under T. U. Walter (then redesigning the Washington Capitol) and in 1858 set up a New York atelier, where Frank FURNESS was among his pupils. His many New York projects included the Stuyvesant Apartments (1869-70), which introduced into America the Parisian concept of upper-income urban flats, the mainly cast-iron Roosevelt Building (1873-4), the Tribune Building (1873-6), for a time the city's tallest commercial structure, and the elaborate French Renaissance W. K. Vanderbilt house (1882). Hunt's many country mansions ranged from the vernacular "stick style" Griswold house to the Petit Trianon-inspired Marble House; other commissions included university buildings, the design of the World's Columbian Exhibition in Chicago (1891-3), and monumental pedestals, notably for the Statue of Liberty. He was a founder member and later president of the American Institution of Architects and received the RIBA's Queen's Gold Medal.

☐ J. N. A. Griswold House, Newport, Rhode Island, 1861-3. Statue of Liberty base, New York, 1881-6. Marble House, Newport, 1888-92. Biltmore House, Asheville, Carolina, 1888-95. US Military Academy, West Point, 1889-93. Metropolitan Museum, New York (façade), 1895-1902.

▷ Paul R. Baker, *Richard Morris Hunt*, Cambridge, Mass., 1980. Susan R. Stein (ed.), *The Architecture of Richard Morris Hunt*, Chicago, 1986. BP

INWOOD Henry William

b. London, 1794; d. at sea, 1843.

English architect remembered for his Greek Revival churches. He trained under, and subsequently worked with, his father, **William Inwood** (*c.*1771-1843), a surveyor. He visited Athens in 1819, subsequently publishing a description of the Erechtheion that became a standard work. He used his Athenian drawings and plaster casts for the design of the new St Pancras Church, a commission won in a limited competition and built at immense cost. While the configuration of the west front was developed from GIBBS's St Martin-in-the-Fields, the building's uncompromisingly neo-Greek character was established by an absence of internal vaulting and an archaeological approach to detail (much of it moulded in terracotta); sources were the Erechtheion (the caryatid porch and Ionic order), the Choragic Monument of Lysicrates, and the Tower of the Winds. Criticized by COCKERELL for its "bad taste...ignorance and presumption", it was admired by others for its elegance and scholarship. The Inwoods designed two other London churches in Greek style, and several, inexpensively, in Gothic (St Mary, Somers Town, was used by PUGIN in *Contrasts* to exemplify modern debasement). H. W. Inwood exhibited at the RA from 1809 and was a member of the Society of Antiquaries. He was shipwrecked on a journey to Spain.

Henry Inwood, St Pancras Church, London, 1819–22

☐ St Pancras New Church, London, 1819-22. All Saints, Camden Town, London, 1822-5. St Peter, Regent Square, London, 1822-5. St Mary, Somers Town, London, 1824-7.

▷ H. W. Inwood, *The Erechtheion at Athens...*, 1827; *The Resources of Design in the Architecture of Greece, Egypt, and other Countries...*, 1834. John Summerson, *Georgian London*, London, 1945. BP

ISOZAKI Arata

b. Oita, Kyushu, Japan, 1931.

Architect who succeeded his mentor Kenzo TANGE as the leading creative figure in Japanese architecture after 1970; he is equally important as a writer and theorist and has been the leading interpreter for Japanese designers of outside trends and movements. He studied under Tange at the University of Tokyo (1950-54), joining Tange's team and Urtec (1954-63); in 1963 he established his own practice. He married the sculptor Aiko Miyawaki in 1972. His work in the late 1960s was influenced by Metabolism, but mannerism is already present at this early stage in the exaggerated expression of the structural members. His joint Core System (1960) influenced Tange. The Oita Prefectural Library illustrates his Metabolist sympathy, as do later works such as the Kitakyushu City Museum of Art (1972-4). The greatest work of this period is Gunma Prefectural Museum of Fine Arts,

Arata Isozaki, Los Angeles Museum of Contemporary Art, 1983

Takasaki City (1971-4), which applied the cube as metaphor for culture. Gunma is an explicit summary of Isozaki's subsequent method, which is mannered and self-conscious in its appropriation and transformation of influences drawn from such diverse sources as the Vienna Secession, Marcel Duchamp and ARCHIGRAM. The Tsukuba Plaza and Hotel (1983) continued the anti-rational themes of disconnection and fragmentation of Gunma. The Los Angeles Museum of Contemporary Art (1983) returned to the quieter, less violently dissonant themes of the Fukuoka Mutual Bank Head Office, Fukuoka City (1968-71). The Palau d'Esports Sant Jordi for the 1992 Barcelona Olympic Games, in which Isozaki attempted to combine the structural and poetic with references to the metaphoricism of Antoni GAUDI is not entirely successful.

□ Oita Prefectural Library, Oita City, Japan 1962-6. Cybernetic environment, Expo 70, Osaka, 1966-70. Gunma Prefectural Museum of Fine Arts, Takasaki City, 1971-4. Kamioka Town Hall, Gifu Prefecture, 1975-7. Tsukuba Civic Centre, 1979-83. Los Angeles Museum of Contemporary Art, USA, 1983. Palau d'Esports Sant Jordi, Barcelona, Spain, 1988-91.

▷ Arata Isozaki, "About my method", *The Japan Architect*, August 1972; "The metaphor for the cube", *The Japan Architect*, March 1976. Philip Drew, *The Architecture of Arata Isozaki*, London and New York, 1982. PD

▷ *see also pp208-9*

JACKSON Daryl

b. Clunes, Victoria, Australia, 1937.

Australian architect noted for his excellent school and college buildings and pleasant functional public swimming pools. He studied architecture at the Royal Melbourne Institute of Technology (1954-6) and the University of Melbourne (1957-8) and then worked in the office of Chamberlin, Powell and Bon, London (1961-3), Paul RUDOLPH, New Haven (1963-4) and SKIDMORE, OWINGS & MERRILL, San Francisco (1964). In 1965 he formed a partnership with Evan Walker which became Daryl Jackson Architects. His pragmatism is both a strength and a weakness: it allows a flexible response to each new commission, but on the other hand, there is no commitment to any single idea. If there is one discernible intention, it is that of creating a pleasing social setting to promote human exchanges. The forms are strongly expressed and often very sculptural, in the Rudolph mould, as in the School of Music, Canberra (1972), with its recreation of the vertical emphasis and physically introverted appeal of LE CORBUSIER's Monastery of Ste Marie-de-la-Tourette.

□ Harold Holt Memorial Swimming Centre, Melbourne, 1967. School of Music, Canberra, 1972. Jackson House, Shoreham, 1978. Swimming Training Halls, National Sports Centre, Bruce, 1983. Australian Film, Television and Radio School, North Ryde, NSW, 1988. Australian Chancery Complex, Riyadh, Saudi Arabia, 1982-9.

▷ *Daryl Jackson: Architecture, Drawings and Photographs*, Melbourne, 1984. PD

JACOBSEN Arne

b. Copenhagen, 1902; d. Copenhagen, 1971.

Widely appreciated Danish architect, somewhat parallel in cultural terms, if not in architecture, to AALTO in Finnish architecture; Jacobsen not only introduced modern architecture (Internationalism) to Denmark but strengthened an internationalist aesthetic that remains recognizably Danish and contemporary. He studied at the Academy of Arts, Copenhagen, graduating in 1928, and ran a private practice from 1930 until his death. Never losing sight of a classical legacy, echoes of ASPLUND, Jacobsen introduced the House of the Future (1929, with Flemming Lassen), a distinctive circular show-house which began a series of remarkably detailed private houses. The signs of an early "critical regionalism" are present here; the International School had arrived. Traditional techniques not only collided with functionalism but crafted Jacobsen's aesthetic and the suitability of scale, detail and project. The Bellevue Seaside development (won in 1932) became a running commentary on his own development as he added to the same site over the years. By the time Jacobsen completed Stelling House in Copenhagen (1937-8) he had demonstrated the shift from the private house to commercial buildings; the influence on Danish architecture and abroad was enormous. Jacobsen became *the* Scandinavian architect; the careful aesthetics, humane detailing and respect for both Asplund and MIES VAN DER ROHE, are best seen in Rødovre Town Hall (1955). Later, with projects abroad, Jacobsen's work developed more rigour and the identifiable, if loose, formalism of the then expanding third-generation International School. Like Aalto again, Jacobsen was interested in the idea of "total design", completing furniture and fittings for industrial production. He was noted for light, delicate

Arne Jacobsen, St Catherine's College, Oxford, 1960

interiors – an ascetic but never sterile style. His wide interest in tectonic scales and total design is demonstrated in the SAS Hotel and Terminal in Copenhagen, where in massing and relieving the mass by reflection, and in the smallest details, Jacobsen achieved lightness and a reflective clarity. It is a lightness within architectonic rigour and has probably been continued best by an architect like UTZON. Jacobsen's simplicity is never simplistic and the classical legacy and control are seen in England in one of the best examples of his work, St Catherine's College, Oxford (1960), where the context for Jacobsen's work was perfect; the traditional feel was answered by his internationalist aesthetic. This became a model for much collegiate architecture in the 1960s and 70s. Like many members of the International School, Jacobsen in the last ten years of his life designed many buildings and projects abroad. His attention to material, his careful echoes of Asplund and Mies, a classical rigour, not nostalgia, and his interpretation of functionalism with regional strength will no doubt be reappraised as each era goes in and out of symbolic and ascetic favour.

□ House of the Future (with Flemming Lassen), 1929. Bellevue Seaside Development, Copenhagen, 1932. Town Hall, Aarhus (with Eric Moller), 1942; Town Hall, Søllerød (with Lassen), 1942. Soholm Terraced Housing, 1950. Munkegaard School, Copenhagen, 1952. Royal Hotel and Air Terminal, SAS, Copenhagen, 1960. St Catherine's College, Oxford, 1960. Tom's Chocolate Factory, Ballerup, 1961. Danish Embassy, London, 1970. National Bank of Kuwait (Project), 1971.

▷ T. Faber, *Arne Jacobsen*, London , 1964. *Arne Jacobsen* (exhibition catalogue), Helsinki, 1968. P. E. Shriver, *Arne Jacobsen, A Danish Architect*, Copenhagen, 1972. L. Rubino, *A. Jacobsen, Opera Completa*, Rome, 1980. RC

▷ *see also pp238-9*

JAHN Helmut

b. Nuremberg, 1940.

Modern architect working in America with the Chicago-based firm of Murphy/Jahn. He trained at the Technische Hochschule in Munich (1960-65) before emigrating to the United States in 1966. He spent a year at the Illinois Institute of Technology studying under MIES VAN DER ROHE and in 1967 entered the office of C. F. Murphy Associates; six years later he became partner and Director of Design. The practice was renamed Murphy/Jahn in 1981. During the 1960s it designed some of the most notable buildings in Chicago in the familiar geometric Miesian idiom. This rigid adherence to pure Modernist doctrine gradually lessened as Jahn began to embrace an architectural philosophy which stressed the intuitive nature of creative rationalism, resulting in a more flexible approach to design. This is an essential tenet of the Post-Modernist movement in America during the 70s and signalled a decisive break with the hitherto unchallenged ideology of the Modernist past. Post-Modernism uses a variable, wide-ranging architectural language to indicate a building's relationship to its context, history or existing vernacular. This rich symbolic code can be understood and appreciated by architects and laymen alike. Jahn's more recent designs such as the Rust-Oleum Headquarters and the State of Illinois Center in Chicago are evidence of a large architectural repertoire.

□ Kemper Arena, Kansas, Missouri, 1974. Rust-Oleum Corporate Headquarters, Chicago, Illinois, 1978. Xerox Centre, Chicago, 1980. State of Illinois Centre, Chicago, 1985.

▷ "Contemporary Architects: Helmut Jahn", *Architecture and Urbanism*, Tokyo, July 1978. Charles Jencks, *Late Modern Architecture*, London and New York, 1980. CS

JEANNERET Pierre

Arnold André Pierre Jeanneret-Gris, b. Geneva, 1896; d. 1967.

Swiss architect who, with his distant cousin and collaborator LE CORBUSIER, was responsible for designing some of the seminal buildings of the Modern Movement. After studying at the Ecole des Beaux Arts in Geneva he joined the Parisian architectural practice of Auguste and Gustave PERRET. From 1921 to 1940 he worked in close collaboration with Le Corbusier, designing with him, amongst other things, the widely influential Pavillon de L'Esprit Nouveau at the 1925 Paris Exposition. The two architects went their separate ways at the onset of the Second World War, Jeanneret joining the Bureau Central de Construction at Grenoble, where he helped to develop rapid construction techniques, employing prefabrication, light metals and wood. After the war he established a practice in Paris, but in 1951 left for Chandigarh, India, where he became director of the Capital Project Office and worked alongside Le Corbusier, Maxwell FRY and Jane Drew, supervising the construction of much of the building, as well as designing all levels of housing and the Governor's Palace. Many Indian commissions followed, the use of reinforced concrete more often reserved for large-scale building whereas unstuccoed brick was used for low-cost housing.

□ 1921-40: see under Le Corbusier. Low-cost housing for the Bureau Central de Construction, Grenoble, 1941-4. Jean Pluet House, Île de Bréhat, France, 1948-9. Technical School, Béziers, (with D. Escorsa and the office of J. Prouvé), 1945-50. Wide range of buildings, Chandigarh, India, from 1951, including Gandhi memorial building (1960) and Library and Administrative buildings (1961).

▷ see under LE CORBUSIER. PP

Thomas Jefferson, Monticello, Charlottesville, Virginia, 1768–82.

JEFFERSON Thomas

b. Shadwell, Virginia, 1743; d. Monticello, Virginia, 1826.

The greatest American architect of his time, though architecture was essentially secondary to his more pressing demands as revolutionary statesman, lawyer, ambassador, farmer and third President of the United States. Jefferson's interest in the arts was encouraged at the College of William and Mary but he received no formal training in architecture. Instead, he assembled an impressive library, including several copies of PALLADIO's *Quattro Libri.* His enthusiasm for Palladio was linked to a great admiration for ancient Rome, which enjoyed honorific status as the birthplace of republican virtue and the seat of a mighty empire. Jefferson recognized the political dimension of such associations and duly employed neo-Roman forms as the basis for many of his civic designs. In 1784-9 he was Second Minister to France, and spent much of his spare time studying her architectural heritage. He was particularly impressed by the Roman temple at Nîmes, the Maison Carrée (16BC), and later, with the assistance of the French architect-antiquarian Clérisseau, constructed a scholarly replica of it as the State Capitol for Virginia – a venture which at that time was unprecedented in its Neo-Classical authenticity. From the mid-1970s he employed and worked with his distinguished contemporary Benjamin H. LATROBE.

□ Monticello, Charlottesville, Virginia, 1768-82 (remodelled 1796-1809). Virginia State Capitol, Richmond, 1785-99. Campus Buildings, University of Virginia, Charlottesville, 1817-26.

▷ Thomas Jefferson, *Autobiography*, New York, 1959. Frederick Doveton Nichols, *Thomas Jefferson's Architectural Drawings*, Charlottesville, 1961. William O'Neal, *Architecture in Virginia*, New Yor, 1968. Desmond Guinness and Julius Trousdale Sadler Jr, *Mr Jefferson – Architect*, New York, 1973. MC

▷ *see also pp226-7*

JENNEY William le Baron

b. Fair Haven, Conn. 1832; d. Los Angeles, 1907.

Influential Chicago-based architect, often credited with the creation of the skyscraper – the most potent symbol of the modern metropolis. Jenney studied at the Phillips Academy in Andover, Massachusetts, and subsequently at the Lawrence Scientific School in Harvard. In 1853 he travelled to Paris to enrol at the Ecole Centrale des Arts et Manufactures. The school propagated the theoretical doctrine of J. N. L. DURAND and emphasized both engineering and empiricism. Durand believed in structural honesty and argued that all buildings should express their structure truthfully and not attempt to conceal or deceive through the contorted elaboration of the façade. Jenney's work reflected this rigorously pragmatic approach, and his Chicago office (opened in 1868) attracted the most promising architects of the day including Louis SULLIVAN, Daniel BURNHAM, William HOLABIRD and Martin Roche. William Mundle was brought in as a partner in 1891, followed by Elmer Jensen in 1905. It was Jenney's development of a fireproof steel skeletal structure capable of withstanding the attendant loading of a tall building which finally established the skyscraper as an identifiable typological form. His Home Insurance Building (now demolished) is often claimed as the first true metal-framed high-rise building.

□ Leiter Building, Chicago, 1879. Home Insurance Building, Chicago, 1884-5. Sears Roebuck & Co. Store, Chicago, 1890-91. Ludington Building, Chicago, 1891.

▷ William le Baron Jenney, *Principles and Practices of Architecture*, 1869. Carl Condit, *Chicago School of Architecture – A History of Commercial and Public Building in the Chicago Area, 1875–1925*, Chicago, 1964. Francisco Mujica, *History of the Skyscraper*, Paris, 1929. MC

▷ *see also pp232-3*

JENSEN-KLINT Peder Vilhelm

b. Copenhagen, 1853; d. Copenhagen, 1930.

Danish vernacular architect and theorist who believed in the importance of traditional craftsmanship. Jensen-Klint originally trained as a building engineer, graduating from the Technical University of Denmark in 1877. He then entered the Royal Academy in Copenhagen to become a painter, but eventually turned his energies towards architecture. Jensen-Klint made extensive studies of Danish vernacular building, believing that traditional methods, materials and craftsmanship were the fundamental basis of architecture. In an age where theory-toting academic architects were prominent, Jensen-Klint took the opposite view, stressing the need for architects to be active participants in the building process. His first house, the Holm Villa (1896), is a testimony to his Expressionistic philosophy, drawing its inspiration from natural organic forms rather than pre-determined abstract principles. Jensen-Klint's most important work is the Grundtvig Church and estate in Copenhagen, an enlarged version of a vernacular village church, evocatively constructed in the Danish brick tradition. Jensen-Klint was hugely influential in Danish architectural circles: many others adopted his philosophy of design, in a movement which became known as the Danish Functional Traditional. His son **Kaare Klint** (1888-1954), carried on the ideas of his father during the 1940s and 50s and also went on to become one of Denmark's leading furniture designers.

□ Holm Villa, Copenhagen, 1896. Grundtvig Church, Copenhagen, 1913-30.

▷ Peder Vilhelm Jensen-Klint, *Bygmesterskolen*, Copenhagen, 1911. Knud Millech, *Danske Arkitektur stromninger: 1850-1950*, Copenhagen, 1951. MC

JOHNSON Philip Cortelyou

b. Cleveland, Ohio, 1906.

One of the most controversial and prolific figures in c20 American architecture and architectural criticism. Johnson received an AB in architectural history from Harvard University in 1930, and upon graduation became the Director of the Department of Architecture at the Museum of Modern Art, New York. In that capacity, he co-curated with Henry-Russell Hitchcock the seminal *Modern Architecture* exhibition at MOMA (1932) which introduced European modern architecture and the works of pioneers such as LE CORBUSIER, MIES VAN DER ROHE and Walter GROPIUS to a wide American audience for the first time. Building on the MOMA show, Johnson and Hitchcock co-authored *The International Style: Architecture since 1922* (1932), which, filtering out the social and political dimension of European modernism, effectively codified the principles of modern architecture on stylistic grounds for the American audience. In the late 1930s, Johnson used his personal wealth and influence to champion the cause of several modernist architects, notably Mies van der Rohe, about whom he would prepare an important monograph in 1947 and with whom he would later join forces in the design of the Seagram Building in New York City. During this period, Johnson established himself as a visible fixture in eastern architectural circles. In 1940 Johnson returned to Harvard's Graduate School of Design to be trained as an architect under Marcel BREUER. He received a B.Arch in 1943 and practised architecture in Cambridge, Massachusetts, from 1942 to 1946, when he moved back to New York to serve again as Director of Architecture at MOMA. He returned to private practice in 1954, establishing partnerships with Richard Foster (1964-7) and with John Burgee (as "Johnson/Burgee Architects" 1967-83 and as "John Burgee with Philip Johnson" since 1983). He has been a trustee of MOMA since 1958 and received the AIA Gold Medal (1978) and the Pritzker Architecture prize (1979). As an architect, Johnson is most widely respected for his work in the early 1950s while still under the immediate influence of Mies van der Rohe. His own residence in New Canaan, the Glass House, is regarded as a milestone of American International Style modernism. In the 1960s and 70s he emerged as one of the premier apologists for the Post-Modern movement in architecture. No doubt his training as an historian and curator made him comfortable with Post-Modernism's reliance on historical allusion and eclecticism. His design for the AT&T Building (1979) takes Post-Modernism to its logical – or, some would say, illogical – conclusion with its imposition of an abstracted Chippendale crown on a New York City skyscraper. Thanks to this design and to his apparent willingness to alter his fundamental architectural principles every few decades, he has been repeatedly criticized for showing more interest in style than in substance. His legacy has still to be put in perspective, but he is apt to be remembered more as a provocateur than as a designer. However he is perceived, it will be noted

Philip Johnson (with John Burgee), NCNB Center, Houston, 1984

GLASS HOUSE, New Canaan, Conn.

The Glass House, designed by Philip Johnson and completed in 1949, was, and still is, a startling piece of Modernist domestic design. Set in beautiful park-like landscaping, the simple steel-framed single-storey, rectangular building with its glass walls is almost totally transparent. The only solid piece of its construction is the cylindrical, brick-built, central bathroom tower. However, the use of full-height sliding wall panels similar to those found in Japanese architecture secures a degree of additional privacy for the building's occupants. Johnson acknowledged many influences in his design from the Classicist Palladio to Modernist Mies van der Rohe.

that, as a man of affluence, erudition, and energy, he has never hesitated to act as an advocate for causes he espouses.

□ Philip Johnson House, New Canaan, Conn., 1949. Seagram Building, New York (with Mies van der Rohe and KAHN and Jacobs), 1958. Museum Building, Munson-Williams-Proctor Institute, Utica, New York, 1960. Painting Gallery, Philip Johnson House, New Canaan, Conn., 1965. Pennzoil Place, Houston (with John Burgee, and Wilson, Morris, Crain and Anderson), 1976. AT&T Headquarters, New York, 1979 (with John Burgee). NCNB Center, Houston (with John Burgee) 1984.

▷ Philip Johnson, *Writings*, foreword by Vincent Scully, New York, 1979. Henry-Russell Hitchcock, *Philip Johnson: Architect 1949-1965*, New York and London, 1966. *Johnson/Burgee: Architecture*, text by N. Miller, London, 1980. Carleton Knight III, *Philip Johnson/John Burgee: Architecture*, New York, 1985.

DP

▷ *see also pp234-5*

Inigo Jones, Queen's House, Greenwich, London, 1616–19

JONES Inigo

b. London, 1573; d. London, 1652.

English classical architecture might seem to be pedantic and wanting in invention, but when it is realized that Jones introduced it to a country still in the realms of Gothic survival and half-timbering its importance may be allowed. Early in the C17 he had been fortunate to journey abroad – on missions with the Earl of Rutland to Denmark and to Italy. He was always to be in royal notice, for he excelled in staging elaborate masques at the Court of James I (1603-25), often in collaboration with Ben Jonson. In 1610 he was appointed Surveyor to the short-lived Henry, Prince of Wales. He may have done a little work then at St James's Palace, but the Prince's death brought a seeming end to such promise. However, in April 1613 he was granted the reversion of the place of Surveyor of the King's Works. This coincided with Jones's second Italian journey, in the entourage of the "collector Earl" of Arundel. They visited northern Italy, looking at PALLADIO's villas, and spent the winter of 1613-14 in Rome and its environs. The notes and marginalia in Jones's copy of the 1570 edition of Palladio's *Quattro Libri* (in Worcester College, Oxford) show his growing mastery of the theory and grammar of classical architecture. With such a background he was the obvious choice, at his return to London, for the post of Surveyor-General to the Office of Works. In James I he had a king ready to build a palace at Whitehall on a lavish enough scale. The Banqueting House in Whitehall, the Queen's House at Greenwich and the Queen's Chapel at St James's Palace show Jones as the careful student of both Andrea Palladio and Vincenzo SCAMOZZI. Between 1625 and 1640 Jones was concerned principally with work on two major London sites: the repairing and remodelling of St Paul's Cathedral, and the designing of Covent Garden for the Earl of Bedford. At the former all his work, which included a great Corinthian portico, was later destroyed in the Fire of London (1666) and subsequently demolished to clear the site for Wren's new church. St Paul's Church at Covent Garden survives but was rebuilt, following Jones's design, after a fire of 1795. Jones's late years followed the tragic decline in the fortunes of his royal master Charles I. He served as a royalist and after capture his estates were sequestered. However, having hidden money he was able to leave a modest fortune when he died.

□ Queen's House, Greenwich, London, 1616-19 (completed by 1635). Banqueting House, Whitehall Palace, London, 1619-22. St Paul's Church, Covent Garden, London, 1631-3, rebuilt 1796-8.

▷ J. Lees-Milne, *The Age of Inigo Jones*, London, 1953. John Summerson, *Inigo Jones*, Harmondsworth, 1966. J. Harris, S. Orgel and R. Strong, *The King's Arcadia: Inigo Jones and the Stuart Court*, London, 1973.

GB

JONES Owen

b. London, 1807; d. London, 1874.

Key figure in the development of Victorian design in the latter half of the C19. The son of a Welsh furrier and antiquary, Jones began his architectural training in 1825 as an apprentice to Lewis Vulliamy, (1791-1871). He subsequently enrolled at the Royal Academy, but in 1830 embarked on a four-year study tour through the countries of the Mediterranean. His extensive itinerary included the Spanish city of Granada, where he and a young French architect, Jules Goury, carried out a measured survey of the Moorish citadel, the Alhambra. These detailed investigations led Jones to the development of a theoretical treatise on colour which attracted great interest and proved influential in his appointment as Superintendent of the Works for the Great Exhibition of 1851. The following year Henry Cole invited him to join the government's new Department of Science and Art, where he compiled his seminal work, *The Grammar of Ornament*. It catalogues and illustrates the decorative motifs of diverse cultures and quickly established itself as the bible of eclecticism.

□ Crystal Palace, London (interior decoration), 1850-51. St James Hall, London, 1855-8. Crystal Palace Bazaar, London, 1858. Eynsham Hall, Oxford, 1872.

▷ Owen Jones and Jules Goury, *Plans, Elevations, Sections and Details of the Alhambra*, London,

1836-45. Owen Jones, *The Grammar of Ornament*, London, 1856 (reprinted New York, 1982). Michael Darby and David Van Zanten, *Marble Halls*, London, 1973. MC

JOURDAIN Frantz

b. Antwerp, 1847; d. Paris, 1935.

Belgian-born Arts & Crafts architect and writer who played a leading role in the development of French Modernism. Jourdain spent his school years at the prestigious Lycée Henri IV in Antwerp, and between 1862 and 1867 studied under Jules Vallès, a prominent social revolutionary who encouraged him to develop a questioning approach to art and architecture. In 1867 Jourdain was admitted to the Ecole des Beaux Arts in Paris, where he studied for three years before enlisting for the Franco-Prussian War. He began to practise architecture in earnest *c.*1886, and by 1890 had become a celebrated and articulate spokesman for reform within the art and design establishment. His search for a modern French style based on a renewal of French spiritual and aesthetic principles led him to criticize the stifling influence of Greece and Rome within institutions such as the Ecole des Beaux Arts. Jourdain's theories and polemical writing gave an important impetus to the emerging French Modern movement before the First World War. In his buildings he attempted to synthesize the French national tradition of gracious ornament with modern technological demands. His most successful work is the Samaritaine department store in Paris, which united technology, decoration and materials in an elegant seven-storey building. He also completed a number of château restorations and continued to be active in both writing and design until the late 1920s.

□ Château of Verteuil (restoration), 1893. La Samaritaine, Paris, 1891-1907. Moët et Chandon Pavilion and Perfumery, Exposition Universelle, Paris, 1900.

▷ Robert Rey, *Frantz Jourdain*, Paris, 1923. Franco Borsi and Ezio Godoli, *Paris 1900*, New York, 1978. CS

Filippo Juvarra, La Superga, Turin, 1718–21

JUVARRA Filippo

b. Messina, 1678; d. Madrid, 1736.

The most gifted and prolific architect of C18 Italy, with a particular mastery in designs of colossal scale. He had an international reputation which he justly deserved. Trained as a silversmith, he worked in Rome under Carlo FONTANA before his appointment (1714) in Turin as royal architect to Vittore Amedeo II, Duke of Savoy and King of Sicily. His early works are relatively sober and reflect his experience in Rome. La Superga, a monumental domed votive church fronting a monastic complex, recalls, for example, elements from RAINALDI's Santa Agnese. On the other hand, the equally restrained royal Palazzo Madama is modelled appropriately enough on the garden front of LE VAU's Versailles. The success of these works relies heavily on a simplicity of composition that is quite unlike the works of Juvarra's great predecessor GUARINI. A basic simplicity also underlies the layout of Stupinigi, a palatial residence of unprecedented scale in Italy that is planned around a hexagon as a coherently articulated complex of pavilions and links. Late works reveal a new exploration of a more skeletal kind of architecture (Stupinigi's Great Hall; Carmine), a direction which now may owe something to Guarini and perhaps also to buildings in Central Europe. Interiors are now conceived in terms of piers and ribs with visible wall surfaces daringly eaten away by a multitude of openings.

□ Venaria Reale, near Turin, 1714-26. La Superga, near Turin, 1717-31. Palazzo Madama, Turin, 1718-21 (interrupted). Royal Hunting Lodge, Stupinigi, near Turin, 1729-33. Chiesa del Carmine, Turin, 1732-6.

▷ V. Viale (ed.), *Mostra di Filippo Juvarra*, Messina, 1966. S. Boscarino, *Juvarra Architetto*, Rome, 1973. N. Carboneri, *La Superga*, Turin, 1979. DH

KAHN Albert

b. Rhaunen, Germany, 1869; d. New York, 1942.

Entrepreneurial American architect who specialized in factory and industrial design. Kahn's family emigrated to the United States in 1880, and four years later he joined the architectural practice of Mason and Rice, working his way up to become the firm's principal resident architect and subsequently chief designer. In 1891 he visited Europe on a $500 scholarship award. Five years later he established a short-lived partnership with George W. Nettleton and Alexander B. Trowbridge, which was dissolved *c.*1900, following Nettleton's death and Trowbridge's acceptance of a prestigious academic post as Dean of Cornell University. Kahn set up his own practice in 1902 and was subsequently joined by his brothers Julius and Moritz. Early industrial projects such as the Packard Motor Car Company Plant, Detroit (1903-10), were of a conventional multistorey design, but in 1906 Kahn achieved a breakthrough with his single storey, top-lit modular design for the George N. Pierce Plant in Buffalo, New York. Ironically, the design was never intended as a prototype for assembly-line production, being developed simply to achieve even lighting conditions and planning flexibility, but it rapidly became the model for American factory design. The combination of single-storey practicality and streamlined assembly-line production was eventually achieved with the River Rouge Plant in Michigan (1917-39) for car manufacturer Henry Ford. America's emergent motor industry was quick to realize the economic potential of Kahn's simple, engineering-based solutions. His huge factories were evocative symbols of the nation's growing industrial capabilities. Unlike his contemporaries Peter BEHRENS and Antonio SANT'ELIA, Kahn was not inclined to romanticize the machine; he remained an architectural pragmatist. By the late 1930s his office employed a staff of 600 and was responsible for almost a fifth of America's architect-designed factory and industrial buildings.

Albert Kahn, The Steel Foundry Company, Lima, Ohio, 1938, drawing

□ George N. Pierce Plant, Buffalo, New York, 1906. Ford Motor Company, River Rouge Plant, Dearborn, Michigan, 1917-39. Chrysler Corporation Half-Ton Truck Plant and Export Building (Dodge Division), Warren, Michigan, 1938.

▷ Detroit Institute of Arts, *The Legacy of Albert Kahn*, Detroit, 1970. Grant Hildebrand, *Designing for Industry: The Architecture of Albert Khan*, Cambridge, Mass., 1974. Leland M. Roth, *A Concise History of American Architecture*, New York, 1979.

CS

KAHN Louis I.

b. Saarama, Estonia, 1901; d. New York, 1974.

One of the foremost architects of the second half of the C20. He went to the United States in 1905, and having mastered the Beaux-Arts-inspired curriculum of Dean Paul Cret, he graduated with honour from the University of Pennsylvania in 1924. In the 1920s and early 30s, he worked first as a draughtsman and later as head designer in a succession of Philadelphia-based firms. Most notably during this period, Kahn was Chief of Design for the Sesquicentennial Exhibition (1925-6) in his capacity as senior assistant in the Philadelphia City Architect's office. During the Depression, he was particularly active in the design of public assisted housing. From 1935 Kahn was in private practice until his death in 1974. He was associated with George HOWE in 1941, with Howe and Oscar Stonorov in 1942, and with Stonorov alone 1943-8. He was Design Critic and Professor of Architecture at Yale University from 1947 to 1957, when he accepted a similar appointment at his alma mater in Philadelphia. Kahn received the AIA Gold Medal (1971) and the RIBA Gold Medal (1972) and was elected a member of the American Academy of Arts and Letters (1971). In his teaching and practice, Kahn profoundly influenced a generation of architects. He brought to both endeavours a talmudic questioning of the first principles of architectural design. This fundamental enquiry led him to dwell on the relationship between the underlying Form of a project and its Design. Kahn's architecture is notable for its simple, platonic forms and compositions. Through the use of brick and poured-in-place concrete masonry, he developed a contemporary architecture of great power and monumentality. At the same time, his buildings invariably display a keen sensitivity to the nuances of site conditions through the artful manipulation of natural light. While rooted in the International Style Modernism of his age, Kahn mined both the Beaux-Arts education of his youth and a deeply felt aesthetic impulse to develop a personal architectural

Louis Kahn, Kimbell Art Museum, Fort Worth, Texas, 1966–72

vocabulary of forms that has been a point of departure for many subsequent architects. Projects such as the Salk Institute and the Kimbell Art Museum, masterpieces of the reconciliation of Form and Order through inspired construction, are among the most studied works of architecture of the last half-century. Noted for his cryptic pronouncements and aphoristic remarks, Kahn often spoke of his desire to discover "what a material wants to be". The diligence and depth of his search set him apart from his colleagues and ensures Kahn's lasting recognition as one of the masters of c20 architecture.

□ Yale Art Gallery, New Haven, Connecticut, 1951-3. Richards Medical Research Building, University of Pennsylvania, Philadelphia, 1957-64. Salk Institute, La Jolla, California, 1959-65. New Capital of Bangladesh, Dacca, 1962-74. Kimbell Art Museum, Fort Worth, Texas, 1966-72. Library and Dining Hall, Phillips Exeter Academy, New Hampshire, 1967-72. Center for British Art and Studies, Yale University, New Haven, 1969-74.

▷ Vincent Scully Jr, *Louis I. Kahn*, New York, 1962. Romaldo Giurgola and Jaimini Mehta, *Louis I. Kahn*, Boulder, Colorado, 1975. Alexandra Tyng, *Beginnings: Louis I. Kahn's Philosophy of Architecture*, New York, 1984. Heinz Ronner and Sharad Jhaveri (eds.) *Louis I. Kahn: Complete Work 1935-1974*, Basel, 1987. DP

KENT William

b. Bridlington, 1685; d. London, 1748.

Kent's work as an architect did not start until the early 1730s. By then English Palladianism was well established through the activities of Lord BURLINGTON and Colen CAMPBELL. Whilst he might have been successful as a Baroque architect (his interiors have overtones of that style), Kent was an ardent Palladianist. The exteriors of his buildings obey in providing pediments, columns and the trappings of a classical repertory. He is said to have been apprenticed *c.*1700 to a coach-painter in Hull, but three gentlemen, Sir John Chester, Sir William Wentworth and Burrell Massingberd, decided to promote his studies in Italy. He travelled there in 1709, and was soon busy trying to become a painter, studying in the studios of Giuseppe Chiari and Benedetto Luti and travelling extensively. In 1713 he was awarded the Pope's medal for painting. It was as a painter that he was brought back to England in 1719 by Lord Burlington; they had first met in Italy five years previously. In London Kent painted various ceilings at Burlington House for his new patron, and he was also employed by the Duke of Chandos and by Earl Tylney. With Lord Burlington's support he even supplanted the Sergeant Painter, Sir James Thornhill, for the painted decorations needed in the new state rooms at Kensington Palace. But as a "history-painter" Kent was really inferior to Thornhill and showed his real abilities only when he turned to architecture and landscape design. In 1726 Burlington, anxious for Kent's advancement, saw to it that he was given a seat at the Board of Works as its Master Carpenter. It was from this position that Kent got involved in work on a number of public and private commissions, as various as designs of furniture and silver, a royal barge for Frederick, Prince of Wales, and internal decorations for Lord Burlington at Chiswick House, at Houghton Hall (home of the Prime Minister, Sir Robert Walpole) and at Holkham Hall for the Earl of Leicester. Lord Burlington had also arranged that Kent should edit his collection of the designs of Inigo JONES, which, with the incorporation of a few designs by both Burlington and Kent, was issued in 1727. Kent's place in the history of landscape gardening is an assured one. He combined bridges, arches, "eye-catchers" of various kinds with the careful siting of statuary. The surrounding park was the foil: stretches of studied informality befitting depiction on the canvases of Claude or Poussin.

□ Burlington House, London (internal decorations), mid-1720s. Chiswick House, Middx. (painting etc.), 1726-9. Houghton Hall, Norfolk (internal decorations), 1726-31. Stowe House, Bucks. (various garden buildings), from 1730. Holkham Hall, Norfolk (decorations and garden buildings), from 1734. Rousham, Oxon. (garden buildings), 1738-41. 22 Arlington Street, London, 1741-50. 44 Berkeley Square, London (includes a fine staircase), 1742-4. Horse Guards, Whitehall, London (not built till 1750-59).

▷ William Kent, *Designs of Inigo Jones*, 1727. John Vardy, *Some Designs of Mr Inigo Jones and Mr William Kent*, 1744. Margaret Jourdain, *The Work of William Kent*, London, 1948. Michael Wilson, *William Kent*, London, 1984. GB

DE KEYSER Hendrick

b. Utrecht, 1565; d. Amsterdam, 1621.

Perhaps the most important Dutch sculptor of the early c17 and an accomplished architect, rivalled only by his contemporary

William Kent, Holkham Hall, Norfolk, 1738–41

Lieven de Key. The bulk of his work is located in Amsterdam, where he was appointed municipal architect in 1594. His architectural œuvre is broad and stylistically varied but his reputation rests principally on two influential churches, the Zuiderkerk and the Westerkerk. Both church towers still act as city landmarks today, but they reflect a significant shift in the Dutch architectural profession during the twenty years separating their completion. The Zuiderkerk is a studied example of the picturesque Dutch Renaissance tradition and the first Protestant church designed specifically to focus attention, not on the altar, but on the pulpit. The Westerkerk, however, betrays the stylistic traits of the imminent move towards Classicism. De Keyser's completed projects formed the basis for an illustrated book, *Architectura Moderna*, published in 1631 by Salomon de Bray, providing a contemporary record of this versatile architect.

□ Zuiderkerk, Amsterdam, 1606-14. Town Hall, Delft, 1618. Nooderkerk, Amsterdam, 1620-38. Westerkerk, Amsterdam, 1620-38.

▷ Salomon de Bray, *Architectura Moderna ofte Bouwinga van osten tyt*, 1631 (facsimile edition, Soest, Holland, 1971). Jakob Rosenberg, Seymour

Slive and E. H. Ter Kuile, *Dutch Art and Architecture: 1600 to 1800*, Harmondsworth, 1966. Henry-Russell Hitchcock, *Netherlandish Scrolled Gables of the 16th and early 17th Centuries*, New York, 1978. MC

KIESLER Frederick

b. Vienna, 1890; d. New York, 1965.

Leading C20 figure in the world of stage and scenic design. Kiesler studied at Vienna's Akademie der Bildenden Kunst and Technische Hochschule. After a brief collaboration with Adolf LOOS in 1920, he joined the Dutch avant-garde *De Stijl* group, where Piet Mondrian's theories on Neo-Plasticism proved highly influential. In 1925 Kiesler designed Austria's contribution to the celebrated Exposition Internationale des Arts Décoratifs et Industriels Modernes in Paris. The following year he emigrated to the US and established a brief partnership with Harvey Wiley Corbett in New York. From 1928 he divided his time between the Juillard School of Music, where he was Director of Stage Design 1934-57, and Columbia University's School of Architecture, where he was an associate professor and directed the Laboratory for Design Correlation 1937-42. Kiesler's abiding obsession was a visionary, if rather nebulous, concept for the "Endless" – a continuous space denying all limitations and restrictions between both performers and their audience, man and his environment.

□ Film Guild Cinema, New York, 1930. Universal Theatre, Woodstock, 1933. Art of This Century Gallery, New York, 1942. Shrine of the Book, Hebrew University, Jerusalem, 1959.

▷ Frederick Kiesler, *Inside the Endless House – Art, People and Architecture: A Journal*, New York, 1966. Ulrich Conrads and Hans Sperlich, *The Architecture of Fantasy*, New York, 1962. R. L. Held, *Endless Innovations – Frederick Kiesler's Theory and Scenic Design*, Michigan, 1982. Nora Phillips, *Frederick Kiesler*, New York, 1982. MC

KLENZE Leo von

b. Schalden, Brunswick, 1784; d. Munich, 1864.

The architect of Neo-Classical Munich; after SCHINKEL, the greatest C19 German architect. After initial studies with GILLY in Berlin he worked in Paris in the ateliers of Percier and Fontaine and became familiar with French Neo-Classical architectural ideas. In 1816 he was appointed court architect in Munich by Crown Prince Ludwig, who was King of Bavaria from 1824 until his abdication in 1848. A period of intense building activity transformed Munich with new buildings and ambitious urban planning. Klenze advocated the continued relevance of ancient Greek architecture in his writings, and in the most individual of his Munich projects, e.g. the Neo-Classical Glyptothek (Museum of Antique Sculpture) and the Propyläen. However, in other work, e.g. the Pinakothek (Picture Gallery), he chose a Renaissance style, which he was also obliged to adopt for the frontages of the great new N axis laid out in 1817 (later Ludwigstrasse). Klenze's buildings are monumental; he believed that architecture should reflect the moral conscience of the nation, as suggested by the Grecophile philosopher and historian J. J. Winckelmann. The Walhalla near Regensburg, based on the Parthenon and designed as a monument for the German people, is perhaps his most famous work.

□ Leuchtenberg Palace, Munich, 1816-21. Glyptothek (Museum of Antique Sculpture), Munich, 1816-31. Ministry of War, Munich, 1826-30. Königsbau Residenz, Munich, 1826-35. Pinakothek (Picture Gallery), 1826-36. Allerheiligen-Hofkirche, Munich, 1826-37. Walhalla (Temple of Fame), near Regensburg, 1830-42.

Leo von Klenze, Walhalla (Temple of Fame), Regensberg, 1830–42, drawing

Festsaalbau, Residenz, Munich, 1833. Törring Palace, Munich (rebuilding), 1836. Addition to the Hermitage, St Petersburg (Leningrad), 1839-51. Befreiungshalle (Hall of Liberation), Kelheim, Bavaria, 1842-63. Ruhmeshalle (Hall of Fame), Munich, 1843-54. Propyläen, Munich, 1846-60.

▷ O. Hederer, *Leo Von Klenze – Persönlichkeit und Werk*, Munich, 1964, 1981. D. Watkin, *German Architecture and the Classical Ideal 1740-1840*, London, 1987. TC

▷ *see also pp220-21*

DE KLERK Michel

b. Amsterdam, 1884; d. Amsterdam, 1923.

The most important and influential architect of the so-called Amsterdam School, a loose-knit "expressionistic" group that existed from 1913 to 1925. He trained as an architect in the office of Eduard Cuypers from 1898 to 1910. Like most Dutch architects of the period, he was also influenced by H. P. BERLAGE and had a considerable interest in and sympathy for the work of the English Arts & Crafts or "Free School" of architects and designers. However, he was not able to find work in England. With J. van der Mey (1878-1949) and close associate Piet Kramer (1881-1965), he co-designed the exuberantly decorative Scheepvaarthuis (1912-16), considered the first building of the Amsterdam School. He resolutely refused to act as leader of the School, although others acknowledged his pre-eminent position. After his death at the early age of 39, five issues of the magazine *Wendingen*, the school's mouthpiece, were devoted to his work. His first major project was the housing block on the Vermeerplein, Amsterdam, followed by the better-known Spaarndammerplantsoen for the same client. This, the most expressionistic of all his structures, was a tripartite housing block, also for the Eigen Haard Housing Association, which culminated in a corner block known as *Het Schip* (The Ship), a transcendental Dutch symbol from the country's Golden Age as well as reflecting artisanal craftsmanship of the highest order. De Klerk was also a superb artist and draughtsman.

□ Housing block, Hillehuis, J. Vermeerplein, Amsterdam, 1911. Scheepvaarthuis, Amsterdam (with Van der Mey and Kramer), 1912-16. Housing blocks, Spaarndammerplantsoen, Amsterdam, 1913 (including the third block for the Eigen Haard, Zaanstraat, 1917-21).

Michel de Klerk, Spaarndammerbuurt housing, Amsterdam, 1913–19

▷ The chief record of De Klerk's work is in *Wendingen* magazine, Amsterdam, 1924-6. Dennis Sharp, "Michel de Klerk and the Eigen Haard Development", in *GA Houses*, Tokyo, No. 3, 1979. Wim de Wit, *The Amsterdam School*, Cambridge, Mass., 1983. DS

▷ *see also pp230-31*

KORN Arthur

b. Breslau, 1891; d. Vienna, 1978.

German Modern Movement architect, town-planner and much-respected teacher. He studied architecture in Berlin, where he worked until he was eventually forced away by Nazism. After working for a period with Erich MENDELSOHN he joined with Sigfried Weitzmann in practice in 1923. They built one of the first examples of the new architecture after the war, the Goldstein House, Berlin (1922-4). Their most celebrated building was the Fromm Rubber Company, Friedrichshafen, with steel frame and glass bricks. Korn wrote on glass construction during this busy period as a practitioner. Later he wrote largely on town-planning. He became secretary of the Novembergruppe and from 1926 was a member of the Berlin Ring of architects. After an initial visit to London in 1934 with Walter GROPIUS, he settled there in 1937, working for a period with F. R. S. YORKE. Later he became thoroughly involved in teaching, firstly at Oxford and then at Hammersmith and the Architectural Association School, London, where he taught for over 21 years and inspired generations of post-war architects and planners. In the late 1930s he, with others, prepared the MARS Plan for London and acted as Secretary of the MARS Town Planning Committee, which published its controversial plan in the *Architectural Review* in 1942. His ideas were based on the concept of "Survey, Analysis and Plan" developed by Geddes, Mumford and others, but Korn streamlined it into his own version, "Concept and Interpretation", e.g. allowing the work of individual architects to fill in the detailed proposals of the conceptual town plan.

□ Villa Goldstein House, Berlin-Charlottenburg, 1922-4. Villa Wasservogel, Berlin-Charlottenburg, 1924. Fromm Factory, Friedrichshafen, 1928-9. Town Centre Competition, Haifa (1st Prize), 1939.

▷ A. Korn, *Glas im Bau und als Gebrauchsgegenstand*, Berlin, 1929 (Eng. trans. London, 1967); *History Builds the Town*, London, 1953. Dennis Sharp (ed.), *Planning and Architecture: Essays presented to Arthur Korn*, London, 1967. DS

▷ *see also pp234-5*

KOTĚRA Jan

b. Brno, 1871; d. Prague, 1923.

Founder of the Modern Movement in Czech architecture. He graduated in 1897 from the Academy of Fine Arts in Vienna, where his professor was Otto WAGNER. He was called as a professor to the School of Decorative Arts in Prague in 1898 and taught there until 1911. From 1911 to 1923 he was a professor at the Academy of Fine Arts in Prague. As chairman of the Mánes Club, as a teacher and architect he ranked among the leading representatives of Czech culture in the early C20. His philosophy was influenced by the Modern Style of Vienna, by folk architecture, and by the English Arts & Crafts movement. After a trip to Holland and England in 1905 he developed a typical, red-brick-based rational style. His art culminated in the Town Museum of Hradec Králové, East Bohemia (1906-12), whose asymmetrical composition shows the influence of Frank Lloyd WRIGHT. As a teacher, he educated two generations of Czech architects: the Cubist group (GOČÁR, Novotný), and then the Functional group (FUCHS, Krejcar, Benš, etc.). It was thanks to Kotěra that Czech architecture freed itself from its provincialism and dependence on Vienna and became an important centre of the European avant-garde.

□ Peterka House, Prague, 1899-1900. S.V. U. Mánes Exhibition Pavilion, Prague 1901-2. National House, Prostějov, 1905-7. Water tower, Prague-Michle, 1906-7. Town Museum, Hradec Králové 1906-12. Chamber of Commerce and Trade Pavilion, Jubilee Exhibition, Prague, 1907-8. Own villa, Prague, 1908-9. Laichter Publisher House, Prague, 1909. Slavia Bank, Sarajevo 1911-12. Mozarteum, Prague, 1911-13. Lemberger Palace, Vienna, 1913-14. Stenc Summer Villa, Všenory, 1921.

▷ Bohuslav Fuchs, *In margine umoleckého edkazu Jana Kotěry*, Brno, 1972. Karel B. Mádl, *Jan Kotěra*, Prague, 1922. Otakar Novotný, *Jan Kotěra a jeho doba*, Prague, 1958. Vladimír Slapeta, Pavel Marek, *Národní dum v Prostějově*. Prostějov, 1978 (3rd ed. 1984). VS

KRAMER Ferdinand

b. Frankfurt-am-Main, 1898; d. Frankfurt, 1985.

American Modernist architect and industrial designer. After an early education at the Oberrealschule in Frankfurt, Kramer's architectural training began in earnest in 1919, when he attended the Bauhaus in Weimar under Walter GROPIUS and Adolf Meyer. This was followed by three years at the Technische Hochschule in Munich studying with Theodor Fischer. Kramer's first job was with Ernst MAY's City Planning office in Frankfurt, a post he combined with industrial design commissions for various companies. He was in private practice in Frankfurt from 1925 to 1930, when he was forbidden to work by the German government because his wife was Jewish. This ban continued until 1938, when Kramer emigrated to the USA, becoming a naturalized American citizen in 1945. Between 1938 and 1952 he worked in New York, where he was inspired by the technological ingenuity of American industrial production methods. Following his return to Germany in 1952, Kramer embarked upon the most important work of his career, which consisted of twenty-three institute and lecture-hall

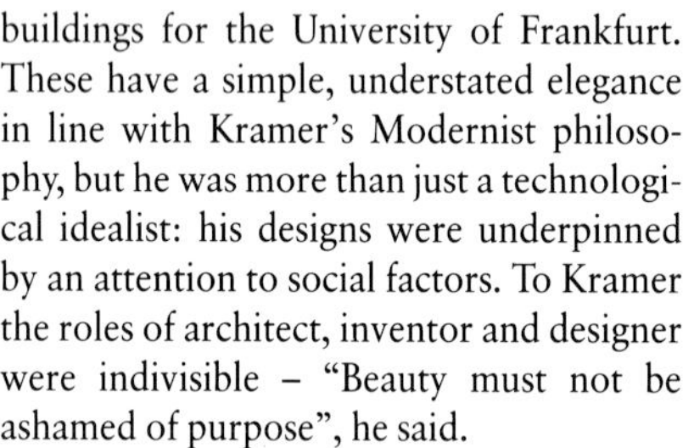

buildings for the University of Frankfurt. These have a simple, understated elegance in line with Kramer's Modernist philosophy, but he was more than just a technological idealist: his designs were underpinned by an attention to social factors. To Kramer the roles of architect, inventor and designer were indivisible – "Beauty must not be ashamed of purpose", he said.

□ Westhausen Residential Development, Frankfurt-am-Main, 1929. Various institute and lecture-hall buildings, University of Frankfurt, 1952-64.

▷ Henry-Russell Hitchcock and Philip Johnson, *The International Style – Architecture since 1922*, New York, 1932. "Ferdinand Kramer – 85 Years Old", *Bauwelt*, Berlin, Jan. 1983. CS

KUROKAWA Kisho

b. Aichi Prefecture, Japan, 1934.

Possibly the most articulate Japanese architect at work today, whose mature work, although invariably semantically coherent, often involves a complex layering of meanings that result in an architecture of implicit suggestion not brash over-statement. Kurokawa graduated from Kyoto University in 1957 and then studied at the Graduate School of Tokyo University under Kenzo TANGE. His early rejection of orthodox Modernism and the West's obsession with the mechanical analogy led to the founding in 1960 of a determinedly Japanese avant-garde movement known as the Metabolists. The group, which included Fumihiko Maki (b. Tokyo, 1928), hoped to propagate a philosophy of radical change. However, following its initial success at Expo 70 in Osaka, where it designed several exhibition buildings, the group splintered and individual members returned to private practice. Many of Kurokawa's buildings explore the notion of *engawa*, the "inbetween space", where public realm and private space coexist in harmony. His recent architecture has achieved considerable international acclaim and secured a series of prestigious commissions. He abhors any retreat to traditionalism but argues that the synthesis of different countries and their respective cultures offers the most appropriate response to the contemporary malaise.

Kisho Kurokawa, Municipal Museum of Art, Nagoya, 1987, with sculpture by Alexander Calder in the foreground

□ Nakagin Capsule Tower, Tokyo, 1972. Saitama Prefectural Museum of Modern Art, Urawa, 1982. Koshi Kaikan Centre, Toyama, 1986. Municipal Museum of Art, Nagoya, 1987. Municipal Museum of Contemporary Art, Hiroshima, 1988.

▷ Kisho Kurokawa, *Metabolism in Architecture*, London, 1977; *Rediscovering Japanese Space*, New York, Tokyo, 1988; *The Architecture of Symbiosis*, New York, 1988. Philip Drew, *The Third Generation*, New York, 1972. MC

▷ *see also pp208-9*

LABROUSTE Pierre François Henri

b. Paris, 1801; d. Paris, 1875.

Most important of the "romantic rationalists". He enrolled at the Ecole des Beaux Arts in 1819 under Vaudoyer and Lebas, winning the Grand Prix in 1824, and then studied at the French Academy in Rome (1824-30), where he developed his ideas with a like-minded group of architects variously termed "romantic rationalists" or "romantic radicals". He fell out with the Beaux Arts over his restoration study (1828) of the ancient Greek temples at Paestum, not as ideal monuments but actual buildings of a somewhat decadent style. Despite this his breakthrough came in 1838 with the Bibliothèque Sainte-Geneviève, which has always been recognized as one of the great masterpieces of C19 architecture, innovatory and forward-looking in its planning, its reinterpretation of classical detail and its decorative scheme as well as its internal use of cast iron. Labrouste believed that architecture should reflect society. But as well as the rationalism and techniques of industrial society, his work also embodies the ideals of the romantic writer Victor Hugo, who believed that architecture is a form of communication, like literature, and that in "organic phases" of construction it expressed a coherent body of social belief.

□ Project for a *cour de cassation*, 1824. Restoration study for Paestum, 1828. Ridèle and Brunet Tombs, Montparnasse Cemetery, Paris, 1837. Bibliothèque Sainte-Geneviève, Paris, designed 1838-9, built 1843-50. Collège Sainte-Barbe, Paris (with Théodore Labrouste), 1840-41. Seminary, Rennes, 1853-75. Bibliothèque Nationale, Paris, 1854-75. Hôtel Fould, Paris, 1856-8. Clugny Tomb, Fontenay-aux-Roses, 1856. Hôtel Thouret, Neuilly-sur-Seine, 1860. Hôtel Rouvenet, Neuilly-sur-Seine, 1861. Paris-Lyon-Méditerranée Railway Administration Offices, Paris, 1862. Hôtel Vilgruy, Paris, 1865. Zolla Tomb, Montparnasse Cemetery, Paris, 1865.

▷ A. Drexler (ed.), *The Architecture of the Ecole des Beaux-Arts*, Cambridge, Mass., 1977. R. Middleton (ed.), *The Beaux-Arts and Nineteenth-Century French Architecture*, London, 1982. TC

▷ *see also pp220-21*

LARSON Henning

b. Copenhagen, 1925.

One of Denmark's elder statesmen of modern architecture. He received his architectural education at the Royal Academy of Fine Arts, Copenhagen, and the AA, and did his postgraduate training at MIT. In the early part of his long career he worked with both Arne JACOBSEN and Jørn UTZON before commencing practice on his own account. In 1968 he was appointed professor of architecture at the Danish Royal Academy. His practice became well-known for extensive competition wins, both locally and internationally; two in particular in the 1960s were widely published, a second prize for the University of Berlin and the University of Trondheim, which was built. The four-storey, marble faced, monumental Ministry of Foreign Affairs at Riyadh received wide international acclaim and an Aga Khan Award (1989). It imaginatively combines traditional Islamic urban concepts (citadel, street, bazaar, etc.) with international modern forms. A further Saudi commission followed with the Danish Embassy building. In Denmark the Community Centre and Library at Gentofte is a more recent project, as is the *Nation* Building, Nairobi.

□ St Jorgen's Hill School, Roskilde (with Brüel, Borfne, Busch and Selchau), 1958-9. Trondheim University, Norway, 1970-77. Ministry of Foreign Affairs, Riyadh, Saudi Arabia, 1979-84. Town and Community Centre, Gentofte, 1987. Danish Embassy, Riyadh, *c.*1987. *Daily Nation* office building, Nairobi, Kenya, from 1989.

Sir Denys Lasdun, National Theatre, London, 1965–76

▷ *New Danish Architecture*, London, 1968. Tobias Faber, *Danish Architecture*, Copenhagen, 1978. DS

▷ *see also pp244-5*

LASDUN Sir Denys

b. London, 1914.

A key second-generation British Modern Movement architect. He trained at the AA School, London, graduating in 1934, and worked initially in association with Wells COATES (1934-7) before joining LUBETKIN and the TECTON group, where he remained until the firm was dissolved in 1948 (he was a partner from 1946). During a partnership with Lindsey Drake (1949-58), Lasdun designed such widely published projects as Hallfield School, Paddington (1951), and clusters of flats at Bethnal Green (1952-5) as well as luxury apartments in St James's (1958). Denys Lasdun and Partners was established in 1960 with Alexander Redhouse and Peter Softley (now called Denys Lasdun, Peter Softley and Partners). Lasdun sees architecture as a "microcosm of the city". His personal design language evolved through many schemes and is about the urban landscape and the way his buildings fit it. It is reinforced by his continual regard for the work of LE CORBUSIER and is based on "routes" (e.g. at the University of East Anglia), the layering of spaces – particularly horizontal levels – and the use of concrete, as well as on nature and its structure and metaphors. He was knighted in 1976 and received the RIBA Royal Gold Medal in 1977.

□ 32 Newton Road, Paddington, London, 1937-8. Hallfield Primary School, Paddington, 1951. LA flats, Bethnal Green, London 1952-5. Apartments, 26 St James's Place, London, 1958. Royal College of Physicians, Regent's Park, London, 1960. National Theatre, London, 1965-76. University of East Anglia, Norwich, 1967-76. European Investment Bank, Luxembourg, 1975.

▷ Denys Lasdun (ed.), *Architecture in the Age of Scepticism*, London, 1984. W. J. B. Curtis, *A Language and a Theme: The Architecture of Denys Lasdun and Partners*, London, 1976. DS

▷ *see also pp240-41*

LATROBE Benjamin Henry

b. Leeds, Yorks., 1764; d. New Orleans, Louisiana, 1820.

Founder of the American architectural profession and instigator of the Greek Revival in the United States. Son of a Moravian minister, Latrobe left England in 1776 and commenced his education at the Moravian Pedagogium in German Silesia. He may also have attended Leipzig University. Interested in engineering, he developed a taste for architecture after travelling round Germany, France and Italy. On his return to England he worked first as an engineer for John Smeaton and then as an architect for S. P. COCKERELL, assisting him on the Admiralty Building in Whitehall, London. Latrobe greatly admired Sir John SOANE, and he may have been familiar with the work of LEDOUX. The fashion for Greek Revivalism had already begun when Latrobe emigrated to America in 1796. He quickly established himself in influential circles, completing a number of houses in Richmond, Virginia, and the Richmond Penitentiary, which put President Thomas JEFFERSON's philosophy of humane penology into practice. In 1798 Latrobe travelled to Philadelphia, where his work on the Bank of Pennsylvania and Philadelphia Water Works are the first examples of Greek Revivalism in America. In 1803 Jefferson summoned him to Washington to complete the United States Capitol, a project which preoccupied him for the rest of his life. However, his Neo-Classical Cathedral in Baltimore (1804-18) is generally considered his best work. Latrobe was the first fully trained architect to work in America and taught and encouraged others. His pupils, STRICKLAND, Robert Mills and William Small, continued working in the Greek Revival style throughout the 1820s and 30s.

□ Bank of Pennsylvania, Philadelphia, 1798. Philadelphia Water Works, Philadelphia, 1799. US Capitol, Washington DC (with others), 1803-17. Baltimore Cathedral, Baltimore, Md, 1804-18.

▷ Talbot F. Hamlin, *Benjamin Henry Latrobe*, New York, 1955. Paul F. Norton, *Latrobe, Jefferson and the National Capitol*, New York & London, 1977.

CS

▷ *see also pp226-7*

LAUGIER Marc Antoine

b. Manosque, 1713; d. Paris, 1769.

Influential Neo-Classical theorist. Laugier was trained as a Jesuit priest and received a humanist education. He went to Paris in 1744 and gained a reputation as a critic and preacher. But after being unwittingly embroiled in political controversy he not only had to leave Paris but opted to leave the Jesuits and worked as editor of the *Gazette de France* and in the diplomatic service. Laugier was a prolific and successful writer but it is for his *Essai sur l'architecture* (1753) that he is best known. There had been various demands since the beginning of the century for a return to a classical lucidity where the

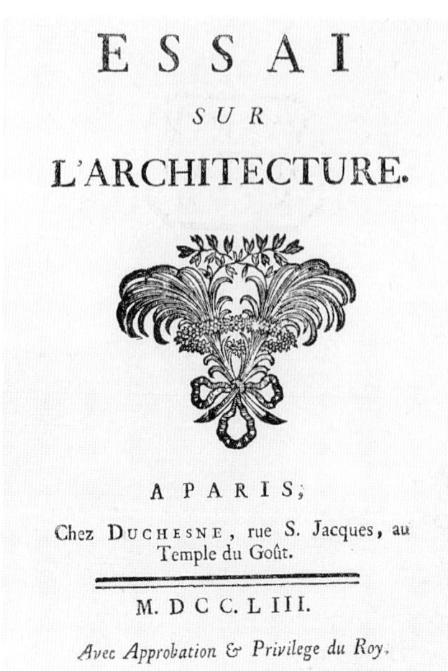
ESSAI
SUR
L'ARCHITECTURE.

A PARIS;
Chez DUCHESNE, rue S. Jacques, au Temple du Goût.

M. D C C. L III.
Avec Approbation & Privilege du Roy.

Marc-Antoine Laugier, title page to Essai sur l'architecture, *1753*

orders were functional rather than decorative. It had long been understood that Greek architecture had evolved from timber structures, but following the hints in VITRUVIUS Laugier postulated the primitive hut fashioned from branches as the origin of the classical temple – to make a compelling image of the way in which "simple nature" and primitive antiquity should be norms for the architect. This combination of rationality and sophisticated yearning for rusticity is central to C18 Neo-Classicism. Laugier's essay was very widely read and influenced amongst others SOUFFLOT and SOANE. For LE CORBUSIER, Laugier's primitive hut was a frequently quoted paradigm.

▷ Marc-Antoine Laugier, *Essai sur l'architecture*, 1753, tr. W. and A. Herrmann, Los Angeles, 1977. A. Braham, *The Architecture of the French Enlightenment*, London, 1980. R. D. Middleton and D. Watkins, *Neo-classical and Nineteenth Century Architecture*, New York, 1980.

TC

LE CORBUSIER

Charles-Edouard Jeanneret-Gris, b. La Chaux de Fonds, Switzerland, 1887; d. Cap Martin, France, 1965.

The most important and influential architect of the C20. Swiss by birth and trained as an artist in his home town under a fastidious teacher, L'Eplattenier, Charles-Edouard Jeanneret (he adopted the pseudonym Le Corbusier only in the early 1920s) was a remarkably talented pupil. He travelled widely in the Near and Middle East, and worked his way through a study tour of Germany at a time when the ideas for a new architecture were being formulated. In 1908-9 he went to Paris to attend classes with Auguste PERRET. Paris later became his *métier*: he was absorbed in the cultural and artistic life of the great city as an editor, a writer, architect and artist. His dedication to the synthesis of the arts – particularly sculpture, painting and drawing and designing – never wavered. His early work, like that of his most important contemporary, Frank Lloyd WRIGHT, was related to nature but also owed much to the famous French theorists Charles Blanc and Auguste Choisy. He began his career as an architect in his native town, building Villa Schwob, an early example of reinforced-concrete construction, in 1916. He had by that time also worked out his basic building diagram, the so-called Maison-Domino, a prototype for mass production with free-standing pillars and rigid oversailing floors. In 1917 he settled in Paris, where, together with his painter and writer colleague Amédée Ozenfant, he issued his Purist manifesto *Après le Cubisme* (1918). With the poet Paul Dermée they edited together a new review, *L'Esprit Nouveau*, from 1920 to 1925, the year in which Le Corbusier won international recognition for the small pavilion of the same name at the 1925 Paris Expo. Two years earlier his book *Vers une architecture*, mainly culled from articles in *L'Esprit Nouveau*, had appeared in French: it was to have worldwide repercussions, the most discussed architectural text of the age. It was translated into German in 1926 and English in 1927, and is still in print. Other influential texts followed, including *L'Art décoratif d'aujourd'hui*, *Urbanisme*, *Le Peinture moderne* (all 1925), *Précisions* (1930), *La Ville radieuse* (1935) and the books on harmonious proportions, *Le Modulor* in 1954 and 1958. From 1922 he worked as an architect in conjunction with his cousin Pierre JEANNERET, and that year they exhibited the Maison Citrohan at the Paris Salon, together with proposals for a city of three million people. Among the early executed domestic projects are the Vaucresson Villa (1922), the Maison La Roche (1923), Maison Cook at Boulogne-sur-Seine (1926), Villa Stein at Garches (1927) and the internationally renowned house and apartment block at the 1927 Stuttgart Werkbund Exhibition, the Weissenhofsiedlung (1927), the Villa Savoye, Poissy (1928-9), and the Clarté Flats in Geneva (1932). These houses, mainly for wealthy clients but not necessarily expensive structures, established the form language of the new rational architecture, which seems to epitomize its definition as a *machine à habiter* ("a machine for living in"). Public buildings included the Swiss Pavilion in the University of Paris (1930-33) and the masterly Cité de Refuge for the Salvation Army in Paris (1929-33). In international competition Le Corbusier did not fare well and complained ceaselessly that he was constantly compromised. He did, however, see the Centrosoyus Building in Moscow built, although he failed to realize his schemes for the League of Nations

Le Corbusier photographed in his Paris studio

in Geneva (1927), the Palace of Soviets (1931), and United Nations, New York (largely carried out by HARRISON & ABRAMOVITZ). He produced town-planning schemes for many parts of the world, often as an adjunct to a lecture tour. In these schemes the routes of mankind (vehicular and pedestrian) and the functional zones of the settlements were always emphasized and eventually embodied in the principles underlying "The Athens Charter", issued as a result of the CIAM Congress IV in 1933. The famous *Ville radieuse*, more personal, humanistic and megalomanic, was issued in book form in 1935. During the Second World War he produced little, emerging with his utopian *Propos d'urbanisme* of 1945 and some years later the fruit of his mathematical meditations in the form of the *Modulor*. In 1947 he began work on his monumental Unité d'habitation at Marseille, completed in 1952. A prototype block of over 300 flats, it had internal streets, duplex maisonettes and internal shopping malls. It was followed by further examples in Berlin, Nantes, Meaux etc. Although relieved of their dominant rectangularity by sculptural roof-lines and highly coloured walls, these massive post-war dwelling blocks received justifiable criticism, although they were also plagiarized throughout the world. As if to contrast with their megalomanic scale, Le Corbusier's post-war small-scale poetic essays in architecture caught many designers unaware of his potentiality as an inventor of rich, new and varied forms. His Maisons Jaoul (1951-5) were a revelation of vernacular materials, brute concrete (*béton brut*) and articulated structure. The Monastery of Ste Marie de la Tourette at Eveux-sur-l'Arbresle (1957-60) and the splendid free-shaped pilgrimage chapel of Notre Dame du Haut at Ronchamp (1950-55) changed the direction of architectural and liturgical thinking. Towards the end of his career Le Corbusier was appointed architect for the public buildings at Chandigarh, the new capital city of the Punjab in India (1952-64), and worked closely with Maxwell FRY and Jane Drew, who with others did a number of infrastructure buildings. This episode ran parallel to the more inspired work carried out at Ahmedabad, where his clients included the wealthy Sarabhai family. With the Shodan House (1956) and the Mill Owners Association (1951-9) some of his early design themes

UNITÉ D'HABITATION, Marseille

This huge seventeen-storey block, providing 337 flats and housing some 1700 people, was designed and built in rough shuttered reinforced concrete by Le Corbusier between 1946-50. The block was a prototype for post-war housing and applicable worldwide. Over 130 m (430 ft) long, the building was raised above ground on piloti, *or stilts, creating a monumental effect in its parkland setting. (The building occupied only about one-tenth of the overall site.) The Unité features centrally-placed interior pedestrian "streets" on alternate floors, and a sculptural roof garden. The proportional harmonics of the building were based on Le Corbusier's* Modulor *system.*

were taken up once again, such as the route, the recessed structural column and the expressive staircase and, of course, the flat undecorated plane, most of which formed part of his celebrated five principles of a free architecture which derive from the late 1920s. With Le Corbusier, every building worked within its time as a testimony to his unremitting genius as the architect of the epoch. Much of it, even though this great architect's popularity was marred by his tendency to overstate his case, will prove of lasting significance and value.

□ Various villas in and around La Chaux de Fonds, Switzerland, 1908-16. Maison Citrohan (first project), 1920. Ozenfant Studio, Paris, 1924. Maison La Roche, Paris-Auteuil, 1925. Pavillon de L'Esprit Nouveau, Paris Exposition, 1925. Villa Cook, Boulogne-sur-Seine, 1927. Houses, Weissenhof Estate, Stuttgart, 1927. Villa Stein, Garches, 1927. Villa Savoye, Poissy, 1928-9. Cité de Refuge, Paris, 1929-33. Maison Clarté, Geneva, 1930-32. Swiss Pavilion, Paris, 1933. Ville Radieuse project, 1935. Ministry of Health and Education, Rio de Janeiro, 1936. "Temps Nouveau" Pavilion, Paris, 1937. Unité d'habitation, Marseille, 1945-8. Duval Factory, St Dié, 1946. Notre Dame du Haut, Ronchamp, 1950-55. Projects and plans, Chandigarh, Punjab (with Fry, Drew and Jeanneret), 1951-64. Maisons Jaoul, 1951-5. Ahmedabad villas and Mill Owners Association, between 1954 and 1959. Ste Marie de la Tourette monastery, Eveux-sur-l'Arbresle, 1957-60. Carpenter Centre for the Visual Arts, Cambridge, Mass. (with SERT), 1959-63. Centre Le Corbusier, Zürich, 1963-5. Cultural Centre, Firminy, 1965.

▷ Charles Edouard Jeanneret (Le Corbusier), *Etude du mouvement d'art décoratif en Allemagne*, La Chaux de Fonds, 1912 (reissued, New York, 1968); *Vers une architecture*, Paris, 1923; *Urbanisme*, Paris, 1925; *L'Art décoratif d'aujourd'hui*, Paris, 1925 (1959); *Le Peinture moderne*, Paris, 1926; *Une Maison – un palais*, Paris, 1928; *Précisions: sur un état présent de l'architecture et de l'urbanisme*, Paris, 1928 (1960); *La Ville radieuse*, Paris 1935 (1964); *Quand les Cathédrales étaient blanches*, Paris, 1937; *Les Trois Etablissements humains*, Paris, 1945; *UN Headquarters*, New York, 1947; *Le Modulor*, Boulogne-sur-Seine, 1950; *Modulor 2*, Boulogne-sur-Seine, 1955; *Le Livre de Ronchamp* (*c*.1956, multilingual editions), etc. S. Von Moos, *Le Corbusier: Elements of a Synthesis*, Cambridge, Mass., 1968, 1979. R. Walden (ed.), *The Open Hand*, Cambridge, Mass., 1977. W. Curtis, *Le Corbusier: Ideas and Forms*, London and New York, 1986. For a full bibliography with English and other foreign-language titles, see D. Brady, *Le Corbusier: an annotated bibliography*, New York, 1985. DS

▷ *see also pp234-7, 240-41*

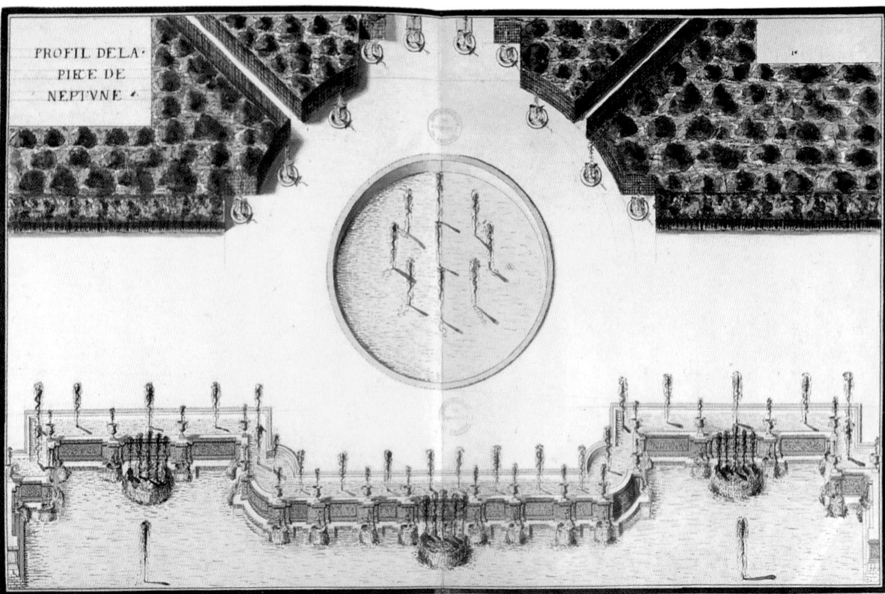

André Le Nôtre, design for park at Versailles, 1661–87

LE NÔTRE André

b. 1613; d. 1700.

Leading French landscape architect of the C17 whose career almost spanned the reign of Louis XIV. He was probably born in Paris, and followed a family tradition to become the third generation of garden designers to the court. He was initially trained in drawing and design by the painter Simon Vouet before taking up his official duties at the Jardin des Tuileries in 1637. Le Nôtre merged the practices of garden designer and architect, eventually becoming a member of the Academy of Architecture (1681). His good fortune with royal patronage led to a lifetime's work on a grand scale that eclipsed all his contempories. The name "Lenôtre" (as it was sometimes written) was synonymous with the Baroque architecture of his time and was influential (in terms of landscaped vistas and symmetry) throughout continental Europe until the end of the C19. His masterpiece is the 15,000-acre park at Versailles, landscaped in a period of four years with a labour force of up to 20,000 soldiers; the buildings and other works took a further 22 years to complete. The huge concept was unified by a complex geometry that ties the extensive layout into harmony with the palace.

□ Vaux-le-Vicomte (his first significant private commission), 1656-61. Versailles, 1661-87. Fontainebleau, 1662-87. Greenwich Park, London, 1662. Chantilly, 1663-88. St-Cloud, 1665-78. Palais des Tuileries, Paris, 1665-87. Grand Trianon, Versailles, 1670-87. Windsor, England, 1698.

▷ Helen M. Fox, *André Le Nôtre, Garden Architect to Kings*, New York, 1962. Julia S. Berrall, *The Garden. An Illustrated History*, New York, 1978. W. H. Adams, *The French Garden 1500-1800*, New York, 1979. Hazleburgh F. Hamilton, *Gardens of Illusion*, Nashville, Tennessee, 1980. AB

LE VAU Louis

b. Paris, 1612; d. Paris, 1670.

Leading French architect of the mid-C17, whose subtle mastery of the Baroque style and practical approach to the demands of his patrons ensured his position over his two main rivals François MANSART and Jacques LEMERCIER. Le Vau's architectural education was supervised by his father, a successful master mason. His early residential work, built during the 1630s and 40s, was largely concentrated on the Ile St Louis in Paris, where his elegant, commodious and innovative *hôtels particuliers* form an exquisite example of domestic urban architecture. He was appointed first architect, counsellor and secretary to Louis XIV in 1654 and four years later succeeded Lemercier as principal architect for the Louvre Palace. His ambitions, however, were frustrated in 1667 when the final designs for the Colonnade were transferred to a committee. Le Vau's extensive œuvre includes a series of impressive châteaux throughout France, the most famous being the Royal Palace at Versailles, where the synthesis between LE NÔTRE's landscaping and Le

Vau's architecture represents *the* quintessential expression of the Baroque era.

□ Hôtel Le Vau, Paris, 1640-42. Hôtel Lambert, Paris, 1640-44. Château of Raincy, *c.*1640-45. Royal Palace, Versailles, 1661-70. Collège des Quatre Nations (Institut de France), Paris, 1662-74. Château of Vaux-le-Vicomte, France, 1656-61.

▷ Anthony Blunt, *Art and Architecture in France 1500-1700*, Harmondsworth, 1953, 1973. Constance Tooth, "Early Private Houses of Le Vau", *Burlington Magazine*, No.109, 1967. Christian Norberg-Schulz, *Baroque Architecture*, Milan, 1971.

MC

▷ *see also pp216-19*

LEDOUX Claude Nicolas

b. Dormans, 1736; d. Paris, 1806.

Leading architect of pre-Revolutionary France, pre-eminent Neo-Classicist. Ledoux came from a provincial bourgeois background. Unusually he was not educated at the Académie but at the private architectural school in Paris established by J. F. BLONDEL, where he was trained in the native Baroque tradition but also exposed to English architecture. Ledoux was qualified as engineer for bridge design and until the Revolution held a number of government positions. He also received fashionable commissions, notably the du Barry Château, which develops the restrained Neo-Classicism of GABRIEL, while the Hôtel Montmorency is a more typical combination of ingenious planning and severely simplified classicism. His dramatic and "visionary" style possibly owes something to the fact that he never went to Rome, relying on the engravings of PIRANESI for his knowledge of Roman architecture. But he did visit England, where he was influenced by the Palladian tradition (*see* PALLADIO), with which he was already familiar, and possibly by the work of Robert ADAM. Much of Ledoux's architecture is practical and self-consciously "functional". The theatre at Besançon (1775-84), was bold and original, featuring a covered pit and also, logically, adapting classical architecture to the needs of a modern theatre with an amphitheatre of three semicircular tiers of seats rising to a ring of Doric columns. But it is the visionary and expressive aspects of his work that are better known. The semicircular plan of the salt works at Arc-et-Senans again shows his interest in geometry, and the buildings themselves are full of metaphor: the director's house, for example, is exaggeratedly rusticated to express the industrial function and to symbolize the power of the state, which had the monopoly of salt distillation. A similar intention lies behind Ledoux's prolific designs for over fifty *barrières* or custom houses, which surrounded Paris and became symbols of the *ancien régime*; their exaggerated use of classical elements seems to anticipate post-modern classicism. The salt works was to form the basis of his frequently illustrated utopian scheme for the ideal town of Chaux. But although he was subject to the irrational and idealist strains of thought that were sweeping France, Ledoux was not a political revolutionary and indeed was imprisoned as a royalist during the Revolution. In contrast to the visionary BOULLEE, Ledoux was concerned with practicalities and accepted the *status quo*.

Claude Nicolas Ledoux, Barrière de la Villette, Paris, 1784–9

□ Café interior, rue St Honoré, Paris, 1762. Cathedral of St Germain (decoration), Auxerre, *c.*1762-1764. Château Hôtel d'Uzes, 1764. Hôtel d'Hallwyl, Paris, 1766-7. Hôtel de Montmorency, Paris, 1769. Château for Madame du Barry, Louveciennes, Paris, 1771-3. Pavillon Guimard, Paris, 1773-6. Theatre, Besançon, 1775-84. Salt works, Arc-et-Senans, 1775-9. Designs for Ville de Chaux, *c.*1780 (published 1804). *Barrières* (custom houses), Paris, 1784-9.

▷ C. L. Ledoux, *L'Architecture considérée sous le rapport de l'art, des mœurs et de la législation*, Paris, 1804. M. Gallet, *Ledoux*, Paris, 1980. A. Braham, *The Architecture of the French Enlightenment*, London, 1980. A. Vidler, *Claude-Nicolas Ledoux*, Cambridge, Mass., 1990.

TC

▷ *see also pp220-21*

LEMERCIER Jacques

b. Pontois, c.1585; d. Paris, 1654.

A leading French architect of the mid-C17, though often considered somewhat pedestrian in comparison with his contemporaries, Louis LE VAU and François MANSART. Born into a family of architects and master masons, he received his early training with his father. After his apprenticeship he spent some years in Rome, where it is thought he worked under Rosato Rosati on S. Carlo ai Catinari. The influence of this early Baroque church is clearly evident in Lemercier's design for the church of the Sorbonne some twenty years later. After returning to Paris in 1615 his first major commission came in 1624 when Louis XIII invited him to complete the construction of Pierre Lescot's Square Court at the Louvre Palace. That same year Lemercier secured the patronage of the man who would eventually become his principal benefactor, Cardinal de Richelieu. The cardinal's wealth and

Jacques Lemercier, Church of the Sorbonne, Paris, 1626–42

importance were such that Lemercier secured a series of prestigious projects, including the Palais Cardinal, the church of the Sorbonne, the enlarging and landscaping of a château at Rueil, and the design and construction of a small town near Richelieu's childhood home in Poitou.

□ Pavillon de l'Horloge at the Louvre, Paris, 1624-41. Palais Cardinal (later the Palais Royal), Paris, 1624-36. Church of the Sorbonne, Paris, 1626-42. Palais Cardinal theatre, Paris, 1639.

▷ Reginald Blomfield, *History of French Architecture*, New York, 1921. Anthony Blunt, *Art and Architecture in France 1500-1700*, Harmondsworth, 1953, 1973. MC

L'ENFANT Pierre Charles

b. Paris, 1754; d. Maryland, 1825.

French émigré architect and engineer who influenced the development of post-Georgian classical style in America. L'Enfant came from an artistic background (his father Pierre was a painter in the service of the French court) and in 1771 became a student at the Royal Academy of Painting and Sculpture, instructed by his father. Despite this artistic pedigree, there is no indication that he had any formal architectural training. In 1777 L'Enfant arrived in America, having volunteered to serve in the American army during the War of Independence. His role was largely non-combative and involved preparing drawings for army training manuals. By 1782 he was in Philadelphia and had turned his attention towards architecture. Four years later he settled in New York and began to design in earnest, remodelling the old City Hall to become the Federal Hall, the first Congress Hall of the new American nation. L'Enfant's most important work, however, was his plan for the Federal Capitol in Washington, which was unique in the way it responded to the site and accommodated the needs of the new government. His visionary design was largely based on the principles of Baroque planning, in particular the layout of Versailles. His introduction of a French classical framework proved an influential model for later generations of American planners and architects, but although his Washington plan was implemented, he was later dismissed from the project after disagreements with the authorities. His last years were spent in reduced circumstances, but he remained a highly respected figure in the American architectural establishment.

□ Federal Hall (remodelling), New York, 1788-9. Plan for the Federal Capitol, Washington DC, 1791.

▷ John W. Reps, *Monumental Washington: The Planning and Development of the Capital Center*, New Jersey, 1967. Paul H. Caemmerer, *The Life of Pierre Charles L'Enfant*, Washington, 1970. CS

LEONARDO DA VINCI

b. Vinci, near Florence, 1472; d. Cloux, near Amboise, 1519.

Although he built little or nothing, Leonardo's many architectural drawings reveal a new concern with form that anticipates the High Renaissance style of BRAMANTE in Rome, and in particular the designs for New St Peter's. Having excelled as a painter in Florence, Leonardo transferred to the ducal court in Milan (*c.* 1481-99), where he became increasingly involved with architecture and engineering and came into contact with Bramante and Francesco di Giorgio. Many of his architectural studies date from around 1488, when he was working on a design for the domed crossing of Milan Cathedral, and these include the rich MS B and MS 2184 (Bibliothèque Nationale, Paris) with their surveys of church designs that were probably intended for an architectural treatise. Most of the designs are for centrally-planned buildings which incorporate both Florentine and Milanese elements and achieve a considerable complexity, with the main domed areas surrounded by a variety of subsidiary spaces. The designs are usually set out carefully in plan but without scaled elevations and sections. Often, however, Leonardo also supplies bird's-eye views of the buildings which explore not so much the details of articulation but the coherent massing of solids in a way that is analogous to some of his studies of figure composition.

▷ C. Pedritti, *Leonardo Architetto*, Milan. P. C. Marani, *L'Architettura Fortificata negli Studi di Leonardo da Vinci*, Florence, 1984. P. Galuzzi (ed), *Leonardo da Vinci, Engineer and Architect*, Montreal, 1987. DH

LEONI Giacomo

b. Venice, 1686; d. London, 1746.

Italian architect of the Palladian school who lived and worked in England. Little is known of Leoni's early life and training. Before his arrival in England *c.*1713, he had worked in Düsseldorf, where he assisted Matteo de Alberti in the building of Schloss Bensberg near Cologne. A disciple of PALLADIO, Leoni published the first English edition of Palladio's *Four Books on Architecture* (1716-20), which proved enormously influential in the Palladian revival in England. However he failed to attract the attention or patronage of Lord BURLINGTON, one of the movement's leading figures. Leoni's architectural output consisted mainly of large country houses, which, unlike the designs of Burlington and his circle, incorporated certain Baroque twists, but his Queensbury House, London, provided a widely copied blueprint for the classic English Palladian town house. In 1726 Leoni published a three-volume translation of *The Architecture of L. B. Alberti.*

□ Queensbury House, London, 1721-3. Lyme Park, Cheshire, 1725-30. Clandon Park, Surrey, 1731-5.

▷ Rudolf Wittkower, "Giacomo Leoni's Edition of Palladio's 'Quattro Libri dell' Architettura'", *Arte*

Giacomo Leoni, Clandon Park, Surrey, 1731–5, entrance hall

Veneta, 1954, No. 8; "English Neoclassicism and the Vicissitudes of Palladio's *Quattro Libri*", 1970, in *Palladio and English Palladianism*, London, 1974. Peter Collins, "New Light on Leoni", *Architectural Review*, 1960, 127. CS

LEONIDOV Ivan Ilich

b. Vlasikh, near Tver, Russia, 1902; d. Moscow, 1959.

Leading but unconforming member of the Russian Constructivist group. He entered the Free Art Studios in Tver in 1920, moving to the Painting Faculty of Moscow Vkhutemas in 1921, and then to the Architecture Faculty under Alexander Vesnin, graduating in 1927. He was a student member of the Constructivists' Union of Contemporary Architects, OSA, later joining the editorial board of its journal. After graduate studies, he worked in 1931 for GIPROGOR (the State Institute for Town Planning) and in 1932 became head of a design studio in Moscow City Soviet. From 1934 he worked on Crimean leisure complexes under OSA co-founder Moisei Ginzburg in a studio of the Heavy Industry Commissariat (NKTP). After war service and jobs in the USSR Academy of Architecture, Leonidov's later years were spent in menial jobs whilst depicting his architectural visions in paintings. He rejected the balanced functionalism of mainstream Constructivist design to emphasize the exploitation of technology. In architecture this meant a boldly high-tech approach beyond the USSR's resources; at the planning scale, it meant maximum use of transport, radio etc. to facilitate dispersal of prismatic building forms in a spatial system that was more Suprematist than Constructivist. From his work Soviet opponents of Modernism coined the label "Leonidovism" to condemn all impractical and therefore "unsocialist" projects. He built virtually nothing, but his graduation and competition projects of the 1920s were highly influential. From the 1930s he pursued a subtle synthesis of his own aesthetic with the historicist demands of Socialist Realism.

Ivan Leonidov, Lenin Institute, Moscow, 1927, project

□ Lenin Institute (graduation project), Moscow, 1927. Sovkino production complex, 1927. Tsentrosoyuz project, 1928. Workers' Club complexes, 1928, 1930. Magnitogorsk new town, 1930. NKTP headquarters, Moscow, 1934. Kislovodsk sanatorium landscaping (partly built), 1937-8. City of the Sun, painted projects, 1943-59.

▷ A. Gozak and A. Leonidov, *Ivan Leonidov: The Complete Works*, London and New York, 1988. CC

LESCAZE William

see Howe & Lescaze

LETHABY William Richard

b. Barnstaple, Devon, 1857; d. London, 1931.

Architect, critic, historian, theorist and teacher who stood at the transition between Arts & Crafts ideas and the development of modern architecture in England. After leaving school at fourteen in Barnstable, he was articled to a local architect, Alexander Lauder, then proceeded, briefly by way of Derby, to Norman SHAW's office in London in 1879. Between then and 1892, when he began his independent practice, he became a close friend and disciple of Philip WEBB and William MORRIS, eventually serving as President of the Arts and Crafts Exhibition Society. He became founding joint principal, with George Frampton, of the Central School of Arts and Crafts in 1894, and was also Professor of Design at the Royal College of Art from 1900. His practice, which included several major country houses, e.g. at Avon Tyrell in Hampshire, The Hurst at Sutton Coldfield, and Melsetter in Orkney, ended with the church of All Saints at Brockhampton in 1902-4; he felt himself unequipped for the challenges of practice in the new century, and thenceforth restricted his activities to teaching, writing and lecturing. He was the principal guide to Hermann MUTHESIUS during that official's studies of British architecture.

□ Avon Tyrell, Hants., 1891. The Hurst, Sutton Coldfield, 1893. Melsetter, Orkney, 1898. Eagle Insurance Building (with J. L. Ball), Birmingham, 1900. All Saints, Brockhampton, Herefordshire, 1902.

▷ William Richard Lethaby, *Architecture, Mysticism and Myth*, London, 1891, (rewritten as articles for *The Builder*, 1928, as *Architecture, Nature and Magic*, and later published London, 1956); *Architecture: An Introduction to the History and Theory of the Art of Building*, London, 1912. Godfrey Ruben, *W. R. Lethaby, His Life and Work*, London, 1986. Robert Macleod, "Lethaby as a Key to Mackintosh" in *Mackintosh and His Contemporaries in Europe and America*, ed. Patrick Nuttgens, London, 1988. RM

▷ *see also pp228-9*

LEWERENTZ Sigurd

b. Bjärtra, Sweden, 1885; d. Lund, 1975.

Deeply original and wilful Swedish modernist, much revered as an "architects' architect". He began his career in mechanical engineering but transferred to building technology at the Institute of Technology, Gothenburg, (1903-8). He worked for a time as a smith, which undoubtedly prepared him for the period later in his life when he supervised every aspect of a building and worked on site. In 1909 he travelled to Italy and then Germany, where he worked in the offices of Theodor Fischer and Richard Riemerschmid before returning to Stockholm and to classes under ÖSTBERG, TENGBOM and Westman at the Klara School. He took up employment with Westman in 1910 but left to commence practice on his own account the year following. In 1914, with his colleague Gunnar ASPLUND, he won the competition for the cemetery in Enskede, and a year later he won first prize for a cemetery in Malmö. He participated in many other competitions over the next decade, receiving first prize for a new theatre in Malmö in 1925 and the premier award in the posters competition (1929) for the Stockholm Exhibition. In 1940 Lewerentz went into window and door production, and it was not until the early 1950s that he came into prominence again, regarded at first with some suspicion but increasingly acknowledged as one of the most sophisticated architects of the C20, "a silent genius", as one critic has put it. Two projects in particular demonstrate this kind of assessment: St Mark's Church, Björkhagen (1956-60), and St Peter's Church, Klippan (1963-6), both of which demonstrate a remarkable originality of thought both spatially and in the use of local natural materials. He was not a radical but a craftsman artist who would demonstrate ideas for building on site with the workmen; he was an architect in control of the building operation who struggled to give birth to an idea both on paper and on site. By all accounts he was not an easy man to work for, or with. But for all the growth of independence in his latter years he must be viewed as one of the catalysts of Nordic Classicism earlier on. His finest building still remains the one with the "impossible perspective": the beautifully proportioned "Chapel of the Resurrection" in the Woodland Cemetery (1925).

□ Woodland Cemetery, Enskede, Stockholm, 1914-34, and "Chapel of the Resurrection", 1922-5. Cemetery Chapel, Kvarnsveden, 1921. Concert Hall, Theatre, Malmö 1927. Crematorium and Chapels, Eastern Cemetery, Malmö, 1943-69. St Mark's Church and Community Hall, Björkhagen, Stockholm, 1956-60. The Petri (St Peter's) Church, Klippan, 1963-6. Flower Kiosk, Eastern Cemetery, Malmö, 1969.

▷ Janne Ahlin, *Sigurd Lewerentz: Architect 1885-1975*, Stockholm 1987. Dennis Sharp, "Unsung Hero", *Building Design*, 18 Sept. 1987. *Sigurd Lewerentz 1885-1975: The Dilemma of Classicism* (exhibition catalogue), London, 1989.

DS

LISSITZKY EL

Lazar Markovich Lissitzky, b. Pochinok, near Smolensk, 1890; d. Moscow, 1941.

Painter, architect and brilliant graphic designer who formed a unique bridge between Russian and European avant-gardes in the 1920s. Barred from Russian higher education because he was Jewish, Lissitzky studied architecture at the Technische Hochschule in Darmstadt (1909-14) and then evacuated for the First World War, at the Riga Polytechnic (1915-16), where he exhibited as a painter, and also worked in book design and graphics. In 1919-21 he taught at the Vitebsk Art School under Chagall and then MALEVICH. From the latter's Suprematism he developed his own concept of the Proun: "the interchange station between painting and architecture." After some participation in agitational art and theoretical debates, Lissitzky spent the years 1921-5 in Germany and Switzerland for tuberculosis treatment. His association with the Erste Russische Kunstausstellung in Berlin (1922), the exhibition which first showed Russian abstraction to the West, led to increasing involvement with the European avant-garde and collaboration on such journals as *Veshch*, *G*, *ABC* and *Merz*. His Prouns and Proun-rooms were shown in European exhibitions, and he was in contact with *De Stijl*, the Bauhaus etc. Returning to Moscow in 1926 he pioneered space-saving furniture design in the Vkhutemas school, for Constructivist housing etc. and produced the Rationalist architects' broadsheet *ASNOVA-News*, which published his Wolkenbügel scheme of "horizontal skyscrapers" for central Moscow. In his later life he entered architectural competitions and wrote architectural journalism, but was most important for his brilliant application of Constructivist and Suprematist aesthetics to typography and graphic and exhibition design.

□ PROUNS, 1919-21. Der Wolkenbügel, Moscow, 1923-5. Soviet section, Pressa exhibition, Cologne, 1928. *Pravda* building, Moscow, 1930.

▷ El Lissitzky, *Russia: the Reconstruction of Architecture in the Soviet Union*, Vienna, 1930 (republished Vienna, 1965 and London/Cambridge, 1970, as *Russia: An Architecture for World Revolution*). S. Lissitzky-Küppers, *El Lissitzky*, Dresden, 1967, London, 1968. S. O. Khan-Magomedov, *Pioneers of Soviet Architecture*, Dresden, 1983, London, 1987.

CC

▷ *See also pp230-31*

LOOS Adolf

b. Brno (now in Czechoslovakia), 1870; d. Vienna, 1933.

Pioneering theorist and exponent of the Modern Movement in Europe. His father's trade of stonemason was to exert a powerful formative influence on the young Adolf Loos; so too were the three years he spent in the USA on completion of his architectural studies at the Technische Hochschule in Dresden. He found integrity in the honest toil of the craftsman and a modern, civilized lifestyle in America. Loos returned to Europe in 1896 to live in Vienna, where he came into contact with the circle of young architects and artists who in the following year were to form the breakaway Secession. He soon became their most forthright and vocal critic, condemning their "fanciful creations" as mere fashion. Loos argued for the lasting quality of design, unhindered by decorative ornament and applied style. The work and materials of the craftsman should not be demeaned by the latest fashions, he argued. Carriages, saddles, bicycles and locomotives were his favoured icons for the modern age; ancient Greece and Rome, England and America served as exemplars. Loos' celebrated essay "*Ornament und Verbrechen*" ("Ornament and Crime") was published in 1908, two years after he had set up a Free School of Architecture in Vienna to gain wider acceptance of his ideas. Loos' architectural work provides an intriguing counterpoint to his theories. His early projects

Adolf Loos, Scheu house, Vienna, 1912–13

owe much to the classical vision of Karl Friedrich SCHINKEL; indeed a classical rationale persists in his projects, even the overtly modern houses of the 1930s. The sequence of projects represents an increasing distillation of a classical model, purifying his buildings of decoration. What remains, however, is the true ornamentation inherent in materials and the manner in which they are crafted: timber, fabrics and particularly marbles.

□ Café Museum, Vienna, 1899. Villa Karma, Montreux, 1903-9. Kärtner Bar, Vienna, 1908. Steiner House, Vienna, 1910. Scheu House, Vienna, 1912-13. Michaelerplatz (Loos Haus), Vienna, 1910. Tristan Tzara House, Paris, 1925. Moller House, Vienna, 1928. Müller House, Prague. 1928-30.

▷ Adolf Loos, *Spoken into the Void: collected essays*, Cambridge, Mass., 1982. Ludwig Münz and Gustav Künstler, *Der Architekt Adolf Loos*, Vienna and Munich, 1964. B. Gravagnuolo, *Adolf Loos – Teoria e opera*, Milan, 1981. IL

▷ *see also pp236-7*

LORIMER Robert Stodart

b. Edinburgh, 1864; d. Gibliston, 1929.

Scotland's leading country house architect of the early C20, who combined the sophistication of his English contemporary Edwin LUTYENS with the rugged simplicity of his native vernacular tradition. He studied for three years at Edinburgh University but left without graduating to take up an apprenticeship in 1884. Later he moved south to London to work with George Frederick BODLEY, a leading figure in the Arts & Crafts movement, but he returned to Edinburgh to establish his own office in 1893 and worked primarily on domestic projects. Lorimer's early houses display a studied informality which fuses elements of both Scottish and English Arts & Crafts to produce a pleasingly picturesque composition. He fostered a close working relationship with local craftsmen and used their skills to realize numerous designs for furniture, stained glass and domestic fittings. Commissions became progressively larger in scale and more eclectic in their stylistic origin. The period immediately after the First World War was overshadowed by his appointment as principal architect to the Imperial War Graves Commission (1918).

□ Wayside House, St Andrews, 1902. Hill of Tarvit House, Fife, 1905. Thistle Chapel, Edinburgh, 1909. Balmanno House, Glenfarg, 1916. National War Memorial, Edinburgh, 1928.

▷ Christopher Hussey, *The Work of Sir Robert Lorimer*, London, 1931. Peter Savage, *Lorimer and the Edinburgh Craft Tradition*, Edinburgh, 1980. MC

LUBETKIN Berthold

b. Tiflis, Georgia, 1901; d. Bristol, 1990

One of a number of highly influential architects who emigrated to Britain from mainland Europe in the 1930s and brought with them a belief and understanding in the modern International Style. Lubetkin studied first in Russia (under Rodchenko, TATLIN and Vesnin), then in Berlin and Warsaw before settling in Paris, attending the Ecole des Beaux Arts amongst other schools. Here, he was able to see first-hand the early experimental work of LE CORBUSIER, at the same time as mastering the use of reinforced concrete under PERRET. A short-lived practice with Jean Ginsberg produced an apartment block, before Lubetkin left for England in 1930. Two years later he helped found the Tecton group with a group of AA graduates, and was actively involved in both the MARS group and CIAM. Highpoint I, Tecton's first major large-scale commission, was widely admired (in particular by Le Corbusier) for its rational organization of high-density living quarters and communal spaces. Its white walls, smooth façades and strip fenestration are the hallmarks of the

Berthold Lubetkin, Penguin Pool, London Zoo, 1933–4

International Style; the team's Penguin Pool of two years earlier is, however, more abstract in conception. The Finsbury Health Centre reveals a plan and elevations dictated by function, a preoccupation seen in the work of one of the firm's later members, Denys LASDUN.

☐ Apartment building, 25 avenue de Versailles, Paris (with J. Ginsberg), 1927-9. Gorilla House and Penguin Pool, London Zoo, 1933-4. Highpoint I, Highgate, London (with Tecton), 1933-5. Finsbury Health Centre, London (with Tecton), 1935-8. Highpoint II, Highgate, London (with Tecton), 1936–8. Hallfield Estate, Paddington, London (with Tecton), 1947-55.

▷ B. Lubetkin, *Finsbury Health Centre*, London, 1938. B. Lubetkin and others, *La Modernité, un Projet Inachevé*, Paris, 1982. Dennis Sharp (ed.), *The Rationalists: Theory and Design in the Modern Movement*, London, 1978. Alastair Service, *The Architects of London*, London, 1979. John S. Allan, *Lubetkin and Tecton*, London, 1981. PP

▷ *see also pp238-9*

LUCAS Colin

see Connell, Ward & Lucas

LURÇAT André

b. Bruyères, 1894; d. Sceaux, 1970.

Radical architect, academic and pioneer within the French Modern Movement. Lurçat's education at the Ecole Municipale des Beaux Arts, Nancy, and the Ecole Nationale Supérieur des Beaux Arts in Paris was interrupted by the First World War. He was in private practice from 1923 to 1934 and from 1937 until his death, and he lectured in architecture at the Ecole des Arts Décoratifs in Paris 1939-43. He was involved in the post-war reconstruction of Paris, both as planner and architect, but his loyalties were divided between architecture and politics. He was founder member of CIAM in 1928, and published his radical manifesto *Architecture* a year later. Influenced by the functionalist doctrines of LE CORBUSIER and Adolf LOOS, Lurçat established his reputation in the mid-1920s with a series of artists' studios in Versailles and Paris. Working with simple forms, practising rationalization and standardization, he remained true to the ideals of CIAM by "putting architecture back on its real plane, the economical and social plane". Lurçat's best work dates from before a disastrous trip to Russia in 1934-6, which broke his spirit and obliged the former radical, who had seen architecture as a means of social change, to tread the middle ground of compromise. The resulting work – mostly housing, schools and town halls – was undistinguished.

☐ Villa Seurat, Paris, 1925-6. Guggenbuhl House, Paris, 1926-7. Hôtel Nord-Sud, Calvi, Corsica, 1930-31. Karl Marx School Complex, Villejuif, 1930-33.

▷ Henry-Russell Hitchcock, *Modern Architecture: Romanticism and Reintegration*, 2nd ed., New York, 1970. Manfredo Tafuri and Francesco Dal Co, *Modern Architecture*, 2nd ed., New York, 1979. CS

LUTYENS Sir Edwin

b. London, 1869; d. London, 1944.

Leading British architect of his generation; after a brilliant beginning in the Arts & Crafts tradition, he committed himself to what he called the "High Game" from 1902, confirmed and set the standard for what became the Edwardian style of architecture, a revival of the classical manner with a strong allegiance to the English Baroque of WREN and his successors. Lutyens became a pupil of Ernest GEORGE in 1887, and met Gertrude Jekyll socially about the time of his commencement of private practice (1889). Although a generation older, she became a close professional collaborator, commissioning Lutyens to design her own house, Munstead Wood, in a garden which she had been establishing (1896), and beginning a succession of houses by Lutyens with gardens by Jekyll, such as Deanery Garden at Sonning, Orchards, Godalming, and Tigbourne Court, Witley, all between 1898 and 1899. All of these houses were in the gentle, easy, informally composed manner of what has since been called the "English Free School". They had, in the manner of Philip WEBB, classical and other historic allusions, always contained, however, in a locally identifiable range of materials and building traditions, organized around the functional disposition of building spaces. Suddenly, with really no forewarning, Lutyens' designs for Heathcote near Ilkley (1906), emerged in a fully developed classical/ Baroque manner in the Doric and Ionic orders. The achievement of this *tour-de-force*, with its comprehensive system of

Sir Edwin Lutyens, Castle Drogo, nr Drewsteignton, Devon, 1910–30

coupled columns and ordered compositional completeness showed an immediate mastery of the classical language of architecture without precedent since C. R. COCKERELL, but achieved, it would seem, without any of his education and background. From this beginning, Lutyens remained committed to the disciplines of the Orders for the rest of his working life. His Doll's House for Queen Mary and the British Embassy in Washington (1928) are typical examples of his developed classical manner. He was knighted in 1918, received the Gold Medal of the RIBA in 1921, and was President of the Royal Academy in 1938.

☐ Munstead Wood, Godalming, Surrey, 1896. Deanery Garden, Sonning, Berks., 1898. Orchards, Godalming, 1898-9. Tigbourne Court, Witley, Surrey, 1899. Heathcote, Ilkley, 1906. St Jude, Hampstead Garden Suburb, London, 1909-11. Castle Drogo, nr Drewsteignton, Devon, 1910-30. Viceroy's House etc., New Delhi, India, from 1912. British Embassy, Washington, DC, 1928.

▷ A. S. G. Butler and Christopher Hussey, *The Architecture of Edwin Lutyens*, London, 1950. Christopher Hussey, *The Life of Edwin Lutyens*, London, 1953. CD

▷ *see also pp224-5*

McKim, Mead & White, Pennsylvania Station, New York, 1902–11

MACKAY David

see Martorell-Bohigas-Mackay

McKIM, MEAD & WHITE

Established 1879. Charles Follen McKim b. Pennsylvania, 1847; d. St James's, New York, 1909. William Rutherford Mead, b. Vermont, 1846; d. Paris, 1928. Stanford White, b. New York, 1853; d. New York, 1906.

A significant New York firm, practising at the end of the C19 and beginning of the C20, which pioneered a more relaxed residential layout (opening the way for Frank Lloyd WRIGHT) at the same time as formalizing civic building. McKim and Mead both worked in the office of Russell Sturgis before forming a loose partnership in New York (joined in 1877 by W. B. Bigelow). White had no formal training but managed to join the firm of H. H. RICHARDSON (as McKim had done) through a family contact, before replacing Bigelow. Initially, the firm designed a number of Shingle-style houses, reaching a geometric purity with the William G. Low House, a low triangular building. For urban houses and civic buildings, the firm looked for inspiration to the classical past – notably the Italian Renaissance – although LABROUSTE's Bibliothèque Sainte-Geneviève in Paris was taken as the starting-point for the Boston Public Library. The Rhode Island State Capitol, built entirely of white marble, served as a model for a whole generation of state capitols and, like many other works of the practice, was embellished with sculptures and paintings. McKim's perfectly formed Pierpont Morgan Library is suitably adorned with inlaid marble floors and sympathetic murals; Pennsylvania Station's façades were left with little detail to facilitate low maintenance, while the interior's dramatic impact lay with huge spaces and a vast glass roof.

□ Henry Villard House, New York, 1882-5. William G. Low House, Bristol, Rhode Island, 1886-7. Goelet Building, New York, 1886-7. Madison Square Garden, New York, 1887-91. Boston Public Library, 1887-98. Herald Building, New York, 1890-95. State Capitol, Providence, Rhode Island, 1891-1903. Columbia University, New York, 1893-1902. Frederick W. Vanderbilt House, New York, 1895-9. Herman Oelrichs House, Newport, Rhode Island, 1897-1902. J. Pierpont Morgan Library, New York, 1902-7. Pennsylvania Station, New York, 1902-11.

▷ A. H. Granger, *Charles Follen McKim: A Study of his Life and Work*, London, 1913. *A Monograph of the Works of McKim, Mead & White*, New York, 1915. Charles H. Reilly, *McKim, Mead & White*, New York, London, 1924. C. Moore, *The Life and Times of Charles Follen McKim*, New York, 1929. Charles C. Baldwin, *Stanford White*, New York, 1931. Leland M. Roth, *The Architecture of McKim, Mead & White*, New York, 1978. PP

MACKINTOSH Charles Rennie

b.Glasgow, 1868; d. London, 1928.

Outstanding Scottish architect, furniture designer, and painter, seen as a pioneer of the Modern Movement and perhaps more importantly, as the greatest flowering of the British Arts & Crafts movement.The son of a superintendent of police, he was apprenticed in 1884 to John Hutchison, architect, and was enrolled at the Glasgow School of Art for evening classes; this was the standard method of training available at the time. In 1889 he became an architectural assistant with Honeyman & Keppie, the firm through which he conducted virtually all his subsequent architectural work. In 1890 he won a travelling scholarship and toured extensively in Italy. His early work, such as the Glasgow Herald Building (1893-5) and Queen Margaret's Medical College (1895), was done with an indeterminate degree of autonomy within Honeyman & Keppie, but the Martyrs' Public School (1895-8) shows some of the maturing characteristics of Mackintosh's principal work, the Glasgow School of Art. This commission, won in limited competition and built in two stages (1897-9 and 1906-9) effectively brackets almost his entire mature architectural output. From his early enrolment at the School of Art Mackintosh had developed a friendship and working relationship with Herbert McNair and the sisters Margaret and Frances Macdonald. Known as "The Four", they exhibited posters, furnishings, and a variety of graphic designs in Glasgow, at the Arts and Crafts Exhibition Society in London, and in Vienna and Turin. The reception in

Vienna in particular was so enthusiastic as to establish Mackintosh by name, reputation, and to a degree by friendships for the rest of his life. In 1900, after McNair and Frances Macdonald had married and removed to Liverpool, Mackintosh and Margaret Macdonald were married. Mackintosh's entry in the 1901 competition for a *Haus eines Kunstfreundes* sponsored by Alexander Koch of Darmstadt in his *Zeitschrift für Innen-Dekoration* was the recipient of a special prize, but more importantly showed to a European audience what he had effectively begun to accomplish in his Windyhill (1899-1901) and what he was to confirm even more assuredly in his design for Hill House, Helensburgh (1902). His continuing commissions for teashops from Miss Catherine Cranston from 1895 onwards gave him a series of opportunities to design everything from furnishings through interiors to napery and murals. In 1913 Mackintosh left the firm of Honeyman, Keppie & Mackintosh, where he had been a partner since 1904, and from then on architectural work virtually ceased for him, apart from minor furnishing, decorative and alteration projects from Miss Cranston, W. J. Bassett-Lowke in Northampton, and a few others. In 1923 the Mackintoshes settled in Port Vendres in the south of France, where he undertook a serious programme of watercolour landscape painting, until his return to London in 1927 for treatment for cancer of the tongue.

□ Glasgow Herald Building, 1893-5. Queen Margaret's Medical College, Glasgow, 1895. Martyrs' Public School, Glasgow, 1895-8. Glasgow School of Art, 1897-1909. Windyhill, Kilmacolm, 1899-1901. Hill House, Helensburgh, 1902. Willow Tearooms, Sauchiehall Street, Glasgow, 1903. Scotland Street School, Glasgow, 1904-6.

▷ Thomas Howarth, *Charles Rennie Mackintosh and the Modern Movement*, London, 1952 (1978). Robert Macleod, *Charles Rennie Mackintosh, Architect and Artist*, London 1968 (1983). Roger Billcliffe, *Architectural Sketches and Flower Drawings by Charles Rennie Mackintosh*, London, 1977; *Mackintosh Watercolours*, London, 1978; *Charles Rennie Mackintosh: The Complete Furniture, Furniture Drawings and Interior Designs*, London, 1979 (1980); *Mackintosh Textile Designs*, London, 1982. Patrick Nuttgens (ed.), *Mackintosh and His Contemporaries in Europe and America*, London, 1988. Pamela Robertson (ed.), *Charles Rennie Mackintosh, The Architectural Papers*, Glasgow, 1990. RM

▷ *see also pp228-31*

MADERNO Carlo

b. Capolago, 1556; d. Rome, 1629.

Outstanding Italian Renaissance architect who laid the foundations for the Baroque movement. Maderno was born on the southernmost tip of Lake Lugano in what is now the Italian-speaking canton of Ticino in Switzerland. By the mid-1570s he had settled in Rome, working for his uncle Domenico FONTANA. Maderno's first great achievement was the remodelling of the façade of the medieval chapel of Santa Susanna, a design in which he rejected the prevailing architectural climate of uninspired Mannerism and established his own disciplined and forceful proto-Baroque style. By the time Santa Susanna was finished (1603), Maderno had been appointed architect of St Peter's in Rome, following in the footsteps of MICHELANGELO, with a commission to complete this most important symbol of the Roman Catholic world. His task involved altering Michelangelo's original centralized plan by adding a nave and a façade. Maderno's nave, one of the largest vaulted spaces constructed before the C19, is his most important interior design, but his other alterations at St Peter's were based largely on the existing elements. Outside Rome, his best work was for the church of S. Domenico in Perugia, where he replaced the Gothic nave vaults which had collapsed. He was also in demand as a designer of chapels and private palaces. Maderno's achievements place him among the foremost Italian architects of the generation before the full flowering of C17 Baroque architecture in Rome under such masters as BORROMINI and BERNINI.

□ Church of Santa Susanna, Rome (new façade and remodelling), 1593-1603. St Peter's, Rome: main façade, 1607-12; nave, 1609-16. Church of S. Domenico, Perugia (restoration), from 1621. Palazzo Lodovisi, Rome, 1622-3.

▷ Nina Caflish, *Carlo Maderno*, Munich, 1934. Howard Hibbard, *Carlo Maderno and Roman Architecture 1580-1630*, Pennsylvania, 1971. CS

MAHONY Marion Lucy

b. Chicago, 1873; d. Chicago, 1962.

The first female architect to graduate from the Massachusetts Institute of Technology; she worked closely with Frank Lloyd WRIGHT and later with her husband Walter Burley GRIFFIN. Marion studied architecture at MIT 1890-94 and after graduation returned to Chicago to work for Dwight Perkins. After a year she joined Wright and worked on a part-time basis at his Oak Park Studio until he left for Europe in 1909. After that she moved to the offices of Hermann von Holst (1875-1955), who had acquired much of Wright's practice. In 1911 she married Griffin, whom she had met at Wright's studio and for whom she was to produce some exquisite competition drawings for his winning design for the new Australian capital city, Canberra (1912). She had excelled at this kind of presentation, and many famous Wright drawings were rendered by her, including some of those in the famous Wasmuth portfolio. Now she did the same for a man she was to call a genius. She was right: Griffin was an extraordinarily talented designer who gave Australia a fine city plan and some remarkable buildings. They lived in Australia from 1914 until Griffin's sojourn in India, where he died in 1937. By this time they were living in an elegant estate of houses at Castlecrag, north of Sydney. Mahony had produced a theatre in a dell at Castlecrag for the production of anthroposophical dramas in a community that had become closely identified with Rudolf STEINER's spiritual and aesthetic teachings. After Griffin's death she returned to her native Chicago, a somewhat sad and disappointed woman whose vitriolic outpourings in numerous volumes of unpublished memoirs, *The Magic America*, now languish in a New York collection.

□ Independent commissions include: Robert Meuller House, Decatur, Illinois, 1910; All Souls Church, Evanston, Illinois, 1912-13. Her renderings can be found in F. L. Wright, *Ausgeführte Bauten und Entwürfe*, Berlin, 1910, and later publications on Wright's work.

▷ James Birrell, *Walter Burley Griffin*, Brisbane, 1964. D. Van Zanten, "The Early Work of Marion Mahony Griffin", in *Prairie School Review*, Vol. III, No.3, 1966. DS

MAILLART Robert

b. Berne, 1872; d. Geneva, 1940.

Swiss engineer, best remembered for his series of forty reinforced concrete bridges built in the first forty years of the C20. His engineering qualification from ETH Zürich (1894), was followed by experience with Swiss engineers. His own construction firm, established in 1902 in Zürich, moved to Russia in 1912, but collapsed with the Russian Revolution (1917). Maillart thenceforth worked as a consulting engineer based in Geneva, in association with Lucien Meisser and Ernst Stettler. Maillart's designs are rooted in the fusion of theoretical knowledge and the flair to create structural forms that turns reinforced concrete into the most expressive modern material. The constructional basis stems from flat or curved concrete slabs that can be reinforced to dispense with the need for beams or solid arches in bridges. In Maillart's hands these concepts produced some of the most beautiful structures of the C20. There is one major building from Maillart's days as contractor engineer, a sanatorium in Davos (1907), and some buildings demonstrating mushroom and shell framing.

□ Bridges (all in Switzerland): Rhine, Tavanasa, 1905; Tschiel, Donath, 1925; Salginatobel, Schiers, 1929-30; Rossgraben, Schwarzenburg, 1932; Schwandbach, Berne, 1933; Thur, Feisegg, 1933; Footbridge, Wulfingen Winterthur, 1934; Arve, Geneva, 1936-7. Buildings: Queen Alexandra Sanatorium, Davos, 1907; Warehouse, Chiasso, 1924-5; Zementhalle, Zürich Exposition, 1939.

▷ Max Bill, *Robert Maillart*, Erlenback-Zürich, 1947. AB

MAKOVECZ Imre

b. Budapest, 1935.

Prominent figure in the current re-emergence of an identifiable vernacular architecture for Hungary after a prolonged period of post-war Socialist Realism. Makovecz's deep respect for local topography, traditions and materials was fostered during his early years spent assisting his father in the restoration of war-damaged wooden buildings. He graduated from the Technical University of Budapest in 1959 and worked in a succession of different state offices before taking up an appointment with the National Forest Organization in 1977. Despite official inertia and the doctrinaire Modernism of the time, Makovecz completed a series of modest buildings which embodied his aspirations for organic and anthropomorphic architecture. His ideological stance attracted several younger architects and led to the formation of the Makovecz Group. His approach eschews the sentimental and rejects the empty replication of historical forms. Although Makovecz's architecture evokes the past, it is informed by contemporary values and a keen awareness of the cultural identity of his native Hungary.

□ Cultural Centre, Sarospatak, 1974-80. Mortuary Chapel of Farkasret Cemetery, Budapest (with Gabor Mezel), 1977. Cultural Centre, Jaszkisen, 1982-4. Forest Culture House, Visegrad, 1986.

▷ Imre Makovecz, *Art Almanac*, Budapest, 1977. Attila Komjathy, *Imre Makovecz*, Budapest, 1977. Janos Frank, *Imre Makovecz*, Budapest, 1979. "Imre Makovecz", *World Architecture*, 2, 1989. MC

▷ *see also pp242-5*

MALEVICH Kazimir Severinovich

b. Kiev, Russia, 1878; d. Leningrad, 1935.

Russian avant-garde painter who devised the energy-based theory of "non-objectivity" called Suprematism. Malevich's scanty formal education included brief periods at the Kiev Drawing School (1895-6) and the Moscow School of Painting, Sculpture and Architecture (1904-5). He then spent five years based in the private studio of F. Rerberg in Moscow, exploring the sequence of recent and current styles before evolving his own "supreme abstraction" around 1914, and exhibiting frequently. After the 1917 Revolution he was given a senior position in the official art administration of the Education Commissariat (Narkompros) then spent 1919-21 teaching at the Vitebsk Art School. Here in 1920 he formed his group of "Affirmers of the New Art" called Unovis. In 1922 he left for Petrograd, becoming director of the avant-garde art research institute Ginkhuk after the departure to Moscow of his rival TATLIN. In 1927 he made a lecture tour to Germany, visiting the Bauhaus, where Moholy-Nagy edited one of his texts for publication as a Bauhausbuch with unhelpful crudeness. In 1936 his work was presented in the USA at MoMa's show of "Cubism and Abstract Art". After his own development through realism, impressionism and cubism, Malevich developed a particularly clear concept of artistic "styles" and languages as "systems" of meaning, each mediated by its own formal conventions. Suprematism was the most advanced of these, corresponding to an urbanized, technological cognition in which all objects had been dissolved down to "units of energy" in a cosmic or mental space. Its formal language of floating geometrical elements and his own cubic sculptural "arkhitektons" have offered powerful paradigms for architectural composition.

□ Suprematist paintings, 1914-27. Suprematist arkhitektons, 1919-23.

▷ L. A. Zhadova, *Malevich*, Dresden, 1978, London, 1982. W. Beeren and J. Joosten (eds.), *Malevich 1878-1935*, Amsterdam/Leningrad, 1989. C. Cooke, "Malevich: from Theory into Teaching", *Art & Design* (London), No. 5/6, 1989. CC

MANSART François

b. Paris, 1598; d. Paris, 1666.

Pre-eminent master of the idiosyncratic French Renaissance tradition in which classical conceptions of order disciplined the essentially diversified, predominantly vertical, masses bequeathed by the Middle Ages to both religious and secular build-

François Mansart, Château de Maisons, nr Paris, 1642–51, interior

ing types. Mansart was trained in the traditional craft context by his father, a carpenter, his uncle, a mason and contractor, and his brother-in-law, a sculptor. Unlike many of his contemporaries, notably Jacques LEMERCIER, he does not seem to have travelled to Italy or, indeed, ever to have left France. Mansart completed the transition from the decorative Mannerism of the late C16 to the full maturity of French classicism, begun by Salomon DE BROSSE after the prophetic example of Pierre Lescot and Philibert DELORME. In such works as the châteaux of Balleroy, Blois (the Orléans Wing) and Maisons, he gave the fullest expression to the qualities generally associated with the rational spirit of the French C17: concentration by the elimination of inessentials, clarity combined wth subtlety, richness of form but restraint in ornamentation, obedience to a strict code of rules but flexibility within them. Although the planning of these châteaux is conservative in retaining the traditional alignment of rooms in single file (*enfilade*), much of Mansart's work reveals an individualistic command of techniques which were soon to become hallmarks of the Roman High Baroque: vigorous contrast in the contours of walls and the profiles of masses, colossal scale, alignment of varied space shapes to provide rich vistas, vertical perspectives and dramatic lighting (as in the Orléans Wing at Blois, the church of the Val de Grâce in Paris, the chapel at Fresnes, the projects for the east wing of the Louvre and for the Bourbon chapel at St Denis). The principle of varying the plasticity of the order in concert with variation of the wall plane – a characteristic Roman High Baroque way of producing movement in a façade after the example set by MADERNO at Santa Susanna – was not new to France. Lescot and Delorme had seen in it the key to the solution of the basic French problem of binding *pavillons* and *corps de logis* together into a consistent whole, at once effecting transition from one mass to another in the interest of unity and expressing distinction between the masses in the interest of variety. This approach, developed by de Brosse to ensure the subordination of the parts in a hierarchically ordered whole, was fundamental to Mansart's conception of monumentality. His virtuosity in varying the expression of strictly correct orders was most spectacular at Blois and Maisons. It recommended him to C18 academic classical authorities like J. F. BLONDEL as the supreme master of the French tradition.

□ Feuillants Church, Paris (façade), 1623. Château de Berny, 1623. Château de Balleroy, 1626(?). Church of the Visitation, Paris, 1632-4. Château de Blois (Orléans Wing partly realized), 1635-8. Hotel de la Vrillière, Paris, 1635-8. Château de Maisons, 1642-51. Hôtel Tubeuf, Paris (alterations), 1644-5. Château de Fresnes (alterations and chapel), 1644(?)-1660. Convent of the Val de Grâce, Paris (partially realized), 1645-6. Hôtel de Jars, Paris, 1648-50. Hôtel de Guenegaud (Nevers), Paris (remodelling), 1648-52. Château de Gesvres, 1650s(?). Hôtel de Guenegaud (des Brosses), Paris, 1653. Church of the Minimes (façade), Paris, 1657-65. Hôtel de Carnavalet, Paris (alterations), 1660(?)-1661. Projects for the Louvre, from 1662. Bourbon Chapel, St Denis, from 1662. Hôtel d'Aumont staircase, Paris, 1665.

▷ A. Blunt, *François Mansart and the Origin of French Classical Architecture*, London, 1941. A. Braham and P. Smith, *François Mansart*, London, 1973. CT

▷ *see also pp218-19*

MARKELIUS Sven

b. Stockholm, 1889; d. Stockholm, 1972.

Prominent Swedish Modernist architect, city-planner and designer. He studied at the Technical College and Academy of Fine Arts in Stockholm and began his architectural career in the office of Ragnar ÖSTBERG. In the mid-1920s, after working in the Neo-Classical vein, Markelius became interested in the "New Architecture", revising the designs for his Gothenburg Town Hall along Functionalist lines. He became a great admirer of LE CORBUSIER. It is recorded that he was the "first Swedish architect to design in the International Style of the 1930s". His Swedish pavilion at the New York World Fair (1939) was well received, and his own house at Kevinge (1945) was a much-admired example of 30s regional Modernism. After years as a private architect he served as Director of City Planning for Stockholm (1944-54); he prepared the regional plan for Stockholm and was responsible for the design and development of satellite towns such as Vallingby and the traffic plan for Räcksta. After his retirement from the public office he recommenced architectural practice and in 1962 was awarded the RIBA Gold Medal.

Sven Markelius

□ House designs for the Stockholm Exhibition, 1930. Helsingborg Concert Hall, 1926-32. "Collective House" in John Ericssonsgaten, Stockholm, 1933. Swedish Pavilion, New York World Fair, 1939. His own house, Kevinge, 1945.

▷ Stefano Ray, *Il Contributo svedese all'architettura contemporanea e l'opera di Sven Markelius*, Rome, 1969. Eva Rudberg, *Sven Markelius, 1889-1972*, Stockholm, 1990. DS

▷ *see also pp238-9*

MARTORELL-BOHIGAS-MACKAY (MBM)

Oriol Bohigas, b. Barcelona, 1925.
Josep Martorell, b. Barcelona, 1925.
David Mackay, b. Eastbourne, Sussex, 1933.

Spanish partnership whose architecture adopts and reuses traditional patterns, while drawing on the rich architectural heritage of GAUDI and "Modernismo" in Barcelona. The partnership between Martorell and theorist writer Bohigas was formed after they completed their studies at the Barcelona School of Architecture (1943-51); the two were founder members of "Grupo R". Mackay, who studied at the Northern Polytechnic, London (1951-8) qualified in Spain and joined Martorell and Bohigas in Barcelona in 1962. MBM's architecture is strongly regional in flavour and sure of its own cultural identity. "Realism", which Bohigas summed up with the word "pessimism" – meaning the acceptance of the world as it actually presents itself to us and not as we might wish it to appear – is a leading idea in MBM's architecture, which has concentrated on housing, whether private houses or public group housing developments. This theory of "pessimism" in architecture entails, among many things, a taste for the critical, the contemporary and the ambiguous.

☐ Hereder House, Tredos, Vall d'Aran, Spain, 1967-8. La Salut housing block, Sant Feliu de Llobregat, 1969-73. Bonanova Housing, Plaza de la Bonanova, Barcelona, 1970-73. Thau School, Carretera de Esplugues, Barcelona, 1972-4. Marti l'Huma housing block, Sabadell, Barcelona, 1974-9. Canovelles House, Canovelles, Barcelona, 1979-81. Mollet housing block, Barcelona, 1983-7. Nestlé Office Building, Esplugues de Llobregat, Barcelona, 1982-7. Park, Crueta del Coll, Barcelona, 1981-7. Olympic Village Project, Barcelona, from 1988.

▷ K. Frampton, *Martorell, Bohigas, Mackay, 1954-1984,* Milan, 1984. "Martorell/Bohigas/Mackay", *El Croquis* 34, July 1988. "Martorell/Bohigas/Mackay", *Architecture & Urbanism,* 225, June 1989.

PD

MAY Ernst

b. Frankfurt-am-Main, 1886; d. Hamburg, 1970.

German Functionalist architect and town-planner responsible as City Architect for the "New Frankfurt" in the 1920s and 30s. He studied under Fischer and Von Tiersch at the Munich Technical High School but continued his studies in London in Raymond UNWIN's Hampstead Garden Suburb office. He admired the ideas of Ebenezer Howard and the embryonic Garden City Movement, and later attempted to co-ordinate their concepts with his Modernist views of the new city.

Ernst May, Oceanic Hotel, Mombasa, 1950–58

In 1925 he became City Architect and planner to Frankfurt, where he produced his main project and many celebrated schemes in conjunction with carefully built up teams of professionals from a number of disciplines. He also directed the influential town-planning journal *Das neue Frankfurt* 1926-31. He was a member of CIAM and organized its first major congress at Frankfurt in 1929 on "existence minimum" dwelling. These minimum efficiency standards, which included the space- and labour-saving kitchen designs of G. Schütte-Lihotsky and much built-in furniture, were necessary to achieve a massive building target of 15,000 living units in 6 years. In 1931 May left Frankfurt for the USSR, where for three years he directed multi-disciplinary teams (or "brigades", as they were called) planning new settlements in the Urals, Armenia and Western Siberia as well as suburban estates and satellite towns around Moscow. Magnitogorsk was one of his best-known projects. He left somewhat disillusioned with Stalinism but unable to return to Germany, because of Hitler; in 1934 he set up as a farmer in Tanganyika, but was soon tempted back into architecture. He settled in Kenya, where he built the functionalist Delamere Flats and his own house in Karen. He established a successful commercial practice in Mombasa. He became a British citizen in 1942. After a contretemps with the Kenya architects' association he left the country in 1952 to become consultant to the *Neue Heimat,* for which he planned the garden city of Kranichstein near Darmstadt.

☐ Suburban and workers' housing layouts in and around Frankfurt-am-Main, including Praunheim, Römerstadt, Westhausen etc. (many with Ferdinand Kramer), 1925-31. Delamere Flats off Kenyatta Ave., Nairobi, from 1939. Town-planning scheme for Kampala (with Christopher Pearce), 1945-7. Oceanic Hotel, Mombasa, Kenya, 1950-58. HH The Aga Khan Maternity Hospital and a School, Kisumu, Kenya, 1950-61. Cultural Centre, Moshi Uganda, Tanzania, *c.* 1953.

▷ The journal *Das neue Frankfurt* (1926-31) and numerous articles in technical and international magazines: see C. Borngräber *et al.* in the special issue of *AA Quarterly*, London, Vol. II, No. 1, 1979, on May's work, and J. Bueckschmitt, *Ernst May: Bauten u. Planungen,* Stuttgart, 1963. See also D. Sharp, "The Modern Movement in East Africa", *Habitat International,* Vol. 7, No.5/6, 1983.

DS

MAYBECK Bernard Ralph

b. New York, 1862; d. Berkeley, California, 1957.

Eclectic American architect who developed a strong regional Californian style. Maybeck was raised in New York, the son of German immigrants; his father was a cabinet maker. In 1882 he went to Paris to study architecture at the Ecole des Beaux Arts in the atelier of Jules Louis André. He was also impressed by the work and theories of VIOLLET-LE-DUC with their emphasis on medievalism combined with the need to embrace new technology. Following two relatively unproductive periods working in New York and Kansas City, Maybeck moved to San Francisco in 1890 and joined the firm of A. Page Brown. By 1894 he had his own practice in Berkeley, and was also teaching at the University of California and the Mark Hopkins Institute of Art in San Francisco. He gradually developed a regionally inspired architectural language which combined eclecticism in the use of symbols and decoration with expressive timber construction. The best single example of what was known as the "Bay Region" style is the First Church of Christ Scientist in Berkeley, which mixes industrially produced materials with craftsmanship of the highest order. This relationship between decoration and structure is clearly derived from Gothic principles and the teachings of Viollet-le-Duc, but Maybeck was not limited to one style, believing that each architectural problem demanded its own solution. Examples of this diversity range from the fantasy structure of the Palace of Fine Arts in San Francisco to experiments in early prefabricated bungalows. He was awarded the Gold Medal of the American Institute of Architects (1951).

☐ Hearst Hall, Berkeley, California, 1899. First Church of Christ Scientist, Berkeley, 1910-12. Palace of Fine Arts, San Francisco, 1913.

▷ Esther McCoy, *Five Californian Architects*, New York, 1960. Kenneth H. Cardwell, *Bernard Maybeck – Artisan, Architect, Artist,* Santa Barbara, California, 1977.

CS

MEAD William Rutherford

see McKim, Mead & White.

MEIER Richard Alan

b. Newark, New Jersey, 1934.

One of the main figures of American neo-Modernism who sprung to fame in 1975 with the "New York Five". Meier's purist "shining white" architecture has helped transform museum design in the 1980s. He was educated at Cornell University, graduating in 1957, and worked in various offices, including SKIDMORE, OWINGS & MERRILL and Marcel BREUER. He commenced practice in 1963. Meier's allegiance to purism, particularly to the heroic period of LE CORBUSIER, provides a unifying theme in his development. The spatial qualities and relationship between parts of his buildings are best demonstrated in the Atheneum, New Harmony, and in the latest work at the J. Paul Getty Museum, Los Angeles (projected 1984-95), which built on earlier villa designs.

□ Domestic designs: Jerome Meier House, Essex Fells, New Jersey, 1965; Smith House, Darien, Conn., 1965-7; Hoffman House, East Hampton, New York, 1966-7; Saltzman House, East Hampton, 1967-9; House at Old Westbury, New York, 1960-71. Public works: The Atheneum, New Harmony, Ind., 1975-9. Bronx Development Center, New York, 1976; Museum of Decorative Arts, Frankfurt, 1979-85; High Museum of Art, Atlanta, Georgia, 1980-83; Siemens HQ, Munich (project), 1983; Des Moines Art Center Addition, Iowa, 1982-5; J. Paul Getty Museum, Los Angeles, 1984-.

▷ J. Rykwert (intro.), *Richard Meier Architect*, London & New York, 1985. AB

Richard Meier, Museum of Decorative Arts, Frankfurt, 1979-85

MELNIKOV Konstantin Stepanovich

b. Moscow, 1890; d. Moscow, 1974.

Leading Russian avant-garde Modernist of great formal inventiveness. Born to a peasant family, he was apprenticed to heating engineers who put him through the Moscow School of Painting, Sculpture and Architecture in painting (1905-11) and then architecture (1912-17). After the 1917 Revolution he worked in Moscow City Soviet's studio for a New Moscow Plan, returning to his old school, now the Moscow Vkhutemas, to teach part-time in 1921-3. Having made a reputation with early exhibition buildings he worked on personal commissions during the 1920s, mainly for Moscow workers' clubs. In 1933 he became head of a design studio in Moscow City Soviet, but, always an individualist, he was even less tolerant of compulsory collaboration in official bureaux than other avant-gardists. In 1937 he was expelled from the profession by the First Congress of Soviet Architects in 1937, and, though later partially rehabilitated, he lived in isolated and enforced idleness in his unique Moscow private house till his death. Melnikov rejected theory and any suggestion of "method" in design, insisting on the primacy of "intuition" and the necessity for a single generating idea to express the social and symbolic "essence" of a building. His early teaching sought a middle way between Classicism and "Leftist modernism", drawing compositional and perceptual principles from architectural tradition. His competition projects of the early 1930s responded to official demands for explicit historicism by obscure formal symbolism and hypertrophied monumentality.

Konstantin Melnikov, Rusakov workers' club, Moscow, 1927

□ Makhorka pavilion, Moscow, 1923. USSR Pavilion, Paris, 1925. Rusakov workers' club and others for Frunze and Kauchuk factories, Moscow, 1927; Svoboda and *Pravda*, Moscow, 1928; Burevestnik, Moscow, 1929. Three Moscow bus garages, 1926, 1929. Private house, 1927. Palace of Soviets, Moscow, 1931. Heavy Industry Commissariat, NKTP, Moscow, 1934.

▷ S. F. Starr, *Melnikov*, Princeton, NJ, 1978. A. Strigalev and I. Kokkinaki (eds.), *K. S. Melnikov*, Moscow, 1985. A. Wortmann (ed.), *The Muscles of Invention*, Rotterdam, 1990. CC

▷ *see also pp230-31*

MENDELSOHN Erich

b. Allenstein, East Prussia (now Poland), 1887; d. San Francisco, 1953.

Key post First World War German architect whose buildings and ideas had a worldwide influence. The son of a merchant, he seemed to be destined for a career in economics, but the creative lure of architecture soon became too strong. He went to Berlin then Munich, the centre of the almost worn-out Jugendstil, for his training as an architect. He was soon caught up in the revolutionary *milieu* of Expressionism. Kandinsky, Marc, Klee and von Jawlensky – later the "Blue Four" – were at that time examining the emotional impact of their new ideas in painting. This emotional emphasis formed a basis for Mendelsohn's own architectural credo. Indeed his manner of design – working up an architectural idea from an expressionistic-type sketch – as well as his personal philosophy of "Dynamism" (with roots in Nietzsche) demonstrated at a very early stage an attitude to design

EINSTEIN TOWER, Potsdam

The epitome of Expressionist architecture, Mendelsohn's Einstein Tower (1919–24) was designed as a laboratory for use by the world famous physicist Albert Einstein. The earliest designs for this practical and symbolic monument date from the mid-war years and it went through many transformations. It was largely conceived as a reinforced concrete structure without any historical overtones. The scientific telescope is situated in the cupola. Due to lack of cement at the time the building had to be partly constructed in brick and then its whole surfaces rendered in cement.

"...recognized that the elastic qualities of the new structural materials, steel and reinforced concrete, must by necessity produce an architecture entirely different from anything known before", one commentator wrote. The Einstein Tower, still standing in Potsdam, is a great symbolic monument to the physicist as well as a kind of sarcophagus to the "Expressionist" interlude in modern architecture (1910-23). It established Mendelsohn's Expressionist reputation. He soon moved away from this kind of architecture and began a whole new series of bold projects for offices, factories and houses. Towards the end of the 20s he built the magnificent "Universum" Cinema on the Kurfürstendamm, now a theatre but originally part of a large estate development. He met Frank Lloyd WRIGHT in 1924 on his first trip to the USA. Later he had to flee from Nazi Germany in 1933, firstly to England, where he settled until 1939 – the year he changed his name to Eric and received British citizenship – then to Palestine and eventually to the USA in 1941. In England he was for a time a partner of Serge CHERMAYEFF, with whom he won the competition for the De La Warr Pavilion at Bexhill-on-Sea. He built up a good general practice in both Palestine and America but always had time to lecture to students and contribute informative articles to the press.

☐ Astrophysical Observatory (Einsteinturm), Potsdam, Germany, 1919-24. Hat Factory, Steinberg, Herrmann Co., Luckenwalde, 1921, 1923. *Berliner*

Erich Mendelsohn (with Serge Chermayeff), De La Warr Pavilion, Bexhill-on-Sea,

that was both idiosyncratic and brilliant. His insight into the form problems of modern architecture remained unique. Mendelsohn drew directly on no historical models and his buildings during the formative years appear free from the stylistic overtones of the work of his contemporaries. It was also free from eclecticism. Sketch by sketch he put together a drama of line and form that explored the worlds of plasticity and architectural symbols. A romantic by conviction, he took an almost Wagnerian delight in producing "operatic" sketches based on music: charcoal *Agnus Dei*, graphic cathedrals to his god of music, J. S. Bach. The early sketches, many of them produced at the front in the war on odd scraps of paper, were the inspiration for his buildings. Mendelsohn

Tageblatt offices, Berlin, 1921, 1923. Sternefeld House, Berlin, 1923-4. Schocken Stores, Stuttgart (1926-8) and Chemnitz (1928-9). Universum Theatre (*Schaubühne*), Berlin, 1926-8. Petersdorff Store, Breslau (now Wroclaw, Poland), 1927-8. German Metalworkers Federation Building, Berlin, 1929-30. Own House, Am Rupenhorn, Berlin, 1929-30. Columbus House, Berlin, 1931-2. De La Warr Pavilion, Bexhill-on-Sea, Sussex (with Chermayeff), 1934-5. Cohen House, London (with Chermayeff), 1935-6. Various projects in Palestine, 1936-41. Maimonides Hospital, San Francisco, 1946-50. Various synagogues, community centres, houses and projects in the US.

▷ Erich Mendelsohn, *Structures and Sketches*, London, 1924 (reprinted from Wasmuth's *Monatshefte*, 1924); *Amerika: Bilderbuch eines Architekten*, Berlin, 1926; *Russland, Europa, Amerika*, Berlin, 1929; *Das Gesamtschaffen des Architekten*, Berlin, 1930. A. Whittick, *Eric Mendelsohn*, London, 1940. B. Zevi, *Erich Mendelsohn: Opera completa*, Milan, 1970. DS

▷ *see also pp238-41*

MERRILL John O.

see Skidmore, Owings & Merrill.

MICHELANGELO BUONARROTI

b. Caprese, near Florence, 1475; d. Rome, 1564.

One of the key innovators of the C16 and a fountainhead of inspiration for post-Renaissance architects. To his many followers it was Michelangelo who had thrown off the shackles of classical dogma and given authority to a freer and more imaginative approach to architectural composition. Michelangelo trained as a sculptor but had also achieved unprecedented success as a painter before turning to architecture relatively late in his career (*c.* 1515) to undertake a series of prestigious papal commissions. An interest in architecture, however, is already apparent in his Sistine Chapel ceiling (1508-12), and in the designs for a monumental tomb for Pope Julius II (from 1505; eventually abandoned). From these, his earliest works of architecture are a logical development, since they were also conceived as settings for sculpture. In design, these works grow out of late C15 Florentine traditions. The basic framework of the New Sacristy in S. Lorenzo, for example, is a modification of BRUNELLESCHI's Old Sacristy in the same church. The inventive

Michelangelo Buonarroti, Laurentian Library, S. Lorenzo, Florence, 1524–57

and free-styled detailing of the side tombs and portals, where architectural elements are assembled for visual effect rather than structural logic, is decisively different in character but is in fact heavily indebted to the decorative ensembles of Donatello and other earlier sculptors. In the Laurentian Library vestibule, the sculptural exploitation of architectural forms now monumentalizes the whole basic conception, with a staircase filling almost the entire space and wall-columns (rather perversely) recessed into deep cavities. In projects of truly monumental scale, Michelangelo was equally able. Invention is now always subordinated to the needs of overall composition, which to Michelangelo was analogous with the symmetry and articulation of the human body. On the Capitoline Hill, he built a new palace to mirror the refaced Palazzo dei Conservatori opposite, the two matching buildings with their influential giant pilaster orders deferring to the taller (refaced) Palazzo dei Senatori at the head of the piazza. In his completion of St Peter's, a curtain wall of giant pilasters binds the building's angular perimeter but also provides a visual link between the lower levels and the vertical thrust of the enormous ribbed dome above, the design of which was Michelangelo's crowning achievement.

□ Medici Chapel (New Sacristy), S. Lorenzo, Florence, 1519-34. Laurentian Library, S. Lorenzo, Florence, 1524-57. Capitoline Palaces, Rome, from 1539. Continuation of St Peter's, Rome, 1546-64. Porta Pia, Rome, 1561-4. Santa Maria degli Angeli, Rome, from 1561.

▷ J. S. Ackerman, *The Architecture of Michelangelo*, London, 1961 etc. D. Summers, *Michelangelo and the Language of Art*, Princeton, 1981. M. Hirst, *Michelangelo and his Drawings*, New Haven, 1988. DH

▷ *see also pp214-15, 218-19*

MICHELOZZO DI BARTOLOMMEO

b. Florence, 1396; d. Florence, 1472.

Creator of the Florentine type of urban palazzo. Trained as a sculptor, Michelozzo became a bronze caster at the mint. From 1417 he spent seven years as an assistant in GHIBERTI's workshop, and then shared a studio with the sculptor Donatello until 1438. Michelozzo was also kept busy over a period of 30 years with Cosimo de' Medici's commissions (including three villas), and loyally shared his patron's exile in Venice during 1433-4. Increasingly engrossed in architectural design, his most influential work was the Palazzo Medici in Florence, begun 1444. The imposing, elemental grandeur of its rusticated masonry courses at street level, and the airy elegance of its central atrium, made it the prototype palazzo for the rich new ruling class of Florence. Michelozzo

Michelozzo di Bartolommeo, Sacristy, S. Marco, Florence, 1437–43

was employed on the rebuilding of the church of the Santissima Annunziata (altered in the C16) and took over as chief architect of the Cathedral when BRUNELLESCHI died in 1446. In his later years he worked mainly in Milan, Pistoia and Dubrovnik (Ragusa). Michelozzo was a transitional designer who spread the Renaissance principles of Brunelleschi and ALBERTI in all his projects, but who retained obvious traces of a medieval approach lurking in the details.

□ Palazzo Medici, Florence, begun 1444. Villa Medici, Caffagiolo, 1451. Villa Medici, Fiesole, 1458-61. S. Marco, Florence: Sacristy, 1437-43, Cloisters and Library, 1441. Santissima Annunziata, Florence, 1444-55.

▷ Harriet M. Caplow, *Michelozzo*, New York and London, 1977. R. W. Lightbown, *Donatello and Michelozzo: an artistic partnership*, London, 1980.

JRC

▷ *see also pp212-13*

MIES VAN DER ROHE Ludwig

b. Aachen, 1886; d. Chicago, 1969.

Famous for his much-misunderstood dictum "Less is More", Mies van der Rohe sought to create contemplative, emotionally neutral spaces through an architecture based on material honesty and structural integrity. The first seeds of this austere vision of architecture may have been planted when Mies attended mass as a schoolboy in the Palatine Chapel, Aachen. Early employment in the family stonecarving business gave him an appreciation of materials that was to endure throughout his life. Following an apprenticeship in the office of Bruno Paul in Berlin, he entered the studio of Peter BEHRENS in 1908 and stayed there, with a brief intermission, until early 1912. Under the influence of Behrens, Mies discovered the combination of Prussian Classicism and advanced structural techniques that was to determine his subsequent development. An important model was provided by SCHINKEL, whose clearly articulated architectural language, based on a simple post-and-lintel construction, was to be rivalled by Mies in the C20 materials of steel and glass. Although never intimately involved with the glass fantasists of post-1918 German Expressionism, Mies created the most powerful early icons of the glass architecture of the future with his proposals for an office tower on Friedrichstrasse, Berlin (1921), and for a thirty-storey glass skyscraper (1922). Mies's sympathy for the aesthetic credos of both Russian Constructivism and the Dutch *De Stijl* group explains his involvement with the magazine *G*, launched in July 1923 by EL LISSITZKY, Hans Richter and Werner Graeff. In the second issue, Mies described his current scheme for a concrete office building as follows: "The office is a building of work, of organization, of clarity, of economy...The materials are concrete, steel, and glass. Reinforced concrete buildings are naturally skeletal constructions...skin and bone buildings." While this office project was firmly ordered by Classical axiality, Mies's contemporary projects for a Concrete Country House (1923) and a Brick Country House (1924) have open plans strongly reminiscent of *De Stijl* paintings, with wall panels and windows arranged as vertical planes around which internal and external spaces can flow without interruption. Mies made a major contribution to the architectural polemics of the late 1920s as artistic director of the Werkbund-sponsored Weissenhof project, in which a model estate was constructed on a site outside Stuttgart as a test-bed for the white, functionalist housing of "Neues Bauen". In addition to designing the site-plan and an apartment block, Mies commissioned house designs from sixteen leading Modernists, including GROPIUS, SCHAROUN, BEHRENS, Bruno and Max TAUT, OUD, STAM, and LE CORBUSIER. A sensuous delight in flowing space and highly finished materials can be admired in the Barcelona Pavilion (1928-9), a single-storey building set on a travertine podium, with a grid of chrome-plated columns and vertical planes of onyx and coloured glass. With the curved steel frame of the Barcelona chair, designed for the same occasion, Mies achieved a timeless minimalist elegance. As Director of the Bauhaus, Mies supervised the last two years of the school's life in Dessau (1930-32) and the final year of its existence in Berlin (1932-3). Deprived of regular employment, and with few prospects in the hostile environment of Nazi Germany, he looked to a future in the USA. He moved to Chicago in 1938, and commissions rapidly followed, most notably a master-plan for the IIT campus (1940-41), in which a series of modestly scaled and immaculately detailed buildings are set in a loosely axial relationship, to create an oasis of calm and repose amid the disorder of the Chicago suburbs. The Farnsworth House (1946-51) – a single-

Ludwig Mies van der Rohe, Seagram Building, New York, 1954–8

storey glazed box floating on a steel frame above a meadow in rural Illinois – achieved similar results in a more propitious setting. Over the last two decades of his life, Mies realized his vision of a monumental "skin and bone" architecture in a series of designs that established an international model and standard for the urban office block: the Seagram Building, New York (1954-8), Federal Center, Chicago (1959-64), and the Dominion Center, Toronto (1963-9). Mies's design for the New National Gallery in Berlin (1962-7) provides a fitting coda to a life dedicated to the notion of a universal architecture, reduced to its essentials.

□ Riehl House, Berlin-Neubabelsberg, 1907. Project: Kröller-Müller House, Wassenaar, Holland, 1912. Project: Office Building, Friedrichstrasse, Berlin, 1921. Project: Glass Skyscraper, 1922. Wolf House, Guben, 1925-7. Monument to the November Revolution: Karl Liebknecht, Rosa Luxemburg, Berlin-Friedrichsfelde, 1926. Site planning and apartment building, Weissenhof Estate, Stuttgart, 1927. German Pavilion, Barcelona Exhibition, 1928-9 (rebuilt 1986). Tugendhat House, Brno, 1928-30. Model House and Apartment, Berlin Building Exhibition, 1931. Project: Reichsbank, Berlin, 1933. Project: Resor House, Jackson Hole,

GERMAN PAVILION, Barcelona

Like the Eiffel Tower earlier this world famous pavilion by the German architect Ludwig Mies van der Rohe was symbolical rather than useful. A beautiful single-storey object, it drew crowds at Barcelona's International Exhibition in 1929, who were fascinated by the pavilion's clean-cut appearance with its black marble walls, diamond-shaped chromium columns and fluid, spatial layout. The inner courtyard featured a fine sculpture of a female dancer by Kolbe; also on display were the equally celebrated steel and leather Barcelona chairs. These elements are incorporated in the replica on the original site.

Wyoming, 1937-8. Preliminary Plan for Campus of Armour Institute of Technology, Chicago, 1939. Master Plan, Illinois Institute of Technology, Chicago, 1940-41 (implemented 1942-57). Farnsworth House, Plano, Illinois, 1946-51. 860-880 Lake Shore Drive Apartments, Chicago, 1948-51. Crown Hall, IIT, Chicago, 1950-56. Seagram Building, New York, 1954-8. Project: Bacardi Office Building, Santiago, Cuba, 1957. Federal Center, Chicago, 1959-64. New National Gallery, Berlin, 1962-7. Lafayette Towers, Lafayette Park, Detroit, 1963. Dominion Center, Toronto, 1963-9. Project: Mansion House Square and Tower, London, 1967.

▷ Philip C. Johnson *Mies van der Rohe*, London, 1978. Franz Schulze, *Mies van der Rohe*, Chicago and London, 1985. Wolf Tegethoff, *Mies van der Rohe: The Villas and Country Houses*, Cambridge, Mass., 1985. Fritz Neumeyer, *Mies van der Rohe: Das kunstlose Wort*, Berlin, 1986. IBW

▷ *see also pp232-7, 240-41*

MORRIS William

b. Walthamstow, London, 1834; d. London, 1896.

Principal founder of the Arts & Crafts movement, poet, political activist, and the most important C19 artist in craft-based media. He was educated at Marlborough School and Exeter College, Oxford, and spent a year in architectural articles to G. E. STREET, where he initiated a lifelong friendship with Philip WEBB, Street's chief assistant. In 1859 Webb designed for Morris the Red House at Bexleyheath, and in seeking to furnish it appropriately Morris recognized the "shoddiness" of contemporary furnishings and fittings. In response he, together with Rossetti, Burne-Jones, Webb, Madox Brown and others, founded the firm of Morris, Marshall, Faulkner & Co. as a producer of furniture, fabrics, wallpapers, and stained glass. In 1877 Morris was a prime mover in the establishment of the Society for the Protection of Ancient Buildings, as a counter to the destructive policy of "restoration" then in vogue. From this time he became increasingly politically active, and became a founder and leader of the Socialist League. He established the Kelmscott Press in 1890, designing lettering and borders, and publishing English classics as well as his own and contemporaries' writings. Morris's idea of art as "the expression of man's joy in his labour" was the great forming principle which inspired a generation of disciples.

▷ William Morris, *A Dream of John Ball*, London, 1888; *News From Nowhere*, London, 1891; *Gothic Architecture*, London, 1893. J. W. Mackail, *The Life of William Morris*, London, 1899. Paul Thompson, *The Work of William Morris*, London, 1967. RM

MOSER Karl

b. Baden, 1860; d. Zürich, 1936.

Highly respected teacher and mentor, considered the founding father of Swiss Modernism. He was educated at the ETH, Zürich (1878-82), and later at the Ecole des Beaux Arts, Paris. He worked first in Zürich and then in SW Germany, in partnership with Hans Curjel, based at Karlsruhe (1887-1915). Moser returned to Zürich in 1915 to take up teaching at his former college (ETH). Recognition for his achievements came in 1928 with election as first President of CIAM. Moser was influenced by the eclectic movements at the turn of the century, his eleven church designs, built 1891-1931, ranging from Gothic and Romanesque (reminiscent of H. H. RICHARDSON) to the Vienna Secession. The latter tendencies can be seen in his public commissions, such as the University and Museum of Fine Arts, Zürich. All Moser's work is distinguished by a powerful handling of interior spaces, whatever the style. His last building (St Antonius, Basel, 1925-31) was his most significant, bringing together the various trends in one simplified statement expressed both internally and externally in a new material, exposed reinforced concrete.

Karl Moser, Church of St Antonius, Basle, 1925–31

☐ St John's, Berne, 1891-3. Bankhaus Homburga, Karlsruhe, 1898-1901. Museum of Fine Arts, Zürich, 1907-10. Zürich University, 1911-14. Badischer Bahnhof, Basel, 1912-13. St Antonius, Basel, 1925-31.

▷ H. Kienzle, *Karl Moser 1860-1936,* Zürich, 1937.

AB

MOYA John Hidalgo

see Powell & Moya.

MURCUTT Glenn Marcus

b. London, 1936.

Australian architect admired for creating an identifiably Australian idiom in domestic architecture. He spent his childhood in the Morobe district of New Guinea, which gave him a sympathy for simple primitive qualities. As a youth, he was introduced by his father to the architecture of MIES VAN DER ROHE and the thought of Henry David Thoreau. He studied architecture at the University of New South Wales (1956-61), then worked with Bill Lucas (1957), Neville Gruzman (1958-9) and John Allen (1962). The years 1962-4 were spent travelling. After five years (1964-9) in the office of Ancher, Mortlock, Murray and Woolley, he established a practice in Sydney in 1970. As well as Mies van der Rohe, Murcutt's other formative influences included CODERCH and the Maison de Verre by Pierre Chareau, work seen in 1973. In an initial exploratory phase (1970-73) he established his mastery of the Miesian idiom. His second phase (1974-83) opened with the Marie Short house, Crescent Head (1974-5), and culminated in the 1983 Ball-Eastaway house at Glenorie. Murcutt's houses are a mixture of common sense and lyricism, using simple shed-like forms which resemble open verandas – the European pavilion converted into a recognizably Australian thin veranda-house.The Magney house, Bingi Point, Moruya (1985), with its expressive wave-shaped metal roof, marked a new level of confidence and maturity far in advance of previous work.

☐ Marie I. Short farmhouse, Crescent Head, NSW, 1974-5. Two houses, Mt Irvine, NSW, 1977-80. Local History Museum and Tourist Information Centre, South Kempsey, NSW, 1981-2. Sydney Ball & Lyn Eastaway house, Glenorie, NSW, 1980-83. Tom Magney house, Bingi Point, Moruya, NSW, 1983-4.

▷ P. Drew, *Leaves of Iron*, Sydney, 1985. PD

MUTHESIUS Hermann

b. Thüringen, 1861; d. Berlin, 1927.

Influential German architect involved in educational reforms in art and architecture, author of *Das englische Haus*. Often referred to as the turn of the century's most celebrated cultural spy, Muthesius spent some eight years as a diplomat in the Prussian Embassy in London (1896-1904). He monitored new developments in railway, house and church design, investigated new educational trends and wrote numerous reports, many of which were modified and issued, in German, as sumptuous books, some with illustrations commissioned from leading British photographers. His book, *The English House*, was published in three parts in Berlin, 1904-5. In 1905 he returned to Germany via the USA and the St Louis Fair. He inspired the formation of the Deutscher Werkbund, although he did not attend its inaugural meeting in Munich in 1907. A successful, if somewhat limited, architect in his own right, he designed a number of domestic buildings in Berlin, including the family home and other Berlin villas and estates at Dresden, Hellerau, Duisburg and Altes Gleinicke. The earlier houses (1906-8) all have essential features drawn from English examples. His later houses show a stronger German impulse without jettisoning *das englische Stil*. Muthesius was a convinced Anglophile who promoted this interest in cultural circles throughout the Reich until, with the growing threat of war, enthusiasm waned around 1912-13. In 1914, he took up a strong position against individualism in art and architecture, in particular in an attack on the Belgian Henri VAN DE VELDE. Muthesius advocated the development of standards and types, i.e., a rational approach to design and architecture. This was meant to elevate German products to the realm of cultural artefacts and consolidate the Werkbund's position as a body that brought together artist and designer, manufacturer and propagandist. With the rapid growth of mass-production over the following years, particularly in relation to the war effort in Germany, Muthesius proved correct in his views; the later Functionalist movement designs, e.g. GROPIUS's Model Factory (1914) and the estates for Berlin and the New Frankfurt, indicate their validity.

☐ Houses for Heinrich Jacob Neuhaus, 1906, Schweitzer, 1908; his own house, 1906, and the

Hermann Muthesius

house for Hermann Freudenberg, Berlin–Nikolassee, 1907-8. Later houses, for Schonstedt, Duisburg, *c.*1910, Klamroth, Halberstadt, *c.*1910, Cramer and Mertens, both in Berlin, 1911-15. Commercial work: Kersten and Tuteur department store, Berlin, 1912-13; silk weaving mill for Michels & Cie, near Potsdam, 1912.

▷ Hermann Muthesius, *Die englische Baukunst der Gegenwart,* Leipzig, 1900; *Stilarchitektur u. Baukunst,* Mullheim-Rühr, 1902; *M. H. Baillie Scott* and *C. R. Mackintosh* in the series "Meister der Innen Kunst", Darmstadt, London, 1902; *Das englische Haus,* 3 vols., Berlin, 1904-5 (English-language version ed. Dennis Sharp, *The English House,* London, New York, 1979). Julius Posener, *Hermann Muthesius 1861-1927,* Berlin, 1977. D. Sharp (ed.), *Hermann Muthesius 1861-27* (exhibition catalogue with contributions by J. Posener and Muthesius's son Eckart), London, 1979. DS

▷ *see also pp228-9*

MYLNE Robert

b. Edinburgh, 1733; d. London, 1811.

Pre-eminent Scottish architect, engineer and surveyor of the late C18, the most celebrated member of an influential family dynasty of master masons. After completing his apprenticeship in 1754, he sailed from Leith on an extended study tour of continental Europe. While in Rome he was awarded a prestigious prize for drawing by the Accademia di S. Luca (much to the chagrin of his contemporary Robert ADAM). On returning to Britain, Mylne quickly established a thriving practice in London with influential connections throughout the country. His design for the first Blackfriars Bridge, London (1760-69), making bold use of elliptical arches, proved controversial and drew fierce criticism. He was appointed surveyor to St Paul's Cathedral in 1767 but his most representative work was carried out at Inveraray in Scotland at the invitation of the 5th Duke of Argyll (1769). His remit included the layout of the model town, the construction of numerous new buildings and the decoration of the principal rooms in the Duke's castle.

□ Cally House, Kirkcudbrightshire, 1759-63. St Cecilia's Hall, Edinburgh, 1762-5. Maam Steading, Inveraray, 1790. Double Church, Inveraray, 1795-1802.

▷ Rev. Robert Scott Mylne, *The Master Masons to the Crown of Scotland*, Edinburgh, 1893. A. E. Richardson and Lovett Gill, *Robert Mylne – Architect and Engineer*, London, 1955. Ian Lindsay and Mary Cosh, *Inveraray and the Dukes of Argyll*, Edinburgh, 1972. MC

John Nash, Church of All Souls, Langham Place, London, 1822–5

NASH John

b. London, 1752; d. East Cowes, 1835.

England's greatest town-planner, dazzling London in the early C19 with his daring terrace schemes and parks. His father died when he was still a boy but he entered the office of the architect Sir Robert Taylor "in a subordinate capacity". He soon became a draughtsman but by 1777 was yearning to set up on his own. He began full of hopes, but within five years was bankrupt and settled in Carmarthen. It took him over ten years to set up a good practice, to return to London, and to form a distinctive style, attractive to patrons. Whilst living in Wales he interested himself in the activities of Thomas Johnes and Uvedale Price. Johnes had created a fine romantic landscape at Hafod in Cardiganshire, a triangular castellated house near Aberystwyth and had designed for Price, who was the author of an important *Essay on the Picturesque* (1796). Through Price, Nash was probably introduced to Richard Payne Knight, a landscape gardening theorist, who lived at Downton Castle near Ludlow, a "picturesque" and irregularly planned house – the prototype of the country house castle. Nash started to provide clients with this kind of house, a castle outside, perhaps, but with some variation, perhaps in Italianate form or even, if they desired it, a Gothic folly (as at Clytha) or a group of delightfully picturesque cottages (as at Blaise Hamlet, near Bristol). Back in London, Nash soon joined in partnership with the successful landscape gardener Humphry REPTON, the idea being to transform old-fashioned country houses into fine modern ones within an attractive, newly designed park. Nash had also come to the attention of the Prince Regent, who asked him to design a conservatory at Carlton House. In 1806 Nash started his important work on the Crown's Marylebone estates, forming what became known as the Regent's Park. He surrounded it with fine houses with stuccoed exteriors in elegant terraces, and designed a broad new street, Regent Street, running north to south. Along its route he also designed the Church of All Souls, Langham Place (1822-4). When James WYATT died (1813), Nash was the Prince Regent's choice for Surveyor-General of the Board of Works. He was then primarily responsible for Carlton House, Kensington and the Royal Lodges in Windsor Great Park. He also did amazing work in remodelling the Royal Pavilion at Brighton. When the Prince became King George IV (1820) Nash was also asked to reconstruct Buckingham

Palace. The expenditure on this became a national scandal, and when the King died in 1830 Nash's career was at a virtual end. He could compose on the grand scale, but he could not avoid the odium of criticism which brought his great reputation to its lowest point.

□ Royal Pavilion, Brighton, Sussex (remodelling), 1815-21. Planning of Regent Street and Regent's Park, London, 1818-27. Haymarket Theatre, London, 1820-21. Church of All Souls, Langham Place, London, 1822-5. Buckingham Palace, London, (remodelling), 1825-30.

▷ Sir John Summerson, *John Nash, Architect to King George IV*, 2nd ed. London, 1949. Terence Davis, *John Nash, the Prince Regent's Architect*, London, 1973. Nigel Temple, *John Nash and the Village Picturesque*, London, 1979. GB

▷ *see also pp220-21*

NERVI Pier Luigi

b. Sondrio, Lombardy, 1891; d. Rome, 1979.

The most influential reinforced-concrete design engineer of the century. Trained as an engineer at Bologna University, he began work as an engineer and contractor there in 1923. His first major commission, won in competition in 1927, was for the elegant 35,000-seat municipal stadium in Florence. From the early 1940s he developed ideas for a *ferro cemento* which combined qualities of strength, simplicity and grace, as can be seen in the great concrete ribs of the single-storey exhibition hall in Turin (1948-9). For the Rome Olympics, Nervi designed the Palazzo and the Palazzetto of Sport, with the architects PIACENTINI and Vitellozzi respectively. He was constantly in demand as an engineering consultant, working with BREUER and Zehrfuss on the UNESCO Building in Paris (1953-8), with PONTI on the Pirelli Tower, Milan (1955-8), and SEIDLER on his Sydney Tower (1976). He held the view that the professions of architecture and engineering were indivisible in the production of good building and deemed a knowledge of building, nature and construction essential to understanding the efficiency of materials and their use. His work as a theorist, recorded in numerous printed lectures and books, attracted a wide following. He can be said to have ensured the success of reinforced concrete as the main structural material of the day. He was awarded Gold Medals by the RIBA, the AIA and the Academie d'Architecture. In the years 1946-61 he was professor of engineering at Rome University.

□ Cinema, Naples, 1927. Municipal Stadium, Florence, 1932 (1927-32). Aeroplane Hangars, Orvieto, 1935-8, and Orbetello and Torre del Lago, 1940-43. Exhibition Building, Turin 1948-9. Palazzo and Palazzeto dello Sport, Rome, 1956-9. Pirelli Tower, Milan, 1955-8. Palazzo del Lavoro, Turin, 1961. Papal Audience Chamber, Vatican City, 1971.

▷ P. L. Nervi, *Structures*, London, New York, 1956; *Aesthetics and Technology in Building*, Cambridge, Mass., 1965. G. C. Argan, *Pier Luigi Nervi*, Milan, 1955. J. Joedicke, *Works of Pier Luigi Nervi*, London, 1957. A. Pica, *Pier Nervi*, Rome, 1969. DS

Pier Luigi Nervi, Exhibition Hall, Turin, 1948–9

W. E. Nesfield, Kinmell Park, Denbighshire, 1866–74

NESFIELD William Eden

b. Bath, 1835; d. Brighton, 1888.

English domestic architect, one of the most distinctive and inspired exponents of the "Queen Anne" style. Son of a landscape gardener and educated at Eton, he was articled in 1851 to William Burn, in whose office he met Richard Norman SHAW, and in 1853 to his uncle Anthony Salvin (1799-1881). He toured Europe in 1857-8 and set up in practice on his return. From 1863 to 1876 he shared an office with Shaw (they were in partnership 1866-9). Though they designed individually, their styles developed collaboratively; with Philip WEBB, they were at the forefront of the generation that repudiated the moral earnestness of "high" Victorian Gothic, and spearheaded the cultural eclecticism of the Aesthetic movement. In the early 1860s Nesfield and Shaw shifted from a STREET-like Gothic to a picturesque "Old English". This in turn merged into the "Queen Anne" style, inspired by "builder's classical" of the late Stuart period, the domestic buildings of WREN, and a heterogeneous array of Elizabethan, Flemish, Dutch, French and Japanese sources. Nesfield possessed an independent income and, uninterested in expanding his practice or in compromising his ideas, accepted commissions only from those who could appreciate (and afford) his inventive exuberance.

□ Cloverley Hall, Shropshire, 1864. Kinmel Park, Denbighshire, 1866-74. Lodge, Kew Gardens, London, 1867. Lodge, Broadlands, Romsey, Hants., 1870. Bodrhyddan, Flintshire, 1872-4. Laughton Hall, Essex, 1878.

▷ W. Eden Nesfield, *Specimens of Mediaeval Architecture, 1862*. Alastair Service (ed.), *Edwardian Architecture and its Origins*, London, 1975. BP

Johann Balthasar Neumann, Residenz, Würzburg, 1719–44, Kaiser Hall

NEUMANN Johann Balthasar

b. Cheb (Eger), 1687; d. Würzburg, 1753.

A master of Baroque and Rococo design in southern Germany. Born in Bohemia, he was apprenticed to a metal founder, migrating in 1711 to Würzburg. His talents were spotted early and first applied to military engineering. He was taken up by the ruling member of the Schönborn family (Prince Bishops of Würzburg and much else), working on fortifications, 1717-18, and then, 1719, on the first stage of the new Residenz of the prince bishop. Neumann quickly distinguished himself and soon was in charge of a brilliant and cosmopolitan team of architects, artists and craftsmen (including the Venetian painter G. B. Tiepolo for ceilings and murals). Neumann's ability to handle the Baroque idiom in splendid style, and his organizational talent, commended him to his employer, and to his employer's relatives in high places elsewhere. In the late 1720s Neumann designed the parish church of Wiesentheid im Steigerwald, the priory church of Holzkirchen, and the Benedictine abbey of Münsterschwarzach on the Rhine. In 1744 (the year the Residenz was completed) he designed his masterpiece, the pilgrimage church of Vierzehnheiligen, N of Bamberg. In this unconventional structure, involving intersecting ovals in plan, Neumann created an exceptional sense of delight and surprise. The death in 1746 of his patron the prince bishop led to three years of demotion, but reinstatement followed in 1749. Neumann's last great work, the large abbey church of Neresheim in the Swabian hills (begun 1747) is more tranquil in effect, and suggests that in his sixties Neumann was taking a more classical direction.

□ Residenz, Würzburg, 1719-44. Priory church, Holzkirchen, 1726-30. Parish church, Wiesentheid im Steigerwald, 1727. Benedictine abbey, Münsterschwarzach, 1727-42. Pilgrimage church, Vierzehnheiligen, 1742-53. Abbey church, Neresheim, 1747-53.

▷ Max von Freeden, *Balthasar Neumann – Leben und Werk*, Würzburg, 1953. Christian F. Otto, *Space into Light, the Churches of Balthasar Neumann*, New York, 1979. JRC

▷ *see also pp218-19*

NEUTRA Richard

b. Vienna, 1892; d. Wuppertal, Germany, 1970.

A seminal but second-generation international architect of the Modern Movement based in the USA. He graduated in 1917 from the Technische Hochschule, Vienna, where he had been taught by Adolf LOOS, and was influenced by Otto WAGNER. He worked for Erich MENDELSOHN in 1921-2 and emigrated to the USA in 1923. He met Frank Lloyd WRIGHT in 1924 at Louis SULLIVAN's funeral. He lived with SCHINDLER in his experimental King's Road House and collaborated with him in several proposals, including the League of Nations Competition. One of Neutra's earliest designs, the Health House for Dr Lovell in Los Angeles (1929), was prophetic and is perhaps his finest work. Using a light metal frame and stucco, he established a modern regionalism for Southern California. Later houses were increasingly light and effortless in appearance, with wall-sized sliding glass doors continuing architectural space into a carefully arranged landscape. His dramatic domestic images of flat industrial architectural surfaces juxtaposed against outdoor textures were popularized by the photography of Julius Shulman. The influential aesthetic and weightless spaces of the Modern Movement were sited in the soft atmosphere of the Hollywood Hills by Neutra. His professional intensity was reinforced by the family participation of his wife Dione from 1922, and his son Dion as a partner from 1965. A partnership with his protégé Robert E. Alexander (1949-58) produced a number of completed larger buildings less distinguished than Neutra's elegant and open custom houses. He was a prolific writer, traveller, draughtsman and speaker, and the titles of his books imply an organic commitment to architecture not present in his thin, cool, controlled built works. But his missionary dedication to the rationale of modern architecture as an international social force in the betterment of mankind was among the most passionate.

□ Lovell Health House, Los Angeles, 1929. Silverlake Research House, Los Angeles, 1933, 1964. Von Sternberg (Ayn Rand) House, San Fernando Valley, California, 1936. Kaufmann Desert House, Palm Springs, California, 1946. Hall of Records, Los Angeles (with Robert E. Alexander), 1964.

▷ Richard Neutra, *Wie Baut Amerika*, Stuttgart, 1926, Los Angeles, 1979; *Richard Neutra, Buildings and Projects* (Vol. I, 1922-50; Vol. II, 1950-60; Vol. III, 1961-6), New York etc., 1951-66; *Mysteries and Realities of the Site*, New York, 1951; *Survival Through Design*, New York and London, 1954. JC

▷ *see also pp232-3*

NIEMEYER Oscar

b. Rio de Janeiro, 1907.

Brazil's leading Modernist architect, planner and academic. Between 1930 and 1934 Niemeyer attended the Escola Nacional de Belas Artas in Rio de Janeiro. He then joined the team of Brazilian architects collaborating with LE CORBUSIER on a new Ministry of Education and Health in Rio de Janeiro. This proved an important and formative experience, and Niemeyer's early work reflects an eagerness to apply Corbusian principles. In 1939 he designed the Brazilian Pavilion for the New York World's Fair (with Lucio COSTA), but it was not until 1942 that he undertook his first major work – a group of recreational buildings at Pampulha in S Brazil, including his famous Church of St Francis of Assisi. These embody an anti-rational, highly expressive style which owed much to the sinuous sculptural quality of Brazilian Baroque architecture. In 1956 Costa won the competition for the design of Brazil's new capital, Brasilia, and Niemeyer was appointed architectural adviser to Nova Cap, the organization charged with implementing

Oscar Niemeyer, Government Buildings, Brasilia, 1957–64

the plans. The following year he became its chief architect, designing most of the city's important buildings, including the Presidential Palace, Congress Building and the National Theatre. This was the crowning achievement of Niemeyer's career, giving free rein to his imaginative, modern symbolism. He continued to work on designs for Brasilia until 1964, when a right-wing coup led him to spend some years of exile in France (he was a card-carrying Communist). Towards the end of the 1960s he resumed his career in Brazil, teaching at the University of Rio de Janeiro and working energetically in private practice. He was awarded the Gold Medal of the American Institute of Architects (1970).

☐ Ministry of Education and Health, Rio de Janeiro (with Lucio Costa, Le Corbusier and others), 1936-45. Pampulha Recreational Facility, Belo Horizonte, 1942-7. Government Buildings, Brasilia, 1957-64. Communist Party Headquarters, Paris, 1967-72.

▷ Oscar Niemeyer, *Oscar Niemeyer*, Milan, 1975. Rupert Spade, *Oscar Niemeyer*, New York, 1971. Nelson W. Sodre, *Oscar Niemeyer*, Rio de Janeiro, 1978. CS

OLBRICH Joseph Maria

b. Silesia, 1867; d. Düsseldorf, 1908.

A leading member of the Vienna Secession, responsible for developing a rectilinear form of Art Nouveau that grew from, as well as adorned, monumental forms. After studying architecture at the Academy of Fine Arts in Vienna (winning the Rome Prize in his third year), Olbrich worked in Otto WAGNER's office (largely on the Stadtbahn), where he was joined by Josef HOFFMANN, then travelled widely in Europe. On returning to Vienna he helped to form the anti-traditionalist exhibiting forum, the Secession. Intent on creating "new" art, the Secessionists looked, in particular, to British architects, notably Charles Rennie MACKINTOSH and BAILLIE SCOTT. The Secession Building is an example of Olbrich's mastery of combining monumentality with delicacy: the formality of the stucco building is lightened by the ornate, organic detailing of the gilded dome. In 1899 Olbrich was invited by the Grand Duke of Hesse to help establish an Artists' Colony at Darmstadt in Germany. There he designed a number of private houses, creating his own brand of "woody" Art Nouveau. Despite a short working life and a relatively small output, his designs were an inspiration to first-generation architects of the Modern Movement, notably Frank Lloyd WRIGHT.

☐ Under Wagner, work on Hofpavillon at Schönbrunn, Vienna, *c.*1888. Secession Building, Vienna, 1897-8. Haus Baur, Vienna, 1899. Ernst Ludwig Haus and other houses, Darmstadt, 1899-1901. Haus Olbrich, Darmstadt, 1900-1901. Gluckert Haus, Darmstadt, 1900-1901. Exhibition

Joseph Maria Olbrich, Secession Building, Vienna, 1897–8

Gallery, Darmstadt, 1900. Hochzeitsturm (Wedding Tower), Darmstadt, 1906-7. Tietz Department Store, Düsseldorf, 1906-8. Opel workers' house, Darmstadt, 1908.

▷ J. M. Olbrich, *Architektur* (3 vols), Berlin, 1901-14. Joseph A. Lux, *Joseph Maria Olbrich*, Berlin, 1919. Giulia Veronesi, *Joseph Maria Olbrich*, Milan, 1948. Karl H. Schreyl, *Joseph Maria Olbrich*, Berlin, 1972. Ian Latham, *Olbrich*, London, 1980. Peter Haiko and Bernd Krimmel, *Joseph Maria Olbrich Architecture*, London, 1988. PP

OLMSTEAD Frederick Law

b. Hartford. Conn., 1822, d. Boston, Mass., 1903.

Prophetic landscape architect and writer who inspired "City Beautiful" and the National Parks Movement in the USA. Because of an asthmatic condition, he had private tutoring instead of formal education, a limitation compensated by extensive travel to Europe and the Far East. A wide-ranging curiosity and openness characterized Olmstead's approach to life. His career embraced advocacy, journalism and the practical work of creating natural and urban parkland. He admired the design of PAXTON's Birkenhead Park, Liverpool, which he visited in 1847, and his partners included the English architect Calvert Vaux for many projects. The firm established by Olmstead in 1858 continues today. It is difficult to summarize the Olmstead achievement. His major creation is Central Park, New York City (commenced 1858), and without his foresight, the creation of National Parks would never have occurred. The inspiration is now worldwide. The formation of urban parkland to ameliorate city life is a corollary to his National Parks idea, which continues with the current movement for "greening our cities".

□ Central Park, New York (with Vaux), from 1858. Campus and village for Berkeley (College of California); also Mountain View Cemetery, Oakland. 1860s. Yosemite National Park and Mariposa Big Tree Grove, 1864. Riverside West, Chicago (with Vaux), 1868. Capitol Grounds, Washington DC, 1874. Mount Royal, Montreal, 1882. Stanford University, Palo Alto (with Shepley, Rutan & Cooledge), 1886. Niagara Falls Reservation (with Vaux), 1887. Rochester Park System, New York, 1888. World Columbian Exposition (with MCKIM, MEAD & WHITE), 1893.

▷ F. L. Olmstead Jnr and T. K. Hubbard (eds.), *F. L. Olmstead 1822-1903* (2 vols.), Cambridge, Mass., 1937. AB

Ragnar Östberg, Town Hall, Stockholm, 1913–23

ÖSTBERG Ragnar

b. Vaxholm, 1866; d. Stockholm, 1945.

Leading Swedish National Romantic architect. The son of a family of actors, he became a noted stage designer as well as a painter, etcher and professor (1922-3) at the Swedish College of Arts. During his early career he travelled widely, studying architecture and drawing it. For a time he worked in the office of J. G. Clason. Östberg's reputation rests firmly on his unique work on the Stockholm Town Hall, which has been described as one of the greatest buildings of the century. In this design he effectively combined "National" elements with diverse eclectic sources, including those he assimilated from the work of T. E. Collcutt (1840-1924) in South Kensington. He received the Gold Medals of both the AIA and the RIBA. When he received the latter in 1926 (the first Swedish architect to do so) it was in the presence of the Prince of Wales, an unprecedented event which underlines the strength of his reputation. Among his later works he built the Swedish Maritime Museum, which is really the last work of Swedish monumental classicism.

□ Town Hall, Stockholm, 1913-23. Helsingborg Crematorium, 1920-28. National Maritime Museum, Stockholm, 1934.

▷ Ragnar Östberg, *Stockholm Town Hall*, Stockholm, 1929. H. Robertson, "Ragnar Östberg", *RIBA Journal*, Nov. 1926, and a review of "The Naval Museum" in *The Architect and Building News*, 17 Jan. 1936. Hakon Ahlberg, *Swedish Architecture of the 20th Century*, London, 1925. DS

OTTO Frei

b. Siegmar, Saxony, 1925.

German architect who was responsible for bringing the tent into the C20; it was his special gift to see minimal lightweight structure as liberating and a bridge to natural or organic structure. He attended Schadow School, Zehlendorf, Berlin (1931-43), as a trainee mason, and served in the Second World War as a fighter pilot. After a period of compulsory labour service, he trained at the Technical University of Berlin (1948-50) under Freese, Bickenbach and Jobst. He established a studio at Zehlendorf (1952-8), later founding the Development Centre for Lightweight Construction, Berlin (1957); its activities were transferred to the Institute for Lightweight Structures, Stuttgart, in 1964. The tent manufacturer Peter Stromeyer was an important influence and supporter of Otto's career. In the 1950s, at a time when the static analysis of such complex surfaces was still in its infancy, Otto used models to define and test more complex shapes. Prior to the mid-1960s, Otto's textile pavilions consisted of the primary membrane elements composed in an additive series. The Pavilion of the Federal German Republic at the 1967 Montreal exposition was the earliest executed example to include a picturesque asymmetrical arrangement. The roofs of the main stadium and indoor arenas for the 1972 Munich Olympic Games, designed by Günter BEHNISCH with Otto as roof design consultant, realized an entirely new scale for this type of structure, and led to the pioneering of purely mathematical computer-based procedures for determining their shape and behaviour. Otto also developed a type of convertible roof with a variable geometry. Since 1972, he has concentrated increasingly on the examination and understanding of biological structures, at the same time carrying on research into grid shells and other topics. He is not an architect as the term is commonly understood, but an experimenter and catalyst who prefers to work with others.

□ Riverside Shelter and Dance Pavilion, Cologne, 1957. Pavilion of the Federal Republic of Germany at Expo '67, Montreal, Canada, 1965-7. Roofs for the Stadium and Arenas, Olympiapark, Munich, 1967-72. Retractable roof, Open-Air Theatre, Bad Hersfeld, 1968. Institute of Light Surface Structures, Vaihingen, 1968. Timber grid shell Multi-Purpose Hall and Restaurant, Mannheim, 1975. Aviary, Munich Zoo, 1980.

▷ Frei Otto, *Das hangende Dach*, Berlin, 1954; *Structures: Traditional and Lightweight*, New Haven, Conn., 1961; *Zugbeanspruchte Konstruktionen*, Vol. 1, Frankfurt-Berlin, 1962. C. Roland, *Frei Otto*, London, 1972. P. Drew, *Frei Otto: Form and Structure*, London, 1976. PD

Frei Otto, Olympic Stadium roof, Munich, 1967–72

OUD Jacobus Johannes Pieter

b. Purmerend, Holland, 1890;
d. Wassenaar, 1963.

Pioneer Dutch Functionalist architect and writer. J.J.P. Oud was educated at the Arts and Crafts School, Amsterdam, and trained as an architect at the Technical University, Delft. For a time he worked for Theodor Fischer in Munich before settling in Leiden, the home of Theo van DOESBURG, where the *De Stijl* movement originated in 1917. He became a member of the group for a while but later, in a brief autobiography, *Mein Weg in "De Stijl"*, written in the 1950s, he recalled the ambiguities of his membership. In 1918 he became Municipal Housing Architect for Rotterdam, retiring in the early 1930s owing to poor health. In 1933 he commenced practice on his own account. As a young socialist and propagandist for social housing he had been at the centre of the international architectural "Functionalist" tendency in Holland. He prepared numerous magazine articles, acted as a correspondent for Soviet architectural journals, and contributed a book on Dutch architecture to the *Bauhausbücher* series (1926). As one would expect, his best-known architectural works are for housing schemes in rapidly developing port and estate areas such as the Hook of Holland (1926-7) and the celebrated Kiefhoek development in Rotterdam (1928-9). He contributed a row of terrace houses to the Werkbund Exhibition on the Weissenhof, Stuttgart (1927). During and after the Second World War he became involved in larger commercial projects, but these never achieved the clarity of architectural expression of his early pioneer housing, which for many epitomized the best of the new architecture with their elegant curved white walls and flat roofs.

J. J. P. Oud, Housing Estate, Hook of Holland, 1926–7

□ Various housing schemes including those at Spangen, 1918-19; Oud-Mathenese, 1922; the housing estate at the Hook of Holland, 1926-7; row houses at the Weissenhofsiedlung, Stuttgart, 1927; the Kiefhoek development, Rotterdam, 1928-9. Shell Building, The Hague, 1938-42. Convalescent home near Arnhem, 1952-60.

▷ J. J. P. Oud, *Holländische Architektur*, Munich, 1926; *Mein Weg in "De Stijl"*, n.d. (1960). H.- R. Hitchcock, *J. J. P. Oud*, Paris, 1931. W. Fisher, *J. J. P. Oud: Bauten 1906-1963*, Munich, 1965. DS

▷ *see also pp234-5*

OWINGS Nathaniel A.

see Skidmore, Owings & Merrill.

P

SAN GIORGIO MAGGIORE, Venice

The superbly theatrical site, facing the Doge's palace across the water, inspired one of Andrea Palladio's most memorably dramatic façades. Soaring columns on giant plinths raise up the entablature above the quay-side piazza, all in dazzling white and lit – as is the interior of the church – by the play of reflected light from the ripples on the lagoon. Palladio's staginess is also evident in the rather awkward way a piece of wall has been added to join the sides of the entablature to the wings fronting the side aisles. Designed in 1565, earlier than the Redentore (begun 1576), the façade of San Giorgio was only completed in 1607–10, thirty years after Palladio's death.

PALLADIO Andrea

b. Padua, 1508; d. Vicenza, 1580.

Architect and theorist who embodied Renaissance architectural thought in the second half of the C16. The son of Pietro della Gondola, he was enrolled as assistant in the Vicenza guild of masons and stone-cutters in 1524, sponsored by the architectural stonemasons Giovanni da Porlezza and Girolamo Pittoni, with whom he retained a working relationship for more than 20 years. In 1538, through their involvement in the remodelling of the Villa Cricoli, he met the patron and amateur architect Giangiorgio Trissino, who took him under his wing and gave him the classical name Palladio. Palladio's first independent project was the Villa Godi, Lonedo (*c.*1538-1542). He was in Rome with Trissino in 1541 and again from 1547 to 1549; following Renaissance tradition, he earnestly studied and recorded the ancient buildings. In 1549 he obtained the commission for the Basilica (town hall) in Vicenza and surrounded the existing Gothic structure with a vast two-tiered stone loggia, a splendid homage to classical tradition. From 1550 to 1556 Palladio worked with Daniele Barbaro on a new edition of VITRUVIUS. By now his architectural projects were many and frequent, particularly palaces and villas for the aristocracy of Venice and Vicenza. One of his most successful domestic buildings is the Villa Barbaro at Maser (*c.*1555), with frescoes by Paolo Veronese; but his best-known villa is the Rotonda (Villa Capra) at Vicenza (*c.*1551), a perfectly symmetrical building with a circular domed central hall. He began to work on religious buildings in the 1560s, his best-known churches, both in Venice, being S. Giorgio Maggiore (1565) and the Redentore (1576), with strong relief façades and simple and severe single naves. In 1570 he published his theoretical work *I Quattro Libri dell 'Architettura*, and, on the death of SANSOVINO, was appointed architectural adviser to the Venetian Republic. He died in Vicenza while working on the Teatro Olimpico, an interesting reinvention of the classical theatre, covered but preserving the curved *cavea* and architectural stage setting. Although Palladio was influenced by his contacts with thinkers such as Trissino and Barbaro and architects such as SANMICHELE and SERLIO, his formative drives seem to have been of a more independent and personal nature. Directly linked to the theoretical and experimental tradition of ALBERTI and BRAMANTE, Palladio's practice of building and theory of architecture merge into one single activity, where the principles relating to art come from experience but, being based more generally on nature, are subject to continuous revision. His reinterpretation of Vitruvius's legacy becomes a fully experimental achievement of the sacred and civil types of architecture, both in his country villas and city palaces and in his conjuring up the modern church out of the old temple. Palladio's influence has been enormous in Italy as well as abroad, at first in France and then in its massive spread into C18 Britain. Palladio's vast production may lack some of the monumental grandeur of other important architects, but his name, over four centuries later, is still synonymous with a most successful and lasting way of restating ancient classicism.

☐ Villa Godi, Lonedo, *c.*1538-1542. Basilica (town hall), Vicenza, 1549. Rotonda (Villa Capra), Vicenza, *c.*1551. Villa Barbaro, Maser, *c.*1555. S. Giorgio Maggiore, Venice, 1565-1610. Redentore (Church of the Redeemer), Venice, 1576. Teatro Olimpico, Vicenza, 1580.

▷ Andrea Palladio, *The Four Books of (Andrea Palladio's) Architecture*, 1570 (facsimile of the 1738 English edition, New York, 1965); *Palladio Drawings*, ed. Lionello Puppi, New York, 1990. James S. Ackerman, *Palladio*, Harmondsworth, 1966. Gian Giorgio Zorzi, *Le Ville e i teatri di Andrea Palladio*, Venice, 1969. Lionello Puppi, *Andrea Palladio*, tr. P. Sanders, London and New York, 1975. GV

▷ *see also pp214-17*

PAXTON Sir Joseph

b. Milton Bryan, nr. Woburn, Beds., 1801; d. Sydenham, 1865.

English landscape gardener and architect, whose pre-eminence in conservatory construction led to his greatest achievement, the Crystal Palace erected for the International Exposition in 1851. A farmer's son, he was apprenticed as gardener to the Chatsworth estate, rising to head gardener (1826) and manager to the Duke of Devonshire's estates (1832). Paxton had no formal education in gardening or design, his gifts being those of shrewd observation and deduction. There was also a connection with the Royal Horticultural Society gardens at Chiswick, his horticultural expertise culminating in 1849 with the first propagation under glass of the Victoria Amazonica, hence his knighthood in 1850. Paxton's constructional interest in glasshouses had commenced at Chatsworth with a series of buildings to provide "forcing frames" for espalier trees; these designs dating from 1828 still stand, just W of the former Great Conservatory (1836/40), designed with Decimus BURTON. The latter glasshouse was the largest built at the time, measuring 84m (277 ft), with a span of 37m (123 ft), rising 20m (67 ft). It incorporated a glazing system perfected by Paxton involving slotted hardwood bars constructed on a ridge-and-farrow system between combined beam and gutter elements (made from laminated timber). The layout provided minimal shading, as compared with the usual array of purlins at frequent centres. The Crystal Palace competition had produced designs that were quite impracticable in terms of expenditure or time; Paxton's submission was irregular, having arrived after the closing date, but it was heralded with publication in the *Illustrated London News*. Paxton's ruse was successful, and tenders from Fox & Henderson agreed, with a four-month programme for covering 7 ha. (18 acres) of land. The resultant building was a masterpiece of prefabrication which invoked the judgement from the writer Lothar Bucher (1851) that "the Crystal Palace is a revolution in architecture from which a new style will date". Paxton's remaining years were dedicated to planning projects, helped by his presence in the House of Commons as MP for Coventry (1854-65). One of his most remarkable ideas was for a covered ring road in London, lined by shops and housing, with railways running along the upper structure.

☐ Garden works at Chatsworth House, Derbyshire (including the Great Conservatory, 1836-40), 1826-44; sundry works for the Chatsworth Estate, gate houses, cottages, including Russian Cottage (1855) Swiss Cottage (1839) and other works at Edensor. The Slopes, Buxton, Derbyshire (layout for park and proposals for housing), 1840s. Birkenhead Park, Cheshire, 1843-7. Schools at Pilsey and Stavely, 1844-9. Burton Closes, Bakewell (house and grounds), 1845-8. Rowsley and Matlock Stations, 1850. The Crystal Palace, Hyde Park, London, 1851. Transfer of the Crystal Palace to Sydenham and layout of park, S London, 1852-4. St Anne's, Baslow, Derbyshire (restoration), 1852-3. Mentmore House, Bucks., 1852-4, for the Rothschilds; followed by a further mansion for them at Ferrières, France (both in conjunction with G. H. Stokes). Pavilion and related gardens, Buxton, 1871. Projects: Crystal Palace schemes for New York and Paris, 1850s; Great Victorian Way, 1855; Thames Embankment Improvements, 1864-70.

▷ Violet R. Markham, *Paxton and the Bachelor Duke*, 1935. G. F. Chadwick, *The Works of Sir Joseph Paxton*, London, 1961. AB

▷ *see also pp222-3*

I. M. Pei, National Gallery of Art, Washington, 1978

PEI Ieoh Ming

b. Canton, China, 1917.

American-naturalized architect known for his large scale and sophisticated glass-clad buildings including the controversial glass pyramid at the Louvre Museum, Paris. Pei left China aged 18 and studied architecture at MIT and then under GROPIUS at Harvard. He became an instructor then assistant professor at Harvard before joining Webb & Knapp Inc., New York (1948-55). In 1955 he founded I. M. Pei & Partners, New York, which in 1979 became Pei, Cobb, Freed & Partners. Pei frequently works on a large scale and is renowned for his sharp, geometric designs. He first achieved recognition for the Dallas Municipal Center (1966-78), which is built of concrete and resembles an upturned pyramid wedged into the ground. It is heavier in style than subsequent buildings, such as the 60-storey John Hancock Tower in Boston, a slender glass-clad tower on a rhomboid plan described by the critic Charles Jencks as an "ice-blue skyberg". The fascination for pyramids surfaced again at the National Gallery of Art's East Building (1978), where the simple stone and brick gallery is given interest in the roof constructed of small glass pyramids. One of Pei's most startling structures is the Bank of China, Hong Kong (1984-8), which has a shaft of fractured triangular shapes that look like a dented space frame. Towards the top the skyscraper is finished with an off-centre spire topped by two slender communications towers resembling skyward-pointing chopsticks. Pei's greatest triumph is the large glass pyramid at the Cour Napoléon outside the Louvre, Paris. The structure in the courtyard is, as it suggests, the tip of an iceberg; below is a vast subterranean hall through which visitors pass to the Metro, shops and galleries.

□ Dallas Municipal Center, 1966-78. John Hancock Tower, Boston, Mass., 1973-7. East Building, National Gallery of Art, Washington DC, 1978. J. F. Kennedy Library, South Boston, Mass., 1979. Bank of China, Hong Kong, 1984-8. Morton H. Meyerson Symphony Center, Dallas, 1989. Louvre pyramid, Paris, 1989.

▷ Bruno Suner, *Ieoh Ming Pei*, Paris, 1984. FS

PELLI Cesar

b. Tucuman, Argentina, 1926.

US-based architect, known best for his vast shimmering towers used as corporate headquarters. After training at the Universidad Nacional de Tucuman and the University of Illinois Pelli worked at Eero SAARINEN & Associates (1954-64) and then became director of design at Daniel, Mann, Johnson & Mendenhall, Los Angeles, for four years. He stayed in Los Angeles and worked for Victor Gruen from 1968 to 1976, when he founded Cesar Pelli & Associates in New Haven. He describes himself as "a pragmatist" who feels that "there is strength and energy flowing" in everything including the energy in his projects themselves. Pelli designs almost exclusively on a large scale. His projects display his fascination for abstract, crystalline glass shapes which are shot through with lines of coloured stone or metal. One of his earliest successful projects was the Pacific Design Center in Los Angeles (1975-6). This enormous, long, low glass block, nicknamed locally "The Blue Whale", has its smooth, shiny surfaces broken by geometric protrusions; a continuous glass arch runs along the top and the wall tops are completed by a glass overhang. Pelli is also known for the "peel-back" effect he created in structures such as the Bunker Hill Project and the World Financial Center Towers by staggering the glass walls of the buildings to reveal further walls inside. One of Pelli's largest projects is the massive 240m (800 ft) tall – central glass-and-steel tower at London's Canary Wharf.

□ Pacific Design Center, Los Angeles, 1975-6. Bunker Hill Project, Los Angeles, 1980. World Financial Center Towers, New York, 1982-7. Four Leaf Towers, Houston, 1983-5. Canary Wharf, London, 1989-91.

▷ Paul Goldberger *et al.*, *Cesar Pelli: Buildings and Projects 1965-1990*, New York, 1990. FS

PERRAULT Claude

b. Paris, 1613; d. Paris, 1688.

Controversial figure of the late C17 whose radical theories signalled the birth of French Rationalism, which in turn established a framework for the European Enlightenment. Perrault's professional background was not in architecture but medicine. He graduated as a physician in 1642 and practised in Paris as well as teaching at the medical faculty, where he held the chair of physiology and anatomy. He was a founding member of the Académie des Sciences (1666) and in 1673 published a celebrated translation of VITRUVIUS which established his intellectual credibility. This seminal work was augmented some years later by the publication of *Ordonnance...*, which finally shattered Renaissance concepts concerning proportion and beauty. Rejecting the traditional notion of a strict interrelationship between musical and architectural harmony, Perrault argued that architecture should adopt a more flexible approach and abandon the rigid criteria governing the classical orders. Establishment figures and the Académie d'Architecture dismissed these theories as anarchic, and as a result Perrault actually built very little and devoted the last ten years of his life to scientific research.

Cesar Pelli, Canary Wharf, London, 1989–91, artist's drawing

□ Observatoire, Paris, 1667-72. East façade of the Louvre, Paris (in collaboration), 1667-74.

▷ Claude Perrault, *The Ten Books of Architecture by Vitruvius*, Paris, 1673; *Ordonnance...* Paris, 1683. Wolfgang Hermann, *The Theory of Claude Perrault*, London, 1973. Joseph Rykwert, *The First Moderns*, Cambridge, 1980. Robin Middleton and David Watkin, *Neoclassical and 19th Century Architecture*, New York, 1980. MC

PERRET Auguste

b. Ixelles, Belgium, 1874; d. Paris, 1954.

First architect to exploit reinforced concrete architecturally. The son of a prosperous builder, Perret entered the Ecole des Beaux Arts in 1891 but never took his diploma because he would be unable to be a contractor. He and his brother Gustave inherited their father's building company and experimented with *béton armé*, which had been pioneered by Hennebique in industrial buildings (variously called "reinforced concrete" or "ferro-cement": concrete threaded with steel which gives it strength in torsion and compression). They quickly established a reputation as the leading French building contractor in the material. Their first project, at 25 *bis* rue Franklin, Paris, was the first multistorey concrete building and used reinforced concrete ingeniously to exploit a difficult site. It introduced to the interiors a novel open-plan arrangement and was the first building where the con-

Auguste Perret, Apartment buildings, 25 bis *Rue Franklin, Paris, 1903–4*

crete frame is clearly expressed on the exterior, although it is used rather like a timber construction (Perret's architecture is often termed *trabeated*) and sheathed in ceramic tiling with decorative infilling. Similarly, the Théâtre des Champs Elysées uses a technically brilliant concrete frame but inside a classical masonry shell which had been designed by VAN DE VELDE complete with *belle époque* decoration. The revolutionary aesthetic and technical possibilities were fully exploited at the Church of Notre Dame du Raincy, where a shallow-vaulted concrete shell is supported on slender columns; the walls are non-load-bearing glass screens set in precast concrete frames. It was the first major use of exposed ferro-cement but it also looks to the past and is really the fusion of Gothic and classical elements which French architectural theorists had long called for. At rue Raynouard, Paris, the structural elements were cast *in situ* and the concrete frame was exposed. Where funds allowed, Perret removed the cement film of cast concrete to reveal the aggregate and express the structure of the material; he had a concern with detail and texture, alien to Modernism, which culminated in the search for a "national-classic" style in his later work, e.g. Mobilier National. Perret was steeped in the thought of the French rational and classical tradition. He saw a connection between natural forms, the symmetry and order of the classical grid and his structural system of concrete. "The great buildings of our time consist of a skeleton ... like the skeleton of an animal." He therefore saw concrete as a superior form of construction to masonry. But because he also saw each element as separate he did not use it to form a structural whole in the way systematized by LE CORBUSIER and GROPIUS.

☐ Casino, St Malo, 1899. Apartment buildings, 25 *bis* rue Franklin, Paris, 1903-4. Garage Marbœuf, 51 rue de Ponthieu, Paris, 1905. Théâtre des Champs Elysées, Paris, 1911-13. Docks of Casablanca, Morocco, 1915. Church of Notre Dame, Le Raincy, 1922-4. Apartment building, 51 rue Raynouard, Paris, 1930-32. Mobilier National, Paris, 1934-5. Plan of Le Havre, 1956. Church of St Joseph, Le Havre 1952.

▷ A. Perret, *Contribution à une théorie de l'architecture*, Paris, 1952. P. Collins, *Concrete: The Vision of a New Architecture; study of Auguste Perret and his precursors*, London, 1959. TC

PERUZZI Baldassare

b. Siena, 1481; d. Rome, 1536.

Follower of BRAMANTE and outstanding pioneer of early Mannerism in Rome. Initially a painter in his birthplace, from 1501 he was in Rome, where his first architectural work is one of his most celebrated, the Villa Farnesina in Trastevere (1509-11). He had many private and ecclesiastical commissions in Rome and elsewhere for both buildings and decorative painting schemes. From 1520 he was associate architect of St Peter's with Antonio SANGALLO THE YOUNGER, continuing MICHELANGELO's and BRAMANTE's designs. During the Sack of Rome in 1527, he slipped home to Siena to escape a heavy ransom and was made architect to the cathedral there. He was gradually drawn to Rome again from 1531 onwards and was confirmed as joint architect for St Peter's. His design for the Palazzo Massimo alle Colonne (begun 1532) on an awkward corner site in Rome is a masterpiece of inventiveness. The small number of his completed buildings does not detract from the importance of Peruzzi's theoretical and design work, much of which survives on paper. He developed the handling of multiple perspective in drawing, did stage designs and clever trompe-l'œil decorations, and even adapted late Gothic forms in the façade of S. Petronio, Bologna. He wrote a commentary on VITRUVIUS and an architectural treatise of his own. See also SERLIO.

Baldassare Peruzzi, Villa Farnesina, Rome, 1509–11

☐ Villa Farnesina, Trastevere, Rome, 1509-11. Palazzo Massimo alle Colonne, Rome, 1532-6.

▷ P. Pouncey and J. A. Gere, *Raphael and his Circle*, London, 1962. JRC

▷ *see also pp214–15*

PIACENTINI Marcello

b. Rome, 1881; d. Rome, 1960.

Italian Rationalist/Fascist architect, planner, academic and writer. The son of the respected Italian architect Pio Piacentini, he studied at the Accademia di S. Luca in Rome and from 1906 onwards worked independently in private practice in Rome, gradually establishing his reputation with a series of buildings such as the Cinema al Corso, which revealed an experimental interest in Modernism. By the time Piacentini had completed the Neo-Classical Palace of Justice in Messina (1928) he was regarded as a leading figure in the architectural establishment. In 1920 he became professor at the Scuola Superiore di Architettura in Rome, and the following year he founded the magazine *L'Architettura* with Gustavo Giovannoni. Following the Fascist seizure of power, Piacentini found himself the leading exponent of state architecture. His blend of sparse Neo-Classicism with monumental overtones became the dominant style of Fascist buildings and during the 1930s he worked on three of the most significant commissions in Rome at that time – the Master Plan (1931), the University of Rome (1932-3) and the satellite town for the Esposizione Universale di Roma (1937-43), which was abandoned because of the Second World War. Although Piacentini was a political opportunist, he was not a dedicated Fascist and made discreet attempts to support the emerging cause of Italian Rationalism through his powerful position in the architectural establishment. However, his attitude to Rationalism remained ambivalent and his own experiments with Modernism were really no more than stylistic exercises, without social or political conviction.

☐ Palace of Justice, Messina, 1912-28. Cinema al Corso, Rome, 1915-17. Master Plan of Rome, 1931. University of Rome (with others), 1932-3.

▷ Luciano Patetta, *L'architettura in Italia 1919-1943: Le Polemiche*, Milan, 1972. Bruno Zevi, *Storia dell'architettura moderna*, 5th ed., Turin, 1975. CS

PIANO Renzo

b. Genoa, 1937.

Leading Italian architect and designer concerned with technological innovations and environmentally balanced buildings. From 1959 to 1964 Piano studied at the Milan Politecnico, where he subsequently taught until 1968. In 1970 he set up in partnership with the English architect Richard ROGERS and undertook a number of commissions in Italy and England, including the PATScentre in Cambridge in 1975. The practice's most important work, however, was its winning entry for the Place Beaubourg competition for a national arts centre in the middle of Paris, organized by the French government in 1973 (the Pompidou Centre). The imposing six-storey design takes the metaphor of "cultural machine" to its technological extreme by placing the structural skeleton and colour-coded servicing elements on the outside of the building. Piano's use of technological function as a point of departure characterizes the work of what has become known as the "High-Tech" group of architects. This movement includes English designers such as Norman FOSTER, Nicholas Grimshaw and Michael Hopkins. However, Piano's desire to achieve a particular aesthetic quality is tempered by a concern for accommodating the user's needs. In his later work Piano has continued the structural experiments of the Pompidou Centre, applying them to a range of social and civic projects such as the residential quarter at Corciano in Perugia, the museum building for the De Menil Collection in Houston, Texas, and, most recently, a new football stadium in Bari, S Italy, built for the 1990 World Cup. The Stadio Nuovo continues Piano's fruitful collaboration with the English engineer Peter Rice of Ove Arup and Partners.

☐ Centre Beaubourg, Paris (with Richard Rogers and Peter Rice), Paris, 1973-7. PATScentre Research Laboratories and Workshops, Cambridge, England (with Richard Rogers), 1975. Experimental residential quarter, Corciano, Perugia (with Peter Rice), 1978-82. Museum for the De Menil Collection, Houston, Texas, 1981. Stadio Nuovo, Bari (with Peter Rice), 1990.

▷ "Renzo Piano", *Architecture d'Aujourd'hui*, Feb. 1982. Dino Massimo, *Renzo Piano: progetti e architettura 1964-1983*, Paris and Milan, 1983. Paul Goldberger (intro.), *Renzo Piano: Buildings and Projects 1971-1989*, New York, 1989. CS

▷ *see also pp240-41, 244-5*

PIETILÄ Reima

b. Turku, Finland, 1923.

Finnish architect who represents a clear lineage from AALTO and SONCK yet has diverged to produce an architecture with *genius loci* strength and architectonic significance. He graduated in 1953 and worked briefly with Helsinki City before winning the competition for the Finnish Pavilion at the Brussels World Fair (1957). In 1960 he set up joint practice with his second wife, **Raili Pietilä** (*née* Paatelainen). Pietilä's tireless exploration began with the "form of form" (Brussels 1958, Venice Pavilion Projects 1959) collaborating with Aulis Blomstedt and working closely with *Le Carré Bleu*. Between 1958 and 1961 Pietilä won three important competitions: Kaleva Church, the Dipoli Students' Centre and the Finnish Embassy in New Delhi. These are a series of remarkable free-form designs but never simple expressionist studies. Pietilä began to distance himself from the more rational studies of his Finnish colleagues. Isolation at home caused him to work abroad, e.g. the Sief Palace Buildings in Kuwait (1972-82). Much of this work and its cultural semiotics came back into his later Finnish projects, the Hervanta Cultural Centre and Lieksa Church. Always interrogating, always oscillating between theory and praxis, a discipline for his development of form, Pietilä was Professor of Architecture at Oulu University between 1973 and 1979, but ceased teaching to concentrate on a second series of intense works, equally remarkable for their breadth, architectural innovation and cultural significance, culminating in the Residence for the President of Finland.

☐ Finnish Pavilion, Brussels, 1958. Dipoli, Otaniemi, 1966. Kaleva Church, Tampere, 1966. Cultural Centre, Hervanta, 1979-86. Lieksa Church 1979. Sief Palace Buildings, Kuwait, 1972-82. Tampere Main Library, 1984. Finnish Embassy, New Delhi, 1986. Residence for the President of Finland, Helsinki, 1993.

▷ Reima Pietilä, *The Morphology of Expressive Form*, Helsinki, 1958. C. Benincasa, *Il Labirinto del Sabba*, Bari, 1979. M. Quantrill, *Pietilä: Architecture, Context and Modernism*, Helsinki, 1984. R. Connah, *Writing Architecture*, Cambridge, Mass., and London, 1989. RC

▷ *see also pp240-41, 244-5*

PIRANESI Giovanni Battista

b. Mogliano di Mestre, near Venice, 1720; d. Rome, 1778.

One of the foremost visionaries and advocates of Neo-Classicism, immensely influential in the formulation of a new taste which was carried beyond Italy to France and was brought to Britain by his protégé Robert ADAM. Piranesi trained as an architect in Venice, where he also studied stage design. Having first travelled to Rome in 1740, he settled there in 1744, and there embarked on the series of seminal publi-

Giovanni Battista Piranesi, Engraving of ruins of Hadrian's Villa, 1771

cations, meticulously illustrated with his spectacular engravings, that were to establish his reputation. His early views of Rome are heavily indebted to the topographical manner of Canaletto and other Venetians, although many, especially those of ancient ruins, are infused with a new grandeur by skilful manipulation of perspective and resort to dramatic atmospheric effects. The influence of ancient Rome is particularly striking in the famous series of fantastic views of prisons, the *Carceri*. In composition, they depend on the tradition of stage set design that had been perfected by Ferdinando GALLI DA BIBIENA, but the sheer scale and drama of the awesome architecture reflect an entirely new response to the classical heritage. Piranesi's attitude to architecture is most clearly expressed in his subsequent writings. He championed the cause of Roman and Etruscan against the rival claims of Greek architecture, and laid particular emphasis on constructional and technical prowess; but he also warned against slavish imitation and valued a creative inventiveness appropriate to a modern age. He exercised his own inventive powers in his numerous reconstructions of ancient buildings which reveal a creative imagination more vivid and more all-encompassing even than his famous C16 predecessor Pirro Ligorio (*c.*1510-1583). For real buildings, however, Piranesi's designs were few. The most far-reaching were his proposals for the Lateran, which involved adding an enormous new apse with hidden top-lighting enclosing a semicircular colonnade. The interior of the remodelled Santa Maria del Priorato, with its ribbed vaulting, recalls BORROMINI, whom Piranesi admired. The planar exterior, like the peripheries of the nearby Piazza de'Cavalieri, incorporates a rich antiquarian decoration within a sober classical framework. Piranesi also produced a series of equally inventive chimneypiece designs for English patrons.

□ Piazza de'Cavalieri di Malta, Rome, 1764-6. Santa Maria del Priorato, Rome, 1764-6. Designs for remodelling of S. Giovanni Laterano, Rome, *c.* 1765.

▷ G. B. Piranesi, *Prima Parte di Architettura e Prospettive*, 1743; *Invenzioni Capric di Carceri*, 1748 (modified and reissued *c.*1760); *Vedute di Roma*, *c.* 1748; *Antichità Romane*, 1748; *Della Magnificenza ed Architettura de'Romani*, 1761; *Il Campo Marzo dell'Antica Roma*, 1762; *Parere su l'Architettura*, 1765; *Pianta di Roma e del Campo Marzio*, *c.*1774; *Différent Vues...de Pesto*, 1778. A. Giesecke, *Giovanni Battista Piranesi*, Leipzig, 1911. H. Foçillon, *Giovanni Battista Piranesi, 1720-1778*, Paris, 1918. A. Hind, *Giovanni Battista Piranesi, a Critical Study*, London, 1922. J. Wilton-Ely, *The Mind and Art of Giovanni Battista Piranesi*, London, 1978.

DH

POELZIG Hans

b. Berlin, 1869; d. Berlin, 1936.

Leading architect in Germany in the early part of the C20, who, as teacher and practitioner, influenced both Expressionist and Functionalist pupils and followers. He was trained as an architect at the Technische Hochschule in Berlin-Charlottenburg, where later he became a full professor. In 1899 he moved to Breslau, where he took up a teaching appointment at the Academy, of which he also later became director. At the turn of the century it was an important centre of art and architectural education in Germany and among Poelzig's celebrated colleagues were the architect philosopher Auguste Endell and Moll. An idiosyncratic, individual and Expressionist architect, he designed an unusual watermill project with shaped walls and windows in 1908. One of his first major projects was a striated corner concrete office block in Breslau. The year 1913 saw the opening of Max Berg's Centennial Hall, Breslau, and the large-scale planning scheme Poelzig had planned with him for the city's Centennial Exhibition. At the end of the First World War he became closely associated with the general artistic movement of Expressionism working on films like *Der Golem* and the creation

Hans Poelzig, Grosses Schauspielhaus, Berlin, 1919–20

of Max Reinhardt's "Theatre of 5000" to form the new *Grosses Schauspielhaus*, converted from the C19 Schumann Circus building in the centre of Berlin. The memorable, sculpted, cavernous interior of this building, with its stalactite forms, is often referred to as the epitome of architectural Expressionism. Poelzig designed a number of other schemes along the same lines, again for Reinhardt, with various projects for his proposed Salzburg Festival Hall. He was active as a vice president of the German Werkbund and once building activity began again in Germany, after 1923, he produced some fine housing estates and other more conventional buildings.

☐ Office Building, Breslau (now Wroclaw, Poland), 1912-13. House of Friendship Project, Istanbul, 1917. Grosses Schauspielhaus, Berlin, 1919-20. Salzburg Festival Hall Projects, 1922-3.

▷ Hans Poelzig, *Der Architekt*, Stuttgart, 1931. H. G. Scheffauer, "Hans Poelzig", *Architectural Review*, Oct. 1923. Theodor Heuss, *Hans Poelzig: Bauten und Entwürfe*, 1939, and *Lebensbild eines Baumeisters*, 1955. See also "Hans Poelzig and Formenrausch" in D. Sharp, *Modern Architecture and Expressionism*, London and New York, 1964. The definitive text is J. Posener, *Hans Poelzig: Gesammelte Schriften und Werke*, Berlin, 1970. DS

PONTI Gio

b. Milan, 1891; d. Milan, 1979.

Influential Milanese architect who acted as a catalyst for the rejuvenation of Italian design after the Second World War. Ponti served two years in the Italian army before enrolling at Milan's Politecnico in 1918. Having graduated in 1921, he collaborated with Emilio Lancia (1927-33) and Antonio Fornaroli and Eugenio Soncini (1933-45). Later he worked in partnership with Fornaroli and Alberto Rosselli (1952-76). Ponti developed an elegant modernity within his designs which eschewed the extremes of either committed rationalism or academic Neo-Classicism. He returned to the Politecnico as professor of interior design (1936-61), promoting an essentially humanistic approach to design as a fusion of pragmatic rationalism within the classical tradition. His œuvre encompasses not only architecture but also furniture and industrial design, town planning, graphics, ceramics, painting and scenic design. He was also founding editor of the influential periodical *Domus* (1928-41, 1948-79).

PIRELLI TOWER, Milan

Gio Ponti's elegant masterpiece, the Pirelli Tower in Milan (built 1956–8), played an important role in rejuvenating Italian design after the Second World War. The 33-storey building, distinguished by its tapering sides and smooth, regular façades, was one of the first European skyscrapers to depart from the rectangular block form and thus avoided imitating American models. It was also a counterblast to the "curtain wall" high block. The architectural critic Charles Jencks described the building as a "skywedge". The tower, which is 126m (415ft) high, was completed in collaboration with the innovative structural engineer, Pier Luigi Nervi, who abandoned the usual steel cage construction in favour of a bold structural skeleton consisting of a double vertebrae form with floors suspended in-between and lifts running through the central core. The tower was completed with a shiny metallic cladding.

☐ Montecatini Building, Milan, 1936. RAI Offices, Milan, 1938. Pirelli Tower, Milan (in collaboration), 1956-8. Cathedral, Taranto, 1971. Museum of Modern Art, Denver, 1972.

▷ Gio Ponti, *Amate l'architettura*, Milan, 1957; *In Praise of Architecture*, New York, 1960. Nathan Shapira (ed.), *The Expression of Gio Ponti*, Minneapolis, 1967. Lisa Licitra Ponti, *Gio Ponti – The Complete Works 1923-78*, London, 1990. MC

POWELL & MOYA

Established 1946. Sir Philip Powell, b. Bedford, 1921. John Hidalgo Moya, b. Los Gartos, California, 1926.

Important post-war British architectural partnership. They studied at the Architectural Association School, London, when Sir Frederick GIBBERD was principal, and on graduating in 1944 they both joined his office. Gibberd's undogmatic Modernism was to become an important influence. They founded the partnership after winning a competition for the Pimlico housing scheme, a redevelopment of thirty-three acres next to the Thames (1946-62). In 1951, for the Festival of Britain, they designed the "Vertical Feature", or *Skylon*, an attempt to symbolize progress in post-war Britain. Powell & Moya have a significant place in post-war British Modernism and have designed a wide range of buildings, often associated with public provision and the welfare state. However, the practice was not part of the "brutalist" movement but sought instead a "modernist vernacular", producing distinct design solutions for different contexts. For example, several of their buildings in Oxford and Cambridge use traditional material in a Modernist idiom.

☐ Churchill Gardens Estate, Pimlico, London, 1946-62. Skylon, Festival of Britain, South Bank, London, 1951. Mayfield School, Putney, London, 1956. Festival Theatre, Chichester, Sussex, 1961. Wycombe General Hospital, High Wycombe, Bucks., 1966-75. Cripps Building, St John's College, Cambridge, England, 1967. British Pavilion, Expo 70, Osaka, Japan, 1970. Museum of London, 1976. Queen Elizabeth II Conference Centre, London, 1986.

▷ R. Maxwell, *New British Architecture*, London, 1972.

PROUVÉ Jean

b. Nancy, 1901; d. Nancy, 1966.

French pioneer in the use of industrial techniques in building. Although he received some education in engineering, Prouvé was trained principally as a metal worker. In 1923 he established his own works in Nancy, which was reorganized in 1931 for the production of prefabricated building products. Prouvé believed that problems of form could be tackled only by coming to terms with industrialization. He had a close working relationship with various architects, including LE CORBUSIER, and helped to develop the new building tradition in which construction was based on industrial design and production. He was responsible for the design of the first totally industrialized building (1936-7), and after the Second World War was involved in the mass-production of houses based on the total prefabrication of building components. In 1954 he moved to Paris, where he worked as an independent designer and consultant. Prouvé's name is particularly linked with the use of lightweight sheet metal, often ridged for strength and rigidity, a theme which has been exhaustively explored by High-Tech architects, although Prouvé was as concerned with space and proportion as with the refinement of industrial detailing.

□ Roland Garros Aero-Club, Buc, France, 1936-7. Maison du Peuple, Clichy, France, 1938-9. Prototypical Emergency Houses, France, 1939. Houses, Meudon, France, 1950. Pump Room, Evian, France, 1956. Free University, Berlin-Dahlem, Germany (detailing), 1963-73. Ecole Nationale d'Architecture, Nancy, 1969-70.

▷ R. Banham, "Jean Prouvé: the thin metal detail", *Architectural Review* 131, April 1962. B. Huber and J. H. Steinegger (eds.), *Jean Prouvé Prefabrication: Structures and Elements*, London and New York, 1971. TC

PUGIN Augustus Welby Northmore

b. London, 1812; d. Ramsgate, 1852.

Initiator and principal theorist of the serious phase of Victorian Gothic architecture. The son of a French *émigré* draughtsman, **Augustus Charles Pugin** (1762-1832), and an Englishwoman, Catherine Welby, Pugin was trained by his parents in a small, informal school for architectural illustrators and architects which they conducted privately. His public work of writing, drawing, and the designing of buildings began in 1835 with the completion and publication of *Examples of Gothic Architecture*, a work his father had left incomplete at his death. In the same year, 1835, Pugin became a convert to Catholicism, a commitment which overwhelmed and conditioned all his future undertakings. The publication in 1836 of *Contrasts: or, a Parallel between the Noble Edifices of the Fourteenth and Fifteenth Centuries, and Similar Buildings of the Present Day: shewing the Present Decay of Taste: Accompanied by appropriate Text* brought him instant notoriety, and determined the extremes of opinion which were to face him and his work for the rest of his life. The argument was premissed on the idea that the arts and artefacts of society were dependent for their quality on the nature of the society that produced them: that, by a series of extrapolations, Gothic architecture was Christian architecture, that society must rediscover its ancient relationship with the Church for the rediscovery of the heart of true architecture, that the Reformation broke not only the link between divine revelation and society, but that the architecture it promoted was pagan, not only in its classical beginnings, but in its subsequent development. In both his designing and his subsequent writing, such as *The True Principles of Pointed or Christian Architecture* (1841), Pugin sought to explore and to manifest the ways in which the Catholic links could be re-established, the ways in which the God-given principles could be explored by means of the archaeology of the remaining Gothic buildings, and used as the principles for modern building. His building work from 1835 onwards, beginning with St Marie's Grange, near Salisbury, for his own young family, encompassed in the seventeen years until his death designs for more than one hundred buildings. He was retained to work with BARRY on his entry for the competition for the new Houses of Parliament, and subsequently designed and detailed much, perhaps nearly all, of the fabric of the superstructure under Barry's direction. He designed furnishings and fitments for many other architects as well as for his own commissions, he wrote eight major books and many articles and pamphlets, and his frenetic energy was matched by a witty but uncompromising intolerance of any view but his own.

□ Scarisbrick Hall, Lancs., from 1836. Alton Towers, Staffordshire, from 1837. Roman Catholic Cathedrals at Birmingham, 1839-41, and Nottingham, 1842-4. Our Lady and St Wilfred, Warwick Bridge, Cumberland, 1840. Bilton Grange, Rugby, 1841-6. St Giles, Cheadle, Staffs, 1841-6.

▷ A. W. N. Pugin, *Contrasts*, 1836; *The True Principles of Pointed or Christian Architecture*, 1841; *Apology for the Revival of Christian Architecture in England*, 1843. M. Trappes-Lomax, *Pugin, a Medieval Victorian*, 1932. RM

▷ *see also pp224-5, 228-9*

PURCELL & ELMSLIE

Established 1913.

American architectural partnership which developed its own interpretation of the Prairie School tradition. **William Gray Purcell** (b. Chicago, 1880; d. California, 1965) was brought up in the Oak Park district of Chicago and went on to study architecture at Cornell University. After graduating in 1903 he worked for a succession of architectural firms, including a short spell with Louis SULLIVAN. In 1906 he travelled to Europe with a Cornell colleague, George Feick, and on their return they established the firm of Purcell & Feick in Minneapolis. By contrast, **George Grant Elmslie** (b. Huntly, Scotland, 1871; d. 1952) came from a large Scottish farming family who emigrated to Chicago in 1884. Three years later he entered the office of J. Lyman Silsbee, where he met Frank Lloyd WRIGHT. In 1888 he was engaged by Adler and Sullivan, eventually becoming chief draughtsman after Wright's departure. Elmslie continued his association with Sullivan until 1909; subsequently he joined the practice of Purcell & Feick, which then became Purcell & Elmslie following Feick's departure in 1913. Though the careers of both partners were intrinsically bound up with Sullivan, Wright and the American Arts & Crafts movement, their buildings express a highly personalized vision of the Prairie School tradition. Like Sullivan, Purcell & Elmslie designed a series of banks throughout the Midwest, the largest being the Merchants Bank of Winona. Other civic work included the Woodbury County Courthouse in Sioux City, which ranks as the largest public building to be designed in the Prairie School style. Purcell & Elmslie also completed a number of variations on the American Arts & Crafts basic two-storey family residence. In 1922 the firm was dissolved, both partners continuing to work separately. Ill-health took its toll on Purcell, while Elmslie's career virtually ended with the onset of the Depression.

□ Merchants Bank, Winona, Minnesota (with George Feick), 1911-12. Edison Shop, San Francisco, 1914. C. T. Backus House, Minneapolis, 1915. Woodbury County Courthouse, Sioux City, 1915-17.

▷ David Gebhard, *Purcell and Elmslie: Architects* (exhibition catalogue), Minneapolis, 1953. Carl W. Condit, *The Chicago School of Architecture*, Chicago, 1964. H. A. Brooks, *The Prairie School*, Toronto, 1972. CS

RAINALDI Carlo

b. Rome, 1611; d. Rome, 1691.

Responsible for some of the most spectacular designs of Baroque Rome. He trained as an architect with his father Girolamo (1570-1655), with whom he had planned the influential Santa Agnese. The design was altered when the work was given briefly to BORROMINI (1653-5) before returning to Carlo; the scenic conception of the building, twin towers framing the tall dome that rises from a Greek-cross layout, was theirs. Carlo's masterpiece, Santa Maria in Campitelli, has a complex twin-focused interior which is monumentalized by an abundance of engaged columns that frame the successive spaces, a highly plastic approach to design reminiscent of Pietro da CORTONA. The grandiose facade, inspired by Cortona, is an interlocking composition based on columnar tabernacles which achieves an unprecedented depth. Even more dramatic is Rainaldi's remodelling of the Piazza del Popolo, one of the most ambitious urban projects of the period. A pair of porticoed and domed churches, which appear virtually identical although one is in fact oval, were built in the angles of three radiating streets, providing a splendid spectacle to greet the visitor at the entrance to Rome.

□ Santa Agnese in Piazza Navona, Rome, from 1652. S. Andrea della Valle, Rome (façade), 1661-5. Santa Maria in Campitelli, Rome, 1662. Piazza del Popolo, Rome, 1662.

▷ R. Wittkower, *Studies in the Italian Baroque*, London, 1975. DH

▷ *see also pp218-19*

RAPHAEL (RAFFAELLO SANZIO)

b. Urbino, 1483; d. Rome, 1520.

A considerable innovator who established the basic language of variety and decoration that was to characterize Italian architecture for the remainder of the c16. Raphael was well established as the leading painter in Rome before becoming papal architect on the death of BRAMANTE in 1514. His views on architecture are made explicit in a famous letter addressed to his patron Leo X which criticizes the quality of ornamentation in Bramante's pioneering buildings. Several of Raphael's buildings provide a critique of his predecessor's. The Chigi Chapel resembles the crossing of Bramante's St Peter's, but in miniature and heavily ornamented. Palazzo Branconio, similarly ornamented, abandons the straightforward regularity of Bramante's innovatory Palazzo Caprini. Its three storeys form an animated counterpoint with one another, the tabernacled windows of the main living floor alternating with niches provocatively positioned over the ground-floor half-columns. Raphael's response to the example of Antiquity, more penetrating than that of any previous architect, was to exert a profound influence over the next generation. In the papal Villa Madama, the monumental planning as a series of terraces derives from Roman villa complexes. The enormous vaulted loggia recalls the halls of Roman baths, and the sumptuous plaster and paintwork revives Roman decoration studied in the Golden House of Nero and elsewhere.

□ Continuation of St Peter's, Rome, from 1514 (little realized). Chigi Chapel, Santa Maria del Popolo, Rome, *c.*1515. Villa Madama, Rome, from 1516 (unfinished). Palazzo Branconio dell'Aquila, Rome, 1518-20.

▷ S. Ray, *Raffaello Architetto*, Rome, 1974. C. L. Frommel *et al.* (ed.), *Raffaello Architetto*, Milan, 1984. DH

▷ *see also pp214-15*

Raphael (Raffaello Sanzio)

RAYMOND Antonin

b. Kladno, Bohemia, 1888;
d. Langhorne, Pennsylvania, 1976.

Czech architect who took the International Style to Japan. Raymond graduated from the Technical University of Prague and emigrated to the USA in 1910. At Taliesen in 1916 he met Frank Lloyd WRIGHT, and in 1919 he went to Japan with him to assist in the construction of the Imperial Hotel. In 1921 he opened his own practice in Tokyo. With his first commission, the Tanaka House, the orientation and respect for climate and culture that characterize his design discipline were established. In 1937 Raymond journeyed to India to initiate the dormitory at the Sri Aurobindo Ashram, a major work of bioclimatic sensibility, beautifully detailed in modern permanent materials built in a remote location. In 1938 he opened an office in New York. He returned to his Tokyo office in 1945 and maintained an international practice with Ladislav Rado. Raymond's internationalism was informed by traditional Japanese houses and crafts. His lean functional architectural detailing is celebrated in his influential 1937 book. Yet his early post-war work shocked Japanese colleagues with its rational refinement. Although a painter and associated with avant-garde artists and composers, Raymond believed that personal expression was inappropriate in modern architecture. In continuing the traditional Japanese embrace of a refined nature his architecture spanned from the years before the Bauhaus to the green and ecological standards of the late C20.

□ Raymond House, Reinanzaka, Tokyo, 1923. St Paul's Church, Kanuizawa, Nagano, Japan, 1934. Golcond Dormitory, Pondicherry, India, 1937-41. Reader's Digest Building, Tokyo, 1949-52. Campus, Nanzan University, Nagoya, 1960-66.

▷ Antonin Raymond with Noemi Raymond, *Architectural Details*, Tokyo, 1937, New York, 1938. Antonin Raymond, *An Autobiography*, Rutland, Vermont and Tokyo, 1973. JC

REIDY Affonso Eduardo

b. Paris, 1909; d. Rio de Janeiro, 1964.

Innovative French-born Modernist architect and planner who lived and worked in Brazil. Although born in France, Reidy grew up in Brazil and began his architectural training in 1927 at the Escola Nacional de Belas Artes in Rio de Janeiro. He obtained his diploma in 1930 and the following year joined the school's teaching staff. From 1936 until 1943 he worked on the design of the new Ministry of Education and Health, the first government-sponsored Modernist building in Brazil, which brought international recognition to the country's emerging Modern Movement. Like Oscar NIEMEYER, Reidy was profoundly influenced by the theories of LE CORBUSIER, who spent some time lecturing and working with the Ministry of Education and Health project team in 1936. After this exposure to Modernist principles, Reidy began to fight against the pervasive influence of academic colonialism which dominated Brazilian architecture until the 1930s. In 1947 he was appointed to the Department of Public Housing and went on to design a project for low-income housing in Rio's Pedregulho district, in the form of a distinctive serpentine structure which followed the existing contours of the site. The scheme incorporated centralized community facilities in the best Corbusian tradition. Another housing development, in the Gávea quarter, was designed along similar lines. Both projects demonstrated a new tropical regionalism, which exploited difficult site conditions and made use of indigenous materials. Reidy's final work was the Museum of Modern Art in Rio de Janeiro, built on reclaimed land in Guanabara Bay. It consists of a glazed exhibition hall supported by a series of concrete ribs, in a daring display of Modernist structural aesthetics which typifies Reidy's innovative approach. His work represents an important application and development of Corbusian ideals in Brazil.

□ Ministry of Education and Health, Rio de Janeiro (with Lucio COSTA, Oscar Niemeyer, Le Corbusier and others), 1936-43. Pedregulho Housing Project, Rio de Janeiro, 1947. Gávea Residential Development, Rio de Janeiro, 1950-52. Museum of Modern Art, Rio de Janeiro, 1954-60.

▷ Klaus Franck, *The Works of Affonso Eduardo Reidy*, New York, 1960. CS

Humphry Repton, design for garden at Sheringham Hall, Norfolk

REPTON Humphry

b. Bury St Edmunds, 1752; d. Aysham, Norfolk, 1818.

Influential landscape gardener who sought by text and example to continue the vision of Capability BROWN, and became the most eloquent and best-remembered exponent of the "Picturesque" in English landscape. He was intended for a mercantile career, but in 1755 received a legacy which allowed him for a time to become a dilettant and writer. His first works were illustrative (views drawn for Blomefield's *History of Norfolk*, 1783); later he published essays covering a wide theoretical range. In the late 1780s Repton's reduced circumstances led him to explore a professional life. His early designs for clients included landscape improvements to Catton (1789) and Sheffield Park (1791). Many garden and landscape works were to follow. The creative process was developed through pattern books prepared for each task at a cost to the client of 5 guineas per day and called "Red Books". Repton's influence is encapsulated in these "Red Books"; over 400 design studies were prepared for landscape improvements, with "before-and-after views" and well-argued cases for acceptance. These publications, coupled with Repton's interest in architecture, had a significant role in the development of the Regency style as demonstrated by his partner John NASH in the completion of Regent's Park and in the remodelling of St James's Park. Many of Repton's landscape works have been modified out of recognition; the best surviving examples are listed below.

□ Blaise Castle, Avon, from 1796. Luscombe, Devon, from 1799. Ashridge, Herts., early 1800s. Sezincote, Glos., from 1805.

▷ Humphry Repton, *Sketches and Hints on Landscape Gardening*, 1795; *Observations on the Theory and Practice of Landscape Gardening*, 1803; *Fragments of the Theory and Practice of Landscape Gardening*, 1818. Christopher Hussey, *The Picturesque*, London, 1924, Hamden, Conn., 1967. Dorothy Stroud, *Humphry Repton*, London, 1962. AB

RICHARDSON Henry Hobson

b. Louisiana, 1838; d. Brookline, Mass., 1886.

Prolific American architect who developed a highly personal style which reinterpreted various European influences.

H. H. Richardson, Trinity Church, Boston, 1872–7

Born in Priestly Plantation in Louisiana, H. H. Richardson was the son of a Bermuda merchant. He first developed an interest in architecture at Harvard College, and after graduation (1859) went to Europe. In 1860 he was admitted to the Ecole des Beaux Arts in Paris – at the time only the second American architect to achieve this distinction. However, the American Civil War interrupted his studies and he was forced to support himself by working for French architectural practices. On his return to the United States, Richardson settled in New York (1865), and worked in partnership with Charles Gambrill (1867-78). Most of his early commissions came from New England, and in 1874 he moved to Brookline, Massachusetts. After the dissolution of his partnership, he practised on his own. His early designs display a number of European influences, notably the French Second Empire style of his Western Railroad Offices (1867-9) and the Agawam National Bank (1869-70), and the English medieval idiom of Grace Church (1867-9) and the Church of the Unity, his first commission (1866-9). He also attempted to reinterpret current themes in American architecture and was attracted by the energy of the recent Romanesque Revival. This, combined with his first-hand knowledge of the robust, organic French Romanesque churches provided the key to much of his subsequent work. The first major example was Brattle Square Church in Boston (1870-72), where simplicity, scale and structural vitality are combined with skilful use of quarry-faced masonry – a technique Richardson continued to exploit with great expressive power. He won the design for Trinity Church (1872-7), also in Boston, which brought Richardson to national prominence and marked the flowering of his creative powers. He soon became involved in the completion of the New York State Capitol at Albany (by Thomas Fuller). Richardson's contribution enhanced his professional reputation in the field of civic architecture, and he received three more commissions on the strength of it, the most important of which was the Allegheny County buildings, Pittsburgh (1883-8). Here he exploited his Beaux-Arts training with a classically symmetrical plan and the visual drama of the sweeping main hall and staircase recall the grandeur of PIRANESI's interiors. Richardson's capacity to produce powerfully functional buildings reached a peak with the Marshall Field Wholesale Store in Chicago, completed in 1887. Here Richardson transformed a practical, commonplace solution into an architectural work of great strength and coherence, which was extolled by his contemporaries, notably Louis SULLIVAN. His many domestic architectural commissions combined the English Queen Anne style with organic form and texture. Richardson's innovative use of timber shingles as a wall covering was taken up by MCKIM, MEAD & WHITE and others, forming the basis of the most original development in C19 American domestic architecture. Richardson's career was characterized by an extraordinary spiritual energy and a complete dedication to his craft. He was an outstanding innovator and one of the first American architects to exert any influence on developments in Europe, as the "Richardsonian" style gained popularity worldwide.

□ Church of the Unity, Springfield, Mass., 1866-9. Grace Church, Medford, Mass., 1867-9. Western Railroad Offices, Springfield, 1867-9. Agawam National Bank, Springfield, 1869-70. Brattle Square Church, Boston, Mass., 1870-72. Trinity Church, Boston, 1872-7. Watts Sherman House, Newport, Rhode Island, 1874-5. New York State Capitol, Albany, from 1875. Allegheny County Courthouse and Jail, Pittsburgh, 1883-8. Marshall Field Store, Chicago, 1885-6.

▷ Mariana Griswold Van Rensselaer, *Henry Hobson Richardson and His Works* (2nd ed. 1888), New York, 1969. Lewis Mumford, *Sticks and Stones: A Study of the American Architecture and Civilization* (1924), 2nd ed., New York, 1955. Henry-Russell Hitchcock, *Richardson as a Victorian Architect*, Baltimore, 1966. Vincent Scully, *The Shingle Style and the Stick Style*, New Haven 1971.

CS

▷ *see also pp226-9, 232-3*

RIETVELD Gerrit Thomas

b. Utrecht, 1888; d. Utrecht, 1964.

Leading architect of the *De Stijl* group. Rietveld was a born constructor yet his abiding achievement was not in the field of structural logic but in the abstract construction of space. He started work at the age of 11 in his father's joinery business and after his apprenticeship in 1906 worked in the jewellery studio of C. J. Beeger. In 1911 he set up his own cabinet-making firm, which he continued to run until 1919. It was during this period that he also studied architecture, part-time, under P. J. Klaarhamer and became acquainted with B. van der Leck and R. van t'Hoff, who were among the founding members of *De Stijl*. In 1917, Rietveld produced the Red Blue Chair, which, in the words of Colin St J. Wilson, "signalled the most radical change in architecture for five hundred years". Rietveld's contribution to the *De Stijl* movement was crowned by the house he designed with and for Mrs Schröder-Schräder in Utrecht (1924), signifying the ultimate achievement of Neo-plasticism, unique in the free and variable use of space. This was to be seen "not with an aesthetic purpose but only to provide us with a more direct experience of reality". Although the *De*

THE SCHRÖDER HOUSE, Utrecht

A joint effort between architect and client, most credit must be given to architect and joiner Gerrit Rietveld in developing this bold new modern house (designed and built 1924). One of the first major projects of the "New Architecture" of the 1920s it nevertheless was a translation of De Stijl *principles into building terms. It employed the primary colours of the artistic movement of* De Stijl *and also used its recessive effects in three dimensional terms. The top floor of the house was originally defined as a storage area in order to allow for an entirely free and partitioned space. Had it been designated as a bedroom floor it would not have been allowed under building codes.*

Stijl movement could not sustain itself, Rietveld's profound understanding of dynamic spatial ideas continued to be demonstrated, with varying degrees of success, throughout his life. In the late 1920s serious architectural developments in the Netherlands centred on the concepts of "dematerialization" and principally the work of J. DUIKER. It was a leaning towards this newer influence that generated Rietveld's group of terrace houses near the Schröder-Schräder house in 1930. It should be noted that in 1928 Rietveld was one of the founder members of CIAM at La Serraz, where he would have felt the rising pressures of Purism. The 1930s and 40s were much less productive for Rietveld, but two distinguished achievements were the Zig Zag Chair of 1934 and the cinema at Utrecht of 1936. Between 1942 and 1958 Rietveld taught variously at the Academie van Beeldende Kunsten at Rotterdam and The Hague, the Academie van Beeldende Kunst en Kunstnijverheid at Arnhem and the Academie voor Bowkunst, Amsterdam. The sculpture pavilion of 1954 at Arnhem (rebuilt at Otterlo in 1965) saw Rietveld's continuing concern with Neo-plastic space. 1954 also was the year of his first large-scale commercial building, the Julianahal at Utrecht. During the 1950s Theo M. Brown was working on the definitive biography of Rietveld (1958), which probably re-established Rietveld as an architect of international importance; from then until his death in 1964 and beyond, commissions were more plentiful. Among the late works of note are the 1956-68 Gerrit Rietveld Academy, Amsterdam, several houses, including Ilpendam and Heerlen, the Zonnenhof Museum, Amersfoort, and Rietveld's final posthumous work, the Vincent Van Gogh Museum, Amsterdam. In 1963 Rietveld was elected an honorary member of the Bond van Nederlandse Architecten and in 1964 was awarded an honorary degree by the Technische Hogeschool in Delft.

□ Red Blue Chair, 1917. Jewellery shop, Amsterdam 1922. Schröder-Schräder house, Utrecht, 1924. Garage and chauffeur's house, Utrecht, 1927. Terrace houses, Utrecht, 1931, 1934. Terrace houses, Vienna, 1932. Music School, Zeist, 1933. Private houses, The Hague, 1936. Cinema, Utrecht, 1936. Holiday house, Brenkelerveen, 1941. Private house, Velp, 1951. Sculpture pavilion, Arnhem/Otterlo, 1954-6. Exhibition hall, "Julianahal", Utrecht, 1954-6. Gerrit Rietveld Academy, Amsterdam, 1956-68. Zonnenhof Museum, Amersfoort, 1958-9. Private house, Ilpendam, 1959. Vincent van Gogh Museum, Amsterdam, 1963-73. Private house, Heerlen, 1964.

▷ G. T. Rietveld, *Nieuwe Zakelijkheid in der Netherlandsene Architectkuur*, Amsterdam, 1932; *Rietveld, 1924, Schröder Huis*, Amsterdam, 1963; contributions to *De Stijl*. Theo M. Brown, *The Work of G. Rietveld, Architect*, Utrecht, 1958. C. St J. Wilson, "Gerrit Rietveld, 1888-1964", *Architectural Review*, Vol. 136, Dec. 1964. Theo M. Brown, "Rietveld's Eccentric Vision", *Journal of the Society of Architectural Historians of Great Britain*, Vol. 24, No. 4, 1965. A. Buffinga, *G. Th. Rietveld*, Amsterdam 1971. *G. Rietveld, Architect* (exhibition catalogue), London, 1972. F. Bless, *Rietveld 1888-1964: Ein biografie*, Amsterdam and Baarm, 1982.

CD

ROCHE Martin

see Holabird & Roche

ROCHE & DINKELOO

Established 1966.

Innovative American architectural partnership of designer and technologist. **John Dinkeloo** (b. Holland, Michigan, 1918; d. Fredericksburg, Virginia, 1981) was educated at the University of Michigan School of Architecture. After working for SKIDMORE, OWINGS & MERRILL, he joined the firm of Eero SAARINEN in 1950, becoming a partner five years later. In 1966 he co-founded Kevin Roche, John Dinkeloo and Associates, based in Hamden, Connecticut. **Kevin Roche** (b. Dublin, 1922) was educated in Dublin and Illinois. After work experience with Michael Scott and the United Nations Planning Office in New York, he joined the Saarinen firm in the same year as Dinkeloo. Saarinen's death in 1961 left Roche and Dinkeloo with such unfinished projects as the TWA Terminal at John F. Kennedy Airport, New York (1952-62). The model partnership of designer and

Roche, Dinkeloo & Associates, Ford Foundation Headquarters, New York, 1963–8

technologist was established in 1966 and enjoyed instant success with the Ford Foundation Headquarters in New York. Roche was the principal designer; Dinkeloo specialized in construction and technology. Together they produced some of America's most provocative civic and corporate architecture of the 1960s and 70s. Dinkeloo's technical virtuosity combined with the bold simplicity of Roche's designs gave many of their buildings a unique sculptural quality. Their work was characterized by a meticulous problem-solving approach and careful consideration of planning in relation to the surrounding environment. They were early innovators of urban public space, introducing interior courtyards into a number of build-ings and even constructing the Oakland Museum (1961-8) entirely underground. Their architecture was often executed on a vast scale – or designed to look as though it was, taking its cue from the powerful imagery of American industrial building and the corporate view of the world.

☐ Oakland Museum, Oakland, California, 1961-8. Ford Foundation Headquarters, New York, 1963-8. Knights of Columbus Headquarters, New Haven, Conn., 1965-9. Hotel and office building of the United Nations Development Corporation, New York, 1969-75.

▷ Robert Stern, *New Directions in American Architecture*, revised ed., New York, 1977. John O'Regan and Shane O'Toole (eds.), *Kevin Roche, Architect: The Work of Kevin Roche, John Dinkeloo and Associates*, Dublin, 1983. CS

ROGERS Richard

b. Florence, 1933.

British exponent of "High-Tech", Late Modern architecture. He was educated at the AA School, London and at Yale University. He and his first wife, Sue, were in dual husband-and-wife partnership with Norman and Wendy FOSTER (Team 4). Their first work, the Reliance Controls Factory at Swindon, England (1966-7), an innovatory high-tech industrial building, received considerable attention. In contrast to Foster, who went on to develop a refined engineering-based high-tech architecture which is almost classical, Rogers's designs are more exuberant. The Pompidou Centre, Paris (1973-7), with Renzo PIANO, which established his international reputation, is an inside-out building: the structure and servicing is on the exterior to achieve uninterrupted flexible interior spaces. The brightly coloured pipes and funnels replace the detail and decoration of traditional façades but are determined by functional requirements and intended to present an industrial appearance. In many ways, Rogers is one of the heirs to the functionalist tradition; he is interested in the crossover of new technologies into the building industry, which is continued in his other well-known work, the controversial Lloyds Building (1979-84). But his concern with total flexibility and overt technical imagery has been termed Late Modern. In his most recent work he has returned to the images of the early Modernists, notably MENDELSOHN.

☐ Reliance Controls Factory, Swindon, Wilts. (with Team 4), 1966-7. Centre National d'Art et de Culture Georges Pompidou, Paris (with Renzo Piano and Peter Rice), 1973-7. Lloyds Building, London, 1979-84. INMOS Factory, Newport, S Wales , 1980-82. Securities Market, Billingsgate, London, 1985-9. European Court of Human Rights, Strasbourg, 1989.

▷ *Richard Rogers and Partners, An Architectural Monograph*, London, 1985. Bryan Appleyard, *Richard Rogers, A Biography*, London, 1986. D. Sudjic, *New Architecture, Foster, Rogers, Stirling*, London, 1986. "Richard Rogers, 1978-88", *Architecture and Urbanism*, Dec. 1988. TC

▷ *see also pp224-41, 244-5*

ROOT John Wellborn

see Burnham & Root

ROSSI Aldo

b. Milan, 1931.

Influential Italian architect and urban theorist who initiated the contemporary school of Rational architecture during the 1960s and 70s. He graduated from the Milan Politecnico in 1959 and joined the Milanese magazine *Casabella-Continuità*, later serving as its editor (1961-4). Rossi has held academic positions at a variety of architecture schools, including Milan's Politecnico, Zürich's ETH, New York's Cooper Union, and Venice's Instituto Universitario di Architettura. His international reputation was first established in 1966 with the publication of his theoretical treatise *L'Architettura della città* (*The Architecture of the City*). The perennial theme in all his written work has remained the city – its monuments, morphology and urban typology. These preoccupations are evident within his architectural œuvre, which focuses on nostalgia and memory, exploiting a vocabulary of forms largely derived from the traditional buildings of Rossi's youth – arcades, galleries, grain silos and farm buildings of the Lombardy countryside. His approach to design not only emphasizes the autonomy of architecture within a given culture but also stresses the importance of a poetic transformation of dogmatic Rationalism.

☐ Gallaratese Quarter, Milan, 1969-70. Elementary School, Fagnano Olona, 1972-6. Teatro del Mondo, Venice, 1979. Social housing, Berlin (with Gianni Braghieri), 1981-8. Hotel Il Palazzo, Fukoka, 1988-90.

▷ Aldo Rossi, *The Architecture of the City*, Cambridge, Mass., 1966, 1982; *A Scientific Autobiography*, Cambridge, Mass., 1981; *Selected Writings and Projects*, Dublin, 1983. Francesco Moschini (ed.), *Aldo Rossi: Projects and Drawings 1962-79*, New York, 1979. MC

RUDOLPH Paul Marvin

b. Elkton, Kentucky, 1918.

Prolific American Modernist architect and draughtsman. He began his education at the Alabama Polytechnic Institute, going on to become a pupil of Walter GROPIUS at Harvard. After graduating in 1947, he entered into a partnership with Ralph Twitchell in Florida which lasted until 1952. Rudolph has subsequently practised on his own in Boston, New Haven and New York. He was Chairman of the Department of Architecture at Yale University (1958-65). His early career coincided with the American building boom of the 1950s and 60s, which swamped his office with an immense and diverse volume of work. From 1952 to the present he has worked on commissions in America, Europe, the Middle East, Africa and the Far East. Rudolph's design is a synthesis of the Modernist ideas of LE CORBUSIER, WRIGHT and Louis KAHN, although more recently he has come to question the precepts of the Modern Movement. His buildings are characterized by their powerful sculptural quality, sweeping monolithic forms and intricate interior spaces. He has also shown interest in the problems of urban design and completed a succession of large-scale projects, most of which remain unexecuted, including the Lower Manhattan Expressway Project (1967-72) and the Buffalo Waterfront Development (1969-72). Rudolph continues to be preoccupied with the notion of an industrialized, "plug-in" city and has devised several schemes featuring a series of mobile residence pods held in place by a steel framework connected to mechanical and electrical services. His unbuilt Graphic Arts Center project for New York proposed that "mobile homes be used as C20 bricks". Rudolph's work remains highly personal, competitive and uncompromising. "Architecture is a personal effort", he once remarked.

□ Art and Architecture Building, Yale University, New Haven, Conn., 1958-62. Interdenominational Chapel, Tuskegee Institute, Alabama, 1960-69. Southeastern Massachusetts Technological Institute, North Dartmouth, Mass., 1963. Graphic Arts Center and Apartments, New York (project), 1967.

▷ Paul Rudolph, *Paul Rudolph: Drawings*, ed. Yukio Futagawa, Tokyo, 1972. Sybyl Moholy-Nagy, *Introduction to the Architecture of Paul Rudolph*, New York, 1970. Rupert Spade, *Paul Rudolph*, New York, 1971. CS

Richard Rogers & Partners, Lloyds Building, London, 1979–84

RUSKIN John

b. London, 1819; d. Coniston, 1900.

The art critic of the C19, his outpourings of judgement and opinion dominate the second half of the century. The only child of a successful sherry merchant, he was dominated by his mother to the exclusion of normal youthful relationships. He was educated at Oxford. Seeking to defend the work of J. M. W. Turner, Ruskin launched himself into art criticism with *Modern Painters* (1842), a work he was to revise and expand for seventeen years. His most influential works on architecture were *The Seven Lamps of Architecture* (1849) and *The Stones of Venice* (1851-3). The former was primarily a reiteration of the ideas of PUGIN, released from their sectarian context; the latter, in particular the chapter "On the Nature of Gothic", was one of the most influential documents of the C19. It was this chapter which inspired William MORRIS and his friends in the establishment of the Arts & Crafts movement. To Ruskin is due the credit for secularizing the Gothic Revival and, at a much lower level, the proliferation of Venetian ornament indiscriminately throughout the country in the middle of the C19. His writings on the shortcomings of industrial society and the significance of art in the life of the nation enlarged and disseminated the views of Pugin across all levels of Victorian society. *Unto This Last* (1862), published originally in the *Cornhill Magazine* (1860), was fundamentally a tract on political economy, and later writings and lectures extended his assaults on the social and economic anomalies of Victorian society.

▷ E. T. Cook and A. Wedderburn (eds), *The Works of John Ruskin*, 39 vols., London, 1903-12. Kenneth Clark (ed.), *Ruskin Today*, London, 1964. Quentin Bell, *Ruskin*, London, 1978. RM

▷ *see also pp224-5, 228-9*

SAARINEN Eero

b. Kirkkonummi, Finland, 1910;
d. Ann Arbor, Mich. 1961.

In a period of developing modern architecture in America, Eero Saarinen became the architect's architect. He went to the USA in 1923 with his father, Eliel SAARINEN, whose practice he joined in 1937 after study in Paris and at Yale University. Saarinen's remarkable range and his instinctive use of colour, form and material are best explained by his early interest in sculpture. Architecture became a sculptural expression; romance was celebrated not balked. After winning the (Jefferson Memorial Gateway Arch) Competition (1948), he began a series of architectural exercises of intensity and expression, adapting ingenuity, sculpture and pragmatism to every project. In 1956 the MIT Auditorium and Chapel indicated Saarinen's double resolutions: sculptural form and restraint. He showed how he could handle the international vocabulary with aplomb and then swerve towards an expressionism of breathless curves and cantilever returns mocking much of the mediocre concrete gymnastics of the period. The TWA terminal at Kennedy Airport (1962) will remain one of this century's iconographic greats, though it is

Eero Saarinen, TWA Terminal, Kennedy Airport, New York, 1962

perhaps surpassed in clarity by Dulles Airport. But Saarinen's rigour, craft and professionalism have seldom been betered.

□ Jefferson Memorial, St Louis, 1948-64. MIT Auditorium and Chapel, 1956. Ingalls Hockey Rink, Yale, 1956-9. TWA Terminal, Kennedy Airport, New York, 1962. Dulles Airport, Washington DC, 1958-62. CBS Building, New York, 1983 (completed posthumously).

▷ Eero Saarinen, *Eero Saarinen on his Work, 1947-64*, New York, 1962; "Function, Structure and Beauty", *Architectural Association Journal*, July-August 1957; "Six Broad Currents of Modern Architecture", *Architectural Forum*, July 1953. G. Dorfles, "Eero Saarinen", *Zodiac* 8, 1961. A. Temko, *Eero Saarinen*, New York, 1962. *Eero Saarinen* (special issue), *A + U*, 1984. E. Hauser, *Saarinen*, Hamburg, 1984. RC

▷ *see also pp240-41*

SAARINEN Eliel

b. Rantasalmi, Finland, 1873;
d. Michigan, 1950.

Finnish architect who, by preserving a rigour from Art Nouveau and never quite succumbing to the full sentiment, produced exacting structures and restraint – especially at Cranbrook Academy of Art, Michigan – which can be seen to pre-empt many of the concerns of later Finnish architects. He studied at Helsinki Polytechnic, graduating in 1897, and from 1896 to 1907 was in partnership with Herman Gesellius and Armas Lindgren, perhaps the most important practice in Finland. In 1923 he emigrated to the USA, where he began another extensive career, designing, and then teaching at Cranbrook. He joined in partnership with his son, Eero SAARINEN, in 1937. Though Saarinen's cultural significance is greater than SONCK's, it is important to see them together in the early stages of the so-called National Romantic movement. Saarinen's early monumentalism owed more to OLBRICH and the Vienna Secession movement. His work expressed a natural and, we could say, a Nordic refinement of the more fluid Art Nouveau from Europe. But it was never a mere restrained adaptation of, say, VOYSEY. Material, form and culture played a more solid picturesque and symbolic role in Saarinen's work. The amalgam of local Finnish farm settlements with the emerging Arts & Crafts elements echoed also H. H. RICHARDSON and WEBB (the Red House). The peak of a demanding eclecticism and timely internationalism in this picturesque period was undoubtedly the Finnish Pavilion at the Paris World Fair (carried out with Gesellius and Lindgren, 1900). The excess and flair of such borrowing and adaptation, tinged with an untutored symbolism, might also account for some of Saarinen's later second-thought refinements. Already by 1902, with Hvittrask, a clearer development of the vernacular was achieved, emphasized again by the Helsinki Railway Station project (1904). Saarinen subsequently revised the station; a stronger, cleaner massing occurred, with, however, the beginnings of that systematic heaviness: all front and interior. We get a further clue to Saarinen's subsequent direction and neat monumentalism in his Chicago Tribune Competition design (1922), which,

Eliel Saarinen, Railway Station, Helsinki, 1914

though placed second, led him to emigrate to the USA. In 1925 his calm monumental restraint emerged in the Cranbrook project which was to occupy him for years. Saarinen indicated just how well an abstracted classical style could suit the Finnish sensibility. And though this sensibility was interrupted by the arrival of Functionalism in Finland, Cranbrook indicates what is now being seen as a consistent link with the Minimalism and the thematic drive to overcome frivolous decoration seen in the 1960s and 70s. The links back to ASPLUND and Saarinen should be clear.

□ Finnish Pavilion, World Fair, Paris, 1900. Hvittrask, Kirkkonummi, 1902. Suur-Merijoki Country House, Viipuri, 1902. Nordic Bank Building, Helsinki, 1904. Finnish National Museum, Helsinki, 1910. Helsinki Railway Station, 1914. City Plan for Greater Helsinki, 1918. Tribune Tower, Chicago, 1922. Berkshire Music Centre, Tanglewood, Mass., 1938. Cranbrook Academy of Art, Michigan, 1941. Tabernacle Church of Christ, Columbus, Indiana, 1942. Civic Centre, Detroit, 1947.

▷ Eliel Saarinen, *The City: its growth, its decay, its future*, New York, 1943; *Search for Form*, New York, 1948. A. Christ-Janer, *Eliel Saarinen*, Chicago, 1948. Hausen, Herler *et al* (eds) *Eliel Saarinen*, Otava, Helsinki, 1991. RC

SAFDIE Moshe

b. Haifa, 1938.

Canadian/Israeli architect whose design for a prefabricated "Habitat" at the Montreal Expo 1967 brought him instant fame. Trained at McGill University, Montreal (1955-61), he spent two years in Louis KAHN's office before commencing in practice on his own account in 1964. He has had offices in Montreal, from whence came the remarkable "Habitat" housing experiment for the 1967 Expo, in Jerusalem and more recently in the USA, where he now lives and holds a Harvard professorship. "Habitat" was the result of a way of thinking about cellular housing initially developed as a student thesis, but after its maturation at Montreal – which proved horrendously expensive and difficult to construct – Safdie introduced it to other parts of the world, including two unbuilt projects for New York and a completed more economic "Habitat" unit in Puerto Rico (1968-72). His Israeli period produced a number of impressive urban insertion projects, including a Rabbinical College, Jerusalem (1971-9), and various town-planning schemes for quarters in Jerusalem. In 1982 he commenced work on the prestigious Canadian Government project for the country's new National Gallery, which opened in 1988 in Ottawa.

□ Habitat, Expo 67, Montreal, Canada (158 flats), 1966-7. Habitat Projects: New York, 1968; Puerto Rico, 1968-72; Tropacao Tropaco, US Virgin Isles, and a further New York Project, both 1970. Yeshivat Porat Joseph Rabbinical College, Jerusalem, 1971-9. Desert Research Institute (and Ben Gurian Archives) in the Negev, 1974. National Gallery of Canada, Ottawa (Parkin/Safdie), 1982-8.

▷ Moshe Safdie, *Beyond Habitat*, New York, 1970; *For Everyone a Garden*, Cambridge, Mass., 1974. DS

▷ *see also pp242-3*

SANGALLO THE YOUNGER Antonio da

b. Florence, 1483; d. Florence, 1546.

Builder and engineer more than an imaginative or innovative architect, he resisted the "mannerism" with which so many others endeavoured to emulate MICHELANGELO. This Antonio was nephew to the brothers Giuliano da SANGALLO and Antonio da Sangallo the Elder, with Cordiano as his surname within the Sangallo clan. Trained by his uncles, he went into the family firm's design, engineering and sculpture business. He accompanied Giuliano to Rome in 1503 and stayed there most of his life, enjoying the patronage of several popes. The Sangallos' efficient infrastructure enabled him to take on commissions for a large number of clients – some of them in distant places – while still playing a part in the insatiable enlargement of St Peter's, where he succeeded RAPHAEL as master of the works in 1520. He designed the Palazzo Farnese in Rome, completed by Michelangelo *c.*1547.

□ Palazzo Farnese, Rome, begun 1515. Palazzo Palma-Baldassini, Rome, *c.*1520.

▷ G. Giovannoni, *Antonio da Sangallo il Giovane*, Rome, 1959. JRC

▷ *see also pp214-15*

SANGALLO Giuliano da

b. Florence, c.1443; d. Florence, 1516.

Somewhat conservative designer at the opening of the High Renaissance period. Born into the Florentine Sangallo clan of fine craftsmen in wood specializing in inlay, picture frames and model-building, Giuliano (family name Giamberti) went to Rome in the 1460s. There he became involved in the papal plans for modernizing the city. While still primarily a sculptor, Giuliano took the opportunity of studying and drawing the major remains of the imperial Roman buildings, especially the great vaulted baths (*thermae*). Back in Florence (*c.*1470) he set up as an architect. His Roman studies showed in the villa commissioned by Lorenzo the Magnificent at Poggio a Caiano. Giuliano also designed the Greek-cross church of Santa Maria delle Carceri at Prato, where the all-over marble cladding depicted, rather than embodied, Roman details. Further visits to Rome (1503, 1513) disappointed his hopes of papal commissions, and showed him how far architecture had moved since his friends BRAMANTE, MICHELANGELO and RAPHAEL started working in the city. In 1515 he entered the Florentine competition for the façade of S. Lorenzo with designs that impressed Michelangelo. For some 18 months before his death, Giuliano held the mastership of the works at St Peter's, Rome, jointly with Bramante at first, and then with Raphael.

□ Villa del Poggio a Caiano, 1480-85. Santa Maria delle Carceri, Prato, 1485. Palazzo Gondi, Florence, 1490-94.

▷ G. Marchini, *Giuliano da Sangallo*, Florence, 1943. JRC

▷ *see also pp212-13*

Jacopo Sansovino, Old Library of St Mark's, Venice, 1537–54

SANMICHELE (SANMICHELI) Michele

b. Verona, c. 1484; d. Verona, 1559.

A prolific, if rather pedestrian, designer, much of whose work for clients in Venice and the mainland (Veneto) was a compromise between Venetian and Tuscan influences, delegated to assistants from his workshop. Descended from a long line of Lombard stone-cutters, Sanmichele went to Rome at the age of sixteen (in 1500) and was trained by the circle of papal architects which included BRAMANTE. Strongly influenced as an engineer and town-planner by Roman examples, Sanmichele collaborated with Antonio da SANGALLO THE YOUNGER. As a military architect, he worked in the Venetian overseas empire (Dalmatia, Corfu, Cyprus, Crete). After the traumatic Sack of Rome (1527), Sanmichele, like many other artists drawn there by the opportunities offered by the papal court, went home. In Verona, from the age of 43, he carried out commissions in and around the city, especially for palazzi of novel design (e.g. Bevilacqua). A theme inspired by Bramante's Tempietto in Rome shows in Sanmichele's circular sanctuary screen in Verona Cathedral and his own version of the Tempietto in the hospital (*lazzaretto*) near Verona. His civil works included erecting (or, as in Verona, demilitarizing) fortifications, and designing gateways.

□ Palazzo Canossa, Verona, *c.*1530. Palazzo Bevilacqua, Verona, *c.*1530. Verona Cathedral (sanctuary screen), 1534-41. Palazzo Grimani at S. Luca, Venice, from 1557.

▷ Eric Langenskiöld, *Michele Sanmicheli, the architect of Verona*, Uppsala, 1938. L. Puppi, *Michele Sanmicheli*, Padua, 1971. JRC

▷ *see also pp214-15*

SANSOVINO Jacopo

b. Caprese, near Florence, 1486; d. Venice, 1570.

Architect whose work, with that of the younger architects of late C16 Venice whom he trained, gives the city much of the character that survives today. Born Jacopo Tatti, he adopted the surname of his teacher, Andrea Sansovino, and followed him to Rome in 1503. Like Giuliano da SANGALLO, he first became known as a sculptor, and restored classical pieces in Rome. After the Sack of Rome (1527) he joined the exodus of artists from Rome and settled in Venice, where he was on friendly terms with the painter Titian and the poet Pietro Aretino. He designed the Palazzo Corner (Ca' Grande), the Old Library of St Mark's, and the porch (*loggietta*) at the foot of the Campanile on St Mark's Square. He also carved the giants at the top of the staircase in the courtyard of the Doge's Palace.

□ Palazzo Corner (Ca' Grande), Venice, 1533. Old Library of St Mark's, Venice, 1537-54. Loggietta, Campanile, St Mark's Square, Venice, 1537-40.

▷ D. Howard, *Jacopo Sansovino: architecture and patronage in Renaissance Venice*, New York, 1975, London, 1987. JRC

▷ *see also pp214-15*

SANT'ELIA Antonio

b. Como, 1888; d. Monfalcone, 1916.

Only two years before his tragic death in the First World War, Sant'Elia had published a spirited manifesto accompanied by a collection of visionary drawings which were to become some of the most potent architectural images of the C20. He studied architecture in Como, receiving a diploma in 1905, at the Accademia di Brera in Milan and subsequently at the Scuola di Belle Arti in Bologna, where he

Antonio Sant' Elia, Hydro-electric power plant, 1914, project

received his diploma in 1912. Early influences included both Vienna Secession and *Stile Liberty* architects, but it was a fascination for the soaring skyscrapers of Chicago and New York which provided the inspiration for the drawings of Sant'Elia's utopian metropolis – the *Città Nuova*. His drawings evoke a Brave New World where the machine is omnipotent and the city consists of monumental towers and stark abstract forms. In 1912 he joined with several radical Milanese architects, including Mario Chiattone and Marcello Nizzoli, to form the *Nuove Tendenze* group, which rejected the dogma of history in order to embrace technology and the future. Sant'Elia contributed to the group's first exhibition some two years later. His preface to the catalogue, entitled the *Messaggio*, was slightly reworked and published under the title *Manifesto of Futurist Architecture*. This seminal document echoed much of the Futurists' propaganda by attacking the anachronisms of the past and calling for a new order focused on the machine age.

□ Memorial to the War Dead (designed, after a sketch by Sant'Elia, by Enrico Prampolini, completed by Giuseppe TERRAGNI and Enrico Prampolini, Como, 1933). Almost 300 drawings and projects.

▷ Ulrich Conrads, *Programs and Manifestoes on 20th Century Architecture*, Cambridge, 1970. Caroline Tisdall and Angelo Bozzolla, *Futurism*, London, 1977. Luciano Caramel and Alberto Longatti, *Antonio Sant'Elia – The Complete Works*, New York, 1987. MC

▷ *see also pp230-31*

SCAMOZZI Vincenzo

b. Vicenza, 1548 or 1552; d. Venice, 1616.

Late Renaissance theorist, eclectic architect and theatre designer. In his youth he took part in the activities of the Accademia Olimpica in Vicenza, guided and influenced by his father, Giandomenico Scamozzi. In 1569 he was sporadically in Venice. In 1574 he read VITRUVIUS, jotting down an abundance of notes and actively accepting Vitruvius's statement *Architectura est scientia*. In 1578 he went to Rome, where he spent eighteen months making a careful study of ancient buildings. In a second visit to Rome (1585) and on journeys through Austria, Hungary, Germany, France and Switzerland (1559 and 1604) he developed his eclectic view of previous architectural styles, learning from and admiring buildings such as the Gothic cathedral which were generally despised by his contemporaries. Many believe that PALLADIO was the dominant influence on Scamozzi, perhaps because he carried on projects originally started by the master (the Villa Rotonda, Teatro Olimpico etc.), but his debt to SERLIO was probably far greater; no doubt, though, that in his maturity he achieved a personal and independent style. He is mostly quoted and remembered as the author of one of the later and comprehensive Renaissance treatises on architecture (*L'Idea dell'architettura universale* – 6 books out of 10 planned) published in Venice in 1615, the year before his death. He sees the building as "a scientific habit lodged in the architect's mind", stressing with originality the independence and fullness of intellectual creation vis-à-vis the practical act. As "author" of a considerable number of projects and buildings, from Palazzo Godi in Vicenza (1569) to Palazzo Contarini in Venice (1609), he is rather aptly summed up by Milizia's judgement (in *Memorie degli architetti antichi e moderni*, 1785, Vol. II): "simple, majestic and correct". He was prepared to diverge from Palladio, for example at the Teatro Olimpico, where, in contrast to Palladio's adherence to Vitruvian ideas, Scamozzi tried to integrate the stage setting into the theatrical space. In his theatre at Sabbioneta (1588-90), the first Italian building meant to house a theatre with its own façades, it is clear from the surviving description of the (demolished) stage that Scamozzi rejected the architectural proscenium of Palladio's Olimpico. Scamozzi's Villa Molino alla Mandria (1597) is almost an antithesis to Palladio's Villa Rotonda. The most characteristic of his town palaces are the Palazzo Galeazzo Trissino al Corso in Vicenza and the Palazzo Contarini in Venice, with a Serlian lower part.

□ Palazzo Godi, Vicenza, 1569. Villa Pisani, Lonigo, 1576. Villa Capra (La Rotonda; continuing Palladio's earlier work), Vicenza, 1580-91. Procuratie Nuove, Venice, 1582-93. Stage of Palladio's Teatro Olimpico, Vicenza, 1584-5. Theatre, Sabbioneta, 1588-90. Church and Monastery of S. Nicola dei Tolentini (on building initiated by Palladio), Venice, 1591. Anteroom, Library of S. Marco, Venice, 1591. Palazzo Galeazzo Trissino al Corso, Vicenza, 1592. Palazzo Duodo a S. Maria Zobenigo, Venice, 1592. Villa Duodo, church and 6 chapels of S. Giorgio, Monselice, 1593. Villa Molino alla Mandria, 1597. Salzburg Cathedral (work to), 1607. Villa Trevisan, S. Doria di Piave, 1609. Palazzo Contarini, Venice, 1609. Palazzo Comunale, Bergamo, 1611.

▷ Vincenzo Scamozzi, *Taccuino di viaggio da Parigi a Venezia*, Venice and Rome, 1600 (ed. F. Barbieri, 1959); *L'Idea dell'architettura universale*, 1615 (Books III and VI only ed. J. Browne, London, 1669). Franco Barbieri, *Vincenzo Scamozzi*, Vicenza, 1952. GV

SCHAROUN Hans

b. Bremen, 1893; d. Berlin, 1972.

The most significant German Modernist to establish himself before the Nazi takeover, remain in Germany, then re-emerge to a major career in the 1950s and 60s; he was also the most important German exponent of "Organic" architecture. He studied architecture in Berlin, and spent the First World War years in the reconstruction of East Prussia. Following the October Revolution of 1918 he became a member of Bruno TAUT's Expressionist circle and contributed to the "Glass Chain" correspondence; his lifelong commitment to socialism dates from this time. He became known in the early 1920s for a number of progressive competition designs, was given a chair at the Breslau Arts Academy in 1925, and was elected to the "Ring" in 1926. Owing to economic circumstances, however, he was unable to build until late in the decade, producing a controversial house at the Stuttgart Weissenhofsiedlung of the Deutscher Werkbund (1927). An ingenious block of flats at the subsequent Werkbund Exhibition at Breslau (1929) confirmed his reputation as a bold new talent, and he went on to build several housing projects in Berlin, including a substantial part of Siemensstadt, for which he also determined the master plan. In 1932 Scharoun built the Schminke House at Löbau in Saxony, experimenting with an oblique stair, and discovering a new kind of dynamic interior space which was to become the hallmark of his later work. This was his last work in the Modernist idiom, for as it was completed the Nazis took over. Scharoun remained in Berlin, building more than a dozen private houses, traditional on the outside, yet with extraordinarily fluid spaces within. During this difficult period he consolidated his friendship with the architect and theorist Hugo HÄRING, who became an important influence on his work, and he took part in Häring's art school Kunst und Werk. He was able to re-emerge after the war with a consolidated architectural philosophy and renewed energy, but had to wait to see his ideas fulfilled. In 1946 he was made City Architect of Berlin, but lost the post for political reasons before any of his ideas were realized. He became involved in teaching again, and in 1955 helped refound the Berlin Arts Academy. From the late 1940s he won major competitions, but time and again designs remained unbuilt, the most tragic case being the theatre for Kassel of 1952-3, abandoned after site work had started. Thus Scharoun had to wait until 1963 to see a major public building completed: the Philharmonie in Berlin, a competition winner of 1956. This revolutionary concert hall, with terraces of seats surrounding the orchestra on all sides and a contrasting labyrinthine foyer, became world famous and has been much imitated. It was a turning-point in Scharoun's career, confirming his credibility and bringing him commissions such as the German Maritime Museum in Bremerhaven and the German Embassy in Brasilia. Until his death (1972) he had as much work as he could cope with, and several projects were completed posthumously. While the Philharmonie was under construction two other projects were realized which became prototypes for the later work: the Geschwister Scholl school at Lünen (1958-62) and housing blocks Romeo and Juliet at Stuttgart (1956-9). Both demonstrated Scharoun's concern with an almost aggressive articulation of parts, allowing each classroom or flat a strong individual identity which the user could comprehend. The parts of a building had to be like individuals in a democracy: contributing to the whole yet retaining strong identities of their own. In a period when most architects allowed space to be dictated by the construction grid, Scharoun's work stood out in its specificity and individuality, and many of his ideas retain their relevance today.

□ Schminke House, Löbau, Saxoy, 1932. Philharmonie, Berlin, 1956-63, Romeo and Juliet housing blocks, Stuttgart, 1956-9. Geschwister Scholl school, Lünen, Germany, 1958-62.

▷ Peter Pfankuch (ed.), *Hans Scharoun*, Berlin, 1974. Peter Blundell Jones, *Hans Scharoun: a monograph*, London, 1978. PBJ

▷ *see also pp234-5, 238-41*

Rudolph Schindler, The Translucent House, Palos Verdes, California, 1927, drawing

SCHINDLER Rudolph M.

b. Vienna, 1887; d. Los Angeles, 1953.

First-generation Modernist who emigrated early to the USA, where he worked for a time with Frank Lloyd WRIGHT. His career outside Europe led to lack of recognition but his reputation was rescued by the writings of David Gebhard and Esther McCoy. They consider Schindler the equal of RIETVELD and the followers of *De Stijl*. He was educated in Vienna, at the Imperial Technical Institute (1906-11) and the Academy of Arts under Otto WAGNER (1909-13), graduating with dual degrees in architecture and engineering. He emigrated to the USA in June 1914 and worked at first in Chicago; this was followed by a significant period with Frank Lloyd Wright (1916-23). He was in independent practice in Hollywood, Los Angeles, from 1921 until his death; Richard NEUTRA collaborated with him from 1925. Schindler's early buildings were executed whilst working for others, Hans Mayr and Theodor Mayer (Vienna) and Ottenheimer, Stern & Reichert (Chicago). The experience with Frank Lloyd Wright was not entirely satisfactory but led to Schinder's detailing and supervising a number of remarkable projects for Miss Barnsdall and others. Schindler also engineered the foundations of the Imperial Hotel, Tokyo, which withstood the earthquake (1923). His first key building is the Schindler & Clyde Chase Duplex (1921-2), which was the joint home of the Schindler and Neutra families 1925-31. The working arrangement with Neutra was flexible and clients were shared, hence the contrasting two commissions for the Lovell family, Schindler's Beach House (1926) in reinforced concrete at Newport Beach and Neutra's smooth steel-framed Health House (1929). The striking difference between the two designers is in the use of materials; Schindler's early works were largely reinforced concrete, the difficulty in obtaining adequate workmanship leading to construction with studwork and ply, a cheap vernacular technique in Southern California. Neither concrete, nor ply, nor rendered framing has aged well, and many of Schindler's buildings need conserving. The principal lesson to be learnt from his imaginative designs is the three-dimensional creation of space regardless of material or technical shortcomings. Schindler achieved a vast production of 330 buildings and projects over 40 years.

□ Houses: Schindler & Clyde Chase Duplex, Hollywood, 1921-2; Beach House for Dr Lovell, Newport Beach, 1925-6; Oliver House, Los Angeles, 1933; Walker House, Los Angeles, 1935-6; Lechner House, Studio City, 1948; Tischler House, Bel Air, 1949-50. Apartments: Pueblo Ribera Court, La Jolla, 1923; Manola Court, Los Angeles, 1926-40; Bubeshko Apartments, Los Angeles, 1938-41; Laurelwood Apartments, Studio City, 1948. Offices and shops: Albert Martin Department Store, Los Angeles (with S. A. Marx), 1939-40; Medical Arts Building, Studio City, 1945. Designs: League of Nations (with Neutra), 1926; Translucent House for Miss Barnsdall, 1927; Lockheed, 27 airplane

Interiors, 1938. Works accredited to Schindler while working with Frank Lloyd Wright: Concrete Monolyth Home (project), 1919; Directors House, Olive Hill, Los Angeles, Hollyhock House and Oleanders for Miss Barnsdall, 1920.

▷ Rudolph Schindler, *Collected Papers*, Los Angeles, 1948. Reyner Banham, "Rudolph Schindler: A pioneer without tears", *Architectural Design*, Dec. 1967. "The Least Appreciated: Rudolph Schindler", *Architects' Journal*, 19 Feb. 1969. David Gebhard, *Schindler*, London and New York, 1971. AB

▷ *see also pp232-3*

SCHINKEL Karl Friedrich

b. Neuruppin, Prussia, 1781; d. Berlin, 1841.

Leading exponent of Prussian Neo-Classicism. Following his studies at the Bauakademie in Berlin, where he was taught by Friedrich GILLY, Schinkel travelled to Italy and France (1803-5). He returned to an economically depressed Prussia under French occupation, and worked initially as a painter and stage designer. He painted his first panorama for Karl Wilhelm Gropius in 1806 and had completed a further forty by 1815. Schinkel also produced oil paintings at this time in a romantic manner that drew equally on classical and medieval sources, and created many stage sets, most notably for *The Magic Flute* (1815) and *The Maid of Orleans* (1816). Schinkel was appointed Surveyor to the Prussian Building Commission in 1810 and, following the defeat of the French, he remodelled the city plan and created a series of monumental buildings that expressed the cultural ambitions of C19 Prussia. Disenchantment with the politics of the French Revolution and with Napoleonism turned the Prussian architects against the Neo-Roman manner favoured by the Ecole des Beaux Arts. This aesthetic preference, reinforced by the need for strict economy, led Schinkel to a Neo-Greek style that mirrored the German idealist vision of Athenian Greece as a model of political and moral freedom. The resulting architecture was based on the simplest constructional forms, the column and lintel. Schinkel's first major work in Berlin was the Neue Wache on Unter den Linden (1816-18), a simple cubiform block fronted by a Doric portico. In April 1818 he was commissioned to rebuild the Nationaltheater, and produced a design that gave clear articulation to the three main functions of the building – auditorium, concert hall, reception rooms – within a highly disciplined external system of columns, pilasters and cornices. His most celebrated commission for Berlin, the Altes Museum (1823-30), has as its focus a central rotunda, designed to house antique sculpture, while the colonnaded main façade derives from the Greek stoa. Schinkel was entirely undogmatic in his classicism, however, and provided designs in both classical and Gothic manners for the Werdersche Kirche in Berlin, which was ultimately built in an anglicized brick Gothic style (1824-30). In contrast, the Nikolaikirche in Potsdam used a centralized plan derived from Gilly, and the four small churches built during the 1830s in the north of Berlin were all Neo-Classical. In 1826 Schinkel travelled to England and Scotland, where he was particularly impressed by the architecture of the early Industrial Revolution. The iron frame of a mill in Stroud, Gloucestershire, provided Schinkel with the model for his Bauakademie in Berlin (1831-5), whose frame and infill construction provided a model for the industrial classicism of Peter BEHRENS, and, ultimately, for the steel frame structures of Ludwig MIES VAN DER ROHE. As court architect, Schinkel was responsible for many interiors and summer residences for the Prussian royal family, including a pavilion in the park of Schloss Charlottenburg (1824-5), Schloss Glienicke (1824 on, Grosse Neugierde 1835-7), and the Römische Bäder and Charlottenhof in the park of Sanssouci, Potsdam. Royal connections also prompted the two great schemes of the 1830s: a palace for King Otto von Wittelsbach on the Acropolis in Athens (1834); and a summer residence for the Tsarina of Russia at Orianda in the Crimea (1838). Neither project was built, but Schinkel's brilliant drawings survive to mark a climax in the dialogue between Neo-Classical Prussia and Periclean Athens.

K. F. Schinkel, Charlottenhof, Potsdam, 1826–36

☐ Mausoleum for Queen Luise of Prussia, 1810. Neue Wache, Berlin, 1816-18. Zivilkasino, Potsdam, 1818-24. Schauspielhaus, Berlin, 1818-21. Friedrich Werdersche Kirche, Berlin, 1821-30. Altes Museum, Berlin, 1823-30. Kasino, Schloss Glienicke, near Potsdam, 1824-5. Charlottenhof, Sanssouci, Potsdam, 1826-36. Allgemeine Bauakademie, Berlin, 1831-6. Elizabeth-Kirche, Berlin, 1832-4. Project: Palace for Otto von Wittelsbach on the Acropolis, Athens, 1834. Roman Baths, Sanssouci, Potsdam, 1834-40. Project: Palace for the Tsarina of Russia, Orianda, near Yalta, 1838.

▷ Karl Friedrich Schinkel, *Collection of Architectural Designs* (based on the *Architektonisches Entwürfe* edition of 1866: London, 1981, 1984). August Grisebach, *Karl Friedrich Schinkel*, Leipzig, 1924; reprinted Munich, 1981. H. G. Pundt, *Schinkel's Berlin*, Cambridge, Mass., 1972. David Watkin and Tilman Mellinghoff, *German Architecture and the Classical Ideal 1740-1840*, London, 1987. IBW

▷ *see also pp220-23*

SCOTT Sir George Gilbert

b. Gawcott, Bucks., 1811; d. London, 1878.

The most prolific exponent of the High Gothic revival in Britain. He was articled to James Edmeston (1827-31) and in partnership with W. B. Moffat (*c.*1834-1845). After encountering PUGIN's ideas, he became an early adherent of the new Ecclesiological principles of church design, and also developed an impressive ability to assimilate and combine elements from disparate English and European C13 and early C14 sources. Dedicated to preserving and enhancing the medieval heritage, Scott played a part in the restoration of the majority of the British cathedrals and hundreds of parish churches. Though he advocated a conservative approach, the conspicuous thoroughness of some of his remedial work and his fondness for "correct" but conjectural renewal (e.g. the N portals of Westminster Abbey) later provoked controversy. His secular projects were informed by his very non-Puginian conviction that Gothic was pre-eminently suited to modern building types and construction materials, and he achieved some prominent competition successes. Scott maintained a large practice and undertook over 850 projects. His pupils included G. F. BODLEY, G. E. STREET, and two of his sons. He won a Royal Gold Medal in 1859 and was knighted in 1872.

□ Foreign Office, Whitehall, London, 1862-73. Albert Memorial, London, 1863-72. Glasgow University, 1867. Midland Hotel, St Pancras Station, London, 1868-74. St Mary Abbots Church, Kensington, London, 1869-72. Anglican Cathedral, Edinburgh, 1874-9.

▷ George Gilbert Scott, *A Plea for the Faithful Restoration of our Ancient Churches*, London, 1850; *Remarks on Domestic and Secular Architecture*, London, 1857; *Personal and Professional Recollections*, London, 1879. David Cole, *The Work of Sir Gilbert Scott*, London, 1980. BP

SCOTT Sir Giles Gilbert

b. London, 1880; d. London, 1960.

English architect who occupied an important position between the wars. Grandson of Sir George Gilbert SCOTT, Giles became an assistant to Temple Moore, a pupil of his father, George Gilbert Scott Jr. Here he received a thorough grounding in the Gothic Revival tradition, which is apparent in his work up to 1920. In 1903, aged twenty-two, he won the second round of the competition to design the Anglican Cathedral in Liverpool, a major undertaking which occupied him for the rest of his career and which also reflected his changing attitude to Gothic architecture. After the First World War, Scott undertook numerous secular commissions, including university libraries for both Oxford and Cambridge, and industrial monuments such as Battersea Power Station and the Guinness Brewery at Park Royal, London. These and others displayed a distinctly Modernist approach, as Scott eagerly embraced new construction methods and the "spirit of the times"; Waterloo Bridge (1934-45), for example, is among the first structures to use reinforced concrete. During the period between the wars, Scott was an influential figure in the British architectural establishment, occupying a respected middle ground between the Modernists and those of a more traditional persuasion. Despite his Modernist excursions, Scott maintained a firm belief in the importance of tradition and remained unaffected by the International Style. He was knighted in 1924.

□ Anglican Cathedral, Liverpool, 1903-60 (completed 1980). Battersea Power Station, London (with Halliday and Agate), 1930-34. Cambridge University Library, Cambridge, England, 1930-34. Guinness Brewery, Park Royal, London (with Alexander Gibb and Partners), 1933-51. Waterloo Bridge, London (with Rendel, Palmer & Tritton), 1934-45.

▷ C. H. Reilly, *Representative British Architects of Today*, London, 1931. Gavin Stamp and Glynn Boyd Harte, *Temples of Power*, London, 1979. CS

Sir Giles Gilbert Scott, Battersea Power Station, London, 1930–4, project drawing

SEGAL Walter Kurt

b. Berlin, 1907; d. London, 1985.

Epitome of the small-scale, independent Modern architect whose career links early c20 ideals with late c20 reality. His father was an important painter, and family friends included Tzara, Arp and OUD; MIES VAN DER ROHE, Klee and Kandinsky; also GROPIUS, MENDELSOHN and TAUT, each of whom later asked Walter Segal to work with them. Each was refused. Segal studied in Holland, Berlin (Dip. Arch. 1932) and Zürich, settling in London in 1936. He always tried to work alone, finding assistants as chafing as masters were repulsive to his independent spirit. From his first small house (Ascona, Switzerland, 1932) to his last (Lewisham, London, 1985), his aim was to make convivial dwellings by cost-efficient, simple building which does not alienate the builder and is a pleasure to inhabit. Segal's focus on economy controlled by reason guided his radical reappraisal of house building, developing (a) a completely novel construction system in timber frame and panel, (b) a way of letting clients participate in the house-planning decisions, and (c) opening the building process itself to the future inhabitants. Segal displayed a powerful combination of utter practicality (he calculated all his structural members; his building did not fail) and a wide and firm grounding as an intellectual, which with prodigious energy he brought to bear on the essential c20, post-Freudian goal: working towards an equality without sameness, a less hierarchical world in which each individual's development is encouraged. In his quiet, unalienated practice, Segal offered an attractive model of the authentic professional architect.

□ Timber-frame small houses: competition winner, 1929, Ascona, Switzerland, 1932, Fideris, Switzerland, 1957, Richmond, London, 1959. Developed timber-system houses: Highgate, London, 1963, ten houses, 1969-75 two terrace projects, 1976; self-build houses, Lewisham, London: 11 houses 1977, 13 houses 1985.

▷ Walter Segal, *Planning and Transport*, London, 1945; *Homes for the People* (in collaboration), London, 1946; *Home and Environment*, London, 1948; "Beyond utility: architecture and the id", *The Architect*, March 1971; "Timber Framed Housing", *RIBA Journal*, July 1977. J. Broome, "The Segal Method", *Architects' Journal*, Nov. 1986. J. McKean, *Learning from Segal/Von Segal Lernen*, Basel, 1988.

JM

SEIDLER Harry

b. Vienna, 1923.

International and Modern architect who has sought a modern building culture for Australia. Seidler's output, extending over more than four decades, represents an intelligent and far from rigid application of the tenets of Modernism. He studied at the University of Manitoba (1941-4) and completed his postgraduate studies under Walter GROPIUS at Harvard, where he was influenced by GIEDION's lectures. At Gropius' suggestion, he attended Josef Albers' summer course at Black Mountain College, North Carolina. In the years 1946-8 Seidler was Marcel BREUER's assistant; in 1948 he set off for Sydney, stopping on the way at Oscar NIEMEYER's Rio de Janeiro office. Seidler's first independent work in Australia, a house in Sydney for his mother (1950), had been designed in Breuer's office. During the 1950s Seidler produced more than fifty houses based on this Breuer – New England formula. By the 1960s, with the Australia Square commission, he had moved in the direction of large-scale government and commercial building projects. In the 1980s Seidler designed a remarkable series of office towers for Sydney and elsewhere in Australia. The rigour of his work stems from an unvarying constructional ethic; Josef Albers, Charles Perry, Frank Stella and others in art, and Pier Luigi NERVI in structure have been important influences.

□ Rose Seidler house, Turramurra, 1948-50. Australia Square, Sydney, 1960-67. Own offices, Milsons Point, 1971-3. MLC Centre Tower, Sydney, 1972-5. Commonwealth Government Trade Group of Offices, Barton, Canberra, 1973-5. Australian Embassy, Paris, France, 1973-7. Grosvenor Place, Sydney, 1982-7. Riverside Centre, Brisbane, 1986.

▷ Harry Seidler, *Harry Seidler: Houses, Interiors, Projects*, Sydney, 1954; *Harry Seidler, 1955-63*, Sydney, 1963. P. Blake, *Architecture for the New World. The work of Harry Seidler*, Sydney, 1973. "Harry Seidler", *World Architecture*, 7, 1990.

PD

SEMPER Gottfried

b. Hamburg, 1803; d. Rome, 1879.

Architect of some of the most successful Neo-Renaissance buildings in c19 Europe who also produced a large body of theoretical writings on the origins and nature

Harry Seidler, Australian Embassy, Paris, 1973–7

of architecture which were to have a major impact on the early advocates of Modernist, functional design. Before completing his mathematical studies at Göttingen, Semper is thought to have moved to Munich in 1825 to study architecture with Friedrich von GÄRTNER. A year later, however, he was in Paris, where he worked with Frans Christian Gau and Jacques-Ignace Hittorff. Following a tour to Italy and Greece (1830-33), Semper returned to Germany, where he was recommended by Gau to head the architecture school in Dresden, taking up the position in May 1834. As the first element in a grandiose scheme for a forum in Dresden, Semper designed the Court Theatre (1838-41) on a site adjacent to the Zwinger. Other commissions followed for houses in both Neo-Palladian and Neo-Renaissance styles, for a Moorish, Neo-Romanesque synagogue (1839-40), and for the Picture Gallery that balanced the Theatre in the grand ensemble by closing off the Zwinger court (1847-54). Following the unsuccessful republican uprising of 1849, which he had actively supported, Semper was exiled, living first in Paris (1849-51) and then in London (1851-5). In 1851 he published a comparative theory of architecture under the title *Die vier Elemente der Baukunst* (*The Four Elements of Building*), locating the origins of building in the hearth, the roof, the enclosure and the mound. This prehistory of architecture was apparently endorsed by the primitive huts exhibited at the Great Exhibition of 1851, in which Semper played a peripheral role. Having made contact with the circle around Sir Henry Cole, he was appointed Professor in the Department of Practical Art at Marlborough House, London (1852), and his next publication, *Wissenschaft, Industrie und Kunst* (Science, Industry and Art; 1852), offered a critique of the crisis in design brought about by industrialization. Through the intercession of the composer Richard Wagner, Semper was offered a professorship in 1855 at the new Polytechnic in Zürich, for which he designed a monumental building in a heavily rusticated, Neo-Renaissance manner. Other commissions from this period include the "Sternwarte" in Zürich – a combined observatory, museum and apartment block – and the Town Hall in Winterthur (1865-9), in which two cross-axial blocks are dominated by a strong portico. During 1865-6 Semper worked on various schemes for a festival theatre for Wagner, and his combination of the earlier hemicyclic scheme of the Court Theatre at Dresden with Wagner's demand for a proscenium stage was finally adopted in the built version (by O. Brückwald, 1871-6). In 1871 Semper was entrusted with the rebuilding of the Dresden Court Theatre, destroyed by fire two years earlier, and produced a Neo-Baroque solution worthy of comparison with the monumental group commissioned from Semper for the Ringstrasse in Vienna, and completed by his assistant Carl von Hasenauer (Museums of Art History and Natural History, 1872-81; Burgtheater, 1874-88). Semper's incomplete study *Der Stil in den technischen und tektonischen Künste* (Style in the Tectonic Arts; 1860, 1863), a materialist account of the origins of art and architecture, had a profound impact on the pre-modernist generation of Otto WAGNER and H. P. BERLAGE.

□ Court Theatre, Dresden, 1838-41 (rebuilt 1871-78), Villa Rosa, Dresden, 1839. Synagogue, Dresden, 1839-40. Palais Oppenheim, Dresden, 1845-8. Picture Gallery, Dresden, 1847-54. Albrechtsburg, Dresden, 1850-55. Polytechnic (now Eidgenössiche Technische Hochschule), Zürich, 1858-64. Town Hall, Winterthur, 1865-9. Museums of Art History and Natural History, Vienna, 1872-81. Hofburgtheater, Vienna (with Carl von Hasenauer), 1874-88.

▷ Gottfried Semper, *Gottfried Semper: The Four Elements of Architecture and Other Writings*, tr. Harry Francis Mallgrave and Wolfgang Herrmann, Cambridge, 1989. Wolfgang Herrmann, *Gottfried Semper: Theoretische Nachlass an der ETH Zürich*, Basel, 1981; *Gottfried Semper: In Search of Architecture*, Cambridge, Mass., 1984. Joseph Rykwert, "Semper and the Conception of Style", in his *The Necessity of Ornament*, London, 1982. IBW

SERLIO Sebastiano

b. Bologna, 1475; d. Fontainebleau, 1554.

The first popularizer of architecture in print, author of the first architectural picture books. He went to Rome in 1514 and was a pupil probably of RAPHAEL and certainly of PERUZZI when the latter succeeded the former as associate architect to St Peter's in 1520. Peruzzi accumulated plans and sketches, presumably either for a treatise on the orders, antiquities and perspective or to illustrate VITRUVIUS, but he died and left the drawings to Serlio. (At this time Vitruvius was newly published in Italian and the early C16 information explosion was underway.) Serlio began a project that was essentially new: in the words of his last publisher, it was "to render the art of architecture easy for all". He was the first to harness the new mass-medium potential of printing to architecture, and he published the first printed books where images rather than words were the chief conveyor of information and style in the arts. Some of Serlio's images – for example, the cut-away elevation/section of BRAMANTE's dome for St Peter's (Book 3) or the three famous perspective scenes (end of Book 2) – are memorable. His text is not. He was pedantic rather than intellectual, pragmatic rather than theoretical. His achievement is a pictorial handbook. For the men of architecture, fundamentally pragmatic, unintellectual but with the veneer of learning demanded of them, Serlio was the ideal author (and always more influential on the edges of Renaissance culture – in the Low Countries, the English Midlands or Scotland). His work was a best-seller, and it was the first Italian treatise in English, a century before PALLADIO and then ALBERTI were translated, 160 years before a full Vitruvius in English. Yet no one really needed to translate Serlio; the value was in his images.

Sebastiano Serlio

▷ Sebastiano Serlio, *Tutte le Opere d'Architettura* (in 7 volumes); Vols. 1 and 2, 1543; Vol. 3, 1540; Vol. 4, 1537; Vol. 5, 1547; Vol. 6 and 7, written and drawn *c.*1550: Vol. 7 pub. posthumously 1574, Vol. 6 not till an Mss. facsimile of 1967. *Libro Extraordinario* (drawings of doorcases), 1551. W. B. Dinsmoor, *The Literary Remains of Sebastiano Serlio*, Art Bulletin, 24, June 1942. M. Rosci, *Il Trattato di Architettura di S. Serlio*, Milan, 1967. M. N. Rosenfeld, *Domestic Architecture*, MIT, 1979. J. M. McKean, "An Introduction to S. Serlio", *AA Quarterly*, Vol. 11, No. 4, 1979. JM

SERT Josep Lluis

b. Barcelona, 1902; d. Barcelona, 1983.

Spanish architect, planner and academic who played a leading role in the development of Modern Movement planning theories. Born into an artistic Catalan family, Sert graduated from the Escuela Tecnica Superior de Arquitectura in Barcelona in 1929. He then worked briefly with LE CORBUSIER and Pierre JEANNERET in Paris before setting up his own practice in Barcelona. An idealistic Modernist, Sert helped to organize the first group of architects in Barcelona affiliated to CIAM. The group GATEPAC was concerned with the role of architects in city planning and encouraged teamwork in the design process. In 1937 Sert returned to Paris, where he designed the Spanish Pavilion for the World's Fair. He moved to the USA two years later and from 1941 to 1958 was an associate with the town planning firm of Paul Lester Weiner. In the years 1947-56 Sert became president of CIAM, helping to develop and promote the planning theories of the Modern Movement. He had edited *Can our Cities Survive?* for CIAM in 1942. His own urban housing projects attempted to achieve a balance between various factors – people and cars; the number of dwellings in relation to support services; ideas of community and privacy. In 1953, on the recommendation of Walter GROPIUS, Sert was appointed Dean of the Faculty of the Graduate School of Design and Chairman and Professor of Architecture at Harvard University. He went on to establish the Urban Design Program at Harvard, the first formal professional urban planning degree course in the United States. In 1955 he established his own office in Cambridge, Massachusetts; subsequently he went into partnership with Huson Jackson and Ronald Gourley. During the 1960s and 70s Sert, Jackson and Associates designed numerous private houses, offices and university buildings, including the Martin Luther King Elementary School, Cambridge and the Undergraduate Science Center, Harvard University. In 1981 Sert was awarded the AIA Gold Medal.

□ Spanish National Pavilion (including Picasso's *Guernica*), World's Fair, Paris, 1937. Plan for Bogotá, Colombia (with Le Corbusier), 1951. United States Embassy, Baghdad, Iraq, 1955. Martin Luther King Elementary School, Cambridge, Mass., 1966. Undergraduate Science Center, Harvard University, Cambridge, Mass., 1970. Joan Miró Foundation, Barcelona, 1972-75.

▷ Josep Lluis Sert and CIAM, *Can our Cities Survive?* Harvard, 1942. Josep Lluis Sert and Jaqueline Tyrwhitt (eds.), *The Shape of Cities*, Cambridge, Mass., 1957. Knud Bastlund, *José Luis Sert*, Zürich and London, 1967. Jauma Freixa, *Josep Ll. Sert*, Barcelona, 1979. CS

SHAW Richard Norman

b. Edinburgh, 1831; d. London, 1913.

One of the most prolific and inventive late Victorian architects, who remained both an establishment figure and a setter of stylistic trends into the Edwardian era. He was educated in Edinburgh and articled to William Burn, an Edinburgh architect who had an office in London. In 1858 he joined G.E. STREET as an assistant and in 1863 began his independent practice, with W. E. NESFIELD as partner. As well as a number of well-known country houses, such as Cragside (1870) and, much later, Bryanston (1889-94), he designed a series of major commercial buildings in a wide range of styles with great accomplishment, such as New Zealand Chambers, London (1872), White Star offices, Liverpool (1895-8), and New Scotland Yard, London (1887-90, with a significant design participation from W. R. LETHABY, by then his senior assistant). A Royal Academician from 1877, he was co-editor with T. G. Jackson of the 1892 collection of essays *Architecture, a Profession or an Art?* Shaw's reversion to a ponderous classical manner in his Piccadilly Hotel, London (1905-8) and the houses of Bryanston and Chesters (1889-91), lent great influence to the emergent Edwardian classicism of the early C20.

□ Cragside, Northumberland, 1870. New Zealand Chambers, Leadenhall Street, London, 1872. New Scotland Yard, London, 1887-90. Chesters, Northumberland, 1889-91. Bryanston, Dorset, 1889-94. White Star Offices, Liverpool, 1895-8. Piccadilly Hotel, London, 1905-8.

▷ R. Blomfield, *Richard Norman Shaw R.A.*, London, 1940. A. Saint, *Richard Norman Shaw*, New Haven and London, 1977. RM

▷ *see also pp228-9*

Sinan, Mosque of Sultan Suleyman, Istanbul, 1564

SINAN

Mimar Koca Sinan (Great Architect Sinan) b. Anatolia, 1489; d. Istanbul, 1588.

The greatest of all Ottoman architects, whose architectural career spanned fifty years and the reigns of Suleyman the Magnificent and Selim II. His great mosques are the archetypal image of Turkish Ottoman architecture. Sinan was born of Greek Christian parents. In 1512 he was conscripted as a janissary to serve the Ottoman royal house. He became a cavalry officer, then a construction officer in the army, serving in campaigns in Eastern Europe, Rhodes, Baghdad and Persia, building bridges and fortifications. In 1538 he was appointed Architect of the Abode of Felicity. His contemporary biographer Mustafa Sai records that during his prodigious career he completed 79 mosques, 34 palaces, 33 harams, 50 chapels, 19 tombs, 55 schools, 16 almshouses, 7 madrassahs, 12 caravan serais and numerous granaries, fountains, aqueducts and hospitals. The architecture of the Ottoman empire (1281-1924) was concerned with developing the theme of a mosque with central dome spanning a rectangular base. Domes on cubical bases had existed in Seljuq architecture (1070-1308), but it was the C6 Byzantine Cathedral of Justinian (Santa Sophia) in Istanbul that was the role model for Sinan to challenge and surpass. His aim was to create a perfectly unified interior where the central dome would hover apparently weightless over an inner space composed of continuous surfaces bathed in light. Elements of buttressing and support were mostly projected on the exteriors of Sinan's buildings, allowing the interiors to become harmonious compositions of continuous plane and curvilinear surfaces. The exteriors of his mosques were great pyramidal compositions of dressed stone walls, piers and buttresses with lead capped domes and cupolas articulated by tall slender stone minarets numbering from one to four. His mosques were often part of a complex (kulliyah) comprising schools, baths, guesthouses and hospitals. The Shehzadeh Mosque, Istanbul (1548), described by Sinan as the work of his apprenticeship, explores the support of a central dome by four half domes and four massive free-standing piers. A different approach is used in the Mihrimah Mosque, Istanbul (1547), where the dome is supported by four great arches whose infill walls become a diaphanous screen of windows flooding the interior with light. The Mosque of Sultan Suleyman, Istanbul (1550-57), the work of Sinan's maturity, uses the plan of Santa Sophia as a model and achieves similar proportions. The central dome is counterbalanced by two half cupolas prolonged by apsidal domes, while the arched screens of the two lateral naves allow light to the interior. The evolution of the main elements of support moving further outside the main space, to merge finally with the enclosing rectangular walls, is demonstrated in the Mosque of Sokulla Pasha, Istanbul (1572), the Mosque of Rustem Pasha, Istanbul (1564), and finally in Sinan's masterpiece, the Mosque of Sultan Selim at Edirne (1569-75). Here the dome rests on eight arches whose supporting piers merge with the outer walls to create a huge, undivided, perfectly balanced space.

Mihrimah Mosque, Istanbul, 1547. Shehzadeh Mosque, Istanbul, 1548. Mosque of Sultan Suleyman, Istanbul, 1550-57. Mosque of Rustem Pasha, Istanbul, 1564. Mosque of Sultan Selim, Edirne, 1569-75. Mosque of Sokulla Pasha, Istanbul, 1572.

Ulya Vogt-Göknil, *Living Architecture: Ottoman*, London, 1966. Geoffrey Goodwin, *A History of Ottoman Architecture*, London, 1971 and 1987. Arthur Stratton, *Sinan*, London, 1972. Titus Burkhardt, *Art of Islam*, London, 1976. GM

see also pp206-7

SKIDMORE, OWINGS & MERRILL (SOM)

Established 1936. Louis Skidmore, b. Lawrenceburg, 1897; d. Winter Haven, Florida, 1962. Nathaniel A. Owings, b. Indianapolis, 1903; d. Santa Fe, 1984. John O. Merrill, b. St Paul, 1896; d. Colorado Springs, 1975. Succeeded by Gordon Bunshaft, b. Buffalo, NY, 1909; d. New York, 1990.

Large multi-disciplinary American, now international, architectural firm which evolved a highly successful team approach to design. Louis Skidmore and Nathaniel Owings established an office in Chicago in 1936 and opened a branch in New York in 1937. In 1939 the practice became formally known as Skidmore, Owings & Merrill (SOM) when John Merrill joined it. From the outset, the office was organized on principles adapted from the American business world, which stressed the importance of teamwork and individual responsibility, together with an economical and efficient *modus operandi*. The firm's early years were largely devoted to establishing a multi-disciplinary corporate structure which could satisfy the demands of high-powered commercial clients. The architectural breakthrough occurred in 1952, with the completion of Lever House in New York, by Bunshaft, a slick curtain-walled office slab block in the International Style, which demonstrated SOM's attention to detail and initiated a series of similar developments. The huge scale of buildings undertaken by SOM often demands some form of structural innovation. This is exemplified by buildings such as the John Hancock Center in Chicago, whose structure is conceived as a rigid, rectangular, self-supporting tube, and the Sears Tower, also in Chicago, which consists of

Skidmore, Owings & Merrill, Lever House, New York, 1952

a cluster of framed steel tubes of varying heights. The Hancock Center was also the first large-scale multi-purpose complex to incorporate shops, offices and flats within a single building. SOM have also designed a number of buildings outside the USA, including the Haj Terminal at Jeddah International Airport, the largest tent roof construction in the world, and the National Commercial Bank, Jeddah (1983). More recently, the British office has been involved in overseeing the massive office development at Canary Wharf in London's docklands.

□ Lever House, New York, 1952. John Hancock Center, Chicago, 1970. Sears Tower, Chicago, 1974. Haj Terminal, King Abdul Aziz International Airport, Jeddah, Saudi Arabia, 1982. National Commercial Bank, Jeddah, 1983.

▷ Ernst Danz, *The Architecture of Skidmore, Owings and Merrill: 1950-1962*, New York, 1962. Arthur Drexler and Axel Menges, *The Architecture of Skidmore, Owings and Merrill: 1963-1973*, New York, 1974. C. H. Krinsky, *Gordon Bunshaft of Skidmore, Owings and Merrill*, Cambridge, Mass., 1988. CS

SMIRKE Sir Robert

b. London, 1780; d. Tunbridge Wells, 1867.

Prolific C19 English architect of the Greek Revival, architect of the British Museum. Smirke spent five years travelling in Europe and set up in practice in London in 1805. He was fortunate in having powerful patrons among the ruling Tories, thanks to his father, a prominent figure in the Royal Academy. Lowther Castle was his first important commission, and his reputation was established by the innovative Covent Garden Theatre. By 1815, at the age of thirty-five, he had reached the top of his profession as one of three architects attached to the Office of Works. Smirke was a fashionable and prolific architect; he designed several Neo-Gothic castle-houses, but they are less significant than his Greek Revival works, which are part of the mainstream of European Neo-Classicism. However, despite the success of the British Museum and his London clubs, Smirke never fully achieved a balance between archaeological accuracy and the need to innovate for new building types. His influence was also to channel the Greek Revival away from the geometrical possibilities and abstraction of the cubic forms seen in his early Covent Garden into archaeological copying and revivalism. Technically, however, Smirke was a great innovator and was the first British architect to make use of cast iron and concrete for load-bearing foundations.

□ Lowther Castle, Cumbria, 1806-11. Covent Garden Theatre, London, 1808-10. Luton Hoo, Beds., *c.*1816-1842. British Museum, London, 1823-46. Council House, Bristol, 1824-7. Oxford and Cambridge Club, London, 1836-7.

▷ J. Mordaunt Crook, *The British Museum*, London, 1972; *The Greek Revival*, London, 1972. TC

Alison and Peter Smithson, Golden Lane housing, 1952, photomontage

SMITHSON Peter & Alison

Peter Smithson, b. Stockton-on-Tees, 1923; Alison, b. Sheffield, 1928.

British architects whose polemical ideas have made as big an impact as their buildings. Their work is often associated with an ill-defined and unwarranted derogatory term: Brutalism. Both studied at the University of Durham and worked for a time with the LCC. They began the design of Hunstanton School in 1949-54. This revolutionary design took its clues from MIES VAN DER ROHE buildings and exploiting a "bare bones" aesthetic with exposed steelwork, floor beams and services, an early kind of technological minimalism. Their significant building, the *Economist* Building in St James's, London, came a decade later (1964). It was followed by the Garden Building at St Hilda's College, Oxford, and Robin Hood Gardens, London (1972), and, more recently, the School of Architecture, Bath University (1988-9). Against this background of solid influential buildings, the Smithsons have written and exhibited their projects and ideas. In 1956 as members of the Independent Group they contributed to the *This is Tomorrow* exhibition (revised in 1990 for the ICA travelling exhibition on the Group's work). However, their initial architectural fame as theorists rests most certainly with their involvement with Team 10 and the overthrowing of the old regime in CIAM. Central to all their ideas is the notion of place.

□ Hunstanton Secondary Modern School, Norfolk, 1949-54. "House of the Future", Ideal Home Exhibition, London, 1956. Pavilion for *This is Tomorrow* exhibition, Whitechapel Art Gallery, London, 1956 (ICA, 1990). House for Dr Sugden, Watford, 1957. *Economist* Building, St James's, London, 1964. Garden Building, St Hilda's College, Oxford, 1972. Robin Hood Gardens, London, 1972. School of Architecture, Bath University, 1988-9.

▷ A. and P. Smithson, *Urban Structuring*, London, 1967; *Ordinariness and Light; Urban Theories '52-'60*, London, 1970; *Without Rhetoric*, London, 1973. D. Robbins (ed.), *The Independent Group: Postwar Britain and the Aesthetics of Plenty*, Cambridge, Mass., 1990. DS

▷ *see also pp240-41*

SMYTHSON Robert

b. c.1535; d. Wollaton, 1614.

Undoubtedly the leading English architect of the late C16 and early C17. Smythson built some of the most magnificent and original houses of the Elizabethan era, but very little is known of his birth, background, formal education or professional career. The earliest documentation dates from 1568, when Sir John Thynne appointed him to oversee the rebuilding of his home at Longleat. Smythson's actual contribution to the final design is uncertain, owing to the long and complicated history of the house. Its significance within the development of an English Renaissance style is, however, undeniable and this success earned Smythson the opportunity to design a series of remarkable country houses. His detailing fused elements of SERLIO's *Architecture*, English Gothic and Flemish influences to produce a romantic synthesis of stunning originality, not merely a bland pastiche. Robert was assisted latterly by his son **John** (d. 1634), who is himself credited with the design of several distinguished houses, most notably the rambling Bolsover Castle, Derbyshire (*c.*1612-34).

☐ Longleat House, Wilts., 1572-80. Wollaton Hall, Notts., 1580-88. Hardwick Hall, Derbyshire, 1590-97. Burton Agnes Hall, Yorks., 1601-10. Chastleton House, Oxon., *c.*1602. Wootton Lodge, Staffs., *c.*1610.

▷ James Lees-Milne, *Tudor Renaissance*, London, 1951. Mark Girouard, *Robert Smythson and the Architecture of the Elizabethan Era*, London, 1966. Malcolm Airs, *The Making of the English Country House 1500-1640*, London, 1975. MC

▷ *see also pp216-17*

SOANE Sir John

b. Goring-on-Thames, 1753; d. London, 1837.

Soane's architecture is in a class by itself; original, mannered, with a brilliant control of internal space and light, and a fondness for shallow domes, repeated segmental arches, clerestories, linear ornament and colour. Whether or not it was his humble origin as the son of a Berkshire bricklayer which spurred him, Soane became undoubtedly successful. He trained under George DANCE the Younger, and later Henry HOLLAND, but entered the Royal Academy Schools in 1771. In 1778, on the King's Travelling Scholarship, he left the Academy Schools for Italy. In Rome he became attracted to the service of Frederick Hervey, the Bishop of Derry, an ardent builder with whom he journeyed back to Ireland. However, no work ensued there and in June 1780 Soane returned, disappointed, to England. Then slow years building up a modest practice in East Anglia, but in 1784 marriage to the daughter of a wealthy builder; at his father-in-law's death in 1790 Soane succeeded to money and property. Two years previously he had had the good fortune to be appointed Surveyor to the Bank of England, so he now had financial security and a good post from which to obtain further introductions to wealthy patrons. His practice grew, and became second in size only to that of James WYATT. (His surveyorship of the Bank of England was the "pride and boast" of his life; his work there included the Stock office 1792–3, now destroyed.) Finally, when the Board of Works was reorganized in 1814 Soane was one of the three architects appointed, with responsibility for public buildings, a post which lasted until 1832, when Soane retired and was knighted by William IV. There must have been pleasure in the Soane family when its head was elected Professor of Architecture at the Royal Academy. In 1809 he succeeded his former master, George Dance the Younger, who had failed to deliver the statutory lectures and had resigned. In the year of his election, by contrast, Soane started to deliver his lectures, and he continued to repeat them for the next twenty-five years. In his long life Soane was a great collector of drawings, models, casts, sculptures, paintings and a vast miscellany of objects. He had lived at Lincoln's Inn Fields since 1812 and, obtaining an Act of Parliament in 1833, he left his house to the nation to be a museum "for the study of Architecture and the Allied Arts". It remains so to this day, one of the most fascinating specialized museums in the world.

☐ Wimpole Hall, Cambs., 1791-3. His own house (now Sir John Soane's Museum), Lincoln's Inn Fields, London, 1792-4. Pitzhanger Place, Ealing, London, 1800-1803.

▷ Sir John Soane, *Designs in Architecture...*, 1778; *Plans ... of buildings erected in Norfolk, Suffolk etc.*, 1788; *Lectures in Architecture by Sir John Soane*, ed. A. T. Bolton, London, 1929. Pierre du Prey, *John Soane: The Making of an Architect*, London, 1982. Dorothy Stroud, *Sir John Soane:*, London, 1983. GB

SOLERI Paolo

b. Turin, 1919.

Visionary Italian architect and planner who has created the word "arcology", combining architecture and ecology. Educated in Italy between the world wars, Soleri graduated as a Dottore in Architettura from the Turin Politecnico in 1946. Apprenticeship for sixteen months with Frank Lloyd WRIGHT followed. His first building, the Dome House at Cave Creek, Arizona (1949), was designed and constructed in collaboration with Mark Mills. In Italy from 1950, Soleri worked in Turin and on the Amalfi coast before returning to the USA in 1955. Since 1956 he has worked alone from "Cosanti" studios at 6433 Doubletree Road, Scottsdale, Arizona, with the continuing assistance of apprentices. Soleri's naive but telling penetrations into the conventions of society are a particular response to the horizontal suburban consumptive culture of the surrounding Phoenix metropolitan area. Although early projects were based on bioclimatic principles and later proposals insist on an energy and ecological responsibility, these techniques are less visible than Soleri's Utopian "megastructure" ideas, best seen at Arcosanti, his ongoing urban experiment in Arizona. He is exceptional in expanding the dimensions of design responsibility. Yet with single-structure urbane visions for millions Soleri insists on "miniaturization". In a spiritual quest inspired by Teilhard de Chardin he pursues imploded human and social intensity through three-dimensional density in experimental buildings, visionary proposals and inspired writing and lecturing. His *Architectural Vision* exhibitions were seen in major N American cities in 1970.

☐ Ceramica Artistica Solinene, Vietri sul Mare, Italy, 1953. Cosanti Studios, Scottsdale, Arizona, 1956-74. Proposals for Luxembourg Bridges, 1958; and Space for Peace since 1980. "Arcosanti" under construction since 1970.

▷ Paolo Soleri, *Arcology: The City in the Image of Man*, MIT, 1969; *The Sketchbooks of Paolo Soleri*, MIT, 1971; *The Bridge Between Matter and Spirit is Matter Becoming Spirit*, 1973. JC

▷ *see also pp 244-5*

Sir John Soane, Bank of England, London, 1799, interior drawing

SONCK Lars Eliel

b. Kälviä, 1870; d. Helsinki, 1956.

Prominent and prolific figure in Finland's anxious search for a national identity after the turn of the century. The rise of National Romanticism paralleled that of Jugendstil within continental Europe, and Sonck, along with Eliel SAARINEN, Hermann Gesellius and Armas Lindgren, played a leading role in the creation of this new style. He graduated from Helsinki's Polytechnic Institute in 1894 and found immediate success after winning a major competition for a church at Turku. His architecture reflects the "patriotic" fervour of the time and looks to the country's medieval stone buildings and the wooden villas of the Karelian region for inspiration. Many of his imposing commercial and ecclesiastical buildings incorporate elements of the neo-Romanesque style, similar in spirit to the work of the American architect H.H. RICHARDSON. Sonck turned his back on the rising clamour for a new rationalism within architecture and retreated increasingly into Finland's early history to develop a heavy monumentalism often employing archaic Nordic or Celtic motifs to add a sense of *gravitas*. His long and extremely active career lasted up to the 1950s. His office produced more than 150 schemes.

□ St Michael's Church, Turku, 1894. St John's Cathedral, Tampere, 1902-7. Mortgage Society Building, Helsinki, 1908. Stock Exchange Building, Helsinki, 1911. Mikael Agricola Church, Helsinki (with Arvo Muroma), 1935.

▷ J. Vikstedt, *De finska stadernas byggnadskonst*, Helsinki, 1926. J. M. Richards, *800 Years of Finnish Architecture*, Newton Abbot, 1978. P. Kivinen, *Lars Sonck 1870-1956*, Helsinki, 1981. R. Spence, *Lars Sonck*, London, 1982.

MC

SOUFFLOT Jacques Germain

b. Irancy, Auxerre, 1713; d. Paris, 1780.

Seminal French Neo-Classicist, notable in particular for the Hôtel-Dieu in Lyon and Ste Geneviève (the Pantheon) in Paris. In Rome from *c.*1731 to 1738, he gravitated to the French Academy, where several younger pensionaries were to be associated with the proto-Romantic circle of Pannini and PIRANESI, dedicated to celebrating the glories of the remains of Roman antiquity. At the same time, Roman architecture was being transformed by the Florentines A. Galilei and F. Fuga, the anti-baroque rationalism of Galilei's work at S. Giovanni in Laterano – contemporary with Soufflot's stay – stunning in its impact. On his return to France, Soufflot practised in Lyon and joined the Lyon Academy. He returned to Italy in 1750 in the company of the future Marquis de Marigny, then being groomed for the post of Director General of Royal Buildings. On this trip he made a special study of theatre design and was amongst the first architects to examine the recently rediscovered remains of Herculaneum and the great Greek Doric temples at Paestum. Marigny appointed him to the control of royal building in Paris in 1755 and he was admitted to the Académie Royale de l'Architecture. Soufflot's Roman training aligned him with J. F. BLONDEL and other critics concerned with the threat to progress represented by the "unregulated imagination" which had produced the novelties of the Rococo *genre pittoresque*. His contributions to debates in the Lyon Academy make it clear that, like them, he saw the discipline of the classical rules as essential for progress. Putting progressive principles into practice in his designs for the Hôtel-Dieu at Lyon, he combined a new strictness of line, firmness of form, simplicity of contour and rigorously architectonic concep-

Jacques Soufflot, Ste Geneviève (Pantheon), Paris, 1755–80

tion of detail (associated with the ancient Greek tradition by Academic critics) to produce a more profound *gravitas* than had been characteristic in C18 France – though it certainly was not foreign to the work of his Roman contemporaries. Beyond Greek Doric, Soufflot's extra-Vitruvian interests extended to Gothic, then still largely despised. At Ste Geneviève in Paris, in line with radical reductive theory but recalling experiments going back to Claude PERRAULT, his aim of uniting the lightness of Gothic construction with the purity and order of Greek forms was prophetic of the essential eclecticism of mainstream Neo-Classicism.

□ Hôtel-Dieu extension, Lyon, 1739-48. Archbishop's Palace alterations, Lyon, 1747-9. Loge au Change, Lyon, 1748-50. Theatre, Lyon, 1753-6. Ste Geneviève (Panthéon), Paris, 1755-80. Projects for the Bibliothèque du Roi in the Louvre, from 1755. Sacristy of Notre Dame Cathedral, Paris, 1756-60. Temple, grotto, changes to Marigny's château at Menars, from 1765. Marigny's house at Roule, Paris, from 1769. Ecole de Droit, Paris, 1771-83. Nymphaeum, Bertin park at Chatou, from 1774.

▷ M. Petzet, *Soufflot's Ste Geneviève*, Berlin, 1961. A. Braham, *Architecture of the French Enlightenment*, London, 1980. Caisse National des Monuments Historiques, *Soufflot et son temps* (exhibition catalogue), Paris, 1981. D. Ternois and F. Perez, *Soufflot à Lyon*, Lyon, 1982. CT

▷ *see also pp220-21*

SPENCE Sir Basil

b. Bombay, 1907; d. Eye, Herefordshire, 1976.

Distinguished British Modern architect responsible for Coventry Cathedral. Educated at the Edinburgh School of Architecture and the Bartlett School of Architecture, University College, London, Spence found his first employment as an assistant in the office of Sir Edwin LUTYENS and then worked with William Kininmonth in the Edinburgh office of Rowand Anderson & Paul (1931-3), becoming a partner in the firm (1934-7). He subsequently established his own practice in Edinburgh. A Modernist tinged with Scandinavian eclecticism, Spence had his first success winning the competition to restore Coventry Cathedral (1950), which established his reputation as a leading architect. Coventry was heavily bombed during the Second World War and the cathedral had been reduced to a shell. This important piece of reconstruction coincided with the rebirth of post-war Britain after the austerity of the 1940s, and Spence, forward-looking and innovative, cleverly married new elements with old, opting for a modern form with Gothic aspirations. Consecrated in 1962, Coventry Cathedral featured contributions from artists and craftsmen such as Graham Sutherland, John Piper and Geoffrey Clarke. In subsequent years Spence worked on university projects in Liverpool, Southampton, Nottingham, Edinburgh and the development of Sussex. Despite his preference for traditional materials, Spence endowed his buildings with an individual artistic vision and continued to attract controversy with such projects as the Knightsbridge Barracks, London and the British Embassy in Rome. He was knighted in 1960.

Sir Basil Spence, Coventry Cathedral, 1950–62

□ Coventry Cathedral, 1950-62. Sea and Ships Pavilion, Festival of Britain, 1951. Sussex University, Brighton, 1962. Chancellory of the British Embassy, Rome, 1971. Cavalry Barracks, Knightsbridge, London, 1970.

▷ Basil Spence and Henry Snoek, *Out of the Ashes: A Progress through Coventry Cathedral*, London, 1963. Basil Spence, *New Buildings in Old Cities*, Southampton, 1973. D. Daiches, *The Idea of a New University: An Experiment in Sussex*, London, 1964. CS

STAM Mart (Martinus Adrianus)

b. Purmerend, Holland, 1899; d. Goldach, Switzerland, 1986.

An underrated architect of the Heroic Period of the Modern Movement. He studied at the Dutch State School for Draughtsmanship (1917-19) and was employed by several local architects until 1922, when he travelled to Berlin and met Bruno TAUT and EL LISSITZKY. In 1924 he returned to Switzerland, where he had previously established links, and worked with Karl MOSER in Zürich and A. Jetten in Thun. During this period he founded, with El Lissitzky, Hans Schmidt and Emil Roth, the avant-garde journal *ABC*. His Swiss-Dutch links were dominant in his life. In Holland he was a member of the *De Stijl* group with the architects OUD, RIETVELD and DUIKER and the painters VAN DOESBURG and Mondrian. He was also a prominent member of Opbouw. His most notable buildings were all of his early period and include the terrace houses at the weissenhof Werkbund Exhibition in Stuttgart (1927), where he also introduced his tubular steel cantilever chair; the "Hellerhof" group in Frankfurt-am-Main: the old people's home with Werner Moser and Ferdinand KRAMER. The most important single contribution was his work as job architect for the Van Nelle factory at Rotterdam with the BRINKMAN and VAN DER VLUGT studio (1925-31): it was the clarity of vision, precise planning and detailing of Mart Stam that made this the outstanding building of Dutch Rationalism. In 1927 he was working with Ernst MAY, and in 1928 he was present at the first CIAM Congress. At this period he taught briefly at the Bauhaus. The opportunities which were then presenting themselves in Russia attracted the European avant-garde and, in 1930, Stam together with Ernst May, Hannes

Meyer and Hans Schmidt, travelled to Moscow, where they worked chiefly on urban planning, producing schemes for Magnitogorsk, Makejerka and Orsk, and Stam produced designs for the open-air theatre at Oeral. In 1934, the political climate in Russia was beginning to become oppressive, and Stam returned to Amsterdam. Subsequently he was Director of the Institute of Applied Art until 1948, when he took up the appointment of Director of the Academy of Figurative and Applied Art at Dresden. From 1950 to 1952 he directed the Academy of Fine Arts in East Berlin. He then returned to Amsterdam, where he practised until 1966; little is known of this period. During his last twenty years he lived a secluded life in Switzerland, but built there at least two modest houses in the local vernacular, one at Arcengo, Tessin (1966) and one at Hilterfingen (1969).

□ Van Nelle Factory, Rotterdam (with Brinkman and Van der Vlugt), 1925-31. Terrace houses, Weissenhofsiedlung, Stuttgart, 1927. Montessori School, Amsterdam (with W. van Tijen and C. Stam-Besse), 1935. Terrace houses, Amsterdam (with W. van Tijen and C. Stam-Besse), 1937.

▷ Mart Stam, *ABC* Nos. 1, 2 and 3/4, *Modernes Bauen*, Zürich, 1924-8 (reissued Delft, 1969). G. Oorthuys, *Mart Stam: Documentation of his work 1920-65*, London, 1970. *Bouwkundig Weekblad* Vol. 87, No. 23, 23.12.69: special issue on Mart Stam. English version, London, 1970. *Forum* Vol. 28, Nos. 1 and 2, April 1983: "Traces of Stam". *Bauwelt* Vol. 77, No. 13, April 86: article by Alfred Roth. *Domus* No. 673, June 1986: obituary by Alfred Roth. CD

▷ *see also pp230-31, 234-5*

STAROV Ivan Yegorovich

b. Moscow, 1744; d. St Petersburg, 1808.

Founder of the simple, antique-inspired Empire style of Russian classicism, and one of its spatially most original exponents. From a church family, Starov entered the new Moscow University's *gymnasium* (secondary school) in 1755, and then from 1758 was among the first pupils in the new Academy of the Three Arts (later Academy of Arts), soon transferring with the school to St Petersburg (Leningrad). He was consistently top student in architecture under Vallin de la Mothe and Alexander Kokorinov, and his gold-medal scholarship to Europe (1762) led to five years under Charles de Wailly in Paris and one in Rome; he returned to St Petersburg in 1768. From 1772 he worked in the Commission for Masonry Building of St Petersburg and Moscow (the planning and development office for all Russian towns), and in 1786-9 he was chief architect of the Office of Her Imperial Majesty's Buildings and Parks. A keen teacher, he became a professor at the Academy School in 1785 and its Deputy Director in 1794. A series of great country house complexes showed Starov's spatial inventiveness and formal originality within a pure Greek canon novel to Russia. French clarity from de la Mothe combined with Kokorinov's concern for local conditions and site to reproduce brilliantly free interpenetrations of internal spaces and the larger landscape, in particular through circular and oval plan elements, bold three-dimensional use of columns and an equally new clarity in overall form.

□ Bogoroditsa and Bobriki houses near Tula, 1771-6. Nikolskoe-Gagarino, near Moscow, 1773-6. Taitsy, near Leningrad, 1774-80. Cathedral of Alexander Nevsky Lavra, Leningrad, 1774-90. Country houses for Potemkin in Ladoga area, 1778, and Tauride Palace, Petersburg 1782-9. Pella complex for Catherine the Great, 1784-90. Voznesenskoe estate, Ladoga area, 1794.

▷ G. Heard Hamilton, *The Art and Architecture of Russia*, London, 1954. V. and A. Kennet, *The Palaces of Leningrad*, London, 1973. D. A. Kyuchariants, *Ivan Starov*, Leningrad, 1982. CC

STEINER Rudolf

b. Kraljevec, Austria, 1861; d. Dornach, Switzerland, 1925.

Philosopher and spiritual teacher who developed a new style of architecture for his Anthroposophical Society. He was a Goethe and Nietzsche scholar, largely self-educated, who developed an interest in the polarity between science and nature. Educated at the Vienna Technical College, he embarked on a lifetime's search to bridge the knowledge gap between matter and spirit, an idea that was thoroughly explored in his unconventional architecture towards the end of his life. He admired the German architect Gottfried SEMPER, having been taught by one of his disciples, Josef Baier, but he viewed Semper also as a material functionalist and one who "led everything artistic back to technique". Steiner was more interested in intuition, creativity and clairvoyance. He gave a series of lectures on architecture at Dornach in 1914 during the building of the First Goetheanum, which was destroyed by fire (1921-2). These and subsequent talks form the basis of Steiner's new style in architecture, which his followers adhere to. There has been a revival of interest recently in Steiner's ideas which is closely associated with "organic architecture".

□ First Goetheanum, Dornach, Switzerland, and various adjacent buildings, including Haus Duldeck (1917), the Glasshouse, Boiler House, etc. First design (only) of Second Goetheanum, Dornach, 1925-*c*.1967.

▷ Rudolf Steiner, *Wege zu einem neuen Baustil*, 1926 (tr. as *Ways to a New Style in Architecture*, London, 1927); *Der Baugedänke des Goetheanum*, Stuttgart, 1958. C. Kemper, *Der Bau: Studien zur Architektur u. Plastik des ersten Goetheanum*, Stuttgart, 1966. Erich Zimmer, *Rudolf Steiner als Architekt*, Stuttgart, 1970. Rex Raab *et al.*, *Eloquent Concrete*, London, 1979. DS

STERN Robert A. M.

b. New York, 1939.

Prolific New York Post-Modern classicist. On finishing his studies at Columbia, New York and Yale (1965), Stern became a designer with Richard MEIER (1966) and subsequently worked as a planner for New York City. He set up his own practice with John Hagmann in 1969, and since 1972 has been principal of Robert A. M. Stern Architects. He has held professorships at Yale and Columbia and represented the USA at the Venice Biennales of 1976 and 1980. He is perhaps best known for a number of exclusive country houses. Earlier works such as the Westchester Residence made allusion to aspects of classical architecture in a Modernist context, but his later designs have come to look more historical. He was an early and important theoretician of Post-Modernism and in his book *Modern Classicism* seeks to explain the continuity of the classical tradition and the relationship to his own Post-Modern classicism, which he has defined as "a modern traditional approach that stresses the importance of cultural and physical context".

□ Westchester Residence, New York, 1974-6. Residence at Farmneck, New York, 1980-81.

Residence at Millneck, New York, 1981-2. Observatory Hill Dining Hall, University of Virginia, Charlottesville, 1982-4. Villa, New Jersey, 1983-8. Berkeley Street, Boston, Mass., from 1986. Point West Place, Framingham, Mass., 1983-5.

▷ Robert A. M. Stern, *New Directions in American Architecture*, London, 1969, New York, 1977; *Modern Classicism*, London and New York, 1988. P. Arnell and T. Bickford, *Robert A. M. Stern: Buildings and Projects 1965-80*, New York, 1981. L. F. Rueda, *Robert A. M. Stern: Buildings and Projects 1981-86, New York, 1986.* TC

STIRLING James

b. Glasgow, 1926.

Internationally known, controversial and multi-faceted British architect. Stirling trained at Liverpool University (1945-50), where the syllabus was based on Beaux-Arts principles. He began work with Lyons, Israel & ELLIS in London (1953-6) and met James Gowan, with whom he worked in partnership (1956-63). They produced a small number of influential buildings, such as the low-rise flats of Ham Common (1957), whose style, derived from LE CORBUSIER's later works and Peter and Alison SMITHSON, started a trend for brick used with exposed concrete. Their major building, the Engineering Faculty building at Leicester University (1959-63), won international attention for its "Constructivist" tower and bold contrasts of industrial red bricks and large areas of glazing. It was to provide the model for a similar concept at Cambridge (1964-7) and Oxford (1966-71). The former sealed Stirling's controversial reputation and was vilified on aesthetic and utilitarian grounds. At one point it was threatened with demolition but has now been renovated. From 1963 to 1971 Stirling was in practice on his own. He is an active teacher and became well known in the USA from whence he received a number of commissions. There were also a number of quintessentially 1960s buildings such as the Olivetti Centre and some housing at Runcorn New Town. Since 1971 Stirling has been in partnership with Michael Wilford. His later work appears more formalist, influenced by the historicism of Post-Modernism. He has aligned himself increasingly with a populist, somewhat witty form of Post-Modern classicism. His Staatsgalerie, Stuttgart, is a melange of arbitrary-seeming modern construction and randomized quotation of historical elements. The design for the Mansion House scheme was more composed, but an unkind critic compared it to an art deco radio. Stirling has always been wilfully experimental, and there is little consistency in his approach or references. Perhaps because of the Beaux-Arts nature of his training he has always admitted to this essential wilful nature of his creative decisions, so that the historicity of his "late work" is no more contrived than the modernity of his former work.

NEUE STAATSGALERIE, Stuttgart

The Neue Staatsgalerie by Stirling & Wilford (1977–84) stands as one of the great public monuments of Post-Modernism. It succeeds in fusing a number of eclectic architectural elements such as Egyptian motifs, classical Roman references and brightly coloured Modernist handrails and balustrading. The elements are contained in a concrete frame building clad in contrasting bands of ashlar. While the plan, with a large circular well cut out of it, evokes Schinkel's Altes Museum, the Staatsgalerie's spatial devices are derived from Cubism, Le Corbusier and Alvar Aalto. Sitting well in its dense urban context, the polychromatic gallery draws visitors inside past its bold, undulating glass front wall and then through a complex sequence of galleries to the central focus – an open courtyard containing a large open-topped drum used as a sculpture courtyard. The Neue Staatsgalerie also plays an important role in an urban context, and has helped to establish the identity of the museum area of the city.

□ Flats, Ham Common, London, 1957-9 (with James Gowan). Engineering Department, Leicester University, 1959-63 (with James Gowan). History Faculty Library, Cambridge, 1964-7. Andrew Melville Hall, St Andrews University, Scotland, 1964-8. Florey Building, Queen's College, Oxford, 1966-71: housing, Runcorn, Cheshire, 1967-9. Olivetti Training Centre, Haslemere, Surrey, 1969-72. Stirling, Wilford and Associates: Fogg Art Museum, Harvard (wing), 1979. Wissenschafts-zentrum, Berlin, 1979-87. Staatsgalerie, Stuttgart, 1980-83. Clore Gallery Extension, Tate Gallery, London, 1980-86. Mansion House scheme, London, 1988. Biennale Bookshop, Venice, 1989.

▷ James Stirling and L. Krier, *Buildings and Projects of James Stirling*, London, 1975. James Stirling, *Buildings and Projects*, New York, 1984. R. Banham, *The New Brutalism*, London 1966. "Recent work of James Stirling and Associates", *A+U* 1990. TC

G. E. Street, Royal Courts of Justice, London, 1869–82

STREET George Edmund

b. Woodford, Essex, 1824; d. London, 1881.

A leading British practitioner and theorist of High Victorian Gothic. After three years in the office of Owen Carter of Winchester, he worked in SCOTT's London office 1845-9. He practised in Oxford (1852-6) and subsequently in London. A

member of the Ecclesiological Society, he was Oxford diocesan architect (1850-81). His earliest buildings used English Gothic as their source, but by the mid-1850s his viewpoint, articulated in *Brick and Marble in the Middle Ages*, had became Ruskinian and eclectic. His buildings reflected his belief that modern needs could be met through a vigorous synthesis of French ecclesiastical architecture (which he regarded as "the noblest and most masculine") and the more hybrid forms and secular applications of Italian Gothic. Like RUSKIN, he advocated constructional polychromy (he used it powerfully at St James-the-Less), and his emphasis on materials and organic decoration anticipated the Arts & Crafts movement and influenced William MORRIS, Philip WEBB, and Norman SHAW, who were among his pupils. For his major work, the rebuilding of the Royal Courts of Justice, Street produced a complex and irregularly picturesque synthesis of C13 English, French and Italian forms. He received the RIBA Gold Medal in 1874.

□ Cuddesdon College, Oxon., 1853-4. St James-the-Less, Pimlico, London, 1859-61. SS. Philip and James, Oxford, 1860-66. St Mary Magdalen, Paddington, London, 1868-78. Royal Courts of Justice, Strand, London, 1869-82.

▷ G. E. Street, *Brick and Marble in the Middle Ages; Notes on a tour in North Italy*, 1855; *Some Account of Gothic Architecture in Spain*, 1869. A. E. Street, *Memoir of George Edmund Street RA*, London, 1888 (reprinted New York, 1972). BP

▷ *see also pp228-9*

STRICKLAND William

b. Navesink, NJ, 1788; d. Nashville, Tennessee, 1854.

Versatile and prolific American architect and engineer, best known for his Neo-Classical public buildings. Strickland studied architecture and engineering under LATROBE (1801-*c.*1805) and worked as a theatre set painter in New York before setting up in practice in Philadelphia (*c.*1818). He visited Europe for the first time in 1838. His early buildings were varied in style and included the Gothic Philadelphia Masonic Hall (1808-11) and the somewhat Middle-Eastern Temple of New Jerusalem (1816-17). The Neo-Classical style of his maturity, developed from Latrobe, was distinguished by a conscientious use of Greek vocabulary based on Stuart and Revett's *Antiquities of Athens* (published in five volumes 1762-1830). He achieved fame with his competition-winning design for the Second Bank of the United States, similar in plan to Latrobe's Bank of Pennsylvania, and fronted by an octastyle Doric portico modelled on the Parthenon. He went on to design further commercial and administrative buildings, theatres and churches, and also undertook major engineering projects, including the "Mixed System" (combined railroad/canal) of Eastern Pennsylvania, several other railroads, the Fair Mount dam, and the Delaware Breakwater.

□ Second Bank of the United States, Philadelphia, 1818-24. United States Mint, Philadelphia, 1829-33. Philadelphia Exchange, 1832-4. State Capitol, Nashville, Tennessee, 1849-59.

▷ Agnes Addison Gilchrist, *William Strickland, Architect and Engineer 1788-1854*, New York, 1950, 1969. BP

▷ *see also pp226-7*

SULLIVAN Louis Henry

b. Boston, Mass., 1856; d. Chicago, Illinois, 1924.

Proponent of an American architecture who was in the vanguard of the Modern Movement. As a boy, Sullivan discovered the power and mystery of life in Boston and on family farms. A year in architecture at the Massachusetts Institute of Technology (1872-3) was followed by several months in draughting jobs with FURNESS and Hewitt in Philadelphia, and a similar short employment with William Le Baron JENNEY in Chicago. In July 1874 Sullivan embarked on his only trip to Europe. He studied in the Vaudremer studio at the Ecole des Beaux Arts in Paris, and one year later rèturned to Chicago, where he worked in a variety of situations. In 1883 the announcement of Adler and Sullivan confirmed his full partnership with **Dankmar Adler** (1844-1900), a productive arrangement which lasted until 1895, when Adler withdrew. Based on Sullivan's comment that "Adler was essentially a technician, an engineer, a conscientious administrator...", the usual assumption is that he was the skilled engineer to complement Sullivan's flair as designer and theorist. But Adler's work "shows a strength, simplicity and straight forwardness together with a certain refinement which reveals the true architect", according to John Root, another premier architect of the Chicago School (see BURNHAM & ROOT). The Auditorium Building, Chicago (1887-90), was the partnership's first major triumph and the city's tallest building. The soaring and delicate auditorium, which seated 4,200, was embedded in a robust multipurpose speculative office block and a 400-room hotel. In contrast, the same cubic power with more refined decorative surfaces is evident in the tiny Getty Tomb (1890). The partners' two most familiar skyscrapers (usually credited only to Sullivan), the Wainwright Building, St Louis (1890-91), and the more vertical Guaranty Building, Buffalo (1894-6), verify Sullivan's essay, "The Tall Office Building Artistically Considered" (1896); each is "a proud and soaring thing, rising in sheer exultation... from bottom to top...without a single dissenting line". Sullivan's most important protégé, Frank Lloyd WRIGHT, was an apprentice in the office between 1888 and 1893. Yet Sullivan's solo swansong, the Schlesinger & Mayer Department Store (now Carson Pirie Scott), Chicago (1898-1904), is a handsome modern white block based on the horizontal proportions of the steel frame and the Chicago Window. Its urbane presence was achieved through a series of remodellings

Louis Sullivan (with Dankmar Adler), Guaranty Building, Buffalo, 1894–6

and additions so the store was always kept open. Sullivan's late works, primarily a series of isolated small town banks such as Owatonna, Minnesota (1906-8), and Grinnell, Iowa (1916-18), repeat the theme of his Transportation Building (1891-2) for the Chicago World's Fair: a robust block is penetrated by a great decorated semicircular entrance and window arch. His restless and intricate ornamentation is always contained by the simplest architectural geometries. Sullivan's seminal demonstration of a virile and indigenous architecture with a native expression was paralleled by his active participation in professionalism. Both as an organizer and director of various architectural groups as well as a formal theorist on aesthetics, he propounded "the spirit of the time" and "the genius of the people". Sullivan as both philosopher and conscience became the most influential force in the concurrent Chicago School with its birth of the skyscraper in "commercial style". But Sullivan's "form ever follows function" always went beyond direct functional or structural expression. Sullivan's commitment to the organic, evident in the stylized nature forms of often lush ornamented surfaces, characterized his creative artistry and lively dedication to architecture as art, and nature as source: "...the complexity of Nature... is steadily revealing a unitary impulse underlying all men and all things". Sullivan died destitute in a Chicago hotel shortly after seeing the first copies of *The Autobiography of an Idea* and *A System of Architectural Ornament*. His obituary in the *New York Times* called him "the Dean of American architects".

□ Adler and Sullivan: Auditorium Building, Chicago, 1887-90; Wainwright Building, St Louis, 1890-91; Guaranty Building, Buffalo, 1894-6. Sullivan: Transportation Building, Chicago, 1891-2; Schlesinger & Mayer Department Store (Carson Pirie Scott Store), Chicago, 1898-1904.

▷ Louis Sullivan, "The Tall Office Building Artistically Considered", *Lippincotts Magazine*, 57, 1896; *Kindergarten Chats*, New York, 1918, 1934, 1947; *The Autobiography of an Idea*, New York, 1924, London, 1956; *A System of Architectural Ornament*, New York, 1924. H. Morrison, *Louis Sullivan – Prophet of Modern Architecture*, New York, 1935, 1952. S. Paul, *Louis Sullivan – An Architect in American Thought*, Englewood Cliffs, NJ, 1962. H. Duncan, *Culture and Democracy*, Totowa, NJ, 1965. R. Twombly, *Louis Sullivan*, Chicago, 1986. JC

▷ *see also pp226-7, 232-3*

TANGE Kenzo

b. Osaka, Japan, 1913.

The leading architect in Japan for a quarter-century after the Second World War. Tange studied at the University of Tokyo, graduating in 1938, and worked for Kunio Maekawa (1938-41) before returning to his alma mater to study city planning in the graduate school (1942-5). He became assistant professor of architecture in 1946 and received a D.Eng. in 1959. In 1961 he became the principal of Kenzo Tange + Urtec (now called Kenzo Tange Associates). He was professor of urban engineering at the University of Tokyo from 1963 to 1974, when he became a professor emeritus. A second-generation Modern Movement architect, Tange attempted in the first half of his career to meld Modernism – particularly the Modernism of LE CORBUSIER – with traditional architectural forms, producing some of the most striking works of C20 Japanese architecture. In the late 1960s he repudiated his earlier regionalism and became an exponent of an abstract internationalist style, which he has displayed in numerous projects, particularly in the Middle East and South Asia. He has been consistent, however, in his concern for a clear structural order, and his formal virtuosity has rarely been questioned. As an urbanist, he attempted to give physical coherence to the city by the introduction of so-called "megastructures", huge structures accommodating services and transportation, and he was closely associated with (but never a member of) the Metabolist movement, which adopted a similar approach. He was also influential as the teacher of many leading third-generation Japanese architects, including Arata ISOZAKI, Kisho KUROKAWA, and Fumihiko Maki. He has received the gold medals of the RIBA (1965), the AIA (1966) and the French Academy of Architecture (1973) and the Pritzker Architecture Prize (1987).

Kenzo Tange, City Hall Complex, Tokyo, 1991

□ Hiroshima Peace Center, Hiroshima, 1955. Kagawa Prefectural Government Office, Takamatsu, 1958. Kurashiki City Hall, Kurashiki, 1960. Tokyo Plan, 1960. Tsukiji Redevelopment Plan, Tokyo, 1964. Yoyogi Olympic Gymnasiums, Tokyo, 1964. City Centre Reconstruction Project, Skopje, Yugoslavia, 1966. Press and Broadcasting Centre,

Yamanashi, 1967. Shizuoka Press and Broadcasting Centre, Tokyo, 1967. Festival Plaza, Expo 70, Osaka, 1970. Institute of Architecture and Urbanism, Oran, Algeria, 1976. Overseas Union Bank Centre, Singapore, 1980. City Hall, Tokyo, 1991.

▷ Kenzo Tange, Walter Gropius, and Yasuhiro Ishimoto, *Katsura: Tradition and Creation in Japanese Architecture*, Tokyo and New Haven, 1960. Kenzo Tange, Noboru Kawazoe, and Yoshio Watanabe, *Ise: Origin of Japanese Architecture*, Tokyo, 1962, Cambridge, Mass., 1968. Udo Kultermann, *Kenzo Tange 1946-1969: Architecture and Urban Design*, Zürich, 1970, London and New York, 1972. HW

▷ *See also pp208-9*

TATLIN Vladimir Evgrafovich

b. Moscow, 1885; d. Moscow, 1953.

Russian avant-garde artist whose work with materials was a major inspiration to the Constructivist movement in architecture and design. Tatlin trained at the Moscow School of Painting, Sculpture and Architecture (1902-4) and at Penza Art School (1904-10), often breaking his studies to work as a sailor on merchant ships. From 1908 he became increasingly involved with avant-garde painters and futurist writers in Moscow, Odessa and St Petersburg, exhibiting widely and designing for the theatre. In 1913-14 he started to make and exhibit abstract compositions he called "Selections of materials". After the 1917 Revolution he became deeply involved in official work for the new Soviet Education Commissariat (Narkompros), using artists and art as a force for public awakening. At the same time he was developing his own theory and aesthetic of a socially useful art of "real materials in real space" in Moscow and Petrograd/Leningrad "institutes" of avant-garde art and design research. His quasi-architectural project of 1919 for a Monument (actually, headquarters) of the Third Communist International became one of the canonical images of Russian avant-garde architecture and of international Modernism. During the 1920s Tatlin taught variously in Petrograd/Leningrad, Kiev and the metal- and woodworking faculty of the Moscow Vkhutemas. The courses propagated his theory of "the culture of materials" as a design principle based on the inner behavioural and loading capacities of material rather than formal abstractions. During the anti-modernist years of the 1930s and after, he lived in obscurity in Moscow, painting and further developing his flying-machine project.

□ "Counter-reliefs: Selections of materials", 1913-17. Monument to the Third International, project, 1919. "Letatlin" flying machine, 1929-32 and thereafter. CC

▷ T. Andersen (ed.), *Vladimir Tatlin* (catalogue), Stockholm, 1968. L. A. Zhadova (ed.), *Tatlin: Complete Works and Documents*, Budapest, 1984, London, 1988. CC

▷ *see also p230-31*

TAUT Bruno

b. Königsberg, 1880; d. Istanbul, 1938.

Key pioneer German avant-garde architect and theorist, associated initially with the Activist group of Expressionists and later with the new objectivity or social functionalism. Trained briefly in Königsberg and Berlin-Charlottenburg, Taut worked in Theodor Fischer's office in Stuttgart (1904-8) before opening his own firm in Berlin (1910). He ran a busy practice with office and exhibition projects before the First World War. He completed his famous Glass Pavilion for the Werkbund Exhibition, Cologne, in 1914. A year earlier he had designed the Steel Industrial Pavilion for the Leipziger Fair. Both buildings were erected in conjunction with his partner Franz Hoffmann, although the Glass Pavilion was the product of a close collaboration between Taut and his mentor, the Expressionist poet Paul Scheerbart (1887-1915). After the war, Taut became the virtual leader of the Berlin architectural avant-garde. In 1918 he had assumed chairmanship of the Arbeitsrat für Kunst, with responsibility for shaping the "Architectural Programme" of that year. In 1919 he saw the publication of drawings prepared during the war depicting a visionary Utopia under the title *Alpine Architektur*. He issued his Expressionist supplement *Frühlicht* as part of a planning magazine in Berlin (1920-21) and as a "Glass Chain" publication in its own right from Magdeburg (1921-2) after he had become the City Architect. In 1923 he returned to Berlin to recommence practice with his brother **Max Taut** (1887-1967) and Hoffmann. He produced his book *Modern Architecture* in English in 1930 for the Studio Press. By the end of the 1920s Taut had become well known as

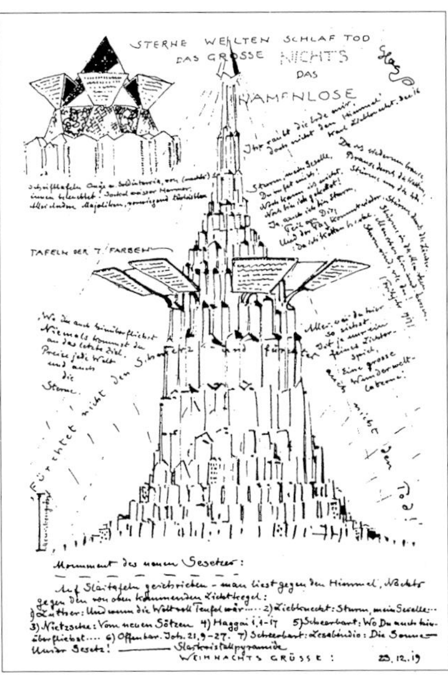

Bruno Taut, "Glass Chain" drawing, 1919

a propagandist of the *Neue Sachlichkeit* or the "New Objective" architecture. He built many estates in Berlin, including "Onkel Tom's" Estate, subsequently often using Marxist colours for the exterior faces. He left Germany for the USSR in 1932 and a year later went to Japan, where he stayed until 1936. He eventually died in Istanbul in 1938, the year in which he had entered the competition for a new parliament building in Ankara.

□ Steel Industries Pavilion, Leipzig, 1913. Garden City "Am Falkenberg", Berlin, 1913-14. Glass Pavilion, Werkbund Exhibition, Cologne, 1914. General Plan for Magdeburg, 1921. Housing Estates: Berlin-Tegel, 1924-32; Berlin-Britz, 1925-30; Berlin-Zehlendorf ("Onkel Tom's" Estate), 1926-31 etc.

▷ Bruno Taut, *Die Stadtkröne*, Jena, 1919; *Alpine Architecture*, Hagen, 1919; *Frühlicht*, 1920-21; *Die neue Wohnung*, Leipzig, 1924; *Bauen*, Leipzig, 1927; *Modern Architecture*, London, 1930. K. Junghans, *Bruno Taut 1880-1938*, Berlin, 1970. Dennis Sharp (ed.), *Glass Architecture/Alpine Architecture*, London, 1972. I. Boyd Whyte, *Bruno Taut and the Architecture of Activism*, Cambridge, 1982. DS

▷ *see also pp230-31*

TENGBOM Ivar Justus

b. Vireda, Sweden, 1878; d. Stockholm, 1968.

Influential early C20 Swedish architect and teacher. Tengbom began his architectural studies at the Chalmers Technical

Institute in Göteborg in 1894 and went on to attend the Academy of Art in Stockholm, where he received the Gold Medal in 1901. Between 1900 and 1906 he travelled extensively round Europe, including among his many ports of call Denmark, where he became familiar with the simple classicism of Martin Nyrop and Hack Kampmann. Tengbom was in practice with Ernst Torulf (1903-12) and then later with his son Anders, and was active in the Royal Building Administration; he became its director in 1924. He also embarked upon an academic career, joining the Academy of Art as professor in 1916 and subsequently becoming its president. Tengbom was an enormously influential teacher and practitioner both in Sweden and abroad. His principal contribution was the development of a modernized Neo-Classicism which combined historical, functional and traditional elements within an elegant whole. Tengbom's career reflected a move away from the early National Romantic style of the Hogalid Church (designed in 1911) to the simple cubic mass of the Stockholm Concert Hall (1923-6). From 1920 to 1930 his work pre-empted the stripped classicism which emerged as a potent force in Europe and America during the 30s. Tengbom's distinguished reputation was enhanced by numerous honours, including the RIBA Gold Medal (1938).

□ Hogalid Church, Stockholm, designed 1911, executed 1917-23. Concert Hall, Stockholm, 1923-6. Swedish Match Company Headquarters, Stockholm, 1926-8. City Palace Offices, Stockholm (with Nils Ahrsom), 1930-32.

▷ G. E. Kidder Smith, *Sweden Builds*, New York and Stockholm, 1956. Simo Paavilainen, *Nordic Classicism 1910-1930*, Helsinki, 1982. CS

TERRAGNI Giuseppe

b. Meda, 1904; d. Como, 1943.

Leading Italian Rationalist and GRUPPO SETTE member from Como. Terragni studied at the Technical College, Como (1917-21), before carrying out his architectural training at the Milan Polytechnic (1921-6). He opened an office in Como with his brother Attilio in 1927 and they remained in practice until the war. Their work was exhibited at the Monza Biennale in 1928 at the same time as the founding of the avant-garde but politically Fascist Gruppo Sette, of which he was a member from the outset. His first major building was the Russian Constructivist-inspired Novocommun Flats, Como (1927-8). This was followed by his most elaborate and famous work, the Casa del Fascio (now the "People's Palace") in Como (1932-6). This building served as a place for Fascist rallies but in architectural terms is undoubtedly one of the masterpieces of international Modernism in Italy, with its simple trabeated geometrical construction, asymmetry and cool white appearance. Its simplicity, however, belies its thorough theoretical framework and the respect it shows for the humanistic traditions of the Renaissance. In the 1930s Terragni contributed an artist's house to the first Milan Triennale, designed the Antonio Sant'Elia School in Como and a further Casa del Fascio, in Lissone (1938-9). The last work in his short career was the Casa Frigerio, Como, completed in 1940.

□ Project for Gas Works, Rome, 1927. Apartments, Novocommun, Como, 1927-8. Salone of the Year, Exhibition of Fascist Architecture, Rome, 1922. Casa del Fascio (now Casa del Popolo) Como, 1932-6. Tominello House (with Lingeri), 1933, followed by other houses with the same collaborator. Sant'Elia Kindergarten, Como, 1937. Danteum (with Lingeri), Rome, 1937. Casa del Fascio, Lissone (with A. Carminati), 1938-9. Casa Giuliani Frigerio, Como, 1939-40.

▷ M. Labò, *Giuseppe Terragni*, Milan, 1947. Bruno Zevi, "Omaggio a Giuseppe Terragni", *L'architettura*, No. 153, 1958; (ed.), *Giuseppe Terragni*, Bologna, 1980. T. Schumacher, "From Gruppo 7 to the Danteum", *Oppositions*, New York, No. 9, 1989. DS

▷ *see also pp238-9*

TESSENOW Heinrich

b. Rostock, 1876; d. Berlin, 1950.

Influential German architect and teacher whose simple, modern classical work brought Dresden-Hellerau Garden City to international attention. Coming from a construction background – his father was a contractor – he began his career as an apprentice carpenter before entering the School of Building, Leipzig, and eventually the famous Technical High School in Munich, where he studied under Von Tiersch (1901-2). Up to 1910, when he began his initial work in Hellerau, he held a number of teaching posts. In the years 1913-18 he taught in Vienna, returning to Hellerau for a further two years before his much longer stint as a professor at the Technical High School in Berlin, where he stayed until his eventual retirement. It was in the period just before and after the First World War that Tessenow made his mark. In the first period at Hellerau he worked closely with the Eurhythmist and dance teacher Jacques Dalcroze, designing the Theatre and Institute Dalcroze worked in (1910-11). His simple, traditional, Arts & Crafts, humanistic approach, welded to a more severe Germanic Greek Hellenistic monumental style, proved a happy conjunction. When conveyed through his beautiful open line drawings it made a significant contribution to the Garden City movement, to the extent that Louis de Soissons, one of the British movement's chief architects, adopted similar forms for Welwyn Garden City in the mid-1920s. As a teacher Tessenow became well-known internationally, influencing LE CORBUSIER to a limited degree and producing many generations of students who followed his precepts. He has enjoyed a revival of interest recently in Italy and Germany.

□ Houses and the Dalcroze Institute and Theatre, Dresden-Hellerau, 1909-11. Saxony County School, Dresden-Klotzsche (with O. Kramer), 1925-7. School, Kassel, 1927-30. Swimming Pool, Berlin, 1927-9.

▷ Heinrich Tessenow, *Der Wohnhausbau*, Munich 1909; *Hausbau und dergleichen*, Berlin, 1917; *Handwerk und Kleinstadt*, Berlin, 1919. G. Wangerin and G. Weiss, *Heinrich Tessenow: ein Baumeister 1876-1950*, Essen, 1976 (includes a full bibliography). J. Posener, "Two Masters, Hans Poelzig and Heinrich Tessenow...", in *Lotus International* 16, 1977. DS

TESSIN Nicodemus the Elder and Younger

Nicodemus Tessin the Elder,
b. Stralsund, 1615; d. Stockholm, 1681.
Nicodemus Tessin the Younger,
b. Nyköping, 1654; d. Stockholm 1728.

Influential Swedish Baroque architects, father and son in a family originating in Pomerania. The elder Nicodemus, who like other architects of his time graduated from military engineering, later collaborated with the court architect Jean de la Vallée (1620-96). Queen Christina sent him on a continental tour (1651-3), from which he returned full of French and Italian influences. His design for Kalmar Cathedral was inspired by VIGNOLA's

Nicodemus Tessin, Drottningholm Palace, Stockholm, begun 1662

church of the Gesù in Rome. His numerous country palaces for the nobility tended to follow French models. Sweden was at the time enjoying new wealth and great-power status in Europe, and had ambitions for grandeur to match. An outburst of building gave native-born architects their chance. Drottningholm Palace just outside central Stockholm, Sweden's answer to Versailles, was designed jointly by both Tessins. The younger Nicodemus trained under BERNINI, and introduced a Roman Baroque style diluted to suit Swedish conditions. He was appointed court architect in 1681. When the old royal castle in Stockholm was destroyed by fire in 1697, he was commissioned to design a completely new Royal Palace on the site. This was accompanied by a grandiose scheme for rebuilding the surrounding area of the city, which was only partially carried out much later.

□ Kalmar Cathedral, 1660. Drottningholm Palace, Stockholm, begun 1662. Royal Palace, Stockholm, 1697-1750. JRC

TESTA Clorindo

b. Naples, 1923.

Prominent Latin-American architect who employs a rigorously empirical approach to the process of architecture. He studied at the Faculty of Architecture and Urbanism of the National University of Buenos Aires at a time when the academic curriculum was still dominated by the Beaux-Arts tradition. After graduating in 1948 he joined the Buenos Aires Regulating Plan but left the following year for Italy, where he spent three years pursuing an abiding interest in painting. On returning to Argentina he established a private practice, but he prefers to work with a diversity of colleagues on individual projects. Thus his work defies easy classification, but it is often characterized by a boldness of form and spatial manipulation also seen in his paintings and sketches. The use of a heavily textured concrete finish in his competition-winning design for the project at La Pampa, Santa Rosa, is often credited as the first Brutalist building in Argentina. His best-known work, the Bank of London in Buenos Aires, a huge concrete structure dominating a narrow street, is often cited as the city's most important C20 building.

□ Civic Centre and Bus Terminal, Santa Rosa (with Boris Dabinovic, Augusto Gaido and Francisco Rossi), 1955-63. Bank of London and South America, Buenos Aires (with SEPRA), 1959-66. National Library, Buenos Aires (with Francisco Bullrich and Alicia Cazzaniga de Bullrich), 1962-84; unfinished (1990). Government Hospital, Ivory Coast, 1979.

▷ Julio Llimas, *Clorindo Testa*, Buenos Aires, 1962. Francisco Bullrich, *New Directions in Latin-American Architecture*, New York, 1969. Damian Bayon and Paolo Gasparini, *The Changing Shape of Latin-American Architecture*, Chichester, 1979. *World Architecture 5* (special issue), 1990. MC

THOMSON Alexander

b. Balfron, Scotland, 1817; d. Glasgow, 1875.

Last and most original of the few great Neo-Classic architects. Employed in architecture from the age of 14, he worked with John Baird from 1836 until he set up in his own practice in Glasgow in 1849. Thomson's quest was for the timeless essence of classical architecture on to which he would build his forms for the third quarter of the C19. Technically his work is highly inventive but only to serve his rhetorical and formal goals in the manipulation of surfaces and spaces. The range of his invention is remarkable, stretching from endless decorative devices to the formal separation of the planes of structural columns and timber-framed glazing on the façades; the design of dynamically rhythmical façades and tightly geometric proportions; masterly interior effects of complex spaces through daring use of structure and subtle borrowed light. Uniquely among his contemporaries, Thomson's buildings (the most original British architecture in the century

Clorindo Testa, Bank of London and South America, Buenos Aires, 1959–66

between SOANE and MACKINTOSH) fit their city context, clarifying the urban form of Glasgow.

☐ Double Villa and Holmwood Villa, Glasgow, 1856-7. Caledonia Road and St Vincent Street churches, Glasgow, 1856. Moray Place, Glasgow, *c.*1857. Cairney Building, Glasgow, 1860. Queens Park Church and Great Western Terrace, Glasgow, 1867. Ellisland Villa and the Egyptian Halls, Glasgow, 1871.

▷ Alexander Thomson, "An enquiry as to the appropriateness of the Gothic style..." (lecture given on 7 May 1866, most recently published in *College Courant* (Glasgow University), 6-7, 1954); "Four lectures on architecture" (to the Glasgow School of Art, 1874; *The British Architect*, 1 May, 5 June, 24 July, 30 Oct. and 20 Nov. 1874). J. McKean, "The Architectonics and Ideals of Alexander Thomson", *AA Files*, London, No. 9, Summer 1985; "La Città di Alexander Thomson", *Glasgow Forma e Progetto della Città*, ed. R. Bocchi, Venice, 1990. JM

▷ *see also pp220-21*

THUMB FAMILY

Michael Thumb, b. Bezau, Austria, c.1640, d. 1690; Christian Thumb, b. Bezau, 1683, d. 1726; Peter Thumb, b. 1681, d. 1766.

Austrian architects and masons. **Michael Thumb** was a founder of the Austrian Voralberger school of architects, noted mainly for a large series of Benedictine monastries in SW Germany and Switzerland, which marked the eventual triumph of German elements over Italian in S German Baroque architecture. Michael Thumb's most important work was the Obermarchtal Church, which demonstrated a pure application of his Baroque spatial concepts and was enhanced by contributions from several renowned artists and craftsmen. Michael's brother **Christian Thumb** also designed and supervised the construction of two major Baroque churches at Schussenried in Bavaria (1700) and Giessen in central Germany (1701). **Peter Thumb**, Michael's son, developed a more sophisticated and inventive manner than his father, culminating in the pilgrimage church of Birnau on Lake Constance (1745-58), and the library in the monastery at St Gallen (1758-67). The latter is characterized by its dramatic agility and marks a transition from Baroque to Peter Thumb's own distinctive Rococo style.

☐ Michael Thumb: Church, Obermachtal, 1686. Christian Thumb: church, Schussenried, 1700; church, Giessen, 1701. Peter Thumb: Neu Birnau Pilgrimage Church, Bavaria, 1745-58; St Gallen Library and Abbey Church, Switzerland, 1758-67.

▷ Henry-Russell Hitchcock, *Rococo Architecture in Southern Germany*, London, 1968. CS

TOWNSEND Charles Harrison

b. Birkenhead, 1851; d. Northwood, 1928.

Highly individualistic architect of the English Arts & Crafts movement who transcended the movement's largely domestic aspirations and developed a personal vocabulary more appropriate to the demands of the metropolitan environment. Townsend was articled to a Liverpool architect (1870) but moved south with his family to London in 1880. He worked with William Eden NESFIELD (a former partner of Richard Norman SHAW) but by 1888 had set up in private practice. In the same year he joined the Art Workers' Guild, founded in 1884 as a forum for artists, architects and craftsmen united in their antipathy towards the prevalent taste for Historicism. Its influence proved crucial in Townsend's search for a progressive architectural expression; he was elected Master of the Guild in 1903. His reputation rests primarily on three celebrated projects in London, the Bishopsgate Institute, Horniman Museum and Whitechapel Gallery. Each offers a dramatic example of how mass and form could be sculpted to evoke a modern, organic, free-style architecture which was both original and monumental. Each also reveals Townsend's debt to the principal exponents of North American Romanesque, Henry Hobson RICHARDSON and Henry Wilson. After 1902 Townsend received no major commissions, largely because of his reluctance to adopt the contemporary fashion for classicism.

☐ Bishopsgate Institute, London, 1892-5. Horniman Museum of Ethnology, London, 1896-1901. Whitechapel Gallery, London, 1899-1901. Church of St Mary, Great Warley, Essex, 1902. Village Hall, Panshanger, Herts., 1910.

▷ Nikolaus Pevsner and J. M. Richards (eds.), *The Anti-Rationalists*, London, 1973. Alastair Service (ed.), *Edwardian Architecture and its Origins*, London, 1975. MC

Charles Harrison Townsend, Whitechapel Gallery, London, 1899-1901, detail

U

UNWIN Sir Raymond

b. Rotherham, Yorks., 1863;
d. Connecticut, USA, 1940.

British architect and town planner who put his social-welfare beliefs into practice by designing, with his partner Barry Parker, decent small dwellings and putting his mind to the perennial problems of town planning. Educated at Oxford, Unwin went on to study engineering and architecture, becoming acquainted early on with William MORRIS and his work. The first dwellings by Unwin and Parker (his partner from 1896) are direct descendants of the Arts & Crafts tradition; their schemes for New Earswick (for Rowntree) and Letchworth Garden City betray similar roots while formalizing the "garden-suburb" principles. From 1907 Unwin and Parker largely followed their own careers, Unwin's interests in town planning reflected in his influential book *Town Planning in Practice*. As well as lecturing, he worked for various government departments and was President of the International Federation for Housing and Town Planning (1928-31) and the RIBA (1931-3). He was knighted in 1932.

□ St Andrew's Church, Barrow Hill, Derbyshire (largely alone), 1893. With Parker: C. F. Goodfellow House, Northwood, Staffs., 1899-1902. Co-op housing, St Botolph's Avenue, Sevenoaks, Kent, 1903-6. New Earswick, York, from 1901. Letchworth Garden City, Herts., from 1903. Hampstead Garden Suburb, London, 1906-7.

▷ Raymond Unwin, *Cottage Plans and Common Sense*, London, 1902; *Town Planning in Practice*, London, 1909. William Ashworth, *The Genesis of Modern British Town Planning*, London, 1954. Walter Creese, *The Search for Environment*, New Haven, Conn., 1966; *The Legacy of Raymond Unwin*, Cambridge, 1967. Mark Swenarton, *Homes for Heroes*, London, 1981. PP

Sir Raymond Unwin (with Barry Parker), Letchworth Garden City, Herts, 1903, drawing

UTZON Jørn

b. Copenhagen, 1918.

Danish Modern architect. He studied at the Academy of Arts, Copenhagen, under Kay FISKER and Steen Eiler Rasmussen (1937-42), and spent the war years 1942-5 with Gunnar ASPLUND. In 1946 he visited Alvar AALTO in Helsinki. He travelled in Europe (1947-8) and the USA and Mexico (1949), then established his practice in Copenhagen (1950) working with other architects on competitions. In 1956 his design for the Sydney Opera House won first prize. Utzon worked from Hellebaek until 1962 when he moved to Sydney, Australia; in 1966 he returned to Denmark following his resignation from the project, which was completed by others. In 1972 Utzon moved permanently to Mallorca in Spain. He is at his best when designing structures beside the water, as with the Sydney Opera House (1956-73) and his own magnificent house, "Can Lis", on Mallorca (1971). The Kuwait National Assembly Complex (1971-9, completed 1983), his most important work after the Opera House, uses the forms of the bedouin black tent for its monumental concrete hanging roofs. The Bagsvaerd Church hides its voluptuous shell vaults behind austere concrete and white-tiled stepped façades crowned by triangular skylights. The humanism and sensitivity of Utzon's domestic architecture are best expressed in the anonymous, self-effacing but subtle group housing of the late 1950s and his own house on Mallorca. He gave Modern architecture a new poetic dimension that marked an influential departure from the functionalism of the 1950s while it built on the broad Scandinavian foundation of Asplund, JACOBSEN and Aalto, by adding the quality of "cultivated intimacy".

□ Sydney Opera House, Sydney, Australia, 1956-73. Kingohusene Housing Estate, near Elsinore, Denmark, 1957-60. Architect's house, Santanyi, Mallorca, Spain, 1971. Kuwait National Assembly Complex, 1971-83. Bagsvaerd Church, Copenhagen, 1976.

▷ Jørn Utzon, "Additive Architecture", *Arkitektur* 1, 1970. "Jørn Utzon and the Third Generation" in S. Giedion, *Space, Time and Architecture*, 5th ed., 1966. P. Drew, *Third Generation*, Stuttgart, 1972. "Can Lis" and "Jørn Utzon on Architecture", *Living Architecture*, No. 8, 1989. PD

▷ *see also pp240-41, 244-5*

VANBRUGH Sir John

b. London, 1664; d. London, 1726.

English Whig architect and playwright. Vanbrugh's architecture, an art on which he gave the impression of alighting by mere chance, is composed of unusual elements. There is always a dramatic massing of the parts and the recess, advance and "movement" of the façades. In busy silhouette are towers and turrets that might belong to a medieval or an Elizabethan past. John Vanbrugh's family moved to Chester *c.* 1667, when he was three years old, probably to escape from a London ravaged by plague and fire. Little is known of him until he received an army commission in 1686. The tedium of garrisoning Guernsey led him to resign and to set out on other travels, which may have included secret duties for the government of William and Mary. In any case he was imprisoned for four years in France. What he was able to see, however, probably had an influence on his later architectural work. After his release, he returned to England, more weary army duty, and the start of his career as a dramatist. And soon came an exciting new commission in a vastly different role – Comptroller of His Majesty's Works (1702). He was now Sir Christopher WREN's principal colleague.

How had he come to be an architect? In 1699 Charles Howard, 3rd Earl of Carlisle, who was to become a great friend to Vanbrugh, had asked him to design his new Yorkshire house. The Earl had rejected earlier plans from the competent but difficult William Talman. It was Lord Carlisle, as First Lord of the Treasury, who arranged that Vanbrugh should replace Talman as Comptroller. This was a post to launch a career and soon Vanbrugh was the favourite architect of the Whig aristocracy. Castle Howard was rising fast. Then a great house, to be named Blenheim, was promised to the 1st Duke of Marlborough by a nation grateful for his victories over the armies of Louis XIV and others. Vanbrugh became the Duke's architect; but he reckoned without the interference of the irascible Duchess. At each step, over many years, she argued with everyone. Work finally stopped in 1716 and Vanbrugh was dismissed; the faithful HAWKSMOOR and others did their best to bring it all to an uneasy, if still mighty, conclusion just before Vanbrugh's death. There were of course also less complicated tasks. Some medieval castles, such as Lumley and Nottingham, were remodelled. Other early structures, such as Kimbolton and Grimsthorpe, were given "something of the castle air". Arcades and encircling forecourts (as at Blenheim, Seaton Delaval and Grimsthorpe) were set off by heavy ringed columns, giant doorways, and deep-cut rustication of the stonework. Vanbrugh was knighted in 1714.

□ Castle Howard, Yorks, 1699-1726. Blenheim Palace, Oxon., 1705-16. Kimbolton Castle, Leics., 1707-10. King's Weston, Bristol, 1712-14. Eastbury Park, Dorset, 1718-24. Seaton Delaval, Northumberland, 1720-28. Grimsthorpe Castle, Lincs., 1722-6.

▷ Kerry Downes, *Vanbrugh*, London, 1977; *Sir John Vanbrugh; A Biography*, London, 1987. Geoffrey Beard, *The Work of Sir John Vanbrugh*, London, 1986.

GB

▷ *see also pp218-19*

Sir John Vanbrugh, Seaton Delaval, Northumberland, 1720–28

VASARI Giorgio

b. Arezzo, 1511; d. Florence, 1574.

The designer of the Uffizi buildings, Florence, but no longer appreciated as a painter, Vasari is best and rightly remembered as the author of the most readable source book on the lives of the Renaissance artists. At 13 he went to Florence, where he trained under MICHELANGELO and Andrea del Sarto. He carried out mural commissions all over central Italy and in 1554 was engaged by Cosimo I de' Medici, for whom he created an innovative scheme for govern-

Giorgio Vasari, The Uffizi, Florence, 1560

ment offices *(uffizi)* in 1560 – now the famous art galleries of that name. During his travels as a younger man, Vasari had sought out and interviewed as many of the surviving giants of the Renaissance as he could, or people who remembered them personally. From this material he wrote the engaging and entertaining biographies, starting with the painter Cimabue, which were published in 1550. His treatise on the art techniques of his time is a valuable source for research.

□ Uffizi, Florence, 1560.

▷ *Le vite de' più eccellenti architetti, pittori et scultori italiani (Lives of the Outstanding Italian Architects, Painters and Sculptors),* 1550 (revised, 1568); *Vasari on Technique*, Dover Books, New York, 1960. Marcia B. Hall, *Renovation and Counter-Reformation*, Oxford, 1979. JRC

VAUBAN Sébastien Le Prestre de

b. Vauban, 1633; d. Paris, 1707.

French C17 military architect, engineer and town-planner. Vauban received his early education in a Carmelite college. In 1655 he obtained an engineer's commission in Louis XIV's army and two years later he masterminded siege operations against the Spanish-held town of Montmédy. His success in this campaign marked the end of his military apprenticeship, and he went on to develop the skills which were to make him the most distinguished military architect of the C17, travelling the length and breadth of France to repair and improve the kingdom's defences. In 1703 he was made a Maréchal de France. His skill lay in his ingenious adaptation of traditional fortification principles rather than the invention of new ones. A practical builder and a brilliant technician, his most famous fortifications are those of Lille, Maubeuge and Neuf-Brisach. His architectural prowess is best appreciated in the monumental simplicity of ramparts (e.g. at Oléron and Bayonne) and his gateways, which include the Baroque grandeur of the Porte de Paris at Lille and the simple severity of the Mons Gate at Maubeuge. He also designed individual buildings (e.g. churches at Givet and Briançon), and restored the châteaux of Auney and Usse.

□ Citadel, Lille, 1668. Enceinte, Maubeuge, 1678-81. Aqueduct of Maintenon, 1684-5. New city foundation, Neuf-Brisach, 1689-99.

▷ Reginald Louis Blomfield, *Sébastien Le Prestre de Vauban: 1633-1707*, London, 1938. CS

VAN DE VELDE Henry

b. Antwerp, Belgium, 1863;
d. Oberagen, Switzerland, 1957.

Architect whose greatest mission in life was to secure the redemption of the modern world from its own ugliness. He was born the son of a wealthy chemist and set out as a painter, influenced by the French Pointillists. But by the late C19 his admiration of RUSKIN, MORRIS and VOYSEY led him to turn his talents to design. His first built project was his own family home, the Villa Bloemenwerf at Uccle near Brussels. Here he worked in a style crossbred between the English Arts & Crafts movement and his own Flemish. Van de Velde designed almost every item in the house, from furniture and cutlery to his own wife's clothes; such was his fastidiousness that he is reputed to have advised his wife on the colour coordination of the food she served. Van de Velde was an idealist and firmly believed that society could be reformed through excellent design. He declared that "Ugliness corrupts not only the eyes, but also the heart and mind." His family house was admired by his friends Toulouse Lautrec and the businessman Samuel Bing, who invited Van de Velde to design the ornate interiors for his Parisian shop, the Maison de l'Art Nouveau. The shop interiors, together with designs for the imperial barber Haby in Berlin, made Van de Velde one of the main influences on the Art Nouveau movement. In 1901 he was invited to Weimar as consultant to the crafts industries of the Grand Duchy of Saxe-Weimar; five years later he became director of the new Grand Ducal School of Arts and Crafts. Once at the school Van de Velde set about remodelling it along the lines of MACKINTOSH's much-admired Glasgow School of Art, where tuition was given in workshops rather than studios. With the advent of the First World War Van de Velde was obliged to leave Germany and was eventually replaced at the school by Walter GROPIUS, who renamed it the State Bauhaus. Van de Velde drew praise for his designs for the Werkbund Exhibition Theatre, Cologne, (1914), a great sweeping structure of concrete of which Erich MENDELSOHN said "Only Van de Velde with his theatre is really searching for a new form. Concrete is used in the Art Nouveau style, but strong in conception and expression." In his later life he opened the Institut Supérieur des Arts Décoratifs in Belgium in 1927, and then designed the Modernist-style Kröller-Müller Museum in Otterlo.

Henry Van de Velde, Grand Ducal School of Arts and Crafts, Weimar, 1906

☐ Villa Bloemenwerf, Brussels, 1894-5. Grand Ducal School of Arts and Crafts, Weimar, 1906. Cologne Werkbund Exhibition Theatre, 1914. Kröller-Müller Museum, Otterlo, Holland, 1937.

▷ H. Voet, *Geschichte meines Lebens*, Munich, 1962, 1986. M. Culot and D. Sharp, *Henry Van de Velde: Theatre Designs 1904-14*, Brussels and London, 1974. Leon Ploegaerts and Pierre Puttemans, *L'œuvre architecturale de Henry Van de Velde*, Quebec, 1987; Klaus-Jürgen Sembach, *Henry Van de Velde*, London, 1989. FS

▷ *see also pp230-31*

VENTURI Robert

b. Philadelphia, 1925.

Key ideologue of Post-Modernism, author of *Complexity and Contradiction in Architecture*. Venturi was educated at the Episcopal Academy, Philadelphia, and at Princeton, graduating in 1950. He worked in the offices of Eero SAARINEN and Louis KAHN before founding his own practice in 1958. In 1964 he formed a partnership with John Rauch, and in 1967 he married Denise Scott Brown, who joined the partnership the same year. Venturi has held a number of academic appointments and has attracted worldwide attention as an architectural writer. He is an important practising architect, but it is as an architectural thinker that he has had enormous influence. He redirected critical discussion and effected a change in sensibilities by his analysis of architecture in terms of the key-words of *complexity* and *contradiction,* stressing the importance of ambiguity and multiple meanings in appreciating architecture. He *"likes"* complexity and, in contrast to the "great Modernists", propounds an architecture which is contextual, symbolic and decorated. He suggests that function/ structure and symbolism/decoration should be allowed to go their own way, "allowing function to be truly functional – as it couldn't be, ironically, when form followed function". Venturi believes that decoration should reflect cultural meanings and diversity. But because modern technology and historical symbols rarely harmonize, such symbolism is almost always "redundant" and is used ironically in his work. But he does not advocate the indiscriminate borrowing from the past of much Post-Modern Classicism, and indeed in his work decoration is not confined to classical elements. Although he sees himself as belonging to the Western classical tradition, he claims "the rules have changed". Wider cultural and social issues underpin his architectural writing; he rejects the label "populist" but in *Learning from Las Vegas* Venturi shifted from an intellectual critique of Modernism in terms of "complexity" and a cool ironic acceptance of "honky-tonk" elements, to a full blown justification of the kitsch of high capitalism – which he has insisted on seeing as a kind of vernacular. Venturi is thus an essential figure in the populist aesthetic of the recent Post-Modernism.

☐ Friends House for Elderly, Philadelphia, 1960-63. Vanna Venturi House, Chestnut Hill, Pa, 1962. Franklin Court, Philadelphia, 1972-5. Best Products, Catalogue Show Room, Oxford Valley, Penn., 1977. House in New East, Delaware, 1978. Molecular Biology Building, Princeton, NJ, 1983-5. Sainsbury Wing (National Gallery Extension), London, 1987-91.

▷ Robert Venturi, *Complexity and Contradiction in Architecture*, New York, 1966, London, 1977. R. Venturi, D. Scott Brown and S. Izenour, *Learning from Las Vegas*, Cambridge, Mass., and London, 1972. Robert Maxwell and Robert A. M. Stern, *Venturi and Rauch*, London, 1978. TC

VIGNOLA Giacomo Barozzi da

b. Vignola, near Modena, 1507; d. Rome, 1573.

By his writings, which were standard works all over Europe for several generations, as much as by the fine craftsmanship of his buildings, Vignola refined the vocabulary of classical architecture at a time when the aesthetic experiments of Mannerism were being outmoded by the Counter-Reformation messages of Baroque. He studied painting at Bologna under Sebastiano SERLIO, and moved to Rome in 1530. Abandoning painting, he got a job on the Vatican palace project in 1534, learning architecture from PERUZZI and Antonio da SANGALLO THE YOUNGER among others. His grounding in classical building methods was acquired at the "Vitruvian Academy", on behalf of which he visited France in 1541. He worked in Bologna (1543-50) and in 1546 was employed by the Farnese Duke of Parma and Piacenza; after MICHELANGELO broke with the Farnese family in 1549, Vignola also completed interior details in the Palazzo Farnese in Rome. He was taken on to the papal staff in 1551. His greatest projects are the Palazzo Farnese at Caprarola and the extremely influential aisle-less Jesuit church in Rome, the Gesù, begun before 1568 and completed after his death. Appointed "second architect" on St Peter's in 1564, he was in full control from 1566, continuing Michelangelo's designs.

☐ Tempietto di S. Andrea, Rome, *c.* 1550. Palazzo Farnese, Caprarola, begun 1559. Il Gesù, Rome, begun 1568. S. Anna dei Palafrenieri, Rome, begun 1573.

▷ *Regola delle cinque ordini d'architettura (Rules of the Five Orders of Architecture)*, 1562. J. Pope-Hennessy, *Italian Renaissance Sculpture*, London, 1958. JRC

▷ *see also p216-17*

VINGBOONS (VINCKEBOONS) Philip

b. Amsterdam, 1607/8; d. Amsterdam, 1678.

Leading exponent of Dutch domestic classicism. Vingboons was born into an artistic Dutch family; his father was a painter and his brothers were an architect and engraver. He was influenced by Jacob VAN CAMPEN's unpretentious and economic use of classicism for civic and domestic buildings. Vingboons worked for the prosperous Amsterdam merchant class, creating a new version of the town house with symmetrical planning and simple elevations. The Poppenhuis shows a clear debt to van Campen with its giant order and pedimented central section. Vingboons also designed a number of country houses, but his output is confined to the domestic field: as a Roman Catholic he was automatically excluded from obtaining commissions for public buildings and churches. In 1648 and 1674 he published two folios with engravings of his works which were very influential, especially in England.

☐ Poppenhuis, Amsterdam, 1642. 364-370 Herengracht, Amsterdam, 1662. Vanenburg House, Putten, Gelderland, 1664.

▷ I. H. van Eeghen, "De famile Vingboons-Vingboons", *Oud Holland*, 1952. CS

VIOLLET-LE-DUC, Eugène Emmanuel

b. Paris, 1814; d. Lausanne, 1879.

Influential French theorist, promoter of modern construction techniques and

Eugène-Emmanuel Viollet-le-Duc, portrait by Monvoisin, 1834

restorer of ancient buildings. Viollet-le-Duc was an original thinker and individualist and broke with tradition in his early life by refusing to enrol at the Ecole des Beaux Arts and follow the usual entry into the architectural profession. During his early career Viollet-le-Duc became a protégé of the writer Prosper Mérimée, who was inspector general of the French National Monuments and Historical Antiquities. After the 1830 Revolution there was a revival of interest in the national heritage and Viollet-le-Duc undertook many commissions to restore buildings, including the church of Vézelay and the Sainte-Chapelle and Notre-Dame in Paris. These were followed by a massive project to renovate the entire ancient walled city of Carcassonne. As a scholar and theorist Viollet-le-Duc promulgated, through his books, the latest building techniques, such as iron frameworks and brick in construction. In his forward-looking *Entretiens* (1858-72) he promoted the idea that "In architecture, there are two necessary ways of being true. [A building design] must be true according to the programme and true according to the methods of construction." He remained vague on precisely how this truth should be found, but felt passionately that each age should develop its own architecture to "conform to the needs and customs of the times". Also in *Entretiens* he foreshadowed the burgeoning of the Art Nouveau style by calling for a "sinewy" architecture to incorporate the use of iron for lighter structures. But, although he earned a reputation for daring thought, his own drawings were cumbersome and often inelegant, and few of his designs were ever built.

☐ Restoration work: Vézelay Church, 1840; Sainte-Chapelle, Paris, 1840; Notre-Dame, Paris, 1844; the medieval walled town of Carcassonne, from 1844 onwards. Built works: flats at the rue de Liège, Paris, 1846-8; house at the rue de Douai, Paris (1857-60).

▷ Viollet-le-Duc's most influential published works were the *Dictionnaire raisonné de l'architecture française du XIe au XVIe siècle*, Paris, 1854-68, *Entretiens sur l'architecture*, Paris, 1858-72, and *Habitations modernes*, 1875. Ivo Tagliaventi, *Viollet-le-Duc e la cultura architettonica dei revivals*, Bologna, 1976. P. Mardaga, *Viollet-le-Duc 1814-1879* (essays), Brussels, 1980. Sir John Summerson and others, *Viollet-le-Duc*, London, 1980. FS

▷ *see also pp228-9*

VITRUVIUS POLLIO

b. c. 90 BC; d. c. 20 BC.

Roman architect, engineer and theorist of the C1 BC, author of the treatise *De Architectura*. We have very little information about his life, and most of the details we have come from his treatise. The Rome of Vitruvius was the centre of exchanges between Greek and Latin architects, and he might easily have had some part in these reciprocal activities. His expertise in machinery of war was employed by Julius Caesar, and he probably took part in his campaigns as military architect for about ten years till Caesar's death (44 BC). It is perhaps due to these prolonged absences from the great city that some of his ideas might have seemed old-fashioned in the new Rome of Augustus. As a practical architect we know of only one of his works (and only through his own writings), the Basilica of the Forum at Colonia Julia Fanestris (contemporary Fano), of which he gives a very detailed description, including precise measurements, but of which not a single archaeological trace remains. Vitruvius's importance is in his authorship of *De Architectura*, which is (with a few minor exceptions) the only treatise on architecture that has survived from classical antiquity. He himself tells us (preface, Book VII) that his was certainly not the first Latin treatise. But, unlike preceding authors, from whom he freely borrowed, he tried in *De Architectura* to organize the various topics systematically. It consists of ten books. Book I deals with architecture in general: the tasks and qualities of the architect, the limits and nature of architecture, choice of sites etc. Book II moves from the origin and development of building to various materials employed, their characteristics and to the structures. In Books III and IV Vitruvius deals with single buildings, and it is here that he mentions the perfect proportions of the human figure which can be inscribed in the circle and in the square (the suggestive image to which Renaissance Man would go back again and again). Book V looks at public buildings, including the Roman forum, basilica and theatre, Book VI at private buildings and their siting according to the nature of the place and their proportions. Book VII deals with floors, plaster, mosaics, wall paintings (including a small treatise on the use and preparation of colours). Book VII completes the treatise on architecture, Books VIII, IX and X being mostly concerned with civil and military engineering. The treatise survived by being copied and recopied by successive amanuenses, but it was almost forgotten till its rediscovery at Montecassino in 1414 by the humanist Poggio Bracciolini. It was first published *c.*1486, followed by an illustrated edition in 1511, an Italian version in 1521 and then in French and German translation in the 1540s. With ALBERTI and his successors, right through to the Baroque era, the theoretical and practical influence of Vitruvius's treatise grew and spread; BRAMANTE, SERLIO, PALLADIO, SCAMOZZI etc. all tried to squeeze from *De Architectura* the innermost secrets of ancient architecture.

☐ Basilica, Fano.

▷ Vitruvius, *De Architectura*. The *Editio princeps* is dated Rome, *c.* 1486; subsequent English editions include J. Gwilt, London, 1826, and the well-known H. M. Morgan, Cambridge, Mass., 1914. GV

▷ *see also pp176-7*

VAN DER VLUGT & BRINKMAN

Established 1925.

Prominent Dutch exponents of the International Style, whose design for the Van Nelle factory in Rotterdam is one of the most important buildings of the C20.

C. F. A. Voysey, Perrycroft, Colwall, Herefordshire, 1893

Johannes Andreas Brinkman (b. Rotterdam, 1902; d. Rotterdam, 1949) studied at the Technical University, Delft, before going into partnership with his father Michiel Brinkman in 1921. **Leendert Cornelis Van der Vlugt** (b. 1894; d. 1936) studied at the Academy of Fine Art, Rotterdam, before entering into the partnership with Brinkman in 1925. Both men were closely aligned with contemporary intellectual and avant-garde movements in Holland and belonged to the influential Rotterdam group Opbouw. The remit for the group, formed in 1920, was to promote Functionalism as the only true expression of a modern industrialized society. Fellow Opbouw member Mart STAM joined the office in 1926 and contributed to the early success of the partnership. Their buildings represent a poetic interpretation of the rigorous tenets of the *Neue Sachlichkeit* (new objectivity) which eschewed aesthetics and all extraneous decoration. After Van der Vlugt's death Brinkman worked with Johannes Hendrik VAN DEN BROEK from 1937 until his retirement in 1948.

□ Van Nelle Offices, Leiden, 1925-7. Van Nelle Factory, Rotterdam (largely Stam), 1926-30. Boeve House, Rotterdam, 1932-4. Bergpolder Flats (with Willem van Tijen), Rotterdam, 1933-4. Feyenoord Stadium, Rotterdam, 1934-6.

▷ J. B. van Loghem, *Bouwen Holland*, Amsterdam, 1932. J. B. Bakema, *Leendert Cornelis Van der Vlugt*, Amsterdam, 1968. Donald Grinberg, *Housing in the Netherlands*, Rotterdam, 1977. MC

▷ *see also pp234-5*

VOYSEY Charles Francis Annesley

b. Hessle, Yorks., 1857;
d. Winchester, 1941.

British designer of relatively small but widely publicized houses which had a great interest in continental Europe at the turn of the century. The son of a clergyman who had been at the centre of one of the C19's famous heresy trials and who subsequently founded a sect not unlike early Unitarianism, Voysey retained his father's rather generalized Deism throughout his working life, and saw in his architecture the opportunity of expressing simplicity, harmony and order as a spiritual exercise. He joined J. P. Seddon as an articled pupil in 1874 and subsequently spent a year with George Devey before launching his own practice in 1882. Designed on Puginian principles, these roughcast, long-windowed, low-roofed houses were published from 1888 in *The Architect* and from 1889 to 1918 in *The British Architect*. Their relative simplicity and horizontal emphasis brought a new and wholly superficial appraisal as being in some way anticipatory of the "International Style", and on the strength of this Voysey was awarded the Gold Medal of the RIBA the year before his death. He designed wallpapers and fabrics in considerable quantity as well as furnishings, all in a simple Arts & Crafts manner.

□ Perrycroft, Colwall, Herefordshire, 1893. Broadleys, Lake Windermere, Lancashire, 1898-9. Moor Crag, Lake Windermere, 1898-9.

▷ C. F. A. Voysey, *Reason as a Basis for Art*, London, 1906; *Individuality*, London, 1915. David Gebhard, *Charles F. A. Voysey*, Los Angeles, 1975. Duncan Simpson, *C. F. A. Voysey, An Architect of Individuality*, London, 1975. RM

▷ *see also pp228-9*

WAGNER Otto

b. Penzing, near Vienna, 1841;
d. Vienna, 1918.

Highly influential figure, through teaching, writing and projects, in the development of modern architecture and planning; founder of the so-called Wagner School. He began his architectural training at the Technische Hochschule in Vienna in 1857, attended the Berlin Bauakademie 1860-61 and returned to Vienna to study under Siccardsburg and van der Nüll at the Academy of Fine Arts. In 1894 he was appointed professor and head of a special school of architecture at the Academy of Fine Arts, and his inaugural lecture, published under the title *Moderne Architektur,* was one of the earliest manifestos to call for an architecture based on purpose and employing modern materials and construction methods. Wagner's earliest projects, primarily urban apartment blocks, were highly accomplished exercises in the classical styles favoured at the time: the High Renaissance of Florence and Tuscany. His reputation was such that in 1890 he was asked to prepare a new city plan for Vienna, but the only part of the grandiose project to be built was the Stadtbahn, the urban rail network, for which he designed most of the stations. These buildings, notably the twin pavilions on the Karlsplatz, are clear exercises in modern construction and functional planning, but they also carry the decorative motifs of the Secession style and retain the urban monumentality of Wagner's classical training, an aspect that was to remain throughout his late career. Encouraged by the radical work of his students – the most talented of whom, such as Joseph OLBRICH and Josef HOFFMANN joined his atelier – Wagner moved further towards the design of buildings which embodied the very principles he taught. The adjacent apartment buildings on the Linke Wienzeile are far removed in their inventiveness and plastic qualities from his early apartments restrained by classical rules. The Steinhof Church, with its Secession-style embellishments, develops a more integrated approach to built form and constructional detail. But the Post Office Savings Bank, which occupies a triangular city block, is the major testament to Wagner's eminence among early C20 architects. This remarkable synthesis of plan, space and materials is centred on a main hall, brightly lit by a steel-framed glazed vault above, and partly floored in glass blocks to light rooms below. Ornamentation deemed unnecessary is dispensed with altogether, and materials are employed to great effect in their natural state and simplest forms.

☐ Länderbank, Vienna, 1882-4. Villa Wagner I, Vienna, 1886. Stadtbahn stations, Vienna, 1894-9. Ankerhaus store, Vienna, 1895: apartment houses on the Linke Wienzeile, 1898-9. Steinhof Church, Vienna, 1902-7. Post Office Savings Bank, Vienna, 1903-6. Lupus Sanatorium, Vienna, 1908-13. Villa Wagner II, Vienna, 1912-13.

▷ Otto Wagner, *Einige Skizze, Projekte und ausgeführte Bauwerke* (4 vols.), Vienna, 1890-1922; *Moderne Architektur*, Vienna, 1896. J. A. Lux, *Otto Wagner*, Munich, 1914; H. Geretsegger and M. Peintner, *Otto Wagner 1841-1918*, Salzburg, 1964. IL

POST OFFICE SAVINGS BANK, Vienna

Built in two phases in 1903–6 the Vienna Post Office Savings Bank is Otto Wagner's most technically advanced building and most mature work of architecture. It epitomizes the state of modern architecture in Vienna in the early years of this century with its extensive use of new materials, especially aluminium, its neat rational structure and well-lit spaces. The exterior is covered in light-coloured marble panels held in place by metal-studded bolts set out in a decorative, pattern-like Jugendstil *framework. Internally, the barrel-vaulted banking hall proved remarkably successful, with its transparent roof, white walls and exposed steel structure. The building also incorporates a fresh air circulation system for both the offices and the public space.*

WAHLMAN Lars Israel

b. Hedemora, Sweden, 1870; d. 1952.

Swedish architect much influenced by the English Arts & Crafts movement; best-known for his Engelbrekt Church, Stockholm (1906-14). He studied at the Royal Institute of Technology, Stockholm, where later he was Professor of Building Science (1912-35). He travelled extensively in the Northern and Low countries, though it was not until 1924 that he visited the USA. He drew inspiration from many sources, including Art Nouveau and the medieval ideas inherent in the English Arts & Crafts movement. His Hjularöd Castle, Scania, and the Toloholm Villa, Halland, built at the end of the C19, had obvious Anglo-Saxon overtones and their interiors owe something to architects like M. H. BAILLIE SCOTT. Wahlman's work contributed a rich turn-of-the-century ecleticism to Swedish architecture which ranged from this Arts & Crafts detailing through to the use of original constructional ideas and Moorish-style detailing. His own house in Stocksund closely followed traditional timber-jointing techniques, something that he was to pick up later in his celebrated competition entry for the large and impressive Engelbrekt Church, Stockholm. It was completed in 1914 on a prominent site in brick with granite trimmings and a harmoniously tiered steeple tower. Internally the church consists of a number of great parabolic arches with recessed timber roofs. Wahlman designed many other churches throughout Sweden and also practised as a landscape designer.

☐ Hjularöd Castle, Scania, 1894-7. Wahlman House, Hedemora, 1900-1901. Lars Wahlman residence, Stocksund, near Stockholm, 1906. Engelbrekt Church, Stockholm, 1906-14. Göteborg Botanical Gardens, 1921-3.

▷ S. I. Lindt, B. Romans and Nils Sterner, *Werk av Lars Israel Wahlman*, Stockholm, 1950. See also H. O. Anderson and F. Bedoire, *Swedish Architecture: Drawings 1640-1970*, Stockholm, 1986. DS

WALLOT Paul

b. Frankfurt-am-Main, 1841; d. Langenschwalbach, 1912.

Late C19 German architect, who is best known for the Reichstag in Berlin. Wallot studied architecture in Berlin under two influential Prussian architects and academics, Richard Lucae and Martin Gropius. The latter was professor at the Bauakademie and director of the Kunstschule. The prevailing architectural climate of the second half of the C19 reflected the bourgeois ambitions of the Bismarckian empire in a spate of buildings executed in dark brick with stone trim and fussy metallic detailing. This nationalistic mode lasted well into the C20, and Wallot's early work in Frankfurt shows that he had absorbed its influence. His career reached a watershed in 1884 when he won the competition for the Reichstag building in Berlin, his overwhelmingly monumental Neo-Baroque design owing more to VANBRUGH than BERNINI. This and other buildings formed part of a general revival of Neo-Baroque taste which began to challenge the established order. The Reichstag took ten years to build and was intended to symbolize the power and grandeur of the New Reich (ironically the Reichstag was destroyed by fire in 1933 during Hitler's rise to power and reconstructed during the 1970s). This commission brought Wallot fame and established his reputation, also earning him a teaching post at the Art Academy in Dresden. He was an influential teacher; his students included Heinrich Straümer, the noted architect and engineer.

□ Store, Offices and Residence, Frankfurt-am-Main, 1882. Reichstag, Berlin, 1884-94. House, Darmstadt Artists' Colony, 1901. President of the Reichstag's Residence, Berlin, 1903.

▷ W. Mackowsky, *Paul Wallot und seine Schuler*, Berlin, 1912. CS

WARD Basil

see Connell, Ward & Lucas

WARE Isaac

b. c. 1707, d. London, 1766.

A leading English architect of the Georgian era, though his importance derives chiefly from his books, which were enormously influential. A man of humble origins, Ware spent his early years (1721-8) as an apprentice to the highly respected architect Thomas Ripley; he later secured the position of draughtsman with His Majesty's Office of Works and at his death held the titles of clerk itinerant, secretary and clerk of works. After 1745 his parallel career in private practice proved equally successful and resulted in a series of prestigious projects. His close association with Lord BURLINGTON is reflected in the strict Palladian formality of his façade treatment, but his interiors often exhibit more catholic tastes, including French Rococo and Gothic. The common-sense pragmatism of Ware's architectural œuvre is also a characteristic of his written work. His 1738 edition of PALLADIO's *Quattro Libri* gave English readers their first accurate translation of this seminal work, and his encyclopedic *Complete Body of Architecture* was an invaluable compendium encompassing both theory and practice, lavishly illustrated with Ware's own designs.

□ St George's Hospital, London, 1733. Chesterfield House, London, 1748. Wrotham Park, Middlesex, 1754. Amisfield House, East Lothian, 1756.

▷ Isaac Ware, *Designs of Inigo Jones*, 1733 (Farnborough, reprinted 1971); *A Complete Body of Architecture*, London, 1756. Isaac Ware (translator), *The Four Books of Architecture – Andrea Palladio*, London, 1738. MC

WATERHOUSE Alfred

b. Liverpool, 1830; d. London, 1905.

Eminent English Victorian architect. A Quaker by birth, Waterhouse was educated at the Grove House Friends' School in Liverpool. In 1848 he became an assistant to Richard Lane in Manchester; after five years' training he made an extensive trip around Europe, returning to set up practice in Manchester in 1854. Success in the 1858 competition for the Manchester Assize Courts brought him national recognition, and he went on to design Manchester Town Hall. His best known London work is the Natural History Museum, executed in a Romanesque variant, unlike his Manchester buildings, which display their allegiance to mainstream Gothic. By working in both the Gothic and classical idioms Waterhouse succeeded in exploiting the stylistic divide of the High Victorian era. He was also willing to exploit new building material such as structural ironwork and terracotta. But his real skill lay in his ability to devise simple plans of great clarity, as exemplified by works such as the Prudential Assurance Building and the National Liberal Club, both in London.

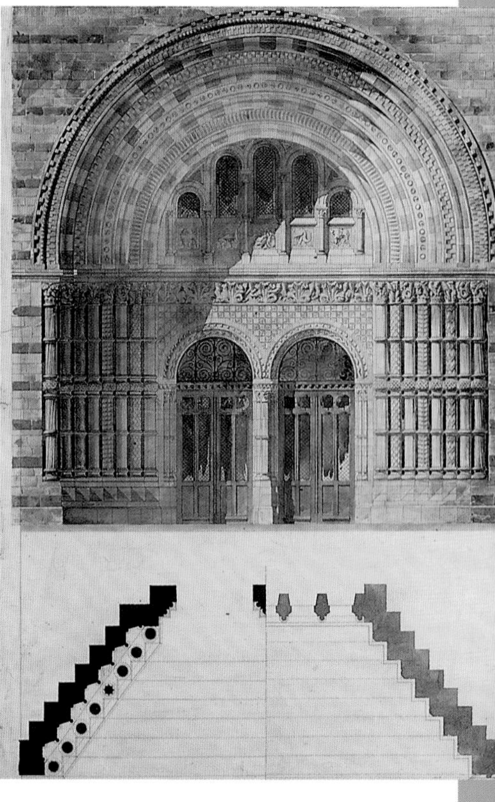

Alfred Waterhouse, Natural History Museum, London, 1871–82, drawing of main entrance

□ Assize Courts, Manchester, 1858-64. Town Hall, Manchester, 1867-77. Natural History Museum, London, 1871-81. Prudential Assurance Buildings, London, 1876-9. National Liberal Club, London, 1884-7.

▷ M. Girouard, *Alfred Waterhouse and the Natural History Museum*, New Haven and London, 1981. CS

WEBB Sir Aston

b. London, 1849; d. London, 1930.

Capable and prolific British designer of public buildings and institutions. Unrelated to Philip WEBB and in many respects his professional opposite, he was articled to R. R. Banks and Charles Barry (Jr.), set up in practice in 1873 and from 1882 was in partnership with **Edward Ingress Bell** (1837-1914). His reputation was founded on a flair for effective large-scale design and on a confident stylistic versatility which was given full scope in an epoch of institutional expansion. The first of many competition successes was his design for the Birmingham Law Courts in an early French Neo-Renaissance manner. Subsequent work ranged from Italian/Byzantine at Birmingham University to Elizabethan at

Christ's Hospital; from the unambiguous imperialism of Admiralty Arch (reflecting the almost universal official preference for eclectic Neo-Baroque during the Edwardian period) to the variegated motifs of the Victoria and Albert Museum façade. Regarded as the leading architect of his generation, he was knighted in 1904 and received the RIBA Royal Gold Medal (1905) and the American Gold Medal (1907).

□ Law Courts, Birmingham, 1886-91. Royal Services Institute, Whitehall, London, 1893-5. Christ's Hospital School, Horsham, Sussex, 1893-1902. Britannia Naval College, Dartmouth, Devon, 1899-1905. Victoria and Albert Museum, London (façade), 1899-1909. Admiralty Arch, London 1901-11. Birmingham University, 1906-9. Royal School of Mines, London, 1909. Buckingham Palace, London (façade), 1913.

▷ Alastair Service (ed.) *Edwardian Architecture and its Origins*, London, 1975. Alastair Service, *The Architects of London*, London, 1979. BP

WEBB Philip

b. Oxford, 1831; d. Worth, Sussex, 1915.

As close friend of William MORRIS, friend and mentor to W. R. LETHABY, the chief technical adviser and instructor to the Society for the Protection of Ancient Buildings, and the designer of a relatively few but hugely influential major houses Webb became the principal instrument through which the Arts & Crafts movement developed and promulgated its architectural ideas to the following generation. Webb was educated at Aynho in Northamptonshire, and did articles with a firm of builder-architects in Reading after which he moved to London and was employed by G. E. STREET, eventually becoming his senior assistant. In this capacity he met and befriended William Morris, who joined the firm for a year. Morris commissioned Webb to design the Red House at Bexleyheath for his own occupancy, and this commission was followed by other houses. Webb insisted on undertaking no more than one commission at a time, and his approach to the design issue was to enter the spirit and object of building as entirely as possible. His work represented a disciplined secularizing of Gothic Revival principles.

□ Red House, Bexleyheath, 1859. Arisaig, Inverness-shire, 1862. Smeaton Manor, Yorks., 1874. Clouds House, Wilts., 1879-86. Standen, East Grinstead, Sussex, 1892. Rounton Grange, Yorks., 1898.

▷ W. R. Lethaby, *Philip Webb and His Work*, 1935 (London, 1979). RM

▷ *see also pp228-9*

William Wilkins, Downing College, Cambridge, 1806–22

WEINBRENNER Friedrich

b. Karlsruhe, 1766; d. Karlsruhe, 1826.

The dominant figure within the German school of Neo-Classicism at the beginning of the C19. After studying mathematics and architecture at the Academy in Vienna, Weinbrenner travelled to Berlin and Italy, returning in 1797 to take up the position of building inspector in Karlsruhe, where his influence became considerable. His œuvre included several important civic buildings and also a series of model dwellings which private contractors were obliged to copy. Weinbrenner shared with Goethe an unshakable faith in the Classical ideal, believing that Truth and beauty could be found only in antiquity. His vision of a new German architecture, founded on early Greek and Roman examples, was instrumental in his decision to open a private architecture school at his Karlsruhe home in 1800. Many of his students, such as Wimmel and Hubsch, were to become influential in their own right and the school was later incorporated into the main University.

□ Ettlinger Tor, Karlsruhe, 1803. Margrave's Palace, Karlsruhe, 1803-14. St Stephen's Church, Karlsruhe, 1808-14. Town Hall, Karlsruhe, 1811-25.

▷ Friedrich Weinbrenner, *Architectonisches Lehrbuch*, Tübingen, 1810-17. Arthur Valdenaire, *Friedrich Weinbrenner*, Karlsruhe, 1926, 1976. David Watkin and Tilman Mellinghoff, *German Architecture and the Classical Ideal*, London, 1987. MC

WHITE Stanford

see McKim, Mead & White

WILKINS William

b. Norwich, 1778; d. Cambridge, 1839.

English architect and classical scholar who pioneered the Greek Revival in Britain. The eldest son of an architect, Wilkins took a joint degree in classics and mathematics at Gonville and Caius College, Cambridge (1796-1800). He was elected to the Society of Antiquaries and travelled round Sicily, Greece and Asia Minor as University Scholar. On his return in 1807 he published *Antiquities of Magna Graecia*, which paved the way for the archaeological Greek Revival. But his approach was rather smug and doctrinaire, and he was later to be outwitted and upstaged by his leading rival, Sir Robert SMIRKE. Wilkins's first major commission was for Downing College, Cambridge, of historical significance as the first true university campus comprising separate buildings arranged around a central lawn. He was presented with several opportunities to develop his Greek Revival style in London: University College, St George's Hospital and the National Gallery, but none of these major commissions was well received. In particular, the patchy façade of the National Gallery served only to lower Wilkins's reputation and highlight his failure to subordinate the parts to the whole. The scheme was, however, dogged by financial constraints. Wilkins also undertook a parallel career as a Gothicist, his most important works being additions to Trinity, King's and Corpus Christi colleges in Cambridge. After 1830 Wilkins's health and career declined. In 1837 Wilkins gained Pyrrhic consolation in being elected to the Royal Academy as Professor of Architecture.

□ Downing College (incomplete), Cambridge, 1805-22. New Court, Trinity College, Cambridge, 1821-7. New Quadrangle, Corpus Christi College, Cambridge, 1822-6. New Buildings and Screen, King's College, Cambridge, 1823-8. St George's Hospital, London, 1826-8. University College, London, 1826-30. National Gallery and Royal Academy, London, 1832-8.

▷ William Wilkins, *The Antiquities of Magna Graecia*, London, 1807. R. Windsor Liscombe, *William Wilkins 1778-1839*, London, 1980. CS

WILLIAMS Sir Evan Owen

b. London, 1890; d. London, 1969.

Eminent British structural engineer/architect who produced outstanding reinforced concrete buildings during the inter-war period. He was educated at Tottenham Grammar School and studied engineering at London University. From 1905-11 he was articled to the Electrical Tramways Co., London and in 1912 was appointed engineer/designer for the Trussed Concrete Company (later Truscon). In 1919 he commenced his own consultancy. He was appointed chief consulting civil engineer to the British Empire Exhibition, Wembley in 1923 working with Maxwell Ayrton. He was knighted for his services. Williams began work on his celebrated "Wets" Building for the Boots Company – and the layout of their new factory at Beeston, Nottingham – in 1929, completing it in 1932. He was also involved in work on the Pioneer Health Centre at Peckham, London and as the design engineer on three buildings for the Daily Express Newspaper Co. in London, Glasgow and Manchester (in conjunction with architects Ellis and Clarke). These buildings were seen as essentially "functional" structures but were sheathed with external decorative curved black glass walls developed by Williams, emphasizing their modern appearance. In the postwar years he turned his attention to developing the first plan for Britain's motorway system and the M1 in particular (opened 1959).

□ "Palace of Industry" and other buildings, British Empire Exhibition, Wembley, 1923-5. Boots Factory buildings at Beeston, Nottingham, 1929-32, 1937-8. *Daily Express* Buildings: Fleet St., London, 1932, Glasgow, 1937 and Manchester, 1939. Pioneer Health Centre, Peckham, London, 1934. Design projects for Ministry of Transport and M1 Motorway London-Birmingham, 1945-59; BOAC Hangar, London Airport, 1950-54. *Daily Mirror* Building, London (with Anderson, Forster and Wilcox), 1959.

▷ Owen Williams, *The Philosophy of Masonry Arches*, London, 1927. David Cottam, *Sir Owen Williams 1890-1969*, London, 1987. See also Dennis Sharp, "Utopian Engineering; Sir Owen Williams' 'New Architecture'", *Architecture and Urbanism*, (Tokyo), No 3, 1985, pp. 33-46. DS

▷ *see also pp238-9*

Sir Owen Williams, Boots Factory, Beeston, Nottingham, 1929–32, project drawing

WOOD John the Elder and Younger

John Wood the Elder, b. Bath, 1704; d. Bath, 1754. John Wood the Younger, b. Bath, 1727; d. Batheaston, 1781.

John Wood the Elder was a prominent figure in English Palladianism during the first half of the C18. Son of a builder, he began his apprenticeship as a joiner in London at the age of twelve. He later moved into property speculation and in 1725 commenced his lifelong association with the city of Bath. He completed several major buildings and created a sequence of majestic urban spaces, inspired by Rome which were to elevate his native city (alongside Edinburgh) as the quintessential example of Georgian elegance. John Wood the Younger proved a dutiful son and provided his eccentric father with a dependable yet creative partner who enabled several of the former's most ambitious schemes to reach fruition, including the world-famous Royal Crescent and the Assembly Rooms.

□ John Wood the Elder: Queen Square, Bath, 1728-36; Prior Park, Bath, 1731-64; The Exchange, Bristol, 1741-3. John Wood the Younger: Royal Crescent, Bath, 1767-75; Assembly Rooms, Bath, 1768-71; Hot Baths, Bath, 1775-8.

▷ John Wood the Elder, *The Origin of Building or the Plagiarism of the Heathens Detected*, 1744. John Wood the Younger, *A Series of Plans for Cottages or Habitations of the Labourer either in Husbandry or the Mechanic Arts*, 1781. Tim Mowl and Brian Earnshaw, *John Wood – Architect of Obsession*, Bath, 1988. MC

WOODWARD Benjamin

see Deane & Woodward

WREN Sir Christopher

b. East Knoyle, Wilts., 1632; d. London, 1723.

The best-known and probably the greatest of English architects. This reputation is earned for his brilliant design of St Paul's Cathedral, London, and the ingenuity of his City churches. Wren was born into a clerical household in Wiltshire. His father was appointed Dean of Windsor in 1634. From Westminster School the young boy spent some three years in London before going as a Gentleman Commoner to Wadham College, Oxford (1649). At Oxford he was soon involved with a group of brilliant scholars, who later formed the nucleus of the Royal Society. Serving as assistant to an eminent anatomist, Wren was at once immersed in new and experimental scientific learning. Astronomy seemed a logical progression for his active mind, and an early interest in working models, diagrams and charts were useful to an eventual architect. Wren's advancement was ever rapid: Gresham Professor of Astronomy in London in 1657, at the age of twenty-five, Savilian Professor of Astronomy at Oxford four years later. In 1663, Wren's uncle, the elderly Bishop of Ely, asked him to design a new chapel for Pembroke College, Cambridge. Architecture was an easy accomplishment to a brilliant scientist. The important Sheldonian Theatre at Oxford, with its great painted ceiling, unsupported by columns, followed; then a new building for Trinity College, Oxford (1668), a visit to Paris in 1665 to survey its "most esteemed fabrics" – always there was more work, with its attendant problems. In London the Great Fire of 1666 gave chance for Wren to present a scheme to rebuild the City. Utopian in concept, it was only partly realized. But there was also need for the rebuilding of St Paul's Cathedral and the replacement of so many damaged churches. Here lay Wren's major work for the rest of the C17 and beyond. In March 1669 Charles II had appointed Wren Surveyor-General of the King's Works (a post held in earlier years by Inigo JONES). This meant the supervision of all work on the royal palaces; because of this increasing commitment to architecture Wren resigned his Oxford professorship in 1673, when he was knighted. St Paul's was also now involving continual time and thought, with the final "Warrant Design" not being approved by the King until 1675. Furthermore, with only two surveyors to help, there were fifty-two churches in the City of London to design or supervise in some way. Most were on awkward, constricting sites. Each demanded an original spatial solution. All of them were given a fine tower and a soaring thin spire, but each had subtle, and often distinct, differences. Wren died, in his own words, having "worn out (by God's Mercy) a long life in the Royal Service, and having made some Figure in the world". He was buried in February 1723 in the crypt of his greatest work, St Paul's Cathedral, where a monument was later erected to his memory.

□ Supervision, and sometimes design, of 52 London City churches, *c.*1670-90. St Paul's Cathedral, London, 1675-1710. Royal Hospital, Chelsea, 1682-92. Royal Hospital, Greenwich, 1696 onwards.

▷ Stephen Wren, *Parentalia, or Memoirs of the Family of the Wrens*, 1750. *The Wren Society*, 20 vols., 1924-43. Kerry Downes, *Christopher Wren*, London, 1971. Geoffrey Beard, *The Work of Christopher Wren*, London, 1982. GB

▷ *see also pp218-19*

Sir Christopher Wren, St Mary-le-Bow, London, 1680

WRIGHT Frank Lloyd

b. Richland Center, Wisconsin, 1867; d. Phoenix, Arizona, 1959.

The best-known and most talented architect of the C20; an American with Welsh ancestry. He was inspired by his mother to become an architect. Boyhood summers on his uncle's farm embued a love of nature. Wright's first building dates from 1886. In that year, as a young man, he was cited as job architect of Unity Chapel, Helena Valley, Wisc., designed by J. L. Silsbee. From then until his death he produced countless architectural projects; in 1974 it was estimated that some 433 buildings remained extant. His own publication output was phenomenal and he and his pupils, admirers, writers and critics produced about 2000 noteworthy items. Wright became a legend in his own lifetime; his lifestyle and extra-marital affairs scandalized America. He was claimed as the model for the character of Howard Roark in Ayn Rand's novel *The Fountainhead*; it was also rumoured that he was a near communist. He had to fall back on farming as a way of surviving during lean times. The first period of his career was connected to the indigenous Prairie School and followed his short apprenticeship to his *Lieber Meister* Louis SULLIVAN of Adler & Sullivan. Wright's family houses for middle-class businessmen, with "gently sloping rooves, low proportions, quiet skylines", initiated a spatial revolution, where rooms were not box containers but were volumes overlapped and interpenetrated. In 1909, with his lover Mrs Mamah Cheney (*née* Borthwick), Wright travelled to Europe, where his early work was published in Berlin by Ernst Wasmuth (1910-11). It had a profound influence on continental architects. In 1913 Wright was in Japan, where he secured the Imperial Hotel commission. It brought him fame when it failed to collapse in the 1923 Tokyo earthquake. Wright's own world, however, had collapsed in 1914 in the most appalling circumstances when he was building Midway Gardens, Chicago; Mrs Cheney and her two children were murdered. Apart from the Imperial Hotel he did little work until the textile block houses for the Los Angeles area of the mid-1920s. These include the famous Millard House. Some of the West Coast houses were supervised

"FALLING WATER", Bear Run, Penn.

"Falling Water" (Frank Lloyd Wright, 1936) is often referred to as the most beautiful and inventive modern house in the world. Originally it was designed as a weekend house for a wealthy client, Edgar Kaufmann Sr. Today it is a much visited landmark building which straddles a precipitous site combining the familiar simple terraced form of Modernism with natural materials in keeping with the local environment. It perches above a ravine with a spectacular waterfall feature. A giant rectangular cantilever projects out over the falls and a suspended staircase connects the living room to the ground. Further terraces project from the third-floor bedrooms emphasizing the building's horizontality and its complex play of interlocking spatial penetrations.

Frank Lloyd Wright

during construction by his son, Lloyd Wright. A year later he began the most important relationship of his life with Olgivanna Hinzenberg, a Gurdejieff disciple, whom he married in 1928. The second most successful period of Wright's career followed, with many important houses, including the two Taliesins, Kaufmann's "Falling Water" and the Johnson Wax Company offices in Racine, Wisconsin, and the Johnson house, "Wingspread". Wright believed in and promoted an "organic" architecture and way of life within a framework that was democratic, even at times utopian (e.g. the Broadacre City and Mile High projects, and his "Usonian" houses – a concept of modest dwellings close to earth, for the average American). During his "international" period of the 1930s, he visited the USSR and gave the Princeton and Sulgrave Manor lectures, which effectively summarized his philosophy. In 1941 he received the RIBA Royal Gold Medal. In the post-war period large-scale projects followed, including the Guggenheim Museum, New York, Marin County Court and offices as well as more houses, theatres, churches, and auditoria.

□ Prairie School houses in and around Chicago, Illinois, including Oak Park (Unity Temple, Own Studio and House (now museum), Fricke, Martin Gale and Cheney Houses etc.); River Forest (Winslow, Roberts Houses etc.) and Riverside (Coonley Residence etc.), from 1890. Imperial Hotel, Tokyo, Japan, 1915 (Annexe, 1916). Millard House "La Miniatura", Pasadena, California, 1923. Taliesin III, Spring Green, Wisc., from 1925; Taliesin West, Scottsdale, Arizona, from 1937. S. C. Johnson and Son Offices, Racine, Wisc., 1934 (Research Tower, 1944). Edgar J. Kaufmann Sr Residence "Falling Water", Bear Run, Penn., 1935 (Guest House, 1938). Solomon R. Guggenheim Museum, 5th Avenue, New York, 1956. Grady Gammage Memorial Auditorium, ASU, Tempe, Arizona, 1959.

▷ F. L. Wright, *An Autobiography*, London, New York and Toronto, 1932 (new eds. 1943, 1977). See also *On Architecture*, 1941, and *The Future of Architecture*, 1953 (his major lectures). W. A. Storer, *The Architecture of Frank Lloyd Wright*, Cambridge, Mass., 1974. R. L. Sweeny, *Frank Lloyd Wright: An Annotated Bibliography*, Los Angeles, 1978. Edgar Tafel, *Apprentice to Genius: Years with Frank Lloyd Wright*, New York, 1979 (now reissued as *Years with Frank Lloyd Wright*, New York). Brendan Gill, *Many Masks: A Life of Frank Lloyd Wright*, New York, 1987. JC/DS

▷ *see also pp228-9, 232-3*

WYATT James

b. Weeford, Staffs., 1746;
d. Camden, London, 1813.

The most conspicuous and fashionable English architect of his generation. He was in Italy 1762-8 and studied in Venice under the Palladian architect Antonio Visentini. After returning to London he won immediate fame with the Oxford Street Pantheon (1770), an astounding timber-domed Neo-Classical assembly room partly inspired by Hagia Sophia in Constantinople. From then on he was constantly in demand, and his panache as a designer was such that his patrons usually forgave his lateness and erratic supervision. Fundamentally eclectic and pragmatic in his approach to style, he borrowed from both ADAM and CHAMBERS, was equally at ease with Palladianism and Neo-Classicism, and became the leading practitioner of picturesque Gothic. Indeed, his Gothic flair, demonstrated first at Lee Priory (1782) and most spec-

James Wyatt, Heveningham Hall, Suffolk, c. 1780–84, dining room

tacularly at Fonthill Abbey (1797-1807; tower collapsed 1825), earned him a reputation as a medieval expert, but his radical restoration work at Hereford, Salisbury, Lichfield and Durham Cathedrals was deplored by antiquaries, and later provoked PUGIN's epithet "Wyatt the Destroyer". He was elected R A in 1785 and succeeded Chambers as Surveyor-General and Comptroller of the Office of Works in 1796. He was killed in a coaching accident. The Wyatt dynasty included James's son **Benjamin Dean Wyatt** (*c.*1775-1850) who designed the Drury Lane Theatre, London, and nephew, Sir Jeffrey WYATVILLE.

☐ Heaton Hall, Manchester, 1772. Radcliffe Observatory, Oxford, 1773-94. Heveningham Hall, Suffolk (interior), *c.*1780-84. Oriel College Library, Oxford, 1788. Castle Coole, Northern Ireland, 1790-97. Dodington House, Glos., 1798-1808. Ashridge, Herts., 1806-13.

▷ Anthony Dale, *James Wyatt*, Oxford, 1936, 1956. John Martin Robinson, *The Wyatts: An Architectural Dynasty*, Oxford, 1979. BP

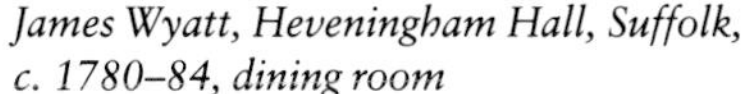

WYATVILLE Sir Jeffrey

b. Burton-on-Trent, 1766; d. London, 1840.

Adaptable and industrious English architect, best known for his remodelling of Windsor Castle. Wyatville was the second son of Joseph Wyatt, a Staffordshire mason and architect. He was apprenticed to his uncles – Samuel and James WYATT – in London and subsequently set up his own practice. He also established a partnership with John Armstrong, a carpentry contractor, thus enabling him to act as a contractor and supplier on numerous projects. The bulk of Wyatville's work consisted of improvements and additions to country houses; he built up an impressive list of aristocratic patrons. He was a competent classical architect – as demonstrated by his alterations and interiors for Chatsworth House – but also specialized in Neo-Gothic and Tudoresque mansions. His most notable work is his restoration and remodelling of Windsor Castle, commissioned by King George IV in 1824. He gave the building a picturesque silhouette by raising the Round Tower and designed a series of sumptuous interiors for the private apartments, which transformed the historic castle into a comfortable royal palace. His country house designs did not achieve the virtuosity of the best of his uncle's work, but he was both versatile and industrious. He changed his name to Wyatville when he began work on Windsor Castle and was knighted for his endeavours in 1828.

☐ Chatsworth House, Derbyshire (additions and interiors), 1818-41. Windsor Castle, Berks. (restoration and remodelling), 1824-40.

▷ Derek Linstrum, *Sir Jeffrey Wyatville: Architect to the King*, Oxford, 1972. John Martin Robinson, *The Wyatts: An Architectural Dynasty*, Oxford, 1979. CS

YORKE Francis Reginald Stevens

b. Stratford-upon-Avon, 1906; d. London, 1962.

Pioneer of the Modern Movement in England and founding partner of YRM, a practice which continues to enjoy an enviable reputation in the British architectural scene. Yorke studied architecture and town planning at the University of Birmingham before setting up in private practice in 1930. Principal influences include LE CORBUSIER and MIES VAN DER ROHE, and from the outset Yorke's work reflected the aspirations of a committed Modernist. For example he was an early member of the MARS Group (1933), an early exponent of reinforced concrete (1933) and a partner alongside ex-Bauhaus tutor Marcel BREUER (1935). Although this partnership was dissolved after two years (when Breuer accepted Walter GROPIUS's invitation to teach at Harvard), they completed several influential commissions which established Yorke's position in the vanguard of British Modernism. The YRM partnership, formed in 1944, with Eugene Rosenberg and Cyril Mardall, secured a succession of important public sector commissions throughout the 1950s and 60s. During the war Yorke became a member of William Holford's team of architects that designed army and internment camps and other structures for the War Ministry. Yorke died at the early age of 55 in 1962 but his influential, discursive and important books that record the growth of the Modern Movement in architecture in England remain the chief sources for the whole period.

□ Gidea Park Housing, Essex (with William Holford), 1933. House, Clifton (with Marcel Breuer), 1936. Gatwick Airport (phase 1), Sussex, 1957. US Embassy, London (with Eero SAARINEN), 1960. Leeds Polytechnic (stage 3), 1960.

▷ F. R. S. Yorke, *The Modern House*, London, 1934; *The Modern Flat*, London, 1937. F. R. S. Yorke and Colin Penn, *A Key to Modern Architecture*, London, 1939. Reyner Banham (intro.), *The Architecture of Yorke, Rosenberg, Mardall*, London, 1972. MC

▷ *see also pp238-9*

Yorke, Rosenberg & Mardall, Barclay School, Stevenage, 1950, with sculpture by Henry Moore in the foreground

ZAKHAROV Andreyan Dmitrievich

b. St Petersburg (Leningrad), 1761;
d. St Petersburg, 1811.

Leading Russian classicist of the early c19. Son of a minor admiralty official, Zakharov entered the preparatory school of the Academy of Arts in 1767, ultimately graduating from its Architecture School in 1782 with the gold medal. The prize took him to Paris for four years under J.F.T. Chalgrin and to Italy. On his return he taught at the Academy from 1787, becoming senior professor of architecture in 1803. He was appointed chief architect to the admiralty in 1805. His early work for various establishments was eclectic, including a Neo-Gothic church at Gatchina. Large urban scale characterized other early projects, including an unrealized one for unifying all buildings of the Academy of Sciences into one grandiose structure, and a highly successful one for developing the tip of Vasilevsky Island with a Bourse complex and related new urban space. The two characteristics came together in his redevelopment of the whole admiralty complex in central Petersburg. Replicating the needle-like gilded spire of the previous complex (by I. K. Korobov), Zakharov wove an original and eclectic synthesis of Classical motifs into the most powerful of all architectural expressions of Russia's imperial power, with volumes of great geometrical clarity, subtle regulation of vast elevational lengths through recession and the play of columnar and flat-wall surfaces, and with superbly scaled symbolic and narrative sculpture. The result was a world-class model of true classical continuity between a city-planning concept, the architectural language and the narrative potential of public art.

Andreyan Zakharov, The Admiralty, Leningrad, 1806–23

□ Monastery church at Gatchina, near St Petersburg (Leningrad), 1800. Development plan for Bourse site, Leningrad, 1803-4. Mizhuev mansion, Fontanka 26, Leningrad, 1804-6. St Andrew's Cathedral, Kronstadt naval base, 1806-17. Admiralty complex, Leningrad, 1806-23.

▷ A. N. Petrov *et al.*, *Pamyatniki arkhitektury Leningrada*, Leningrad, 1976. W. C. Brumfield, *Gold in Azure*, Boston, Mass., 1983. CC

2

ARCHITECTURE AND THE HISTORY OF IDEAS

EARLIEST ARCHITECTURE

Tracing the beginnings of architecture from Neolithic times

Architecture has always been commonly regarded as one of the arts. Incorporating as it does the arts of both painting and sculpture, it has indeed been called the "mistress" art. But unlike the other arts it alone is useful in the ordinary sense of the word. Unlike pictures, poems, sculpture and music, it protects us from the rigours of the environment. In it, artistic expression and functional fitness are inextricably mixed together. Architecture is also recognized as having a socio-political function, reinforcing the authority of those who seek to organize the society in which they live. For architecture represents an influential picture of the ideal world, drawing mankind along various paths of social develop-ment and evolution.

At its most basic, the term "architecture" can also be used to describe any structured object. In this sense the cathedral, the bicycle shed, and even the pine tree, the ants' nest or the sea shell could all be described as architecture. This view is a useful stimulant to our appreciation of built form even if we take the more conventional view and believe that architecture only correctly describes a building which does more than serve a basic function and delights the senses, such as the great temples and palaces and other habitable products of the famous designers.

As there is no universally agreed definition – even the Concise Oxford English Dictionary is rather vague, defining architecture as "... thing built, structure, style of building, construction" – architecture may be taken to mean any habitable building with a form dictated by considerations beyond pure utility. The earliest surviving examples of stone-built architecture date back six thousand years but the roots of architecture go back further still. The tendency for mankind to organize its communities and habitations into meaningful shapes seems instinctive, like the drive to make pictures, to dance or to sing. Impermanent architecture probably flourished (within the limits of its builders' resources) for many millennia until human resources made it possible to give architecture a more lasting and permanent expression. Archaeologists recording evidence of neolithic settlements have uncovered evidence of fairly extensive village complexes. Lines of post-holes preserved in the old layers of clay give a clue to the kind of structures these prehistoric people built. However, there is little evidence of the "architecture" of these peoples in the sense of the aesthetic effect sought after and the means by which it was achieved, and while the traces are of intense academic interest, they supply us with little information as to how the building actually looked. However, this ephemeral architecture is not entirely lost to us beyond all conjecture. In order to imagine some of its probable forms, we need only look at the contemporary building of cultures with strong neolithic roots.

(DNS)

▲ *Indonesian village house. This illustrates the same human needs as the "long house" opposite but the similar materials are used in a very different way. Here the roof curves up, turning the gable end into a dramatic forward-leaning peak below which can be seen the horizontal line of the upper floor and ground floor entry. The two flanking screens, each of four carefully shaped vertical, and three horizontal, wooden members, are not just a fence but part of the whole, dramatic, architectural composition.*

▶ *This ambitious mud building seems at first sight to imitate the stone buildings of cultures with more resources, but in fact stone architecture itself simply imitates earlier buildings in more easily managed materials. The roughly plastered mud is an effective protection against the West African sun. The long water spouts are intended to carry water clear of the walls to avoid erosion. They show how the design has been adapted to meet the shortcomings of the materials.*

▲ *Gate in the old city, Kano, Nigeria. This is constructed from one of the earliest building materials: mud brick. The plastic massing of the material gives a feeling of protection and shelter – one of the most persistent ideas expressed by architecture down the ages.*

▲ *The skin tent of the American Indians was lightweight and portable, but can still be called architecture. Its strictly disciplined form and cultural significance are emphasized by the totem decorations on the surface.*

▲ *Traditional "long house", Sarawak, Malaysia. Although contemporary, this building exhibits characteristics evident in man's earliest structures. The regular post supports, simple roof slope and pattern of uniform smaller parts combine to create a timeless arrangement.*

EGYPT AND MESOPOTAMIA

The legacy of ancient pyramids, palaces and temples

Some 5000 years ago the small but rich tribal communities that lived along the Nile and the Tigris-Euphrates river systems fused into big single power blocks. These national communities possessed the wealth to enable them to build structures the size and permanence of which have hardly been equalled since. The most famous of architectural symbols – the pyramids of Egypt – were really the centrepieces of large complexes, with areas for state ceremony, temples and shrines, workshops, offices and stores. Although these elements have largely disappeared, at the most ancient pyramid of all, the step pyramid, built at Sakkara near modern Cairo (*c.* 2650 BC), enough remains to give a fairly clear idea of the pyramid complex.

In the millennia that followed the building of the step pyramid, whenever political stability brought prosperity Egypt's national resources were employed to raise huge structures to pay homage to the gods in heaven and to stabilize social organization on earth.

When the building of huge pyramids passed from fashion, temples took their place as symbols of power. These consisted of an inner shrine with concentric layers of buildings and courts. Some are relatively modest, others breathtakingly spectacular. The biggest, the Temple of Kons at Karnak, had columns up to 25 m (80 ft) high; the great ceremonies of religion and state took place in its many courts and halls. Thousands of priests were attached to the temple, a combination of gigantic abbey and state ministry. As with all Egyptian buildings, the walls, ceilings and often the columns were decorated with depictions of the life of the gods, often carved in low relief and painted. Further adorned with pylons and obelisks, these buildings bear witness to the importance of architecture in the social organization of the nation.

In the north in Mesopotamia along the banks of the Tigris and the Euphrates and the irrigated river plain beyond, the temples and palaces were probably just as spectacular as their Egyptian counterparts, but a shortage of stone in this area meant that the temples and palaces were built of mudbrick. Following their destruction by the Mongols in the 13th century AD, these monuments largely vanished. Only great mounds of earth and accumulations of the glazed bricks that once decorated their outer surface remain as testimony of the past prosperity of the plain.

The accumulations of wealth and power in this part of the world led to the development of empires striving to gain supreme control and to spread their influence and culture from the eastern Mediterranean to the Persian Gulf. By 500 BC Persia was the strongest of these and added its own artistic tradition to existing architectural influences. Greece and the islands of the Aegean Sea were inaccessible to the armies of these empires. Although independent, they were able to benefit from the trade and cultures of Egypt, Mesopotamia and Persia, and develop an architecture which although similar in stylistic roots was radically different in terms of scale and purpose. (DNS)

▶ *Step Pyramid Sakkara, Cairo* c. *2650* BC. *Originally conceived as a simple tomb, the ambitions of its builders increased the size of the step pyramid in successive layers. Around it was built a complex of temples, funerary chapels and royal residential quarters. These buildings and the vast outer wall that enclosed them, although built of stone, closely followed the form of buildings made from less permanent materials, such as mud, brick and palm logs.*

▲ *Glazed reliefs from Ishtar gate, Babylon, 604–562* BC. *The mud-brick walls of Mesopotamian temple shrines were sometimes decorated with a veneer of burnt brick, carved in relief and decorated with coloured glazes. This late example shows how the style persisted through the centuries.*

▼ View of courtyard, Temple of Isis, Philae, 283–247 BC. This temple is a late addition to a long tradition of Egyptian temple building. Columns were used both internally and to provide colonnades round the courtyards, while pairs of tapering towers (pylons) gave dramatic emphasis to the main doorways.

▼ *Reconstruction of a typical Mesopotamian palace. The architects of ancient Mesopotamia lacked a good supply of stone. They relied not on columns and stone beams as the Egyptians had done, but on massive mud-brick walls pierced where necessary with arched openings. The roofs were either supported by wooden beams or brick vaults. A typical Mesopotamian palace stood on a raised platform and had high outer walls, its arched entries flanked by towers.*

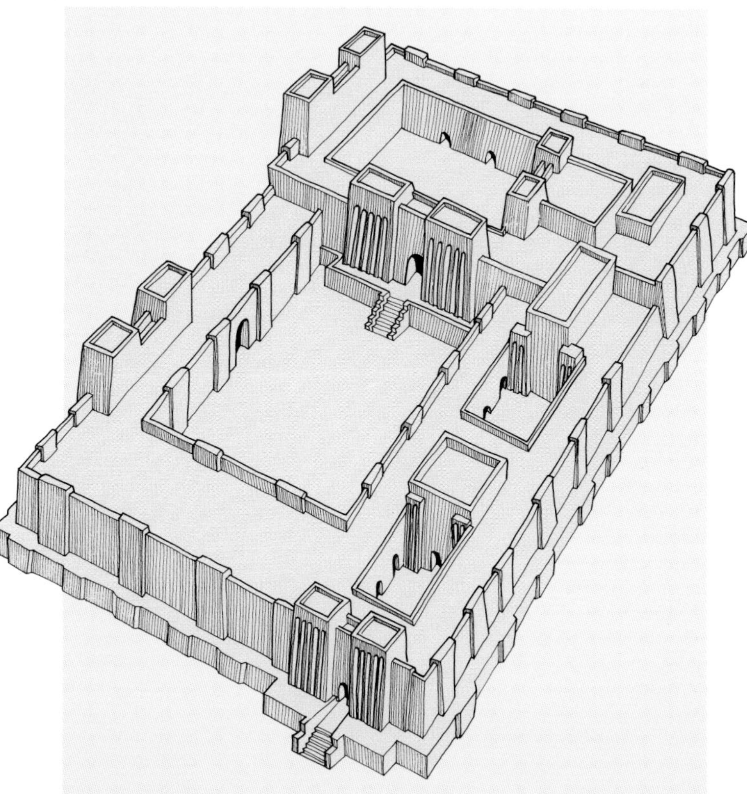

▶ *Reconstruction of the entry hall complex of the step pyramid, Sakkara. Elegant polished granite columns imitate supports of reed bundles, and overhead the stone ceiling is laboriously carved in the form of palm logs. This shows that before the earliest architecture known to us stretched a tradition of ambitious structures in less permanent materials.*

THE AEGEAN CIVILIZATION

Cretan, Mycenaean, Etruscan and early Greek architecture

Out of the immediate military reach of the great empires of Egypt, Babylonia, Assyria and Persia lay the Aegean coast (now western Turkey), the Aegean islands and the valleys of the hilly Greek peninsula beyond. The communities here developed their own small economies and benefited from the cultural and technological advances of the big empires while remaining politically independent.

The island of Crete had a flourishing Bronze Age civilization as early as 2000 BC, probably as a result of its position on the sea route between the wheat-producing lands on the Black Sea and Egypt. Cretan (sometimes also known as Minoan) art was both decorative and elegant, and flourished until around 1400 BC. Unlike the art of the old empires, which was primarily religious or political and concerned with glorifying the gods and the rulers, it focused on the decorative forms of nature in the form of graceful athletes and dancers. Although there were strong religious elements in the work, artists seemed preoccupied with the creation of beauty for its own sake rather than religion. Cretan architecture, with its air of stylish luxury, gives the same impression. It remained as a characteristic of the Classical architecture which flourished round the shores and islands of the Aegean in the succeeding age.

From around 1400 BC the mainland states were under the control of the Mycenaeans, who created an architecture that was both monumental and sophisticated, and which showed great engineering skill. Their work was a forerunner of Greek Classical architecture.

The continuity of architectural development in the Aegean was interrupted by a series of catastrophes. Crete vanished as the dominant power, perhaps partly the result of earthquakes, and waves of invasions by peoples from the north followed. The invaders, who established themselves in central Greece, were known as the Dorians while on the peninsula of Attica (the state of Athens), on the islands and on the Turkish coast, the original inhabitants, known as Ionians, generally prevailed. They all spoke Greek, worshipped the same gods and participated in the development of an Iron Age culture which in the succeeding centuries produced Classical art and architecture.

By the 6th century BC, just across the Aegean in central Italy, the Etruscans were producing an architecture in some ways similar to the Dorian, or Doric, builders of central Greece. Building largely in wood and baked clay, using stone only for foundations, their temples possessed individual features which were to contribute in the future to the essential character of Roman, as distinct from Greek, architecture. The Etruscans used the arch freely and their temples were built to be seen from the front only: a form that was less sculptural than that of Classical Greek architecture but more dramatic. This distinction between the architecture of the Greek and Italian peninsulas remained into the centuries that followed. (DNS)

▲ *Etruscan tomb, Chiusi, 6th century BC. A carved stone container for human remains represents a building with an arched entry. The arch was not used in Greek architecture, where the emphasis was traditionally on the vertical columns and horizontal beam, but it was readily used by the Etruscans. Later it became important in Roman architecture.*

◀ *The Lion Gate, Mycenae, 13th century* BC. *The entry to the citadel at Mycenae on the Greek mainland has a 1m (3ft) thick beam spanning the opening. This use of massive stone is a typical feature of Mycenaean architecture.*

▶ *A reconstruction of an Etruscan temple. The Etruscans built in wood with columns and beams. Unlike the Greek temples which were designed to be seen from all points of view, Etruscan buildings were intended to be seen from the front. It was this feature, as well as the arch, that made Etruscan architecture so radically different from that of the Greeks.*

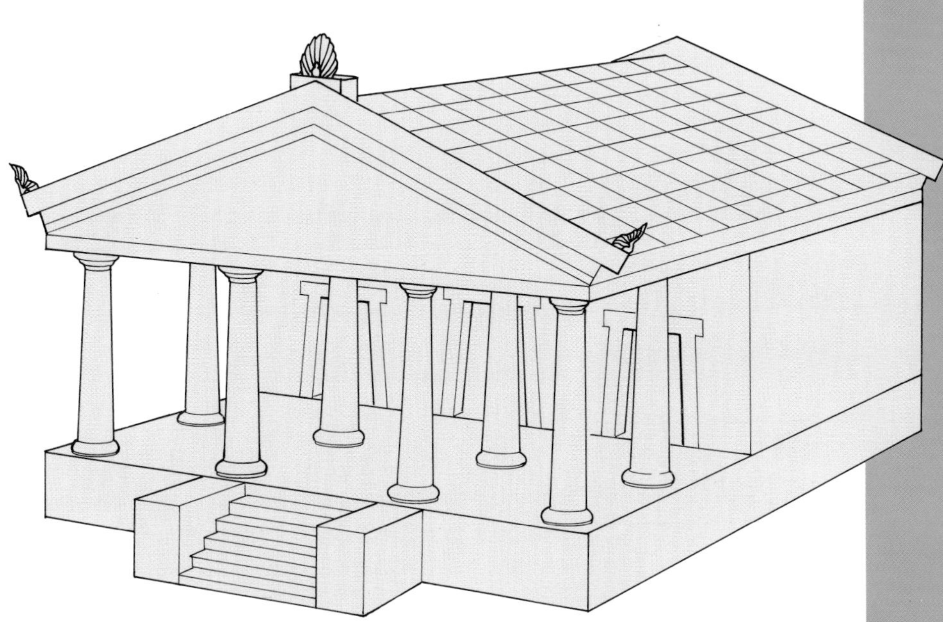

▲ *Temple of Apollo, Corinth, mid 6th century* BC. *These columns with spreading cushion capitals are early examples of the Doric style. Unlike the shafts and other features they do not look as if they could have had a wooden prototype. The popular view that the Doric style was wholly derived from wooden prototypes has to be regarded with some reserve.*

◀ *Palace of Knossos, Crete, c. 1500* BC. *Sometimes known as the palace of Minos, this is a spectacular structure covering several acres of land. Rising in parts to two and three storeys it had sumptuous interiors with rooms for royal ceremonies, a grand staircase and luxurious bathrooms. The columns, tapering toward the base, are a characteristic feature of the Cretan (or Minoan) style.*

CLASSICAL GREECE

Evolution of the Orders and the "golden age" of Classical architecture in Greece

About 500 BC the Persian empire was at its height, dominating the lands of the once powerful Babylonian empire (now Iraq and Syria) and Egypt. It then began acquiring the Ionian Greek kingdoms on what is now the Turkish coast of the Aegean Sea. The states of the Greek peninsula, Dorian and Ionian alike, became drawn into the conflict. When the Greeks emerged triumphant in 479 BC, they celebrated their success with widespread building activity, and the creation of many now-famous temples. The designing of these temples was a carefully considered act and it was usual for Greek architects to publish a written account of the rationale behind their work. This practice led to the rules governing the design being systemized; they were eventually perpetuated in a later age by Roman authors, especially VITRUVIUS. In his treatise *De Architectura* Vitruvius outlines the principles of these rules, telling us that the Greek architects determined the approximate size of the temple by reference to the site and resources and then selected a suitable column size to determine all other dimensions, such as the size and depth of mouldings, in terms of a "module" derived from the thickness of the column at the base. Thus a column shaft might be seven or eight modules high, the capital above that another module, the beam (architrave) that rests on the capital yet another module, the frieze above the architrave perhaps one or one and a quarter more, and the cornice above that yet another one. In even the smallest parts of the building, for example, the individual mouldings which together made up the cornice were presented as fractions of the module.

The module thus became a means of controlling the proportional relationships of the various parts of the building which constituted what was termed the "Order". In Greek Classical architecture there were two main orders – Doric and Ionic, illustrated opposite. The temples usually consisted of a windowless room (the *naos*), lit from the doorway, containing the image of a god. Opening from the back of this structure there was sometimes a second smaller room (the *cela*). The structure was usually surrounded by a line of columns which were the principal architectural feature of the building. The plan was usually a simple rectangle about twice as long as it was wide. Circular temples also occurred.

What gave the classical buildings of Greece an overwhelming beauty was their simple uniformity, the emphasis on precision and refinement of form and above all the relationship of the Greek temples with the sunshine of the Mediterranean landscape. The remains of the Greek work and the influence of its Roman imitations has led to 5th-century Greece being called an architectural golden age, and has inspired recurrent revivals of "classical" architecture down to the present day.

(DNS)

▲ *Tholos of Marmaria, Delphi, 380 BC. As well as rectangular temples the Greeks built circular ones, beginning a tradition which was to continue as an influence throughout the history of Classical architecture. Here the Doric Order is adapted to the circular form. The three restored columns, complete with entablature, are a good illustration of this Order.*

▶ *Temple of the Wingless Victory* (Nike apteros), *Athens, 426 BC. Perched on a rocky spur of the Acropolis, this little temple, only 7m (23ft) high, can be recognized as Ionic by the curling volutes of its capitals. The relative smallness of Greek temples of the Classical period enabled them to be the subject of perfectionist refinement in the treatment of details, surfaces and proportions.*

▲ *The Parthenon, Athens, 447* BC. *This has all the features of the Doric Order in their perfection. It was designed by Ictinos and Callicrates. Largely destroyed in the 17th century its ruins still display the crisp precision aimed at by its designers. The work of the master sculptor, Phidius, can be seen in the western frieze along the top of the wall of the* naos *(central room housing the image of the god).*

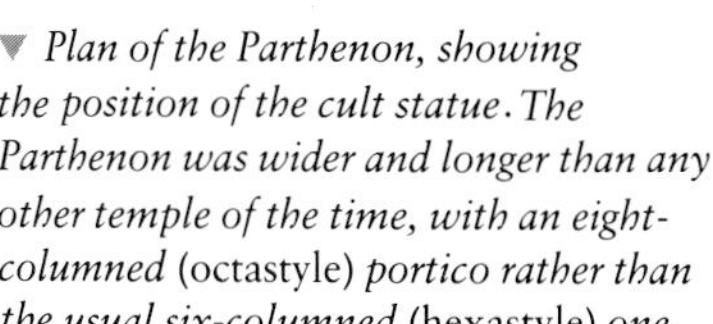

▼ *Plan of the Parthenon, showing the position of the cult statue. The Parthenon was wider and longer than any other temple of the time, with an eight-columned* (octastyle) *portico rather than the usual six-columned* (hexastyle) *one.*

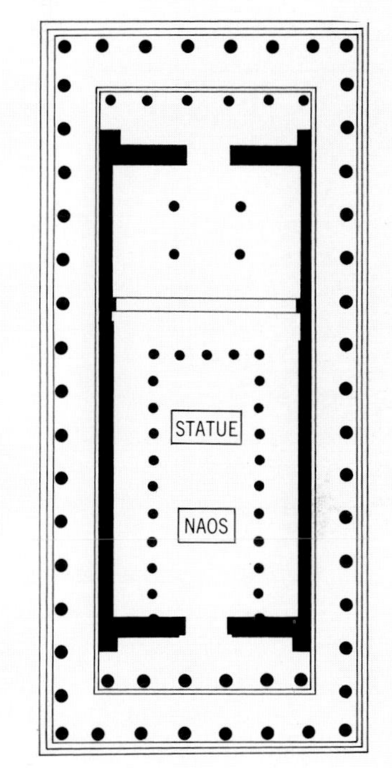

▶ *Doric (right) and Ionic (far right) Orders. The Greeks constantly refined the details of their architecture. The assemblage of base, column, capital and beam, frieze and cornice were exactly prescribed and the treatment of doors was also specified. This was known as the "Order" and each Order was thought to have its own mood. The Doric Order was thought to be masculine and severe, the Ionic more slender and elegant.*

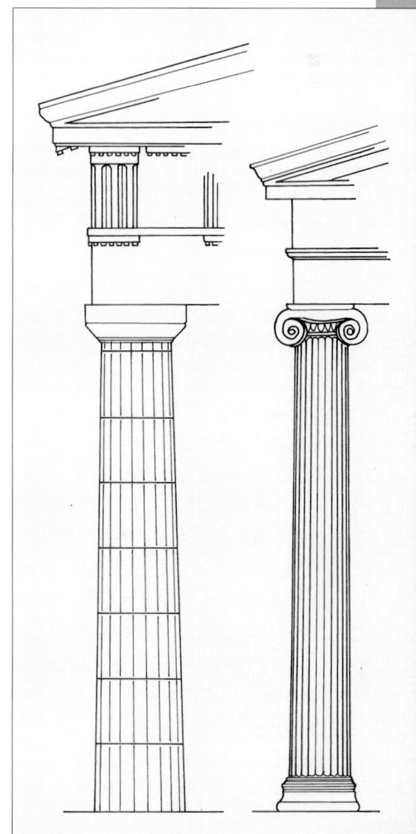

HELLENISTIC ARCHITECTURE

Alexander the Great and the spread of Classical architecture

Although the defeat of the invading Persians early in the 5th century BC gave the Greek people unchallenged prosperity and established them as the major power in the eastern Mediterranean, the individual states which composed the Greek nation never succeeded in uniting politically. Bitter disputes inevitably led to them all being swallowed up by one aggressive military power, Macedonia, in the 4th century BC, led by the Greek-speaking king Alexander the Great (356–323 BC). He followed the subjugation of Greece with the conquest of the three great empires of the East – Babylonia, Egypt and Persia. In all the areas under his control, Alexander promoted Greek learning and language. After his death these regions – prosperous and densely populated – were ruled by Greek dynasties. As a result, Greek science, art and of course architecture were deliberately fostered in the Near East, while in Greece the influence of eastern luxury and wealth encouraged a more flamboyant architectural style.

Even before the Alexandrian conquests, the new Greek cities on or near the Turkish coast had started ambitious building programmes. The Ionic Temple of Diana at Ephesus (begun 356 BC) and the temple of Apollo near Miletus (335 BC) were on a truly grand scale, the latter with columns about 20m (65ft) high. It too was Ionic but had some columns of the Corinthian Order, which was to become a favourite of Hellenistic architects. The last great Corinthian building of the epoch, the Olympieion, was built at Athens, where once Doric and Ionic had been the usual Orders for temples.

The Corinthian Order resembled the Ionic in terms of base shaft, architrave and cornice, but it was slightly more slender. In place of the Ionic curling volutes, the capital had an arrangement of the serrated leaves of the acanthus plant. This form was probably not derived from wooden or stone constructional members but cast-bronze prototypes created by craftsmen in Corinth. Its popularity reflected the love of refinement, luxury and naturalistic representation which characterized all the arts of the period.

Cities in the expanded Greek world were provided with colonnaded open spaces for markets and meetings, stadia for foot races and hippodromes for chariot racing. Theatres were usually built to take advantage of a hollow hillside, the spectators sitting in circular tiers up the hill. At Athens the theatre of Dionysus (330 BC) could accommodate 30,000 people. These enormous public buildings were followed in domestic architecture with a greater interest in complexity. In addition to the ancient divisions in Greek domestic architecture between a men's area and women's one, courtyards, sometimes enclosing gardens, were added, leading to rooms with specific functions. In the houses of the richer citizens, these rooms were increased in size until they became grandiose colonnaded halls, decorated with marble and mosaics. The heroic scale of these houses was typical of the Hellenistic age. (DNS)

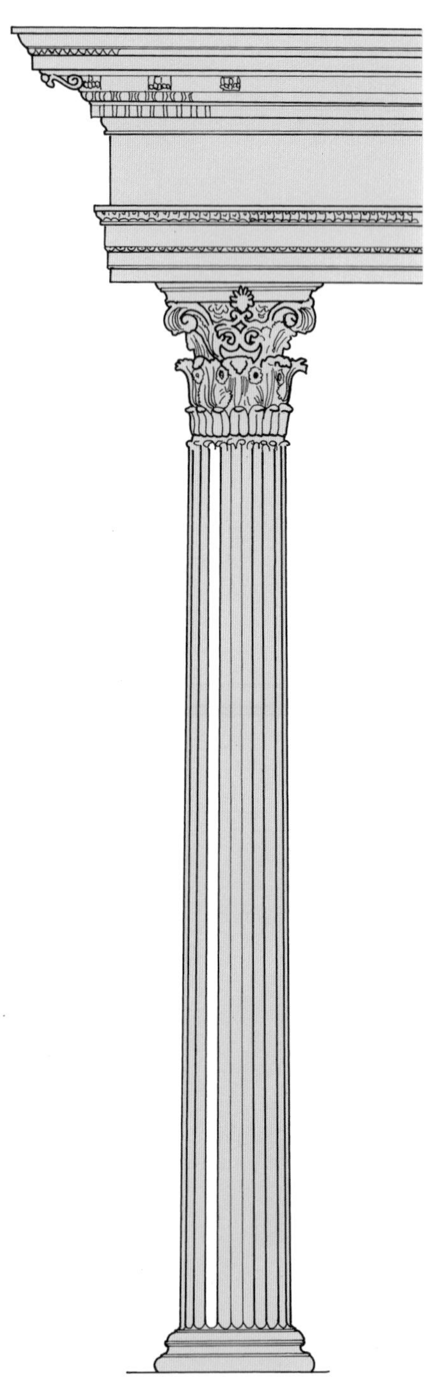

▲ *Corinthian Order. Although introduced to architecture in Classical times, this became a favourite with later Hellenistic architects. The capital has two circles of acanthus leaves, with four volutes projecting at each corner. Between the volutes, there are coiled tendrils and a flower-head. Slender and richly decorated, it expressed the mood of the last phase of Greek architecture.*

◀ *Rock-cut tomb, Petra, Jordan, mid-1st century* AD. *In its later developments Hellenistic architecture was cut and modelled according to the Greek order. The serenity of Classical architecture was exchanged for exaggerated and dramatic effects. Although the columnation remains regular, the entablature is shaped into independent forms, emphasized by the treatment of the gable.*

▲ *The Olympieion, Athens, begun in 174* BC. *The columns are 17.5m (56ft) high, close to the upper limits for columned structures in the ancient world. Athenian temples of the earlier Classical period were usually smaller. The Parthenon, for example, had columns only 10.5m (34ft) high.*

▲ *Theatre at Delphi, 350* BC. *The Greeks' preoccupation with geometrical form is evident in the design of this theatre. In spite of its ruined state, it was clearly once a spectacular and glamorous public space. Its position takes advantage of a naturally hollow hillside site, as was usual with Greek theatres.*

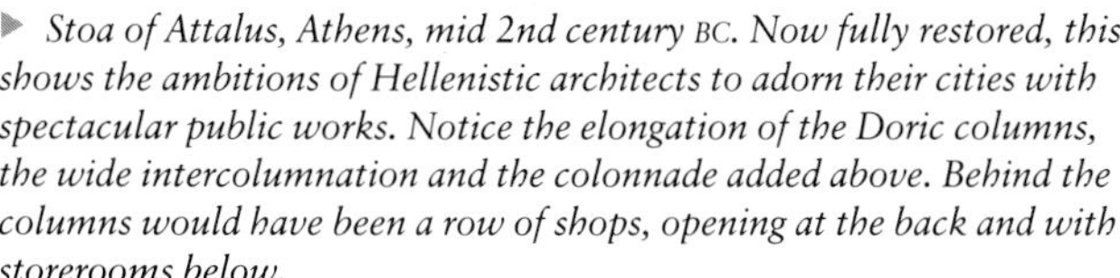

▶ *Stoa of Attalus, Athens, mid 2nd century* BC. *Now fully restored, this shows the ambitions of Hellenistic architects to adorn their cities with spectacular public works. Notice the elongation of the Doric columns, the wide intercolumnation and the colonnade added above. Behind the columns would have been a row of shops, opening at the back and with storerooms below.*

THE ARCHITECTURE OF ROME

Public and private Roman architecture from the 1st century BC

As Greek architecture ran its course from archaic to Classical, and from Classical to Hellenistic, a small community in central Italy grew to great power. While Alexander was conquering the East, Rome was establishing herself as a dominant force in Italy. Before the beginning of the 1st century, her armies had over-run Greece. As a result, the Romans became acquainted with cities of fine marble public buildings, splendid colonnaded urban spaces and luxurious private houses, all of which influenced their later architecture.

Architecture in Rome, then, had two sources – the attractive Greek heritage and the local Italian tradition reaching back to the Etruscans. From the Italian tradition came the exploitation of the arch, often in daring and ingenious ways. Also possibly derived from Etruscan architecture is an emphasis on the fronts of buildings, which became a key feature of Roman urban architecture. Etruscan architecture is also supposedly the source of the Tuscan Order, which together with the Corinthian became the favourite Order of Roman architects. It is a simplified Doric Order, well suited to the coarse limestone produced in Roman quarries. With both Orders Roman architects tended to use smooth, unfluted columns made from a single piece of stone. These polished monoliths were ideal vehicles to show off the colour and veining of the stone, and also encouraged the use of rare marbles.

Roman architects, in pursuit of dramatic effect, exploited the hilly slopes of Rome to produce buildings of overwhelming grandeur. Unlike the Greek model, the traditional Roman house did not create separate sets of rooms for men and women. The early Romans lived simple lives, in houses which consisted of an entry room or covered courtyard, called the *atrium,* and beyond it a room for the family, known as the *tablinum*. In later times it became the formal reception room, and beyond it a garden court with a range of columns, the *peristyle*, was introduced – an idea imported from Greece. Round the peristyle were added luxurious rooms for family use inspired by the domestic architecture of the Hellenistic world.

The Romans excelled in the creation of public buildings. Free from the restrictions of religious tradition, they could use their engineering ability to vault the wide spaces as they saw fit. At Rome they built a succession of colonnaded urban spaces *(fora)* which were a setting for great public halls (*basilicas*). The most spectacular buildings of all were the bath-houses *(thermae)* each covering a wide expanse of ground with domed and vaulted central buildings housing the heated baths, surrounded by gardens with gymnasia, lecture halls and libraries. The chief emphasis of Roman urban architecture was on grandeur – to glorify the empire and encourage its maintenance and perpetuation. Even the open spaces of the city were articulated by ceremonial arches and monumental columns or statues. (DNS)

▲ *Peristyle, Roman house, Pompeii, 1st century* AD. *Although the peristyle was originally a feature of Greek houses, the Romans adopted it with enthusiasm. Even quite modest houses often had a tiny garden courtyard, with the principal living rooms of the family opening out around it.*

▲ *Maison Carrée, Nîmes, France, 16* BC. *One of the best-preserved Roman temples, this is built in the Corinthian style. The temple can only be approached from the front, a characteristic feature of Roman design. The temple's monumentality is exaggerated by a high, solid base, or podium, which is 4m (12 ft) off the ground.*

◄ *The Colosseum, Rome,* AD *75. Built with stone facings on Roman concrete, it has an applied screen of columns added to Roman arches. From the base up, the Orders used are the Tuscan (a Roman version of Doric), Ionic and Corinthian. Notice the smooth monolithic shafts of the Roman columns in the foreground.*

◄ *The Pantheon, Rome,* c. AD *126. The greatest of all surviving temples, it demonstrates the great Roman structural achievement: mastery of the dome. The temple has a diameter of 43m (142 ft). The temple is illuminated solely by a circular, unglazed opening 8m (26 ft) in the crown. This famous 18th-century painting of the interior is by Pannini.*

▲ *The arch of Titus, Rome,* AD *81. Giant columns, obelisk and arches gave drama, focus and direction to the spaces which were a vital part of the design of the city. Their rich decoration of relief sculpture celebrating the triumphs of Rome was framed in architectural details based on the Greek Orders.*

IMPERIAL ROMAN ARCHITECTURE

The grand architecture of imperial Rome spreads across the Empire

It was not only the art of Greece which provided an example to be followed by the Romans. The military conquests of Alexander the Great demonstrated the possibilities of the expansion of a small state on an imperial scale. Like Alexander, the Romans had a trained and disciplined army, but unlike Alexander's successors they had a highly developed sense of national purpose and public duty which helped to make their imperial venture long lasting.

During the first century BC the Romans over-ran all the countries around the Mediterranean. To the west and north-west, Spain, France, England and Wales were subdued. To the north and north-east, they took Switzerland and the territory south of the Danube; to the east, they subdued Greece, the Black Sea coast and the territory that comprises modern Turkey, Syria, Iraq, Jordan and Palestine, while to the south they occupied Egypt and the North African coast as far as Morocco.

It was the Roman policy to bring to the peoples of this great Empire the benefits of peace and organized administration. As a visible confirmation of this end, they endowed their provinces with spectacular architectural works. These works were of two kinds. Firstly the practical forms, which included military defence work, forts, walls and towers as well as docks and harbours, warehouses and markets, and bridges, aqueducts, dams and irrigation works. Although primarily feats of engineering, these often also embodied architecture of great beauty and grandeur. Secondary elements of the great Greek-inspired architectural assemblage that constituted the city of Rome were duplicated in any Roman city of importance. Theatre and amphitheatre, basilica, temple and bath-house were built on a lavish scale and often set in colonnaded public spaces. After the collapse of the Empire, many of these buildings survived over the centuries that followed. Even when their marble casings were stripped away for other works, the enduring quality of their concrete core has preserved hints of the size and scale of these great public works.

In the Italian countryside beyond Rome and throughout the Empire at large could be found the domestic expression of Roman architecture. This was the Roman country house or villa. Apart from those few miraculously preserved in the lava of Vesuvius, the others have to be largely imagined from their appearance in contemporary wall paintings and descriptions in Roman literature. The villas, although sometimes grandiose, were closely related to their natural setting. Roman life was lived close to nature. As the writings of Cicero and Pliny make clear, it is the view to the fields, the hours of sunlight a room enjoys, the closeness of a terrace to the breaking waves of the sea, or the way the villa extends into the garden that were such important elements in the domestic architecture of the time. (DNS)

▲ *Pont du Gard, Nîmes, late 1st century* BC. *This aqueduct was part of a canal system built to carry fresh water to the city from springs 50km (30 miles) away. A lead-lined tunnel in the top row of arches carried the water across a river valley that lay between the source of the water and Nîmes.*

▶ *Basilica of Constantine, Rome,* AD *310-13. Basilicas were used as law and business centres and structurally form a link between Classical and Byzantine architecture. The huge scale of such public buildings made them powerful reminders of the benefits and security of being part of a great empire.*

▲ *Theatre at Orange, France, c.* AD *50. This is typical of the many theatres built in provincial towns all over the Empire. In front of rising tiers of semi-circular stone seats a permanent backdrop was built in the form of an architectural screen of the columns of different Orders in successive storeys. In front of this, the plays were performed.*

▲ *The sanctuary at Baalbeck, Lebanon, early 1st century to* AD *250. This illustrates the scale of building made possible by eastern wealth. Note the use of the Corinthian Order. The sanctuary forms part of an impressive temple complex, which stands as testimony to the power of Roman rule.*

THE EARLY CHRISTIAN ERA

Hardship, invasion and decline from the fourth century AD

As the Roman Empire distintegrated amid war and rebellion, living standards in western Europe declined precipitously, and so did the population – to a third of what it had been. Poverty and lawlessness were universal. Marauding pirates converged on the West from Africa, Scandinavia and the Russian Steppes, pillaging deep into the European heartland. The Eastern Roman Empire retained its central organization, and even expanded for a while under Justinian before being decimated by the Moslem armies. Though Christianity survived in what is now Greece and Turkey, centuries were spent simply battling for survival. For obvious reasons, the castle was the dominant architectural form in these times. Perched on crags and surrounded by defensive moats and battlements, the castle provided a base from which its occupants either plundered the countryside or beat off attacks from rivals.

Stone churches were rare in western Europe, and towards the East most builders reused the Roman materials close to hand, such as bricks and broken marble. The few churches that remain from this period are beautiful in their simplicity. Lacking in pomp and fashionable gloss, they are among the purest examples of architecture left to us. A good example is Germigny-des-Prés in central France, which was designed as a cube surrounded by four semi-cylindrical chapels with domical vaults. These perfect Platonic solids are juxtaposed in a lovely but unostentatious arrangement. It is an architecture of purity and meditation within the surrounding storm.

In Constantinople in the 4th century AD, Justinian's architects built the largest church ever known, Hagia Sophia, or the Church of Holy Wisdom, as massive and awe-inspiring as the pomp of his expanded Empire. The charming little church of SS. Sergius-and-Bacchus nearby was a model for the greater building.

When Charlemagne followed Justinian's example centuries later, and recreated the Roman Empire in the West, he naturally looked to the East for inspiration. His palace church at Aachen (AD 796–814) is also a centralized building, symmetrical in every direction but proportionally much taller. The soaring height foreshadows later developments in Western architecture.

The basis of this architecture was the wall. As in all earlier periods, it was the thickness and weight of the walls that kept the vaults, the massive domes and the roofs in their place; openings were simply holes cut through the walls. The bigger or the taller the building, the more massive the walls and the smaller the openings. It was a stable architecture – weighty, permanent and secure – in direct contrast to the uncertain times in which it was created. (JJ)

▲ *Santa Maria Fuori, Rome,* c. AD *370. This is a typical empire church, based on the basilica, where the judge sat under a domed apse and the people coming for justice stood in a colonnaded hall. Its architectural style accorded well with the beliefs of Christianity, in which believers were supplicants before Christ the judge. The repetitive columns help create a feeling of stability in uncertain times.*

▶ *SS. Sergius-and-Bacchus, Constantinople (now Istanbul),* c. AD *530. This has a symmetrical plan under a large dome, with a first-floor gallery. The central space revolves around the spectator, whose attention is drawn towards Heaven by the well-lit dome, while the aisles and first-floor gallery, only partly glimpsed, suggest unrecorded mysteries.*

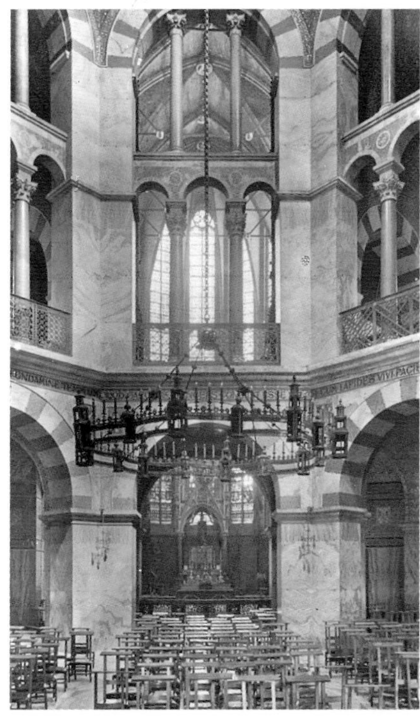

◀ *The Palatine Chapel, Aachen, AD 796–814. Domed and galleried like its Eastern prototypes, this building reflected Charlemagne's unfulfilled desire to recreate the glories of ancient Rome.*

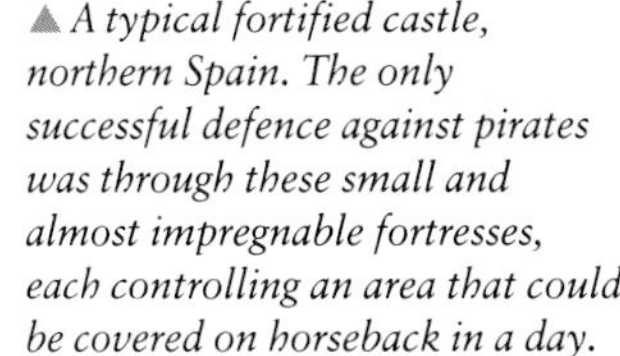

▲ *A typical fortified castle, northern Spain. The only successful defence against pirates was through these small and almost impregnable fortresses, each controlling an area that could be covered on horseback in a day.*

▼ *Private chapel, Germigny-des-Prés, Loire region, AD 806. The central square symbolized the earth, the circular dome the spirit, and the four flanking chapels the four gates and rivers of Paradise.*

ROMANESQUE AND BYZANTINE

The growth of the church as a refuge and sanctuary, 900-1150

Times began to improve in the West after 900. The climate was gradually becoming warmer, lengthening the growing season, and the population began to expand again. The raiders settled down, the Vikings being granted Normandy. The Arab sorties across the Mediterranean were curbed and the Huns turned to agriculture. Very slowly, people began to build again in stone, but the craft of masonry had to be learnt from the beginning.

The basic style of building did not change. St Etienne in Nevers, like Germigny-des-Prés, was assembled from the same cubes, cylinders and spheres, though it was considerably larger. The wall was still the predominant architectural element. Its impervious surfaces were emphasized by paintwork. The interior was dark and peaceful. Lighting came from hundreds of candles that threw uneven and mobile shadows onto the painted walls, a flickering light that brought the figures of saints and sinners to life.

It was in Durham, England, one of the most northerly towns in Christian Europe, that the first real move was made towards a new kind of architecture. Previously all stone vaults covering public spaces had been as plain surfaced as the walls, and the junctions between the curved surfaces were marked by a crease or groin. A year or two before 1100, ribs were laid under these groins for the first time. These transformed the ceiling from an undecorated plane into a patterned surface that was to trigger the most profound changes in architecture over the years. What had begun as a builder's device eventually became the inspiration for the whole building.

The rib is a line, whereas the groin vault and the walls below are surfaces. Sinuous and fluid, the presence of the rib encouraged builders to feel the space in a more graphic way. In time the shafts became thinner, the number of ribs were multiplied and the structural elements reduced until the interior became a playful web that both enlivened the surface and denied its mass. This turned out to be one of the most important characteristics of the later Gothic style.

Meanwhile, in the Greek Orthodox East, centralized domical and wall-based architecture had become firmly established, and was to continue up to our own day.

As prosperity grew trade increased, and a new class emerged – the merchants who lived in walled towns to protect their goods. Gradually their growing wealth enabled them to seek political independence from the bishops and princes who had ruled them. Municipal and democratic government was born in the medieval towns.

Man's final judgement at the hands of the all-male Trinity was expected to be severe, masculine and impartial, unsoftened by forgiveness, as the austere sculpture of Moissac shows. People were terrified by the belief that, no matter what one did, there was little chance of salvation for most. (JJ)

▲ *Monastery, Gracanica, Serbia, 1300s. Barrel vaults, centralized domes with lanterns, and squared unadorned walls characterized most Greek Orthodox churches. There was little change over the centuries under the bureaucratic and ritualistic regime of the Byzantine Empire.*

▼ *The nave, Durham Cathedral, 1096–1132. It was here, amongst the massive Norman columns and arches, that the ribbed vault was first introduced, heralding the new Gothic style, to be developed in France.*

▶ *The town walls, Carcassonne, 1100s, restored in the 1850s. Towns, like castles, were dotted across the landscape, separated by little more than trees and farms and the occasional hamlet. No-one, even in the largest city, was more than fifteen minutes walk from nature.*

▲ *The interior, St Etienne, Neuvy-Saint-Sépulchre, 1040s–1120s. In imitation of the church of the Holy Sepulchre in Jerusalem, many circular churches were built with annular (ring-shaped) barrel vaults and a central stone vault. This building has 11 columns with deeply sculpted capitals.*

▲ *Abbey church of St Pierre, Moissac. The figure of Christ in the Last Judgement Portal, c. 1120, is a literal interpretation of the apocalypse. It creates a remote, unbending and altogether terrifying image of the final judgement on life.*

▶ *Interior of choir, St Etienne, Nevers, c. 1070–1100. A painting of Christ in Judgement once decorated the dome, and the gold and blue painting must have made the upper part of the choir seem like Heaven itself. The thin columns below seem to push the eye of the beholder upwards into the celestial zone, but the little triforium helps to separate it from our own mortal one.*

THE MYSTIC AGE

The birth and development of the Gothic in Europe, 1130-1240

Around 1130 a significant change occurred in the Christian religion. The Virgin Mary was gradually introduced as the intercessor in Church stories of the soul's Judgement, thus bringing an element of feminine sympathy and forgiveness to a prospect that had hitherto been cloaked in terror. People suddenly had hope; they could be saved if they appealed to the Virgin. This seems to have released an enormous reservoir of positive and creative energy and vitality which transformed the architecture of a very traditional community for ever.

During the next century, mainly in the limestone region of northern France called the Paris Basin, five crucial inventions set the stage for all the architecture of the next three centuries. Firstly, shafts which had once been thick enough to support the load over them were transformed into decoration by being made incredibly thin (as at the Abbey of Braine). Like the rib-vaulted ceiling, the whole wall was now turning into a bundle of energy rather than mass. Secondly, thinness was emphasized by making buildings taller. Separated from their supporting role, these elegant ribs and shafts transformed the upper part of the interior into a suspended canopy. These churches were no longer safe citadels or even symbols of Paradise; the people of the 12th century held to a mystic faith that the church was not just *like* Heaven, it actually *was* God's promised world. Thus the vault was suspended from His realm, while the emaciated shafts became the tassels that hung from the corners of this Holy Tabernacle. No wonder the master mason, who was capable of creating this Paradise on earth, was so highly regarded.

The third innovation was stained glass. By replacing the painted wall with glass, previously inert matter became translucent. Although the glass was dark, and the weak light shed little illumination inside, it completely transformed the walls. The light seemed to come from within the very core of the stone, making it glow as though in proof that the church was the Celestial City.

As the mass of the inner wall surfaces was obliterated, the solidity of the outside was also broken up. The buttress, which had given additional support to the wall where it was most needed, was moved away to the perimeter of the building, and arches set between the two to transmit the loads to the outside. By moving the massive stonework needed to support the roof away from the windows, the amount of stone around the thinning shafts that hung from the vaults could be reduced and vast windows installed.

Tracery, first invented at Rheims around 1220, finally turned the window itself into another surface pattern. The combination of the canopied vaults, the thin elements ranging over the surface, the stained glass set in, the traceried windows and the flying buttresses, had the effect of dematerializing the masonry so the entire building appeared to belong to another mystic universe. All these inventions stretched technical expertise to the limits, and compelled masons to improve their skills greatly. (JJ)

▲ *Exterior of apse, Soissons Cathedral, c. 1180–1220. The flying buttresses are clearly a necessary part of the structure, and the ambulatory chapels fit neatly in between them. The windows have been made as wide as possible. A just balance has been struck, if only for a moment, between aspiration and earthiness.*

◄ *Eastern ambulatory and chapels, Rheims Cathedral, 1210–1220s. Protected by the vaults, even huge spaces appear humane in scale. These windows contain the first tracery, later to be filled with the spectacular stained glass that transformed the interiors into shimmering reliquaries.*

▲ *Flying buttresses, Chartres Cathedral, 1212–1224. These are in the corner between the south transept and the choir. The arches carrying the vault thrusts from the transept pass through those from the choir, an extraordinarily precise and sophisticated arrangement which shows how well the master masons understood the forces and thrusts within the building.*

◄ *Stained glass window, Chartres Cathedral, 13th century. Dramatic, intense and at the same time sombre, the intention of the windows was not to shed light on the interior, but to break up the mass of the wall. The glass became stonework transformed into energy that vibrated and glistened in the sun, almost speaking with the voice of God.*

► *Interior of the crossing, Abbey of Saint-Yves, Braine, c. 1180–1210. This is the first classic Gothic building, with spacious aisles, a continuous triforium and large clerestory windows. This is a confident style of architecture, in which there is no trace of the earlier need for reassurance.*

COURT GOTHIC

The spread of the Gothic tradition across Europe, 1230-1360

The extraordinary period of invention ended as the increasingly hot, dry climate burnt the fields and desiccated the northern French vineyards which had funded much of this work. As the population continued to increase in spite of worsening conditions, ordinary people became poorer and wealth was increasingly concentrated among the kings and nobility. Where earlier churches expressed the spirit of the abbeys and the towns, much French architecture of the next century or two originated in the Court. France was by now the most populous country in Europe, and her society and culture was the most prestigious. Foreigners eagerly adopted the new "Opus Francorum" and spread the Court Gothic style throughout northern Europe and Spain. In the 1240s one country after another either imported French masons or sent their men to France to emulate what had been done there. They were most excited by la Sainte-Chapelle, the royal chapel built by King Louis for the Crown of Thorns, a holy relic from the Byzantine Empire.

In England the solid Norman architecture was replaced with much lighter structures. Sometimes whimsical, seldom pompous, the new style appealed to the people over the Channel. The great traceried windows were so beguiling that whole walls of earlier churches were ripped out in order to make those glorious fantasies in thin stone and stained glass as large as possible.

Unlike their prototypes in France, little sense of structure permeates English Gothic. The thin ribs and shafts in the Paris area, although decorative, always relate to their structural purpose, with ribs running from one support to another and arches remaining as arches without being disguised by heavy decoration. In England, however, the master masons often let pattern run its own course with little regard for the purpose behind it; the French called it *cosmétique*.

The French style hardly touched Italy, as that region was so pervasively influenced by the many Roman remains. Milan cathedral was built only after a long controversy between French and German masons who had been brought in to advise the locals who had no experience of or even interest in the new style.

It is symptomatic of the times that the quantity of construction throughout the whole of Europe in the century before the Black Death of 1348 was hardly more than that in the Paris Basin alone during the previous century. The Black Death marks a crucial watershed in architectural development. The population had trebled since the turn of the millennium, yet there was still no shortage of virgin lands to till. The plague killed one in three people within a few short months, and the style of architecture changed to suit. (JJ)

▶ *Interior, Beauvais Cathedral,* c. *1220–1250. The incredible sense of height not only elevates the spirits, but gives the impression of separating this world from the next. It is helped by the glazing of the back of the triforium and the absorption of what was once a meditative zone into the heavenly clerestory.*

▲ *West façade, Léon Cathedral, Spain,* c. *1250–1303. The international triumph of the* Opus Francorum *produced magnificent clones throughout Europe, built either by masters from the north of France or by locals who had studied there.*

▶ *North transept, Wells Cathedral,* c. *1310–1319. Playfulness and decoration disguise both form and structure to create a casual, almost unreal, atmosphere. These great English buildings were more costume-dress than construction.*

▶ *Exterior, la Sainte-Chapelle, Paris, 1238–1244. Light, elegant and superbly crafted, this was one of the first examples of the Court style. King Louis, the only king to become a saint, possessed the wealth and reputation to inspire every court in Europe, and this little chapel became a model for the new style.*

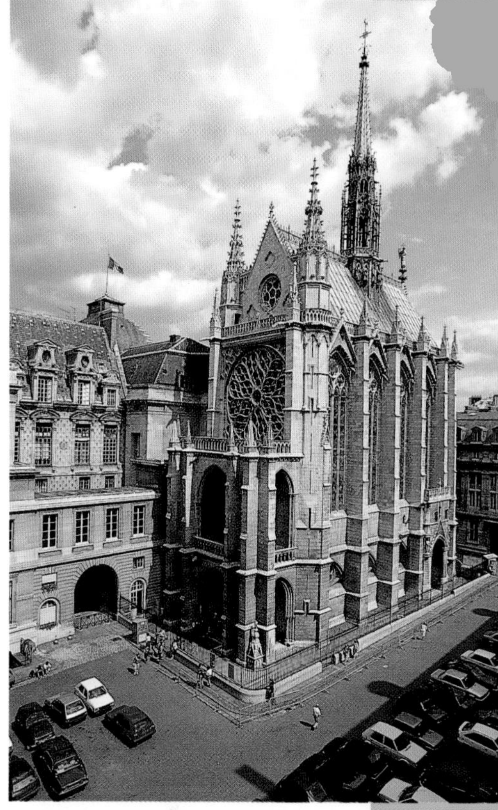

▲ *Interior, la Sainte-Chapelle, Paris, 1238–1244. The vaults restrain space in a seemingly effortless way, and the acres of stained glass, gilded arches and gem-encrusted spandrels give the whole interior the look of a gigantic reliquary.*

BOURGEOIS GOTHIC

Flamboyant virtuosity and the triumph of cleverness

The Perpendicular style, with its fan vaults and thin screen-like walls, was the English reaction to the Black Death. While the French were still crushed by the Hundred Years War (1337–1453) they built almost nothing, but when they did they created in the flamboyant style of St Maclou and the Beauvais Cathedral transepts stunning feats of architectural virtuosity.

In the East the centres of architectural excellence moved into the Hanseatic trading towns along the Baltic coast, and to the mining areas of central Europe. Everywhere masons developed a very sophisticated architecture, exquisitely carved and often looking as if it had been designed without much effort. The mouldings and the way different elements penetrated one another as they crossed over was handled with great intelligence – and ambiguity. The supreme clarity of earlier buildings was replaced with an uncertainty in both function and structure.

The work is both clever and humane, reflecting the new learning of the Reformation. Castles were no longer the pre-eminent lay construction; now there was a demand for colleges of learning, great and often ostentatious mansions and flamboyant town halls. Examples are the Oxford colleges, the house of the great Belgian banker, Jacques Coeur at Bourges, and the huge Hôtel-de-Ville at Rouen with its exuberantly decorated chimneys and an ornate court not much smaller than the king's at Fontainebleau.

The reduced population, now living off the best land, generated an economic boom, especially after 1450, from which the whole of Europe benefited. Both princes and merchants wanted clear, usable and interesting architecture that would extol their material virtues and comforts. They were not interested in the inspired mystic work of earlier times nor did they want sombre interiors in which the light only filtered lingeringly through dark stained glass. They wanted to be able to read their prayer books, and ordered grey glass that turned their churches into practical meeting places.

Before being replaced by the regenerated Classical style coming from Italy, medieval architecture went out in a blaze of excitement and virtuosity. Vaults became woven nets, often with ribs detached from the surface to be left suspended, functionless, in space. Sometimes they did not meet their shafts, but were cut off in mid-span. In the ceilings and tracery of Kutna Hora in Czechoslovakia the diamantine geometry was twisted and curved like shimmering flames of pure energy. There was little in this bravura display to quiet the pilgrim's soul, and decadence, as always, heralded an imminent change. (JJ)

▲ *Vault of nave, Saint Barbara, Kutna Hora, Czechoslovakia, c. 1530. After centuries of relative unimportance the Bohemian and Bavarian masons produced exciting late Gothic work some decades after the last examples had been completed in the West.*

◀ *Self-portrait of Adam Kraft, Saint Lorenz, Nuremberg, 1495. This typical medieval master mason proudly displays the tools of his trade, the pick and bolster. A confident man, he supports with ease the full weight of the priest delivering his sermon in the pulpit above.*

▲ *South transept rose window, Beauvais Cathedral, c. 1500–1520. This is movement for its own sake. The eye moves hither and thither across the surface, and even the fretwork within the centre throws the eye outwards, to be caught by the weaving flames before being brought inwards again.*

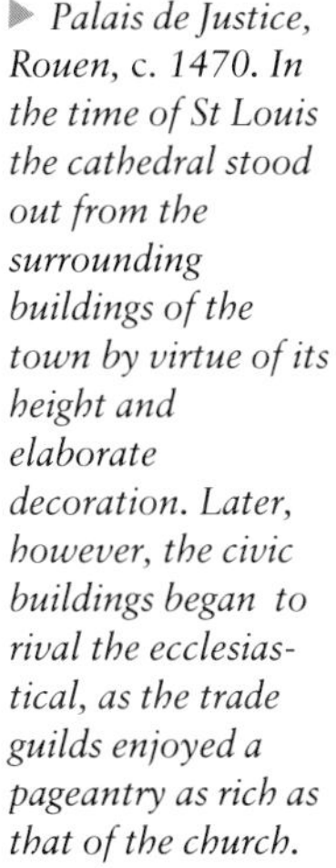

▶ *Palais de Justice, Rouen, c. 1470. In the time of St Louis the cathedral stood out from the surrounding buildings of the town by virtue of its height and elaborate decoration. Later, however, the civic buildings began to rival the ecclesiastical, as the trade guilds enjoyed a pageantry as rich as that of the church.*

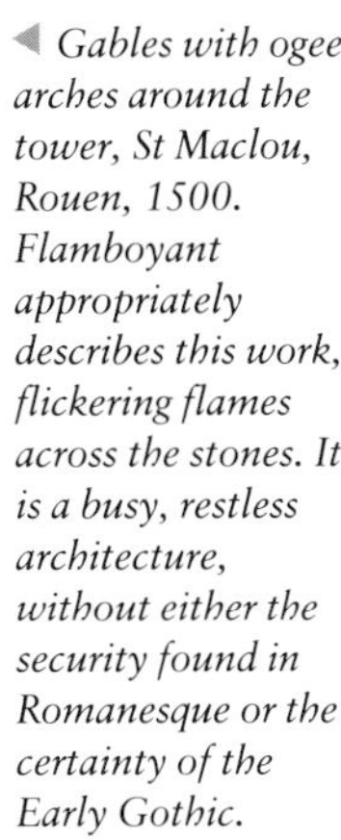

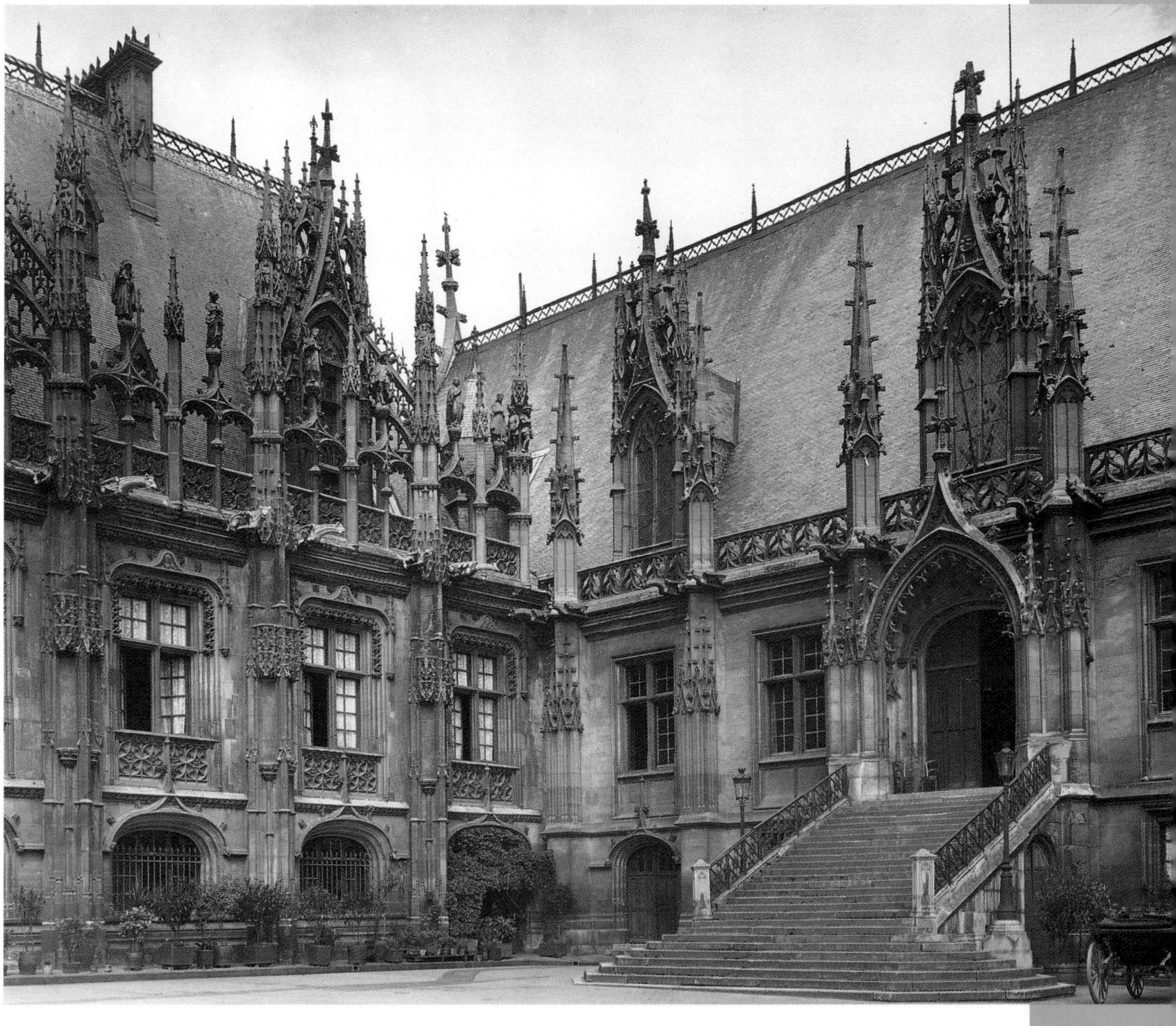

◀ *Gables with ogee arches around the tower, St Maclou, Rouen, 1500. Flamboyant appropriately describes this work, flickering flames across the stones. It is a busy, restless architecture, without either the security found in Romanesque or the certainty of the Early Gothic.*

PRE-COLUMBIAN ARCHITECTURE

The earliest civilizations in Central and South America

Pre-Columbian architecture reached its greatest level of achievement in two cultural zones: Meso-America (comprising much of Mexico and Central America) and the Andean region. It was a unique, symbolic architecture, always based around ceremonial centres. These two geographical environments were very different, but in both cases exterior spaces were adroitly exploited, with little attention paid to interior ones.

In Meso-America, a number of ceremonial sites were built between 1200BC and AD200, each under a theocratic regime. Among these ancient centres are La Venta and Cuicuilco, both with circular pyramids. From AD200, during what is known as the Classic Period, diverse cultures emerged in different stages and at different sites. They share several features, such as urban centres composed of buildings with taluses (sloping walls) and superimposed panels that included sloping front steps with struts. Two important settlements in the high plateau region are Xochilcalco and Teotihuacan, the latter a huge urban complex sustaining a considerable population. Further south the Zapotec centre of Monte Albán, and the Mayan's Palenque and Tikal, were also very important.

Typical of Meso-American architecture are plazas surrounded by monumental pyramids, crowned by temples or altars in honour of a particular cult. There were also palace complexes and areas for ball games, which had cult significance. With the rise of military and imperialistic states after AD900, ceremonial building complexes shared their importance with buildings representing power and trade. In the high plateau region Tula became the dominant city, and later on there was a series of kingdoms, among which the most outstanding was Tenochtitlán, the island capital of the Aztecs. Important sites in the south included Mitla, representative of the Mixtec culture, and Chichén Itza and Uxmal, two of a large number of Mayan cities.

The varied cultures of the Andean region were less developed, having no writing system. Their architecture was thus less elaborate and monumental, but their ceremonial centres are nevertheless full of interest. The greatest of the earliest civilizations flourished at Chavín de Huántar, in the 10th century BC. During the first eight centuries AD the Mochica culture extended far to the north; evidence of this can be seen in the adobe pyramids they built at different intervals. Tiahuanaco, a stone-built complex in the highest point of the central region, was the centre of a period of expansion about AD500. With the decline of the Tiahuanaco, the kingdom of the Chimu flourished; their capital, Chan-Chan, was built entirely of adobe. The most important central nucleus of the region was the Incan Empire, which rose to power around AD1200 and was based around the Central Andean Plateau. Cuzco, its capital, and other cities such as Ollantaytambo and Machu Picchu were of particular importance for defensive purposes. (LN)

▲ *Machu-Picchu, Peru, c. 15th century. The Incas, who controlled a huge area, built this as a border fortress, situating it on a mountain over 2000m (6000ft) high. The city walls were constructed in huge blocks of stone, carefully organized so that they could be fitted together without mortar. The complex consists of rooms for the nobility, military quarters, warehouses and agricultural terraces.*

▶ *Tikal, Guatemala, 3rd-9th centuries AD. The builders of this Maya ceremonial complex were clearly concerned with achieving symmetry in both the monumental buildings and in their location. A desire for vertical emphasis is manifested in the numerous pyramids, crowned with a temple and characteristic cresting. Particularly outstanding, due to their height and the fineness of their architecture, are Temple I, known as the Giant Jaguar, and Temple IV, both located in the Great Plaza of the North Acropolis.*

▶ *Teotihuacan, Mexico, 3rd-9th centuries AD. This was the most densely populated and influential ceremonial centre in Meso-America. The buildings are of monumental proportion and numerous palaces are located around the centre. Particularly noteworthy are the Pyramids of the Sun (the largest in America) and the Moon and the Citadel complex, which houses the Temple of Quetzalcoatl.*

◀ *Uxmal, Mexico, 9th-15th centuries AD. This great ceremonial centre is dominated by the Pyramid of the Prophet. Two palatial buildings, the Quadrangle of the Nuns and the Governer's Palace, are organized around central patios and lavishly decorated with fine carvings. The dominant motif is the mask of the raingod, Chac.*

▲ *Monte Albán, Mexico, 2nd-9th centuries AD. Monte Albán was built by the Zapotecs over a period of more than 2000 years. Its buildings are grouped around a large plaza. The earliest buildings (Temple of the Dancers and the Observatory) are undecorated; later structures are more elaborated and incorporate the use of lintels and a "scapulary" panel. There is also a court for playing the ancient ball game.*

SUB-SAHARAN AFRICA

Environment and resources in the shaping of Africa's traditional architecture

Unlike many other parts of the world, Africa has comparatively little surviving historical architecture. There are exceptions, like the extraordinary Coptic churches of Lalibela, Ethiopia, which were hewn out of the living rock by 13th-century African Christians. Early travellers from Europe gave accounts of African cities, including a 16th-century description of the splendid palace of Benin (Nigeria) with bronze birds on its steep roofs and plaques decorating its entrance. But a number of towns were destroyed by Europeans during the "struggle for Africa" in the late 19th century. One remarkable ruin is the walled "acropolis" of Great Zimbabwe, built in the 15th century. In plan it is not dissimilar to a large, traditional mud-walled compound but it owes its survival to the use of stone in its construction. Generally there is little stone building on the African continent, and the use of less permanent materials means that most examples of African traditional architecture have been built in this century.

It is evident that traditional African architecture is shaped by many inter-related factors: the climate, the physical environment, the material resources available, and the social systems and economies of its 5000 peoples. So, for example, the nomads who live in the desert, with its occasional oases and thin vegetation, have to move frequently with their flocks or camels. As permanent dwellings are inappropriate, many nomads live in tents, varying in profile, size and structure. The membranes are made of woven cloths, grass mats or skins, sewn together and stretched over pole frames, like the tents of the Tuareg tribes of the central Sahara. When the group moves to fresh, if sparse, grazing, the tents are dismantled and carried by the animals.

Not all nomads use tents: in the southern desert of the Kalahari, the San (Bushmen) live by hunting animals and gathering berries and roots, their dwellings being temporary brush shelters. There are hunter-gatherer peoples in the forests, like the Mbuti (pygmies) of Zaire, whose leaf-covered domes last for several months. Semi-sedentary cattle-herding peoples like the Maasai of Kenya build *manyattas* – circular settlements of dung-plastered huts. Some of the peoples of the African grasslands build large, hooded Council houses, covered with trimmed thatch. Others build with grass: the Zulu *indlu* is a domed dwelling like a finely made inverted basket.

Forest-dwelling farmers in Central and West Africa have the timber to make more substantial houses. Timber-framed roofs have rafters and purlins lashed in place with bark strips and then thatched; side walls of poles are packed with mud, their surfaces mud-plastered. Rectangular in plan, many have pitched or hipped roofs; so do the houses built by the Asante (Ghana) with layers of packed red earth. These dry rock-hard, though the walls are subject to erosion in the tropical rains. The extremes of climate often cause deterioration, but although many of the structures are impermanent, the building traditions endure, meeting the needs of their occupants. (PO)

▲ *Rock-hewn church, Lalibela, Ethiopia. One of 10 carved under the direction of King Lalibela of Ethiopia, the 13th-century patron of the Coptic church, the form of this church shows strong Classical and Moslem influences.*

▶ *(Above right) Palace building, Great Zimbabwe. Completed in the 15th century, the vast enclosure has walls nearly 10m (33ft) high which surrounded shrines, huts and granaries, overlooked by a massive conical tower.*

▲ *Ibibio village street, south-west Cameroon. The houses in this village in a forest clearing have pole frames, palm-thatched roofs, and deep eaves to provide shade. The villagers farm the nearby forest.*

▲ *Tuareg tents, near Agades, Niger. They include a tent cloth stretched from poles (foreground), a skin tent over a curved frame (right), and a domed tent, covered and screened with straw mats (beyond).*

▲ *Zulu kraal, South Africa. The former traditional domed, grass-covered dwelling is being replaced by the more popular thatched, cylindrical house type which is widely distributed.*

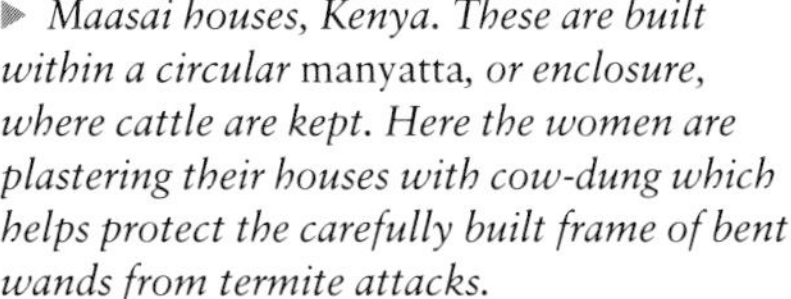

▶ *Maasai houses, Kenya. These are built within a circular* manyatta, *or enclosure, where cattle are kept. Here the women are plastering their houses with cow-dung which helps protect the carefully built frame of bent wands from termite attacks.*

AFRICAN SYMBOLISM

Decoration and meaning in African indigenous architecture

Cylindrical dwellings with conical thatched roofs are widely spread in Africa, grouped round cattle *kraals* in the south or scattered in farms in the east. Beautiful examples of mud architecture can be found in the West African savannah. The Kassena of Burkino Faso hand-mould their huts like pottery, linking them with curving walls. Such compounds are clusters of similar one-roomed sleeping huts for the extended families, each wife having her own kitchen and granaries. Smooth-plastered houses may be boldly decorated in earth colours. Among many societies the decorations have religious significance, depicting deities or symbolizing values, as in the sacred Mbari shrines of the Ibo, resplendent with sculptured figures. Further north in Nigeria, the Hausa display their status, wealth or devotion by enriching the façades of their houses with moulded and painted motifs that are part-Islamic, part-popular art in style.

The full significance of many mouldings and paintings is not evident: a crocodile could represent, say, a lineage or a mythical clan ancestor. Often there is no decoration to symbolize such beliefs, but they may be expressed instead in the arrangement of the compound. Numerous cultures are hierarchical: stratified by age, with male peer groups moving to eventual authority as elders and living together in communal houses. Kings like the Kabaka of Buganda had royal residences; the great palaces of the Yoruba chiefs were one-storeyed and situated close to the housing of the commoners, symbolic both of power and of their relation to their people.

Symbol systems are frequently expressed in architecture: few are more profound than that of the Dogon, the cliff-dwelling desert farmers of Mali. Although apparently random, the plan of their settlements is anthropomorphic, the men's Council house symbolizing the head, the Clan houses representing the chest, and the altars signifying the genitals. Dwellings of other tribes, like those of the Fali of northern Cameroon, are no less symbolic of their beliefs.

The conversion of some African peoples to Islam led to the adoption of square plans under North African influence, and the building of mosques. Many of these mosques are of a type particular to sub-Saharan Africa, with moulded forms and bristling pinnacles. Conversion to Christianity meant the suppression of many animist beliefs and the building of churches, some made of corrugated iron despatched from Britain. There have been many pressures for change – urban, industrial and commercial development have had their impact on African cities. But in spite of the noise, the pollution and the congestion, a lively popular art thrives on many buildings.

Traditional building exists in rural areas throughout Africa. The architecture is seldom monumental or deliberately imposing, but instead offers a valuable alternative: responsive to climate, built of local materials, appropriate to local economies, modest in scale, often beautiful in form and decoration, expressive of the values, and symbolic of the many and diverse cultures that create it. (PO)

▲ *Decorated entrance, Hausa merchant's house, Kano, northern Nigeria. This marks the transition from public to private spaces. The motif is the* daga *or the continuous knot, which is symbolic of eternal life.*

▶ *(Above right) Protective* Nommo, *or ancestral figures, are carved on the door to the home of a Dogon village headman. On the right of the wall the* kanaga *device symbolizes simultaneously a mythical crocodile and a bird, and the double placenta from which good and evil are believed to come.*

▶ *Dogon village, Mali. The Dogon live on the rock-fall of the Bandiagara escarpment in the Mali desert. House compound and village layouts suggest an ancestral being, with granaries and stables signifying arms and legs.*

▼ *Cinema, Zaria, Nigeria. It is decorated with brightly painted patterns, the designs deriving from traditional secular motifs often used on house façades.*

◀ *Ancient caravan entrepôt, Oualata, Mauretania. The Kounta women of Oualata paint their courtyard walls with arabesque designs. Oualata is built of stone, though the walls are rendered with earth.*

EARLY INDIAN ARCHITECTURE

The Hindu, Jain and Buddhist traditions of the Indian subcontinent

Throughout the history of civilization India has commanded a central position in the world trade routes, which acted as arteries for the exchange of ideas and information between East and West. Indian lotus pattern motifs, for example, can be seen in the famous Persian palaces of Persepolis (5th to 6th centuries BC) and evidence of Greek styles of architecture and decoration is to be found in the Buddhist caves at Gandhara, North Western India (3rd century AD).

Some of the earliest architectural remains in India date back to the Indus Valley civilization, from about 3000 BC. Their two capital cities – Mohenjo-daro and Harappa – were carefully planned on an orthogonal grid with large communal buildings and grain stores built out of baked brick. Later, when the Indus Valley civilization was destroyed, apparently by the Aryan invaders from the north around 1500 BC, a new religious culture – Hinduism – came into being and with it a change in the architectural style. The myriad of gods and goddesses mentioned in the *Rig Vedas* (ancient Sanskrit hymns) embellish Hindu temples all over India.

Hinduism embraces an infinite number of religions, the most significant being the Jain and Buddhist faiths which emerged in the 5th century BC. Monolithic stone constructions with delicate paintings and sculpture are characteristic of Buddhist architecture. The domed stupas of the Buddhist monuments are easily recognizable and some of the earliest examples of this form are to be found in Sanchi in central India, dating from the 3rd century AD. The processional route through intricately carved gateways and finally circling the stupa is a theme which continued and spread with the faith to South East Asia, China and Japan.

Jain and other Hindu temples are generally more intricate in design than the Buddhist ones. The geometry and proportion of the architecture is very sophisticated, with several levels of meaning. For example, perambulatory routes through a central axis punctuated with gateways eventually lead to a small, dark inner sanctum (the *garbagriha* or womb chamber), which is located under a monolithic tower (*shikara*), representing the cosmic sacred mountain of the Hindu faith. The sculptures and patterns that cover these temples do not obscure the complex three-dimensional geometry of the basic temple design but enhance the composition rather like chords in music.

Hindu, Jain and Buddhist traditions were the main forces shaping the architecture of the subcontinent until the spread of Islam. Regional styles developed and reflected the stability and strength of the rulers, while trade continued to be an important stimulus. The different sects and religions always coexisted despite sporadic religious purges, and the dominating religion of the ruling classes did not preclude the existence of other religions. The diversity of religions and subcultures which coexisted resulted in an architectural style which drew on an immensely varied palette for its inspiration. (YS)

▲ *Khajuraho, Central India, 9th-12th centuries AD. There are some 25 temples still standing at Khajuraho, the erotic sculptures on which are world famous. There is great variety and boldness in the portrayal of the various coital positions combined with very delicately detailed expressions.*

◀ *Ajanta Caves, the Deccan, Central India, 2nd-1st centuries* BC *and 5th century* AD*. A series of breathtaking manmade caves housing temples and monasteries in the horseshoe sweep of a rocky outcrop. The rock has been sculpted out to imitate timber forms of construction and decoration. Many of the caves have spectacular painted scenes depicting court life with exquisite detail.*

▶ *Dilwara, Mount Abu, Western India 11th-15th centuries* AD*. Dilwara, an important place of pilgrimage for Jains, has spectacular marble and stone temples. The complex geometric forms are adorned with finely carved sculptures and intricate patterns.*

▲ *Borobudur, Central Java, Indonesia. The immense stone Buddhist shrine designed with a four-square base and elaborately carved stone archways and staircases is thought to have been built at the end of the 8th century* AD*. The geometric system ordering the architectural forms is Indian in derivation.*

▶ *Stupa 1, Sanchi, Madhya Pradesh, Central India, 3rd-1st centuries* BC *and 5th century* AD*. This, the largest and earliest stupa, has been enlarged and added to many times. It has fine processional gate-ways, balustrades and railings. The stone carving imitates the timber construction which is a common feature in many Buddhist monuments.*

LATER INDIAN ARCHITECTURE

Commerce and craftsmanship: monuments of Indian architecture from AD 1000

The most significant development in Indian architecture this millenium was precipitated by the spread of Islam after AD 1000, although the extent of Moslem dominance varied tremendously. There were many different regional kingdoms, but not all had Moslem rulers, and each region developed its own distinctive style of architecture. Jain and other Hindu religions coexisted with Islam and some of the finest temples and palaces were built during the height of Moslem rule. They include those in the 18th-century city of Jaipur, Rajasthan, and the temples in the city of Patan, Gujarat, dating from the 16th century. New cults and religions also emerged with their own architectural forms of expression, such as the Golden Temple at Amritsar (from 1579) – the sacred centre of the Sikh religion.

The architectural achievements during Moslem suzerainty were remarkable. The earliest significant monument was the Qutb Minar complex in Delhi (*c.* 1197) but undoubtedly the finest structures – including the Taj Mahal (1632–54) – were built during the period of Mughal rule under Shah Jahan.

Often temples were dismantled and the elements reassembled to build mosques, such as the one at the Qutb Minar complex. Typical of early mosque architecture are large *hypostyle* halls, with their forests of columns, and enclosed courtyards. Vaulted construction was also developed and one of the largest clear-span structures in the world was built in Bijapur (Deccan) where the dome above Muhammad Adil Shah's tomb spans some 40m (125ft). The sensuous animal and human carvings of Hindu temples were replaced with carefully proportioned calligraphy, arabesque and vegetal decorative forms, and new decorative techniques such as external ceramic tile and *pietra dura* were developed.

Some of the most significant examples of non-Moslem palatial and temple complexes can be seen at Vijayanagar (1336–1565). Further south the temple building tradition continued at sacred sites like Madura and Srirangam. Although Sri Lanka was the only corner of the subcontinent where Buddhism retained its dominance, magnificent Buddhist monuments were erected in South East Asia.

By the 17th century, European influence on Indian architecture had grown with the increase of trading activities of the Portuguese, French, British and Dutch. The Europeans introduced a predominantly classical architectural language into their factories and official buildings which incorporated elements of the Greek Orders. Under Portuguese influence in Goa a more flamboyant Baroque style developed, as can be seen in the Church of the Immaculate Conception (1541) in Panaji. In 1858 the British East India Company ceded control to the British Government and the grand imperial monuments of the ensuing Raj were built in a curious Anglo-Indian style, best described as a mix between the Albert Hall and the Taj Mahal. (YS)

▲ *Qutb Minar, Delhi, 1199. The majestic 72.5m (220 ft) high minar in finely carved red sandstone is part of a mosque and tomb ensemble erected by one of the first major Moslem rulers in Northern India. Most of the stone elements for the buildings were re-used from the Hindu temple which had stood on the site.*

▶ *Fatehpur Sikri, Agra, Northern India, 1569–74. The city – commissioned by Akbar, the founder of the Mughal Empire – was built in less than a decade using highly organized prefabricated methods of construction. The architecture can be compared to the tented forms of the mobile Mughal encampments. Here the tent poles and awnings are transcribed into red sandstone.*

▶ *Taj Mahal, Agra, 1632–54. One of the wonders of the world, the Taj Mahal was constructed as a tribute of love from the Mughal Emperor Shah Jahan to his wife Mumtaz Mahal (who lies buried here). It is remarkable for the perfect proportions of the main structure and its ancillary buildings, the paradise garden setting, the complex hydraulic devices and the fine* pietra dura *decoration.*

▼ *Sidi Said Mosque, Ahamadabad, Gujarat, Western India, 1515. The craftsmanship of the Gujarati stonemasons is legendary. In their hands, stone could be turned to lace as these mosque panels demonstrate. With the absorption of Gujarat into the growing Mughal Empire, many of the stonemasons moved to the new Mughal capitals, such as Fatehpur Sikri.*

▲ *Tomb of Rukn-i Alam, Multan, Northern India (Pakistan), 1320-24. The octagonal plan, carved brickwork, glazed external tiles and carved woodwork make this Moslem tomb one of the most elegant and advanced constructions of the time.*

EARLY ISLAMIC ARCHITECTURE

Mosques, madrassahs and palaces under the early caliphates

The religion of Islam was born in the deserts of Arabia in AD 622 with the revelations of the prophet Mohammed and embodied in the Koran, the Holy Book seen by Moslems as the source of divine knowledge, the law, and the correct way of living. After the death of the Prophet Mohammed in AD 632, Arab armies expanded this new proselytizing religion by campaigns against the decaying Byzantine empire and the vast eastern territories of the Sassanian Empire. Within fifty years the banner of Islam held sway over lands stretching from Central Asia to Spain. The Umayyad caliphate, established in Damascus in AD 660, undertook the first great Islamic building projects such as the Dome of the Rock in Jerusalem AD 690 and the Friday Mosque in Damascus (AD 709). These projects drew heavily on inherited regional building traditions, using predominantly stone architecture and mosaic tile decoration. During the 8th century faith in Islam united peoples of diverse religious, ethnic and cultural backgrounds. Regional styles of Islamic architecture evolved, influenced by climate, available construction materials and pre-Islamic building traditions. Craftsmen were attracted to centres of political power and there was a cross-fertilization of ideas via the silk routes that linked the Mediterranean with Asia.

The Abbasid caliphate that supplanted the Umayyad was centred in Baghdad (AD 754–1258) and saw a flowering of building activity including the circular city in Baghdad in AD 762; the city of Samarra, in AD 836; the Friday Mosque of Al Mutawakkil, Samarra, in AD 847; and the Al Mustansiriyah Madrassah, Baghdad, in 1233. Architecture was mainly brick with carved terracotta and stucco decoration.

A characteristic of Islamic architecture is the importance given to the expression of enclosed space; mosques, madrassahs, houses and palaces were designed around courtyard spaces. Formal elements such as domes, iwans (vaulted porches), arcades, arches and minarets were used on many different types of building to define and connect interior space. During the 9th century a typical North African style of mosque architecture evolved, consisting of arcaded aisles surrounding an open rectangular courtyard, one side of which was developed as a horizontal prayer hall (as in the mosque of Kairouan, AD 836, and at Ibn Tulun, Cairo).

The weakening of the Abbasid caliphate led to converted nomadic Turkish tribes from Central Asia setting up independent Seljuk states in Persia (1038-1194) and Anatolia (1070–1308). The iwan (large vaulted porch), the monumental tomb-tower and the cylindrical minaret were introduced. An important development was the introduction of the four-iwan courtyard plan, which became universal for mosques and madrassahs. There was an emphasis on large domed interiors, complex brick patterning (as in the Tomb of the Samanids, Bukhara, 10th century) and carved terracotta and turquoise glazing. These elements were interpreted in stone in Seljuk Anatolia (at the Mosque of Ala-ad-Din, Konya, 1156). (GM)

▲ *Friday Mosque of Al Mutawakkil, Samarra, AD 847. The largest mosque in the Islamic world had a huge rectangular courtyard and prayer hall surrounded by monumental bastioned walls exhibiting a recessed frieze. The 50-m (164-ft) high spiral minaret resting on a square base was influenced by the ruined ziggurats of past Mesopotamian societies.*

▶ *Friday Mosque, Cordoba, AD 784. The height of this prayer hall is achieved by a subtle combination of antique columns supporting raised piers from which spring a double tier of horseshoe arches using alternating brick and stone voussoirs. A forest of arcades recalls the endless repetition of a palm grove.*

◀ *Mosque of Ibn Tulun, Cairo, AD 876. Monumental brick arcades of alternating ogival arches and piers with applied columns surround a square courtyard. The exquisite stucco frieze, crenellated parapets and spiral staircase of the minaret reveal the influence of Mesopotamian craftsmen. The domed structure covering the ablution fountain is 13th-century Mamluk.*

▶ *Friday Mosque, Damascus, AD 709–715. The earliest mosque of significance in the Islamic world uses green and gold mosaic extensively. This pre-Islamic Byzantine decorative tradition depicts towns, landscapes and vegetal motifs. The horizontal two storey arcades surrounding the* sahan *(courtyard) contrast effectively with the verticality of the minaret set on axis with the main prayer hall opposite.*

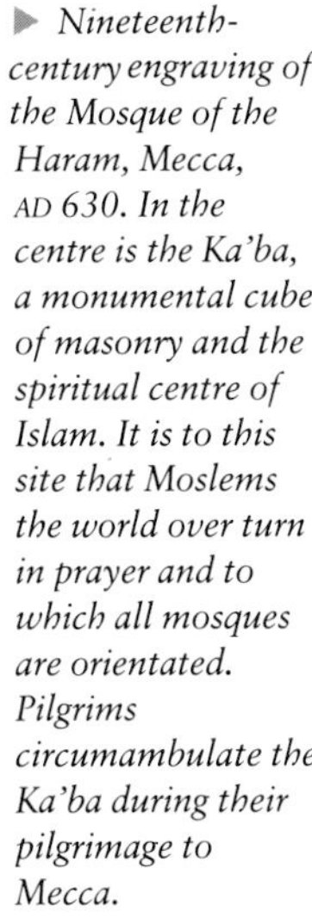

▶ *Nineteenth-century engraving of the Mosque of the Haram, Mecca, AD 630. In the centre is the Ka'ba, a monumental cube of masonry and the spiritual centre of Islam. It is to this site that Moslems the world over turn in prayer and to which all mosques are orientated. Pilgrims circumambulate the Ka'ba during their pilgrimage to Mecca.*

LATER ISLAMIC ARCHITECTURE

Elaborate splendour and symbol in Islamic form and decoration

The great Islamic civilizations of the 13th century were almost completely destroyed by the Mongol invasions and the ravages of Timur (or Tamerlane). In central Asia, the rule of Shah Rukh, Timur's successor, began a brilliant era with the building of the Madrassah of Ulugh Beg, Samarkand in 1417, Gur-i-Emir, Samarkand in the 15th century and the Kalyan Mosque, Bukhara in 1514.

Under the Il Khan dynasty established by the Mongols in Persia, the use of colour in buildings developed, in the form of painted glazed tiles reflecting a characteristically Persian emphasis on surface as opposed to structure.

In Spain, before the Islamic states fell to the *Reconquista* in 1492 the Nasrids of Granada (1248–1492) had evolved an architecture of elaborate decorative effects using stone, stucco, brick, painted tiles, multi-lobed arches and muqarnas (stalactite vaulting), which was brilliantly displayed in the Alhambra Palace (13th-14th centuries).

Orthodox Islam proscribes the use of human imagery in art. This together with the nomadic Arab's fascination with abstraction and rhythm as demonstrated in their poetry and music, led to the creation of a distinctive Islamic style of decoration in buildings. Geometric ornament was used to frame and border major architectural elements. The cursive vine of pre-Islamic origin evolved into the arabesque: infinite patterns developed from repeated spirals. Walls, vaults and domes were covered in geometric and arabesque decoration and muqarnas, dissolving tectonic forms and enhancing the feeling of unlimited space. The symbolism of the Arabic script inspired the art of calligraphy, and inscriptions from the Koran were used as important decorative elements in mosques throughout the Islamic world, using the geometric Kufi and the cursive Nashki scripts.

The Ottoman empire, founded in 1281 in Anatolia and centred in Constantinople (now Istanbul) after the conquest of the city in 1453, was to absorb most of the western Islamic world until the 20th century. The concept of the hemispherical dome built over a rectangular chamber and buttressed by half domes and smaller apsidal domes resulted in the characteristic Ottoman mosque with its colonnaded courtyards and tall slender stone minarets. In Constantinople, SINAN produced a brilliant diversity of mosque designs. His mosques, together with the use of Iznik tiles in such magnificent complexes as the Topkapi palace and the 17th-century Sultanahmet Mosque, characterize Ottoman architecture.

In Persia the Safavid dynasty (1501–1732) made their capital at Isfahan, creating the Masjid-i-Shah in 1612, the Friday Mosque in the 17th century and the Sheikh Lutfallah Mosque in 1617. Here an architecture of iwans, domes, arcades and minarets displayed radiant mantles of turquoise, blue and yellow glazed tiles combining calligraphy, geometric and arabesque decoration. (GM)

▲ *Gur-i-Emir (Timur's Tomb), Samarkand, 15th century. Timur's mausoleum formed part of a complex of buildings originally flanked by four minarets. The ribbed dome is raised high on a drum over an octagonal chamber containing the cenotaph. A Kufi inscription surrounds the drum.*

◄ *Qansuh al-Ghuri, Cairo, 1504. This Mamluk caravanserai surrounds a large rectangular courtyard. The lower arcaded floors were used as stores and workshops. Upper floors were three-storey apartments for travelling merchants and pilgrims. The timber mashrabiyah screens for ventilation and privacy are set in stone walls.*

◄ *Madrassah-Mosque-Mausoleum of Sultan Hasan, Cairo, 1356. This Mamluk complex is surrounded by a fortress-like wall. The entrance portal with its muqarnas vault is angled to enter a four-iwan central courtyard, which is cubic in form.*

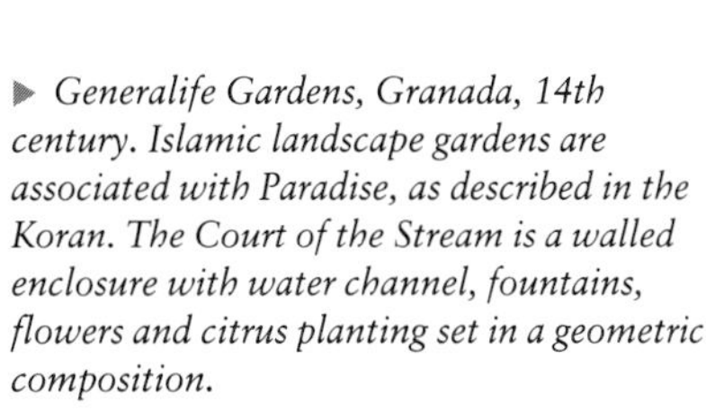

► *Generalife Gardens, Granada, 14th century. Islamic landscape gardens are associated with Paradise, as described in the Koran. The Court of the Stream is a walled enclosure with water channel, fountains, flowers and citrus planting set in a geometric composition.*

◄ *Court of the Lions, Alhambra Palace, Granada, 13th and 14th centuries. This courtyard, as an outdoor living space, uses axial water channels to link internal spaces. These are partly enclosed by arcades and porticoes of colonnettes supporting exquisitely carved, lace-like arches with perforated muqarnas decoration, effecting a subtle transition from form to space and light.*

► *Masjid-i-Shah (Shah Mosque), Isfahan, 1612. This four-iwan mosque displays a brilliantly composed sequence, from its skewed entry gate flanked by minarets leading to a prayer hall with iwan arch, minarets, and pointed dome set on a drum. The main elements are covered in an array of arabesque patterns in turquoise, blue and yellow tiles.*

JAPANESE ARCHITECTURE

From the very earliest shrines to concrete, glass and steel

Japan has a distinct architectural tradition despite its debt to foreign cultures. What Japan has learned from others, it has re-interpreted in ways more congenial to the national sensibility. In particular, there is a feeling of oneness with nature evident both in the close integration of buildings with the landscape and in the direct expression of materials. No buildings that predate the introduction of mainland culture survive, but the oldest Shinto shrines, such as Ise Shrine, are believed to preserve an ancient architectural style.

Seventh-century Japan was enamoured of the civilization of the Asian continent, and palaces, residences and Buddhist temples, not to mention entire cities, came to be built in the Chinese style. Subsequent centuries, however, witnessed a process of Japanization. In the case of the aristocratic residence, what had started as a very formal, axial arrangement evolved into the *shinden*-style residence of the 10th century, an asymmetrical ensemble of interconnected pavilions overlooking a garden centred around a pond.

The interiors of temples and residences grew more complex as spaces to accommodate worshippers and visitors developed. The *shoin*-style residence, which was perfected in the late 16th century, possessed rooms completely floored with rush *(tatami)* mats and defined by sliding doors and paper-covered screens, also sliding. The rooms and the gardens, mediated by verandas and overhanging roofs, were spatially continuous. The *sukiya* style, a more informal variant of the *shoin*, incorporated features of the rustic tea-ceremony hut such as earthern walls and barked wood columns. The *sukiya*-style residence is what is generally thought of today as the traditional Japanese house.

After the 1868 Meiji Restoration, Japan opened itself to the West as wholeheartedly as it had to China in earlier times. Japanese architects gradually mastered Western building technology and design, and produced Neo-Classical landmarks. In the 20th century, even as eclecticism slowly gave way to Modernism, there were demands for an indigenous architectural style. During the 1930s and 1940s – a period of militant nationalism – the Imperial Crown style provided otherwise conventional modern buildings with traditional pitched roofs. Again, in the 1950s and early 1960s Japanese architects, disillusioned with strict Functionalism, attempted to suggest the look of traditional architecture with varying degrees of sophistication.

In the 1960s, as the Japanese economy underwent intensive growth, a movement called Metabolism advanced futuristic proposals for new cities organized around enormous infrastructures. The energy crisis of 1973 was only one of the factors that finally led to general disenchantment with such ambitious schemes. Since the 1970s, the most creative Japanese architects, in reaction to Metabolist hubris, have tended to work at the scale of individual buildings. Their works do not resemble traditional architecture in detail or overall form, but suggest continuity with the past through such means as an integration with nature and the rejection of ornamentation. (HW)

▲ *The Inner Shrine of Ise Shrine, Ise, Mie Prefecture. The shrine is dedicated to the legendary ancestress of the imperial family, and preserves the style of ancient Shinto shrines. It has been periodically reconstructed on alternate adjoining sites since the 7th century. The most recent reconstruction was in 1973.*

▲ *Katsura Detached Palace, Kyoto. This 17th-century villa for imperial princes is considered the finest example of* sukiya*-style architecture. The main building is notable for its elegant geometry and unpainted wood members. It and the ancillary pavilions and belvederes are visually integrated with an extensive tour-style garden.*

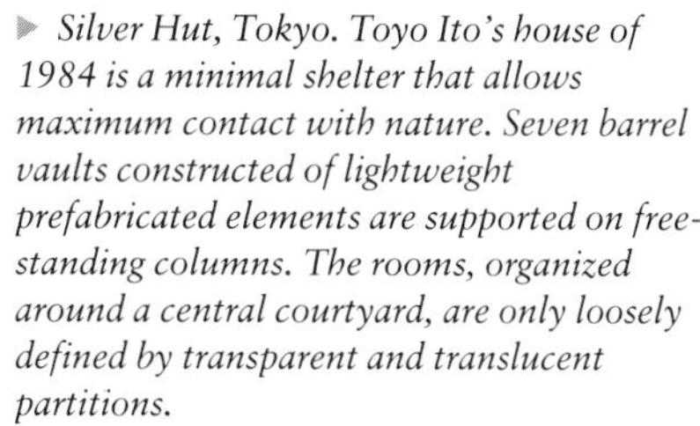

▶ *Silver Hut, Tokyo. Toyo Ito's house of 1984 is a minimal shelter that allows maximum contact with nature. Seven barrel vaults constructed of lightweight prefabricated elements are supported on free-standing columns. The rooms, organized around a central courtyard, are only loosely defined by transparent and translucent partitions.*

◀ *Church on the Water, Tomamu, Hokkaido. Designed by Tadao Ando and built in 1988, this is a wedding chapel. Ando's stark and uncompromising space, defined entirely by exposed concrete, steel and glass, brings people face to face with nature and could be said to express not so much Christian as pantheistic beliefs.*

◀ *The western precinct, Horyuji, Ikaruga, Nara Prefecture. Probably dating from the late 7th century, this includes some of the oldest wooden buildings in the world. Based on the style of China's Six Dynasties period (*AD *220–589), Horyuji nevertheless has an asymmetrical site plan that is believed to be a Japanese innovation.*

▶ *Yoyogi Gymnasiums, Tokyo. The buildings were designed by Kenzo Tange with engineer Yoshikatsu Tsuboi for the 1964 Olympics. The post-war search for a modern architectural idiom that evoked traditional forms culminated in these two suspended structures with sweeping curves and asymmetrical plans.*

THE CHINESE TRADITION

The principles of Chinese religious and secular architecture

Both grand and domestic Chinese buildings have used the courtyard plan almost universally since the Bronze Age (*c.* 1700 BC). Temples and palaces consisted of a series of linked courtyards and even the smallest domestic buildings had a single walled courtyard. In domestic architecture the courtyard was important since it protected the family's property and enclosed its women (who were not supposed to venture beyond the home according to the rules of Confucian morality). It also symbolized the inward-looking nature of family worship, based on the ancestral shrine in the central bay of the main, northern wing of the building.

From the very earliest period, demonstrated by the excavated timber remains at Hemudu dating from *c.* 5000 BC, Chinese architecture relied upon timber as its major structural material. The characteristic stepped post-and-lintel form of building developed quickly. Miniature ceramic house-models, made to place in tombs, and stone carved pillars *(que)* of the Han dynasty (206 BC to AD 220) indicate that the bracketing that was to characterize later building was already developed. To protect the timbers from the rain, the roof eaves projected beyond the pillars and were supported on brackets placed on top of the columns, as can be seen in the late 7th-century AD Nan chan Temple. Subsequent subtle changes in style were limited, mainly affecting roof forms and decoration and the size and number of brackets. In 1103, the *Ying zao fa shi* (Building Standards) were published by the Imperial Ministry of Public Works. This set out the proportions of Song brackets; derived from one part of the bracket these determined a building's relative size.

The buildings within the walled enclosures were erected on a stone or brick platform. The columns supporting the brackets and timbers of the double-pitched roofs were set in carved stone bases and determined the number of bays in each wing (always uneven, from three to nine). The major areas of decoration were the lattice windows of the façade and the roof tiles. The roof was considered vulnerable to evil spirits so ceramic figures of frightening dragon-heads were set at either end. Sumptuary laws dictated the use of colour: imperial buildings were roofed with yellow glazed tiles, temples and the homes of nobles with green glazed tiles and the roofs of ordinary houses had grey unglazed tiled roofs. The use of scarlet doors and columns was restricted to the nobility while ordinary houses had timbers painted dark red or brown.

Regional variation in architectual style is most noticeable in domestic buildings. The simple grey-roofed courtyards of Peking contrast with the elaborate house-garden complexes of Suzhou which include garden pavilions, pools and mock mountains. Whitewashed southern Chinese courtyard houses are almost completely enclosed, with only a small opening in the roof to ventilate the halls and stone-flagged court below. Their gable-end walls were stepped and curved and some southern buildings, like the North temple pagoda, Suzhou, have elaborately up-turned eaves. (FW)

▲ *North temple pagoda, Suzhou. The temple was founded in the 3rd century AD, with the most recent major reconstruction being after a fire in 1570. The nine-storey timber pagoda is in the southern style with up-turned eaves, a style restricted to pagodas and southern garden pavilions, for which the town of Suzhou is famous. Pagodas, based originally on the Indian stupa reliquary which was often the central building in a Buddhist pagoda, were introduced to China sometime during the Han dynasty (206 BC–AD 220) at the same time as the religion.*

▲ *Rural houses, outskirts of Peking, 1976. Oriented towards the south, these rural buildings consist of a single five-bay wing with a courtyard enclosure in front. The houses are of the characteristic timber-frame construction with apron walls and attractive lattice windows above. Patterns incorporated in the lattice include auspicious symbols like the "double happiness" character and interlocked coins or, since 1949, in the case of an army family, the emblem of the People's Liberation Army.*

▲ *Courtyard houses, central Peking, early 1980s. City planning in China was based on a grid plan. Cities were walled and, ideally, rectangular with barbican gates on all sides. Peking, laid out in its present form during the Ming dynasty (1368–1644), is a perfect example. The main hall in a domestic courtyard was to the north, with subsidiary wings to east, west and, sometimes, south.*

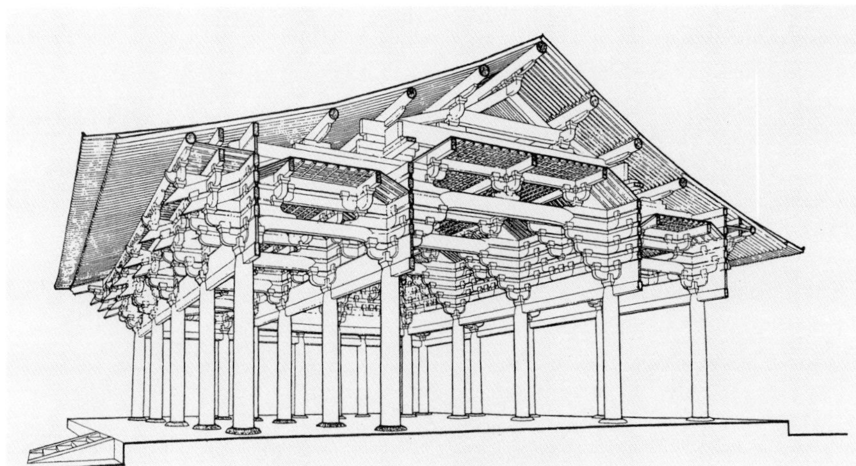

◀ *Cross-section of timber frame, main hall, Fo guang temple. Dating from AD 857, this has a far more elaborate bracketing system than the Nan chan hall and supporting eaves that project some 4m (13ft). The building is seven bays wide and four bays deep. The two side bays have brick apron walls and a simple grid lattice window above; the other bays have strong, studded wooden doors which could be opened to reveal the Buddhist figures inside. Some of the beams and ceiling areas were painted.*

▶ *The Nan chan temple hall, built between AD 618 and 782 on a Buddhist holy mountain, is the earliest standing timber-frame building in China. It is three bays wide and three bays deep but the central bay is broader than the side bays. Standing on a stone and brick platform, it has a grey-tiled single-eaved hip-gable roof with incurling acroteria (known as "owls' tails").*

EARLY RENAISSANCE

Local traditions and the revival of Ancient Rome in 15th century Italy

Renaissance architecture began in the Republican city of Florence with the revolutionary work of Filippo BRUNELLESCHI at the beginning of the 15th century. His buildings were conceived not so much as a revival of the ancient Roman heritage but rather as a reassertion of Italian values to counter the preference that prevailed during the previous century for North-European Gothic. Brunelleschi's designs took as their immediate models the buildings of the pre-Gothic period, such as the Florentine Baptistry (11th century) or Pisa Cathedral (begun 1063), even though Brunelleschi's selection and repetition of architectural motifs was now rather closer to the example of Classical antiquity.

Other architects working in early Renaissance Florence profited at least as much from an exploitation of medieval traditions as they did from a study of ancient monuments. In MICHELOZZO's three-storey Palazzo Riccardi-Medici (begun 1444), which established the basic format of the palace façade for the rest of the century, the rusticated stonework and round-arched windows divided by columns derived from recent Florentine traditions and only the projecting top-cornice depended on ancient prototypes. It was not long, however, before the patrons of Leon Battista ALBERTI in Rimini and Mantua, as well as aristocratic patrons elsewhere in Italy, recognized the political effectiveness of building in a more wholeheartedly Roman manner. Basic models, such as temple fronts, triumphal arches, audience halls and the vaulted halls of bath complexes, were then increasingly adapted for the design of whole buildings.

There are two major typological innovations of the period. The first is the small free-standing centrally planned church, usually destined to house a venerated object, usually a miraculous image, which became increasingly common from the 1480s. The second is the villa; the deliberate revival of the villa or country retreat of the ancient Romans, which became firmly established with Giuliano da SANGALLO's Villa Medici at Poggio a Caiano (*c.* 1485). Large-scale urban development was rare but notable exceptions include Bernardo Rossellino's remodelling of the area around the central piazza at Pienza with its new cathedral, Papal palace and public buildings (begun 1459), and Biagio Rossetti's new suburb of Ferrara, which included several major churches and palaces (1492).

Local traditions played a major part in the regional development of early Renaissance architecture, and these were to a great extent conditioned by the availability of materials. Stone was plentiful in much of central Italy, but scarce in the north where brick and terracotta continued to predominate. In Milan and Venice, however, stone was obtainable at a price, and it was here that the large workshops of a new generation of talented sculptor-architects, notably Giovanni Antonio Amedeo, Pietro Lombardo and Mauro Codussi, produced some of the most inventive works of the period, such as the splendid Certosa di Pavia (Amedeo, begun 1491). (DH)

▲ *S. Spirito, Florence, begun 1436, Brunelleschi. A basilican design of unprecedented regularity with square bays and semi-circular chapels. The four colonnaded arms of the cross-shaped layout meet at a domed crossing as they do in Pisa Cathedral, designed over two centuries earlier. In elevation, all Gothic elements have been discarded.*

▲ *Villa Medici, Poggio a Caiano, near Prato, c. 1485, da Sangallo. Conceived in imitation of the villas of the ancient Romans, the building is raised on an arcaded podium and the main entrance is treated as a pedimented portico. The accommodation is arranged in separate apartments around a central barrel-vaulted hall.*

▲ *Palazzo Riccardi-Medici, Florence, begun 1444; extended 1680, Michelozzo. The building stands on a prestigious corner site and is organized more or less symmetrically around a central colonnaded courtyard. Both the plan and the three-storey rusticated elevations were extensively drawn upon in subsequent palace designs.*

◀ *Pazzi Chapel, S. Croce, Florence, begun 1429, Brunelleschi. The building served as a chapter house with the ledge around the larger space for seating and a separate space for the altar. Brunelleschi's highly restricted vocabulary of pilasters, round arches and other classical motifs established the prevailing style in Italy for the rest of the century.*

◀ *S. Andrea, Mantua, 1470, Alberti. The awesome vaulted interior is based on the Roman Basilica of Maxentius, while the imposing pedimented façade is inspired by ancient Roman temples and triumphal arches. The design is well suited to a construction of brick and stucco, the only materials readily available.*

HIGH RENAISSANCE

The Classical language of architecture at its fullest expression

The works carried out by Donato BRAMANTE in Rome at the beginning of the 16th century established a new outlook which influenced the direction of architecture for the next 100 years. In this Bramante resolutely reaffirmed the authority of antiquity and bequeathed a group of austere and imposing buildings and projects which would provide points of departure for his many followers. Following Bramante's death, the new style was developed and defined by his followers, RAPHAEL, Baldassare PERUZZI and Antonio da SANGALLO, before being transferred to northern Italy by GIULIO ROMANO, SANSOVINO and SANMICHELI. There, the new style was adapted to local conditions, and it evolved into a coherent and universal Classical language that finds its fullest expression in the work of Andrea PALLADIO in Vicenza and Venice, where it was seized upon and avidly promoted by the wealthy upper classes.

Side by side with the mainstream Classical tradition, other architects developed more individualistic approaches, most notably MICHELANGELO who attached more importance to invention than many of his contemporaries. Michelangelo attracted many imitators in Florence and Rome, but his approach was developed perhaps most profitably in the work of Galeazzo Alessi and especially Pellegrino Tibaldi during the second half of the century in Milan. Yet other designers, in particular Pirro Ligorio, paid greater attention to the variety offered by ancient architecture itself, although antiquarian trends gradually waned in the wake of the new intellectual climate of the Counter-Reformation.

The most ambitious schemes of the period were undertaken in Papal Rome: most notably the rebuilding of St Peter's (begun 1506) initiated by Bramante, but also Michelangelo's remodelling of the Capitoline Palaces (begun 1539), and the new network of streets masterminded by Domenico FONTANA (*c.* 1590). During the century, there were considerable changes in both religious and domestic architecture. In church design a changed layout appropriate to the new Reformist movements was established: a nave with side chapels and a domed crossing with short transepts. Both Giacomo Barozzi da VIGNOLA's Gesù in 1568 and Andrea Palladio's Redentore in 1576 conform to this new type, and they also reveal the renewed importance that began to be attached to the façade. The Redentore façade is innovative with a central temple front, although the Gesù façade (redesigned by Della Porta in 1571), a two-storey arrangement emphasizing the portal, was more influential. In domestic architecture, the greatest changes were in the field of villa design. One type to emerge, the palatial villa retreat, often set in spectacularly landscaped grounds, is associated in particular with the Papal Court of Central Italy. Another, the farmyard-villa, is more characteristic of northern Italy, and combines the utilitarian aspects of the conventional farmhouse with the comforts of gracious living. In the hands of Palladio, who established the genre, these complexes are clad in Classical attire and achieve a truly palatial grandeur. (DH)

▲ *Il Gesù, Rome, 1568, Vignola; façade by Della Porta 1571. The mother church of the Jesuits was perhaps the most influential of the Renaissance. The splendid façade, as modified by Della Porta, is a conventional two-storey format, but the Orders are arranged to emphasize the portal.*

▼ *Tempietto, S. Pietro in Montorio, Rome, 1502, Bramante. The building marks the supposed site of St Peter's execution. The revolutionary design, conceived as a circular temple, surmounted by a Christian drum and dome, is the earliest application of the correct Doric Order to a Renaissance building.*

◀ *Palazzo Grimani, Venice, c. 1556, Sanmicheli. The stone façade is one of the most imposing on the Grand Canal. Pilaster Orders are applied to all three storeys, but their spacing is determined by the tripartite planning characteristic of Venice and the need to gain as much internal light as possible.*

▲ *St Peter's, Rome. Begun by Bramante in 1506, this was largely completed under Michelangelo. The rebuilding of the most hallowed church of Catholicism was by far the largest undertaking of the period. The undulating curtain wall with its giant Order and imaginative detailing belongs to Michelangelo, as does the soaring ribbed dome.*

▲ *Villa Barbaro, Maser, near Padua, c. 1555, Palladio. The residential block at the centre is marked by a temple front and is joined to more utilitarian structures at either side. The buildings are shelved into the hillside with a secluded garden terrace and fountain house behind.*

◀ *Il Redentore, Venice, 1576, Palladio. This was built to commemorate the lifting of a terrible plague. The white stone façade is innovative in its arrangement, with the central area taken up by an applied temple front with a coupled smaller pilaster Order extending out to the wings which correspond with the lower side chapels.*

RENAISSANCE CLASSICISM

The new architectural style spreads north to the rest of Europe

The example of Italy was carried north to the rest of Europe in various ways. Already, by around the beginning of the 16th century, a number of Italian sculptor-architects had settled in northern European cities, and had begun to introduce the Renaissance style, and some architects, notably the Frenchman Philibert DELORME, had journeyed to Italy to become fully acquainted with recent developments. For many, however, knowledge of Italy was acquired only at secondhand, sometimes from drawings of key buildings, but most usually from published treatises, especially those of Sebastiano Serlio (from 1537), Giacomo Barozzi da VIGNOLA (1568) and Andrea PALLADIO (1570), which all ran into many editions. For other architects, especially Inigo JONES in England and Jacob VAN CAMPEN in Holland, Palladio's treatise was to provide the impetus for them to travel to Italy, as many architects, notably the British Palladians, were to do subsequently. Thus "High Renaissance" Italy soon established the basic language of architecture for the rest of Europe, which in Britain and France underlay subsequent developments into the 18th century.

A great variety of regional styles developed during this early period in accordance with localized building traditions, stone predominating in France and southern Europe, and wood and brick construction in the Low Countries, England and the North, and these produced very different approaches. The continuing cultural orientations and systems of patronage of individual nations gave rise to classical reinterpretations of well-established building types: the hospitals and university buildings of Spain, the town halls and guild buildings of the Low Countries and Germany, and the private hôtels and châteaux of France and the country homes of England.

In church design, Catholic countries turned in particular to Italian models such as Vignola's Gesù and stressed the façade. Protestant countries needed to develop new designs and their churches are much less assuming, conceived as simple congregational spaces, perhaps with side-galleries. The new tradition was developed in particular in Holland, where the plain but inventive brick-built structures were often elaborated externally with ornamental steeples. The most ambitious projects of the period were those conceived under royal patronage. For Philip II of Spain, a new royal palace was erected at El Escorial near Madrid (1562–82), and was combined with a monastery in an enormous rectangular complex. For the kings and queens of France a succession of châteaux were built or restored, including the Palais de Fontainebleau, which attracted a number of Italian designers. In Paris royal works included the remodelling of the Louvre begun by Louis LE VAU in 1546, and subsequently the Palais des Tuileries (destroyed) and DE BROSSE's Italianate Palais de Luxembourg (1615–24). Even more ambitious were the plans for an enormous palace complex at Whitehall in London for Charles I of England; although only a fragment, Inigo Jones's Banqueting House was finally realized (1619–22). (DH)

▲ Chapel, Château d'Anet (Normandy), begun 1541, Philibert Delorme. The chapel with its four tall arches recalls Raphael's Chigi Chapel which Philibert would have studied during his stay in Rome, although it is now adapted to a circular plan.

► Banqueting House, Whitehall, London, 1619–22, Inigo Jones. The building, part of the Royal palace, is one of the first to be directly influenced by Renaissance Italy. The two-storey exterior recalls the palaces of Palladio, and the arrangement is repeated in the double-cube interior which was used for the staging of court masques.

▶ *East façade, the Louvre, Paris, c. 1667, Le Vau in collaboration with Claude Perrault and Charles Le Brun. Classical orthodoxy remains the dominant tradition in French architecture, and the new Louvre façade with its free-standing columns and pediment provides one of its most monumental and dignified examples.*

▶ *Wollaton Hall, Nottinghamshire, 1580–85, Robert Smythson. The four-towered arrangement recalls earlier castles, but the most immediate model is a woodcut in Serlio. The Classical Orders here combine with traditional mullioned windows. The banqueting room above the central hall takes advantage of the splendid views.*

▲ *El Escorial, near Madrid, 1562–82, Juan Bautista de Toledo and Juan de Herrera. The front half of this enormous multi-functional complex is dominated by the Italianate domed church of St Lawrence, preceded by a spacious atrium. From the king's quarters immediately behind the church a window overlooks the high altar.*

THE BAROQUE

The triumph of drama and spectacle in Rome and beyond

Baroque architecture was brought to fruition in 17th-century Papal Rome and in many ways it is the final culmination of the earlier Renaissance. It is manifested in a series of truly spectacular projects by the architects Gianlorenzo BERNINI, Francesco BORROMINI and Pietro da CORTONA which reflected the new political power of the papacy, as well as the renewed confidence of the whole church. As in previous centuries, the new directions in architecture were subsequently mirrored over the rest of Italy, and then across the length and breadth of Europe. However, the influence of the Italian Baroque was felt most strongly on church design in the Catholic states, and on the projects of the royal and princely courts.

The great works of Roman Baroque architecture are typically large-scale, dramatic and exuberant in character, but there is a considerable variety of individual styles. The more conventional and classical manner of Bernini and later architects, such as Carlo RAINALDI and Carlo FONTANA, represents the main stream of development, but the more individualistic and inventive approach of Borromini, which owes much to the works of MICHELANGELO, was to influence Guarino GUARINI in Turin and provided the germ for the 18th-century Rococo movement led by Johann Balthasar NEUMANN and the ASAM brothers in Germany and Central Europe. Meanwhile, in Spain and Portugal traditions were more insulated, although the buildings with their astonishingly elaborate decoration are no less spectacular.

The key projects of the Roman architects were to provide the basic models for major buildings in Europe for well over a century. St Peter's, recently completed with the addition of Carlo MADERNO's nave (1606–12), provided the prototype for several other great domed churches of the 17th and 18th centuries: FISCHER VON ERLACH's Karlskirche in Vienna (begun 1716), Francois MANSART's Val-de-Grâce (begun 1645) and Jules HARDOUIN-MANSART's Les Invalides (begun 1620) in Paris, and even Sir Christopher WREN's Protestant St Paul's Cathedral (1675) in London. New developments in the design of church façades, in particular the resourceful use of convex and concave elements pioneered by Cortona and Borromini and a more exciting handling of columns were to have a universal appeal to architects working in Catholic states. In palace design, the impetus also came initially from Roman architects whose ideas were taken up in LE VAU's Versailles: Neumann's Residenz at Würtzburg (begun 1719), Hildebrandt's Upper Belvedere (1721–2) in Vienna, as well as in royal palaces as far afield as Stockholm and St Petersburg (Leningrad). The great piazzas of Baroque Rome by Cortona, Rainaldi and Bernini would also soon be echoed by similar projects in other major cities, most notably Hardouin-Mansart's Place Vendôme (begun 1698) in Paris. A taste for grandiose planning was ultimately to sweep across Europe, the debt to Baroque Italy still being dimly reflected in the great scenic complexes of Restoration England, such as VANBRUGH and HAWKSMOOR's Blenheim Palace (begun 1705). (DH)

▲ *Vierzehnheiligen Pilgrimage Church, begun 1743, Neumann. The cross-shaped plan, based on a series of ovals, recalls published designs by Guarini. The slender piers, the ribbed vaulting and delicate painted decoration, give the building an air of insubstantiality.*

▲ *Blenheim Palace, Oxfordshire, begun 1705, Vanbrugh and Hawksmoor. Many of the basic themes recall much earlier buildings of Palladio's, especially the tall pedimented central block, the linking elements and the corner pavilions, but the massing of the complex design creates a magnificence that is truly Baroque.*

▲ *Chapel of the Holy Shroud, Turin Cathedral, begun 1667, Guarini. Above the nine-bay chapel, three pendentives carry a six-bay drum which is covered by a remarkable dome. The dome is more or less conical in section and is constructed as a series of superimposed arches which admit an almost mystical light.*

◀ *S. Carlo alle Quattro Fontane, Rome, begun 1634, Borromini. The building is highly unconventional in both overall design and detail. The plan is based on an oval with four apses, and the applied Order which runs into the apses supplies an additional plasticity, as do the niches inserted in the minor bays.*

◀ *St Paul's, London, begun 1675, Christopher Wren. The towered façade recalls Roman models such as Borromini's Sant' Agnese, although the arrangement also follows that of many medieval English cathedrals. The dome, unlike that of St Peter's, its ultimate model, is lifted so it can dominate the composition from in front.*

A NEW VIEW

Neo-Classicism and the architecture of the industrial revolution

The Romantic era, which fundamentally changed the way Western culture perceived its art and architecture, was born 200 years ago alongside the first industrial age. Late 18th-century revolutionary France and America took the noble republics of the Greeks and Romans as their architectural models. But the hard rationalism, clarity and logic behind Neo-Classical architecture ensured that it outlived republican France's fashion for the antique. This was an architecture of geometry and purity rather than of ornament and luxuriance.

In the following decades the Classical language of architecture was used in a self-consciously picturesque way to dress the modern capitals of northern Europe in classic costume. Ambitious building schemes were put into effect in St Petersburg and Copenhagen, the new Prussian capital Berlin, and Edinburgh, the "Athens of the North" which counterbalanced Britain's commercial metropolis in the south.

This architecture of the first industrial age was indeed an "international style". Although it did not outwardly display the sinew and fibre of industry – it was unseemly to show off muscle and brawn – it made sense to benefit from new industrial developments, and many architects exploited the latest technical possibilities. Nets of iron, for example, could be used for reinforcing masonry, and new theories of structure allowed this to be calculated. Cast iron could be used for framing, not just as columns (in compression). And when formed in trusses (to withstand bending and tension) it could carry a roof over wide spans. There were also developments in piped services; in glass as a walling material; in mill-sawn timber and mass-produced nails, and much more. All these were utilized but politely hidden behind the accepted language of architecture. Jacques SOUFFLOT's mid-18th-century Ste Geneviève in Paris had iron-reinforced masonry, and Leo von KLENZE's early 19th-century Walhalla near Regensburg, a copy of the Parthenon, had a pioneering iron-frame roof. The great early 19th-century classicist Karl SCHINKEL drew designs for immense sheets of glass held unframed between masonry columns, unbuildable until thirty years later when Alexander THOMSON pioneered such "direct glazing" in his own classicist architecture.

In general architects were much more concerned with giving recognizable clothing to the new forms of assembly than in celebrating the materials of industrial development. In the early 19th century there was a demand for a huge variety of new building types as the story of architecture broadened to embrace commercial, social and public buildings rather than just palaces, churches and dwellings. Exchanges, offices, institutions for health, incarceration or education, municipal libraries and – most of all – museums, mushroomed without precedent. As Marx and Engels noted in *The Communist Manifesto* (1847) "the bourgeoisie [has] accomplished wonders far surpassing Egyptian pyramids, Roman aqueducts and Gothic cathedrals. In a word, it creates a world after its own image." (JM)

▲ *St Vincent Street church, Glasgow, 1856–9, Alexander Thomson. This is magnificently formed urban architecture; a Greek temple with porticoes at the ends surmounts its built acropolis – and yet expertly exploits the Glaswegian four-storey residential street pattern within which it sits. Inside, the preaching hall is both rich and austere, a sense of archaic strength coming from the open trussed roof and surrounding rectangular columns, forming one of the mid-19th century's most remarkable interior spaces.*

▶ *Brighton Pavilion, 1815, John Nash. This exotic confection built for the Prince Regent rejected the international style of Classicism. Like the other examples of its period, the Brighton Pavilion exploited the new possibilities of metal structures both practically (it has a massive cast-iron substructure) and expressively (the cast-iron columns in the kitchen have metallic palm-frond capitals).*

▶ *Director's Stables, Royal Saltworks, Chaux (Arc-en-Senans), Burgundy, 1775. This building formed part of Claude Nicolas Ledoux's Classical but highly expressive circular plan for a total industrial community. Building work was brought to a halt by the French Revolution.*

▼ *Berlin Museum, 1823–8, K. F. Schinkel. This steel engraving is from Schinkel's drawing of the outstanding element in his building. The two floors are linked to each other, and inside to outside, by the inspired device of opening the stair space, which is deep in the plan, to the front of the building, behind the double colonnade.*

▲ *Bibliothèque Nationale, Paris, 1862–8, Henri Labrouste. The bookstacks, under a glass roof, are stacked four storeys high with light filtering down through open, grid-iron floor panels in a completely new utilitarian aesthetic. The reading room, by contrast, sits under the most elegant canopy of nine terracotta and glass domes held on 16 suspended iron columns.*

BUILDER AND ARCHITECT

Pioneers of construction in a world of new needs and new materials

The pilgrimage church of Vierzehnheiligen, one of the great masterpieces of the Baroque, was completed in 1772, the same year as the Coalbrookdale iron bridge. Today the bridge must receive nearly as many pilgrims, as it symbolizes the new industrial age – the birth of our times. Although a pioneering bridge is not architecture, any more than was the equally pioneering Eiffel Tower in Paris a century later, such structures have had an enduring influence, as images, on architects.

Another type of new building that became instantly attractive to the cultured Romantics was the factory, or "mill". Produced for entirely practical purposes and at a distance from architectural culture, it tended not to disguise its straightforward use of the latest constructional developments. K. F. SCHINKEL, when visiting England, sketched not the Neo-Classical monuments but the new Mersey docks and the smoking chimneys of Dudley. This was the other face of Romanticism, in which industry and technology were seen as the honest production of the industrial age's "noble savages", and it has echoed through architectural culture ever since.

Towards the middle of the 19th century there were rapid developments in methods of organizing the erection of structures, usually formed in metal. The products were not regarded as "architecture", nor were they usually the work of architects. Some, such as the glasshouses and metal roofs of J. C. Loudon, were the common-sense designs of self-taught men while others, like the great train sheds or town markets, were the work of engineers. Brunel designed a war hospital for the Crimea in prefabricated wooden elements, which were shipped to the Dardanelles and erected at Renkioi very speedily. It was a magnificent exercise in rational planning, being uniquely air conditioned and sanitary.

Sometimes architects were involved, working in collaboration with an ironfounder. The hand of the architect John Baird can be clearly discerned in Gardner's warehouse in Glasgow, but the Palm House at Kew, although credited to Decimus BURTON, is really the masterpiece of his Irish ironfounder, Richard Turner. For Paddington Station, Brunel, as the entrepreneur and engineer, specifically commissioned M. D. Wyatt as his architect to add the façade of culture.

London's Crystal Palace was designed by entrepreneurs with acute understanding of new contractual and organizational practices (in engineering rather than in architecture), of mass production and of competitive tendering. It also was produced at a distance from architectural culture; unashamedly straightforward and structurally uninspiring, the process of its production was planned with radical commonsense, simply aggregated to an arbitrary size which produced the eventual astounding glass-clad space. Architects were bowled over by it, but none could emulate it. Yet it is these glazed, iron-framed "umbrellas", epitomized in the glazed arcades which followed, which provide the one memorable architectural form of the era. (JM)

▲ *Boathouse, Sheerness, 1858–60. Designed by Colonel Greene, a military engineer, this was probably the first multi-storey building to be completely framed in iron, both inside and out. It remains one of the most elegant, allowing its date to be mistaken for a century later. It is also the first building to use H-shape columns and I-shape beams, which later became a universal standard.*

▶ *Oriel Chambers, Liverpool, 1864. One of the most original structures in England, Peter Ellis Jnr's Oriel Chambers was an early example of glass and stone architecture. The minor bay windows that protrude from the façade like fish scales lie between vertical pillars of stonework that end in finials. The building puzzled the Victorians, and after completing it Ellis did little else.*

► *Crystal Palace, London, 1850–51. Designed by Paxton and Fox, this building employed no architect, was huge, and went up unbelievably fast, within a low budget. Although structurally conservative it was the first public building to omit references to the past.*

◄ *Galleria Vittorio Emanuelle II, Milan, 1865–77. Designed by Giuseppe Mengoni and built with English capital, this vast covered space (the main entrance as high as the adjoining cathedral nave), epitomizes the outstanding urban architecture of the age. Here, as under Eiffel's glass roof of the Bon Marché in Paris, the new bourgeois needs for display and consumption met perfectly.*

▲ *Gardner's Warehouse, Glasgow, 1855–6. The ironfounder Robert McConnell designed the frame and held the patent on the iron beams, but architect John Baird produced the unmatched architectural refinement and restraint. Optical subtleties include the changes of window form between floors (for example, the arches flattening as the storeys deepen), and the four-arch bays on the narrow side façade (left) which increased the perspective effect.*

THE SEARCH FOR STYLE

Historical emblems and styles in an age of new technology

Architectural form combines both instrument and emblem. Its instrumental role is that of allowing certain human actions to take place within it, which the building will either encourage or limit in specific ways. Its emblematic aspect is the way in which the building's imagery and quality of surface and space enhance these activities and make them memorable. Great architecture usually holds these two elements in an integrated balance.

As the 19th century progressed, the emblematic side of architecture became diffused. It was under threat from both the new technological building world which ascribed little importance to it and from an accompanying loss of faith in the need for "one true style". Lightly adopted styles were used with considerable abandon, often only reflecting a weak association of ideas, such as "Classical" for learning or "Gothic" for religion. Many were troubled by this and fine architects felt hopelessly lost. "In what style should we build?" moaned one German, and the question summed up the dilemma. In England, A. W. N. PUGIN and then John RUSKIN argued for true principles in design and moral rules for honest building. Their exemplar was medieval ecclesiastical society and its buildings; true Gothic, they believed, would be an appropriate reflection of an honest modern society. But this approach to design, in which it was treated as a moral issue (an attitude which reappeared later in Modernism) could not ultimately prevail, and the so-called Battle of the Styles continued to be fought.

The engineering exploitation of new situations, however, was self-confident enough to ignore any concern for cultural reference. The completely new forms, such as stations, exhibition halls, exchanges and arcades, which were unprecedented in spatial terms as well as rich in constructional ideas, were virtually drained of architecture's traditional emblematic role. More importantly, they were usually also rather crude as instruments.

Architects, on the other hand, sometimes designed a brilliant instrument, but went too far with the emblematic content. Charles GARNIER's Opéra in Paris, for example, is a magnificent and complex articulation of a difficult requirement, but the building's lavish ornament is at odds with its precisely articulated form.

This looseness of emblem which decorated so much 19th-century architecture is seen both in the fashion for the exotic styles brought back from the colonies and in the exported imperial culture. Through the century Britain built in Bombay an "Ionic" mint (1829), a "Doric and Corinthian" town hall (1825–33), "Early English" high courts, a "Renaissance" telegraph office, a "Venetian gothic" secretariat (1874), a "15th-century French decorated" university hall and finally a "14th-century Flanders" library designed by Scott. Meaningless fancy-dress, it was particularly tasteless, given India's own ancient cultural heritage.

(JM)

▲ *St Andrew's Scots Kirk, Calcutta, c. 1820. Later colonial exportation tended to offer a tasteless mixed salad of the most bombastic and inappropriate kind. But early in the century, the new settlements in India as in the new cities of North America were exports of considerable elegance. St Andrew's in Calcutta has been described as one of the finest Regency churches anywhere.*

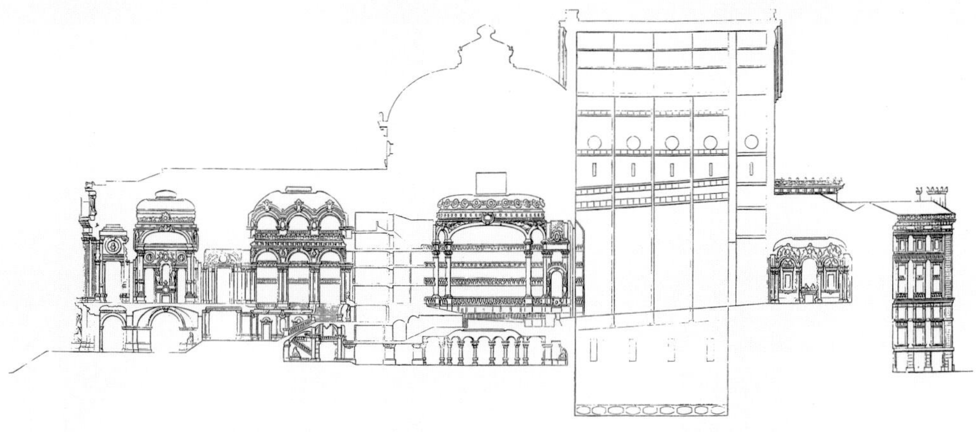

◀ ▲ *Paris Opéra, 1861–74, Charles Garnier. Section drawing (above) and façade (left). This is an immensely carefully worked out three-dimensional essay in architectural condensation, through* porte cochère, *entrance hall, stairs up and then down into the balconies which hang into the hall. There is a great, tall, front foyer, an inner foyer so much lower and wider, emphasizing the drum, the beating heart of the theatre. From the doors in the drum, up the steps, into the wedge which allows disrobing and then focuses attention on the amazingly close stage, behind and above which lie equally complex service spaces.*

▲ *Viceroy's house (now President's House), New Delhi, Edwin Lutyens. In 1911 Britain decided to build a new Indian Imperial city; Calcutta was largely "classic"; Bombay largely "gothic" but should New Delhi be "oriental"? Lutyens decided on a Classical tradition with Indian trimmings.The building was erected 1920–31. This watercolour shows the north elevation.*

◀ *Proposed "gothic" cathedral for Colombo, Sri Lanka, 1861, Carpenter. Along with William Butterfield, Carpenter was the favourite architect of the Ecclesiological Society, an evangelistic pressure group, in whose magazine this project was illustrated in 1861.*

AMERICAN COLONISTS

Tradition and innovation in early North American architecture

The English colonists in North America were neither adventurers nor the rulers of great and ancient peoples. Unlike various colonizers down the ages, they had no need to impress the native people, nor did they have a strong local tradition to fit into. They were simple, hard-working people, often craftsmen, seeking a better life across the sea. There was little stone suitable for building, and there was no lime, which ruled out brick building, but there was abundant timber. As a result, the architecture of North America is largely in wood.

By the time of the War of Independence (1775–83), a strong tradition of timber-frame building had grown up, whether for public buildings, churches or houses. Wood-built towns, simple and well-planned, with the buildings often faced in shingles, can still be seen on the Eastern Seaboard of the early states. A Classical look became fashionable, and wooden villas and plantation mansions in the Palladian style multiplied. It was an undogmatic Classicism, since the columns of porticoes could be much slimmer than their stone prototypes. Thomas JEFFERSON used Ionic capitals because his slave carpenters were not skilled enough to carve Corinthian ones.

Jefferson, however, was a man of the Enlightenment, and he and other internationally aware architects like Benjamin LATROBE and William STRICKLAND produced a rational and romantic Classicism – planned cities and masonry architecture. With these men, the United States had entered the international arena, and the seeds were sown for its leading role in architecture half a century later.

But timber building continued, and a vital development in this context was that of the balloon frame, devised by G. W. Snow, a civil engineer, in the village of Chicago in 1832. Thanks to mass-produced nails and machine-sawn sticks, the old heavy sections of wood and complex joints were things of the past. Balloon framing is credited with enabling the rapid expansion of settlements like Chicago and San Francisco in the middle of the century.

The North American "heritage" of forests, frontier-folk and shingle-clad cottages was readily kept alive in more sophisticated times. In the 1840s, Andrew Jackson Downing, architect, landscape designer and influential writer, advocated the exploitation of wood, and in the later decades of the century a "shingle style" was led by architects like H. H. RICHARDSON and MCKIM, MEAD & WHITE. They produced large mansions, informally and picturesquely planned, linked to the English free style (see pages 228-9).

In the city, however, Richardson (who had studied with Henri LABROUSTE in Paris in the 1870s) built in stone, as did Louis SULLIVAN after him, on a scale where issues of style were dwarfed by sheer monumental form. And this form was to have a metal frame, hydraulic lifts, central heating, air-conditioning and telephone intercom, as in Adler & SULLIVAN's vast Auditorium (1886). Balloon-framed Chicago had been wiped out by fire in 1871; what replaced it was the skyscraper, the second urban artefact to be invented in Chicago. (JM)

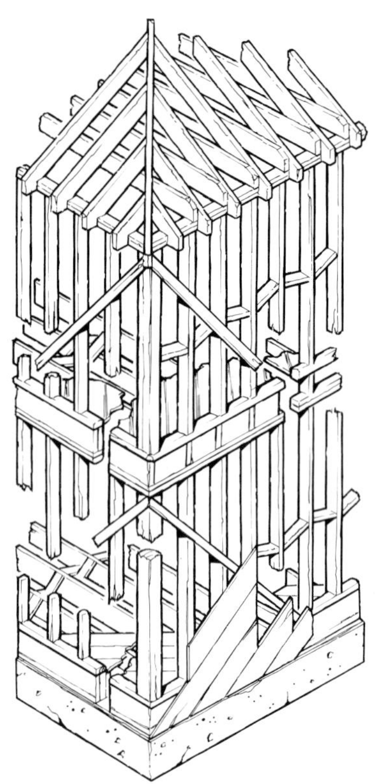

▲ *Balloon framing. The first known use of the balloon frame dates from 1833; in the 1860s it cut building cost by 40 per cent and increased building speed immeasurably. In essence, the balloon frame is a cage of long sticks covered with a skin of clapboarding, forming a continuous structural web. These boxes were easily put together with hammer and nails, making the role of the skilled carpenter redundant.*

◀ *Provident Life and Trust Building, Philadelphia, 1879, Frank Furness. Much more than "muscular gothic", this has an extra-ordinary vigour and sense of scale, the American equivalent of the work of William Burges in Castel Coch, Wales, or even Antoni Gaudí in Palau Güell, Barcelona.*

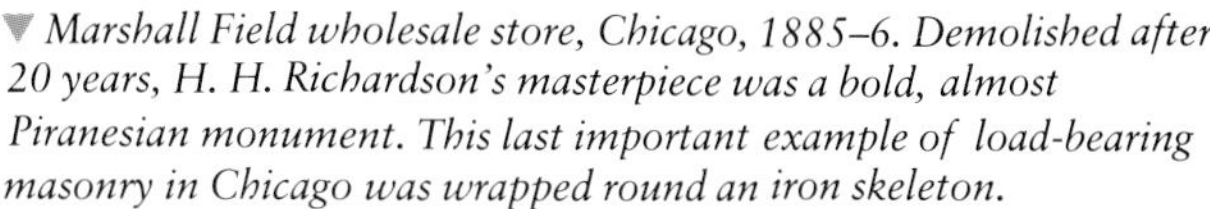

▼ *Marshall Field wholesale store, Chicago, 1885–6. Demolished after 20 years, H. H. Richardson's masterpiece was a bold, almost Piranesian monument. This last important example of load-bearing masonry in Chicago was wrapped round an iron skeleton.*

◀ *Reliance Building, Chicago, 1890–95, Burnham and Root. This was the most refined and advanced skyscraper of its time. The light-coloured terracotta cladding is reduced to a minimum, the cap on the top is the thinnest of slabs and there is no cornice. This potentially infinite grid image – chopped off at an arbitrary height – is the three-dimensional equivalent of US city planning.*

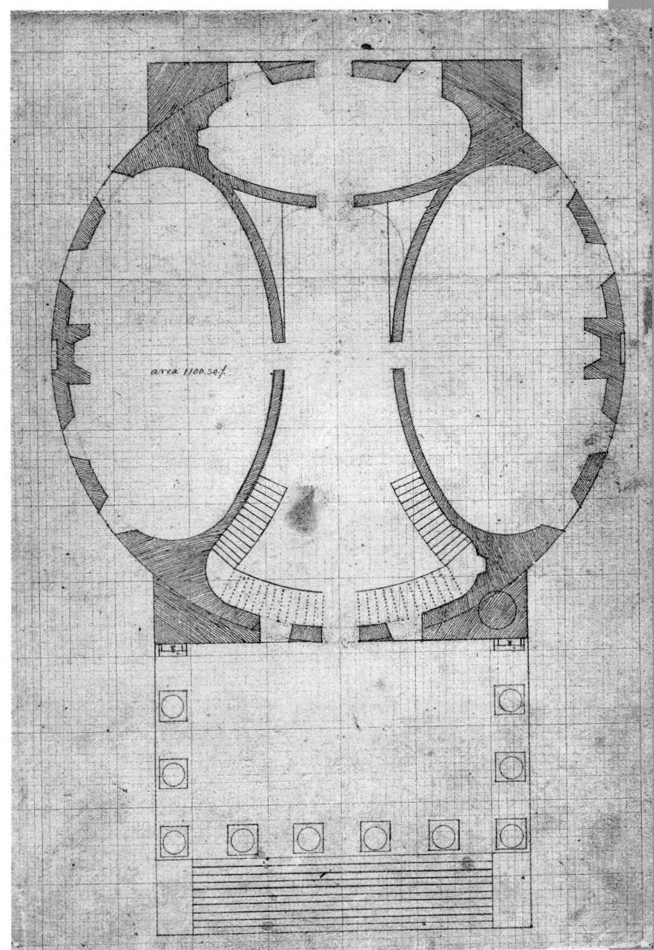

▲▼ *University of Virginia Rotunda, Charlottesville, 1821, elevation and plan. Thomas Jefferson's architectural drawings, the first to use squared paper, show the rationalist idea, the use of sphere and cube, behind the built form.*

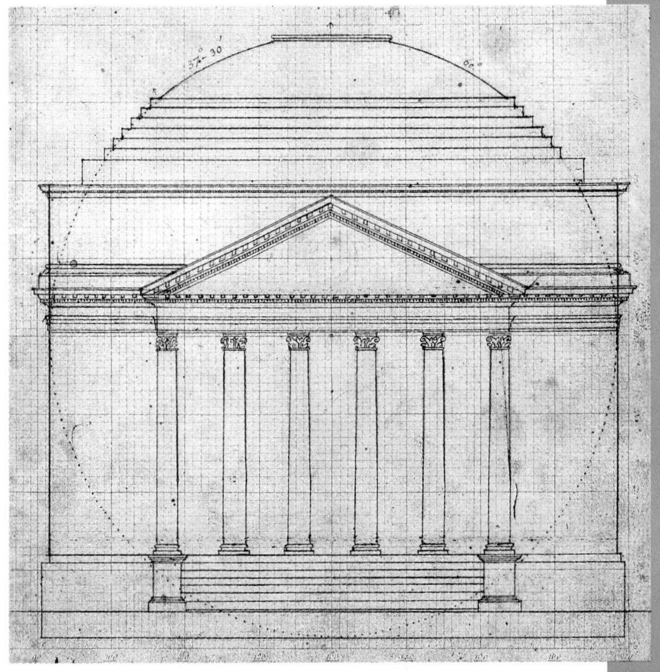

TOWARDS OBJECTIVITY

Architectural honesty and the growth of "Free Style" building

Throughout the middle decades of the 19th century architects lacked a clear view of their role. Nevertheless, William BUTTERFIELD and G. E. STREET in England built magnificent urban churches quite unlike anything previously known; Alexander THOMSON in Scotland and Henri LABROUSTE in France both produced masterworks of genuinely urban architecture for the bourgeois industrial cities. These might exploit technology and material, but without worrying about its being suitably clothed, or they might exploit the conventional language of architecture, but not become over-anxious about the "right" style. At the same time an architecture with a rather different meaning was beginning to appear. Since the 1830s there had been powerful arguments (initially in England) for an "honest", "organic" and "true" architecture, coupled with an anti-industrial mood which encouraged the use of sensible traditional detailing and commonsense forms. Windows, for example, could now be allowed to cluster as required, and be large or small according to the needs of each room, rather than being elements in the abstract geometry of a façade. The whole design of a building would be informed by the process of its production and by its intended occupation.

The ideas often produced better books than buildings, from A. W. N. PUGIN's *True Principles* (1842) via John RUSKIN, Andrew Jackson Downing (in the USA) and William MORRIS to VIOLLET-LE-DUC's *How to Build a House* (1874). Originally based on the precedent of medieval building, this stream of ideas was swollen by the Arts and Crafts Movement, centred around Morris, and the structural rationalism advocated by Viollet-le-Duc which was based on the concept that the best architecture grows directly from straightforward, logical building. Gradually the search for "a style" assumed a less central position and the copying of Gothic shapes died away, but these design principles held centre stage until the turn of the century. It was these concepts that formed the ideas of Norman SHAW and Philip WEBB, then of William LETHABY, BAILLIE SCOTT and C. F. A. VOYSEY, of Parker & UNWIN in England; of Charles Rennie MACKINTOSH in Scotland, Frank Lloyd WRIGHT in America and many more.

The most influential book of the time, extolling the houses of the British domestic architects, was Hermann MUTHESIUS' *Das Englische Haus (The English House)*, published in Berlin in 1904/5. After the First World War new designers took up Muthesius's principles without relying on the images he had illustrated. These principles, such as "unassuming naturalness" and "absolute practicality", where form responded to and intimated its use, both helped channel the notion of *sachlichkeit* (uneasily translated as "objectivity") central to the work of Walter GROPIUS and the Bauhaus (see pages 234-5) and led to the organic "functional" tradition of the German architects Hans SCHAROUN and Hugo HÄRING who talked, as had Lethaby, of "building" rather than of "architecture". (JM)

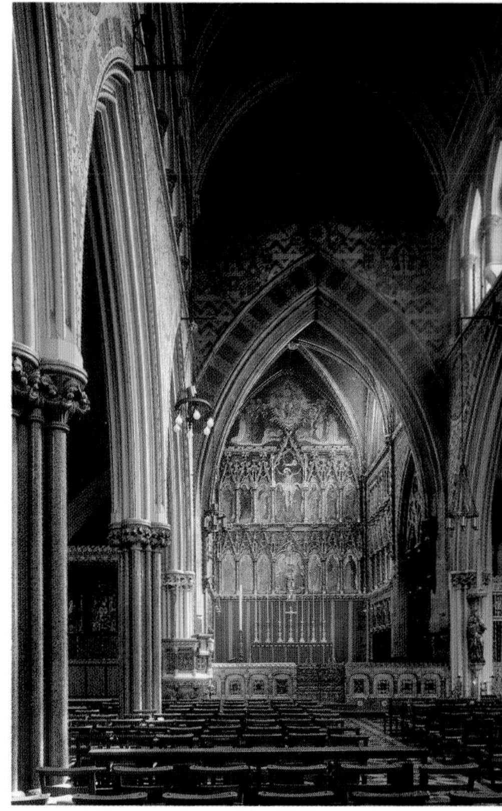

▲ *All Saints church, Margaret Street, London, 1850–59, William Butterfield. The model church of the Ecclesiologists, this was the first bright red brick building in London for an age. Boldly patterned in black outside, inside the polychromy explodes in a blaze of richly varied materials, surfaces and decoration.*

► *Hill House, Helensburgh, Scotland, 1914. This is the domestic masterpiece of Charles Rennie Mackintosh. An Edwardian suburban mansion, in the English country house plan and layout, transformed by Mackintosh's magic with colour, surface and decoration into a series of unique interior spaces. The shell around it is based on a reinterpretation of the Scottish 17th-century "Z-plan tower" (for nursery, service and staff rooms) and the 18th-century wing, with the larger public rooms overlooking the Clyde to the south.*

▼ Red House, Bexleyheath, England, 1859, Philip Webb and William Morris. This fits within the honest tradition embraced by A. W. N. Pugin, G. E. Street and William Butterfield. It eschewed formal façades and concentrated on "realism". All the earlier ecclesiastical imagery was discarded; instead, the asymmetric plan responds directly to its purpose, and is expressed externally in the variety of roof forms and window shapes.

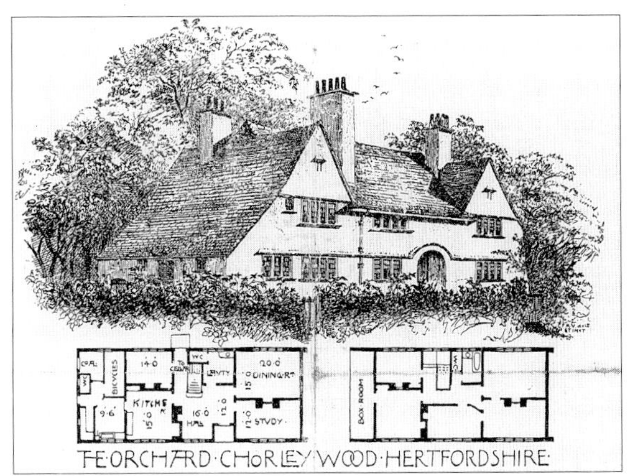

◀ "The Orchard", Chorleywood, Hertfordshire. C. F. A. Voysey built this house for himself in 1899. Based on local craftsmanship and skills, its light interior was enhanced by the unusual pale colour scheme.

▲ All Saints church, Brockhampton, England, 1902, by Lethaby, epitomizes a "functional tradition" far richer than that of engineering, as it embraces style as well. It is very carefully sited, formed from an in-situ reinforced concrete vault which is exposed internally, and with walls of local masonry. The interior is enriched with tapestries designed by Burne-Jones and woven by Morris & Co some time earlier.

ROMANTIC REVOLUTIONARIES

New directions in Europe: Art Nouveau, Futurism, Constructivism

At very much the same time as the "free-style" stream and often linked with it, were others who broke with past historicism. As architects struggled to liberate themselves from the ponderous and overdressed style associated with the period after the Franco-Prussian War a new sensibility began to appear, particularly at the regional centres of European culture. In some cases this was explicitly linked with a resurgence of local cultural (and often political) identity. Scandinavians, Finns, Catalans and Scots were at the centre of this new romantic nationalism. Its structures are often rational and sometimes daring. But the central concern was for expressive form-making. Rich and sinuous, but never overweight, it combined immediacy and power in the handling and modelling of surface and texture. Nowhere is this more obvious than in Charles Rennie MACKINTOSH's Glasgow School of Art.

In Belgium and France, this mood opened out into Art Nouveau, epitomized by the work of Henry VAN DE VELDE and Victor HORTA. Similar imagery formed part of a *fin-de-siècle* reaction to the decrepit Austro-Hungarian empire as "Jugendstil" and "Secessionstil", while in Catalunya the fruits of the romantic nationalist movement were known as "Modernismo".

It was the brief, brilliant dance of a guttering candle, dying out even before the new world of Cubism, *De Stijl* and Futurism (or the Great War itself) could extinguish it. But in Scandinavia and outer European centres, away from the cultural centres of the 20th-century avant-garde, romantic nationalism thrived a little longer. It can be seen in the Amsterdam housing of Michel DE KLERK up to the 1920s, and more importantly in Jože Plečnik's many buildings carefully inserted in the fabric of Ljubljana. Meanwhile in England the romantic strains of Elgar's music were echoed in brick and timber by the finest English architect of the time, Edwin LUTYENS.

The obverse of the romantic nationalist coin was a romantic-revolutionism. Italian Futurism's leading architect, Antonio SANT'ELIA, a marvellously talented visionary who strongly influenced LE CORBUSIER, was killed in 1917 aged 29 before he could build. A German group of expressionists led by Bruno TAUT immediately after the First World War translated Utopian dreams into crystalline glass forms, which remained on paper. Revolutionary architecture first found physical expression in Russia with the work of a brilliant group including Vladimir TATLIN, EL LISSITZKY, the Vesnin brothers, Moise Ginzberg and especially Konstantin MELNIKOV. Fading there with the death of Lenin in 1924, this self-styled "objective" and "scientific" architecture is seen even more clearly in the work of a Swiss group (centred on Hans Schmidt, Hannes Meyer, Hans Wittwer, Mart STAM and Alfred Roth) who called for images of lightness and transparency, under the motto "building x weight = monumentality". (JM)

▼ *Design for a rural kiosk, c. 1924, Alexei Gan. This typical project from the heroic moment of Constructivism (between 1917 and the death of Lenin) shows the romance of revolution. "Let us take over the healthy bases of art – colour, line, materials and form – into the field of practical construction!" proclaimed Gan (essentially a typographer) in his manifesto* Constructivism *(1922). This is a wooden 'agitprop' construction, with dynamic form and imagery which incorporates graphic messages, radio loudspeakers and a film screen; all to act as – and symbolize – the introduction of new world into Russian villages.*

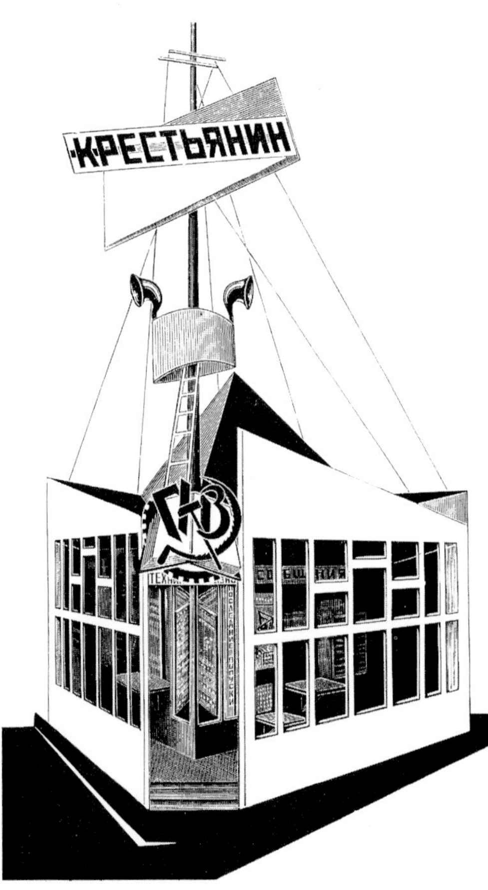

▶ *League of Nations competition entry, Geneva, 1926–7, Hannes Meyer and Hans Wittwer. Using modular, prefabricated construction, the designers claimed their building to be an "objective solution" to the problem and to "symbolize nothing". But it has the hallmarks of scientific romance: glazed lifts (seen in various Russian Constructivist projects, but not built for half a century) and political engineering towards a new morality.*

▲ *Entrance façade, School of Art, Glasgow, 1897–1909, Charles Rennie Mackintosh. The north side, with its huge studio windows and formal, if asymmetric, geometry is clearly the front. The muscular handling of form owes much to traditional Scottish architecture, however, the influence of continental Art Nouveau can be detected in the detailing, such as the curved ironwork brackets on the first floor.*

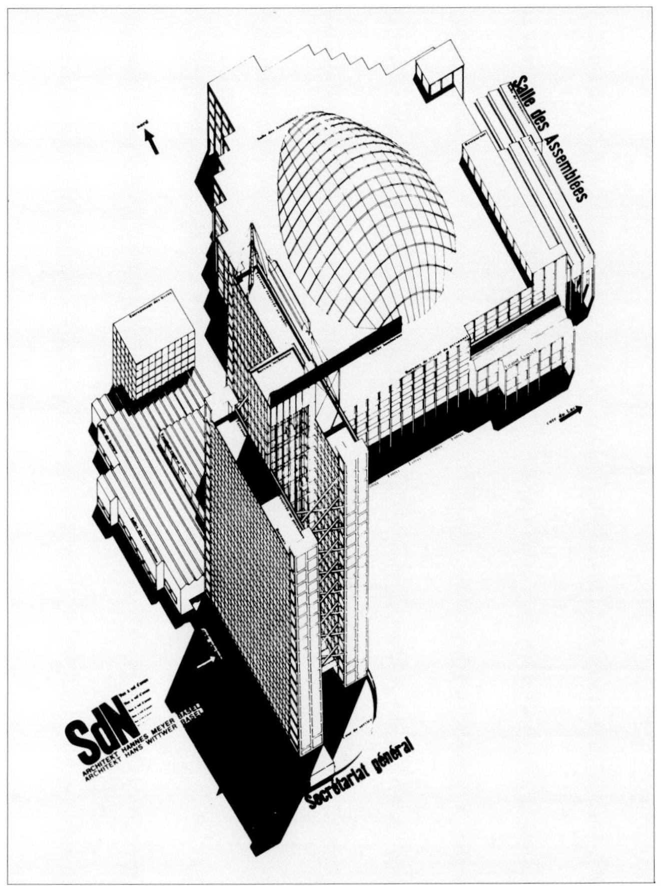

▲ *Tassel House, Brussels, 1892, Victor Horta. Horta's first important work, commissioned when he was 31, this fine terraced town house heralded Art Nouveau. The top-lit main stair ascends with graceful elegance and complex geometry – only 6 of its 26 treads are perpendicular to the stair's main axis. Serpentine designs mingle floor mosaic, wrought iron balustrade, wall decoration and structural iron capitals, all combining to exemplify the Symbolist vision of an "artificial paradise".*

▲ *Palau de la Música Catalana, Barcelona, 1905–8, Domènech y Montaner. While Domènech is a lesser figure than Gaudí, his contemporary, this magnificent, exuberant work clearly displays its cultural importance. "Bold, coarse and rich" it may be, as Hitchcock commented, but its use of metal and glass is very advanced technically.*

THE AMERICAN PATH

The Chicago school and the work of Frank Lloyd Wright

American architecture in the first four decades of this century, if perceived as having any continuity at all, is held together by the least typical of all its architects, Frank Lloyd WRIGHT. In the closing decades of the previous century, the multi-storey commercial building had not only been invented in technical terms, but also developed to become the key architectural form of its time. This achievement was almost exclusively due to a "Chicago school" of first-rank designers: William le Baron JENNEY, H. H. RICHARDSON, the partnerships of HOLABIRD & ROCHE, and BURNHAM & ROOT, and the towering figure of Louis SULLIVAN, who mastered the skyscraper structure and its form in the Guaranty Building, Buffalo (1894).

Wright was never much interested in the skyscraper, despite serving his apprentice years with Sullivan; his concerns with interior space were quite different. By 1900, Wright's villas for his rich suburban neighbours were developing a recognizable physiognomy. They hug their flat prairie sites yet float on the surface, with dramatic terraces and low-pitched roofs. These "Prairie Houses", formed part of a genuinely new interior architecture, from Wright's Willitts House (1901), with its pinwheel core of fireplaces to his Robie House (1909), with its progression up towards the hearth. His interior space, no longer formed of box-like rooms with single purposes, made an overlapping and interpenetrating whole, defined by screening, changes in ceiling height, and a person's position in the space.

Wright was as fascinated with geometry as the European architects discussed on pages 236–7. His work is far from the pure formal concepts of MIES VAN DER ROHE, and closer to the overlapping, densely layered spaces of LE CORBUSIER. It is perhaps closest of all – in its mix of timeless values (such as the sense of enclosure and the sense of centre) and the completely new ways of forming them – to Adolf LOOS. Wright was 20 years earlier.

Between the World Wars there was more interesting architectural development in tiny, shadowy Finland than in the immense and centre-stage USA. Wright went increasingly his own way and European developments only seemed noted by emigrés. The best architecture came from two of these, both Viennese – Richard NEUTRA and Rudolph SCHINDLER. Schindler's layered, open section in the Lovell beach house predates Le Corbusier's similar and more influential essays – but again these American sparks never really caught fire.

America's late-19th-century dynamism and its open-minded tackling of the consequences of industrialization ran aground on an even stronger national trait – a deep persistent conventionalism. Conservative skyscrapers, a contradiction in terms 20 years earlier, filled the cities in the 1920s. The first architecturally important one since Sullivan, HOWE & LESCAZE's Philadelphia Savings Fund, was built in 1932. After this it took the exodus from Nazism in Europe to bring a revitalizing blood transfusion to American architecture. (JM)

▲ *Schlesinger & Meyer department store (later Carson Pirie Scott) Chicago, 1899 – 1904. Louis H. Sullivan. Over a two-storey base, with beautiful cast-iron decoration around the windows and door, grows this tall department store, with shopping floors right to the top. There is an evenness and balance, and an overall simplicity in the external image, with its regular steel-frame behind white terracotta cladding. But it also demonstrates an exquisite care for ornamentation whenever it is near the eye.*

▶ *Robie House, Chicago, 1906–9, Frank Lloyd Wright. The living and dining spaces, reached by stairs round the hearth, form a linear double core, visually connected above the fires, and by the long narrow walkways by the windows.*

▲ *Lovell beach house, Newport Beach, California, 1925–6, R. M. Schindler. The Viennese pupil of Wagner, Schindler was also influenced by Mackintosh and Loos. This subtle and complex house consists in essence of two tray-like planes which, supported on the external concrete frame, interconnect easily. Dr Lovell and his architect achieved that rare synthesis of health and modernity which was so much part of the Modernist outlook.*

▲ *S. C. Johnson & Son administration building, Racine, Wisconsin, 1936, Frank Lloyd Wright (interior drawing). This is another strangely cut-off workplace. In the main interior space there is (as Hitchcock has observed) "a certain illusion of sky seen from the bottom of an aquarium". This richly inventive building, all red brick and glass tubing, centres on a space filled with slender concrete mushrooms and shaped columns and is lit where one would expect a cornice. Wright designed all the original furniture, manufactured by the "Steelcase" company.*

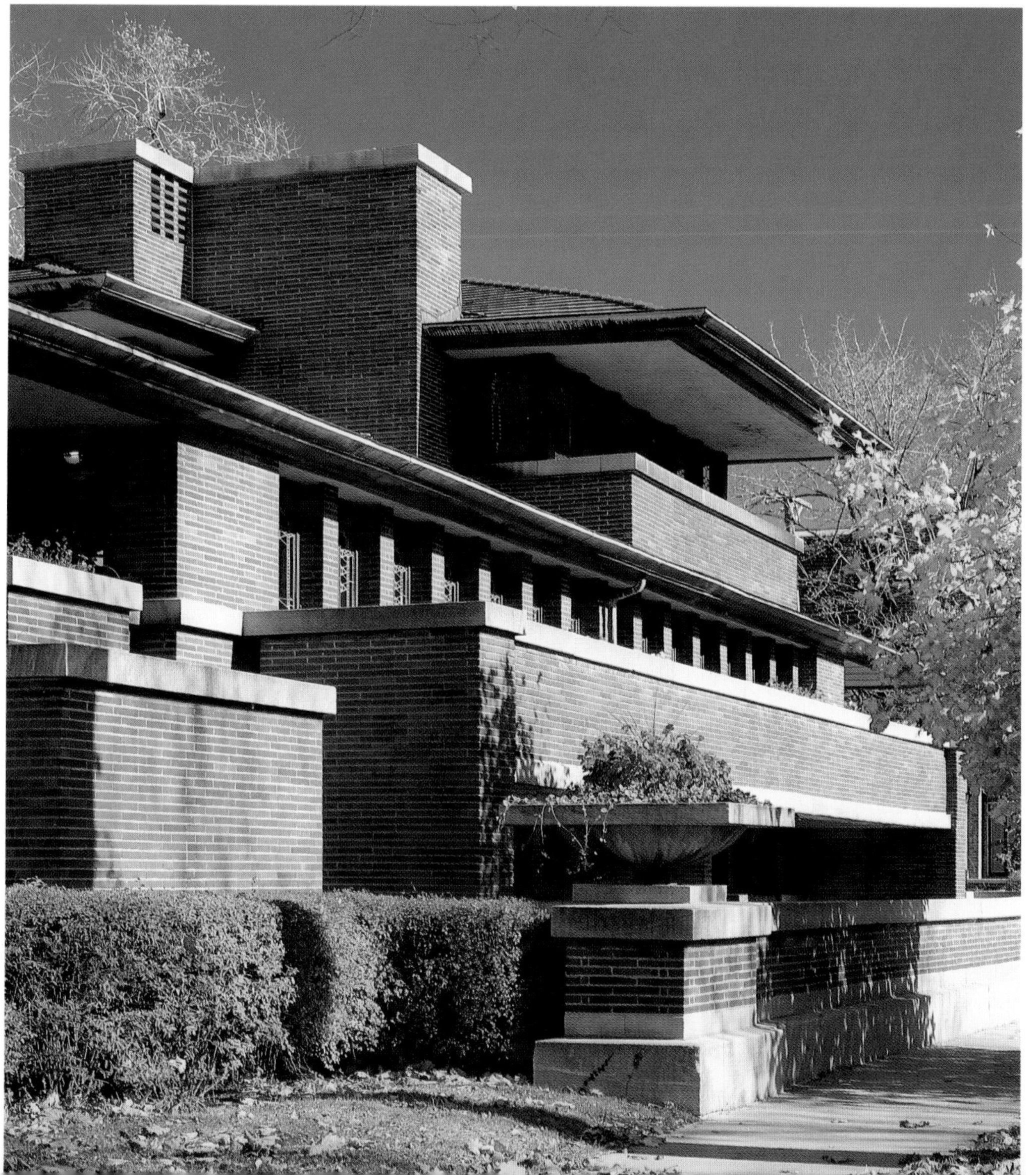

THE MODERN MOVEMENT

The search for a rational and democratic architecture in the 1920s

In one sense, the "Modern Movement" in architecture was born in Weimar Germany and certainly its enduring principles have a post-war optimistic social flavour. Modernism offered a new possibility of rational utility and democratic comfort, centred on the professional skills of planning and construction in an economic and subtle manner. The strength of these concerns inevitably caused the clamour about style to fade into the background. The visual fixation could, it seemed, be broken, and the frame of reference changed. From then on science and technology became increasingly important, as did the social goals of equality of provision and shelter for democratic freedoms. It was a reduced and limited version of this optimistic programme that some called "functionalism".

The first design school to teach on "Modernist" principles was the Bauhaus (1919–33), in Weimar, Dessau and then Berlin. It was inspired by Walter GROPIUS, its first director, who was succeeded by Hannes Meyer and finally by Ludwig MIES VAN DER ROHE. However, few original designers were happy with the term "International Style", coined by Hitchcock and Johnson in the USA, which simply grouped their architecture together by its image. Gropius wrote in 1935: "A Bauhaus style would have been a confession of failure"; LE CORBUSIER in 1936: "Let us abolish schools – the Corbu school together with the Vignola school, I beg you!" No-one, however, was more concerned with the visual than Le Corbusier.

Even those least fixated on the visual were concerned with issues of economy, with lightness and the appearance of lightness. The "polemic of objectivity" led to rigorously rational structures, an excitement with the developing possibilities of steel framing (and new welding techniques), new methods of timber framing, lightweight cladding and mass production. At last architects were taking up the ideas developed by 19th-century engineers.

The other stimulus to a new form of architecture was in the need for new housing. By the 1920s and 1930s, housing was a central concern in the developed European countries: the multiple production of convenient, affordable small dwellings. Massive developments of houses following the Modernist principles outlined above created a completely new type of place, the most outstanding being in Holland and in Germany where, in the late 1920s, much more housing was being built than in France or England.

Model estates like the Werkbund Weissenhofsiedlung, Stuttgart (1927) and the Werkbundsiedlung, Vienna (1932) demonstrated the fundamentally similar intentions of the wide range of contributing designers. Sadly, the subsequent generation of architects, while living in their changed social world, mimicked the *forms* they remembered from this time – white, box-like shapes, flat roofs, long windows, building off the ground and "abstract" compositions, but forgot the underlying purpose behind such transitory emblems. (JM)

▲ *The new Bauhaus building, Dessau, 1925–6, Walter Gropius. The model building of the ethos encapsulated by this pioneer institution. Headed by Gropius from 1919 to 1928, it taught new attitudes to design. It was the first large building to crystallize the new conception of space, with its interlocking cubic forms, its reinforced concrete frame, and curtain walls of glass.*

▶ *Hans Scharoun, house on the Weissenhofsiedlung, Stuttgart, 1927. Mies van der Rohe planned this estate and invited the best architects across Europe to design houses as part of the Werkbund's second exhibition. The first had been in Cologne in 1914, and a comparison between the two exhibitions shows how quickly Modernism had taken hold within just over a decade. The new image is remarkably consistent, despite the wide range of designers involved. Those included Le Corbusier and Gropius, the older Behrens and Poelzig, the more radical Stam and Oud, and the independent young Scharoun who already was interpreting Modernism's new language in a personal and less confined way.*

▶ *Kiefhoek Estate, Rotterdam, 1925–7. The young J.J.P. Oud became Rotterdam city architect in 1918, producing masterly groups of modest terrace houses in the Hook of Holland in 1924–7 and in Rotterdam. The planning is very careful, humane and precise, the form controlled and simple (influenced by De Stijl principles).*

▶ *Fromm Rubber factory, Kopernick, 1930. Arthur Korn designed this neat box, the first steel exposed cage, in a mode later developed by Mies van der Rohe in America. Unlike Mies van der Rohe's buildings, however, this makes use of red steel and white glazed brick.*

▲ *Van Nelle factory, Rotterdam, 1927, Mart Stam for Van der Vlugt & Brinkman. "Modern" architecture came of age with the design of three large buildings: the dynamic Bauhaus; Le Corbusier's tragically rejected League of Nations competition-winning project; and its contemporary, this very different factory. Stam produced a rational masterpiece, exposing the factory's processes (in glazed conveyors) as well as its constructed form.*

THE RANGE OF MODERNISM

Le Corbusier, Mies van der Rohe and the embodiment of Modernism

At the same period in the late 1920s, three houses were designed which encapsulated the differing strands within the new view of architecture, by then often called "Modernism": the Dymaxion House by Richard Buckminster FULLER in the USA; "Les Terraces" outside Paris by LE CORBUSIER for the Stein and de Monzie families; and Haus Moller in Potzleinsdorf, a Viennese suburb, by Adolf LOOS.

Fuller, denying the need for an emblem beyond creating an image of "newness", produced a remarkable metal structure hung from a central core. The project made little allowance for normal domestic habits and needs; instead, it displayed the romance of technology. The intense concentration on elegant technical solutions to rationally stated problems, without being prejudiced by experience, is a Modernist theme which only came to fruition in the last decades of this century with the works of Norman FOSTER.

Loos integrated emblem and instrument in a house with a timeless calm. By reinforcing existing forms of habitation, with slight level changes of both floors and ceilings and the relationship of spaces, it is for the whole body not just the eye. To Loos, the house, while it must contain symbolic and formal values, was neither a work of art nor a spectacle. All these designers were concerned with the making of their buildings. Fuller focused on technology transfer from industry, Le Corbusier on the imagery of new building technology, while Loos reconsidered the domain of craftsmanship.

Le Corbusier used technology to suggest new ways of moving through space and inhabiting it; new senses of enclosure, a new visual language of compressed planes, overlaid forms and virtual transparencies, a feast for the promenading eye. In contrast to Loos, Le Corbusier exploited his skill with publicity. As a result, the Villa Stein/de Monzie, along with the celebrated Villa Savoye at Poissy which was built shortly after it, came to canonize the ideals of Modernism.

These three, so different, not only in their intentions but in their image, left rather worthless the term "International Style". But undoubtedly Le Corbusier reinforced the "International" idea with his memorable *Five Points of Modern Architecture*: (1) Lift the building on columns off the ground; (2) Replace the ground covered by the building's footprint with a roof-terrace; (3) Let long windows stretch across the façade, and from side to side of rooms; (4) Let the plan be free-flowing; (5) Let the façade be a free composition, able to respond to light, views or compositional effect.

Le Corbusier's own series of buildings, from the villa for La Roche, 1923–4, via the Villa Cook of 1926 (which first canonized the "five points"), exploits the polemic without limiting the excitement of the architectural experience. The interior spaces of Ludwig MIES VAN DER ROHE might sometimes seem to "obey" the five points, but the effect is quite different, of pure, calm, almost abstract space. The experience of Le Corbusier's villas, by contrast, is captured by a dynamic *promenade architecturale*. (JM)

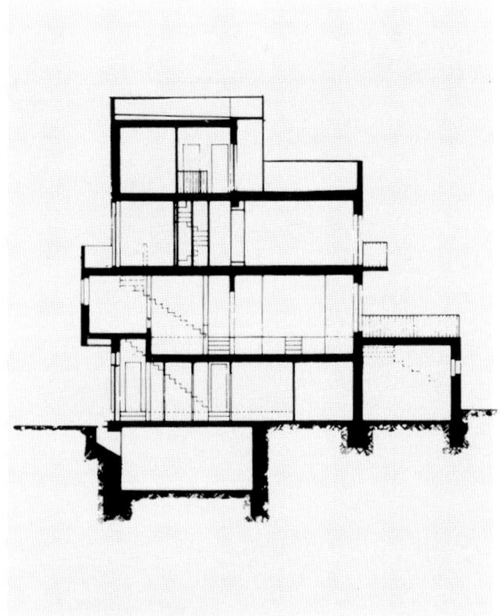

▲ *Villa Savoye, Poissy, nr Paris, 1928-30, Le Corbusier. Neither as grand nor as subtle as the Villa Stein/de Monzie, this villa has a certain jewel-like perfectness which is unique. The main living floor is raised over service quarters, reached up a spine ramp from which one processes further up to the roof terrace. The almost square form is held by a carefully proportioned column-grid and is enclosed by a continuous strip window. It is hollowed out on plan, allowing the living-room wall (vast sheets of sliding glass) to give onto an enclosed roof garden and sun trap.*

◀ ▼ *Haus Moller, Vienna, 1928, Adolf Loos, interior (below) and section (left). Inside the cubic configuration here, Loos planned a careful progression, up stairs off which rooms twist until the core is reached, the large living space on various levels. Opposed to a feverish search for novel forms, Loos dug deep towards a reinterpretation of archetypal place-making.*

▲ *Tugendhat House, Brno, 1930, Ludwig Mies van der Rohe. Contrasting with Le Corbusier's complex dove-tailing of space, Mies aims for a cool purity. The simplicity is highly formalized, its quality residing in the material detail – chrome cruciform columns, dividing screens (away from the structure) of onyx and ebony; and in cleverly worked out technology – the huge window here could descend out of sight to become literally immaterial.*

▶ *Dymaxion House, 1928, R. Buckminster Fuller. At a glance, this project fulfils Le Corbusier's "five points". But Fuller's intentions could not have been more different. It was the prototype of a mass-produced house with the central aim of transferring high scientific capability from the world of weaponry to creative and humane needs. The central core holds all services, with factory-built bathroom units coupled like train coaches. The building is supported off this core which also distributes heat, light and fresh air. The main floor, above the ground floor (reserved for garage and store) has pneumatic furniture and the roof terrace is protected by a duralumin umbrella. Perhaps the clearest image of its distance from human culture is the absence of bedlinen, made obsolete by interior climate control.*

EUROPEAN REALISTS

The spread of Modernism throughout Europe in the 1930s

In the 1930s, the seeds of Modernism were sown throughout Europe and her colonies (notably in East and South Africa). In Scandinavia, the late flowering of national romanticism had given way quite suddenly around 1930 to this new architecture; its acceptance was aided by a link with fundamental social changes. There was a growth in democracy and rapid levelling of living standards. Young architects were given public commissions – Sven MARKELIUS' Helsingborg Concert Hall (1932) is a fine example – while established masters like Gunnar ASPLUND developed a new palette which was graceful and translucent. Asplund's pavilions for the Stockholm Exhibition of 1930 were light and elegant but the Law Courts he designed as an addition to the Town Hall of Gothenburg, with their beautifully transparent courtyard, are probably a greater achievement.

In Denmark, Arne JACOBSEN produced fine work, ending the decade by winning the Aarhus town hall competition; but it was Alvar AALTO in Finland, also born at the turn of the century, who dominated the new architecture. There his master works of the decade are his first major projects: the Paimio Sanitorium and the Viipuri Library.

With the sanitorium Aalto extended Modernism's notions to include the physical and psychological needs of the building's occupants. The design is anti-mechanistic, deeply responsive to both the site and its inhabitants. But in all these works – the Gothenburg courtyard, the Aarhus council chamber, the Viipuri lecture room, the Helsingborg hall – there remained a certain romance, and undogmatic concern to create a new form of place-making.

In Italy Modernism found a different expression. Rational, rather puritanical and under fascist directives, the best works were Giuseppe TERRAGNI's Casa del Fascio and Giovanni Michelucci's Florence station. Stalin's Russia offered little opportunity for architecture, no more than did Hitler's Germany. But the pre-Nazi houses of Hans SCHAROUN were noteworthy. Few but exquisite, with a truly functional and unrestricted planning, they were based "on man's conscious need for form as the frame of his free existence" (Raymond McGrath).

In England it was the refugees from Europe who led the new architecture into the 1930s; Berthold LUBETKIN, from Russia, built the Highpoint flats in London (1933–5); while Erich MENDELSOHN, Walter GROPIUS, and Marcel BREUER each collaborated on interesting if minor buildings. Their partners (CHERMAYEFF, FRY and YORKE respectively) carried on the torch when they all soon left Britain, and with a handful of young designers like Wells COATES and CONNELL, WARD & LUCAS, English architecture was soon able to offer a more varied European fare of very reasonable standard. Other lesser designers included Thomas Tait, with his jazzy tower and fine treetop restaurant at the 1938 Empire exhibition and, standing apart from the architects, was the work of an unusual engineer, Owen WILLIAMS, whose remarkably free-thinking, independent works included sleek black glass newspaper buildings in London, Manchester and Glasgow. (JM)

▲ *The Schminke house, Saxony, 1932–3, Hans Scharoun. This country house represents a high point in Scharoun's work in the 1930s. It had to fit a site overlooked to the south but with gardens and a natural view to the north east. Raymond McGrath wrote in 1934: "The design has the smooth quality of a machine without being in any way like one, is solid and at the same time delicate, moving and at rest. . ."*

▶ *(Above right) The Concert Hall, Helsingborg, Denmark, 1925–32, Sven Markelius. One of the first great public halls of Scandinavian Modernism, its simple form was arrived at, in 1930, after a succession of Neo-Classicist proposals.*

◄ *TB Sanatorium, Paimio, Finland, 1929–31, Alvar Aalto. This masterwork was Aalto's first major opportunity to show how Modernism's notions could be extended to include the physical and psychological needs of the occupants of his buildings. Very subtly arranged two-person wards and open sun-decks showed great care for the needs and the environment of the patient, offering privacy, identity, heat and light; Aalto's hand can be clearly seen in all the surfaces, fittings and furniture.*

▲ *Casa del Fascio, Como, 1932–6, Giuseppe Terragni. Austere and rational, this magnificently controlled form (based on a regulating geometry) offered remarkable spaces behind one of Modernism's most intellectually pleasing façades.*

▲ *Highpoint apartments, Highgate, London, 1933, Lubetkin and Tecton. Initially planned as accommodation for workers in the developer's factory, Highpoint was the first of two blocks of flats. They soon became the beacon of modern civilized urban living in London. Every flat has a sense of space, sunlight and privacy, as well as economic compactness within the larger community.*

POST-WAR ARCHITECTURE

The old generation gives way to the new Moderns

The past four decades have seen one of the largest building programmes in history. The world has literally been reshaped. This extensive building programme began with the need to rebuild, renew and reinstate after the ravages of the Second World War. Housing took priority, and from an architectural point of view, it appeared there was stylistically only one way to go: along the lines of the pre-war international Modern Movement. "Modernism" had set out new "scientific" ways of building. Most importantly it offered the attraction of mass and serial production, as well as industrial and prefabrication processes – nothing could have been more appropriate and useful in a period that demanded fast, efficient and economic building. New, large-scale housing projects, schools, hospitals, and offices appeared everywhere. New towns were started and soon a growing private market for town centre redevelopment established itself in the Western countries. However, because of the complexity of the projects, architecture became more a teamwork activity. But its aspirations still lay with the so-called pioneers of modern architecture: GROPIUS, MENDELSOHN, MIES VAN DER ROHE and LE CORBUSIER.

An ideological clash among generations occurred in the Modern Movement's co-ordinating organization CIAM in the mid 1950s. A group of younger architects felt that the older Modernists were too doctrinaire and that their architecture was both impersonal and inflexible. Thus, CIAM was superseded by "Team 10", which included Aldo VAN EYCK (Holland), Georges Candilis (France), Ralph ERSKINE (Sweden), Reima PIETILÄ (Finland) and Alison and Peter SMITHSON (Britain). The latter were closely associated with the social content of architecture, with questions of "identity" in buildings and the so-called "New Brutalism". This term seems to have derived from two main sources: Le Corbusier's use of *beton brut* and its tough appearance, and the exposed services and materials of its key monument, a new school at Hunstanton, Norfolk, in 1957 by the Smithsons. The term is also often applied to the unadorned raw concrete of buildings like the London South Bank complex (including Denys LASDUN's National Theatre). It heralded one aspect of a new era, while another was the "free-form" design of Le Corbusier's Ronchamp Chapel, the originality and freshness of which surprised even the young revolutionaries. It led to a host of free architectural compositions from SAARINEN's TWA terminal in New York, and UTZON's Sydney Opera House, to Ton Albert's HMB buildings in Amsterdam.

The Pompidou Centre in Paris by PIANO and ROGERS represented a break in another direction. As a museum it was to be viewed as a cultural "machine". One of the first major essays in the new "High-Tech" manner, it was rooted in the science fiction ideas of the British ARCHIGRAM group of designers. Engineering, or High-Tech, architecture carries on the Modernist tradition of the simple functional shed, albeit with external guts or services *à la* Lloyds Building in London, also by Richard Rogers. (DS)

▲ *Sydney Opera House, Sydney, Australia, 1956–1976. Jørn Utzon's Opera House, with its great sail-like concrete ceramic-faced roofs, has been referred to as "the building of the century". Originally won in competition in 1956, it took over 20 years to build after the project had been handed over to other architects. Nonetheless, the building clearly achieved its original promise.*

▲ *Pompidou Centre, Paris, 1969–72. Won in international competition, the design brought immediate fame to the architects Renzo Piano and Richard Rogers. Great external escalators traverse the main façade to Place Beaubourg, while the rear elevation, shown here, presents a more prosaic "services" appearance. Interior spaces are entirely free from columns to ensure maximum flexibility.*

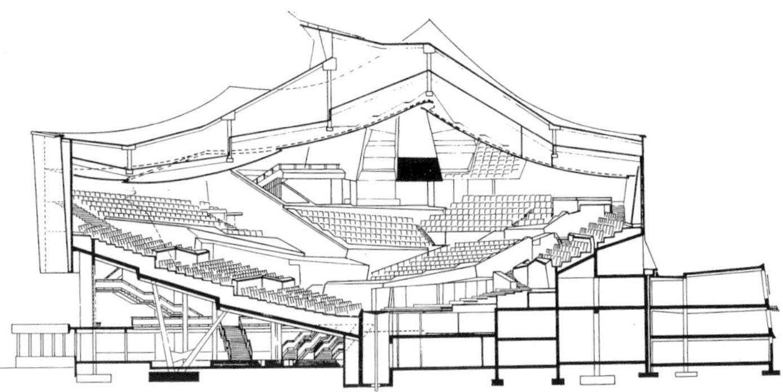

▲ *The Philharmonic Hall, Berlin, 1963, by Hans Scharoun (exterior and section). This is a truly irregular and organic building although it still functions effectively as a concert hall. It is related to an inherent geometrical order that becomes apparent through the interconnected but free-flowing internal spaces.*

▲ *Interior, Hunstanton Secondary Modern School, Norfolk, Peter and Alison Smithson. This was the result of a competition held in 1949 and completed in 1954. It took its cues from buildings by Mies van der Rohe, exploiting a "bare bones" and brickwork aesthetic with exposed steelwork, floor beams and services. It has been referred to as the first British "Brutalist" building.*

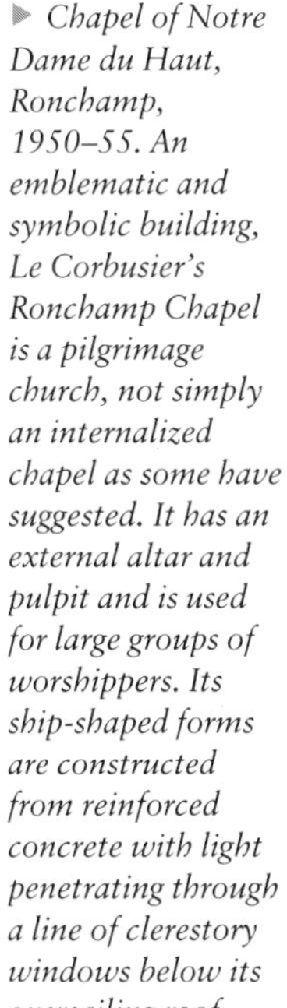

▶ *Chapel of Notre Dame du Haut, Ronchamp, 1950–55. An emblematic and symbolic building, Le Corbusier's Ronchamp Chapel is a pilgrimage church, not simply an internalized chapel as some have suggested. It has an external altar and pulpit and is used for large groups of worshippers. Its ship-shaped forms are constructed from reinforced concrete with light penetrating through a line of clerestory windows below its oversailing roof.*

THE NEW TRADITIONALISTS

Community architecture and the Post-Modernist fashion

By the mid-1970s a wide dissatisfaction had grown up with "Modern" architecture, which began to be viewed as an arrogant imposition of inadequate environmental ideas upon society. Its basic ideals were seriously questioned and eventually its "death" was recorded. It was soon followed by the growth of a fashionable "Post-Modernism" invented by a number of critics and historians as a substitute style. Although it proved insubstantial it did, however, lead to a revival of interest in historicism as an architectural language and a return to Neo-Classicism.

Post-Modern Classicism can be seen in the guise of much overscaled and bulky concrete (often prefabricated) architecture for housing schemes as well as public buildings, in Europe and the USA. The monumental work of the Spanish architect Ricardo Bofill and the American Michael GRAVES is perhaps most closely associated with this form of Post-Modernism. In contrast to this trend there was also a growing fascination with vernacular and regional modern architecture and with what Bernard Rudofsky had described as "Architecture without Architects", the title of his celebrated 1965 MOMA exhibition.

"Free-form" architecture, too, expressed a growing awareness of new values of vernacular and indigenous building materials and traditions, ranging from Japan to Hungary where the Pecs Group and Imre MAKOVECZ exerted considerable influence. Thus, "community architecture" and a closer public identification and participation in design and planning processes proved significant. Many schemes were produced indicating varying approaches to the housing problem, from the early prototypical prefabricated Habitat project by SAFDIE for the Montreal Expo in 1967, to the work carried out by the Belgian architect Lucien Kroll with his student "clients" at Louvain University, as well as the Byker Community project by ERSKINE at Newcastle and Rod Hackney's more conventional people's housing at Macclesfield. The community architecture development led, particularly in England, to a much greater awareness of conservation issues, culminating in the Prince of Wales's general popularity as the movement's "guru" and the bearer of a new vision of architecture.

Thus, as we approach the end of the millennium a curious situation has emerged in architecture: pluralities have been recognised, there is a much wider acceptance of historical precedent (as in the work of the American architects Charles Moore and Michael Graves), and a sensitivity has been displayed in relation to ecology, nature and the organic approach to design. There is also a genuine excitement – particularly among the younger generation – over architecture's new freedoms and opportunities. Internationally, a great interest has been shown in the independent identity of regions and national cultures and this has been reflected in architecture, whilst in the former Communist countries the heavy concrete work of the post-war years is gradually giving way too to a lighter and a much more adventurous aesthetic. (DS)

▲ *Belgian architect Lucien Kroll's housing experiments in the 1970s were based on the idea of participation of users in the design process. His* La Mémé *(Grandmother) scheme of student housing was for the Medical Faculty at the University of Louvain. Seemingly built up in a random manner it provided a series of living cells based on the specific requirements of the first generation of students.*

▲ *The multi-unit reinforced concrete "Habitat" housing was specially "prefabricated" for the Montreal World Exposition in 1967 by the Canadian/Israeli architect Moshe Safdie. Based on a student thesis design, it summarized a whole generation's design philosophy about modern urban living with its well-equipped living pods, private balconies and fine views.*

▼ *Broadgate development, London, by Arup Associates, begun 1981. Built in stages, the first part to be opened (in 1984) was No. 1 Finsbury Avenue, shown here. A feature of the development is the way in which the spaces between buildings are given back to public use with cafés, pubs, an ice rink-cum-theatre as well as fine art works.*

▶ *World Arab Institute, Paris, 1988, Jean Nouvel. One of the so-called* Grands Projets *built in central Paris in the 1980s, the Institute is an innovative building. The south façade overlooks a large courtyard and is dominated by a patterned series of ocular devices that dilate in relation to the sun's power, giving it something of the appearance of an "Islamic screen".*

▲ *Piazza d'Italia, New Orleans, 1975-80, Charles Moore. This wonderfully evocative design for New Orleans acts as a community metaphor for the Italians who live in the city. A central fountain, which incorporates a stream in the shape of Italy, is flanked on either side by "walls" devoted to the development of Attic columns; Doric, Composite, Corinthian and Tuscan are reassembled in fragmentary façades.*

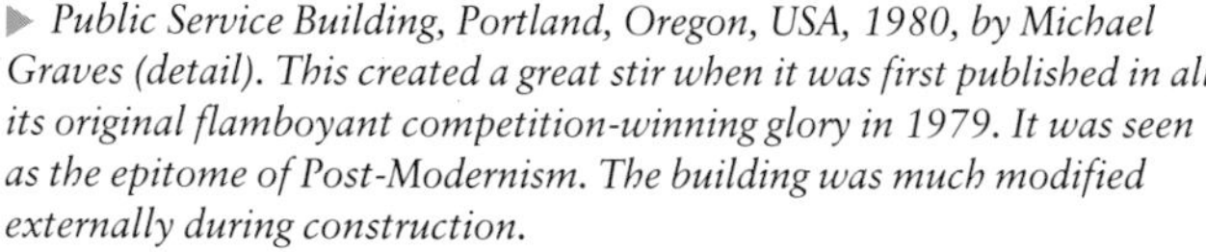

▶ *Public Service Building, Portland, Oregon, USA, 1980, by Michael Graves (detail). This created a great stir when it was first published in all its original flamboyant competition-winning glory in 1979. It was seen as the epitome of Post-Modernism. The building was much modified externally during construction.*

NEW TENDENCIES

From the hippy age to architecture's green revolution

Freedom and liberation were the passwords of the 1960s counter-culture, and that meant freedom to act, sing, draw and design in any way one pleased. This "hippie" era saw the emergence of designers like Buckminster FULLER and Paolo SOLERI as cult heroes. Free forms and bright colours were characteristic of the new Aquarian age. Form was no longer dictated by function but liberated by fashion.

In the 1970s while the Western world cowered behind economic barriers and experienced deep recession, the oil-rich states commandeered the architecture and planning principles of mature Modernism. The Arab countries produced developments (and Utopias) employing the skills of talented Western architects such as Jørn UTZON, Henning LARSON, Reima PIETILÄ, SKIDMORE, OWINGS & MERRILL and James Cubitt. The international promise of modern architecture became a reality in the Middle East.

In poorer developing countries sprawling squatter areas grew into monster slums and the United Nations saw fit to hold influential conferences on environmental issues, as well as setting up a number of regional environmental centres. More generally people began to view the impact of urban expansion and the new technologies on their environment and found it wanting. The narrowing of resources, the burgeoning population question, and the ever-present threat of nuclear war all caused much concern.

The self-build city *Arcosanti* by Soleri in Arizona (begun in 1969) and projects such as the Anthroposophical Seminary in Järna, Sweden (begun in 1976), and the "spiritual" centres in America, Scotland and India all contributed to a new sensibility in their attempts to humanize design. They proved to be small pockets of resistance to the prevailing commercial developments and to doctrinaire Functionalism. In a sense they were also early components of the embryonic "green" movement. They also represented a new interest in "natural" design, and in organic architecture coupled with environmental betterment. Organic architecture, which derives largely from Frank Lloyd WRIGHT, is concerned with respect for natural materials, the sympathetic siting of buildings and new spatial principles, as can be seen in Douglas CARDINAL's Canadian Museum.

In sharp contrast to this tendency is the interest in "Deconstruction": a literary method applied to art and architecture in the work of Zaha Hadid, Rem Koolhaas, Peter EISENMAN and others whose projects were featured in a Deconstructivist exhibition in New York in 1987. It relates in some ways to earlier Soviet Constructivist design with its dynamic planar emphasis, but is also redolent with new ideas.

The strongest tendency of the past decade, however, has undoubtedly been the resurgence of the technically dominated High-Tech mode of design. This is seen particularly in the work of Renzo PIANO and Richard ROGERS, Philip COX, Norman FOSTER, Nicholas Grimshaw and Michael Hopkins whose influence still continues to dominate today's architectural thinking and practice. (DS)

▲ *Dance Studio, The Hague, 1988. The New York Deconstructivist Exhibition held at MOMA in 1988 brought together a disparate group of designers some of whom had built little and many of whom had trained at the AA School in London. Dutch architect and AA graduate Rem Koolhaas's projects included this Dance Studio.*

▲ *The Tourist Village at Yulura, N.T., Australia, c. 1987, is situated in the shadow of the enormous Ayers Rock. Designed by Cox, Richardson and Taylor it uses High-Tech elements to create the impression of a temporary encampment in the desert.*

▲ *Steiner Seminary, Järna, Sweden (begun in 1974). Developing architectural ideas from philosopher Rudolf Steiner's "new style in architecture", the Danish architect Erik Asmussen has produced some distinctive organic buildings at the Steiner Seminary. More than a dozen highly coloured structures have been built in local natural materials (including a library, eurhythmy studios, student facilities and a "nature cure" clinic) on a beautiful site overlooking the Baltic Sea. It is surrounded by organically farmed land.*

▲ *(Above right) Canadian Museum of Civilization, Quebec, 1990. Another organically inspired building draws inspiration from the glacial remnants of Canada's wastelands. Situated along the river's edge at Hull, Quebec, this museum lies opposite the great Parliamentary Buildings in Ottawa. Canadian architect Douglas Cardinal designed his amorphous museum complex with the aid of the latest computer design techniques.*

▲ Arcosanti *is a Utopian prototype for a huge population. A largely self-built project on a mesa site at Cordes Junction, Arizona, USA, it was designed by Paolo Soleri and begun, using voluntary labour, in 1969. It was intended as one of Soleri's first* Arcologies *– settlements designed to bring architecture and ecology together by the use of high-density urban environments and the minimum amount of built-on land. It remains now as a testimony to his notions.*

◀ *The small Hysolar Institute by Günter Behnisch (1987) is devoted to research into solar energy. It is part of Stuttgart University's facilities for environmental research and information and is partly used by a private company. Its stainless steel and glass blocks and façades are made from standard elements but are built up in a multi-angled, almost chaotic, manner giving the appearance of a partly finished, experimental building.*

GLOSSARY OF TERMS, MOVEMENTS AND ABBREVIATIONS

AA: Architectural Association, London, leading progressive school of architecture and association with worldwide membership.

ABACUS: the top slab of a CAPITAL.

ACANTHUS: the plant whose leaf is used as part of the decoration on column capitals of the Corinthian and Composite orders.

ACROTERION (pl *Acroteria):* PLINTH at the apex of a PEDIMENT on which stands a statue or an ornament.

ADOBE: Mud brick baked in the sun, commonly used in Africa, Spain and Latin America.

AIA: American Institute of Architects, Washington DC, USA.

AISLE: a walkway in a church or hall which runs laterally through the building usually parallel to the central nave.

AMBULATORY: circulation or processional space or corridor surrounding the sanctuary of a religious building.

APSE: semicircular or polygonal end of the CHOIR in a church.

ARCADE: a number of arches carried on piers or columns, or a covered passage lined with shops on one or both sides.

ARCH: there are many styles of arch and the design often denotes the period in which a building is designed. The *basket* arch is a half-oval shape and resembles a basket handle; the *four-centred* or *depressed* arch has a curved, squat shape and is frequently found in medieval buildings; the *horseshoe* arch is found in Islamic architecture; the *lancet,* or *pointed,* is high and pointed and features in Gothic buildings; the *lobed* or *clover leaf* has several concave segments; the *Roman* has a semi-circular top; the *ogee* consists of four arcs resembling an upturned boat keel and was introduced in around 1300; a *Tudor* arch is squat in shape and rises to an apex in the centre.

ARCHITRAVE: the lower part of an ENTABLATURE running along the top of the row of columns. It is also commonly used to describe the moulding surrounding a door or window.

ARCUATED: a building whose construction is based around the arch shape in contrast to the POST-AND-LINTEL type.

ART DECO: a style of architecture and decoration named after the 1925 Paris Exposition des Arts Décoratifs, epitomized by use of cubic shapes and angular, dynamic ornamentation.

ART NOUVEAU: general term to describe flowing, sinuous designs based on natural forms, popular in Europe *c.*1895–1906. See JUGENDSTIL, SECESSIONSTIL.

ARTS & CRAFTS: movement for design reform, initially centred around William Morris, which developed in England in the second half of the C19 and was widely influential. In architecture, the movement aimed to abolish historicism and revivalism, and design "honest" buildings that expressed universal values.

AXONOMETRIC: a geometric drawing around an axis which shows a building three dimensionally.

ASHLAR: large, smooth-finished masonry blocks.

ATRIUM: originally a central room or court found in Classical houses. In modern architecture the term is applied to a tall, multi-storey open central area within a building that receives light from above.

AXIAL PLAN: a term used when a building is planned longitudinally, i.e. not a CENTRALIZED PLAN.

BALDACHIN/BALDACCHINO: a canopy over doorway, altar or throne.

BALLOON FRAME: a method of building using a timber frame commonly found in North America and Scandinavia. The construction begins with an enclosure of upright posts against which are nailed horizontal timbers.

BALUSTER: a short post or pillar supporting a rail which in a series becomes *balustrading.*

BAROQUE: exuberant, ornate architecture and interior design which proliferated in Europe *c.*1600–1750.

BASILICA: in Roman architecture a rectangular building, usually a meeting hall, with central nave, two side aisles and often also including galleries. Today the term is applied to a church with a nave and two or more aisles.

BASTION: projecting part of a fortification as a look-out.

BAUHAUS: progressive and radical German school of art and design, headed by architects Walter Gropius, Mies van der Rohe and Adolf Meyer, situated in Weimar, Dessau and Berlin, 1919–32. Exercised an important influence on the development of MODERNISM.

BAY: the vertical division of a building into segments usually denoted by columns or windows.

BDA: Bund Deutscher Architekten (German Association of Architects).

BEAM: horizontal, load-bearing members of a building.

BEAUX ARTS: rich NEO-CLASSICAL style favoured by the Paris-based Ecole des Beaux Arts in C19 France and well into the C20.

BOSS: ornamental projection at the intersection of ribs or beams.

BRACKET: a small supporting piece of stone, wood or metal projecting from a wall.

BRISE SOLEIL: a sun-break, usually of horizontal or vertical slats, used to shade a window.

BRUTALISM: architecture where the rough constructional materials are left exposed; term derived in part from use of *in-situ* concrete (*béton brut*) by Le Corbusier and others.

BUTTRESS: masonry or brickwork which is built against, or projects from, a loadbearing wall to add strength (see FLYING BUTTRESS)

BYZANTINE: art and architecture of Byzantium (Constantinople); term used for eastern Christian art of the C4–14.

CAMPANILE: a bell tower, usually free standing.

CANTILEVER: a horizontal projection from a wall, often balcony or stair, supported at one end only.

CAPITAL: top section or crowning feature of a column, often elaborate. The shape and design denotes the architectural order eg DORIC, CORINTHIAN.

CAROLINGIAN: art based on a Roman revival, which appeared from the C8 to the C10 in Charlemagne's empire – notably the Netherlands, France and Germany.

CARYATID: statue of a draped human figure, usually female, used as a supporting column.

CENTRALIZED PLAN: building design radiating from a central point.

CHAMFERED: bevelled edge of stone or wood.

CHANCEL: part of church in which the altar is placed, also a term used to refer to the entire east end of a church beyond the CROSSING.

Arches

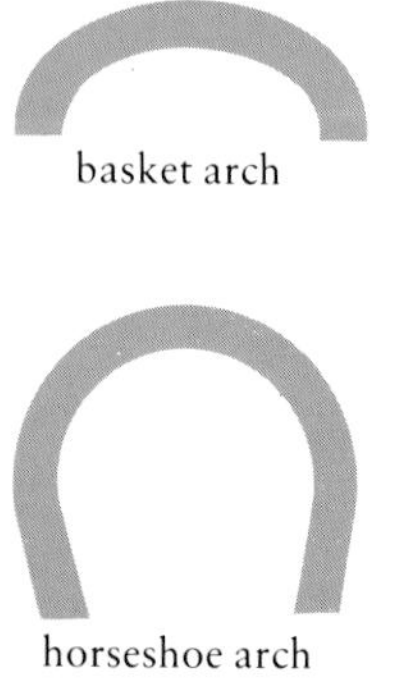

basket arch

horseshoe arch

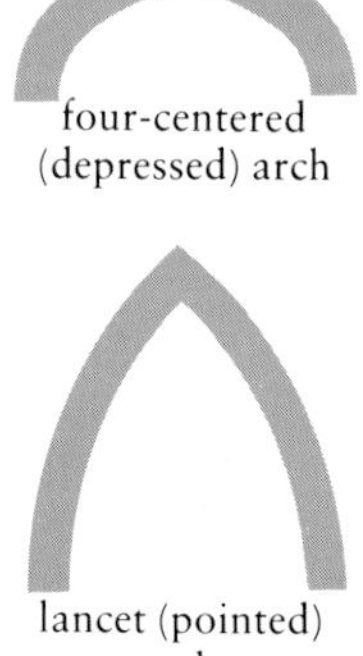

four-centered (depressed) arch

lancet (pointed) arch

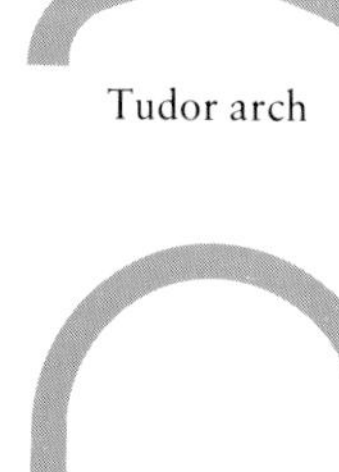

Tudor arch

Roman arch

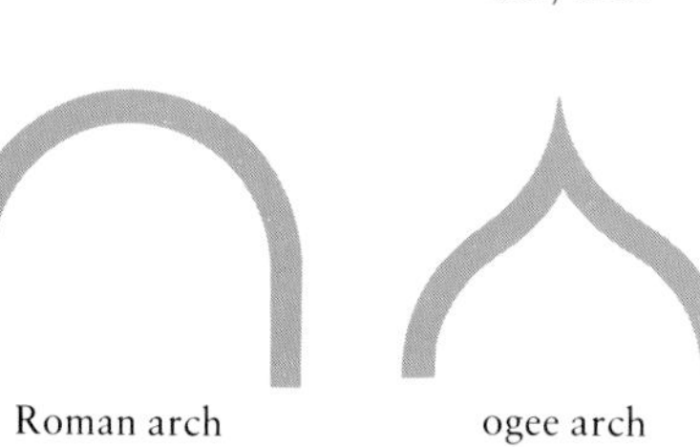

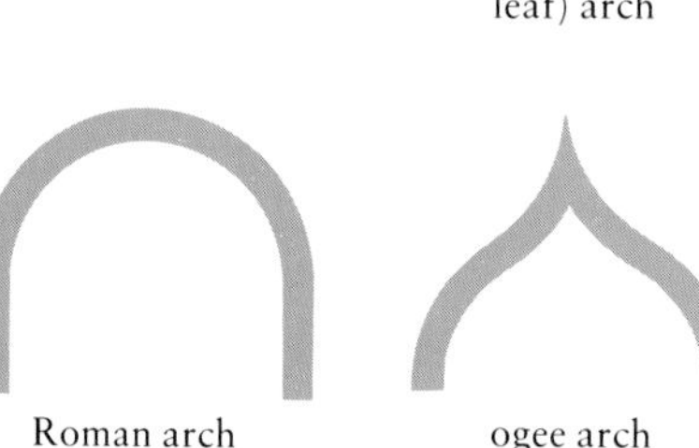

Lobed (clover leaf) arch

ogee arch

CHICAGO SCHOOL: group of architects in Chicago which in the years 1880–1910 invented the steel-frame, multi-storey skyscraper.

CHOIR: portion of the church to the west of the altar used by singers and clergy.

CIAM: Congrès Internationaux d'Architecture Moderne – a liberal, reformist organization of architects, artists and designers founded at La Sarraz in 1928 and which supported MODERNISM. It disbanded in the 1950s.

CICA: Comité Internationale des Critiques d'Architecture, founded in Barcelona in 1979.

CIRPAC: Comité Internationale pour la Résolution des Problèmes de l'Architecture Contemporaine, a group within CIAM, founded in 1929.

CITADEL: a fort usually placed at the corner of a fortified town.

CLADDING: non-loadbearing external envelope or covering to a building.

CLASSICAL: the architecture originating in ancient Greece or Rome, the rules and forms of which were revived to establish the classical RENAISSANCE in Europe in the c15 and c16.

CLERESTORY: range of windows constituting the upper stage of a church above the AISLE.

CLOISTER: a space, usually a quadrangle, surrounded by a COLONNADE or ARCADE opening on to a central courtyard.

COFFERING: recessed panels usually found in ceilings, VAULTS or domes.

COLONNADE: line of columns bearing arches or a horizontal ENTABLATURE.

COLOSSAL ORDER: see GIANT ORDER.

COLUMN: vertical, round pillar or support for an arch or an ENTABLATURE.

COMPOSITE ORDER: see Orders.

CONSTRUCTIVISM: radical arts and architecture movement in post-revolution Russia of the 1920s, concerned with abstract, geometric forms and utilitarian socially orientated design.

CORBEL: a projecting BRACKET, usually of stone, to provide support for a beam.

CORINTHIAN ORDER: see ORDERS.

CORNICE: top section of an ENTABLATURE also used to describe the decorative moulding along the top of a building or wall.

COURSE: horizontal layer of bricks or stone forming part of a wall.

CRENELLATION: parapet or battlements with openings, usually at the top of castle walls.

CROSSING: place in a church where nave and transept intersect.

CROSS-VAULT: see VAULT.

CRUCIFORM: cross-shaped.

CRYPT: underground chamber of a church.

CUPOLA: a domed VAULT crowning a roof.

CURTAIN WALL: in modern architecture, the non-loadbearing skin or cladding on the outside of a building.

DECONSTRUCTIVISM: term derived for the contemporary philosophical/literary movement centred around Jacques Derrida. In architecture it is exemplified by exploded architectural shapes as in the "Deconstructivist" show in New York in 1987.

DECORATED: term for late c13/early c14 British architecture characterized by ornate decoration and the ogee (S-curve) in arches and window TRACERY.

DENTIL: small square block used at regular intervals to form part of a CORNICE.

DE STIJL: Dutch political and creative anti-tradition movement founded by Van Doesberg in Leiden in 1917 (until 1931), whose work is characterized by geometric abstraction, the use of primary colours and the interplay of flat planes.

DOMICAL VAULT: see VAULT.

DORIC ORDER: see ORDERS.

DRUM: vertical wall, usually circular, on which sits a dome.

EARLY ENGLISH: term for English GOTHIC of the c12-late c13.

EAVES: the projection of a roof overhanging the walls.

ELEVATION: the vertical face of a building or a drawing showing a face.

ELIZABETHAN: Late c16–mid-c17 English architecture characterized by symmetrical façades, decorative STRAPWORK and large windows.

ENTABLATURE: section of upper wall or horizontal beam supported by columns consisting of ARCHITRAVE, FRIEZE and CORNICE.

Entablature

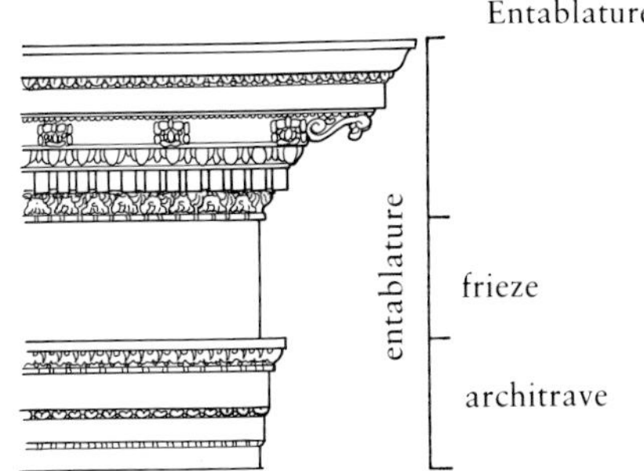

ETH: Eidgenössische Technische Hochschule (Swiss Federal Institute of Technology), Zurich.

EXPRESSIONISM: German movement in the arts which flourished between 1910 and 1924. Its architecture is typified by bold, sculptural, monumental buildings and bizarre Utopian projects.

FAÇADE: the exterior face of a building.

FASCIA: a plain horizontal band usually found in the ARCHITRAVE of an order. Also, a board or plate covering the end of roof rafters.

FENESTRATION: the arrangement of windows in a building.

FENG-SHUI: The ancient art of living in harmony with nature and of planning mankind's relationship with the land. Much used by Chinese architects, builders and developers in the layout of their buildings.

FERRO-CONCRETE: steel-reinforced concrete.

FINIAL: formal ornament on top of a gable, pinnacle etc.

FLAMBOYANT: 19th-century term for late French GOTHIC architecture of the c15-16 characterized by flame-like TRACERY and elaborate carving.

FLUTING: vertical, concave channels cut into column shafts.

FLYING BUTTRESS: an arch or half-arch transmitting the thrust of a VAULT or roof from the upper part of a wall to a support outside

Flying buttress

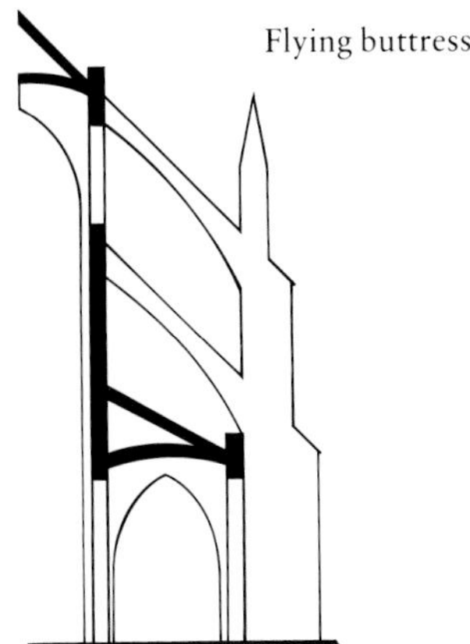

FOLLY: a decorative building, often in the form of a classical ruin, used to enhance a landscape.

FRESCO: method of painting directly on wall or ceiling before plaster dries.

FRIEZE: a horizontal band, often close to the top of a wall or forming the central part of an ENTABLATURE, usually enriched with sculpture or decorative paintwork.

FUNCTIONALISM: basic MODERN MOVEMENT idea that the purpose, or function, of a building can be expressed through its utilitarian plan and unadorned external forms. Derived from German term *Zweck*.

FUTURISM: a European but Italian-based modern art movement originating in the "Speed and War" manifesto published by Marinetti in 1909. Architecture was added to the movement's arsenal in 1914 with Antonia Sant'Elia's "Futurist Architecture" manifesto.

GABLE: triangular part of a wall at the end of a roof, also a triangular canopy above a door or window.

GARDEN CITY: idea formulated by Ebenezer Howard and others and first realized at Letchworth, Herts, in 1903.

GATEPAC: Grup d'Artistes i Tècnics Catalans per el Progrés de l'Arquitectura Contemporànea. Spanish architects group founded by Sert and others associated with CIAM in 1930.

GEORGIAN: the brick and STUCCO urban CLASSICAL-style language in England from the early c18 to the early c19.

GIANT ORDER (also called Colossal Order): can apply to any Order whose columns climb to several storeys high.

GOTHIC: general term for medieval architecture characterized by pointed stone arches, rib VAULTS, great windows of coloured glass and skilful construction to create delicate-looking structures.

GRUPPO 7: group of 7 Italian architects founded in 1926, later known as MIAR.

HALF-TIMBERED: building style consisting of an exposed timber frame with the gaps between filled with brick or plaster.

HELLENISTIC: architecture which developed between 323 BC and 27 BC in the kingdoms, including Greece and northern Egypt, which made the empire of Alexander the Great (356-323 BC). It is typified by rich decoration and sculpture.

HIGH-TECH: a term employed for some architecture dating from late 1970s onwards which displays the technology of supports and services of a building.

HIPPED ROOF: a roof composed of inclining sides and ends.

IAA: International Academy of Architecture.

IBA: German abbreviation for the International Building Exhibition organization to renovate and rebuild West Berlin, 1977-87.

IIT: Illinois Institute of Technology.

INTERNATIONAL STYLE: An American term introduced by Hitchcock and Johnson to describe European MODERNIST buildings of the early inter-war years, 1920-31.

IONIC ORDER: see ORDERS.

ISOMETRIC: accurate, 45°-drawn three-dimensional projection.

IWAN: a term used of Near Eastern and Islamic architecture meaning a rectangular, vaulted hall enclosed by either two or three walls and often leading to a courtyard.

IUA: International Union of Architects.

JUGENDSTIL: German term for ART NOUVEAU, which can be translated as "Youth Style". Its characteristics include naturalistic, whiplash ornamentation.

KEEP: the main tower of a castle, often containing living quarters and storage space to be used in times of siege.

KEYSTONE: the central stone of a semi-circular arch.

LANTERN: small glazed turret on the top of a roof or dome.

LATTICE WINDOW: a window with diamond shaped panes of glass.

LCC: London County Council.

LINTEL: wooden or stone beam across the top of a door or window to support the weight of the wall above.

MADRASA: a Muslim school of theology attached to a mosque.

MANNERISM: High RENAISSANCE tendency (beginning with late Michelangelo and popular throughout c16 Italy, Spain and France) to break the Classical rules, transforming the Renaissance architectural language into a more individual style.

MARS: Modern Architectural Research, a British group of architects associated with CIAM founded in 1933 by Maxwell Fry and Wells Coates.

METABOLISTS: group formed in Tokyo in 1960 whose original members included Kenzo Tange and Kisho Kurokawa. Their projects are characterised by the use of futuristic, mechanical imagery, often using "pods" or cells, in order to "reflect dynamic reality".

MIHRAB: a niche, used for prayer and facing Mecca, in a mosque wall.

MIT: Massachussetts Institute of Technology.

MODERN MOVEMENT or MODERNISM: general terms to describe the new, socially progressive, undecorated, cubic, democratic and functionalist architectural intentions of the first half of the c20.

MOMA: Museum of Modern Art, New York.

MULLION: Vertical post used to divide a window.

MUQARNA: see VAULT.

NATO: Narrative Architecture Today. Group within the AA founded by Nigel Coates.

NAVE: the central, broad walkway in a church. The term is also applied to the entire western section of a church.

NEO-CLASSICISM: revival of the purity and formality of Classical design (mid-c18 – early c19) as a reaction against BAROQUE and ROCOCO extravagance.

NEUE SACHLICHKEIT: roughly translated as the "new objectivity"; the post-Weimar Republic MODERNIST tradition associated with FUNCTIONALISM.

NORMAN: Form of ROMANESQUE architecture in England around the time of the Norman Conquest.

OBELISK: tall, tapering stone shaft finished with pyramidal top.

OCTASTYLE: PORTICO with eight columns.

OGIVE: see ARCH.

OMA: Office of Metropolitan Architecture of Rem Koolhaas.

ORDERS: term describing the classical architectural language of religious and secular buildings in ancient Greece and Rome. There are five principal orders – Tuscan, Doric, Ionic, Corinthian and Composite and each is denoted by a column with decorated ENTABLATURE. The *Tuscan* is primitive looking and derives from ancient Etruscan temples; the *Doric* is more refined than Tuscan and has its origins in ancient Greece but is also found in ancient Roman building; *Ionic* originated in Asia Minor in the mid c6 BC and is distinguished by VOLUTES at the column tops and DENTILS in the CORNICE; *Corinthian* is thought to be an Athenian invention of around c5 BC and is distinguished by ornate ACANTHUS leaf decoration at its crown; the *Composite* is the latest and most elaborate of the orders and combines features from the Corinthian and Ionic orders.

ORGANIC: an architecture closely associated with nature, in terms of landscape, setting, materials and often forms of construction. Used widely in relation to c20 "individualist" and "democratic" thinking by Frank Lloyd Wright and his followers.

PALLADIANISM: style popular in England in early c17, and then in USA, inspired by the work of Andrea Palladio (1508-80).

PEDIMENT: the low-pitched triangular GABLE above an ENTABLATURE in classical architecture. In RENAISSANCE architecture and later it refers to any roof end whether triangular, semi-circular or broken.

PENDENTIVE: concave structure, usually composed of inclining arches, which supports circular dome over square or polygonal base.

PERISTYLE: a line of columns surrounding a building or courtyard.

PERPENDICULAR: late English GOTHIC architecture characterized by tall, stressed verticals, slender supports and large windows.

PIETRA DURA: decorative work using inlaid semi-precious stones to depict geometric patterns etc.

PIER: the solid, structure-carrying areas or pillars between windows, doors or other openings.

PILASTER: shallow, ornamental, rectangular pillar projecting from a wall.

Orders

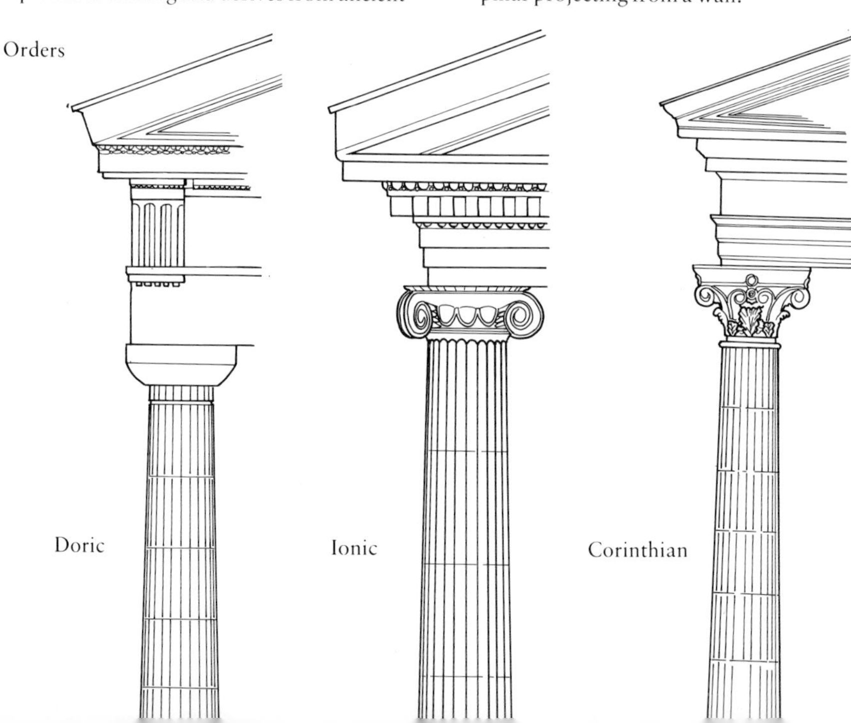

PILLAR: a vertical support which differs from a column in that it does not have to be cylindrical nor conform to the orders.
PILOTIS: term coined by Le Corbusier to describe pillars or stilts upon which a building is raised.
PLAN: the layout of a building drawn in a horizontal plane.
PLINTH: the square base upon which a column sits.
PODIUM: continuous base supporting columns.
POINTED ARCH: see ARCH.
PORTE-COCHÈRE: an entrance large enough for wheeled vehicles to pass through.
PORTICO: covered entrance or centrepiece to a building, often supported on columns.
POST-AND-LINTEL: also known as post-and-beam, a construction method consisting of horizontal beams, or LINTELS, supported on vertical posts.
POST-MODERNISM: mid-1970s reaction to MODERNISM seen as an historical and pictoral style; uses elements from different periods eclectically and sometimes light-heartedly.
PRAIRIE SCHOOL: architecture of the American Midwest, particularly Frank Lloyd Wright and contemporaries at turn of c20, which derived its inspiration from the open flat landscape and natural materials.
PREFABRICATION: manufactured components or entire buildings which are easily transported from factory to site. "Prefab" is the name given to factory-made emergency short life homes, particularly in Great Britain after the Second World War.
PYLON: in ancient Egyptian architecture, the large, chunky pyramidal towers flanking a temple entrance.
QUADRATURA: wall or ceiling painting which deceives the eye into believing objects portrayed are three-dimensional. In the c17-c18 the work was undertaken by travelling painters known as "quadraturisti".
QUEEN ANNE: late c19 style borrowed from c17 brick-built Dutch housing, typified by the designs of Norman Shaw.
RAMPART: a stone or earth wall of defence around a castle or fortified town.
REINFORCED CONCRETE: concrete (a mixture of sand, aggregate and cement) which is given additional tensile strength by incorporating steel rods within its mass.
RENAISSANCE: rebirth of Classical learning in architecture, beginning in mid-c15 Italy, which revolutionized building practice and took inspiration from Classical buildings and writings.
RENDER: the application of STUCCO or cement mortar to the face of a wall to give a continuous smooth finish.
RIB: a projecting band on a ceiling or VAULT.
RIAS: Royal Incorporation of Architects of Scotland.
RIBA: Royal Institute of British Architects.
ROCOCO: the latter phase of the BAROQUE style, highly ornamental yet more delicate than earlier phases.
ROMANESQUE: revival, from the c6 onwards, of Roman Imperial culture characterized by use of round arch and BASILICA plan.
ROMANTICISM: c18 sensibility introducing crucial change in how architecture was perceived and therefore formed.
ROOF LIGHT: a fixed or opening window in a roof.
ROTUNDA: a circular or polygonal building which is usually capped with a dome.
RUSTICATION: masonry with a roughened surface and joints marked by deep grooves.
SECESSIONSTIL: term to describe the ART NOUVEAU-influenced work of the Secession group, established in Vienna in 1897 by avant-garde artists and architects who had seceded from the conservative *Künstlerhaus*.
SECTION: a drawing showing a vertical "cut" through a building.
SERVICES: a term referring to the distribution of all utilities, electrical, gas, heating, hot water, air conditioning ducts, telephone cables, etc, throughout a building.
SHAFTED: a pillar is shafted when it has several thin columns attached.
SHINGLE STYLE: late c19 US underivative free style of domestic architecture typified by the hanging of wooden tiles (shingles) on walls.
SILL: the horizontal member at the bottom of a door or window frame. Sometimes "cill".
SKIN: the outer envelope or surface membrane of a building, brick walls or the glass and steel CLADDING.
SPANDREL: the surface between two arches or ribs in a vault.
STEEL FRAME: constructional method based on a calculated framework of steel, beams, girders, columns and ties.
STRAPWORK: decorative masonry or plaster in the form of interlaced bands; originated in France and the Netherlands and common in Elizabethan England.
STRING COURSE: a moulding or projecting course of stone or brick running horizontally along the face of a building.
STUCCO: smooth plaster or cement rendering to walls, or moulded for ceilings.
STUPA: a simple Buddhist religious monument often containing relics.
TECTON: team founded in London in 1932 by Berthold Lubetkin and others. The most important representative of the INTERNATIONAL STYLE in Great Britain, the group was disbanded in 1948.
TIMBER FRAME: method of construction which is based around a frame of interlocking or connected timber beams.
TRABEATED: building constructed on the POST-AND-LINTEL principle.
TRACERY: ornamental wood or stonework usually found decorating windows.
TRANSEPT: the cross-piece of a CRUCIFORM church at right angles to the body or nave.
TRIFORIUM: a straight, arcaded wall passage facing the nave in a church.
TROMPE L'ŒIL: wall or ceiling painting which deceives the eye into believing objects portrayed are three-dimensional.
TRUSS: a number of members framed together to bridge a space.
TUSCAN ORDER: see ORDERS.
UIA: see IUA.
VAULT: an arched roof or ceiling of stone, brick or wood designed in a number of shapes. The simplest is the *tunnel* or *barrel vault* designed as a continuous semi-circular archway; the *groin vault*, or *cross vault*, is formed by crossing two tunnel vaults; the *domical vault* is a dome consisting of a number of wedge-shaped sections rather like an umbrella; the *rib vault* is a complex structure formed by arched ribs, and the *fan vault* is a geometric weaving of ribs resembling the structure of a fan. The *stalactite vault* (muqarna) is common in Islamic architecture.

Vaults

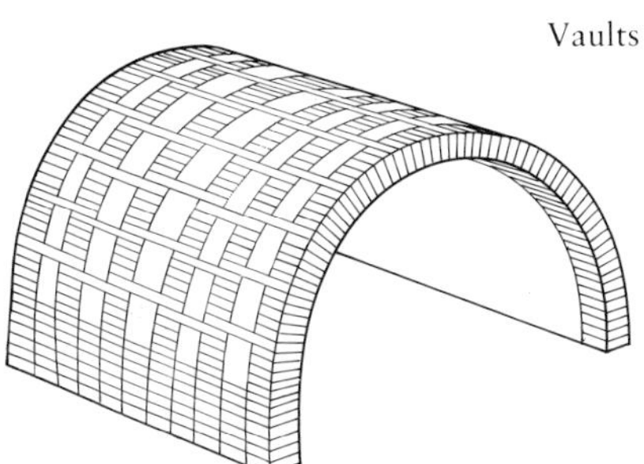

tunnel (barrel) vault

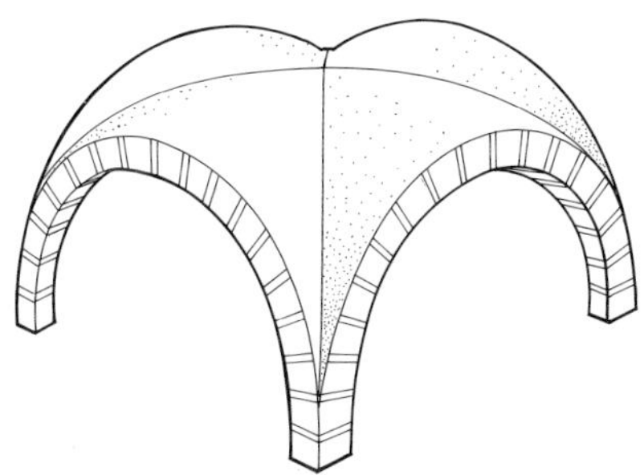

groin (cross) vault

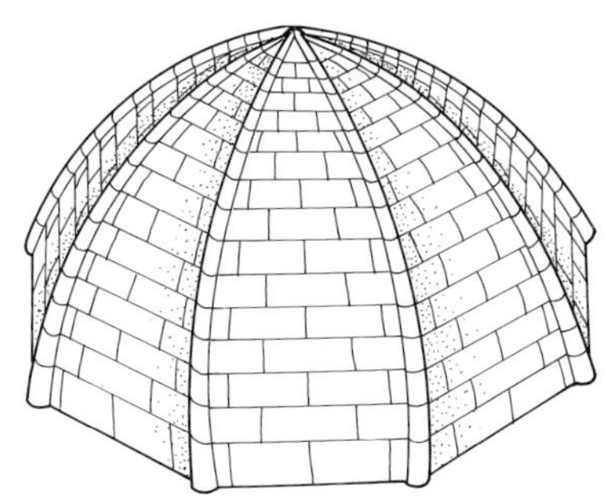

domical vault

VERNACULAR: refers to indigenous or traditional building styles.
VOLUTE: the scroll or spiral decoration featured principally in IONIC capitals.
VOUSSOIR: bricks or stones cut into wedge shapes and placed side by side to form an arch.
ZIGGURAT: a stepped pyramidal structure, with a large base receding to a small top.

INDEX

Main biographical entries are indicated by bold type; pictures and captions in italic